THINK
COMMUNICATION

Third Edition

ISA N. ENGLEBERG
Prince George's Community College

DIANNA R. WYNN
Nash Community College

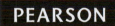

PEARSON

Boston   Columbus   Indianapolis   New York   San Francisco   Upper Saddle River   Amsterdam
Cape Town   Dubai   London   Madrid   Milan   Munich   Paris   Montreal   Toronto   Delhi   Mexico City
São Paulo   Sydney   Hong Kong   Seoul   Singapore   Taipei   Tokyo

Publisher, Communication: Karon Bowers
Director of Development: Sharon Geary
Development Editor: Lai T. Moy
Editorial Assistant: Jennifer Nolan
Senior Marketing Manager: Blair Zoe Tuckman
Marketing Assistant: Karen Tanico
Program Manager: Anne Ricigliano
Project Manager: Barbara Mack
Operations Manager: Mary Fischer
Operations Specialist: Mary Ann Gloriande
Art Director, Cover: Jayne Conte
Cover Design: Bruce Kenselaar
Cover Photos: (far left) A1Stock/Fotolia; (top, left) RATOCA/Fotolia; (bottom, left) Cifotart/Fotolia; (center, right) M.studio/Fotolia; (bottom, right) puckillustrations/Fotolia; (far right) Santhosh Kumar/Fotolia; (center, left) Ronda/Fotolia; (center, top) vladgrin/Fotolia; (top, right) jirikaderabek/Fotolia
Media Production Manager: Diane Lombardo
Media Project Manager: Tina Rudowski
Project Coordination, Text Design, and Electronic Page Makeup: PreMediaGlobal
Printer/Binder: LSC Communications
Cover Printer: LSC Communications

Credits and acknowledgments borrowed from other sources and reproduced, with permission, in this textbook appear on appropriate page within text or on pages 354–356.

Copyright © 2015, 2013, 2011 by Pearson Education, Inc.

Library of Congress Control Number: 2013956210

17 2022

ISBN-13: 978-0-205-94450-7
ISBN-10:   0-205-94450-7

brief CONTENTS

on the cover:

THINK
COMMUNICATION
ENGLEBERG • WYNN 2015

Can You Hear Me Now?
Listening is more than hearing

I Win; You Lose
Interpersonal conflict styles

Let's Stop Meeting Like This
The 5Ws of effective meetings

Tips for Wits
Using humor in a speech

How Many Friends Do You Need?
Online relationships

www.mysearchlab.com

212
Let's Stop Meeting Like This
The 5Ws of effective meetings

291
Tips for Wits
Using humor in a speech

142
I Win; You Lose
Interpersonal conflict styles

116
How Many Friends Do You Need?
Online relationships

59
Can You Hear Me Now?
Listening is more than hearing

detailed CONTENTS

PART ONE: THINK Communication

9

10

13

14

what's new in **THINK** *Communication,* 3e

New Features

Key Objectives

Every chapter in this third edition of *THINK Communication* begins with a list of competency-based Key Objectives directly tied to chapter content. These objectives are also linked to the end-of-chapter Summaries and Test Your Knowledge features, which allow students to assess whether and how well they have learned the theories, strategies, and skills essential for effective and ethical communication. Faculty members can use the same objectives as a basis for assessing student performance and learning.

Mediated Communication in *ACTION*

This new feature in every chapter examines the positive and negative impact of digital communication in our daily lives—from interacting online through social media to working in virtual groups.

Chapter 1. Social Media Madness

Chapter 2. Creating, Deceiving, and Revealing Yourself Online

Chapter 3. The International Digital Revolution

Chapter 4. Listening Online

Chapter 5. How's Your Netspeak?

Chapter 6. Expressing Emotions Online Smart Phone Etiquette

Chapter 7. How Many Friends Do You Need?

Chapter 8. Resolving Online Conflicts

Chapter 9. Are You Tweeting Your Career Away?

Chapter 10. Working in Virtual Groups

Chapter 11. Decision Making and Problem Solving in Virtual Groups

Chapter 12. Web-Based Presentations

Chapter 13. Getting Wiser about Wikipedia

Chapter 14. Master the Microphone

Chapter 15. Fact and Fiction Go Viral

Chapter 16. The Persuasive Power of Social Media

Key Objectives

Chapter-opening vignettes

New feature: Mediated Communication in *ACTION*

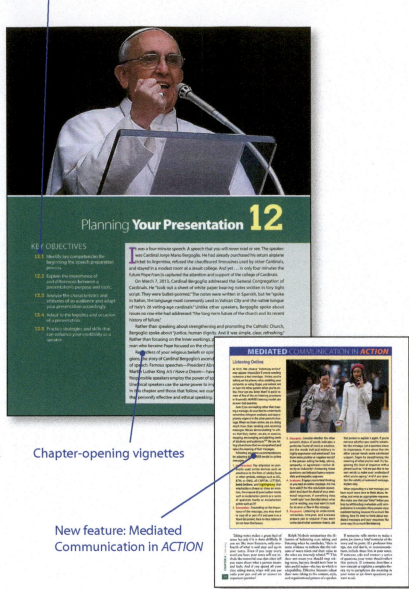

Chapter-Opening Vignettes

New chapter-opening narratives and photos focus on contemporary issues and events:

• Mini-interviews for professional school admission

• Infants lack a sense of "self"

• Race, ethnicity, gender, and age in the 2012 presidential election

• The "You Never Listen" epidemic

• The power of naming

• Love at first sight

• Mark Zuckerberg's interpersonal challenges

• Predicting romantic breakups and divorce

• The millennial generation at work

• Teamwork in Cirque du Soleil

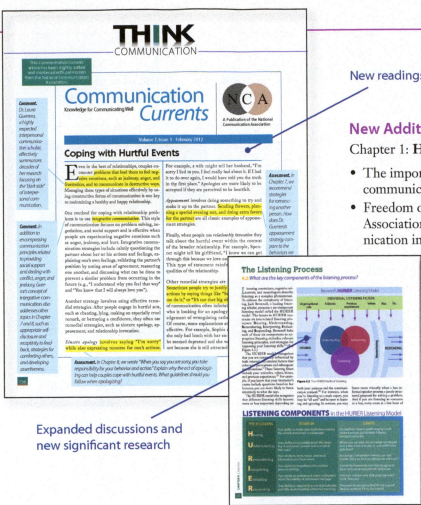

New readings

Expanded discussions and new significant research

New Additions—Chapter by Chapter

Chapter 1: **Human Communication**

- The importance of critical thinking as an essential communication competency
- Freedom of speech and the National Communication Association Credo for a free and responsible communication in a democratic society

Chapter 2: **Understanding Your Self**

- Self-Concept development model focusing on social comparison, social judgments, self-observation, and self-identification
- Self-monitoring and self-presentation competencies

Chapter 3: **Adapting to Others**

- Gender expectations as an intercultural variable
- More intercultural examples, including individualistic words in American political campaigns; male and female interaction in Muslim cultures

Chapter 4: **Listening**

- Expanded discussion of HURIER Model of Listening (Hearing, Understanding, Remembering, Interpreting, Evaluating, Responding)
- New listening research

Chapter 5: **Verbal Communication**

- Powerful and powerless language
- Expanded discussion on the power of naming

Chapter 6: **Nonverbal Communication**

- Mediated communication as a nonverbal variable
- Vocal expressiveness and meaning

Chapter 7: **Understanding Interpersonal Relationships**

- Empathic listening competencies
- Classifying and coping with jealousy

Chapter 8: **Improving Interpersonal Communication**

- New organization that emphasizes interpersonal communication strategies
- Managing and responding to emotions

Chapter 9: **Professional Relationships**

- Communication and professionalism
- Communication and the quality of work
- Interviewing pitfalls and best practices

- National security decision-making and the Osama bin Laden raid
- Language, delivery, and an actor's craft
- The rhetoric of Pope Francis
- Crafting and recrafting messages
- Instructive classroom lectures
- Michelle Obama's homage to Hadiya Pendleton

New Readings from *Communication Currents*

Part Two: "Coping with Hurtful Events" by Laura K. Guerrero

"Even in the best of relationships, couples sometimes encounter problems that lead them to feel negative emotions, such as jealousy, anger, and frustration, and to communicate in destructive ways." This article recommends constructive communication strategies for "maintaining a healthy and happy relationship."

Part Four: "Muhammad Ali's Fighting Words for Justice" by Ellen W. Gorsevski and Michael L. Butterworth

Although Muhammad Ali is best known as a world-class boxer who could "float like a butterfly, sting like a bee," he should also be recognized for the ways in which "his persuasive public performances played a pivotal role in radicalizing the civil rights movement . . . and the anti-Vietnam war movement."

Chapter 10: **Working in Groups**

- Types of conflict in groups
- Group development stages and the group process

Chapter 11: **Group Decision Making and Problem Solving**

- Prerequisites for group deliberation
- Matching problem-solving methods to group goals

Chapter 12: **Planning Your Presentation**

- Audience ethics
- New, contemporary speech excerpts, such as Cardinal Bergoglio's [Pope Francis] address to the general congregation of Cardinals

Chapter 13: **Content and Organization**

- New up-to-date examples of different supporting material
- Selecting appropriate key points for a presentation

Chapter 14: **Language and Delivery**

- Enhancing expressiveness through the vitality, variety, and sincerity of a speaker's delivery
- New contemporary speech excerpts, such as Pakistani teenager Malala Yousafzai's address to the United Nations General Assembly

Chapter 15: **Speaking to Inform**

- New, contemporary examples of misinformation, such as the rumors and reporting errors following the Boston Marathon bombing

Chapter 16: **Speaking to Persuade**

- New contemporary speech and campaign examples, such as First Lady Michele Obama's address to Chicago business leaders on the shooting death of an innocent teenager

New examples and analysis of contemporary presentations and persuasive campaigns

New, contemporary examples and analysis of ethical communication issues

Instructor and Student Resources

Key instructor resources include an Instructor's Manual (ISBN 0-13-377467-8), Test Bank (ISBN 0-13-377461-9), and PowerPoint Presentation Package (ISBN 0-13-374597-X). These supplements are available at www.pearsonhighered.com/irc (instructor login required). MyTest online test-generating software (ISBN 0-13-374645-3) is available at www.pearsonmytest.com (instructor login required). Also available is Pearson's MySearchLab™, a valuable tool to help students conduct online research. Access to MySearchLab is available at no additional cost in an optional package with new copies of this text or for purchase at www.mysearchlab.com (access code required). For a complete list of the instructor and student resources available with the text, please visit the Pearson Communication catalog at www.pearsonhighered.com/communication.

acknowledgments

- This new edition of *THINK Communication* would not have been possible without the talents and dedication of our publishing team. We are particularly grateful to the production editors, graphic designers, photo editors, copy editors, and behind-the-scenes technicians who transformed our revised manuscript into a cutting-edge introduction to communication studies. Thanks go out to Barbara Mack, Anne Ricigliano, Greg Johnson, Katy Mehrtens, Carolyn Arcabascio, Lee Scher, Mark Schaefer, Craig Jones, Tina Rudowski, and Diane Lombardo.

- Four amazing women deserve our thanks. Karon Bowers, our dynamic, multitasking editor in chief at Pearson, is always there for us with her wise counsel, problem-solving acumen, creativity, and sense of humor. We also welcome the return of Lai T. Moy as our development editor *par excellence*. We enjoyed racing Lai to see who would be first to suggest better explanations, more up-to-date examples, engaging and creative approaches, and social media applications to critical communication strategies and skills.

  We are particularly grateful to marketing manager Blair Tuckman and the Pearson sales representatives for demonstrating the many ways in which *THINK Communication* meets the needs of faculty members and their students. This year, we welcomed the e-mails they forwarded to us from instructors and students asking questions and recommending new approaches and examples to enliven the textbook. Our fourth leading lady, Jennifer Nolan, earned her stripes as editorial assistant by responding to our sometimes-desperate requests with patience and speed.

- Insightful reviewers provided many excellent suggestions that make the third edition of *THINK Communication* a better textbook. We salute Leonard Assante of Volunteer State Community College; Ann Duncan of McLennan Community College; Norman Earls Jr. of Valdosta State University; Bernadette Kapocias of Southwestern Oregon Community College; Karl Krayer of Brookhaven College; Dee Ann McFarlin of North Central Texas College; and Laurie Metcalf of Blinn College.

- Most of all, we are indebted to our students and faculty colleagues who have shared their opinions and provided valuable suggestions and insights throughout our careers. They are the measure of all things.

ISA ENGLEBERG, Professor *emerita* at Prince George's Community College in Largo, Maryland, served as president of the National Communication Association (NCA) in 2004 and chaired the NCA Research Board from 1995 to 1998. She has written six college textbooks in communication studies, published more than three dozen articles in academic journals, and made hundreds of convention and seminar presentations. Dr. Engleberg received the Outstand-

ing Community College Educator Award from NCA and the President's Medal from Prince George's Community College for outstanding teaching, scholarship, and community service. She has focused her professional career on improving both the content and teaching of introductory of communication courses at all levels of higher education as well as studying, teaching, and consulting internationally.

DIANNA WYNN is a faculty member at Nash Community College in Rocky Mount, North Carolina. Previously she taught at Midland College in Texas and Prince George's Community College in Maryland, where she was chosen by students as the Outstanding Teacher of the Year. She has co-authored three communication textbooks and has written articles in academic journals. Professor Wynn served as an officer in the Community College Section and a member

of the Legislative Assembly of the National Communication Association (NCA). In addition to teaching and college services, she worked as a trial consultant, assisting attorneys in developing effective communication strategies for the courtroom.

Human **Communication** 1

Let's say your dream is to become a doctor. Your excellent grades make you look great on paper, but to get accepted into medical school, you also need exceptional recommendations from your professors, high scores on your MCATs (Medical College Admission Test®), and a successful interview. Several top medical schools require an additional hurdle—you must demonstrate an ability to communicate effectively with others.

At the Virginia Tech Carilion School of Medicine, applicants participate in nine mini-interviews that test whether candidates have "the social skills to navigate a health care system in which good communication has become critical."[1] Mini-interviews like these have become part of the admission process at other medical schools, such as Stanford and the University of California, Los Angeles. When asked to describe the goal of these interviews, a medical school administrator replied, "[We are trying to] weed out the students who look great on paper but haven't developed the people or communication skills we think are important."[2]

By now you might be saying to yourself, "But becoming a doctor is not my dream." That's not the point. The point is this: regardless of whether you dream of becoming a teacher, a business manager, a chef, an engineer, a musician, a physical therapist, an elected official, or a landscape architect, effective communication skills are critical in all occupations as well as in all professional and social settings.

Communication in Your Life

1.1 *Explain the purpose and impact of human communication.*

Communication is the process of using verbal and nonverbal messages to generate meaning within and across a variety of contexts.[3] The key phrase in this definition is *to generate meaning*. You generate meaning when you speak, write, act, and create visual images as well as when you listen, read, and react to messages.

Your personal, academic, and professional success throughout your lifetime will depend on how well you communicate.[4] Even college faculty members identify communication skills, such as effective speaking, listening, and problem solving as well as working in and leading groups, as essential for every college graduate.[5] When you communicate effectively with others, your personal relationships become richer and more rewarding. Colleagues who express respect for one another and argue constructively are more likely to enjoy productive interactions. Work group members who communicate skillfully with one another are more likely to achieve their goals. Moreover, if you speak early, often, and well, you are more likely to be elected or selected for leadership roles. Finally, in this highly competitive world of ours, effective communication skills can transform you into a dynamic public speaker—one with the potential, knowledge, opinions, talents, and personality to make you stand out from the crowd.[6]

To gauge whether you communicate effectively in a variety of communication situations, ask yourself the following questions:

- *Personal.* Do I have meaningful personal relationships with close friends, relatives, and romantic partners?
- *Professional.* Do I communicate effectively within and on behalf of a business, organization, or work team?
- *Educational.* Do I demonstrate what I have learned in collegiate, corporate, and other training settings?

- *Intercultural.* Do I understand, respect, and adapt to people from diverse backgrounds?
- *Intellectual.* Do I analyze and evaluate the meaning of multiple and complex messages in an ever-changing world?
- *Societal.* Do I critically analyze and appropriately respond to public and mediated messages?
- *Ethical.* Do I apply ethical standards to personal and public communication in a variety of situations?

Executives from Fortune 500 companies claim that the college graduates they employ need better communication skills, as well as demonstrated ability to work in teams and with people from diverse backgrounds.[8] In a 2010 critical skills study, the American Management Association (AMA) put the need for communication skills front and center: "As the U.S. economy begins to show signs of improvement, executives say they need a workforce fully equipped with skills beyond just the basics of reading, writing and arithmetic (the three Rs) in order to grow their businesses." Rather than the 3 Rs, the AMA identifies the four competencies (4Cs)—(1) communication, (2) critical thinking, (3) collaboration, and (4) creativity—as even more essential to organizations and employees in the future.[9]

Know Thy Self

Do You Have the Right Stuff for the Job?

A survey by the National Association of Colleges and Employers (NACE) asked employers to rate the skills they seek in the college graduates they hire.[7] In your opinion, which of the skills in the table below are most important to employers? Rank them in order of preference, with 1 being the most prized skill, 2 being the next most prized skill, and so on. Then rate yourself: Are your skills in this area strong, moderate, or weak?

Now compare *your* rankings with the NACE study results. Numbers indicate rankings, with 1 going to the most important skill, 2 to the next most important, and so on.

Employee Skills	Rank Order	Your Skill
a. Analytical skills	_____	___ Strong ___ Moderate ___ Weak
b. Computer skills	_____	___ Strong ___ Moderate ___ Weak
c. Interpersonal skills	_____	___ Strong ___ Moderate ___ Weak
d. Leadership skills	_____	___ Strong ___ Moderate ___ Weak
e. Oral communication skills	_____	___ Strong ___ Moderate ___ Weak
f. Proficiency in field of study	_____	___ Strong ___ Moderate ___ Weak
g. Teamwork skills	_____	___ Strong ___ Moderate ___ Weak
h. Written communication skills	_____	___ Strong ___ Moderate ___ Weak

Desired skills in college graduates: a (4); b (8); c (2); d (5); e (1); f (7); g (3); h (6)

Think Communication recommends strategies and skills for improving *all* four of these competencies. We focus on communication principles and practices that will help you think critically and ethically, work collaboratively with people from similar and diverse backgrounds, and engage your creative powers to solve problems, engage listeners, resolve disputes, and create memorable messages.

Communication Models

1.2 Use communication models to analyze the communication process.

When we describe the fundamental nature of communication, we often use **communication models**. Communication scholars Rob Anderson and Veronica Ross write, "A model of communication—or any other process, object, or event—is a way of simplifying the complex interactions of elements in order to clarify relevant relationships, and perhaps to help predict outcomes."[10] Communication models

- identify the basic components in the communication process,
- show how the various components relate to and interact with one another, and
- help explain why communication succeeds or fails.

Early Communication Models

The earliest type of communication model, a **linear communication model**, functions in only one direction: A source creates a message and sends it through a channel to reach a receiver. The **channel** represents the various physical and electronic media through which we express messages. Linear models identify several important components but do not address the interactive nature of human communication.

Communication theorists then devised **interactive communication models**, which include the concepts of feedback and noise to show that communication is not an unobstructed or one-way street. When feedback is added, each communicator becomes both the source *and* the receiver of messages. When noise is added, every component becomes susceptible to disruption.

Feedback Any verbal or nonverbal response you can see, hear, or feel from others is referred to as **feedback**. A person giving feedback may smile or frown, ask questions or challenge your ideas, listen intently or tune out.

Another person may nod yes or no, raise his or her vocal pitch and volume when responding, or pat your back. If you accurately interpret feedback, you can assess how well your message is being received and whether you are likely to achieve your purpose. Consider, for example, what the president of a New York marketing and design company For example, consider how much the president of a New York design company said she relied upon feedback: "You *know* when they are with you." Expert communicators are sensitive to listener reactions. They use feedback—whether positive or negative—to evaluate whether and how well they are achieving their purpose, and then they adjust their message accordingly.

Noise Interactive communication models recognize obstacles that can prevent a message from reaching its receivers as intended; in communication studies, this is referred to as **noise**. Noise can be external or internal. **External noise** consists of physical elements in the environment that interfere with effective communication. Noise is often an audible problem: heavy vehicle traffic outside the window, a soft-speaking voice, or a difficult-to-understand accent. However, noise is not limited to just the sounds you hear. An uncomfortably warm room, an unpleasant odor, or even bright and distracting wall designs can interfere with your ability to be an attentive and effective communicator.

While external noise can be any distracting element in your environment, internal noise is a mental distraction within yourself. **Internal noise** consists of thoughts, feelings, and attitudes that inhibit your ability to communicate and understand a message as it was intended. A listener preoccupied with personal thoughts can miss or misinterpret a message. As a speaker, you may be distracted and worried about how you look during a presentation instead of focusing on your message and your audience. Or you may be thinking about your upcoming vacation rather than listening to a coworker's instructions. Such preoccupations can impair your ability to speak and listen effectively.

Encoding and Decoding According to most of the early models, communicators have two important functions: they serve as both the source and the receiver of messages.

Linear Communication Model

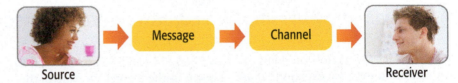

Source → Message → Channel → Receiver

Interactive Communication Model

Source — Channel — Message — Source
Receiver ← Feedback ← Channel — Receiver
Noise

Transactional Communication Model

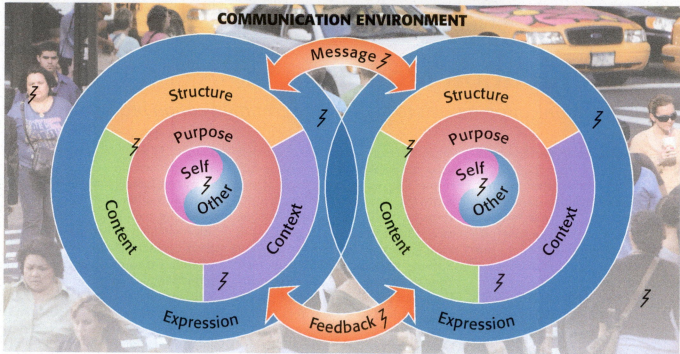

COMMUNICATION ENVIRONMENT

Message

Structure — Purpose — Self — Other — Content — Context — Expression

Feedback

⚡ = Noise

The communication **source** is a person or group of people who create a message intended to produce a particular response. Your message has no meaning until it arrives at a **receiver**, another person or group of people who interpret and evaluate your message. These two actions, sending and receiving, are called *encoding* and *decoding*.

When you communicate with others, you *encode* your ideas: you transform them into verbal and nonverbal messages, or *codes*. Thus, **encoding** is the decision-making process you use

to create and send **messages** that generate meaning.

Decoding converts a *code* or message sent by someone else into a form you can understand and use. Decoding is the decision-making process you use to interpret, evaluate, and respond to the meaning of verbal and nonverbal messages.

Transactional Communication Models

Communication in real time, however, is more complex than the

processes depicted in linear or interactive models. In reality, communication is a *simultaneous* transaction in which we continuously exchange verbal and nonverbal messages, and share meanings. Transactional communication is also fluid, not a "thing" that happens.

Transactional communication models recognize that we send and receive messages simultaneously within specific contexts. Even when we listen to someone, our nonverbal reactions send messages to the speaker.

Communication Contexts

1.3 *Explain the ways in which context affects the meaning of messages.*

In the previous section on communication models, we explain that *all* communication occurs within a **context**, the setting and circumstances in which communication takes place. Although this definition may appear simple—after all, communication must occur somewhere—context is anything but simple. Effective communicators analyze and adapt to the context. Consider, for example, how various contexts affect the implied meaning of the question, "Why are you here?" In addition to the contexts shown in the images on page 6, there are countless other meanings for this question, which changes as the context changes.

There are four types of interrelated communication contexts: psychosocial, logistical, interactional, and mediated.

Psychosocial Context

Psychosocial context refers to the psychological and cultural

environment in which you live and communicate. Consider, for example, your relationship with other communicators, their personality traits, and the extent to which they share attitudes, beliefs, and behaviors. Consider their age, gender, race, ethnicity, religion, sexual orientation, levels of ability, and socioeconomic class.

The psychosocial context also includes *your* emotional history, personal experiences, and cultural background. Thus, if you have a history of conflict with a work colleague, your feelings, experiences, and culture may influence your response to a suggestion made by that colleague.

Logistical Context

Logistical context refers to the physical characteristics of a particular communication situation in terms of its time, place, setting, and occasion. Are you talking to your friend privately or in a busy hallway? Are you speaking informally to colleagues in a staff meeting or welcoming guests to an important event? Can you be heard and your PowerPoint slides be seen from the back of the room?

Interactional Context

Interactional context refers to whether the interaction is between two people, among group members, or between a presenter and an audience.

Psychosocial Context

Logistical Context

Interactional Context

Mediated Context

COMMUNICATION IN ACTION

The Arab Spring

Twitter and its many offspring such as Tumblr and Reddit have been criticized as "dumb," "annoying," "meaningless," and "a monumental waste of time." Others view social media as an incomparable medium for sharing important news, citizen comments, and political opinions. During the 2012 U.S. presidential elections, both candidates used the full range of social media—as did journalists, political action committees, advocacy groups, and voters.

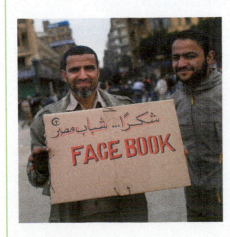

Even more dramatic than a U.S. presidential election, the political uprisings, citizen demonstrations, and public criticism of government actions in other countries have used social networking to plan, inform, and motivate their followers. For example, at the beginning of the Arab Spring uprisings in 2011, social media was celebrated as a tool for political action and democracy building in the Middle East. A 2012 report by the Pew Research Center indicated that in Egypt and Tunisia, two nations at the heart of the Arab Spring, more than sixty percent of social networkers shared their views about politics online.[11]

The Nation, a government-owned English-language newspaper published in Abu Dhabi (capital of the United Arab Emirates, one of the world's largest producers of oil) described the impact of social media. "Nearly 9 in 10 Egyptians and Tunisians surveyed in March [2011] said they were using Facebook to organize protests or spread awareness about

them. [These findings] give empirical heft to the conventional wisdom that Facebook and Twitter abetted if not enabled the historic region-wide uprisings of early 2011."

In studying the Arab Spring uprisings in Tunisia and Egypt, researchers in Australia question the supposed effects of social media. They found that social media such as YouTube helped mobilize mass support in a matter of weeks. Social media did not, however, *cause* the Arab Spring uprisings.[12] Despite the excitement and joy of the Arab Spring, social media was powerless in preventing the tragic events that followed in many Arab countries. Popular protests against the elected regime in Egypt resulted in what some describe as a military coup. The continuing civil war in Syria has claimed more than 100,000 lives. Four Americans died defending the U.S. diplomatic mission in Benghazi, Libya. In 2011, social media gave millions of people a sense of hope and a taste of freedom. Today both hope and freedom persist as a dream rather than a reality in many countries.[13]

"WHY ARE YOU HERE?" THE EFFECTS OF CONTEXT

At the airport

"Why are you here?"
(Meaning: Are you traveling for business or pleasure?)

At the doctor's office

"Why are you here?"
(Meaning: Are you here for your annual physical or because there's a problem?)

On the job

"Why are you here?"
(Meaning: Are you here to train or to explain the design options?)

On Twitter

"Why are you here?"
(Meaning: Are you rejoining us or just lurking?)

We divide the communication that occurs in interactional contexts into three common types of communication: interpersonal, group, and presentational.

Interpersonal communication occurs when a limited number of people, usually two, interact for the purpose of sharing information, accomplishing a specific goal, or maintaining a relationship. Chapters 7 through 9 focus on the fundamentals of interpersonal communication and the strategies and skills needed for effective communication in personal and professional relationships.

Group communication refers to the interaction of three or more interdependent people who interact for the purpose of achieving a common goal. Group communication represents

COMMUNICATION&CULTURE

DOES EVERYONE COMMUNICATE THE SAME WAY?

Do the differences between people outweigh what they have in common? How do these differences affect the way people from different cultures communicate? Carefully consider the following statements about communicative behavior and indicate whether you agree, disagree, or don't have an opinion about them.

Agree	Disagree	I Don't Know	Communicative Behaviors
☐	☐	☐	1. The United States is the most individualistic (independent, self-centered, me-first) culture in the world.
☐	☐	☐	2. Australian students and professors communicate on a first-name basis and expect to have lively class discussions.
☐	☐	☐	3. Women talk more than men do.
☐	☐	☐	4. Men and women communicate very differently from one another.
☐	☐	☐	5. Genetic characteristics explain why African Americans communicate differently from European Americans.
☐	☐	☐	6. Communicators from Asia are more likely to honor their elders and defer the gratification of their needs than are communicators from the United States.

Now think about how you responded to each of these statements. Why did you respond this way? After reading Chapter 3, "Adapting to Others," return to this survey and think about whether you would change any of your answers. If so, why? If not, why not?

more than a collection of individuals who talk to one another; it is a complex system in which members depend on one another. Family members and friends, work groups, neighborhood associations, self-help groups, social clubs, and athletic teams engage in group communication. Chapters 10 and 11 focus on how group communication works and discuss the essential strategies and skills for effective group participation, leadership, decision making, and problem solving.

Presentational communication occurs between speakers and audience members.[14] Presentational communication comes in many forms, from formal commencement addresses, campaign speeches, and conference lectures to informal class reports, staff briefings, and training sessions. You will make many presentations in your lifetime—at school, at work, at family and social gatherings, or at community and public events. Chapters 12 through 16 explain how to create and deliver effective presentations.

Mediated context

Mediated communication occurs when an additional media exists between communicators—usually some type of technology. Personal forms of mediated communication include phone calls, social media posts, and mailed letters. Mediated communication that occurs between a person or group of people and a larger, often remote audience is classified as **mass communication**. Radio, television, film, blogs, and websites are forms of mass communication, as are newspapers, magazines, billboards, and books.

Usually, the person who shares a message using mass communication cannot see or hear how audience members react as they see, read, and hear. All mass communication is mediated, but not all mediated communication—text messages, letters, or greeting cards—is intended for the masses.

Today, it's all about **computer-mediated communication**, which

Media Richness Theory

Richard Daft and Robert Lengel developed the **Media Richness Theory** to explain how the qualities of different media affect communication.[15] The theory also helps explain why your physical presence makes a significant difference in how well you communicate. Let's say you have a message you want to share with a group of people. You can share that message in one of four ways: face to face, written, visual, and virtual.

Face-to-face communication (be it at a party, group meeting, or presentation) is the richest communication medium because you can (1) see and respond instantly to others, (2) use nonverbal communication, such as body movement, vocal tone, facial expressions, and visual images, to clarify and reinforce messages, (3) use a natural speaking

style, and (4) convey your personal feelings and emotions.

In contrast, written, visual, and virtual communication in the form of handwritten notes, a book or magazine, a photograph, a billboard, e-mail messages, text messages, and posts on social media sites are quite the opposite. Readers rely exclusively on printed words and illustrations to interpret the sender's meaning. Thus, a tweet does not let

you hear a person's vocal tone, see a person's facial expressions or have more than 140 characters to understand a complex message. Generally, and particularly when a message is complex or potentially confusing, more media are needed to ensure effective communication. Thus, face-to-face communication is often the most effective because it can engage more of our senses than any other form of communication.

refers to how we interact with others using various networked technologies and software, ranging from simple texting to multimedia communication.[16] Computer-mediated communication also includes SMS (short message services)—communication that occurs through texting, and SNS (social networking sites)—communication that occurs through sites such as Google Hangouts and Pinterest.

Adapt to Others

Improve your personal relationships

COMMUNICATION SKILLS

Prepare and deliver a presentation

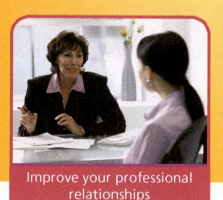
Improve your professional relationships

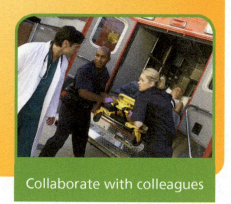
Collaborate with colleagues

Communication Principles and Practices

1.4 *Apply key principles of communication to a variety of contexts.*

Most of us would laugh at individuals who thought they could become a champion tennis player, a professional airline pilot, or a gourmet chef simply by reading a single book. At the very least, you'd have to practice that skill. Likewise, no textbook or classroom lecture *alone* can teach you everything you need to know about initiating a new relationship, resolving a conflict, comforting a person in distress, leading a group, planning a presentation, or responding to tough questions. As we see it, the best way to learn how to communicate effectively is to develop a set of reliable competencies based on validated communication theories, strategies, and skills.

Communication Theories

Theories are statements that explain how the world works. They describe, explain, and predict events and behavior.

Communication theories have emerged from extensive observation, empirical research, and rigorous scholarship. They help you understand *what* is happening when you communicate and *why* communication is sometimes effective and sometimes ineffective.

Learning about theories in isolation, however, will not make you a more effective communicator. Theories do not necessarily tell you what to do, what to say, or how to say it. Nevertheless, without theories, we would have difficulty understanding why or how a particular strategy works or how strategies and skills interact.

Communication Strategies

Strategies are the specific plans of action you use to achieve a goal. The word *strategy* comes from the Greek word *strategia* and refers to the office of a military general. Like great generals, effective communicators marshal their "forces" to achieve a specific purpose: to comfort a friend, resolve a conflict, lead a group discussion, or deliver an inspiring presentation.

However, learning about strategies is not enough. Effective strategies are based on theories. If you don't understand theory, you won't know why some strategies work in one situation and fail in another. Strategies based on theory help you understand when, where, why, and how to use a particular strategy most effectively.

MEDIATED COMMUNICATION IN *ACTION*

Social Media Madness

When academic researchers study computer-mediated communication, they face a host of corporate products such as Facebook, Twitter, LinkedIn, Pinterest, Google+, Meetup, Vimeo, and Squidoo.

There is no question that social media affects the way we communicate. What follows is a short list of the ways in which new social media has helped us:

- To initiate new relationships
- To seek social information about potential relationship partners
- To construct individual or multiple identities
- To manage interpersonal impressions
- To comment on postings, photographs, and relationships
- To aid in relationship reconnections[17]

To understand the full impact of social media, let's take a quick look at two of the most popular: Facebook and Twitter.

Facebook. When Facebook launched in early 2004, no one imagined that it would attract the flood of users that it did. By the end of its first year, CEO Mark Zuckerberg estimated that approximately one million individuals had joined. By 2012 the number of active users had skyrocketed to one billion—*monthly* and *worldwide*. So hugely popular did Facebook become that its popularity inspired its own net lingo, for example, *Facebook fever* (the uncontrollable urge to check Facebook constantly), *Facebooking* (the act of checking and posting on Facebook); *FB* (Facebook), and *wall sniper* (someone who tends to post only negative or controversial comments). Currently, it ranks as the most popular social network, followed by Twitter at a close second, and Pinterest, a newer, image-based networking site.

Twitter. In 2006, two years after Facebook stepped onto the social networking stage, Twitter was launched. Six years later, in 2012, it tweeted that its number of active users had surpassed the half-billion mark.[18] Originally, Twitter asked its users the question, "What are you doing?" Soon, the smart folks at Twitter realized that subscribers were exchanging information, not just about themselves, but about the things, people, and events they cared about. In 2009, Twitter shortened its question by two characters and changed it to "What's happening?" As much as people enjoyed telling others that they were sitting in traffic or climbing a mountain, they were also "witnessing accidents, organizing events, sharing links, breaking news, reporting stuff their dad says, and so much more."[19]

Social Media Controversies. Social media have become much more than a place for personal interactions. In the last decade, we've witnessed its growth and role in helping to report on and respond to major world events: presidential elections and debates; mass protests against governments and dictators, citizen uprisings, popular revolutions, and civil wars; natural and human-caused disasters; and triumphs and failures at the Olympic Games.

But, with this revolution comes a warning that communication scholars refer to as the "dark side" of social media: becoming a cyber victim to sexual solicitation, cyberbullying, cybersex, deception, spying, theft, and invasions of privacy.[20]

So what's your verdict? Do the advantages of social media make it one of the greatest innovations of the twenty-first century? Do the disadvantages, at the very least, moderate your initial verdict or even outweigh the advantages? See whether you can add two more advantages and two more disadvantages to the table that follows.

Advantages of Social Media	Disadvantages of Social Media
1. Convenient: You can contact others no matter where you or they are.	1. Inconvenient: You can disturb and annoy others when you are messaging.
2. Useful: You can share urgent, provocative, and useful information, opinions, and experiences with others.	2. A waste of time: You can waste precious hours by getting sidetracked by what other people are writing about and doing.
3.	3.
4.	4.

Communication Skills

Communication **skills** refer to your ability to accomplish communication goals through interactions with others. Communication skills are the tools or techniques you use to collaborate with a colleague, prepare a meeting agenda, and speak loudly enough to be heard by a large audience. Throughout this book, you will read about and practice many communication skills: how to be more assertive, how to think critically, how to listen effectively, how to resolve conflicts, how to speak clearly, how to organize a message, and how to explain complex concepts or persuade others.

Like strategies, skills are most effective when they are grounded in theory. Without theories, you may not understand when and why to use a particular strategy or skill to your best advantage. For example, in the hope of improving group morale, you may decide *not* to use a structured, problem-solving agenda at a critical meeting. Unfortunately, this may *lower* group morale because your approach to problem solving is disorganized and wastes everyone's valuable time. However, if you are familiar with group communication theory, you will know that using a standard agenda helps a group to follow a series of practical steps to solve problems. In our eagerness to communicate effectively, we may grab ready-made, easy-to-use tricks of the trade, which are inappropriate or ineffective. Enlisting skills without an understanding of theories and strategies can make communication inefficient and ineffective as well as frustrating for everyone.

Communication Competencies

When you understand well-founded communication theories, select appropriate communication strategies, and practice a variety of communication skills, you are ready to transform your understanding, appreciation, and abilities into lifelong competencies.

The term *competency* has become a big deal at all levels of education, from preschool to postgraduate work. Communication competencies are not the same as objectives, or learning outcomes. Rather, competencies are sets of performance standards that go well beyond "the mere attainment of skill." "[They involve] other qualities such as attitudes, motives, personal insightfulness, interpretive ability, receptivity, maturity, and self-assessment."[21] That's a lot to ask of anyone, but well worth the effort. For example, if you are unmotivated to communicate or cannot monitor and accurately interpret your own behavior and how others react to you, all the theories, strategies, and skills in the world will be of no use to you.

Communication competencies are measurable performance standards that require the knowledge, skills, attitudes, and personal qualities essential to the practice of effective and ethical communication.[23] When you master such competencies, effective communication becomes an enduring habit that will last a lifetime.

Study the full-page graphic on the following page. It depicts 7 Key Competencies of Effective Communication matched with a series of questions that can help you understand their scope and significance.

The seven key competencies apply to all types of communication, regardless of whether you are talking to friends, sending an instant message, delivering a speech to a large audience, planning a business meeting, or participating in a videoconference. No matter how well you adapt to others, structure the content of your message, or speak in a melodious voice, you won't achieve your purpose if you do not appreciate how all seven competencies interact with one another every time you communicate. Effective communicators accept the fact that they may never create or deliver a perfect message, but they never stop trying to reach that ideal.

"You never forget how to ride a bike." This popular and true statement applies to many physical skills. Once learned—and assuming there aren't physical or health barriers—you never forget how to swim, ride a horse, ski, surf, drive a car, or use chop sticks. In 2009, neuroscientists identified a nerve cell in your brain that controls the formation of memories for motor skill. Put another way, specific nerve cells help you learn and remember how to do something.[24]

We believe that a similar process is at work when we communicate effectively. Highly competent communicators develop an instinct for knowing what to say, where to say it, when to say it, how to say it, and even whether to speak at all. When learning to communicate more effectively, you should engage three types of learning:

- Knowledge: *What* to do
- Skills: *How* to do it
- Motivation: *Want* to do it

For example, in the case of an interpersonal conflict, these three types of learning can help you manage the quality and outcome of a difficult situation as described in the following paragraph:

If a friend of mine and I have an argument, things may get worse if I don't know what to say or do. However, by studying conflict resolution principles and best practices, I can analyze the conflict and choose appropriate communication strategies (*what* to do) that may help resolve it. But unless I have the skills (*how* to do it) to put those principles into action, I may not resolve the problem and could even make it worse. Finally, even if I learn about and master conflict resolution strategies *and* skills, I also must *want* to resolve the problem. Only then will I be prepared to resolve the argument and preserve a friendship. Equally important, I will be better prepared and know what to do, how to do it, and why to do it, when I face a similar conflict in the future.

> **"** Theories are nets to catch what we call 'the world': to rationalize, to explain, and to master it. **"**
>
> Karl R. Popper, philosopher[22]

The 7 Key Competencies of Effective Communication

1 KNOW THY SELF

2 CONNECT WITH OTHERS

3 DETERMINE YOUR PURPOSE

4 ADAPT TO THE CONTEXT

5 SELECT MESSAGE CONTENT

6 STRUCTURE THE MESSAGE

7 EXPRESS THE MESSAGE

EXPRESSION

- Which channels are most appropriate given your purpose, the other communicators, the context, and the message's content and structure?
- What skills and techniques will improve your ability to express your message?
- How effectively do you express and listen to verbal and nonverbal messages?

STRUCTURE

- What are the most effective ways to organize your message?
- How can your organizational structure enhance attention, comprehension, and interest in others?
- In what order should you share your ideas and information?

CONTENT

- What ideas and opinions should you include in your message to make it clear, effective, and interesting?
- How should you support your ideas and opinions in your message?
- How well do you interpret messages from others?
- Do you listen to and defend the rights of others to express opinions contrary to yours?

SELF

- How do your characteristics, traits, skills, needs, attitudes, values, and self-concept influence your communication goals and style?
- How well do you put aside your personal needs and attitudes when listening to others?
- What is your ethical responsibility as a communicator?

OTHERS

- With whom are you communicating? How do their characteristics, traits, skills, needs, attitudes, and beliefs affect the way they listen and respond?
- How can you better understand, respect, and adapt to others when you communicate with them?
- How well do you listen when interacting with others?

PURPOSE

- What do you want others to know, think, believe, feel, or do as a result of communicating with them?
- How might others misunderstand or misinterpret your purpose?
- Can you identify the intended purpose of other communicators?

CONTEXT

- What role are you assuming in this setting or situation?
- How will you behave in different psychological and interactional contexts?
- How well do you adapt to the logistics of the place where you will communicate and the occasion?

Communication and Critical Thinking

1.5 *Explain the relationship between critical thinking and effective communication.*

Critical thinking puts your mind to work on complex communication problems—from applying for a job promotion to solving a family crisis, from making an effective classroom presentation to critiquing a politician's campaign commercial.[26]

Critical thinking is "reasonable reflective thinking that focuses on deciding" what to believe, do, or say.[25] It can also result in a more meaningful conversation, a more productive group discussion, or a highly persuasive presentation. Critical thinkers are usually highly skilled listeners who know how to accurately hear, understand, remember, interpret, and evaluate messages as well as appropriately respond to others.

Critical thinking puts your mind to work on complex communication challenges such as resolving a family crisis, supporting a grieving friend, conducting an important meeting, expressing your point of view, or critiquing a politician's campaign speech. At every stage of the encoding and decoding process, you will make significant decisions depending on your desire and ability to think critically.

A common misconception about critical thinking is that it means criticizing. The word *criticize* implies judging in order to find fault with something or someone. The word *critical* is a broader term, with a less of a fault-finding implication. *Critical* comes from the Greek word for *critic* (*kritkos*), which means "to question, to make sense of, to be able to analyze."[27] Critical thinking is *not* a way to tear down a statement or belittle someone. Rather, it helps you identify the intended meaning of a message and evaluate the evidence and reasoning used to support that message. Critical thinking also enables you to develop and defend your position on issues.[28]

According to Robert Ennis, a well-respected philosophy professor, skilled critical thinkers exhibit distinct attitudes and skills, as shown in the table to the left.[29]

Before leaving this topic, take a second look at the table. Think critically about the attitudes and skills of critical thinkers. All of these perspectives and abilities exemplify highly competent communicators. In subsequent chapters, you will learn how to apply specific critical thinking skills to help you identify faulty reasoning and create persuasive messages. Equally important, you will learn to appreciate the important role of emotions in making critical decisions.

Attitude and Skills of Ideal *CRITICAL THINKERS*

ATTITUDE	SKILLS
• I want to know the intended meaning of a message.	• I can identify the central purpose of a message.
• I take the communication context and characteristics of other communicators into account.	• I analyze others' reasons for disagreeing with or doubting my claims.
• I am open-minded and withhold judgment when messages seem weak or questionable.	• I respect and appropriately respond to the feelings, information, and opinions expressed by others.
• I am aware of my own and others' beliefs and biases.	• I can judge the credibility of evidence and sources.
• I am willing to take or change a position when the evidence and reasons are sufficient to do so.	• I ask and answer questions effectively.
	• I ask probing questions.

Communication Ethics

1.6 *Practice ethical communication.*

How would you feel if you learned that

- a corporate executive hid lavish, personal expenditures while laying off employees?
- a teacher gave higher grades to students he liked and lower grades to students who annoyed him?
- a close friend shared your most intimate secrets with people you don't know or don't like?
- a politician used a racial slur in private to describe a disgruntled group of constituents?

Most of the above actions are not illegal. They are, however, unethical.

Whereas theories, strategies, and skills focus on questions asking *why*, *what*, and *how* to communicate, you also must answer a *whether* question, that is, whether you should communicate as planned: Is it right? Is it fair? Is it deceptive?[30]

Ethical Communication

Ethical issues arise whenever we communicate because communication has consequences. What you say and do can help or hurt others; can build or destroy your reputation; and can result in justice or injustice. Sadly, the communication competencies we address in this textbook can and have been used for less-than-ethical purposes. Unscrupulous speakers have misled trusting citizens and consumers. Bigots have used hate speech to oppress and discriminate against those who are "different." Self-centered people have destroyed the reputations of their rivals by spreading cruel rumors among friends, colleagues, and members of the public.

In every chapter of this textbook, we include a feature titled Ethical Communication. Each of these features discusses the ethical issues that arise whenever you interact with others in a variety of communication contexts.

Ethics requires an understanding of whether communication behaviors meet agreed-on standards of right and wrong.[31] The National Communication Association (NCA), the largest professional association of communication scholars, researchers, educators, students, and practitioners in the world, provides a Credo for Ethical Communication. In Latin, *credo* means "I believe." Thus, the NCA ethics credo is a set of belief statements about what it means to be an ethical communicator.

Freedom of Speech

The NCA Credo for Ethical Communication emphasizes the strong connection between communication ethics and free speech. Several ethical principles in the credo—"We endorse freedom of expression," "We are committed to the courageous expression of personal conviction," and "We accept responsibility for the short- and

ETHICAL COMMUNICATION

The NCA Credo for Ethical Communication[32]

Questions of right and wrong arise whenever people communicate. Ethical communication is fundamental to responsible thinking, decision making, and the development of relationships and communities within and across contexts, cultures, channels, and media. Moreover, ethical communication enhances human worth and dignity by fostering truthfulness, fairness, responsibility, personal integrity, and respect for self and others. We believe that unethical communication threatens the well-being of individuals and the society in which we live. Therefore we, the members of the National Communication Association, endorse and are committed to practicing the following principles of ethical communication:

- We advocate truthfulness, accuracy, honesty, and reason as essential to the integrity of communication.
- We endorse freedom of expression, diversity of perspective, and tolerance of dissent to achieve the informed and responsible decision making fundamental to a civil society.
- We strive to understand and respect other communicators before evaluating and responding to their messages.
- We promote access to communication resources and opportunities as necessary to fulfill human potential and contribute to the well-being of families, communities, and society.
- We promote communication climates of caring and mutual understanding that respect the unique needs and characteristics of individual communicators.
- We condemn communication that degrades individuals and humanity through distortion, intimidation, coercion, and violence, and through the expression of intolerance and hatred.
- We are committed to the courageous expression of personal conviction in pursuit of fairness and justice.
- We advocate sharing information, opinions, and feelings when facing significant choices while also respecting privacy and confidentiality.
- We accept responsibility for the short- and long-term consequences of our own communication and expect the same of others.

FREEDOM OF *SPEECH*

National Communication Association Credo for a Free and Responsible Communication in a Democratic Society[33]

Recognizing the essential place of free and responsible communication in a democratic society, and recognizing the distinction between the freedoms our legal system should respect and the responsibilities our educational system should cultivate, we members of the Speech Association of America endorse the following statement of principles:

WE BELIEVE that freedom of speech and assembly must hold a central position among American constitutional principles, and we express our determined support for the right of peaceful expression by any communicative means available.

WE SUPPORT the proposition that a free society can absorb with equanimity speech which exceeds the boundaries of generally accepted beliefs and mores; that much good and little harm can ensue if we err on the side of freedom, whereas much harm and little good may follow if we err on the side of suppression.

WE CRITICIZE as misguided those who believe that the justice of their cause confers license to interfere physically and coercively with speech of others, and we condemn intimidation, whether by powerful majorities or strident minorities, which attempts to restrict free expression.

WE ACCEPT the responsibility of cultivating by precepts and example, in our classrooms and in our communities, enlightened uses of communication; of developing in our students a respect for precision and accuracy in communication, and for reasoning based upon evidence and a judicious discrimination among values.

WE ENCOURAGE our students to accept the role of well-informed and articulate citizens, to defend the communication rights of those with whom they may disagree, and to expose abuses of the communication process.

WE DEDICATE ourselves fully to these principles, confident in the belief that reason will ultimately prevail in a free marketplace of ideas.

long-term consequences of our own communication and expect the same of others"—demonstrate the centrality of free speech to our democracy and ethical communication.

The first amendment of the United States Constitution guarantees our **freedom of speech** when it states that "Congress shall make no law respecting an establishment of religion, or prohibiting the free exercise thereof; or abridging the freedom of speech, or of the press; or the right of the people peaceably to assemble, and to petition the Government for a redress of grievances."

Although you are free to say whatever you want (with some exceptions), even if it is false, highly controversial, discriminatory, or inflammatory, there are consequences. If, for example, your claims prove false or unjustified, you can be sued for **defamation**, a false statement that damages a person's reputation.[34] If you say hateful or inflammatory things about someone, you may face hostility and harassment from others as well as sharp criticisms about your character and competence. You may even find your job or career in jeopardy. The best protection of your right to free speech is to make sure that you can back up your opinions with legitimate facts, valid reasoning, and defensible responses to objections.

We strongly recommend that you review the NCA's Credo for a Free and Responsible Communication in a Democratic Society. In addition to presenting a set of belief statements about the nature of free and responsible communication, the credo calls upon "students to accept the role of well-informed and articulate citizens, to defend the communication rights of those with whom they may disagree, and to expose abuses of the communication process."

Are You an Effective Communicator?

How can you become a more effective communicator? Use the five-point scale below to rate the following competencies in terms of their importance to *you*. Circle only one number for each item.

Competencies	Extremely Important	Very Important	Somewhat Important	Not Very Important	Not at All Important
1. Reduce your speaking anxiety	5	4	3	2	1
2. Influence the attitudes and behavior of others	5	4	3	2	1
3. Use humor appropriately	5	4	3	2	1
4. Listen effectively to others	5	4	3	2	1
5. Develop good interpersonal relationships	5	4	3	2	1
6. Hold an interesting conversation	5	4	3	2	1
7. Use your voice effectively	5	4	3	2	1
8. Resolve interpersonal conflicts	5	4	3	2	1
9. Use gesture, movement, and eye contact effectively	5	4	3	2	1
10. Interview for a job	5	4	3	2	1
11. Adapt to people from different cultures	5	4	3	2	1
12. Lead a group or work team	5	4	3	2	1
13. Present visual aids and slides effectively	5	4	3	2	1
14. Tell stories skillfully	5	4	3	2	1
15. Chair or conduct a meeting	5	4	3	2	1
16. Gain audience or listener attention and interest	5	4	3	2	1
17. Prepare and deliver an effective presentation	5	4	3	2	1
18. Explain complex ideas to others	5	4	3	2	1
19. Inspire or motivate others	5	4	3	2	1
20. Assert your ideas and opinions	5	4	3	2	1
21. Participate effectively in a group discussion	5	4	3	2	1
22. Organize the content of a presentation	5	4	3	2	1
23. Begin and end a presentation	5	4	3	2	1
24. Use appropriate and effective words	5	4	3	2	1
25. Develop strong, valid arguments	5	4	3	2	1
26. Interact in business and professional settings	5	4	3	2	1
27. Support and comfort others	5	4	3	2	1

Review your ratings: Circle the competency item numbers next to the skills that you scored as **5**—skills that, in your opinion, are the most important and essential for effective communication. Why did you select these items?

Communication in Your Life

1.1 Define the purpose and impact of human communication.

- Communication is the process of using verbal and nonverbal messages to generate meaning within and across a variety of contexts.
- Effective communication helps you achieve personal, professional, educational, intercultural, intellectual, societal, and ethical goals.

Communication Models

1.2 Use communication models to analyze the communication process.

- Unlike linear and interactional communication models, transactional models depict communication as a *simultaneous* transaction in which we continuously exchange verbal and nonverbal messages and share meanings.
- In a communication transaction, communicators encode and decode messages at the same time.
- Social media has positive and negative effects on how we develop and maintain relationships in mediated contexts.

Communication Contexts

1.3 Explain the ways in which context affects the meaning of messages.

- The four types of communication context are psychosocial, logistical, interactional, and mediated.
- The three interactional contexts are interpersonal, group, and presentational communication.
- Media Richness Theory explains how the quantity and qualities of different media affect communication.

Communication Principles and Practices

1.4 Apply key principles of communication to a variety of contexts.

- Communication strategies and skills are most effective when they are grounded in theory. Without theory, you may not understand when and why to use a particular strategy or skill to your best advantage.
- Effective communicators develop the following key competencies: (1) Know thy self; (2) Connect with others; (3) Determine your purpose; (4) Apply to the context; (5) Select message content; (6) Structure your message; (7) Express the message.
- Competent communicators know what to do and why to do it (theory and knowledge), know how to do it (strategies and skills), and want to do it (motivation and attitude).

Communication and Critical Thinking

1.5 Explain the relationship between critical thinking and effective communication.

- Critical thinking is reasonable reflective thinking that focuses on deciding what to believe, do, or say.
- Critical thinkers exhibit distinct attitudes and skills that also exemplify highly competent communicators.

Communication Ethics

1.6 Practice ethical communication.

- Ethical communication is fundamental to responsible thinking and decision making as well as relationship development and maintenance within and across a variety of communication contexts.
- The National Communication Association Credo for Ethical Communication endorses principles of ethical communication for all communicators.
- The National Communication Association Credo for a Free and Responsible Communication in a Democratic Society sets forth principles that facilitate the free marketplace of ideas.

Key Terms

Channels	Feedback	Mediated communication
Communication	Freedom of speech	Messages
Communication competencies	Group communication	Noise
Communication models	Interactional context	Presentational communication
Computer-mediated communication	Interactive communication model	Psychosocial context
Context	Internal noise	Receiver
Critical Thinking	Interpersonal communication	Skills
Decoding	Linear communication model	Source
Defamation		Strategies
Encoding	Logistical context	Theories
Ethics	Mass communication	Transactional communication model
External noise	Media Richness Theory	

TEST YOUR KNOWLEDGE

1.1 Define the purpose and impact of human communication.

1 This textbook defines *communication* as the process of using verbal and nonverbal messages to generate meaning within and across a variety of contexts. Which term in this definition refers to the various physical and electronic media through which we express messages?

   a. messages
   b. meaning
   c. channels
   d. process

2 Which of the following skills received the *lowest* ranking in the NACE study of skills employers seek in college graduates?

   a. written communication skills
   b. leadership skills
   c. oral communication skills
   d. proficiency in field of study

1.2 Use communication models to analyze the communication process.

3 Linear models of communication

   a. include the concepts of noise and feedback.
   b. function in only one direction: a source creates a message and sends it through a channel to reach a receiver.
   c. recognize that we send and receive messages simultaneously.
   d. illustrate the interrelationships among the key elements of human communication.

4 The encoding process can be described as

   a. the way you feel about others.
   b. the process of minimizing internal noise.
   c. converting a code sent by someone else into a meaningful message.
   d. the decision-making process you use to create messages that generate meaning.

1.3 Explain the ways in which context affects the meaning of messages.

5 Logistical context refers to

   a. the cultural environment in which you live.
   b. your emotional history, personal experiences, and cultural background.
   c. the time, place, setting, and occasion in which you will interact with others.
   d. whether communication occurs one to one, in groups, or between a speaker and an audience.

6 According to Media Richness Theory, which of the following media would be the least rich?

   a. a tweet
   b. a public speech on television
   c. a web seminar using Skype
   d. a group discussion at work

1.4 Apply key principles of communication to a variety of contexts.

7 The authors of your textbook write that you "the best way to learn how to communicate effectively is to develop a set of reliable competencies based on validated communication ____, ____, and ____."

   a. theories, strategies, and skills
   b. psychology, sociology, and philosophy
   c. cognition, psychomotor skills, and affect
   d. feedback, noise, and encoding

8 Which key competency of effective communication focuses on how well you put aside *your* personal needs and attitudes when listening to others ?

   a. Know thy self
   b. Express the message
   c. Determine your purpose
   d. Adapt to the context

1.5 Explain the relationship between critical thinking and effective communication.

9 All of the following answers characterize skilled critical thinking except one. Which answer should not be on this list?

   a. I am open-minded and withhold judgment when messages seem weak or questionable.
   b. I can judge the credibility of evidence and sources.
   c. I rely on my own beliefs and values to judge the truthfulness of a message.
   d. I can identify the central purpose of a message.

1.6 Practice ethical communication.

10 Which principle in the NCA Credo for Ethical Communication is violated if a close friend shares your most intimate secrets with people you don't know or don't like?

   a. We advocate truthfulness, accuracy, honesty, and reason as essential to the integrity of communication.
   b. We strive to understand and respect other communicators before evaluating and responding to their messages.
   c. We advocate sharing information, opinions, and feelings when facing significant choices while also respecting privacy and confidentiality.
   d. We promote access to communication resources and opportunities as necessary to fulfill human potential.

Answers found on page 368.

THINK
COMMUNICATION

This *Communication Currents* article has been slightly edited and shortened with permission from the National Communication Association.

Communication
Knowledge for Communicating Well
Currents

A Publication of the National Communication Association

Volume 5, Issue 3 - June 2010

Examining Communication

O ur communication practices are among the most human of all human behavior. We use words to create messages, and we create meanings from those messages. Humans are social creatures, making the need to communicate essential to our survival, development, and happiness. Too often, communication is thought of as just something we do. However, to fully appreciate communication, let's examine it more closely.

Communication is functional. Communication allows us to create things we need. For example, an organization does not exist until we talk one into existence. For an organization to survive, we must talk about the culture we want to create and develop procedures for procuring and providing products and services. In large organizations and communities, communication can be more difficult as time and geography separate us. For example, you call the utility company to report a disruption of service and get "press 1 for . . ." In this case, what is functional for the utility company (and the people who represent it) is different than your idea of functionality. Often the ways in which we use communication to accomplish a function or do something complicates the conversations we have.

Communication is social. Communication allows us to create and manage relationships with one another. You don't have a boyfriend until you have the talk about being boyfriend and girlfriend. You can't

get a divorce until you (or the lawyer and judge) talk one into existence. Relationships between people are negotiated from talk. Formal relationships become solidified as you accept your role as manager and talk as a manager to your subordinates. The relationship between husband and wife is also negotiated—think of the number of couples who disagree over what is said in their wedding vows. You can't just say, "I do." This simple phrase has to be said after what you vow to do, and after it is said in front of others (or at least a justice of the peace). Informal relationships, such as friendships, are derived from talk that shares personal information. Somewhere in those conversations, acquaintances turn to friendships—but you really don't know you are friends until he or she introduces you with, "Say hello to my friend Jeff."

Communication is symbolic. Communication is not water that can be turned on or off. Its symbolic nature is fluid and dynamic, and, as a result, meanings are not necessarily fixed. Communicators can't give meaning, rather meaning is negotiated through talk with others. This is why your meaning and my meaning can differ, although we agree that you sent me a specific message. "Mowing the grass" said by my dad, I soon learned, did not mean simply pushing the lawnmower around the yard. Rather, through negotiated talk (okay, yelling), I came to understand that mowing the lawn meant

Assessment. *What strategies do you use when you communicate with someone whose race, ethnicity, age, gender, religious beliefs, sexual preferences, political attitudes, or educational level differs from yours?*

(in this order): picking up trash and sticks in the yard, mowing the grass, sweeping grass clippings off the driveway and walk, cleaning the mower, and, finally, returning the mower to where it was stored. Over time, I forgot about the negotiation and was able to use his "mowing the grass" message for this set of tasks. Imagine my surprise when many years later I hired someone to "mow my grass" and he did exactly that. I had failed to negotiate what "mowing the grass" meant.

Communication is cultural. Obviously, we have flattened the world through travel and the use of technology. Beyond these obvious national differences in culture, cultural differences also exist locally. The culture of neighborhoods and regions, age and sex, race and religion, and politics and philosophy complicate communication. We often argue and disagree because our fundamental views of the world are at odds with one another. I announce to my colleagues that I have to go home and "get the kids." I use this phrase even though my kids are dogs. Why? Because it's acceptable to leave the meeting to pick up your children from school, but less acceptable to leave to let the dogs out of the house.

Communication is functional, social, symbolic, cultural, and complicated—whether it is face to face or mediated. However, sometimes we need to accomplish something by communicating, and yet we do not always want to expose ourselves too much to the other person. For example, having a courteous interaction with a retail clerk is sufficient. I do not need to establish a relationship more explicit than clerk-customer with him or her.

Saying "yes" to the clerk's "Did you find everything you need?" is all that is needed (whether I found everything or not).

Sometimes, we don't have the words or messages to express ourselves fully. Not all feelings can be easily labeled; not all experiences can be easily translated. I may feel that something is not right about our relationship, but cannot find a way to express it to you that sounds genuine. After all, communication often appears to be linear, yet feelings, experiences, and meanings can be simultaneously layered: "I love you, but I can't stand you."

Sometimes, we fail to take the time to talk with others in a meaningful way. Time is a precious commodity. When I'm in a hurry, "please" and "thank you" interfere in my making a meeting on time. You come to my office to talk over a problem with me, but I have only 15 minutes before I must be somewhere else. When communication is strained by time and other pressures, people communicate less effectively because they talk at rather than talk with others. Communication is complicated. Communication scholars have studied these complexities, and are learning more about how to communicate more effectively.

Comment. *Remember the following statement from Chapter 1: "Your personal, academic, and professional success throughout your lifetime will depend on how well you communicate." in terms of Dr. Keyton's claims in this article.*

ABOUT THE AUTHOR

Joann Keyton is a professor of Communication and noted Group Communication scholar at North Carolina State University, Raleigh, NC. She is the founding editor of *Communication Currents* (Volumes 1 through 5). This essay appeared in the June 2010 issue of *Communication Currents,* a publication of the National Communication Association.

Comment. *Remember to use the key competencies of effective communication (self, others, purpose, context, content, structure, and expression) to adapt to the complex challenge of generating meaning within and across a variety of contexts, cultures, and channels.*

Assessment. *In light of what you've read in Chapter 1, what should you focus on to communicate more effectively? What specific strategies and skills can help you achieve this goal?*

Understanding **Your Self** 2

What do infants see when they look in a mirror? Unlike children and adults who see and recognize themselves in their reflections, an infant's experience is quite different. Babies do not know that they are seeing themselves—much like birds, dogs, and cats. Infants see "others" and just more of the world in which they live. It is not until they grow to be four or five years old, do they genuinely recognize that they are seeing their own reflections in a mirror.[1] Although the process of fully understanding and expressing the concept of "me,"[2] takes a long time, young children eventually see themselves in a mirror from a first-person perspective. They, like adults, have learned what they look like and how they look to others.

When adults look in a mirror, they may ask themselves, *Am I pleased with what I see? Would I change what I see if I could?* These questions are often directed at more than just the reflection staring back from the mirror—they are also directed at the person beyond the mirror—at the individual self.

In this chapter we look at the impact of self-concept, self-esteem, and self-monitoring on our ability to present ourselves; we also observe how these three aspects of self affect our ability to communicate confidently with others in a variety of circumstances and settings.

Self-Concept

2.1 *Describe your self-concept and how it influences the way you communicate.*

Your self-concept comprises the beliefs you have about yourself. It answers two simple questions: "Who are you?" and "What makes you *you*?" Not only do characteristics such as your age, ethnicity, race, religion, and gender help define who you are ("I am a thirty-year-old, African American, Catholic female"), so do your life experiences, attitudes, and personality traits ("I had life-threatening allergies as a child, have strong feelings about my religion, and enjoy interacting with all sorts of people").

You are always changing or *becoming*. As you change, so does your self-concept. A physically awkward child may grow into a confident and graceful dancer. A middle school student with poor grades and grammar may become a celebrated author.

Where does your self-concept come from? How did you move beyond a lack of self-awareness to a unique sense of self and identity? Although many factors influence the development of self-concept, the following factors are among the most

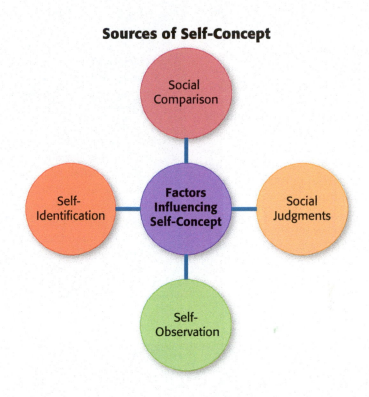

Sources of Self-Concept

- Social Comparison
- Self-Identification
- Factors Influencing Self-Concept
- Social Judgments
- Self-Observation

significant: social comparison, social judgments, self-observation, and self-identification.

Social Comparison

We naturally compare ourselves to others, and when we do, we find ourselves asking, *How do I measure up to other people? Am I smart, funny, and attractive?* You may also wonder whether you are more or less talkative, more or less coordinated, more likely to become angry or less likely to lose your temper. Your answers to these questions influence the way you see yourself.

Social comparison describes how you measure up or judge yourself in comparison to others in your reference groups.[4] **Reference groups** are the groups of people with whom you primarily associate. For example, when you were in high school, you

> **❝** Of all the judgments we pass in life, none is as important as the ones we pass on ourselves. **❞**
> Nathaniel Branden[3]

might have belonged to the popular or elite set, the brainy or geeky group, the artistic or athletic crowd. How did this membership affect your self-concept and the way you saw yourself? What impact did it have on your interactions with others? Such memberships do not go away, but they can change. For example, you may now belong to a social group, campus club, work team, religious fellowship, civic association, or profession staff. Whatever your current reference groups may be, they impact the development and maintenance of your self-concept.

Commercials and advertisements use social comparison to appeal to our desire for a positive self-concept. If you drive *this* car, you'll be popular, rich, and famous—just like the person in the ad. If you use *this* facial cream,

you'll have beautiful skin—just like this model or that movie star. We all compare ourselves to others in terms of our abilities, attitudes, attractiveness, and behaviors: "I'm not as popular as my best friends" and "I got the highest score on the exam."

Social Judgments

Social judgments reflect your interpretation of how people react to you verbally and nonverbally as a powerful determinant of your self-concept. If we grow up being told we are stupid, lazy, ugly, or clumsy we will absorb these perceptions and they will become part of our self-concepts. Thus, we are more likely to think of ourselves as intelligent if a teacher or parent praises our work. We are more likely to think of ourselves as attractive if another person admires the way we look or flatters us with compliments.

How We Make Ourselves Look Good

In order to maintain a positive self-concept, we tend to:

- attribute successes to our own abilities and blame our failures on external factors.
- view facts depicting us unfavorably as flawed.
- forget negative feedback and remember positive feedback.
- compare ourselves to others who make us look good.
- overestimate how many people share our opinions and underestimate how many people share our abilities.
- believe our good traits are unusual while our faults are common.

Self-Concept Continuum
RATE YOURSELF

Attractive	⟵⟶	Unattractive
Respected	⟵⟶	Not respected
Successful	⟵⟶	Unsuccessful
Confident	⟵⟶	Anxious
Good	⟵⟶	Bad
Intelligent	⟵⟶	Unintelligent
Humorous	⟵⟶	Humorless

In addition to how the significant people in our lives judge us, society judges us. Public rewards and recognition influence self-concept—they may come in the form of an academic honor, employee-of-the-month award, job promotion, community-service prize, or a blue ribbon for individual achievement. Such recognition, accompanied by praise and words of encouragement, can boost your self-concept. Unfortunately, the opposite is also true: How would you feel about yourself if you never received positive feedback?

Self-Observation

Self-observation describes the process of interpreting your actual performance (how you look and act) and your behavior (how well you do something) as a basis for your self-concept.[5] If you repeatedly succeed at something, you are likely to evaluate your performance in that area positively. For example, if you were an "A" student in high school, you probably expect to be an "A," or at least a good student in college. Thus, you may be disappointed or distressed if you receive a low grade, and as a result, doubt your academic and intellectual abilities.

We also pay a lot of attention to our appearance and physical abilities. We search for what we consider the ideal—for example, fashion models, movie stars, and professional athletes. When judging how we see ourselves compared to such figures, we have chosen an almost impossible ideal.

Self-Identification

I'm a twenty-five-year-old, single woman who was born in India, graduated from a state college, work as a third-grade teacher in Atlanta, Georgia, and teach English-as-a-second language in my spare time. Such is one woman's description of herself. How would you describe yourself? Regardless of whether you are a third-grade teacher or the person reading this page, **self-identification** is the way in which your self-concept reflects your cultural affiliations, the various roles you assume, and your experiences.

Who would you be if you could not remember your parents or childhood playmates, your successes and failures, the places you lived, the schools you attended, the books you read, and the teams you played for?

Intercultural communication scholar Min-Sun Kim explains that cultures have "different ways of being, and different ways of knowing, feeling, and acting."[6] For example, Western cultures emphasize the value of independence and self-reliance. Most Asian cultures emphasize the value of group membership; the "self" generally is not perceived outside its relationship to the "other." In Chapter 3, "Adapting to Others," we focus on how our personal characteristics and culture shape who we are and how we communicate.

Partly what defines us are our **roles**, the patterns of behaviors we adopt that are associated with an expected function in a specific context or relationship. When you shift roles, your behavior often changes. For example, how do your public roles (student, teacher, mechanic, nurse, manager, police officer, musician) determine your self-view? How do your private roles (child, parent, spouse, lover, best friend) shape your self-concept? Not surprisingly, you learn how to behave in a role largely by modeling others in that role. For instance (and for better or worse) we learn the parenting role from our own parents.

Without past experiences and personal memories, you would have little basis for a coherent self-concept. For instance, vivid memories of traumatic events—the death of a loved one, a serious automobile accident, a life-threatening illness, or an event of greater human impact, such as the 9/11 attacks—influence your identity and determine how you interpret and react to personal circumstances and current events. Who would you be if you could not remember the past experiences that define you?[7]

Creating, Deceiving, and Revealing Yourself Online

Researchers disagree about whether online communication harms or promotes the development of a self-concept. Whereas the anonymous nature of the Internet may encourage intimate self-disclosure in close relationships, it also has the potential for negative outcomes such as deception and flaming.[8] Some researchers go so far as to claim that the endless number of social media communities with constantly changing contexts, significant others, and reference groups make it difficult for anyone to develop a stable self-identity.[9] Others argue that social media provide valuable opportunities to experiment with identities. For example, shy teenagers may feel more confident and comfortable communicating online than in face-to-face interactions. As they "try on" different selves online, positive feedback from virtual others can help them develop a stronger self-concept and a healthier self-esteem.[10]

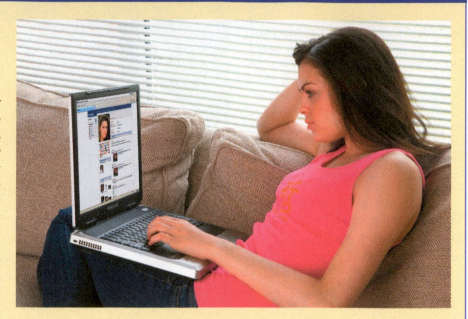

Unfortunately, the absence of *real*, face-to-face interactions makes it easier to distort aspects of your self, as well as to fabricate a false identity. A study of personal characteristics described by participants in online dating services uncovered gender-based misrepresentations. Men were more likely to misrepresent their personal assets (job status, income, intelligence, education). Women were more likely to misrepresent their weight as lower; men were more likely to misrepresent their age as older and their height as taller.[11] Moreover, as many as one-third of online photographs were not accurate. Women were more likely to be older than they were portrayed in their photographs

and their photographs were more likely to be retouched or taken by professional photographers.[12]

A study in Israel found that "frequent [Internet] users deceive online more than infrequent users, young users more than old, and competent users more than non-competent." Interestingly and perhaps most distressingly, "Most people felt a sense of enjoyment while engaging in online deception."[13]

In the world of online dating, a lot of people create an ideal self that has little in common with their real self. On the other hand, being truthful does have its disadvantages. One study found, "online daters often regret it when they do tell the truth, feeling that too much honesty, especially about negative attributes, creates a bad impression."[14] Another study reports that men claiming incomes above $250,000 got 151 percent more replies than men claiming incomes less than $50,000. Other studies have found that women list their age as younger.[15]

Psychologist, Robert Epstein, a writer for *Scientific American Mind*, offers a set of

guidelines for anyone using the Internet to find a romantic partner. Here are three good suggestions:

- Initially, provide vague information about yourself. People will fill in the missing details in a way that will suit their own interests and desires.
- Don't rely on online matching sites. Their methods and results have not been "scientifically validated" or predictive of romantic bliss.
- Be honest. A little exaggeration is expected, but outright lies will backfire.[16]

When you share aspects of yourself online—be they opinions, personal feelings, photos, or the story of your wild summer vacation—remember that once you've hit the submit or send button, your communication is irreversible. Always ask yourself, "Can this message embarrass or hurt me now or in the future? Will it hurt someone else? Would I want my family or a potential employer to read or see this posting?"

Self-Esteem

2.2 *Discuss the major factors that contribute to a person's self-esteem.*

Now that you know something about your self-concept, how do you *feel* about yourself? Are you satisfied, discouraged, delighted, optimistic, or troubled? **Self-esteem** represents your judgments about yourself. Nathaniel Branden puts it this way: "Self-esteem is the reputation we acquire with ourselves."[17] Not surprisingly, your personal beliefs and customary behaviors influence your level of self-esteem.

Studies affirm that people with high self-esteem are significantly happier than people with low self-esteem. They are also less likely to be depressed. One especially compelling study surveyed more than 13,000 college students. High self-esteem emerged as the strongest factor in overall life satisfaction.[18]

Building Blocks of Self-Esteem

Enhancing your self-esteem requires a great deal of thought about yourself and the way you interact with others. The following approaches can help boost your self-esteem as long as you keep in mind that these practices require persistence, honesty, and effort.

Building Your Self-Esteem

- Practice self-assertiveness.
- Practice personal integrity.
- Practice self-talk.

Practice Self-Assertiveness (But Respect the Needs of Others) **Self-assertiveness** describes your willingness and ability to stand up for yourself in appropriate ways in order to satisfy your needs and pursue your goals. Being assertive, however, is not the same as being aggressive or hostile. Don't stand in the way of others when you stand up for yourself.[19]

Some of us might look at assertive people and say, "It's easy for her to be self-assertive, she has good self-esteem."[20] But, it is better to think of this observation in the reverse. The more skilled and confident she is at standing up for her needs, rights, beliefs, and values, the more positive she becomes about herself. In Chapter 7, "Understanding Interpersonal Relationships," we devote a major section to strategies that can help you assert yourself and also respect the rights and needs of others.

Practice Personal Integrity (But Consider Different Perspectives) **Personal Integrity** means behaving in ways that are consistent with your values and beliefs. Go beyond thoughts about what you *should* do; instead, actually do "the right thing." At the same time, remember the right thing for you may not be "the right thing" for someone else. Make sure your actions do not offend or hurt others.[21]

How would you end the following sentence: if I want people to trust me, I _____. If you complete the sentence with a statement such as "I keep the promises I make" or "I practice what I preach" you should have a high level and well deserved sense of self-esteem—you uphold and demonstrate commendable values and beliefs.[22]

Practice Positive Self-Talk (But Listen to Others) **Self-talk** represents the silent statements you make to yourself about yourself. One way to

"I think the answers to a lot of issues come from self-esteem. Young girls and women have to believe they are worth something more, they have to see opportunities for themselves beyond a relationship or beyond what's right there in front of them."

Michelle Obama

self-esteem

Practicing Positive Self-Talk

Read the following example of negative self-talk and its corresponding example of positive self-talk. With your self in mind, provide two examples of negative self-talk and corresponding examples of positive self-talk. Then assess how likely it is you use negative and positive self-talk in the silent statements you make to yourself about yourself.

Negative Self-Talk	Positive Self-Talk
Example: I won't be able to work as quickly as the other members.	Example: I'll do my best, but also ask for help from others if I need it.
Your Example:_____	Your Example:_____
Your Example:_____	Your Example:_____

enhance your self-esteem is to replace negative, self-defeating statements with more positive and productive statements. For example, rather than saying, "I can't handle this; it's impossible!" change the statement into a question such as, "*How* can I handle this?" Not only does this sound more hopeful, it may help you find new possibilities and solutions.[24]

Barriers to Self-Esteem

If, as research claims, people with high self-esteem are significantly happier and more successful than people with low self-esteem, you should probably do everything you can to build your self-esteem. Unfortunately, this task is neither easy nor foolproof.

Imagine you want to build a house. You think you have the right materials and believe you know how to do it. However, if all you have is straw, rather than lumber or bricks, your house may collapse in a gust of wind. If you don't have the knowledge or skills to build a house correctly, it may fall apart or tumble down.

The same is true of building your self-esteem. Unless you are willing to recognize and accept your strengths and weaknesses as part of who you are, your self-esteem may be distorted. Unless you are willing to take responsibility for what you do, how happy you are, and how you achieve your

goals, you may blame everyone but yourself for failures.

Beware of Self-Distortions Not surprisingly, you (and everyone else) have a tendency to distort what happens to you and how you feel about a variety of experiences. All of us tend to remember the past as if it were a drama in which you were the leading player.[25] When asked about high school, many people describe it as "terrible" or "wonderful" when they really mean it *seemed* terrible or wonderful to *them*. When we tell stories about the past, we cast ourselves at the center of action rather than as bit players or observers.

At the same time, your mind tries to protect you from potentially hurtful or threatening feedback from others. These ego-defense mechanisms can lead us into forming a distorted self-image:[26] "What's the big deal about being late to a meeting? She's just obsessed with time and took it out on me. It's no big deal."[27]

High self-esteem will not solve all your personal problems, nor will it automatically improve your ability to communicate effectively and ethically. Educators have learned this lesson, much to the detriment of students. For example, some well-meaning school systems have tried to raise the self-esteem of disadvantaged and failing students by passing them to the next grade. Unfortunately, such

efforts have had no positive effects and demonstrated "artificially boosting self-esteem may lower subsequent academic performance."[28]

Beware of Self-Fulfilling Prophecies A prophecy is a prediction. A **self-fulfilling prophecy** is "an impression formation process in which an initial impression elicits behavior . . . that conforms to the impression."[29] More simply, it is a self-prediction you make that you cause to happen or become true. For example, if girls are told that boys do better in mathematics, they may believe it and stop trying to succeed. As a result, they won't do as well in math as boys, just as predicted.

In one study, researchers administered a math test to different groups of women. Before taking the test, one group of women was told that men and women do math equally well. Another group was told that there is a genetic difference in math ability that explains why women are not as good at math as men. The women in the first group got nearly twice as many right answers as those in the second group. The researchers concluded that people tend to accept genetic explanations as powerful and permanent, which can lead to self-fulfilling prophecies.[30]

In order to minimize the chances of falling into the self-fulfilling prophecy trap, try to answer the following questions:

- What predictions do you make about your own behavior and the responses of others?
- Why do you make these predictions? Are they justified?
- Are you doing anything to elicit the predicted responses?

- What alternative behaviors could help you avoid fulfilling these prophesies?

In her commencement address at Mount Holyoke College, the then president of Ireland, Mary McAleese, said, "When I was in my mid-teens, I announced at home that I had decided to become a lawyer. The first words I heard in response were, 'You can't because you are a woman.'"[31] President McAleese did not let these words and her parents' beliefs become a self-fulfilling prophecy.

Self-Presentation

2.3 *Examine the role of self-monitoring as a prerequisite for effective self-presentation.*

You know from experience that first impressions count. If you don't make a good impression on a first date, it may be your last with that person. Someone you meet on an airplane may eventually offer you a job. If you get off to a good start with someone sitting next to you in class, you may become close friends. And, once you've made a good initial impression on someone, your subsequent behavior can reinforce and maintain that impression or can weaken and even reverse it.

> You don't get a second chance to make a first impression

Self-presentation represents the strategies we use to shape and control the way other people see us—how they perceive, evaluate, and treat us.[32] Sociologist Erving Goffman claims that we assume a social identity that others help us to maintain.[33] Your ability to manage these impressions contributes to people's perceptions of you in social interactions as well as their interpretations of your ability to gain influence, power, sympathy, or approval. It even influences how you see yourself.

Psychologists Mark Leary and Robin Kowalski note that we do this all the time. We "spend billions of dollars on diets, cosmetics, and plastic surgery—all intended to make us more attractive to others. Political candidates are packaged for public consumption." Parents urge children to make a good impression on their neighbors, teachers, and relatives,

and "people become paralyzed at the prospect of speaking or performing in public because they are worried about the audience evaluation of them."[34]

So how do you make a good impression when you present yourself to others? We recommend two strategies: self-monitoring and impression management.

Self-Monitoring

The word *monitor* means to be aware of, to observe, to examine, and to analyze. Thus, **self-monitoring** describes your ability to observe and control how you express yourself verbally and nonverbally when interacting with others.[35] People who are skilled self-monitors adapt to others by appearing and speaking in a socially appropriate manner. High self-monitors can control their facial expressions and body movements, the content of their message, their tone of voice as well as when and how they express emotions.[36] In a sense, they take on the skills

of good actors who portray different roles in different plays. The goal of self-monitoring is to project an image that "impresses others and receives positive feedback."[37]

At first, self-monitoring may seem difficult. The truth is, we monitor ourselves all the time. We count calories to monitor how much food we eat. We check the speedometer on the car to make sure we're not speeding.[38] We look around to make sure we're using the right fork at a formal dinner. Think of self-monitoring as a communication GPS—it tells you when you've gone too far or too long, when you've made a mistake or a wrong turn, when there are rough spots around the corner, and when there's nothing but smooth sailing ahead. By being sensitive to your internal GPS, you can adjust the way you communicate based on what it tells you about your behavior and when it offers positive and negative feedback.

Know Thy Self

Are You an Effective Self-Monitor?

High self-monitors generally answer *yes* to the following questions. Read each question and answer each with *Yes*, *Sometimes*, or *No*. What kind of self-monitor are you?

1. Can you usually tell if you've made a good or bad impression on someone else?
2. Can you modify your behavior and how you express your needs and opinions in different types of situations?
3. Can you accurately identify the emotions you are feeling when interacting with others?
4. Do you compliment others, but also present yourself in a positive light.
5. Are you willing to express your opinions even if you know others will disagree?

Effective self-monitoring helps you realize, "This is anger I'm feeling." It gives you the opportunity to modify or control anger rather than allowing it to hijack your mind and body. Self-monitoring also helps you differentiate emotional responses: love versus lust, disappointment versus depression, and anxiety versus excitement. People who are *high self-monitors* constantly watch other people, what they do, and how they respond to the behavior of others. They are also self-aware, like to "look good," and usually adapt well to differing social situations. On the other hand, *low self-monitors* are often oblivious to how others see them and may "march to their own, different drum."[39]

Impression Management

Impression management is the process we use when trying to influence the images that other people have of us.[40] Here we present five impression management strategies—ingratiation, self-promotion, exemplification, supplication, and intimidation. Each one describes a communicator's desired goal and the reactions and emotions sought in others.[41]

Ingratiation (But Not Phony Flattery) The most common impression management strategy is

ingratiation; the goal of ingratiation is to be liked by others. Ingratiation skills include complimenting others, doing another person a favor, and comforting someone. Complimenting someone with whom you disagree can ease tensions and reopen communication channels. Insincere, phony flattery,

Beyonce and Lady Gaga have created unique public images that differ from one another. What is your overall impression of each pop star?

however, has the potential to damage rather than enhance your image and reputation. Whereas honest flattery ingratiates you with others, phony flattery can have the opposite effect.

Self-Promotion (But Not Bragging) If you want to be seen as competent, you may use **self-promotion**. When you self-promote, you attempt to earn the respect of others. Announcing, "I'm a fast writer" can earn you a place on an important work team that has short-deadline projects and reports. At the same time, *overstated self-promotion*—exaggerating your achievements and skills in order to impress others—may create a negative impression that is difficult to change. And if your actual performance does not live up to your self-promotion, you can create a long-lasting negative impression. No one likes a braggart, so promote yourself honestly and appropriately.

Exemplification (But Not Just in Public) When you hold yourself up as a good example or a model of noteworthy behavior, you are practicing **exemplification**. The goal is to be seen as ethical and responsible. But make sure you practice what you preach. If you claim it's wrong to pirate DVDs, but you photocopy entire books rather than buy them, no one will believe your claims about honesty and moral values. Don't declare you're on a strict diet and then get caught with your hand in the cookie jar.

Supplication (But Not Endless Pleading) **Supplication** describes a humble request or an appeal for help. As a supplicant, you're seeking compassion from others. Appropriate supplication causes other people to feel resourceful and valued. But don't rely on supplication to get someone else to do your work or to earn eternal love and respect; if you cry out for help when you have the resources to handle something on your own, you will soon be ignored and not taken seriously. In other words, don't cry "wolf" unless the wolf is knocking on your door.

Intimidation (But Not Bullying) The goal of **intimidation** is to provoke fear. In order to be seen as powerful, an intimidating person demonstrates a willingness and ability to cause personal harm. Intimidation strategies involve threats to subdue or control others. "If you speak to me that way again, I will file a formal grievance against you." We do not recommend using intimidation in most communication situations. In some instances, however, you may need to protect yourself or to establish your authority and willingness to use power. If others are taking advantage of you, you may need to show them that you won't take it anymore—that you won't be intimidated.

Perception

2.4 *Identify how selection, organization, and interpretation shape perceptions.*

Why does one person experience great satisfaction in a job while another person in the same job dreads it? Why do you find a speech inspiring while another person finds it offensive? The answer to these questions lies in one word: *perception*. Imagine that you and a colleague are chatting after a meeting. You say, "That was a good session. We got through all the issues and ended early." Your friend responds with, "Are you kidding? Didn't you notice that Hector rushed us through the agenda to avoid any serious discussion or disagreement?" What happened here? You both attended the same meeting, but each of you perceived the experience quite differently.

From a communication point of view, we define **perception** as the process through which you select, organize, and interpret sensory stimuli in the world around you. The accuracy of your perceptions determines how well you interpret and evaluate experiences and the people you encounter. At the same time, once you reach a conclusion, it's often difficult to change your perception.

Generally, we trust our perceptions and treat them as accurate and reliable. Even though you run the risk of drawing incorrect conclusions, you would be lost in a confusing world without your perceptions. Not only does perception help you make sense out of other people's behavior, but it also helps you decide what you will say or do. For example, suppose you notice that your boss keeps track of employees who arrive late and leave early, and that she rarely grants these employees the special privileges given to those who put in full workdays. These perceptions tell you that it is a good idea to arrive early and stay late if you want a positive evaluation or a future promotion.

Popular sayings such as, "Seeing is believing," "I call it as I see it," or "I saw it with my own eyes" can lead to false perceptions. As shown in the illustration of the old and young woman to the right, we may be fooled by what we see. Police officers know very well that three witnesses to a traffic accident may provide three very different descriptions of the cars involved, the estimated speed

Old Woman or Young Woman? What you see depends on how your eyes select graphic details, how you organize that information, and how you interpret the results.

When Eyewitnesses Fail to See

The ways in which we select, organize, and interpret what our senses supposedly tell us can have dire consequences. In 2011, the New Jersey Supreme Court issued new rules for using eyewitness testimony given the "troubling lack of reliability in eyewitness identifications." Now, it will be easier for defendants to challenge eyewitness evidence in criminal cases.[43]

As many experienced judges, prosecutors, and defense lawyers know, eyewitness testimony has put innocent defendants in jail and allowed guilty criminals to go free. "Every year, more than 75,000 eyewitnesses identify suspects in criminal investigations. Those identifications are wrong about a third of the time."[44] In his book, *Convicting the Innocent*, law professor Brandon Garrett reports that of the first 250 DNA cases where subsequent DNA evidence found a convicted criminal *not* guilty, 190 of those convictions were based on eyewitness testimony.[45] An overwhelming number of recent studies conclude, "It is perilous to base a conviction on witnesses' identification of a stranger." In a friend-of-the court brief, the American Psychological Association points out that jury members tend to "over believe" the testimony of eyewitnesses.[46]

A tragic and now infamous legal case highlights the risks in relying on eyewitness perceptions. On February 26, 2012, two witnesses to a murder gave the following descriptions to investigators of the Florida Department of Law Enforcement:

> From Witness 6: "There was a black man, with a black hoodie on top of either a white guy or . . . a Hispanic guy with a red sweatshirt on the ground yelling 'help.'"

> From Witness 3: "I just saw this white shirt on top. I tried to stay away and was scared."

These two observers were witnesses in the 2012 Trayvon Martin murder case in Sanford, Florida, in which George Zimmerman (an armed, twenty-eight-year-old multiracial Latino American neighborhood watch coordinator) was accused of shooting and killing Trayvon Martin (an unarmed, black seventeen-year-old teenager).[47]

Barbara Tverksy, a psychology professor at Columbia University, explains we often see things differently than they really are. "At the time something happens, we are trying to make sense of it. I'm not focusing on someone's shirt color or heights. I'm focusing on what's happening and trying to make sense of what's going on." After such events, we try to process what we saw and heard—and that can lead to inaccuracies. "People are more influenced by what they *think* must have happened" rather than what actually happened.[48]

The fatal shooting of Trayvon Martin by George Zimmerman took place on the night of February 26, 2012, in Sanford, Florida.

they were traveling, and the physical characteristics of the drivers. In fact, eyewitness testimony, although persuasive, is often the least reliable form of courtroom evidence.

Selection

You use your senses (sight, sound, taste, smell, and touch) to notice and choose from the many stimuli around you. Your needs, wants, interests, moods, and memories largely determine which stimuli you will select. For example, when your eyes and ears detect something familiar or potentially interesting as you flip through television channels, you stop. Or you may be daydreaming in class, but when your professor says, "The following chapters will be covered on the next test," you find yourself paying full attention again.

The selection process can distort your perceptions in four ways. Although all of us engage in these practices, astute communicators are aware of how selective exposure, selective attention, selective interpretation, and selective recall shape their perceptions.[49]

The Selective Processes
- Selective Exposure
- Selective Attention
- Selective Interpretation
- Selective Recall

Selective Exposure Our tendency to only expose ourselves to messages that are consistent with what we already believe is called **selective exposure**. Some researchers describe selective exposure as a defense mechanism that protects us from messages that threaten our self-concept and self-esteem. Others view selective exposure as a routine process for coping with enormous amounts of information that bombard us every day.[50] As Nate Silver writes in *The Signal and the Noise*, there is so much information available to us, we take shortcuts by "selectively, picking out the parts we like and ignoring the remainder."[51]

Consider the numerous news outlets available to you: Fox News, MSNBC, CNN, *Slate*, *The Huffington Post*, NPR, or one of the traditional networks. Do you rely on just one of these news sources? Do you read the news in just print or online form? Every news source offers different perspectives about issues that affect our lives and the lives of others, and according to selective exposure, we prefer the ones whose perspectives best match ours. In doing so, we exclude other sources that would expose us to different viewpoints, features, stories, music, and so forth.

Selective exposure also guides whom you meet and whom you consider a friend. Are most of your friends the same race, ethnicity, age, and religion as you are? Do they live in similar neighborhoods and live in comparable economic circumstances? Have you travelled abroad and interacted with the people who live in those countries? The diversity of other people with whom you do or do not associate will have bearing upon your self-concept, your self-esteem, your ability to present yourself to others, and most importantly, your attitudes, beliefs, and values.

Selective Attention When we pay attention to messages that are consistent with what we already believe, we engage in **selective attention**. Even if you are exposed to a wide variety of stimuli, you may only pay attention to information you like and agree with. For example, you may pay more attention to news about the candidate you support than the candidate you oppose. You may turn up the volume when you hear the kind of music you like. However, you may turn down the volume or ignore the music you do not like. Because we often tune out what we don't like or agree with, our perceptions may become distorted and difficult to change—even in the face of valid facts and expert opinion.

Selective Interpretation When we alter the meaning of messages so they become consistent with what we already believe, we engage in **selective interpretation**. Thus, even if you expose yourself to a wide variety of messages and do your best to pay attention to them, you may distort their meaning and importance to match your preexisting interests, needs, opinions, beliefs, and values. For example if you attend the religious service of a faith other than yours or one you do not believe in, you may find yourself criticizing, refuting, or even condemning the sermon, despite the fact that the two faiths may share many common beliefs. If a highly qualified person you don't like applies for a job, will you be able to judge that person's application fairly? If a less qualified person you like applies for a job, will you make excuses for that person's second-rate qualifications?

And in the political arena, we all-too-often have a "knee-jerk willingness to attribute irredeemable stupidity and bad motives to opponents . . . [and] pseudo-information is trusted when it clicks neatly into our jigsaw puzzle of preconceptions."[52]

Thus, when we add up the results of selective exposure, selective attention, and selective interpretation, we may be "making allies with those who have made the same choices and enemies of the rest."[53]

Selective Recall When you remember positive and negative messages and experiences in a way that is consistent with what you already believe about yourself and your encounters with others, you are engaging in **selective recall**. Even if you are the one in a billion people who does not engage in selective exposure, attention, or perception, you may fall prey to selective recall. Very often, selective recall prevents us from seeing past experiences realistically,

Is this woman a college student? An instructor? A store clerk? An attorney? A business executive?

such as people who describe their first jobs as either "terrible" or "wonderful." The partners in a bitter break-up may describe nothing but horrible times during the relationship even though their families and friends remember their many years as a loving couple. We tend to remember events and people in a way that matches our ideal selves as expressed in our self-concepts and our level of self-esteem.

Organization

Suppose you see a middle-aged woman wearing a suit walking across campus. You conclude that she is a professor. You also observe a young man entering a classroom wearing a school sweatshirt and carrying a backpack that appears to be loaded with books. You assume that he is a student. You took the information, or stimuli, you observed and categorized it into "professor" and "student." What these two scenarios demonstrate is how *context* influences the way you organize information. For example, you could conclude that a woman in a suit on campus is a professor, but in a different context, you might conclude that she is a business executive. You may conclude that a young man wearing a school sweatshirt and carrying books on campus is a student, but backstage in a theater, you may decide that he is an actor or stagehand.

Perceptual Organization Principles[54]

The Principle	Example
The Proximity Principle: We tend to perceive objects, events, and people as belonging together when they are physically close to one another.[55]	A restaurant host may assume that two people waiting in line to be seated are together. "Two for lunch?"
The Similarity Principle: We tend to perceive elements or people as part of a group if their characteristics are similar.	If your friend from Texas likes country music, you may assume that someone else from Texas also likes country music.
The Closure Principle: We tend to fill in missing elements to form a more complete impression of an object, person, or event.	Do you see four straight lines or a box?
The Simplicity Principle: We tend to organize information in a way that provides the simplest interpretation.	If the sidewalk is wet, we may assume it rained rather than there being a leak in a nearby hose or pipe beneath the sidewalk.

Four organizational principles for categorizing perceptual information.

You sort and arrange the sensory stimuli you select into useful categories based on your knowledge and past experiences with similar stimuli. The above table describes four principles that influence how you organize or categorize perceptual information.

Interpretation

Many factors influence your interpretation of the stimuli you select and organize. Suppose a friend asks you to volunteer your time over the weekend to help build a house for Habitat for Humanity. The following factors may influence your interpretation and reaction to your friend's request:

- *Past experiences.* After volunteering at a soup kitchen last year, you felt really good about yourself.

COMMUNICATION&CULTURE

EAST IS EAST AND WEST IS WEST

The mental process of perception is the same across cultures. Everyone selects, organizes, and interprets stimuli. However, psychologist Richard Nisbett argues that each culture can "literally experience the world in very different ways."[56] Look, for example, at the three objects depicted on your right. Which two objects would you pair together?

People from Western cultures are more likely to put the chicken and cow together because they are both animals. East Asians, however, are more likely to pair the cow and the grass because cows eat grass. According to Nisbett, East Asians perceive the world in terms of relationships, whereas Westerners are inclined to see objects that can be grouped into categories. As Chapter 3, "Adapting to Others," explains, many cultures—and East Asian cultures in

particular—are more sensitive to the context in which communication takes place. As Rudyard Kipling wrote in *The Ballad of East and West*, "Oh, East is East, and West is West, and never the twain shall meet."

Your culture influences what you notice, how you organize that information, and how you interpret information and situations.

Perception-Checking Guidelines
The Martha and George Dilemma

Read the following scenario carefully. Then examine how the perception-checking guidelines and application examples could help a communicator respond fairly and appropriately to this particular situation. Also note that the perception-checking guidelines reflect the seven key competencies of effective communication presented in Chapter 1, "Human Communication."

Your best friend, Martha, has lived with George for three years. Everyone had been expecting them to get married, so you were shocked when Martha told you they'd broken up. Martha explained that she could no longer live with a man who made fun of her "menial" job as a receptionist, comparing it unfavorably to his as a senior marketing director. When he insisted that he control all their finances and refused to tell her how he was spending their money, she couldn't take it anymore and left him. Yesterday, you learned that George has been hired as a consultant to develop a marketing plan for your office. Whether you like him or not, you will have to work with him for the next four weeks.

Communication Elements	Perception-Checking Guidelines	Applying Perception-Checking Guidelines
1 SELF	How could factors such as your personal biases, level of self-awareness, cultural background, or the influence of others affect your perceptions?	How do my feelings about Martha, my biases, my past experiences with George, and my gender affect my perceptions of their breakup and George's character?
2 OTHERS	Do you perceive a situation the same way others do? If not, how can you adapt to their perceptions?	Although I was shocked at George's behavior, I know there are usually two sides to every story.
3 PURPOSE	How does the way you select, organize, and interpret information affect the way you communicate?	When I work with George, I may pay more attention to his mistakes or suggestions I don't like rather than to the job we need to do. I need to be aware of and guard against such assumptions and behavior.
4 CONTEXT	How could the psychological, logistical, and interactional communication context affect your perceptions and the perception of others?	In the office environment, I will do my best to put aside my feelings about George and work with him to get the job done in a professional way.
5 CONTENT	How could your perceptions affect the content you choose for a message?	I won't make comments about Martha. Certainly, I need to avoid commenting about menial jobs, receptionists, and personal finances.
6 STRUCTURE	How could your perceptions affect the way you organize ideas and information in a message?	I will put the job first, and if George begins talking about Martha, I will tell him that discussing personal matters is inappropriate at work.
7 EXPRESSION	How could your perceptions affect the way you express your messages?	I will try to avoid engaging in negative nonverbal behavior such as frowning, avoiding eye contact, or putting more distance between us.

- *Knowledge.* You spent a summer working as a house painter and have a useful skill to contribute.
- *Expectations.* It sounds like fun, and you might meet some interesting people.
- *Attitudes.* You believe that volunteering in the community is important.
- *Relational involvement.* This work is really important to your friend.

These same factors may also lead to inaccurate perceptions. For example, suppose you once volunteered at a homeless shelter and had a terrible experience. The coordinator assigned you the task of washing the sheets and towels every morning and cleaning the bathrooms. As a result, you didn't use your counseling skills and rarely talked to a homeless person. Clearly, your previous experience may have created an unfair or erroneous interpretation and perception of volunteer work.

Perception Checking

Psychologists Richard Block and Harold Yuker point out, "Perception often is a poor representation of reality. Yet it is important to recognize that a person's behavior is controlled less by what is actually true, than what the person believes is true. Perceptions may be more important than reality in determining behavior!"[57]

You can improve the accuracy of your perceptions by pausing to check the basis of your conclusions. **Perception checking** involves noticing and analyzing how you select, organize, and interpret sensory stimuli, whether you consider alternative interpretations, and whether you try to verify your perceptions with others.[58] Perception checking is valuable in everyday life because it helps you decode messages more accurately, reduce the likelihood of misunderstanding or conflict, and respond fairly and appropriately to others.

ETHICAL COMMUNICATION

The Golden Rule Does Not Always Apply

The Golden Rule, "Do to others what you would have them do to you," comes from the New Testament (Matthew 7:12).[59] However, what *you* would do may not necessarily be what another person wants you to do. In his *Maxims for Revolutionists*, playwright George Bernard Shaw wrote, "The golden rule is that there are no golden rules. . . . Do not do unto others as you would that they should do unto you. Their tastes may not be the same."[60] If you wish to follow the Golden Rule, keep in mind these two cautions:

- Consider how another person may perceive the situation differently than you do.
- Look for solutions that would be appropriate and fair from someone else's point of view or culture.

Communication Apprehension and Confidence

2.5 *Practice appropriate strategies and skills to enhance your communication confidence.*

Your self-concept and level of self-confidence directly influence how effectively you communicate.[61] Most of us see ourselves as bright and hardworking. At the same time, all of us have occasional doubts and insecurities. If you lack confidence, you are less likely to share what you know or voice your opinions. On the other hand, when you feel good about yourself, you can engage in a conversation with ease, defend your ideas in a group, and give successful presentations.

Most people experience some anxiety when they are in an important communication situation. In fact, that "keyed-up" feeling is a positive and normal reaction and demonstrates that you care about what you have to say.

Communication Apprehension

The anxiety you may experience when speaking to others is referred to by many names: *speaking anxiety*, *podium panic*, and *stage fright*. We prefer the broader phrase **communication apprehension** which is "an individual's level of fear or anxiety associated with either real or anticipated communication with another person or persons."[62] It occurs in a variety of communication contexts, such as group discussions, meetings, interpersonal conversations, public speaking, and job interviews.

Communication apprehension is not just "in your head"; it is a type of stress that manifests in real physiological responses. Physical reactions such as sweaty palms, perspiring, a fast pulse, shallow breathing, cold extremities, flushed skin, nausea, trembling hands, quivering legs, or "butterflies" in the stomach are the body's response to the release of hormones such as adrenaline.[63]

Communication Apprehension

Since the early 1970s, the study of communication apprehension has been a major research focus in the communication discipline. As communication scholar James C. McCroskey wrote, "It permeates every facet of an individual's life," including major decisions such as career and housing choices, as well as affecting the quality of our communication behavior in a variety of interpersonal, small group, social, educational, work, and public settings.[64]

In the beginning, when McCroskey began studying communication apprehension, he believed that it was a "learned trait, one that is conditioned through reinforcements of the child's communication behavior."[65] More recently, he claimed that a person's environment or situation has only a small effect on that person's level of anxiety. Rather communication apprehension is a personality trait, "An expression of principally inborn neurobiological functioning."[66]

Communication apprehension, concludes McCroskey, "can be reduced by a variety of methods and has already been so reduced for literally

thousands of individuals."[67] In the remainder of this chapter, we provide a deeper understanding of communication apprehension and a variety of methods for reducing its effects.

Communication Confidence

Always remember that in most cases, your anxiety is invisible. We can't see your pounding heart, upset stomach, cold hands, or worried thoughts. Most of us think we display more anxiety than listeners report noticing. However, the fact that your anxiety is often invisible to others does not make it feel any less real to you. Fortunately, there are a number of strategies to reduce your anxiety and help you become a more confident communicator.

> **Strategies for Building Communication Confidence**
> - Prepare
> - Relax, Rethink, Re-Envision
>   - Cognitive Restructuring
>   - Visualization
>   - Systematic Desensitization
> - Practice

Prepare Although you may not be able to predict unexpected situations or anticipate the nature of everyday conversations, you can prepare for many of the communication situations you encounter. For instance, you can prepare for a job interview or performance appraisal, a staff meeting or professional seminar, and a public speech or presentation. When you are prepared, you know a great deal about the ideas you wish to discuss, the others who will be involved, the context of the situation, the content and structure of your message, and how you will express yourself.

Relax, Rethink, Re-vision By learning to relax your body, you can reduce your level of communication apprehension. Consider a variety of meditation techniques or develop short, tension-reducing exercises (deep breathing, quick muscle tensing and relaxing drills) that you can use in the few minutes or seconds before you speak. However, physical relaxation is only half the battle; you also need to change the way you think about communication.[68]

When you have confident thoughts ("I know I can persuade this group to join the Animal Rescue League"), you begin to feel more confident. Three strategies can help you rethink your attitudes, visualize your message, and relax your body:

- **Cognitive restructuring** is a method for reducing anxiety by replacing negative, irrational thoughts with more realistic, positive self-talk. The next time you feel anxious, repeat any one of these positive statements: "My message is important," or "I am a well-prepared, skilled communicator," "I know more about this than the audience does," or "I've done this before, so I'm not going to be as nervous as I've been in the past."

- **Visualization** is a powerful method for building confidence, and it allows you to imagine what it would be like to communicate successfully. Find a quiet place, relax, and imagine yourself walking into the room with confidence and energy. Think about the smiles you'll receive as you talk, the heads nodding in agreement, and the look of interest in the eyes of your listeners. By visualizing yourself communicating effectively, you are mentally practicing the skills you need to succeed while also building a positive self-image.

Sources of COMMUNICATION APPREHENSION

The process of managing communication apprehension begins with recognizing why you feel anxious when speaking to an individual, group, or audience. Although everyone has personal reasons for nervousness, researchers have identified some of the key fears that underlie communication apprehension.[69] Which of these sources best describe your reasons for feeling anxious when engaging in communication or when anticipating communication with another person or persons?

FEAR OF FAILURE

Many researchers claim that the fear of a negative evaluation is the number one cause of communication anxiety.[70] When you focus your thoughts on the possibility of failure, you are more likely to fail. Try to shift your focus to the positive feedback you see from others—a nod, a smile, or an alert look. When you sense that a listener likes you and your message, you may gain the extra confidence you need.

FEAR OF OTHERS

Do you get nervous when interacting with people who have more status or power, education or experience, fame or popularity? Fear of others can be heightened when talking to a powerful person, an influential group, or a large audience. Usually, this fear is based on an exaggerated feeling of being different from or inferior to others. If you don't know much about the people around you, you are more likely to feel apprehensive. Learning more about your listeners can decrease your anxiety. You may have more in common with them than you realize.

FEAR OF BREAKING THE RULES

"Three strikes and you're out" works in baseball, and "What goes up must come down" makes sense in physics, but the rules of communication are not hard and fast and should not be treated as though they are enforceable laws. For example, novice speakers sometimes over-rehearse to the point of sounding robotic for fear of saying "uh" or "um" in a presentation. Good communicators learn not to "sweat the small stuff" and that, sometimes, "rules" should be bent or broken.

FEAR OF THE UNKNOWN

Most people fear the unknown. Performing an unfamiliar or unexpected role can transform a usually confident person into a tangle of nerves. If you are attending an event as an audience member and suddenly are called on to introduce a guest to the audience, you can become very unsettled. Similarly, most people feel stressed when interviewing for a job in an office they've never been to and with a person they hardly know.

FEAR OF THE SPOTLIGHT

Although a little attention may be flattering, being the center of attention makes many people nervous. Psychologist Peter Desberg puts it this way: "If you were performing as part of a choir, you'd probably feel much calmer than if you were singing a solo."[71] The more self-focused you are, the more nervous you become. This is especially true when giving a presentation to an audience. Try to stay focused on your purpose and message rather than allowing yourself to be distracted by the spotlight.

- **Systematic desensitization** is a relaxation and visualization technique developed by psychologist Joseph Wolpe to reduce the anxiety associated with stressful situations.[72] You start with deep muscle relaxation. In this relaxed state, you then imagine yourself in a variety of communication contexts ranging from very comfortable to highly stressful. By working to remain relaxed while visualizing various situations, you gradually associate communication with relaxation rather than nervousness.

Practice The best way to become good at something is to practice, regardless of whether it's cooking, serving a tennis ball, or communicating. You can practice wording a request or expressing an emotion to another person, answering questions in an interview, stating your position at a meeting, or making a presentation to an audience.

In addition to enhancing your confidence, practice stimulates your brain in positive ways. As Daniel Goleman notes in *Social Intelligence*, "Simulating an act is, in the brain, the same as performing it."[73] Practicing

Journalist Candy Crowley received a lot of attention after her stint as a presidential debate moderator, in part because of her devotion to meditation as a way of helping her relax, especially during election season.

communication mentally and physically is as important as practicing the piano or a gymnastics routine. At the very least, communicators should practice what they intend to say to others before they say it.

Know Thy Self

Work Toward Calm Through Systematic Desensitization

The following hierarchy of anxiety-producing communication situations[74] range from least likely to most likely to produce stress. Assess your reactions to find out which of these situations produce the most anxiety; then, as you visualize each context, try to remain calm and relaxed.

1. You are talking to your best friend in person.
2. You are being introduced to a new acquaintance by your best friend.
3. You are talking to a small group of people, all of whom you know well.
4. You are at a social gathering where you don't know anyone but are expected to meet and talk to others.
5. You are asking someone to go to a party with you.
6. You are in a supervisory role talking to someone in a supervisory role about a problem at work.
7. You are presenting in front of a large group of people you do not know well.
8. You are going on a job interview.
9. You are appearing on a television show with other panelists to talk about a topic you know well.
10. You are appearing on a television show and debating another person.

communication apprehension and confidence

Personal Report of Communication Apprehension[75]

The Personal Report of Communication Apprehension (PRCA) is composed of twenty-four statements. Indicate the degree to which each statement applies to you by marking whether you (1) strongly agree, (2) agree, (3) are undecided, (4) disagree, or (5) strongly disagree. Work quickly; record your first impression.

_____ 1. I dislike participating in group discussions.

_____ 2. Generally, I am comfortable while participating in group discussions.

_____ 3. I am tense and nervous while participating in group discussions.

_____ 4. I like to get involved in group discussions.

_____ 5. Engaging in a group discussion with new people makes me tense and nervous.

_____ 6. I am calm and relaxed while participating in a group discussion.

_____ 7. Generally, I am nervous when I have to participate in a meeting.

_____ 8. Usually, I am calm and relaxed while participating in a meeting.

_____ 9. I am very calm and relaxed when I am called on to express an opinion at a meeting.

_____ 10. I am afraid to express myself at meetings.

_____ 11. Communicating at meetings usually makes me feel uncomfortable.

_____ 12. I am very relaxed when answering questions at a meeting.

_____ 13. While participating in a conversation with a new acquaintance, I feel very nervous.

_____ 14. I have no fear of speaking up in conversations.

_____ 15. Ordinarily, I am very tense and nervous in conversations.

_____ 16. Ordinarily, I am very calm and relaxed in conversations.

_____ 17. While conversing with a new acquaintance, I feel very relaxed.

_____ 18. I'm afraid to speak up in conversations.

_____ 19. I have no fear of giving a speech.

_____ 20. Certain parts of my body feel very tense and rigid while I am giving a speech.

_____ 21. I feel relaxed while giving a speech.

_____ 22. My thoughts become confused and jumbled when I am giving a speech.

_____ 23. I face the prospect of giving a speech with confidence.

_____ 24. While giving a speech, I get so nervous I forget facts I really know.

Scoring: As you score each subcategory, begin with a score of 18 points. Then add or subtract from 18 based on the following instructions:

Subscores	Scoring Formula
Group discussions	18+ scores for items 2, 4, and 6; − (minus) scores for items 1, 3, and 5
Meetings	18+ scores for items 8, 9, and 12; − (minus) scores for items 7, 10, and 11
Interpersonal conversations	18+ scores for items 14, 16, and 17; − (minus) scores for items 13, 15, and 18
Public speaking	18+ scores for items 19, 21, and 23; − (minus) scores for items 20, 22, and 24

To obtain your total score for the PRCA, add your four subscores together. Your score should range between 24 points and 120 points. Then examine your score for each of the subcategories. If, for example, your score for the Group subcategory is 20 (which is higher than average), you are probably more anxious than most other people when participating in a group discussion.

Norms for PRCA

	Mean	Standard Deviation
Total score	65.5	15.3
Group	15.4	4.8
Meetings	16.4	4.8
Interpersonal	14.5	4.2
Public speaking	19.3	5.1

Self-Concept

2.1 Describe your self-concept and how it influences the way you communicate.

- Four of the most significant factors that determine your self-concept are: social comparison, social judgments, self-observation, and self-identification.

- Social comparison is the process of evaluating yourself in relation to the groups with whom you primarily associate and to commercial and popular culture messages.

- Social judgments represent how you interpret other people's verbal and nonverbal reactions to you as a basis for your self-concept.

- Self-observation is the process of interpreting your actual performance (how you look and act) and your behavior (how well you do something) as a basis for your self-concept.

- Self-identification is the process of integrating your cultural affiliations, assumption of roles, and unique experiences into your self-concept.

Self-Esteem

2.2 Discuss the major factors that contribute to a person's self-esteem.

- You can improve your self-esteem by practicing self-assertiveness, personal integrity, and self-talk.

- The tendency to distort—either positively or negatively—what happens to you and how you feel about those experiences can distort your self-concept.

- Beware of self-fulfilling prophecies, which are predictions that directly or indirectly cause themselves to become true.

Self-Presentation

2.3 Examine the role of self-monitoring as a prerequisite for effective self-presentation.

- Self-presentation represents the strategies you use to shape the way other people perceive, evaluate, and treat you.

- Self-monitoring represents your ability to observe and control how you express yourself verbally and nonverbally when interacting with others.

- Effective impression management strategies include choosing appropriate forms of ingratiation, self-promotion, exemplification, supplication, and intimidation to achieve your communication goals.

Perception

2.4 Identify how selection, organization, and interpretation shape perceptions.

- Perception is the process through which you select, organize, and interpret sensory stimuli in the world around you.

- Your needs, interests, moods, wants, and memories largely determine which stimuli you will select.

- Four principles that influence how you organize information are the proximity, similarity, closure, and simplicity principles.

- Your past experiences, knowledge, expectations, attitudes, and relationships affect how you interpret and react to people and events.

- When you engage in perception checking, apply perception-checking guidelines and skills linked to the seven key competencies of effective communication.

Communication Confidence

2.5 Practice appropriate strategies and skills to enhance your communication confidence.

- Communication apprehension refers to an individual's level of fear or anxiety associated with real or anticipated communication with another person or persons.

- Sources of communication apprehension include fear of failure, fear of the unknown, fear of the spotlight, fear of others, and fear of breaking the supposed rules.

- Strategies for reducing your level of communication apprehension include (1) preparation, (2) physical relaxation, (3) cognitive restructuring, (4) visualization, (5) systematic desensitization, and (6) practice.

Key Terms

Closure principle	Reference groups	Self-observation
Cognitive restructuring	Roles	Self-presentation
Communication apprehension	Self-assertiveness	Self-promotion
Exemplification	Selective attention	Self-talk
Impression management	Selective exposure	Similarity principle
Ingratiation	Selective interpretation	Simplicity principle
Intimidation	Selective recall	Social comparison
Perception	Self-concept	Social judgments
Perception checking	Self-esteem	Supplication
Personal integrity	Self-fulfilling prophecy	Systematic desensitization
Proximity principle	Self-identification	Visualization
	Self-monitoring	

TEST YOUR KNOWLEDGE

2.1 *Describe your self-concept and how it influences the way you communicate.*

1 Jorge describes himself as a thirty-year-old, single, entrepreneur and tour guide in the Galapagos Islands of Ecuador. What source of his self-concept has he shared?

a. Social comparison

b. Social judgments

c. Self-observation

d. Self-identification

2 Each of the following strategies helps us maintain a positive self-concept except one. Which strategy does not belong on this list?

a. We remember negative feedback and forget positive feedback.

b. We believe our good traits are unusual while our faults are common to many people.

c. We compare ourselves to others who make us look good.

d. We attribute successes to our own abilities and blame our failures on external factors.

2.2 *Discuss the major factors that contribute to a person's self-esteem.*

3 Which of the following is the best example of positive self-talk?

a. I may screw up the presentation I have to make at work, but that's okay.

b. If I had another week to work on this, I'd be better prepared.

c. I've succeeded at this before; I know I can do it again.

d. No one will read this report so it's doesn't matter whether I do a good job writing it.

4 If your guidance counselor or parents tell you that you should become a teacher because you don't have the drive or aptitude to work in corporate management, you may give up your dream of becoming a CEO. What barrier to self-esteem may be responsible for your decision?

a. Self-concept

b. Self-integrity

c. Self-mismanagement and perceptual distortion

d. Self-fulfilling prophecy

2.3 *Examine the role of self-monitoring as a prerequisite for effective self-presentation.*

5 Which of the following statements does *not* belong on the following list of statements made by someone with high self-monitoring skills?

a. I find it unnecessary and difficult to imitate the behavior of other people.

b. I can usually alter my behavior if I think the situation calls for a different kind of behavior.

c. I'm good at reading people's emotions and reactions.

d. I can usually tell when I've said or done something inappropriate.

6 Which impression management strategy can cause other people to feel resourceful and valued?

a. Supplication

b. Self-promotion

c. Exemplification

d. Intimidation

2.4 *Identify how selection, organization, and interpretation shape perception.*

7 This textbook uses the example of eyewitness testimony to illustrate:

a. the power of self-concept.

b. the unreliability of human perception.

c. the role of organization in the perceptual process.

d. the role of self-esteem in the perceptual process.

8 In the waiting room of a doctor's office, the television channel is on a news network you don't like. Rather than watching the news, you decide to sit as far away as you can from the television and read a book. Which of the four selective processes is described in this example?

a. Selective exposure

b. Selective attention

c. Selective interpretation

d. Selective recall

2.5 *Practice appropriate strategies and skills to enhance your communication confidence.*

9 Which strategy for reducing communication apprehension replaces negative, irrational thoughts with more realistic, positive self-talk?

a. Prepare.

b. Use cognitive restructuring.

c. Visualize yourself succeeding.

d. Use systematic desensitization.

10 Which source of communication apprehension is psychologist Peter Desberg describing when he writes: "If you were performing as part of a choir, you'd probably feel much calmer than if you were singing a solo."?

a. Fear of failure

b. Fear of breaking the rules

c. Fear of the spotlight

d. Fear of others

Answers found on page 368.

Adapting to **Others** 3

President Barack Obama's 322 electoral-vote victory over Republican candidate Mitt Romney in the 2012 presidential election shocked many Republicans and astonished many Democrats. It wasn't even close.

Why did Obama win? There are numerous explanations: an improving economy, a less effective Republican campaign, and the incumbency of a sitting president. But the one explanation that both Republicans and Democrats agreed upon was this: Obama succeeded because he and his messages appealed to three key constituencies: minorities, women, and young people.

Black, Latino, and Asian voters accounted for 42 percent of Obama's support but only 10 percent of Romney's. According to the Pew Hispanic Center, 71 percent of Latinos voted for Barack Obama over Mitt Romney's 27 percent. Among women voters in critical swing states, Obama led by 18 percentage points. And of voters in the eighteen to twenty-nine age group, 60 percent voted for Obama and 35 percent voted for Romney.[1]

There is no question that the race, ethnicity, gender, and age of voters played a significant role in the outcome of the 2012 presidential election. Republicans who had counted on older, wealthier, white Americans to secure a victory realized they could no longer rely solely on this group to win a presidential election.

More than ever, the United States is a nation of "others." Modern travel, advanced technologies, and instant communication have brought us closer together in a highly diverse and ever-changing global village. Consequently, we find ourselves communicating with diverse populations within our own borders as well as beyond those borders. This "otherness" is our strength, and our own personal success depends upon our ability to understand, respect, and adapt to the many "others" in our lives.

The Many Faces of Others

3.1 *Assess how the increasing cultural diversity in the United States influences your interactions with others.*

The increasing diversity of the U.S. population affects us in many ways—socially, economically, politically, artistically, and spiritually. According to the 2010 Census, the "face" of the United States continues to change in significant ways. Although the Census Bureau reports that 72.4 percent of the U.S. population is "white or European American," that figure *includes* Hispanic/Latino Americans. When the population of this ethnic group is subtracted from the number of "white or European Americans," white Americans only represent 63.7 percent of the U.S. population—and that number includes North African and Middle Eastern Arabs.

More than half the growth in the total U.S. population between 2000 and 2010 was due to increases in the Hispanic/Latino population—from 13 to 16.4 percent. Close in percentage to Latino Americans were African Americans at 12.6 percent followed by Asian Americans at 4.8 percent and Native Americans at 1.2 percent. Of all population groups, Asians had the fastest rate of growth and non-Hispanic whites experienced the slowest growth. The Census projects that by 2050, 82 percent of the increase in the U.S. population will be due to immigration.[2] By the middle of this century, white Americans will become one of the many minority groups living in the United States.[3]

Defining Culture

When some people hear the phrase *cultural diversity*, they think about skin color and immigrants. Words such as *nationality*, *race*, and *ethnicity* are often used synonymously with the term *culture*. However, the concept of culture is much broader. We define **culture** as "a learned set of shared interpretations about beliefs, values, norms, and social practices that affect the behaviors of a relatively large group of people."[4]

Within most cultures, there are also groups of people—members of **co-cultures**—who coexist within the mainstream society, yet remain connected to one another through their cultural heritage.[5] In the United States, American Indian tribes are co-cultures, as are African Americans, Latino Americans, Asian Americans, Arab Americans, Irish Americans, and the members of large and small religious groups. Given our broad definition of culture, a Nebraska rancher and a Boston professor can have very different cultural perspectives, as would a native Egyptian, a Brazilian, an Indonesian, and a Chippewa tribal member.

Each one of us has an ethnicity, gender, age, religious belief (including atheism), socioeconomic position, sexual orientation, and a variety of abilities. We also live in, or have come from, a certain region or country. Consider the following examples:

- A white, sixth-generation, male, Lutheran teacher whose family still lives in the same Mid-western town as their great grandparents did.

- A fifty-five-year-old Jewish female scientist living in Chicago whose family emigrated from Russia.

- An Islamic, African American female working as a researcher for the federal government in Washington, DC.

All these characteristics contribute to our self-concept as derived from the social categories to which we see ourselves belonging.[6] Although we may identify ourselves as Italian, Vietnamese, Nigerian, or Cherokee, many of us have lost touch with our family history and culture.

Understanding *Your* Culture

Culture affects your life in both obvious and subtle ways. The first step in understanding others is to understand your own culture. As we indicated in Chapter 2, "Understanding Your Self," you derive a significant part of your self-concept from your cultural affiliations, that is, from the cultural groups to which you belong as well as the groups to which you do *not* belong: "I know who I am and that I am *not* you." This is a thoroughly natural feeling. We often divide our world into distinct and opposite groups (men and women, rich and poor, black and white, gay and straight, young and old,

American and foreign) in a way that sets us in opposition with one other. A more constructive approach is to explore your own cultural affiliation and compare it to people from different cultures.

For example, many white people in the United States don't think of their traits or behavior as characteristic of a culture. Because whiteness is a historical norm in the United States, it is difficult to classify it as a culture. Yet as Dr. Rita Hardiman wrote,

> Like fish, whose environment is water, we are surrounded by Whiteness and it is easy to think that what we experience is reality rather than recognizing it as the particular culture of a particular group. And like fish who are not aware of water until they are out of it, White people sometimes become aware of their culture only when they get to know, or interact with, the cultures of people of color.[7]

Understanding *Other* Cultures

If you believe you can live a life in which you avoid people from other cultures, you are fooling yourself. Many remote and formerly all-white towns have been transformed by major influxes of immigrants and migrant workers (Mexican laborers in Garden City, Kansas), immigrant populations (Hmong communities in Manitowoc County, Wisconsin), and religious groups (Orthodox Jews in Postville, Iowa).

Religion is an important aspect of many cultures. In some countries and for many groups, religion *is* the culture, such as Buddhism in Thailand, Islam in Iran, and Judaism in Israel. Occasionally, when religious groups attempt to practice their culture in a secular country, they encounter intolerance. In France, for example, religious attire, including headscarves for Muslim girls, skullcaps for Jewish boys, and crosses for Christian children, has been banned from public high schools.[8] Regardless of your individual religious beliefs, "you must remember that people feel strongly about their religion, and that differences between religious beliefs and practices do matter."[9]

In the 2012 film *Beasts of the Southern Wild*, six-year old Hushpuppy lives with her daddy in Bathtub, a swampy, ramshackle Louisiana settlement cut off from the mainland by a levee. There, black and white residents live cooperatively in both joy and sorrow as they struggle to survive poverty and isolation. When a catastrophic hurricane destroys the settlement, the Bathtub folks resist help from "civilized" rescuers and return to what is left of Bathtub.

Questions of Faith

According to Stephen Prothero, professor of religion at Boston University, many of us are illiterate about our own and others' religions. **Religious literacy** requires an accurate, objective, and respectful understanding of the history, beliefs, principles, and practices of world religions as well as those we encounter in our daily lives.[10] Test your knowledge about a few of the world's major religions by selecting "True," "False," or "I Don't Know" (?) for each of the following items:[11]

T	F	?	1.	Muslims believe in Islam and the Islamic way of life.
T	F	?	2.	Judaism is an older religion than Buddhism.
T	F	?	3.	Islam is a monotheistic religion (belief in one God) just like Christianity and Judaism.
T	F	?	4.	A Christian Scientist believes that disease is a delusion of the carnal mind that can be cured by prayer.
T	F	?	5.	Jews fast during Yom Kippur; Muslims fast during Ramadan.
T	F	?	6.	Jesus Christ was Jewish.
T	F	?	7.	Roman Catholics throughout the world outnumber all other Christians combined.
T	F	?	8.	Sunni Muslims compose about 90 percent of all adherents to Islam.
T	F	?	9.	Hindus believe in reincarnation.
T	F	?	10.	The Ten Commandments form the basis of Jewish religious laws.
T	F	?	11.	Mormonism is a Christian faith founded in the United States.[12]
T	F	?	12.	The Protestant reformer Martin Luther labeled the beliefs of Muslims, Jews, and Roman Catholics as false.
T	F	?	13.	One-third of the world's population is Christian.
T	F	?	14.	One-fifth of the world's population is Muslim.
T	F	?	15.	Hinduism is the oldest of the world's major religions, dating back more than 3,000 years.

Answers: All of the statements are true.

Barriers to Understanding Others

3.2 *Explain how ethnocentrism, stereotyping, prejudice, discrimination, and racism inhibit effective and ethical communication.*

Learning to communicate effectively in the twenty-first century can be a significant challenge. In order to become a more effective and ethical communicator in a multicultural environment, you must avoid or overcome five obstacles that can inhibit your understanding of others: ethnocentrism, stereotyping, prejudice, discrimination, and racism.

Ethnocentrism

Ethnocentrism is the mistaken belief that your culture is a superior culture

BARRIERS
to Understanding Others

Ethnocentrism
Stereotyping
Prejudice
Discrimination
Racism

with special rights and privileges that are or should be denied to others.

Ethnocentric communicators offend others when they imply that they come from a superior culture with superior values. As an ethical and culturally sensitive communicator, you should examine your own ethnocentric beliefs. Begin by investigating how your culture and your culture-based perspectives may differ from others. Then complete the Generalized Ethnocentrism (GENE) Scale at the end of this chapter to assess your level of ethnocentrism.

Stereotyping

Stereotypes are generalizations about a group of people that oversimplify the group's characteristics. When we stereotype others, we rely on exaggerated beliefs to make judgments about an entire group of people. Stereotyping assigns negative or positive traits to *all* members of a group when, in reality, only a few people may possess those traits. A mid-1990s study of college students found that African Americans were negatively stereotyped as lazy and loud and Jews were described as shrewd and intelligent.[13]

You may have heard other common stereotypes such as, "Athletes are poor students," "The elderly are boring," "Latinos are always late," "Women are more compassionate than men," and "Gay men dress with style." Whether negative or positive, all-inclusive generalizations about any group of people result in unfair judgments. When we stereotype others, we cause serious breakdowns in communication.

Intercultural communication scholars Stella Ting-Toomey and Leeva C. Chung claim that the nature of our language creates many stereotypes. Paired words, for example, encourage "either/or" thinking: *straight* or *gay*, *female* or *male*, *black* or *white*, *rich* or *poor*, *old* or *young*, *red state* or *blue state*, *us* or *them*. Such either/or perceptions lead us to interpret the social world as good or bad, normal or abnormal, and right or wrong. When you think in either/or terms, you tend to overlook the fact that people may fall somewhere between extremes.[14] Knowing this can profoundly affect the way you interact with and understand others. In Chapter 5, "Verbal Communication," we devote a major section to the ways in which language reflects gender and cultural biases. We also note how exclusionary language—words that reinforce stereotypes or belittle others—widens the social gap, separating *us* from *them*.

Prejudice

Stereotypes lead to **prejudices**: positive or negative attitudes about an individual or cultural group based on little or no direct experience with that person or group. The word *prejudice* has two parts: *pre*, meaning "before," and *judice*, meaning "judge." When you believe or express a prejudice, you are making a judgment about someone before you get to know that person and learn whether your opinions and feelings are justified. Although prejudices can be positive— "He must be brilliant if he went to Yale"—most prejudices are negative. Statements such as, "A disabled person working on our group project will slow us down" or "He's too old to understand cutting-edge technology" are examples of prejudice based on stereotypes.

Discrimination

Discrimination is how we act out and express prejudice. When we discriminate, we exclude groups of people from opportunities granted to others: employment, promotion, housing, political expression, equal rights, and access to educational, recreational, and social institutions. This form of intolerance makes effective and productive exchanges between diverse groups of people nearly impossible.

Discrimination comes in many forms: discrimination against racial, ethnic, religious, and gender groups; discrimination based on sexual

---

The Characteristics of PREJUDICE

- Biased beliefs about group members that are not based on direct experience and first-hand knowledge[15]
- Irrational feelings of dislike and even hatred for a group
- A readiness to behave in negative and unjust ways toward members of a group

---

ETHICAL COMMUNICATION

Acknowledge Unconscious Biases

The National Communication Association's Credo for Ethical Communication includes the following principle: "We condemn communication that degrades individuals and humanity through distortion, intimidation, coercion, and violence, and through the expression of intolerance and hatred."[16] Practicing this principle, however, can be difficult. Despite claims of "I'm not prejudiced," most of us have positive and negative attitudes about cultural groups based on little or no direct experience with members of that group.

Two Harvard researchers, Mahzarin Banaji and Brian Nosek, have developed an Implicit Association Test (IAT) to help us understand the differences between what we think about others and how we feel about them.[17] The IAT uncovers our often-unconscious opinions about race, ethnicity, gender, age, and religions (which we would refuse to reveal publicly). It asks you to make a series of rapid judgments based on seeing words that describe different cultural dimensions (race, ethnicity, gender, age, religion) that are either positive or negative. The results uncover the real attitudes we may have toward commonly stigmatized groups and concludes that our unacknowledged prejudicial feelings can predict why and how we act in a negatively, biased way toward others.[18]

IAT results also indicate that most individuals, including people of color and other minorities, show a variety of biases they believe they do not have. Banaji and Nosek recommend that when it comes to prejudice, it is less important how biased you are and more important how willing you are to confront your unconscious thoughts about others. When you acknowledge your unconscious biases, you can take steps to confront them, which is the ethical thing to do.[19] To take the IAT for free, go to Harvard's website at https://implicit.harvard.edu/implicit.

barriers to understanding others

orientation, disability, age, and physical appearance; and discrimination against people from different social classes and political ideologies. Recall, for example, the time when black Americans could not drink from the same water fountains, use the same rest rooms, eat at the same restaurants, attend the same schools, or stay in the same hotels as white Americans. Or the time when women could not vote, work in certain jobs, or join male-only business, golf, and social clubs. Or the time when the Chinese were excluded from immigrating to the United States and the Irish were told they "need not apply."

Do any of these discriminatory barriers still exist? To what extent do other groups such as gays, Muslims, migrant farm workers, and disabled Americans face discrimination? When one group restricts the rights of any other group and is unwilling to revise its thinking, communication breaks down and may be irreparably damaged. Without effective interaction with others, we lose the ability to resolve conflicts and accept differences as natural and beneficial.

Racism

Racism is the culminating effect of ethnocentrism, stereotyping, prejudice, and discrimination. Racist people assume that a person with a certain inherited characteristic (for example, skin color) also has negative characteristics and abilities. Racists also believe in the superiority of their own race above all others. In his book *Privilege, Power, and Difference*, Allan Johnson points out that racism is built into the system in which people live and work. It goes beyond the personal and becomes a pattern of privilege and oppression within a society.[20]

Although racism—whether expressed in public settings, in printed material, or on Internet websites—continues to plague the United States, antiracist attitudes and behaviors prevail. For example, on the day of Barack Obama's re-election as president, a group of about 400 University of Mississippi students assembled to protest the outcome. The *Daily Mississippian* student newspaper reported that hundreds of students "exchanged racial epithets and violent, politicized chants." Some shouted, "The South will rise again." A photo posted on Twitter showed an Obama campaign sign being set on fire. In response and on the day after the election, about 600 University of Mississippi students gathered for the "We Are One Mississippi" counter-protest and candlelight vigil. Together, they recited the campus creed affirming "the respect and dignity of each person."[22]

> **❝ Racism** is an attitude, a collection of stereotypes, a bad intention, a desire or need to discriminate or do harm, a form of hatred. **❞**
>
> —Allan Johnson, *Privilege, Power, and Difference*[21]

University of Mississippi students and administrators gather for the "We Are One Mississippi" counter-protest where they recited the campus creed affirming "the respect and dignity of each person."

What Is Your Race?

What is your race? Before you answer, consider a more basic question: Is there such a thing as race?" Intercultural communication scholars Mark Orbe and Tina Harris define **race** as a socially constructed concept that classifies people into separate value-based categories.[23] Unfortunately, many people see race as subdivisions of the human species based on *significant* genetic differences. Many of our ideas about race developed in the eighteenth century when German scientist Johann Friedrich Blumenbach classified humans according to geography and physical differences by using Caucasians as the ideal. The result was a racial ranking of white Europeans first, Malays and Native Americans second, and Africans and Asians last. The following pyramid illustrates Blumenbach's 1795 Geometry of Human Order:[24]

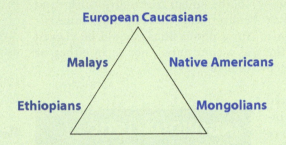

Before the human genome was decoded, most systems of race classification were based on skin color, hair texture, and facial attributes.[25] These classifications led to the separation of people based on skin color: white, yellow, and black.

The genetic definition of race, however, has absolutely *nothing* to do with any physical or behavioral characteristics.[26] Anthropologists, biologists, geneticists, and ethicists emphasize that 99.9 percent of DNA sequences are common to all humans.[27] According to extensive research, pure races never existed and all humans belong to the same species. And this species, *Homo sapiens*, had its origins in Africa.[28]

Race is a socially constructed concept that should be understood as the outcome of ancient population shifts. When race is viewed this way, it becomes a neutral human characteristic, not a motivation to elevate the virtues or power of one group over another.

The Dimensions of Culture

3.3 *Describe the qualities and impact of cultural dimensions on the communication process.*

We owe a great deal to contemporary social scientists such as Geert H. Hofstede, Edward T. Hall, Florence Kluckhohn, Frederick Strodtbeck, the GLOBE Study team, and Shalom Schwartz who have identified important dimensions of culture.[29] Hofstede defines **intercultural dimension** as "an aspect of a culture that can be measured relative to other cultures."[30]

Intercultural communication scholars, Myron Lustig and Jolene Koester, have synthesized significant research on intercultural dimensions into several common dimensions that are fundamental to understanding a culture. "Each dimension can be viewed as a continuum of choices that a culture must make" rather than either/or categories.[31] In this section we first examine four of these dimensions. Then we look at a fifth that cuts across all the other dimensions and focuses on the relationship between culture and communication.

Individualism–Collectivism

Individualism–collectivism may be the most important factor distinguishing one culture from another.[32] **Individualism–collectivism** represents the degree to which a culture relies on and has allegiance to the self *or* the group; whether people are unique and independent *or* similar and interdependent on one another.[33]

Most North Americans value individualism. However, as much as 70 percent of the world's population values interdependence or collectivism. In these societies, the interests

5 DIMENSIONS OF CULTURE

1 Individualism–Collectivism

2 Power Distance

3 Gender Expectations

4 Time Orientation

5 High–Low Context

of the group prevail over the interests of the individual.[34] For instance, once children have completed high school or higher education in the United States, many parents encourage them to strike out on their own—to pursue a career and find their own place to live. However, in many Asian countries, parents encourage their children to stay at home and work until they marry, and once they do, to work for the benefit of the immediate and extended family. See the box to the far right on "Individualistic and Collectivist Countries" for the top-four rankings of countries in each category.[35]

Despite the fact that the United States ranks highest in terms of individualism, not all Americans are individualistic. In fact, many African Americans, Asian Americans, and Latino Americans embrace the traditions and values of collectivist societies. Interestingly, U.S. political parties are often described in individualistic–collectivist terms. The *Wall Street Journal* columnist Peggy Noonan noticed that at the 2012 U.S. presidential conventions, Republican speakers "talked about their own stories, lauded their own history—a whole lot of I, I, I." Democratic convention speakers "were more communal. There was a lot of 'us' and 'we'—we are together, we are part of something, we are united, we are Democrats." Noonan added that the Democrats' "we-ness" seemed "more attractive to a lot of voters in modern, broken-up America."[36]

In another study, a search of words on Google's 1960 to 2008 book database found that U.S. writers are using more individualistic words (self, personalize, unique, all about me, I am special, I'm the best) and fewer collective words (share, united, band together, common good). The conclusion: We are writing and caring "less about community bonds and obligations" and more about ourselves.[37]

The focus on individual achievement and personal rewards in the United States can make interaction with people from collectivist cultures difficult. The typical U.S. communicator's style and behavior may be viewed as arrogant, antagonistic, power hungry, and impatient.

Interestingly, as poor nations gain wealth, they begin to shift toward greater individualism.[38]

Those of us who have taught in other countries or at minority–majority colleges quickly learn that whereas many U.S. students are more likely to ask questions and even challenge our opinions, students from collectivist cultures are more likely to respect and accept what we say. Even so, remember that individualism and collectivism, just like other intercultural dimensions, should be viewed as a continuum, not as an either/or category.

INDIVIDUALISTIC
Culture Characteristics[39]

- "I" is important.
- Independence is worth pursuing.
- Personal achievement should be rewarded.
- Individual uniqueness is valued.

COLLECTIVIST
Culture Characteristics[40]

- "We" is important.
- The needs, beliefs, and goals of the "in-group" (e.g., family, community members) are emphasized above those of the individual.
- Achievements that benefit and foster cooperation in the group are rewarded.

Individualistic and Collectivistic Countries

Power Distance

Is it easy to make a personal appointment with the president of your college or university? Can you simply walk into your boss's office, or do you have to navigate your way through an army of secretaries and administrative assistants? Does our society truly believe in the sentiments expressed in the U.S. Declaration of Independence that all people are created equal? These are the questions addressed in power distance dimension, also labeled the egalitarian-hierarchy dimension.[41]

Power distance refers to the physical and psychological distance between those who have power and those who do not in relationships, institutions, and organizations. It also represents "the extent to which the less powerful members of institutions and organizations within a country expect and accept that power is distributed inequality."[42]

In cultures with **high power distance**, individuals accept major differences in power as normal. It is accepted that all people are *not* created equal. In such cultures, the privileged have much more power and use it to guide or control the lives of people with less power. In a high-power-distance culture, you accept and do not challenge authority. Parents have total control over their children. Husbands may have total control over their wives. And government officials, corporate officers, and religious authorities dictate rules of behavior and have the power to ensure compliance.

In cultures with **low power distance**, power distinctions are

Power Distance

Masculine and Feminine Index

minimized: supervisors work with subordinates, professors work with students, elected officials work with constituents. See the above box on "Power Distance" for the top-ranking countries in each category of this dimension. Despite the fact that the United States claims to be the greatest democracy on earth and an equal opportunity society, it is sixteenth on the list after low-power-distance countries such as Ireland, Sweden, Finland, Switzerland, Great Britain, Germany, Australia, the Netherlands, and Canada.[43]

Power distance has enormous implications for communication. For example, in Australia (a low-power-distance country), students and professors are often on a first-name basis, and lively class discussions are the norm. However, in Malaysia (a high-power-distance country), students show up and are seated *before* class begins; almost no one comes late. Students are polite and appreciative, but rarely challenge a professor's claims. In a high-power-distance culture, you do not openly disagree with teachers, elders, bosses, law enforcement officials, or government agents.

If you compare the figures on individualism–collectivism and power distance, you will notice a strong correlation between collectivism and high power distance and between individualism and low power distance. If you are individualistic and strongly encouraged to express your own opinion, you are more willing to challenge authority. If, on the other hand, your culture is collectivist and your personal opinion is subordinate to the welfare of others, you are less likely to challenge the collective authority of your family, your employer, or your government.

Gender Expectations

All of us—no matter what our culture—have expectations about gender roles. Obviously in terms of biological traits, men cannot become pregnant and are generally stronger and bigger than women. The **gender expectations dimension** focuses on "both expectations about suitable role behaviors," such as assertiveness and nurturing, as well as "expectations about the preferred similarities and differences in the behaviors of men and women."[44]

Hofstede describes the differences in gender expectations as the "desirability of assertive behavior as opposed to these desirability of modest behavior."[45] When the terms *masculinity* and *femininity* are used to describe these dimensions, they refer to societal perspectives rather than to individuals. Koester and Jolene provide a simple but useful continuum to explain this cultural dimension.[46] (See below)

In more masculine societies, men are supposed to be assertive, tough, and focused on material success, whereas women are supposed to be more nurturing, modest, tender, and concerned with the quality of life. In more feminine societies, *both* men and women are nurturing, modest, tender, and concerned with the quality of life. In cultures with an egalitarian gender society, gender roles overlap: Men and women can be assertive and/or nurturing. See the above box on Masculine/Feminine Values for the top-ranking countries under each category.[47]

Hofstede ranks the United States as nineteenth in terms of masculine values coming *after* the countries ranked fourteenth through eighteenth (Columbia, Philippines, Poland, South Africa, and Ecuador).[48] In highly masculine societies, personal success, competition, assertiveness, and strength are admired. Unselfishness and nurturing may be seen as weaknesses. Although women have come a long way from the rigid roles of past centuries, they have miles to go before they achieve genuine equality in cultures with high masculine values.

At the more masculine end of the gender expectation continuum, women have fewer rights and privileges than men do. In countries such as Japan, Austria, and Arab countries with large Muslim populations, men and women are viewed as inherently different "and these differences require dissimilar expectations and treatments."[49] Even if you do not approve of the way women are treated in some cultures, you should do your best to understand and adapt to their customs. For example, the United Arab Emirates website offers the following advice about traveling in a Muslim country: "Men shake hands. Women should wait until the man extends his hand. Pious Muslim men may not shake hands with women.

MEN ARE ASSERTIVE ←	→ MEN ARE NURTURING
WOMEN ARE ASSERTIVE ←	→ WOMEN ARE NURTURING
MEN AND WOMEN ARE EQUALLY ASSERTIVE ←	→ MEN AND WOMEN ARE NOT EQUALLY NURTURING

Culture-Based Gender Expectations

Then U.S. Secretary of State Hillary Clinton and the president of the Republic of Tatarstan, Russia, congratulate newlyweds at an Islamic mosque. How did Secretary Clinton demonstrate her understanding and respect for this country and its people's values?

Pious Muslim women do not shake the hands or touch men who are not in their families. Rather, they might simply put their hand over their hearts to show their sincerity in welcoming the visitor."[50]

Time Orientation

Time orientation is a multifaceted cultural dimension that focuses on time variables such as short and long term; past, present, and future; one-thing-at-a-time and many-things-at-a-time; and the pace of activities. As a result, there are many interpretations of time.

In most parts of northern Europe and North America, time is a valuable commodity. We spend time, save time, waste time, make time, lose time, gain time, and take time outs. As a result, we fill our days and nights with multiple commitments and live fast-paced lives. However, the pace of life in India, Kenya, and Argentina, for example, is driven less by a need to "get things done" than by a sense of

---

Muted Group Theory

Cheris Kramarae's **muted group theory** observes that powerful, wealthy groups at the top of a society determine who will communicate and be listened to. For this reason, women, the poor, and minority groups may have trouble participating and being heard.[51] The following three assumptions in muted group theory explain how women's voices are subdued or silenced in many cultures:

1. Women perceive the world differently than men because of traditional divisions of labor. *Example*:

Homemaker versus bread-winner, nurse versus doctor.

2. Women's freedom of expression is limited by men's dominance in relationships and institutions. *Example*: Women in the United States only gained the right to vote in 1920. The "glass ceiling" still prevents many women from achieving professional advancement.

3. Women must transform their thinking and behavior to participate fully in society. *Example*: Women have become more politically active to make sure that sexual harassment,

date and marital rape, and spousal abuse are seen as serious crimes rather than practices that may be excused or tolerated.

Although muted group theory focuses on women, its assumptions apply to many groups. In the United States, for example, the voices of people of color, recent immigrants, the disabled, and the poor are also muted.

participation in events that create their own rhythm.[52]

Depending on your life and your culture, your view of time may primarily focus on the past, the present, or the future. Hofstede notes that cultures also vary in terms of how and when to achieve goals: **short-term or long-term**. He defines this dimension as fostering virtues oriented toward future (long-term) rewards or fostering virtues related to the past and present (short-term) rewards. If your time orientation is short-term, you may feel as though time, deadlines, multitasking chores, and To Do lists control your life. If you come from a long-term culture, you see time as flexible and that it can suit your needs rather than the other way around.

Are you a Pisces or a Gemini? If you can identify your celestial sign, you are more likely to live in a Western, short-term culture. Were you born in the Year of the Tiger or the Year of the Monkey? If you know the lunar year of your birth and its symbol, you are more likely to live in a far Eastern, long-term culture.

Countries with short-term time orientations such as Pakistan, Nigeria, the Philippines, Canada, and not far behind, the United States, expect quick results from their efforts. They value their leisure time and are more likely to spend than save what they earn. Countries with long-term

time orientations such as China, Taiwan, Japan, and South Korea value persistence, thriftiness, adaptability, and humility. The members of long-term cultures honor elders and value the ability to defer gratification of needs.

High–Low Context Cultures

In Chapter 1, "Human Communication," we defined *context* as the psychosocial, logistical, and interactional environment in which communication occurs. Edward T. Hall sees context as the information that surrounds an event, inextricably bound up with the meaning of the event. He claims that a message's context—in and of itself—may hold more meaning than the words in a message.[54] Like the other four intercultural dimensions, we can place cultures on a continuum from high context to low context.

In a **high-context culture**, very little meaning is expressed through words. In contrast, gestures, silence, and facial expressions, as well as the relationships among communicators, have meaning. In high-context cultures, meaning can also be conveyed through status (age, gender, education, family background, title, and affiliations) and through an individual's informal network of friends and associates.

In a **low-context culture**, meaning is expressed primarily through language. As members of a low-context culture, people in North America tend to speak more, speak more loudly, and speak more rapidly than a person from a high-context culture. Americans and Canadians "speak up," "spell it out," "just say no," and "speak our mind." The figure at the top of the next page depicts high- and low-context cultures and contrasts the characteristics between the two.[55]

High-context communication usually occurs in collectivist cultures in which members share similar attitudes, beliefs, and values. As a result, spoken communication can be indirect, implied, or vague because everyone *gets* the meaning by understanding the context, the person's nonverbal

behavior, and the significance of the communicator's status.

Shirley van der Veur, a former Peace Corps volunteer and now a university professor, relates the following illustration of this concept: A scholar from Kenya was invited to dinner at an American colleague's home. Even though he ate ravenously, not leaving a morsel of food on his plate, the American hosts were not convinced that he liked his dinner because he had not *said* so. In Kenya, if his hosts saw him appreciatively eating his meal, they would know that he was enjoying it without necessarily needing him to express his pleasure verbally.[56]

Edward Hall includes different time orientation as a function of high- or low-context cultures.[57] In high-context cultures, time is viewed as more open, less structured, more responsive to the immediate needs of people, and less subject to external goals and constraints. Schedules and deadlines are not as important; they are frequently broken. If you belong to a high-context culture, you probably find it stimulating to think about several different problems at the same time and feel comfortable holding two or three conversations simultaneously.

In low-context cultures, the opposite is true. Events are highly organized and divided into separate items—one thing at a time. If you belong to a low-context culture, you probably prefer to concentrate on one job before moving to another and may become irritated when someone interrupts you or brings up a personal topic unrelated to the purpose of a discussion or meeting.

Hall maintains that these two time orientations are incompatible and can result in high levels of frustration. Being on time in high-context cultures doesn't have the same significance as it does in the United States, a low-context culture. For high-context people, schedules and commitments, particularly plans for the future, are not firm, and even important plans may change right up to the last minute.[58]

SHORT-TERM TIME ORIENTATION
1. Pakistan
2. Nigeria
3. Philippines
4. Canada

LONG-TERM TIME ORIENTATION
1. China
2. Hong Kong
3. Taiwan
4. Japan

Time Orientations[53]

HIGH-CONTEXT CULTURES

Examples

Chinese
Japanese
South Korean
Native American
African American
Mexican American
Latino American

Characteristics

Implicit meaning
Nonverbal communication
Reserved reactions
Strong in-group bonds
High level of commitment
Time open and flexible

LOW-CONTEXT CULTURES

Characteristics

Explicit meaning
Verbal communication
Reactions on the surface
Flexible group memberships
Low level of commitment
Time highly organized

Examples

German
Swiss
White American
Scandinavian
Canadian

MEDIATED COMMUNICATION IN *ACTION*

The International Digital Revolution

We live in a worldwide digital age. Most of you depend on the Internet to stay in touch with your friends and family members; to take college courses, do research, and ask your instructor questions; to buy products, check your bank account, and make investments; to find a job, succeed in a job, and keep your job; to watch a movie, play a game, and begin or end a romance. But don't start boasting. Even though scientists in the United States invented the Internet, we're falling behind in an international digital revolution. Consider the following: Roughly 20 percent of American adults "do not use the Internet at home, work and school, or by mobile device." That results in about 60 million people "shut off from jobs, government services, health care and education," which in turn hurts individuals and the U.S. economy.[59]

Today the United States ranks about sixteenth in the world when it comes to the speed and cost of our broadband connections.[60] If you only measure the speed of our system, the United States ranks twenty-ninth in the world.[61] Adding insult to injury, Americans pay more for poor quality and slow speed than almost anyone else in the world.

David Cay Johnston, a Pulitzer Prize winning journalist, explained "We're way behind countries like Lithuania, Ukraine and Moldavia. Per bit of information moved, we pay 38 times what the Japanese pay. If you buy one of these triple-play packages that are heavily advertised—where you get Internet, telephone and cable TV together—typically you'll pay what I pay, about $160 a month including fees. The same service in France is $38 a month."[62]

Among highly industrialized, communication-savvy countries, the United States is on the wrong side of a digital divide. Many low-income Americans cannot afford reliable Internet access. If they lived in South Korea, the story would be different. South Koreans "have access to Internet speeds that are more than 200 times faster than what most Americans have, and they can have it for just $27 a month."[63]

So what does this mean to you? It means that you cannot communicate at the same speed with the same quality and at a cheaper price as do people in countries that compete economically with the United States. If all you do is tweet or text your friends, this may not seem like a big problem. But, as Susan Crawford, author of the book *Captive Audience* explains, the problem does more than affect social equality and fairness. The middle class is squeezed by the high price "and poor and rural people are relying on public libraries and McDonald's for free, inferior Wi-Fi access." The bottom line is that the inferior and costly digital system in the United States affects our nation's economic growth and our ability to communicate in a global economy.[64] And that affects you directly—the job you want or hope to keep, the money you earn or want to save, the things you can and cannot afford, and the quality of your life.

So keep tweeting and texting to your heart's content, but remember that your ability to communicate effectively in a sophisticated global economy is in jeopardy unless we "ensure that everyone has cheap, fast, abundant connectivity."[65]

Intercultural Communication Strategies

3.4 *Practice communication strategies and skills that enhance your ability to understand, respect, and adapt to others.*

As a way of understanding the perspectives of "others," we urge you to "see the world through other people's eyes." The fundamental purpose of understanding others—seeing the world as others see it—is to minimize miscommunication and prejudice. Of course learning about and adapting to the many "others" you encounter every day may require changes in long-standing habits of thought and action.

Be Mindful

Mindfulness is both an old and a new concept. The ancient concept can be traced back to the first millennium B.C. to the foothills of the Himalayas, when it is believed that Buddha attained enlightenment through mindfulness.[66] **Mindfulness** involves being fully aware—in your physical body, emotional feelings, and conscious mind—of the present moment without making judgments.

> Mindful communicators understand what they experience *inside themselves* (body, mind, heart, spirit) and pay full attention to what is happening *around them* (people, the natural world, surroundings, events).

Before explaining mindfulness in more detail, let's take a look at its opposite: mind*less*ness. **Mindlessness** occurs when you allow rigid categories and false distinctions to become habits of thought and behavior.[67] For example, you approach a sales counter and say, "Excuse me" to the salesperson. Why did you say that? Did you really mean to apologize for interrupting someone who should have been paying more attention to you in the first place? All of us engage in some mindless behavior without any serious consequences. But when mindlessness occurs in a sensitive communication situation, the results can be detrimental to a relationship or damaging to an important project. For example, after the 9/11 tragedy, many patriotic Muslim Americans suffered mindless stereotyping, prejudice, and discrimination as a result of a larger ignorance about the Islamic faith and culture. If you engage in mindlessness, you are trapped in an inflexible, biased world in which your religion is always right and good; people from other cultures are inferior and untrustworthy; boys will always be boys, and girls will always be girls; and change is a terrible and scary thing.[68]

Mind*ful*ness, in contrast, requires paying attention to how you and another person communicate. It asks you to observe what is happening as it happens, without forming opinions or taking sides as you learn more about someone else.[69] When you are mindful, you recognize stereotypical thinking and prejudices and try to overcome them. Mindfulness gives you the freedom and motivation to understand, respect, and adapt to others.[70]

Be Receptive to New Information Mindful communicators learn more about others and their cultures by being open to new information. Too often, we dismiss another person's belief or behavior as irrational or bizarre when more information about that belief or behavior would help us understand it. Once you learn why observant Muslims and Jews won't eat pork products or why Hindus won't eat the meat of sacred cows even under famine conditions, you may become more mindful and accepting of their customs.

Respect Others' Perspectives In addition to being open to new information, mindful communicators are open to other points of view. Psychologist Richard Nisbett credits a graduate student from China with helping him understand such differences. When he and the Chinese student were working together, the student said, "You know, the difference between you and me is that I know the world is a circle, and you think it's a line. The Chinese believe in constant change, but with things always moving back to some prior state . . . Westerners live in a simpler world . . . and they think they can control events because

INTERCULTURAL COMMUNICATION STRATEGIES

1 Be Mindful

2 Adapt to Others

3 Actively Engage Others

they know the rules that govern the behavior of objects."[71]

When you cling to one way of seeing a person or interpreting an event, you have stopped being mindful. Every idea, person, or object can be many things, depending on the perspective from which it is viewed. A cow is a livelihood to a rancher, a sacred animal to a Hindu, a collection of genes and proteins to a biologist, and a mistreated, living being to members of PETA (People for the Ethical Treatment of Animals).[72]

Adapt to Others

You probably feel most comfortable when you "fit in" with the people around you. To fit in, you may modify the way you talk to family members, friends, colleagues, authority figures, and strangers. For example, two people may be from different areas

RANGE OF THINKING

◄ WESTERN

- Focuses on discovering the basic and predictable nature of objects and events
- Tries to control objects, events, and environments
- Puts things in discrete categories
- Uses formal logical rules
- Insists on the correctness of one belief vs. another

EAST ASIAN ►

- Focuses on the interacting, unpredictable relationships among events
- Doubts that objects, events, and environments are controllable
- Describes relationships and connections, not categories
- Accepts contractions and dissimilar beliefs

of the country, one from Maine and the other from Alabama. When they go "home," their dialects, vocabulary, sentence structure, rate of speech, and even volume change to accommodate their home culture. Yet, in professional settings, their speech may be more formal in style and substance.

COMMUNICATION&CULTURE

WHY DON'T HUNGRY HINDUS EAT SACRED COWS?

Among India's Hindus, cows are a sacred symbol of life. There is no greater sacrilege for a Hindu than killing a cow. At first, this belief may seem irrational, particularly in light of India's food shortages and poverty. If you have visited or seen pictures of India, you've seen cows wandering city streets and sidewalks, highways and railroad tracks, gardens, and agricultural fields. You've also seen pictures of extreme poverty and hunger.

In his book *Cows, Pigs, Wars, and Witches: The Riddles of Culture*, Marvin Harris offers an explanation for Hindus' treatment of cows.[73] Cows give birth to oxen, which are the principal source for plowing fields. Unfortunately, there are too few oxen for India's sixty million farms. Without oxen to plow fields, farmers cannot farm, food shortages result, and people go

hungry. If you kill a cow, you eliminate your source of oxen. During the worst famines, killing a cow only provides temporary relief. Once a cow is killed, there will be no more oxen to plow the field in future years. The long-term effect may be a much more devastating famine. Harris offers this conclusion:

What I am saying is that cow love is an active element in a complex, finely articulated material and cultural order. Cow love mobilizes the latent capacity of human beings to persevere in a low-energy ecosystem in which there is little room for waste or indolence.[74]

In light of Harris's anthropological explanation, you can begin to understand and respect why hungry peasants in India refuse to eat the cows that surround them.

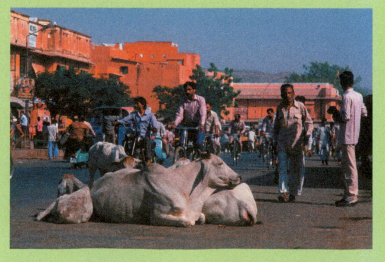

Communication scholar, Professor Howard Giles, encourages us to practice **communication accommodation**.[75] When we communicate with others, we should compare ourselves, and if possible, adapt our behavior to them. For example, if you believe that another group has more power or has desirable characteristics, you may "accommodate" your conversations to the accepted speech behaviors and norms of that group. Here are four of Giles's observations about how effective communicators accommodate others.

1. *Communication similarities and differences exist in all conversations.* Whether you talk to an international student or your grandmother, you will encounter differences.
2. *The manner in which we perceive the communication of others will determine how we evaluate our interaction with others.* Effective communicators avoid stereotyping by carefully listening to others and attentively observing what they do.
3. *Language and behavior convey information about social status and group membership.* Usually, the person or group with more status and power establishes the "accepted" type of talk and behavior. For example, if you are being interviewed for a job by someone who behaves formally, you are likely to behave the same way.
4. *Accommodation varies in its degree of appropriateness, and norms guide the accommodation process.* When a situation is awkward, effective communicators try to accommodate the behavior of the group in that situation. Thus, if you interact with a culture that respects its elders, you may hesitate questioning the views of an older person or senior official. Or when you learn that a particular behavior is *inappropriate*, you will not engage in that behavior. For example, if you and your colleagues are on a deadline at work and they decide to leave the office before they complete the project, you may not leave with them.

Actively Engage Others

Direct, face-to-face interaction with people from culturally diverse backgrounds benefits everyone. You and others may transform long-held negative beliefs about each other's cultures into positive opinions.

One of the most interesting and exciting ways to actively engage others is to travel. Within the United States, visits to San Francisco, New Orleans, Miami, New York, and Washington, DC will put you in touch with, literally, different worlds. Traveling abroad is even more engaging and has long-term benefits. A survey of students who studied abroad found a positive link to career success, a more tolerant worldview, and increased self-confidence. When questioned about their intercultural development and understanding, 98 percent reported that study abroad helped them to better understand their own cultural values and biases.[76]

If you succeed in minimizing your level of anxiety and uncertainty when encountering others, you may discover new worlds with fascinating people who can enrich your life. The fact is, regardless of culture, nationality, gender, religion, age, and ability, all of us share the traits unique to the amazing human condition.

Communication Traits ALL PEOPLE SHARE[77]

We **SMILE** when happy.

We **WAVE** as a greeting.

We **LAUGH** when amused.

We **BLUSH** when embarrassed.

We **CRY** when sad or in pain.

We **FROWN** when concerned or ill at ease.

We adopt a **FETAL POSITION** when dejected, cold, or in a hopeless situation.

We **SHRUG** to express "I don't know."

We **SLUMP** when dejected or tired.

We **STAND STRAIGHT** when alert or confident.

intercultural communication strategies

The Generalized Ethnocentrism (GENE) Scale[78]

Read the following statements concerning your feelings about your and others' cultures. In the space provided, indicate how each statement applies to you by marking whether you (5) strongly agree, (4) agree, (3) are undecided, (2) disagree, or (1) strongly disagree. There are no right or wrong answers. Remember that the word *culture* refers to a learned set of shared interpretations about beliefs, values, norms, and social practices that affect the behaviors of a relatively large group of people—both in the United States and in other countries. Some of the statements may seem similar. Remember, everyone experiences some degree of ethnocentrism. Be honest. Work quickly and record your first response.

_____ 1. Most other cultures are backward compared with my culture.

_____ 2. People in other cultures have a better lifestyle than we do in my culture.

_____ 3. Most people would be happier if they didn't live like people do in my culture.

_____ 4. My culture should be the role model for other cultures.

_____ 5. Lifestyles in other cultures are just as valid as those in my culture.

_____ 6. Other cultures should try to be more like my culture.

_____ 7. I'm not interested in the values and customs of other cultures.

_____ 8. It is not wise for people of other cultures to look up my culture.

_____ 9. People in my culture could learn a lot from people in other cultures.

_____ 10. Most people from other cultures just don't know what's good for them.

_____ 11. People from my culture act strange and unusual when they go into other cultures.

_____ 12. I have little respect for the values and customs of others cultures.

_____ 13. Most people would be happier if they lived like people in my culture.

_____ 14. People in my culture have just about the best lifestyles of anywhere.

_____ 15. My culture is backward compared to most other cultures.

_____ 16. My culture is a poor role model for other cultures.

_____ 17. Lifestyles in other cultures are not as valid as those in my culture.

_____ 18. My culture should try to be more like other cultures.

_____ 19. I'm very interested in the values and customs of other cultures.

_____ 20. Most people in my culture just don't know what is good for them.

_____ 21. People in other cultures should learn a lot from people in my culture.

_____ 22. Other cultures are smart to look up to my culture.

_____ 23. I respect the values and customs of other cultures.

_____ 24. People from other cultures act strange and unusual when they come into my culture.

To determine your ethnocentrism score, complete the following four steps:

1. Add your responses to items 5, 9, and 23.

2. Add your responses to items 1, 3, 4, 6, 10, 11, 12, 13, 14, 17, 20, and 22.

3. Subtract the sum from step 1 from 18.

4. Add results from step 2 and step 3. This is your generalized ethnocentrism score. Scores of more than 55 points indicate high ethnocentrism.

The Many Faces of Others

3.1 Assess how the increasing cultural diversity in the United States influences your interactions with others.

- By the middle of the twenty-first century there will be no majority culture in the United States.
- Culture is a learned set of shared interpretations about beliefs, values, norms, and social practices, that affect the behaviors of a relatively large group of people.
- Co-cultures exist within the mainstream of society yet remain connected to one another through their cultural heritage.
- Many people are not literate about others' religions or about their own religion.

Barriers to Understand Others

3.2 Explain how ethnocentrism, stereotyping, prejudice, discrimination, and racism inhibit effective and ethical communication.

- Ethnocentrism is a belief that your culture is superior to others; stereotypes are generalizations about a group of people that oversimplify their characteristics.
- Stereotypes lead to prejudices, which are positive or negative attitudes about an individual or cultural group based on little or no direct experience.
- Prejudice leads to discrimination, the exclusion of groups of people from opportunities granted to others.
- In the extreme, prejudice and discrimination lead to racism, which justifies dominating and mistreating people of other races.
- When we view race as a socially constructed concept, it becomes a neutral and natural characteristic of people.

The Dimensions of Culture

3.3 Describe the qualities and impact of cultural dimensions on the communication process.

- The individualism–collectivism cultural dimension contrasts independence and personal achievement with interdependence and group values.
- The power distance cultural dimension examines the physical and psychological distance between those with power and those without power.
- The gender expectation cultural dimension focuses on both expectations about suitable role behaviors as well as expectations about the preferred similarities and differences in the behaviors of men and women.
- The time orientation cultural dimension contrasts a short-term orientation that values time as a commodity and concentrate on one job at a time with a long-term time orientation that values flexibility rather than deadlines and is comfortable with distractions and interruptions.
- The high/low-context cultural dimension focuses on whether meaning is expressed in words or through nonverbal communication and the nature of personal relationships.
- The inferior and costly digital system in the United States affects the country's economic growth and your ability to communicate and compete in a global economy.

Intercultural Communication Strategies

3.4 Practice communication strategies and skills that enhance your ability to understand, respect, and adapt to others.

- Effective communicators are mindful; they are receptive to new information and are responsive to and respectful of others.
- Communication accommodation principles help us understand, respect, and successfully adapt to others.
- Finding ways to interact and actively engage people who are different from you and can help you be a better communicator.

Key Terms

Co-cultures	High power distance	Power distance
Collectivism	High-context culture	Prejudices
Communication Accommodation Theory	Individualism	Race
	Intercultural dimension	Racism
Culture	Low power distance	Religious literacy
Discrimination	Low-context culture	Short-term or long-term
Ethnocentrism	Mindfulness	Stereotypes
Gender expectations dimension	Mindlessness	Time orientation
	Muted Group Theory	

TEST YOUR KNOWLEDGE

3.1 *Assess how the increasing cultural diversity in the United States influences your interactions with others.*

1 According to the U.S. Census, between 2000 and 2010, _____ had the *fastest rate* of population growth and _____ had the *slowest* rate of growth.

   a. Non-Hispanic whites; Hispanic whites

   b. Latinos; Asians

   c. Asians; non-Hispanic whites

   d. Immigrants; Latinos

2 All of the following are true statements about religions except one. Which of the following answer is *false*?

   a. Like Christianity and Judaism, Islam is a monotheistic (belief in one God) religion.

   b. Hindus believe in the idea of reincarnation.

   c. Jesus Christ was Jewish.

   d. One-half of the world's population is Christian.

3.2 *Explain how ethnocentrism, stereotyping, prejudice, discrimination, and racism inhibit effective and ethical communication.*

3 When the courts examined a supermarket's hiring record, they found that the company never hired nonwhite applicants for the better-paying job of working at cash registers. Which barrier to understand others does this example exemplify?

   a. ethnocentrism

   b. stereotyping

   c. racism

   d. discrimination

4 A study in the 1990s found that many college students described African Americans as lazy and loud and Jews as shrewd and intelligent. Which barrier in understanding others is demonstrated by the responses in this study?

   a. ethnocentrism

   b. stereotyping

   c. racism

   d. discrimination

3.3 *Describe the qualities and impact of cultural dimensions on the communication process.*

5 Which of the following countries exhibit the most individualism?

   a. Australia

   b. Indonesia

   c. Taiwan

   d. Peru

6 Which behavior is characteristic of a society with feminine values?

   a. Men are assertive, tough, and focused on success; women are more modest and tender.

   b. Men's and women's gender roles overlap.

   c. Women assume almost all of the homemaking and child-rearing responsibilities.

   d. Men assume most homemaking and child-rearing responsibilities.

3.4 *Practice communication strategies and skills that enhance your ability to understand, respect, and adapt to others.*

7 Which behavior demonstrates mindfulness when communicating with people from other cultures?

   a. You recognize your personal prejudices and try to overcome them.

   b. You understand and respect different cultural values.

   c. You are receptive to new ideas and respect other people's perspectives.

   d. You do all of the above.

8 Howard Giles's communication accommodation theory observes that:

   a. The manner in which we perceive the communication of others determines how we evaluate our interaction with others.

   b. Language and behavior convey information about social status and group membership.

   c. Accommodation varies in its degree of appropriateness.

   d. All of the above.

Answers found on page 368.

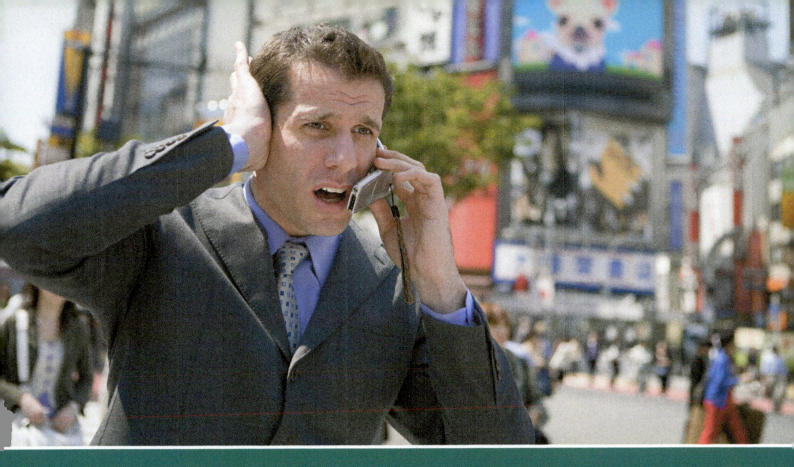

Listening 4

Who is Paul Marcarelli? If you watched any television from November 2001 to September 2011, you heard him repeatedly ask one question: "Can you hear me now?" As the star of Verizon's Test Man commercials, he roamed the country testing the signal on his cell phone.[1]

Of course, the Test Man's question is not just about the range of Verizon's network. It's also about how well people can hear. Humans developed hearing ability as the result of two evolutionary pressures: language and nature. Humans needed to hear in order to recognize and decipher speech sounds. They also needed a way to respond to noises in the natural environment, such as cracks and booms of thunder and the sounds of both edible and of predatory animals.

With the development of hearing came the development of *listening*. Listening requires the careful evaluation of the words and sounds you hear, a critical skill in communication contexts. As *New York Times* science writer, Seth Horowitz, notes that: "*You never listen* [has] become an epidemic in a world that is exchanging convenience for content, speed for meaning."[2]

In this chapter, we examine how to enlist basic components of the listening process as a means of improving your ability to hear, understand, remember, interpret, evaluate, and appropriately respond to a variety of messages.

The Nature of Listening

4.1 *Explain why listening is essential for effective communication.*

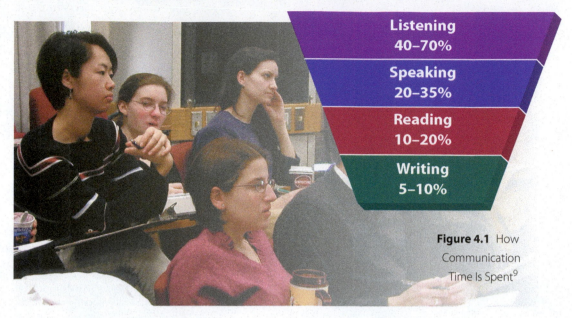

Figure 4.1 How Communication Time Is Spent[9]

Listening 40–70%

Speaking 20–35%

Reading 10–20%

Writing 5–10%

The International Listening Association defines **listening** as "the process of receiving, constructing meaning from, and responding to a spoken and/or nonverbal message."[3] This definition describes the results of effective listening; however, it does not explain *how* the listening process works. Listening—just like speaking, reading, and writing—is a complex process that goes beyond "you speak, I listen." Because many people do not appreciate this complexity, listening may appear to be easy and natural. In fact, just the opposite is true. Hearing is easy (unless there is a genetic, medical, developmental, or environmental impediment). Whereas hearing only requires physical ability, effective listening requires knowledge, skills, and motivation. Listening is hard work, particularly given the thousands of everyday noises that can impair your ability to hear, understand, remember, interpret, evaluate, and respond to others.[4]

Listening is our number one communication activity. A study that accounted for Internet and social media use among college students found that listening occupies more than half of their communicating time.[5] Additionally, effective listening skills are a significant factor in predicting a student's academic success and survival.[6] On the flip side, poor listening is a significant factor in predicting student failure. Although percentages vary from study to study, Figure 4.1 shows how most people divide up their daily communicating time.

In the business world, many executives devote more than 60 percent of their workdays to listening to others.[7] Moreover, listening is often cited as the communication skill most lacking in new employees.[8]

Never underestimate the importance of listening in all aspects of your life. It is much more than our number one communication activity; it is a critical life skill. Graham Bodie, a leading listening scholar claims, "listening is *the* quintessential positive interpersonal communication behavior" because "it connotes an appreciation of and interest in" others.[10]

Bodie explains that the feeling of being listened to or being heard is "an expected part of many relationships from early childhood to the end of life." Good listening is also an important aspect of parenting, marital relationships, sales performances, customer satisfaction, and effective healthcare. Good listeners help others cope with problems, are seen as more likable, attractive, and trustworthy, and are more likely to succeed in a career. Certainly, good listening is a critical component "of managing conflict, succeeding as a leader," and creating a positive business climate.[11] Clearly, in communication contexts, effective listening is as important a skill to develop as effective reading, writing, and speaking.

How Well Do You Listen?

In *The Lost Art of Listening*, Michael Nichols writes, "Listening is so basic that we take it for granted. Unfortunately most of us think of ourselves as

> **Although most of us can hear, we often fail to listen to what others say.**

better listeners than we really are."[12]

For example, immediately after listening to a short talk, most of us cannot accurately report 50 percent of what was said. Without training, we listen at about 25 percent efficiency.[13] And of that 25 percent, most is distorted or inaccurate.[14]

A study of Fortune 500 company training managers concludes, "ineffective listening leads to ineffective performance or low productivity." These same problems also appear in studies of sales professionals, educators, health practitioners, lawyers, and religious leaders.[15]

Listening at home is just as—or more—important. In families the common cry "Nobody around here listens to me!" may come from a frustrated mother, father, or any of the children. Unquestionably, good parenting necessitates good listening. Michael P. Nichols notes, "adolescents need their parents to listen to their troubles, their hopes, and ambitions, even some of their farfetched plans."[16]

When you first meet someone, you form an impression of the person based, in part, on whether she or he appears to be a good listener. Researchers Graham Bodie and his colleagues studied the attributes and behaviors of good listening in such situations. They concluded that when you perceive a listener as attentive (interested, focused), friendly (positive facial expressions and body language), responsive (asking and answering questions), personally engaged (initiates talk, shares personal thoughts), and understanding (seeks commonalities, supportive), they are exhibiting good listening behaviors that are more likely to create a positive impression.[17]

Effective listening is hard work. Researchers note that active listeners register an increase in blood pressure, a higher pulse rate, and even more perspiration.[18] Active listeners try to understand what a speaker is saying, the emotions behind the content, and the conclusion the speaker is making without stating it openly.[19] Effective listening requires the kind of preparation and concentration required of attorneys trying a case and psychologists counseling a client.

Assess Your Listening Habits

As we noted in Chapter 1, "Human Communication," genuine, long-term learning requires *knowledge*, *skills*, and *motivation*. Here we briefly summarize how that applies to listening:

- Knowledge—*What* to do: Unless you understand the principles, importance, and functions of human listening, you may not even know you *need* to listen.
- Skills—*How* to do it: Even if you know you need to listen, you may not have the skill to do it effectively.
- Motivation—*Want* to do it: Knowing you need to listen and knowing how to listen are not enough. Unless you *want* to listen, listening will not become a natural, lifelong practice.

Several listening researchers have applied these three competencies to college students and people working in organizational settings. Research on student listening competencies by Lynn Cooper and Trey Buchanan demonstrate the importance of knowledge, skills, and motivation. They conclude that effective listeners are:[20]

1. open or willing to listen
2. able to read nonverbal cues
3. able to understand verbal cues
4. able to respond appropriately
5. able to remember relevant details

Know Thy Self

Do You Have Poor Listening Habits?[21]

Examine the poor listening habits below and select the response that best reflects how you listen. Notice that we have not included a "never" option because no one is a perfect listener 100 percent of the time.

Poor Listening Habits	How Frequently Do You Listen This Way?		
Defensive Listening. Do you feel threatened or humiliated by critical remarks from others? Do you focus on how to respond to or challenge another person's questions and criticisms rather than listening objectively?	Often	Sometimes	Rarely
Disruptive Listening. Do you interrupt others while they're speaking? Do you exaggerate your responses by sighing audibly, rolling your eyes, shaking your head in a *no*, or obviously withholding your attention?	Often	Sometimes	Rarely
Pseudolistening. Do you fake attention or pretend to listen when your mind is elsewhere, you're bored, or you think it pleases the speaker? Do you nod or smile even though your response has nothing to do with the message?	Often	Sometimes	Rarely
Selective Listening. If you don't like or agree with someone, do you avoid listening or look for faults in what that person says? Do you avoid listening to complex or highly technical information?	Often	Sometimes	Rarely
Superficial Listening. Do you pay more attention to the way other people look or how they speak rather than to what they say? Do you draw conclusions about others' intentions or claims before they've finished talking?	Often	Sometimes	Rarely

If you answered with an honest *rarely* to all of the questions, you are probably a good listener. If you answered *often* or *sometimes*, you may have a gap in your listening knowledge, skills, and/or motivation.

The Listening Process

4.2 *Identify the key components of the listening process.*

Listening researchers, cognitive scientists, and neurologists describe listening as a complex phenomenon. To address the complexity of listening, Judi Brownell, a leading listening scholar, presents a six-component listening model called the HURIER model. The letters in HURIER represent six interrelated listening processes: **H**earing, **U**nderstanding, **R**emembering, **I**nterpreting, **E**valuating, and **R**esponding. Brownell links each of these six components to appropriate listening attitudes, relevant listening principles, and strategies for improving your listening skills.[22] (See Figure 4.2.)

The HURIER model "recognizes that you are constantly influenced by both internal and external factors that color your perceptions and subsequent interpretations." These listening filters include your attitudes, values, biases, and previous experiences.[23] For example, if you know that your instructor's exams include questions based on her lectures, you are more likely to listen attentively to what she says.

The HURIER model also recognizes that different listening skills become more or less important depending on

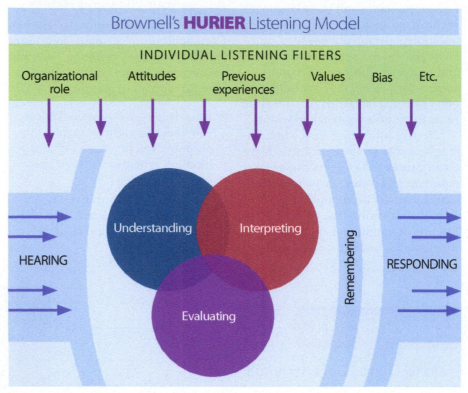

Figure 4.2 The HURIER Model of Listening.

both your purpose and the communication context.[24] For instance, when you're listening to a topic expert, you may be "all ears" and be open to learning and agreeing. In contrast, you may listen more critically when a less informed speaker presents a poorly structured proposal for solving a problem. And if you are listening to someone in a hot, noisy room at a late hour of

LISTENING COMPONENTS in the HURIER Listening Model

TYPE OF LISTENING	DEFINITION	EXAMPLE
Hearing	Your ability to make clear distinctions among the sounds and words in a language	I sometimes have trouble hearing a soft-spoken person, particularly if there's background noise.
Understanding	Your ability to accurately grasp the meaning of someone's spoken and nonverbal messages	When you say wait, do you mean we should wait a few more minutes or wait until Caleb gets here?
Remembering	Your ability to store, retain, and recall information you have heard	Hi George. I remember meeting you last month. Did you end up selling your old truck?
Interpreting	Your ability to empathize with another person's feelings	It must be frustrating and discouraging to have such an unsympathetic instructor.
Evaluating	Your ability to analyze and make a judgment about the validity of someone's message	I see two reasons why that proposal won't work. They are . . .
Responding	Your ability to respond in a way that indicates you fully understanding someone's meaning	You seem to be saying that it's not a good time to confront Chris. Am I right?

the day, it may be very difficult to focus your attention and energy on the task.

Brownell's HURIER listening model highlights six types of listening to ensure that you accurately and appropriately hear, understand, remember, interpret, evaluate, and respond to spoken and/or nonverbal messages. In the following section, we take a more detailed look at the listening components in the HURIER model to help you assess your own and others' listening needs and abilities.

Listening to Hear

Listening to hear is the ability to make clear distinctions among the sounds and words in a language and is the "prerequisite to all listening."[25] Your hearing ability also determines whether you can detect the meaning of vocalized sounds such as a groan or a laugh. Hearing, writes science writer Seth Horowitz, "is your life line, your alarm system, your way to escape danger and pass on your genes."[26]

Most of us rely on seeing as our first and most important sense. But studies have shown that visual recognition, unlike hearing, requires conscious thought. As a result, hearing is as much as ten times faster than recognizing and responding to something you see.[27]

Hearing ability differs from person to person. According to the National Institute on Deafness and Other Communication Disorders, about thirty-six million American adults report some degree of hearing loss. Given that hearing loss is usually gradual and cumulative throughout your life, older adults have greater hearing losses than children and young adults. However, "approximately 15 percent (26 million) of Americans between the ages of 20 and 69 have high frequency hearing loss due to exposure to loud sounds or noise at work or in leisure activities."[28] Researchers at Gallaudet University report that about two to four of every 1,000 people in the United States are "functionally deaf," though more than half became deaf relatively late in life.[29]

Answering the following questions can help you understand why hearing is the gateway to effective listening.

- Do you often ask others to repeat what they've said or misunderstand what they've said because you did not hear them accurately?

- Do you notice nonverbal messages expressed in people's facial expressions, gestures, posture, movement, and vocal sounds (sighs, groans, laughter, gasps)?

Listening to Understand

Listening to understand, also known as *comprehensive* listening, focuses on accurately grasping the *meaning* of someone's spoken and nonverbal messages. After all, if you don't understand what someone means, how can you respond in a reasonable way? For example, an after-class discussion just before finals might begin as follows: "Let's have a party on the last day of class." If you are listening to understand, you may wonder whether the statement means that (1) we should have a party *instead* of an exam, (2) we should ask the instructor whether we can have a party, or (3) we should have a party literally *after* the exam. Misinterpreting the meaning of this comment could result in an inappropriate response.

Asking questions is one of the best ways to make sure you understand the meaning of someone's words and nonverbal behavior.[30] The strategies and questions in the box below constitute a blueprint for understanding what a person means.

Listening to Remember

How good is your memory? Do you ever forget what you're talking about during a discussion? Can you remember a person's name or a phone number if you haven't written it down? Occasionally, everyone experiences memory problems.

Listening to remember is the ability to store, retain, and recall information you have heard. As we noted earlier in this chapter, most people cannot recall 50 percent of what they hear immediately after hearing it. At the same time, your ability to remember directly affects how well you listen.

When we ask students, "How good is *your* memory?" they often answer, "It depends." For example, if you're very interested in what someone's saying you're more likely to remember the conversation, discussion, or presentation. However, if you're under a lot of stress or preoccupied with personal problems, you may not remember anything. Here are just a few suggestions that, with practice, can improve your memory:

- **Repeat.** Repeat an important idea or piece of information after you hear it; say it aloud if you can. For example, if you've just learned that your group project report is due on the 22nd, use this date in a sentence several times ("Let's see how many meetings we need to have before the 22nd"; "We'll need to have our first draft done a week ahead of time—22 minus 7 is 15"). If you're in a situation where it's not appropriate to do this aloud, repeat the information in your mind.

- **Associate.** Associate a word, phrase, or idea with something that

Ask GOOD QUESTIONS to Ensure Understanding

1. **Have a plan.** Make sure your question is clear and appropriate so it will not be misunderstood or waste time.
2. **Keep the questions simple.** Ask one question at a time and make sure it's relevant to the message.
3. **Ask nonthreatening questions.** Avoid questions that begin with "Why didn't you . . . ?" or "How could you . . . ?" because they can create a defensive climate in responders.
4. **Ask permission.** If a topic is sensitive, explain why you are asking the question and ask permission before continuing. "You say you're fearful about telling Sharon about the mistake you made. Would you mind helping me understand why you're so apprehensive?"
5. **Avoid biased or manipulative questions.** Tricking someone into giving you the answer you want can destroy trust. There's a big difference between "Why did we miss the deadline?" and "Who screwed up?"
6. **Wait for the answer.** In addition to asking good questions, respond appropriately to the response you receive. After you ask a question, give the other person time to think and frame an answer.

describes it. For example, when you meet someone whose name you want to remember, associate the name with the context in which you met the person (Jamal in biology class) or with a word beginning with the same letter that describes the person (Brunette Brenda).

- **Visualize.** Visualize a word, phrase, or idea. For example, when a patient was told she might need to take calcium channel blockers, she visualized a swimmer trying to cross the English Channel filled with floating calcium pills.

- **Use mnemonics.** A **mnemonic** is a memory aid that is based on something simple like a pattern or rhyme. For example, the HURIER in Brownell's Model of Listening is an acronym (the first letters for the six components of listening). Many people remember which months of the year have thirty days with the poem that begins "Thirty days hath September. . . ." Thus, by rearranging these memory suggestions, you might be able to remember MARV (**m**nemonics, **a**ssociate, **r**epeat, **v**isualize).

Listening to Interpret

Judi Brownell describes **listening to interpret** (also called *empathic* listening) as "a primary factor in empathic listening, where your ability to recognize and respond appropriately to

---

Remembering Names

Ava is headed to a local coffee shop with her friend Eduard, when she recognizes an acquaintance of hers walking toward them. Ava waves at the acquaintance and pulls Eduard over to meet him. Eduard extends his hand and smiles while Ava introduces the two men: "Eduard, this is Colin, a former colleague of mine. Colin, this is Eduard, a longtime friend." She pronounces each name clearly. After a couple of minutes, Eduard realizes that he cannot recall Colin's name. Eduard does not want to appear rude by asking for Colin's name again, especially because Colin referred to Eduard by name several times during the conversation. Two weeks later, Eduard bumps into Colin again, and Colin greets Eduard by name. Eduard cannot return the honor.

Why do so many of us forget names? In *How to Start a Conversation and Make Friends*, Don Gabor suggests the reason is because we're not *listening* effectively. We're too busy thinking about ourselves, what we're going to say, whether we will make a good impression, and how other people will react to us.[31] Based on Gabor's tips, we suggest six strategies for remembering someone's name during your first conversation:

1. Pay undivided attention to the moment of introduction.
2. Rather than thinking about what *you* want to say, listen for the name and information about the person.
3. Repeat the person's name out loud when you hear it.
4. Think of someone you know or someone famous who has the same name. For example, if you meet someone named Homer, think about Homer Simpson or the epic poet who wrote the *Iliad* and *Odyssey*. If you meet someone who looks like a childhood friend, teacher, relative, or even celebrity with the same name, associate the new person with the name of that person.
5. Link the person's name to a unique characteristic such as a word that begins with the same letter (Strong Sergio, Laughing Lewis, Cooking Cathy), a characteristic word that rhymes with the person's name (Curley Shirley, Slim Jim), or a word that reminds of you of an event (Tom's Toe because you met him the night he broke his toe).
6. Use the person's name several times during the conversation.[32]

emotional meanings is critical."[33] This kind of listening answers the question: How does the other person feel?

Empathic listening goes beyond comprehending what a person means; it involves focusing on understanding someone's situation, feelings, or motives. Can you see the situation through the other person's eyes? How would you feel in a similar situation?

> ❝ [Listening] involves learning how to suspend your own emotional agenda and then realizing the rewards of genuine empathy. ❞
> —Michael Nichols, *The Lost Art of Listening*[34]

By not listening for feelings, you may overlook the most important part of a message. Even if you understand every word a person says, you can still miss the anger, enthusiasm, or frustration in someone's voice. As an empathic listener, you don't have to agree with or feel the same way as others, but you do have to try to understand the type and intensity of feelings they are experiencing. For example, the after-class discussion mentioned earlier might continue as follows: "A class party would be a waste of time!" exclaims Kim. An empathic listener may wonder whether Kim means that (1) she has more important things to do during exam week, (2) she doesn't think the class or the instructor deserves a party, or (3) she doesn't want to attend such a party.

Empathic listening is difficult, but it also is "the pinnacle of listening" because it demands "fine skill and exquisite tuning into another's mood and feeling."[35] Answering the following questions can help you understand the scope of empathic listening:

- Do you show interest and concern about the other person?
- Does your nonverbal behavior communicate friendliness and trust?

- Do you avoid highly critical reactions to others?
- Do you avoid talking about your own experiences and feelings when someone else is describing theirs?[36]

Listening to Evaluate

Listening to evaluate is the ability to analyze and make a judgment about the validity of what someone says. Once you are sure you've comprehended the meaning of a message, ask yourself whether your reasoning is sound and the conclusion is justified. Evaluative listeners understand why they accept or reject someone's ideas and suggestions. They make judgments based on their evaluation of another person's

Empathic listening shows that you care.

message: Is the speaker right or wrong, logical or illogical, biased or unbiased? Should I accept, question, or reject the

ETHICAL COMMUNICATION

Apply the Golden Listening Rule

The **Golden Listening Rule** is easy to remember: *Listen to others as you would have them listen to you.* Unfortunately, this rule can be difficult to follow. It asks you to suspend your own needs and opinions to listen to someone else's.[37]

The golden listening rule is also an ethical listening practice. It reflects a principle in the National Communication Association's Credo for Ethical Communication: "We strive to understand and respect other communicators before evaluating and responding to their message."[38] When you follow the golden listening rule, you communicate your interest, patience, and open-mindedness.

The golden listening rule is not so much a "rule" as it is a positive listening attitude. If you aren't motivated to listen, you won't listen. Effective listeners have made listening an enduring habit by recognizing the importance of good listening, learning effective listening skills, and—perhaps most important of all—*wanting* to listen. An appropriate listening attitude requires a strong motivation to listen and discover.[39] Contrast the six positive listening attitudes that follow with their six negative counterparts:[40]

How Positive Is Your Listening *Attitude*?	
Positive Listening	**Negative Listening**
Interested	Uninterested
Responsible	Irresponsible
Sympathetic	Unsympathetic
Other-centered	Self-centered
Patient	Impatient
Equal	Superior
Open-minded	Closed-minded

speaker's ideas and suggestions? Evaluative listeners are open-minded. They put aside biases or prejudices about the speaker or message when they analyze what they hear in order to arrive at a rational conclusion or decision.

Recognizing that someone is trying to persuade—rather than merely inform—is one of the first steps in improving your evaluative listening. Ask yourself the following questions to determine your ability to listen and evaluate what you hear:[41]

- Do you recognize persuasive communication strategies?
- Can you tell when someone is appealing to your emotions and/or to your critical thinking ability?
- Can you assess the quality and validity of arguments and evidence?

The ability to think critically as you listen and carefully evaluate what someone is saying is a difficult but learnable skill. In later chapters, we focus on the critical thinking skills you need to enhance the quality of communication and to separate the valid from invalid claims you encounter.

Listening to Respond

Listening to respond is the ability to react in a way that indicates you have done your best to fully understand

---

Functions of PARAPHRASING

- To ensure comprehension before evaluation
- To reassure others that you want to understand them
- To clear up confusion and ask for clarification
- To summarize lengthy comments
- To help others uncover their own thoughts and feelings
- To provide a safe and supportive communication climate
- To help others reach their own conclusions[42]

---

what someone says. When you listen to others (and especially if you listen to hear, understand, remember, interpret, and evaluate), you are likely to respond verbally and/or nonverbally. You may ask a question, provide support, offer advice, or share your opinion. You may frown, smile, laugh, shrug, or look confused. Fortunately, there is a critical responding skill that can help you make sure you fully understand someone else's meaning: paraphrasing.

The Nature of Paraphrasing

Paraphrasing is the ability to restate what people say in a way that indicates you understand them.

Knowing how to paraphrase is critical to becoming a highly effective listener. When you paraphrase, you go beyond the words you hear to understand the feelings and underlying meanings that accompany the words. Too often, we jump to conclusions and incorrectly assume that we know what a speaker means and feels.

Paraphrasing is a form of feedback—a listening check—that asks, "Am I right—is this what you mean?" Paraphrasing is not repeating what a person says; it requires finding *new* words to describe what you have heard.

The Complexities of Paraphrasing Paraphrasing is difficult. Not only are you putting aside your own interests and opinions, but you are also finding *new* words that best

> Effective paraphrasing requires mindful listening. Paraphrasing says, "I want to hear what you have to say, and I want to understand what you mean."

Know Thy Self

Paraphrase This

How well do you understand paraphrasing? Read the following three statements and write a response that paraphrases their meaning, as demonstrated in the following example:

Group member: "I get really annoyed when André yells at one of us during our meetings."

Paraphrase: *"You sound as though you become very upset when André shouts at you or other group members. Is that what's bothering you?"*

1. **Friend:** I have the worst luck with computers. The computer I have now has crashed again, and I lost all of my documents. Maybe I'm doing something wrong. Why me?

   Paraphrase: _____

   _____

2. **Colleague:** I dislike saying *no* to anyone who asks for help, but then I have to rush or stay up late to get my own work done. I want to help, but I also want to do my own job.

   Paraphrase: _____

   _____

3. **Classmate:** How on earth am I going to get an A on this exam if I can't even find time to read the textbook?

   Paraphrase: _____

   _____

Type of Paraphrase	Effective Paraphrase: Technique and Example	Ineffective Paraphrase Examples
Martin: "I never seem to get anywhere on time, and I don't know why."		
Paraphrase Content: Find *new* words to express the same meaning. Paraphrase, don't parrot.	"What I'm hearing is that you've tried to figure out why you're often late but can't. Is that what you're saying?"	"Ah, so you don't know why you never seem to get anywhere on time?"
Martin: "People, including my boss, bug me about being late, and sometimes I can tell that they're pretty angry."		
Paraphrase Depth: Match the emotions to the speaker's meaning. Avoid responding lightly to a serious problem and vice versa.	"When you say that people are angry, you sound as though it's become serious enough to put your job at risk or damage your relationships with your boss and coworkers; is that right?"	"In other words, you worry that other people are kind of upset by your lateness."
Martin: "I really don't know . . ."*		
Paraphrase Meaning: Do not add unintended meaning or complete the person's sentence.	"Let me make sure I understand what you're saying. Is it that you don't know why you're always late, or that you wish you had a better idea of how to manage your time?"	". . . how to manage your time?" (*Martin would have finished with "what to do.")
Martin: "I never seem to get anywhere on time and I don't know why."		
Paraphrase Language: Use simple language to ensure accuracy.	"It sounds as though being late has become a big problem at work and you're looking for ways to fix it. Right?"	"Ahh, your importunate perplexities about punctuality are inextricably linked."

Figure 4.3 Types of Paraphrasing

match someone else's meaning. Figure 4.3 shows how a paraphrase can vary in four critical ways: content, depth, meaning, and language.[43]

Paraphrasing says, "I want to hear what you have to say, and I want to understand what you mean." If you paraphrase accurately, the other person will appreciate your understanding and support. Even if you don't get the paraphrase right, your feedback provides another opportunity for the speaker to explain.

Listening to Gender and Culture

4.3 *Describe the ways in which gender and culture influence how we listen.*

Understanding and adapting to the diverse listening skills and styles of others can be a challenging task, particularly when gender and cultural differences are taken into account. Keep in mind that there are many exceptions to the research summaries we present about listening differences. As you read, you may say, "But I know women who don't listen this way." The existence of exceptions does not mean that the general claim is totally false. Diversity research provides useful insights that help explain common differences in listening behavior.

Listening to Gender

Linguist Deborah Tannen, author of the best-selling book, *You Just Don't Understand: Women and Men in Conversation*, examines more than the talking part of a conversation. She also focuses on how women and men listen to one another. Some women complain that their male partners and colleagues don't listen to them. Tannen observes that men sometimes make the same complaint about women. She explains that the accusation "You're not listening" often means "You don't understand what I said" or "I'm not getting the response I want."[44]

Tannen also explains why it may *seem* that men don't listen. Quite simply, many men don't *show* they are listening, whereas women do. In general, women provide more feedback when listening: They provide listening responses, such as *mhm*, *uh-huh*, and *yeah*. And women respond more positively and enthusiastically by nodding and laughing. To a man (who expects a listener to be quiet and attentive), a woman giving off a stream of feedback and support will seem to be "talking" too much for

a listener. To a woman (who expects a listener to be active and show interest, attention, and support), a man who listens silently will seem to have checked out of the conversation. The bottom line is this: Women may get the impression that men don't listen when, in fact, they are listening. Unfortunately, some men really don't want to listen because they believe that it puts them in a weak position compared to women.[45]

Researchers have noted that men often tune out things they can't solve or wonder why they should even listen if there isn't a problem to solve. Women may become more involved and connected to the speaker and see listening as something important to do for the other person.[46]

Although men use talk to establish status, women are more likely to use listening to empower others. Unfortunately, people who listen much more than they talk are often viewed as subordinate and subservient rather than powerful.[47]

Most of the research examining gender-based listening differences needs to be revisited. Would you agree that men listen to the content of what is said, whereas women are more likely to focus on the relationship between the speaker and listener? Do males focus on the facts, whereas females are more aware of the mood of the interaction? Are men more likely to be comprehensive and analytical listeners,

whereas women are more likely to be empathetic and appreciative listeners? Twenty years ago, most researchers would have answered *yes* to these questions. Unfortunately, many of these observations may be little more than conclusions based on limited observations and on our implicit biases. Today as more and more women assume traditionally male roles and jobs and men assume traditionally female roles and jobs, these distinctions may not be as clear-cut as they were even two decades ago. As in the case with many gender issues, our socialization and implicit biases affect our expectations about the way women and men listen.

Listening to Cultures

In Chapter 3, "Adapting to Others," we introduced the concept of high- and low-context cultures. In high-context countries such as Japan, China, and Korea and in African American, American Indian, and Arab cultures, not all meaning is expressed through words. Much more attention is given to nonverbal cues and the relationships among the communicators. As a result, listeners from high-context cultures "listen" for meanings in your behavior and in who you are rather than in the words you say. However, listeners from low-context countries such as Germany, Switzerland, Scandinavia, and the United States focus on words. They expect speakers to be direct.

When people from high-context/low-context cultures interact, misunderstanding, offense, and even conflict may result. In many Asian cultures, the amount of time spent talking and the value placed on talking are very different from what they are in the United States and Latin America.

One line of research points to an interesting difference between what is called a **speaker-responsible language** and a **listener-responsible language**.[48] English is a speaker-responsible language in which speakers provide the specific meaning of a message—what they will talk about and exactly what they want listeners to know or do. You don't have to know much about your relationship with the speaker or the speaker's background to understand such messages. Japanese is a listener-responsible language in which speakers "indicate only indirectly what they are discussing and what they want the listener to know [or do]." In this case, the listener has to fill in the blanks and construct the meaning of the speaker's message based on shared knowledge between the speaker and the listener. For example, whereas you might fail to get the A you deserve if your English composition paper doesn't have a thesis statement, other cultures do not expect such an upfront statement. The thesis is implied; it's up to the listener to connect ideas, figure out the speaker's intentions, and discover the thesis.[49]

COMMUNICATION&CULTURE

THE ART OF HIGH-CONTEXT LISTENING

High-context communicators listen beyond a person's words to interpret meaning by paying close attention to nonverbal cues. Interestingly, the Chinese symbol for "to listen" includes characters for eyes, ears, and heart.

For the Chinese, "it is impossible to listen . . . without using the eyes because you need to look for nonverbal communication." The Chinese listen with their ears as well because they speak a tonal language in which intonation determines meaning. They also claim, "you listen with your heart because . . . [you must sense the] emotional undertones expressed by the speaker." In Korean, the word *nunchi* means that you communicate through your eyes. "Koreans believe that the environment supplies most of the information that we seek, so there is little need to speak."[50]

Chinese symbol for listening

The Personal Listening Styles Controversy

Communication research on listening is dynamic and continues to evolve. In 1995, communication researchers Kittie Watson, Larry Barker, and James Weaver theorized that each of us prefers and uses one or more of four distinct listening styles. They claimed that by understanding your preferred listening style or styles, you "can explore other styles and learn how to adapt [your listening] behaviors accordingly to maximize communication."[51]

Since 2010, researchers Graham Bodie, Debra Worthington, and Christopher Gearhart have been analyzing the personal listening styles concept proposed by Watson, Barker, and Weaver. Their research concludes that the four styles cannot be validated as distinct or separate from one another and do not represent a reliable explanation of listening styles.[52] Bodie and colleagues then provide substantive evidence supporting an alternative set of listening styles as well as a statistically validated instrument to measure those styles. The table in this box lists each set of listening styles.

At first glance, these two sets of listening styles may seem very similar. What makes them different is the way in which each listening style is defined and the instruments used to uncover and measure each style. In light of the original research by Watson, Barker, and Weaver and the analysis by Bodie, Worthington, and Gearhart do your best to answer the following questions:

1. Which style or styles do *you* generally prefer and use when listening to others?
2. If you have a preferred listening style or styles, what are the positive and negative characteristics of that style?
3. How, if at all, can understanding these four styles help you adapt to others?
4. Which of the two lists makes the most sense to you? How can continued research help us better understand the complex task of listening to others?

Bodie, Worthington, and Gearhart take their analysis of listening styles one step further than did Watson, Barker, and Weaver by noting that their scale "taps various goals that listeners have when engaged in situations that call them to be a particular kind of listener." In other words, you may be a task listener when trying to finish a project in cooperation with others, a critical listener while watching a televised election debate, a relational listener when supporting a friend in crisis, and an analytical listener when assessing the validity of an academic presentation. If, as they suggest, our styles may differ depending on the characteristics of the situation and the people with whom we interact, we should try to become proficient in all listening styles, not just the one we prefer or usually use.[53]

Personal Listening Styles Research

Watson, Barker, and Weaver	Bodie, Worthington, and Gearhart
Action-oriented: Focuses on objectives and results; prefers clear and structured messages; focuses on what will be done and who will do it	**Task Listening:** Focuses on completing simple communication transactions effectively and efficiently; describes listeners who need structure
Time-oriented: Focuses on the clock; time and listening are organized in neat segments; wants short answers to question	**Critical Listening:** Focuses on noting inconsistencies and errors when others speak; listens to evaluate what others say
People-oriented: Focuses on feelings, emotions, and understanding others; responds with "we" statements; Interested in understanding, not criticizing	**Relational Listening:** Focuses on understanding emotions and connecting with others; empathic listening
Content-oriented: Focuses on what is said, not who says it; not concerned about feelings; interested in facts, evidence, logic, and complex ideas	**Analytical Listening:** Focuses on withholding judgment about others' ideas in order to consider all sides of an issue before responding

Listening Strategies and Skills

4.4 *Practice effective listening strategies and skills.*

At this point, you should know *why* good listening is essential for effective and ethical communication. You should also have some ideas about how to better hear, understand, remember, interpret, evaluate, and respond appropriately to others. In this section, we introduce several listening strategies and skills that can improve your listening ability in most contexts. When and how you use these strategies depends, in part, on whether you are the speaker or the listener (or both) and whether you are speaking to one person or a large group of people.

Use Your Extra Thought Speed

Most people talk at about 125 to 150 words per minute. But most of us can *think* at three to four times that rate.[54] Thus, we have about 400 extra words of spare thinking time during every minute a person talks to us.

Thought speed is the speed (words per minute) at which most people can think compared to the speed at which they can speak. Poor listeners use their extra thought speed to daydream, engage in side conversations, take unnecessary notes, or plan how to confront a speaker. Conscientious listeners use their extra thought speed to enhance all types of listening.

You can use your extra thought speed to:

- make sure you **hear** what someone says.
- determine the **meaning** of a message.
- identify and summarize **key ideas**.
- **remember** what someone says.
- **empathize** with a person's expressed **feelings**.
- **analyze** and evaluate arguments.
- determine the most appropriate way to **respond** to what you hear.

Listening Strategies and Skills

1 Use Your Extra Thought Speed

2 Listen for Feedback

3 Listen to Nonverbal Behavior

4 Listen Before You Leap

5 Minimize Distractions

6 Take Relevant Notes

Listen to Feedback

One of the most important and challenging communication skills is listening to and providing appropriate feedback to others during a conversation, meeting, or presentation. Feedback, the verbal and nonverbal responses others communicate as they listen, reveals how listeners react—negatively or positively—to you and your message.

All listeners react in some way. They may smile or frown or nod "yes" or "no." They may break into spontaneous applause or not applaud at all. They may sit forward at full attention or sit back and look bored. Analyzing your listeners' feedback helps determine how you and your message affect others. As you speak, look and listen to the ways in which people react to you. Do they look interested or uninterested, pleased or displeased? If you can't see or hear reactions, ask for feedback. You can stop in the middle of a conversation, meeting, or presentation to ask whether others understand you. Soliciting feedback helps you adapt to your listeners and tells your listeners that you are interested in their reactions. It also helps others focus their attention and listen more effectively to your message.

Listen to Nonverbal Behavior

Very often, another person's meaning is expressed through nonverbal behavior (see Chapter 6, "Nonverbal Communication"). For example, a change in vocal tone or volume may be another way of saying, "Listen up! This is very important." A person's sustained eye contact may mean, "I'm talking to you!" Facial expressions can reveal whether a person is experiencing joy, skepticism, or fear. Nonverbal behavior also reveals others' intentions.

A recent study found that children as young as three are less likely to help a person at a later point in time after seeing them harm someone else. What's intriguing about this finding is, "the toddlers judged a person's intention" by observing their nonverbal behavior.

> **" ... next to the words you say, your face is the primary source of information about you and the meaning of your message. "**
>
> —Mark Knapp and Judith Hall[55]

In other words—just like most three-year-olds—many of us can determine others' intentions without hearing them say a single word.[56]

Gestures express emotions that words cannot convey. For example, at the moment during a trial when an attorney makes his final argument to the jury that his client should be acquitted, one juror, almost imperceptibly, moves her head back and forth, signifying "no." When the attorney states that his client had no idea that a crime had been committed, another juror raises one eyebrow with a look that says, "Okay, you've done your best to defend your client, but you and I know he's guilty as sin." In the end, the jury finds the defendant guilty as charged.

> ❝ We must always withhold evaluation until our comprehension is complete. ❞
> —Ralph Nichols[57]

Listen Before You Leap

Ralph Nichols, often called the "father of listening research," counsels listeners to make sure they understand a speaker's message *before* reacting, either positively or negatively. This strategy requires taking time to bring your emotions under control. You may comprehend a speaker perfectly but be infuriated or offended by what you hear. If an insensitive speaker refers to women in the room as "girls" or a minority group as "those people," you may need to count to twenty to collect your thoughts and refocus your attention on comprehensive listening.

If a speaker tells an offensive joke, you may react with anger at the speaker and disappointment with those who laughed. Try to understand the effects of offensive comments and emotion-laden words without losing your composure or concentration.

When you listen before you leap, you are using your extra thought speed to decide how to react to controversial, prejudiced, or offensive comments.

What are students "telling" this instructor (who is reading from his lecture notes)?

Listening before you leap gives you time to adjust your reaction and to clarify and correct a statement rather than offend, disrupt, or infuriate others.

Minimize Distractions

Have you ever attended a lecture where the room was too hot, the seats were uncomfortable, or people in the hallway were talking loudly? Distractions such as loud and annoying noises, poor seating arrangements, foul odors, frequent interruptions, and unattractive décor can make listening very difficult.[58] Other forms of distraction include a speaker's delivery that is too soft, fast, slow, or monotone; an accent that is unfamiliar; or mannerisms and appearance that appear unconventional or distracting.

You can help people listen better by taking action to overcome distractions. For example, when a distraction is physical, you are well within your rights as a listener or speaker to shut a door, open a window, or turn on more lights. In large groups, you may ask permission to improve the group's surroundings. Depending on the circumstances and setting, you can also take direct action to reduce behavioral distractions. If someone is talking or fidgeting while the speaker is addressing the audience, ask that person to stop. After all, if someone is distracting you, he or she is probably distracting others. If someone is speaking too quietly, kindly ask the presenter to speak more loudly.

Take Relevant Notes

Given that most of us only listen at 25 percent efficiency, why not take notes and write down important facts and big ideas? Research has found that note takers recall messages in more detail than non–note takers.[59]

Taking notes makes a great deal of sense but *only* if it is done skillfully.

Good listeners are flexible and adaptable note takers.

listening strategies and skills

If you are like most listeners, only one-fourth of what is said may end up in your notes. Even if you copy every word you hear, your notes will not include the nonverbal cues that often tell you more about what a person means and feels. And if you spend all your time taking notes, when will you put aside your pen and ask or answer an important question?

Ralph Nichols summarizes the dilemma of balancing note taking and listening when he concludes, "there is some evidence to indicate that the volume of notes taken and their value to the taker are inversely related."[60] This does not mean you should stop taking notes, but you should learn how to take useful notes—the key to which is adaptability. Effective listeners adjust their note taking to the content, style, and organizational pattern of a speaker.

If someone tells stories to make a point, jot down a brief reminder of the story and its point. If a professor lists tips, dos and don'ts, or recommendations, include those lists in your notes. If someone asks and answers a series of questions, your notes should reflect that pattern. If someone describes a new concept or explains a complex theory, try to paraphrase the meaning in your notes or jot down questions you want to ask.

MEDIATED COMMUNICATION IN *ACTION*

Listening Online

At first, the phrase "listening online" may appear impossible if you're sending someone a text message. Unless you're talking on the phone, voice-enabling your computer, or using Skype, you cannot see or hear the other person when you're online. How can you listen then? A quick review of five of the six listening processes in Brownell's HURIER listening model can answer that question.

Even if you are reading rather than hearing a message, do your best to understand, remember, interpret, evaluate, and appropriately respond to the other person's message. When we listen online, we are doing much more than sending and receiving messages. We are demonstrating "to others that they matter; we are, in essence, stopping, encouraging, and planting seeds of kindness and optimism."[61] We are letting others know that we comprehend and value the meaning of their messages.

Following are some recommendations for adapting the HURIER model to online messages:

1. **Understand.** Pay attention to commonly used online devices such as emoticons in the form of smiley faces or other symbols, netlingo such as LOL, BTW, or OMG, all CAPITAL LETTERS, **bold letters**, and <mark>highlighting</mark> that emphasize a phrase or show an emotion, the overuse of punctuation marks such as exclamation points or a series of question marks or exclamation points such as !?!?

2. **Remember.** Depending on the importance of the message, you may want to copy all or part of it and save it as a Word document. Face-to-face listeners do not have that luxury.

3. **Interpret.** Consider whether the other person's choice of words indicates a particular frame of mind or emotion. Are the words dull and ordinary or highly expressive and emotional? Are there more positive or negative words? Is the person asking for help, advice, sympathy, or agreement—either directly or indirectly? Answering these questions can help you frame a responsible and empathic response.

4. **Evaluate.** Engage your critical thinking as you read an online message. Are the facts valid? Are the conclusions reasonable? And don't be afraid of your emotional responses. If something does "smell right" (not literally) about what you're reading, you may want to look for an error or flaw in the message.

5. **Respond.** Listening to understand, remember, interpret, and evaluate prepare you to respond. If you don't understand what someone means, ask that person to explain it again. If you're not sure whether you need to remember the message, ask a question about its importance. If you sense that the other person needs some emotional support, begin by paraphrasing the meaning of what you've read. Try beginning this kind of response with a phrase such as, "Let me put this in my own words to make sure I understand what you're saying." And if you question the validity of someone's message, explain why.

When responding to a text message, you have much more time to think about, develop, and write an appropriate response. Also make sure that you "listen" before you leap by withholding evaluation until comprehension is complete. Many people enjoy mediated texting because it's so much like talking. Now it's time to think about mediated messages and your responses the same way: It's so much like listening.

Student Listening Inventory[62]

Use the following numbers to indicate how often you, as a student, engage in the following listening behaviors. The "speaker" can refer to the instructor or another student.

1 = almost never   2 = not often   3 = sometimes   4 = more often than not   5 = almost always

Scoring: Add up your scores to assess how well you think you listen.

Listening Behavior

1. When someone is speaking to me, I purposely block out distractions, such as side conversations and personal problems. _____
2. I ask questions when I don't understand something a speaker has said. _____
3. When a speaker uses words I don't know, I jot them down and look them up later. _____
4. I assess a speaker's credibility while listening. _____
5. I paraphrase and/or summarize a speaker's main ideas in my head as I listen. _____
6. I concentrate on a speaker's main ideas rather than the specific details. _____
7. I try to understand people who speak both directly and indirectly. _____
8. Before reaching a conclusion, I try to confirm fully with the speaker my understanding of the message. _____
9. I fully concentrate when a speaker is explaining a complex idea. _____
10. When listening, I devote my full attention to a speaker's message. _____
11. I apply what I know about cultural differences when listening to someone from another culture. _____
12. I watch a speaker's facial expressions and body language for meaning. _____
13. I give positive nonverbal feedback to speakers—nods, eye contact, vocalized agreement. _____
14. When listening to a speaker, I establish eye contact and stop doing nonrelated tasks. _____
15. I avoid tuning out speakers when I disagree with or dislike their message. _____
16. When I have an emotional response to a speaker or the message, I try to set aside my feelings and continue listening to the message. _____
17. I try to match my nonverbal responses to my verbal responses. _____
18. When someone begins speaking, I focus my attention on the message. _____
19. I try to understand how past experiences influence the ways in which I interpret a message. _____
20. I attempt to eliminate outside interruptions and distractions. _____
21. When I listen, I look at the speaker, maintain some eye contact, and focus on the message. _____
22. I avoid tuning out messages that are complex, complicated, and challenging. _____
23. I try to understand the other person's point of view when it is different from mine. _____
24. I try to be nonjudgmental and noncritical when I listen. _____
25. As appropriate, I self-disclose personal information similar to the information the other person shares with me. _____

Score	Interpretation
0–62	You perceive yourself to be a poor listener.
63–86	You perceive yourself to be an adequate listener.
87–111	You perceive yourself to be a good listener.
112–125	You perceive yourself to be an outstanding listener.

communication assessment

The Nature of Listening

4.1 Explain why listening is essential for effective communication.

- We spend most of our communicating time engaged in listening.
- Most people cannot accurately recall 50 percent of what they hear after listening to a short talk. Without training, we listen at about 25 percent efficiency.

The Listening Process

4.2 Identify the key components of the listening process.

- The six types of listening in the HURIER listening model—hearing, understanding, remembering, interpreting, evaluating, and responding—call for unique listening skills.
- Effective paraphrasing involves restating what others say in a way that indicates you understand their meaning.
- Asking well-planned, appropriate questions can help you understand another person's meaning.
- The Golden Listening Rule is: Listen to others as you would have them listen to you.

Listening to Gender and Culture

4.3 Describe the ways in which gender and culture influence how we listen.

- Adjusting to diverse listening styles, particularly those involving differences in gender and culture is a challenging task that requires understanding, respecting, and adapting to others.
- Adjust the way you speak and listen to people who use a listener-responsible language.

Listening Strategies and Skills

4.4 Practice effective listening strategies and skills.

- Conscientious listeners use their extra thought speed to enhance listening.
- Effective communicators skillfully listen to feedback and nonverbal behavior while also making sure that they withhold evaluation until their comprehension is complete.
- Effective listeners avoid and minimize distractions to themselves and others.
- Adaptability and flexibility are keys to listening and taking useful notes.

Key Terms

Empathic listening	Listening to hear	Paraphrasing
Golden Listening Rule	Listening to interpret	Speaker-responsible
Listener-responsible	Listening to remember	language
language	Listening to respond	Thought speed
Listening	Listening to understand	
Listening to evaluate	Mnemonic	

TEST YOUR KNOWLEDGE

4.1 *Explain why listening is essential for effective communication.*

1. In general, we spend 40 to 70 percent of our communicating time engaged in:
   a. writing
   b. speaking
   c. reading
   d. listening

2. Immediately after listening to a short talk or lecture, most people cannot accurately report _____ percent of what was said.
   a. 10
   b. 30
   c. 50
   d. 70

4.2 *Identify the key components of the listening process.*

3. Listening to interpret refers to:
   a. how accurately you understand the meaning of another person's message.
   b. your ability to evaluate the validity of a message.
   c. your ability to distinguish auditory and/or visual stimuli in a listening situation.
   d. how well you focus on understanding and identifying with a person's situation, feeling, or motives.

4. Read the following statement and a listener's paraphrase that follows. What characteristic of paraphrasing has the listener failed to take into account?

   Grace: My whole family—parents, sisters, and Aunt Ruth—bug me about it, and sometimes I can tell they're very angry with me and how I'm overdrawn at the bank.

   Listener: In other words, your family is angry because you're overdrawn at the bank; am I right?
   a. The listener is not mindful.
   b. The listener is not using new words to express Grace's message.
   c. The listener has not heard Grace's words correctly.
   d. The listener has not asked for confirmation.

4.3 *Describe the ways in which gender and culture affect how we listen.*

5. In general, men tend to listen comprehensively and analytically, whereas women tend to listen _____.
   a. only comprehensively
   b. empathically
   c. empathically and appreciatively
   d. appreciatively and comprehensively

6. _____ is a listener-responsible language in which speakers indicate only indirectly what they are discussing and what they want the listener to know or do.
   a. Japanese
   b. Arabic
   c. English
   d. Spanish

4.4 *Practice effective listening strategies and skills.*

7. Which of the following listening strategies involves using your extra thought speed productively?
   a. Identify the key ideas in a message.
   b. Pay attention to the meaning of a speaker's nonverbal behavior.
   c. Analyze the strengths and weaknesses of arguments.
   d. All of the above.

8. When you "listen" to *evaluate* an online message, which question should you ask?
   a. Are the speaker's words dull, ordinary, expressive, or emotional?
   b. Are there more positive than negative or positive words?
   c. Are the facts valid and the conclusions reasonable?
   d. Is the person asking for help, advice, sympathy, or agreement?

Answers found on page 368.

Verbal **Communication** 5

Our ability "to name" is uniquely human. It has been considered a holy privilege as well as a magical gift. According to the Hebrew Bible, the first honor God confers on Adam is that of naming the animals.[1]

Many names also have interesting histories as well as special meanings. For example, the English name *Dianna* is probably derived from an old Indo-European root meaning "heavenly" and "divine" and is related to Diana, the Roman goddess of the moon, hunting, forests, and childbirth. The name *John* comes from the Greek name meaning "gracious." This name owes its popularity to John the Baptist and the apostle John in the New Testament. All cultures have their own naming traditions. Consider, for example, the story of a Nigerian student named Ifeyinwa:

> In Africa, back in the days when my grandparents were alive, names meant many things and people named their children from events or circumstances. When my father was about six years old, his mother gave birth to twin babies. They did not survive because they were put in a special clay pot and left in the fields until they died. That was the tradition of the land then. It was taboo for a woman to give birth to more than one child at a time. My father named me after this ordeal. My name Ifeyinwa means "child is supreme" and "precious." He knows a child is a precious gift from God and each child is unique in his or her own special ways. I have always loved my name but even more after learning its meaning. I wish to live up to my father's expectations of me and the meaning of my name.[2]

Now consider *your* name. Why did your parents choose this name? Does their choice say something about your family's history or your culture? Why do you like or dislike your name? How has your name affected your life?

Human Language

5.1 *Identify the qualities that make human language unique.*

Humans do not share the remarkable sensory skills of many animals. We cannot track a faint scent through a forest or camouflage our skin color to hide from predators. Many animals also do a much better job of interpreting body movement than we do.[3] Yet what we can do that no other animals can is speak.

Even though other animals use sophisticated communication systems, none can claim the power and complexity of human language. The ability to learn words and to combine, invent, and give meaning to new words makes humans unique among animals.[4]

Researchers estimate that the first humans to speak language, as we know it, lived in East Africa about 150,000 years ago.[5] In a 100,000-year-old skull, anthropologists found a modern-shaped hyoid bone, which fits right at the top of the windpipe and resembles part of the modern apparatus we need to speak. Fully modern language probably evolved only 50,000 years ago.[6] Thus, the ability to speak is relatively new given that our earliest known ancestors lived about 3.3 million years ago in what is now Ethiopia.[7]

> **" The difference between the almost right word and the right word is really a large matter—'tis the difference between the lightning bug and the lightning. "**
> —Mark Twain[8]

Human **language** is a system of arbitrary signs and symbols used to communicate thoughts and feelings. Every language spoken on this planet is a *system*—an interrelated collection of words and rules used to construct and express meaning. In addition to defining words, all languages impose a grammar that arranges words into coherent messages. "The went store he to" makes no sense until you rearrange the words in their proper grammatical order: "He went to the store." "Him go to store" may get the message across, but it does so by breaking several grammatical rules.

When you use language incorrectly, you may risk "derailing your career," as supported by the following examples:

A recruiter refused to recommend a financial manager for the chief financial officer's position because he often said "me and so-and-so," followed by the wrong verb form.

The president of a publishing company rejects sales and editorial candidates when they exhibit grammatically incorrect speech. The president complained that such behavior "reflects a low level of professionalism."[9]

> **" Whatever else people do when they come together— whether they play, fight, make love, or make automobiles— they talk. We live in a world of language. "**
> —Victoria Fromkin and Robert Rodman, linguists[10]

Well-chosen words lie at the heart of effective communication, whether you are chatting with a friend, leading a group, addressing an audience, or writing a novel. In this chapter, we focus on **verbal communication**—the ways in which we use the words in a language to generate meaning, regardless of whether we communicate face-to-face or in cyberspace.[11] We focus on nonverbal communication—how we use message components *other than words* to generate meaning—in Chapter 6, "Nonverbal Communication."

Communication

Sticks and Stones May Break My Bones, but Words Can Hurt Forever

Gary Martin, author and proprietor of *The Phrase Maker* website, explains that the phrase "'Sticks and stones may break my bones but names will never hurt me' is a standard response to verbal bullying in school playgrounds throughout the English-speaking world." He also observes, "It sounds a little antiquated these days and has no doubt been superseded by more streetwise comebacks."[12]

Today, a more appropriate assessment might be, "Sticks and stones may break my bones, but words can hurt forever." In an article titled, "Bullying: When Words Hurt," a woman named Heather recalls, "Even after 18 years, I can tell you her name, describe what she looked like, show you where she lived and tell you all the horrible things she did to me—in detail. She ruined all my memories of fifth and sixth grade. Those two years will always be remembered as the time that Christie tortured me." Of course "she" didn't physically torture Heather. But she did call her names and verbally harassed her.[13]

When a well-known British radio personality was asked to complete the sentence "The unqualified regret you wish you could amend …," he said that he wished he hadn't forgotten what one of his school teachers had taught him. His teacher had told him that you couldn't take back the spoken word. As a radio presenter, he'd said things that he wished he hadn't, not because they'd hurt him, but because they'd hurt others.[14]

Interestingly, a medical study found that words can literally hurt you. When, for example, a doctor or nurse says, "This may hurt a bit," right before you get a shot, the mere mention of it "… may be enough to trigger a pain response in your brain long before any actual pain is felt."[15]

If you're angry or unaware of the negative impact your words have on others, remember the Golden Rule. How would you feel if other people used the same words to describe you and what you do?

Language and Meaning

5.2 *Explain how the nature of language affects meaning.*

When you don't know the meaning of a word, you may look it up in a dictionary. Depending on the word, however, you may find several definitions. Likewise, no two people assign the exact same meaning to the same word.

> **Words do not have meanings; people have meanings for words.**[16]

Signs and Symbols

As noted earlier, all languages are human inventions composed of signs and symbols: The words we speak or write, and the system that underlies their use, have all been made up by people.[17] A **sign** stands for or represents something specific and often looks like the thing it represents. Thus, it has a visual relationship to that thing. For example, the graphic depictions of jagged lightning and clouds on a weather map are signs for a storm.

The Many Meanings of **LOVE**

Consider the many ways in which people define the word *love*.

Love for a romantic partner

Love for family and friends

Love for a pet

Love for a hobby or sport

Love for your country

Common **SIGNS**

Rain

Rain and Lightning

Partly Cloudy

Unlike signs, **symbols** do *not* have a direct relationship to the things they represent. Instead, they are an *arbitrary* collection of sounds that in certain combinations stand for concepts. Nothing in the compilation of letters that make up the word *lightning* looks or sounds like lightning. The letters making up the word *cloud* are neither white and puffy nor dark and gloomy.

You cannot be struck by the word *lightning* or get wet from the word *rain*.

When you see or hear a word, you apply your knowledge, experience, and feelings to decide what the word means. Language scholars C. K. Ogden and I. A. Richards provide an explanation of this phenomenon below. They employ a triangle to explain the three elements of language: the

thinking person, the symbol (or sign) used to represent something, and the actual thing, idea, or feeling being referenced.[19] The triangle does not have a solid base because the symbol and the referent are *not* directly related. The symbol must be mentally processed by a person before it has meaning.

Denotative and Connotative Meaning

One of the great myths about language is that every word has an exact meaning. The truth is just the opposite: just as no two communicators or communication contexts are exactly alike, no two word meanings can ever be exactly the same.[20]

Two linguistic concepts—denotation and connotation—help explain the elusive nature of word meanings. **Denotation** refers to the specific and objective dictionary-based meaning of a word. For example, most of us would agree that a *snake* is a scaly, legless, sometimes venomous reptile with a long, cylindrical body. Plumbers have their own version of a *snake*—a flexible metal wire or coil used to clean out pipes. Each of these "snakes" has a denotative meaning.

Connotation refers to the emotional response or personal thoughts connected to the meaning of a word. Connotation, rather than denotation, is more likely to influence your response to words. For example, just hearing the word *snake* is enough to make some people cringe with fear. Yet, to a serpentologist, the word *snake* evokes fascination and excitement.

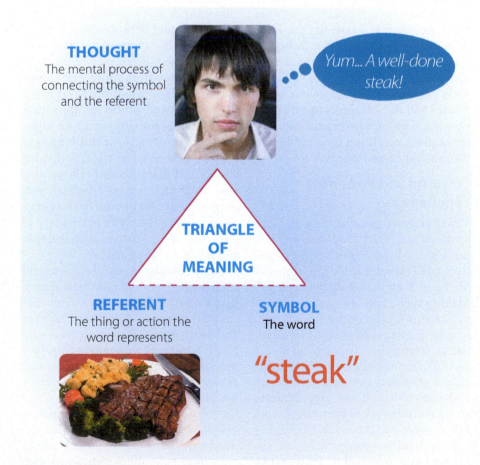

THOUGHT
The mental process of connecting the symbol and the referent

Yum... A well-done steak!

TRIANGLE OF MEANING

REFERENT
The thing or action the word represents

SYMBOL
The word

"steak"

Ogden and Richards's Triangle of Meaning[18]

Three Levels Of MEACONNING

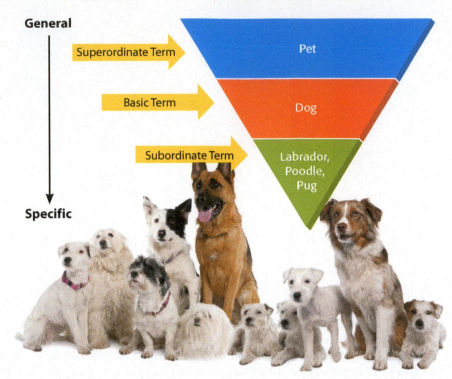

General

→ Superordinate Term → Pet

→ Basic Term → Dog

→ Subordinate Term → Labrador, Poodle, Pug

Specific

For most people, a word's connotation has much more significance than its denotation. Whereas you may tell someone that a *cop* pulled you over and gave you an undeserved ticket, a *police officer* may have helped you with a flat tire. What seems like a neutral word to you can have strong connotations to others.

Concrete and Abstract Words

Your choice of concrete or abstract words significantly affects whether and how well others understand the intended meaning of your message. **Concrete words** refer to specific things you perceive with your senses—things you can smell, taste, touch, see, or hear. The words *table, Paris, giraffe,* and *red rose* are concrete because, unlike *furniture, city, animal,* and *flower,* they narrow the number of possible meanings and decrease the likelihood of misinterpretation.

Abstract words refer to ideas or concepts that usually cannot be observed or touched and often require interpretation. The word *animal* is more abstract than *giraffe* because there are a huge number of different kinds of animals. Moreover, you can see a giraffe in your mind, but what image does an animal conjure up? Both a crayfish and a giraffe are animals. Similarly, words such as *fairness, freedom,* and *evil* can have an almost endless number of meanings and don't specifically refer to something you can see, hear, smell, taste, or touch. The more abstract your language is, the more likely it is that your listeners may interpret your meaning other than the way you intended.[22]

Language has three general levels of meaning that range from highly abstract to very concrete.[23] **Superordinate terms** group objects and ideas together very generally; *vehicle, animal,* or *location* are superordinate terms. **Basic terms** further describe a superordinate term, such as *car, van, truck; cat, chicken, mouse;* or *New England, Deep South, Appalachia.* **Subordinate terms** offer the most concrete and specialized descriptions. The vehicle parked outside is not just a *car,* it is a 1988 red Mercedes sports convertible. The cat purring on your lap is not just a cat; it is a blue-eyed male Siamese cat named Gatsby.

Powerful and Powerless Language

What is your reaction if you hear someone say, "It's a good idea, isn't it?" or "Um … I don't mean to be negative, but I wonder if we might possibly be making the wrong move here." Making such cautious, qualified statements can undercut the importance of your message. Now consider alternative statements: "It's a good idea!" and "We're making the wrong move." These statements express confidence and conviction. They also demonstrate the differences between powerful language and powerless language.

Powerful language is direct, assertive, and persuasive. **Powerless language** is the opposite and conveys uncertainty and a lack of confidence. Despite such stark differences, powerful and powerless languages are not an either/or choice. There may be circumstances and contexts in which a middle ground between these two extremes is more appropriate. Moreover in high-power distance cultures, powerful language from those with power and powerless responses from those without power would be appropriate, even if seemingly unfair. In high-context cultures, powerful language may be perceived as rude, individualistic, and disrespectful. There may also be circumstances in which you purposely use less powerful language to encourage others to participate in a discussion or to feel comfortable endorsing a plan of action.

Early research associated powerful speech with men and powerless speech with women. Subsequent research discounted this claim by noting that men and women use both powerful and powerless speech depending on factors such as culture, status, and context as well as their speaking ability, their intentions, the nature of listeners, and the context.[24] However, two speech habits—ending sentences with an upward tone as though you are asking questions and ending statements with a tag question (e.g., "She showed up late, didn't she?") are generally viewed as characteristics of a female speaking style.[25]

Recent studies pay more attention to the *consequences* of powerful and powerless speech. One study found that powerless language decreases message forcefulness as well as the perceived credibility of the speaker. The use of powerful speech in job interviews creates a more positive impression of the applicant and a higher likelihood of that applicant being hired.[26] Not surprisingly, in computer-mediated discussions, the user of "powerful language is generally perceived as more credible, attractive, and persuasive than the user of a powerless speaking style."[27]

> When the communication goal is significant and personally important, both men and women use powerful language.

Language, Culture, Gender, and Context

5.3 *Describe the ways in which language, culture, gender, and context affect one another.*

"Tall half-skinny half-1 percent hot quad shot latte with whip, please."

There are approximately 5,000 to 6,000 languages spoken in the world, all of them with different vocabularies and rules of grammar.[29] Have you ever tried to talk to or understand someone who speaks very little English? The experience can be frustrating, comical, enlightening, or even disastrous.

In one of Tony Hillerman's mystery novels, a Navaho tribal police officer explains to an FBI agent who cannot come up with anything better than the word *rocks* to describe a murder scene, "It's said the Inuits up on the Arctic Circle have nine words for snow. I guess, living in our stony world, we're that way with our rocks."[30] The words in a language often reflect what is important to the people in a specific culture. Just as there are dozens of words used to describe camels in Arabic languages and snow in Eskimo languages, there are dozens of words in American English to describe different kinds of vehicles or the different kinds of coffee drinks served at a Starbucks. The United States is also host to significant regional differences in vocabulary. For example, a sandwich on a large roll with a variety of meats and cheeses on it may be a *grinder*, a *hero*, a *sub*, a *hoagie*, or a *po'boy*, depending on the area.[31]

IDEA PLAN EXPERIMENT METHOD

The Whorf Hypothesis

A significant and controversial language theory attempts to explain why people from different cultures speak and interpret messages differently from one another. Linguist Edward Sapir and his student Benjamin Whorf spent decades studying the relationship between language, culture, and thought. Whorf's most controversial theory contends that the structure of a language determines how we see, experience, and interpret the world around us. For example, if you don't have a word for red, will you be able to see red or separate it from other colors you do recognize?

In English, we understand the grammatical differences between "I saw the girl," "I see the girl," and "I will see the girl." Whorf observed that the Hopi Indians of Arizona make no past, present, and future-tense distinctions in their language. Therefore, he concluded, they must perceive the world very differently. He also noted that the Hopi have a single word, masa'ytaka, for everything that flies, from insects to airplanes. Does that mean the Hopi cannot think about tomorrow and cannot see the differences between an airplane and a fly? Originally, many linguists believed that the answer was yes. Now linguists understand that the Hopi do think about tomorrow, even if they may lack a word for it.

Like many controversial theories, the Whorf hypothesis (also referred to as the Sapir–Whorf hypothesis) has been accepted, rejected, resurrected, and amended—several

While language does not determine everything we think, it does influence the way we perceive others and the world around us.[32]

times. Today, most linguists accept a more moderate version of the **Whorf hypothesis**: Language reflects cultural models of the world, which in turn influence how the speakers of a language think, act, and behave.[33] For example, in English, terms that end with man, such as chairman, fireman, and policeman, may lead us to view certain roles and jobs as only appropriate for men. Substituting words such as chairperson, firefighter, and police officer may change perceptions about who can hold these positions.

Language and Culture

In Chapter 3, "Adapting to Others," we explained how several cultural dimensions influence the way we communicate. Here we examine two aspects of language—the use of pronouns and the degree of verbal directness—in terms of the ways they are used in different cultures.

Pronouns As we noted in Chapter 3, "Adapting to Others," individualism–collectivism is the most significant cultural dimension that distinguishes one culture from another. Individualistic cultures have an "I" orientation; collectivist cultures have a "we" orientation. Interestingly, "English is the only language that capitalizes the pronoun *I* in writing. English does not, however, capitalize the written form of the pronoun *you*."[34] By contrast, people of the Athabaskan-speaking community

in Alaska speak and think in a collective plural voice. The word for *people*, *dene*, is used as a kind of *we*, and is the subject for almost every sentence requiring a personal pronoun.[35]

When speaking to others, pay attention to the individualistic or collectivist tendencies in the way they use languages. Although frequent use of the words *I*, *me*, and *my* may be common for a group of ambitious and individualistic corporate executives in the United States, the words *we* and *us* might be heard more frequently from African Americans or immigrants from Central and South America, who are more collectivist.

Verbal Directness Most people living in the United States have a low-context, direct way of speaking. In the eyes of other cultures, we get to the point with blunt, straight talk. When we say *no*, we mean *no*! Many

other cultures view direct language as a disregard for others that can lead to embarrassment and injured feelings.[36] For example, at a news conference in Europe, President George W. Bush acknowledged that his all-American speaking style may have been too direct when dealing with the leaders of other nations. "'I explained to the prime minister [Tony Blair of Great Britain] that the policy of my government is the removal of Saddam.' Catching himself, Bush added: 'Maybe I should be a little less direct and be a little more nuanced, and say we support regime change.'"[37]

Most North Americans learn to say yes or no when expressing their opinions; however, Japanese speakers may say *yes* to a suggestion because it is what they believes you want to hear when, in fact, the real response may be *no*.

Language and Gender

Most languages reflect a gender bias. These differences can be minor or major depending on the language and context in which communication takes place.[38] In English, we struggle with the words *he* and *she*. For many years, the pronoun *he* was used to refer to an unspecified individual. Older English textbooks used sentences such as: *every speaker should pay attention to his words*. Other languages have gender-related challenges as well. French, for example, has separate third-person plurals: masculine and feminine versions of *they*. Japanese distinguishes gender in both the first and the second person; they use a different version of *you* for men and women. The language of Finland may have the best solution. All pronouns are gender neutral; there is a single word that means both *he* and *she*.[39]

In Sweden, the movement for gender-neutral pronouns won a victory when "a new pronoun, *hen* (pronounced like the bird in English), was added to the online version of the country's *National Encyclopedia*." *Hen* is suggested as a "gender-neutral personal pronoun instead of he [*han* in Swedish] and she [*hon*]."[40]

A preschool in Stockholm went even further when teachers decided to stop using the pronouns *him* and *her*. Instead, they call the children "friends"—for example, *Your friend wants to play with you* rather than *He wants to play with you*. Masculine and feminine references were abolished when possible. As one of the school directors explained, "We just use the name—Peter, Sally—or Come on, friends!"[41] Dropping gender-based pronouns may work well in Sweden with its more egalitarian, feminine-value culture. What's the likelihood the same approach would be accepted in the United States?

Although some languages, such as Finnish, make very few distinctions between men and women, English favors men over women. Most gender-related word pairings begin with the male term: male and female, boys and girls, husband and wife, Jack and Jill, Romeo and Juliet, Mr. and Mrs.[42] If you doubt this preference, think about the married couples you know.

How do you talk about a couple when using their first names? Is it Juliet and Romeo or Romeo and Juliet; Adam and Eve or Eve and Adam?

Would you address a letter to Mrs. and Mr. Smith?

Unfortunately, because of the male bias in English and in American society, female terms tend to take on demeaning connotations. The connotations of the second word in the following pairings are negative or outdated for women: *governor/governess*, *master/mistress*, and *sir/madam*. Women are also compared with animals: *chick*, *bitch*, *fox*, *cow*, *shrew*, *dog*. One study lists more than 500 English slang terms for the word *prostitutes* but only sixty-five for the men who are their willing clients.[43]

Strategies for AVOIDING GENDER BIAS WITH PRONOUNS

- **Use plural forms.** Instead of saying, "Every speaker should pay attention to his words," consider, "All speakers should pay attention to their words."

- **Avoid using any pronoun.** Instead of using a pronoun at all, consider, "Good speakers pay careful attention to language."

- **Use variations on the phrase "he or she" as well as "his and her."** Instead of saying, "Every speaker should pay attention to his or her words," consider, "Every speaker should pay attention to her or his words."

Gender-Neutral Terms for Jobs and Professions

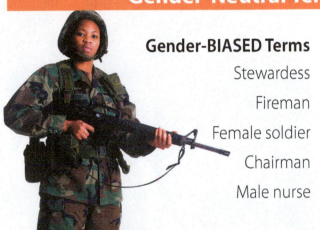

Gender-BIASED Terms	Gender-NEUTRAL Terms
Stewardess	*Flight attendant*
Fireman	*Firefighter*
Female soldier	*Soldier*
Chairman	*Chairperson*
Male nurse	*Nurse*

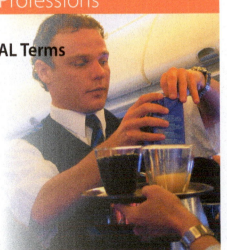

Use gender-neutral terms to describe jobs and professions. In the theater and film industries, for example, the word *actor* is replacing actress for female performers.

Language and Context

What kind of language would you use in a college classroom, at a family member's funeral, at a critical job interview, at a political or pep rally, at home with your parents, or at a party with your friends? There would be subtle and not-so-subtle differences in your choice of words and grammar. We naturally change the way we use language based on our relationships with other communicators, their psychological traits and preferences, and the extent to which they share our cultural attitudes, beliefs, values, and behaviors.

The phrase *code switching* refers to a common strategy for adapting to the many contexts in which we communicate. If you can speak more than one language, you already code switch as you move from one language to another. Here we use the term **code switching** in a broader sense: to describe how we modify our verbal and nonverbal communication in different contexts.

Effective communicators learn to adapt their language to the communication context. Although a swear word would never pass your lips at a job interview, during a church service, or in a formal public speech, you may curse in the company of close friends and like-minded colleagues. In his book *Word on the Street*, linguist John McWhorter notes that many middle-class African Americans typically speak both Black English (the language they may speak at home) and Standard English (the language they may speak among white people), switching constantly between the two, often in the same sentence.[49] For example, a Black English speaker may use double negatives ("He don't know nothing") and delete *to be* verbs ("She fine") within statements made in Standard English. McWhorter also notes that African Americans usually code switch between Standard and Black English when the topic or tone is informal, lighthearted, or intimate. As a result, African Americans are competent in two sophisticated dialects of English.[50]

COMMUNICATION IN *ACTION*

Do Women Talk More Than Men?

One of the great language myths is that women talk more than men. This belief is neither new nor confined to the United States.[44] Consider, for example, the following proverbs:[45]

> Where there are women and geese, there's noise. (Japanese)

> Women's tongues are like lambs' tails—they are never still. (English)

> The woman with active hands and feet, marry her. But the woman with an active mouth, leave well alone. (New Zealand Maori)

Most research studies, however, paint a different picture. A recent study of 400 college students found that the number of words uttered by males and females were virtually the same. An analysis of sixty-three studies of gender differences in talkativeness found that men actually "yakked slightly more than women, especially when interacting with spouses or strangers and when the topic was non-personal." Women talked more with classmates, with parents and children, and in situations where the topic of conversation required disclosure of feelings.[46]

In work settings, men do most of the talking. Even when women hold influential positions, they often find it hard to contribute to a discussion as much as men do. This pattern is also evident in educational settings (from kindergarten through university), where males usually dominate classroom talk. Sadly, when women talk as much as men do, they may be perceived as talking "too much."[47]

When linguist Janet Holmes answers the question, "Do women talk more than men?" she concludes, "It depends." It depends on the social context, the kind of talk, the confidence of the speaker, the social roles, and the speaker's expertise.

Generally, men are more likely to dominate conversation in formal, public contexts where talk is highly valued and associated with status and power. Women, on the other hand, are likely to contribute more in private, informal interactions, when talk functions to maintain relationships and in situations where women feel socially confident.[48]

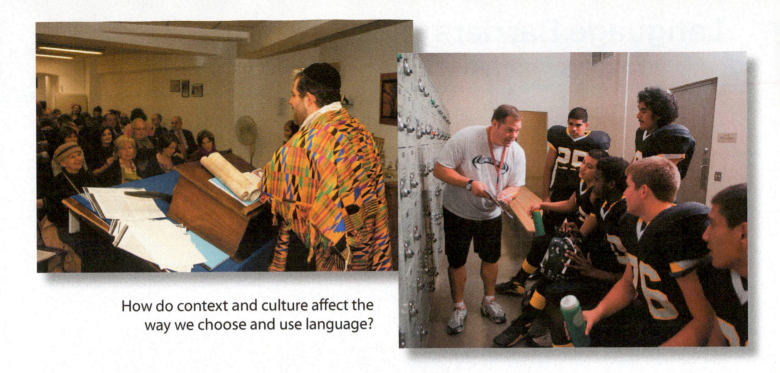

How do context and culture affect the way we choose and use language?

COMMUNICATION&CULTURE

WHEN GOVERNMENTS DICTATE YOUR NAME

In some countries, governments dictate the names a parent can choose for a child. In early 2013, a fifteen-year-old girl in Iceland sued and was granted the right to legally keep her given name, Blaer. Like many other countries, Iceland has an approved list of names that can be given to girls and boys. Blaer, which means "light breeze" in Icelandic, is not on the government-approved list of 1,853 names for female children. Until the court decision ruled in Blaer's favor, she was identified simply as "Girl" in communication with Icelandic officials.[51]

Similar laws are in place in other countries. For instance, in Germany unisex names are banned. In Denmark, parents can pick only from an approved list of 7,000 male and female names. Although unisex names for children are encouraged in liberal Sweden, only 170 are legally recognized. Swedish parents have mobilized and are demanding the right to choose any names they want for their children.[52]

No such restrictions exist in the United States—in fact, allowable names run to the opposite extreme, for example, MoxieCrimeFighter, Fifi Trixibelle, or Heavenly Hiraani Tiger Lily Hutchence—these are all names of children born to U.S. celebrities. Consider,

Icelandic teenager Blaer Bjarkardottir and her mother

too, the Pennsylvania parents who were called into Child Protective Services in early 2013 after ordering a birthday cake for their son Adolph Hitler, brother of daughter JoyceLynn Aryan Nation. Would you have done the same?[53] Later in 2013, a Tennessee judge ordered that a baby's name be changed from "Messiah" to "Martin" because Messiah is "a title that has only been earned by one person, Jesus Christ."[54] Do you agree?

Language Barriers

5.4 *Identify common language barriers that can undermine communication.*

Despite our best efforts to understand the complex relationship between language and meaning, misunderstandings are inevitable. The following are three common language barriers to effective communication: bypassing, exclusionary language, and offensive language.

Bypassing

When two people assign different meanings to the same word or phrase, they risk bypassing each other. **Bypassing** is a form of miscommunication that occurs when people "miss each other with their meanings."[55] If you have ever found yourself saying, "But that's not what I meant," you have experienced bypassing.

Note the problem created in the following example of bypassing: A high school graphic design teacher wrote a letter to Randy Cohen, a former "ethicist" for *The New York Times Magazine*. The teacher explained that students were assigned the task of creating a guitar using Photoshop. A few asked if they could use an online tutorial. The teacher said *yes*, assuming and quite sure they'd merely consult it for help. Three students handed in identical work because they'd carefully followed the tutorial to the letter. The teacher wanted to give each student a "C" on the assignment because the other students created their work from scratch. Thus his question: Should he give them the "C," or is he bound by having given them the okay to use the tutorial?

The ethicist wrote back, saying, "There's something not quite right about penalizing these students for doing what you explicitly permitted them to do. It's a teacher's obligation to be clear about what is and what is not acceptable."[56] The students clearly believed they had permission to use the tutorial to create the guitar graphic, whereas the teacher assumed they would only consult the tutorial for help.

William Haney, an organizational communication scholar, maintains that effective "communicators who habitually look for meanings in the people using words, rather than in the words themselves, are much less prone to bypass or be bypassed."[57]

Euphemisms

When you use a **euphemism**, you substitute a bland, mild, vague, or unobjectionable word or phrase for one that seems too direct, indecent, harsh, offensive, or hurtful. In Victorian England, the word *limb* was used for *leg*, a word that had sexual connotations. Even a chair leg wasn't referred to as such because it might spark thoughts of sexuality. In the United States, we usually ask for directions to the restroom, ladies' room, or men's room rather than the toilet.[58] Some euphemisms substitute letters in a word to make them less offensive. You frequently hear people say "jeeze" instead of "Jesus," "darn" instead of "damn," and "heck" rather than "hell."

Although euphemisms may seem harmless and nothing more than a way to express yourself politely, they have the power to hide intended and mask the truth.

Look at table at the top of the next column. The words in the left column are euphemisms. The words lower down in the right column are often expressed as euphemisms. See if you can fill in the blanks in both columns with either the word the euphemism represents or the euphemism frequently used for the word or phrase.

Euphemism	Definition (What It Means)
Passed away; in God's hands	
Bless her/his heart (Southern expression)	
Downsizing staff	
	Euthanizing a pet
	Pregnant
	Used car

Euphemisms can make tragedies and extreme cruelty seem tolerable. For example, the term *collateral damage* describes unintended casualties and destruction in civilian areas caused by military action. The phrase *friendly fire* refers to attacks that injure or kill a member of your own military or an ally. During and subsequent to the war in Iraq, the word *interrogation* came to mean "information-seeking techniques Americans used on Iraqis in the Abu Ghraib prison." Many critics described these techniques (food and sleep deprivation, water boarding, stress positioning, hooding, and attacking with dogs) as nothing short of *torture*.[59]

Exclusionary Language

Exclusionary language uses words that reinforce stereotypes, belittle other people, or exclude others from understanding an in-group's message. Exclusionary language widens the social gap by separating the world into *we* (to refer to people who are like you) and *they* or *those people* (to refer to people who are different from you). Such terms can offend others. You don't have to be excessive about being "politically correct," using *vertically challenged* for *short*, but you should avoid alienating others and use language that includes rather than excludes. Specifically, avoid mentioning anything about age, health or mental and physical abilities, sexual orientation, or race and ethnicity unless these characteristics are relevant to the discussion.

> Remember that it's not what words mean to you, but what others mean when they use those words.

- **Age.** Instead of *old lady*, use *older woman* or just *woman*.
- **Health and Abilities.** Rather than use terms such as *cripple* or *head case*, use *physically disabled* or *person with an emotional illness*. Do not use the word *retarded* in reference to *mental ability* or *physical ability*.
- **Sexual Orientation.** Never assume that the sexual orientation of others is the same as your own. *Homo*, *fairy*, *fag*, *butch*, and *dyke* are unacceptable; instead, use *gay* or *lesbian*.
- **Race and Ethnicity.** Avoid using stereotypical terms and descriptions based on a person's race, ethnicity, or region, such as *hick*. Use the names people prefer to describe their racial or ethnic affiliations, such as black, African American, Latino/a, Hispanic, and Asian. Avoid identifying race and ethnicity unless it is relevant to the conversation. Rather than saying, "That Polish guy down the block owns several repair shops," say instead, "That man down the block owns several repair shops."

If you doubt that people still use exclusionary language, consider the 2010 election campaign for U.S. senate in West Virginia. The National Republican Senatorial Committee put out a casting ad calling for "hicky-looking blue-collar actors" to play everyday West Virginians. The democratic opponent, Joe Manchin, put out his own ad in response calling the GOP portrayal "insulting" and asserting that Republican candidate John Raese "thinks we're hicks." When the story broke, the Republican committee pulled their ad.[60]

Slang, Jargon, and Gobbledygook

In this section, we look at how some words and phrases in a single language can have special meaning for those who "know" and can interpret that language. These words come and go with the times and circumstances.

Slang Although there is disagreement about the origins of the word *slang*, most linguists agree that slang is a short-lived, group-related, ever-changing, creative and innovative, often playful and metaphorical, colloquial language variety that is below the level of stylistically neutral language.[61] Huh?

> **"Slang is language which takes off its coat, spits on its hands—and goes to work."**
> —Carl Sandburg, American poet[65]

In other words, **slang** consists of informal, nonstandard words or phrases that tend to originate in subcultures (such as teenagers, musicians, athletes, inner-city gangs, railroad workers, prisoners) within a society.

Slang helps language change and renew itself.[62] Many words that began as slang—cool; Uncle Tom and Mr. Charley; booze, bread and dough; and lots of words for toilet (john, head, can, loo, potty)—have ended up in standard usage dictionaries. Just about every surviving slang word has an interesting history. Why, for example, do people say, "Where's the john?" Could it be that the inventor of the first toilet in a home (as opposed to an outhouse) was Sir John Harrington, a member of Queen Elizabeth I's sixteenth century court in England?[63]

Most slang, however, doesn't last long. As Kathryn Lindskoop writes in *Creative Writing*, "It looks foolish when it gets old, when it is slightly misused, and when it is used by the wrong people in a futile attempt to sound hip."[64] In other words, we see nothing wrong with using slang in the right place at the right time with the right people and for the right reasons.

Jargon The specialized or technical language of a profession or homogeneous group is known as **jargon**. English professor William Lutz points out that groups use jargon as "verbal shorthand that allows members to communicate with each other clearly, efficiently, and quickly."[67] In some settings and on some occasions, such as at a meeting of doctors, attorneys, information technology professionals, accountants, or educators, the ability to use jargon properly is a sign of group membership, and it speeds communication among members.

Some speakers use jargon to impress others with their specialized knowledge. For example, a skilled statistician may bewilder an audience by using unfamiliar terms to describe cutting-edge methodologies for establishing causality. In other situations, people use jargon when they have nothing to say; they just string together a bunch of nonsense and hope no one notices their lack of content.[68] Such tactics fail to inform others and often result in misunderstandings and resentment.

Gobbledygook Semanticist Stuart Chase defines **gobbledygook** (the sound of which imitates the nonsense gobbling of a turkey) as "using two or three or ten words in place of one, or using a five-syllable word where a single syllable would suffice." He cites the example of the single word *now* being replaced by the five-word, seventeen-letter phrase *at this point in time*.[69] In his book *Say What You Mean*, Rudolf Flesch contends that long words are a curse, a special language that comes between a speaker and listener.[70]

To demonstrate the value of clear, plain language, John Strylowski of the U.S. Department of the Interior and a frequent speaker at plain language seminars offers several recommendations:

- Never write a sentence with more than forty words.
- Cover only one subject per sentence.
- Don't include information just because you know it. Think about what the reader [or listener] needs.
- Use shorter words and phrases such as "now" rather than "at the present time."[71]

Reports that say something hasn't happened are always interesting to me, because as we know, there are known knowns; there are things we know we know. We also know there are known unknowns; that is to say, we know there are some things we do not know. But also unknown unknowns—the ones we don't know we don't know.[75]

If you doubt the need for plain language, try to decipher the example of gobbledygook to the right used by former Secretary of Defense Donald Rumsfeld:

Offensive Language

During the first half of the twentieth century, many words were considered inappropriate, particularly those that referred to private body parts and functions. Euphemisms flourished. Women went to the *powder room* and men to the *lavatory*. Even the word *pregnant* was once considered improper. Instead, a woman was "in the family way" or "with child." In 1952, Lucille Ball became the first pregnant woman to appear on a television show. The scripts called her an "expectant mother," never using the word *pregnant*. To make certain the language used in the *I Love Lucy* scripts were in good taste, a priest, a rabbi, and a minister reviewed them.[72]

Today you may experience offensive language everywhere—in public, on cable and network television shows, and just a few clicks away on the Internet. Swearing is especially pervasive in modern media, and researchers who study the evolution of language report that swearing or cursing is a human universal.[73] In her book *Holy Sh*t: A Brief History of Swearing*, Melissa Mohr explains that humans have been swearing for as long as they've been talking.[74]

Swear words are words considered taboo or disapproved of in a culture. They should *not* be interpreted literally and are typically used to express strong emotions and attitudes.[76] When we use swear words, we rarely wish, for example, for someone to literally "go to hell" or be "damned." Rather, we express the words as a way of coping with extreme emotion or to release stress.[77] For some, swearing may be a sign of a neurological disorder; in the case of the small percentage of people with Tourette's syndrome, for example, swearing is something that cannot be controlled.[78]

In his book, *Cuss Control: The Complete Book on How to Curb Your Cursing*, James O'Connor wants us to understand why we swear and then learn how to control when and where we use such words. Although swearing can hurt, embarrass, insult and offend others, many of us engage in "recreational swearing."[79] Why? Here are a few of the reasons:

- Swearing is lazy language that is easy to call on.
- Swearing can be fun if it's used humorously or in the right company.
- Our peers (or parents, or bosses, or colleagues, or role models) do it.
- Men swear to show they're naturally aggressive and strong.
- Women may swear to appear equal to and competitive with men.
- Swearing helps emphasize a point.
- Swearing shows we are unhappy or depressed.
- Swearing is a habit we're not motivated to break.[80]

> **❝ Every language, dialect or patois ever studied, living or dead, spoken by millions or by a small tribe, turns out to have its share of forbidden speech. ❞**
>
> —Natalie Angier, science writer, *The New York Times*[84]

Whatever our reasons for swearing, many researchers claim, "cursing is positively helpful, both psychologically and physically: It enables us to express negative emotions without resorting to violence."[81] On the other hand, as swearing becomes more and more common in public and more and more hostile, it has increased the potential of severely hurting others. After describing an incident in which car drivers viciously swore at him, philosophy professor Simon Critchley acknowledged, "It feels really good to swear and really bad to be sworn at." Swearing at someone, he wrote, "always aims at something intimate, something usually hidden, which is why the words are often so explicitly and violently sexual."[82]

There are good reasons to stop swearing or, at least, to control where, when, and with whom you use such language. One study reported that 91 percent of respondents ranked foul language as "the most

Cursing and using sexually explicit language were once taboo on television and not considered ladylike. Although some women now believe swearing is liberating, it remains a stigma in many contexts—for both women *and* men. Pictured here is the foul-mouthed Monica Talbot (played by Dawn Olivieri) in Showtime's *House of Lies*.

ill-mannered type of workplace behavior."[83] People who do *not* swear are seen as more intelligent (because they can find more accurate and appropriate words) and more pleasant (because they don't offend anyone). They are also perceived as effective communicators who have greater control over their emotions.

Language Lessons

5.5 *Practice effective language strategies and skills.*

In the previous section, we emphasized how *not* to use language if you want to be understood and respected by others. Here we take a more positive approach by examining five ways in which you can use language to express messages clearly and appropriately: expand your vocabulary, use oral language, use active language, use *I* and *you* pronouns wisely, and use correct grammar.

Expand Your Vocabulary

How many words do you know? By the age of five, you probably knew about 10,000 words, which means that you learned about ten words a day. Children have an inborn ability for learning languages that diminishes at around age twelve or thirteen. Although children can learn a second or third language with relative ease,

adults struggle to become fluent in a second language.[85]

By the time you are an adult, your vocabulary has expanded to include tens of thousands of words. Not surprisingly, finding the "right" word is a lot easier if you have many words from which to choose. When your ice cream choices are only vanilla or chocolate, you miss the delights of caramel butter pecan, mocha fudge swirl, and even simple strawberry. When you search for words in the English language, you have more than a million choices.

As you learn more words, make sure you understand their meaning and usage. For example, you should be able to make distinctions in meaning among the words in the following groups:[86]

- Absurd, silly, dumb, ridiculous, ludicrous, idiotic
- Pretty, attractive, gorgeous, elegant, lovely, cute, beautiful

Remember, the difference between the almost-right word and the right word is significant. You may not mind being called "silly" but may have serious objections to being called "idiotic." Improving your vocabulary is a lifelong task—and one that will be much easier if you are an avid reader.

Use Oral Language

Usually, there is a big difference between the words we use for written documents and the words we use orally in conversations, group discussions, and presentations.

In his book *How to Win Any Argument*, Robert Mayer writes, "The words you'll craft for a listener's ears are not the same as the words you'll choose for a reader's eyes. Readers can slow their pace to reread, to absorb, and to understand—luxuries listeners don't have."[87] The Crafting Language for the Ear table below contrasts five aspects of appropriate and inappropriate oral language.

Say what you mean by speaking the way you talk, not the way you write.

Use Active Language

Effective communicators use active language: vivid, expressive verbs rather than passive forms of the verb *to be* (*be, am, is, are, was, being, been*). Consider the difference between "Cheating is a violation of the college's plagiarism rules" and "Cheating violates the college's plagiarism rules." The second sentence is stronger and draws attention to the subject.

If the subject of a sentence performs the action, you are using an **active voice**. If the subject receives the action, you are using a **passive voice**. A strong, active voice makes your message more engaging, whereas a passive voice takes the focus away from the subject of your sentence. "The *Iliad* was read by the student" is passive. "The student read the *Iliad*" is active. Because an active voice requires fewer words, it also keeps sentences short and direct. Simply state who is doing what, not what was done by whom.

Use *I* and *You* Language Wisely

The pronouns you use can affect the quality and meaning of your verbal communication. Understanding the nature and power of pronouns can help you improve your way with words.

When you use *I* **Language**, you take responsibility for your own feelings and actions: *I* feel great. *I* am a good student. *I* will not vote for someone who cuts spending on education. Some people avoid using the word *I* because they think it may seem as though they are showing off, being selfish, or bragging. Other people use the word *I* too much and appear self-centered or oblivious to those around them.

Unfortunately, some people avoid *I* language when it is most important. Instead, they shift responsibility from themselves to others by using the word *you*. **You language** can express judgments about others. When the judgments are positive—"You did a great job" or "You look marvelous!"—there's rarely a problem. When *you* is used to accuse, blame, or criticize, however, it can arouse defensiveness, anger, and even revenge. Consider the following statements: "You make me angry." "You embarrass me." "You drive too fast."

When you use *you* language, you are saying that another person makes you feel a certain way rather than accepting that you control how you feel. To take personal responsibility and decrease the probability of defensive reactions, use *I* language even when your impulse tells you to use *you*. Review the three components of *I* Language in the box on the next page. Notice that the 2nd component asks you to describe someone's behavior rather than criticizing or blaming the other person.

Crafting Language **FOR THE EAR**

Oral Style	Say This	Don't Say This
Shorter, familiar words	Healthy	Salubrious
Shorter, simple sentences	He came back.	He returned from his point of departure.
Contractions	I'm not going and that's that.	I am not going and that is that.
Informal, colloquial expressions	Give it a try.	You should attempt it first.
Incomplete sentences	Old wood, best to burn; old wine, best to drink	Old wood burns the best, and old wine is the best to drink.

Then read the examples that demonstrate how the three components of *I* language can help you take responsibility for your own feeling and actions. Also note that the *you* statements are short. The *I* statements are longer because they provide more information about the consequences of someone's behavior.

You Versus I

You Statement
You embarrassed me last night.

I Statement
I was embarrassed last night when you interrupted me in front of my boss and contradicted what I said. I'm afraid she'll think I don't know what I'm doing.

You Statement
What a stupid thing to do!

I Statement
When you turn on the gas grill and let it run, I'm afraid that it will blow up in your face when you light it.

Use Grammatical Language

In his book *If You Can Talk, You Can Write*, Joel Saltzman notes that when you're talking to someone, you rarely worry about grammar or let it stand in the way of getting your point across.

You probably never say to yourself, "Because I don't know if I should use *who* or *whom*, I won't even ask the question." According to Saltzman, when you're talking, 98 percent of the time, your grammar is fine and not an issue. For the 2 percent of time your grammar is a problem, many of your listeners won't even notice your mistakes.[88]

We are not saying that grammar isn't important. However, worrying about it all the time may make it impossible for you to write or speak. If you have questions about grammar, consult a good writing handbook or website. Although most listeners miss or forgive a few grammatical errors, consistent grammatical problems can distract listeners and seriously harm your credibility. Your ability to use grammar correctly makes a public statement about your education, social class, and intelligence.

MEDIATED COMMUNICATION IN ACTION

How's Your Netlingo and Netspeak?

English language scholar David Crystal claims that the development of netlingo and netspeak has "millennial significance. A new medium of linguistic communication does not arrive very often in the history of the [human] race."[89]

Communication scholars describe **netlingo** as an identifiable language developed for Internet communication with the following features:[90]

- **Compounds and blends.** Examples: shareware, netiquette, e- and cyber- anything

- **Abbreviations and acronyms.** Examples: BTW = by the way; THX = thanks; IRL = in real life; F2F = face to face; IMHO = in my humble opinion.

- **Less use of capitalization, punctuation, and hyphenation.** Examples: internet and email, or not capitalizing any words

- **Less use of traditional openings and closings.** Examples: Hi or Hey instead of Dear or using no greeting phrase at all

Netspeak reflects common typographic strategies used to achieve a more sociable, oral, and interactive communication style:[91]

- **Letter homophones.** Examples: RU (are you); OIC (oh, I see); CUL8R (see you later)

- **Capitalization or other symbols used for emphasis.** Examples: YES, * yes *

- **Sound-based and/or stylized spelling.** Examples: cooooool, hahahahaha

- **Keyboard-generated emoticons.** Examples: :-) = smiley; @>—;— = rose; ;-) = winking; :-o = shocked, uh-oh, oh-no)

- Direct requests. Examples: A/S/L for "age, sex, location," GOS for gay or straight?

Netlingo and netspeak are so pervasive, the prestigious *Oxford International Dictionary* publishes the *Oxford Dictionaries Online* four times a year in order to keep up with trends. Below are three new words in the August 2013 edition. By the time you read this, there will be many more.[92]

- **Selfie.** A self-portrait taken with a smart phone.

- **Jorts.** A word that combines *jeans* and *shorts*.

- **Twerk.** Once called the "bump and grind," the *twerk* is a sexually provocative dance usually performed by a female who bends over in a low stance facing away from a male dancer, arches her back, and shakes her buttocks rhythmically.

Some new words are little more than shorthand versions of slightly longer words, as in *srsly* for *seriously*. Others are abbreviations such as TL; DR for *too long; didn't read*.

Netlingo and netspeak are language forms that adapt to online contexts. Like all languages, they will continue to evolve. Even so, there are voices that find online languages both strange and even sinister. Michael Dirda, a Pulitzer Prize–winning book critic for *The Washington Post*, prefaces his remarks by admitting that online language "is not my world." In his opinion, many computer-age words are ugly, "repulsive-sounding terminology." Of all the new words in the *Oxford Dictionaries Online*, he is most distressed by TL;DR. "I sometimes fear that everything I value in the way of literature and scholarship will be casually dismissed with those letters." He acknowledges, however, that most of these words are not "meant to be spoken by actual human beings. . . . They live and breathe only on the tiny screen." To which he adds, "let them stay there."[93]

Be careful when using netlingo and netspeak. Some readers may not "get it." If you send difficult-to-understand messages, readers may ignore it. And too many in one message can make reading difficult and annoying, as well as make you and your writing appear immature.[94]

Writing Apprehension Test (WAT)[95]

Writing apprehension is the fear or anxiety associated with writing situations and topic-specific writing assignments. The following statements will help you to gauge how you feel about using written words to express messages that share your ideas and opinions with others.

Indicate the degree to which each statement applies to you by marking whether you (1) strongly agree, (2) agree, (3) are uncertain about, (4) disagree, or (5) strongly disagree with the statement. Although some of these statements may seem repetitious, take your time and try to be as honest as possible.

_____ 1. I avoid writing.

_____ 2. I have no fear of my writing being evaluated.

_____ 3. I look forward to writing down my ideas.

_____ 4. My mind seems to go blank when I start to work on a composition.

_____ 5. Expressing ideas through writing seems to be a waste of time.

_____ 6. I would enjoy submitting my writing to magazines for evaluation and publication.

_____ 7. I like to write my ideas down.

_____ 8. I feel confident in my ability to express my ideas clearly in writing.

_____ 9. I like to have my friends read what I have written.

_____ 10. I'm nervous about writing.

_____ 11. People seem to enjoy what I write.

_____ 12. I enjoy writing.

_____ 13. I never seem to be able to write down my ideas clearly.

_____ 14. Writing is a lot of fun.

_____ 15. I like seeing my thoughts on paper.

_____ 16. Discussing my writing with others is an enjoyable experience.

_____ 17. It's easy for me to write good compositions.

_____ 18. I don't think I write as well as other people write.

_____ 19. I don't like my compositions to be evaluated.

_____ 20. I'm not good at writing.

Scoring: To determine your score on the WAT, complete the following steps:

1. Add the scores for items 1, 4, 5, 10, 13, 18, 19, and 20.
2. Add the scores for items 2, 3, 6, 7, 8, 9, 11, 12, 14, 15, 16, and 17.
3. Determine your score using the following formula:

   WAT score = 48 − total from step 1 + total from step 2

Your score should be between 20 and 100 points. If your score is less than 20 or more than 100 points, you have made a mistake in computing the score. The higher your score, the more apprehension you feel about writing.

Score	Level of Apprehension	Description
20–45	Low	Enjoys writing; seeks writing opportunities
46–75	Average	Some writing creates apprehension; other writing does not
76–100	High	Troubled by many kinds of writing; avoids writing in most situations

SUMMARY

Human Language

5.1 Identify the qualities that make human language unique.

- The ability to learn words and to combine, invent, and give meaning make humans different from other animals.
- Language is a system of arbitrary signs and symbols used to communicate with others.

Language and Meaning

5.2 Explain how the nature of language affects meaning.

- Whereas signs often look like the thing they represent, symbols are arbitrary collections of sounds that in certain combinations stand for concepts.
- Words have both denotative and connotative meanings and also differ in terms of whether they are concrete or abstract.
- Use different degrees of powerful and powerless language as appropriate.

Language and Culture, Gender, and Context

5.3 Describe the ways in which language, culture, gender, and context affect one another.

- The Whorf hypothesis claims that the nature of your language reflects your culture's view of the world.
- Individualistic cultures have an "I" orientation, whereas collectivist cultures have a "we" orientation.
- Low-context cultures rely on words to convey meaning; high-context, collectivist cultures rely on nonverbal behavior and the relationship between communicators to generate meaning.
- Most languages have a gender bias that privileges men more than women. Avoid gender bias by avoiding male and female pronouns when possible.
- Men tend to talk as much or more than women even though many people believe the opposite.
- Code switching refers to modifying verbal and nonverbal communication during interaction with people from other cultures.

Language Barriers

5.4 Identify the common language barriers that can undermine communication.

- Communicators who look for meaning in words rather than in the people using words are more likely to bypass and be bypassed.
- Exclusionary language uses words that reinforce stereotypes, belittle other people, or exclude others from understanding an in-group's message.
- Euphemisms substitute neutral, polite words for those considered too direct, indecent, or hurtful. Euphemisms can also hide meaning and mask the truth.
- Slang, jargon, and gobbledygook differ in terms of their ability to

enhance relationships and improve understanding.

- People who rarely swear or use offensive language are seen as more intelligent, more pleasant, and more skilled at controlling their emotions.

Language Lessons

5.5 Practice effective language strategies and skills.

- You can improve your way with words by expanding your vocabulary, using oral language when you speak, speaking in an active voice, using the pronouns *I* and *you* wisely, and avoiding gobbledygook.
- An excessive number of grammatical errors in your speech can derail a career or create a negative personal impression.

Key Terms

Abstract words	**Gobbledygook**	**Slang**
Active voice	**I Language**	**Subordinate terms**
Basic terms	**Jargon**	**Superordinate terms**
Bypassing	**Language**	**Swear words**
Code switching	**Netlingo**	**Symbols**
Concrete words	**Netspeak**	**Verbal communication**
Connotation	**Passive voice**	**Whorf Hypothesis**
Denotation	**Powerful language**	**Writing apprehension**
Euphemism	**Powerless language**	***You* language**
Exclusionary language	**Sign**	

TEST YOUR KNOWLEDGE

5.1 *Identify the qualities that make human language unique.*

1 Which word is missing from the following definition of language: human language is a system of arbitrary signs and _____ used to communicate thoughts and feelings.
   a. words
   b. symbols
   c. denotations
   d. connotations

5.2 *Explain how the nature of language affects meaning.*

2 Which of the following words is the most superordinate term?
   a. Caribbean Sea
   b. rain
   c. ocean
   d. liquid

3 Which of the following answers is not a characteristic of powerful language?
   a. Powerful language is direct, assertive, and persuasive.
   b. Powerful language uses more qualifiers, hedges, and disclaimers.
   c. Powerful language enhances a speaker's credibility, attractiveness, and persuasiveness.
   d. Powerful language may be perceived as rude, individualistic, and disrespectful.

5.3 *Describe the ways in which language, culture, gender, and context affect one another.*

4 Which set of words is more common in the language of individualistic cultures?
   a. I, me, my
   b. we, our, us
   c. his, hers, theirs
   d. person, people

5 According to the more modern version of the Whorf hypothesis,
   a. people without a word for "airplane" cannot see airplanes.
   b. primitive people, even with training, cannot understand modern technology.
   c. language reflects cultural models and influences how people think and act.
   d. people without a word for "tomorrow" or "future" cannot plan.

6 Which of the following demonstrates code switching?
   a. using Netlingo online and Standard American English in class.
   b. talking with your hands with a parent and a teacher.
   c. lying about lateness and lying about tardiness.
   d. evaluating a review and assessing a review.

5.4 *Identify the common language barriers that can undermine communication.*

7 All of the following are examples of exclusionary language except:
   a. The man who served us at lunch was very professional.
   b. A little old lady tipped the young man.
   c. Even though she's a cancer victim, she has a very positive attitude.
   d. What do you expect from such left-wing socialist?

8 What language barrier is evident when a woman asks a male waiter, "Where is the powder room?"
   a. bypassing
   b. slang and jargon
   c. euphemism
   d. exclusionary language

5.5 *Practice effective language strategies and skills.*

9 Select the best example of effective oral language:
   a. The libation you desired awaits you in the parlor.
   b. Your perfectly boiled caffeinated beverage is prepared.
   c. The market response from the academic sector proved positive.
   d. Bob and Ray like the book.

10 Which of the following answers is not a component of I language?
   a. Identify your feelings.
   b. Always avoid using the word *you*.
   c. Describe the other person's behavior.
   d. Explain the potential consequences.

Answers found on page 368.

Nonverbal Communication **6**

In Shakespeare's comedy, *As You Like It*, a character exclaims, "Who ever loved that loved not at first sight?"[1] In her song "Just One Look," Doris Troy's lyrics proclaim "Just one look and I fell so hard in love with you."[2] And Peter Gabriel's song "In Your Eyes" declares, "In your eyes I am complete."[3]

Playwrights, poets, artists, and songwriters have long understood the power of eye contact and what happens when one pair of eyes locks on another. They may reveal or withhold feelings; invite attention or turn it away. According to a study conducted at the Face Research Lab at the University of Glasgow in Scotland, you don't need to look like a sexy film star to attract a mate. When study volunteers examined various photographs of faces, they rated the forward-looking subjects who smiled and maintained direct eye contact as the most attractive. "It's really a very basic effect that we are all, at some level at least, aware of—which is that if you smile at people and you maintain eye contact, it makes you more attractive."[4]

Eye contact and smiling are just two forms of nonverbal communication. In this chapter, we look well beyond alluring eyes and captivating smiles to examine nonverbal communication in all of its forms and functions.

Communicating without Words

6.1 *Describe the nature and scope of nonverbal communication.*

Nonverbal communication encompasses behaviors that generate meaning without using words. Researchers estimate that as much as 60 to 70 percent, or about two-thirds, of the meaning we generate may be conveyed through nonverbal behaviors.[5] Whereas verbal communication is expressed solely through language, nonverbal communication may be expressed through physical appearance, body movement, facial expressions, touch, vocal characteristics, clothing, objects, and the communication context.

Everyone uses nonverbal communication. When you are aware of your own nonverbal behavior and are sensitive to others' unspoken messages, you are more likely to experience better social relationships (and, consequently, less loneliness, shyness, depression, and mental illness), better chances of academic and occupational success, a more satisfying marriage, and less stress, anxiety, and hypertension.[6]

Functions of Nonverbal Communication

Because nonverbal communication allows you to send and receive messages through all five of your senses, you have more information to draw on when creating and interpreting messages. Effective nonverbal communication can help you achieve many communication goals, ranging from creating a positive impression to detecting deception.

Creating an Impression As soon as you walk into a room, your physical appearance, clothing, posture, facial expression, and behavior create an impression. These *initial* impressions have a strong effect on how others judge and feel about you.[7] When attorneys prepare witnesses to testify in court, they tell them how to dress and teach them how to look and sound sincere and confident. Experienced courtroom lawyers know that jurors begin forming their opinions of witnesses before witnesses utter a word. Whether it's a first date, a job interview, or a meeting with a new client, nonverbal messages create strong, lasting impressions.

Identifying and Expressing Emotions We rely on nonverbal communication to identify and express the emotional components of a message. For example, if Jason says, "I'm angry," he simply labels an emotion, but his nonverbal behavior—vocal intensity, facial expression, and body tension—tell you how to interpret his anger. Expressing emotions by smiling, laughing, frowning, crying, grimacing, and even walking away from an encounter can make words unnecessary, provided that other person accurately interprets the meaning of the nonverbal cues they see or hear.

Defining Relationships The nature of a relationship is often expressed nonverbally. For example, the closeness and duration of a hug can reveal the level of intimacy between friends. Or a group member may take a central position at the head of a conference table to establish leadership. The simple act of holding hands in public signifies "we are more than just friends."

Establishing Power Do you know people who are influential and persuasive? What kind of nonverbal characteristics do they display? Powerful people often take up more space by having a bigger office or desk. They often touch others more than they are touched. They look at others less frequently unless they want to stare someone down. By using a powerful voice and confident posture, they command attention and influence.

Interpreting Verbal Messages Nonverbal communication provides us with a message about a message, or a **metamessage**, by offering important clues about how to interpret its verbal components. For example,

What do the nonverbal cues in this photograph tell you about this woman?

you may doubt a person who says he's feeling fine after a fall if he winces when he walks. If someone says she's glad to see you but is looking over your shoulder to see who else is in the room, you may distrust her sincerity.

Deceiving Others and Detecting Deception Have you ever tried to hide your feelings from others—whether you're denying wrongdoing or keeping a secret? Of course you have. Great poker players have mastered this skill. However, most of us are amateurs. Our

> **"He that has eyes to see and ears to hear may convince himself that no mortal can keep a secret. If his lips are silent, he chatters with his fingertips; betrayal oozes out of him at every pore."**
> —Sigmund Freud[8]

"innocent" smile may seem false, our gestures may look awkward, our voice may sound shaky, and our persistent toe tapping or knee jiggling may broadcast our anxiety.

Know Thy Self

Can You Detect a Lie?

Most of us aren't very good at detecting lies. According to Judee Burgoon, a noted researcher in human deception, most people's ability to detect deception accurately is equivalent to flipping a coin: about fifty–fifty.[9] Paul Ekman, another leading researcher in deception and nonverbal communication, points out that accurately identifying when someone is lying is further complicated by the fact that there is no single facial expression or body movement that serves as a reliable sign of deceit.[10]

There are, however, liars who involuntarily give themselves away by displaying **leakage cues**, unintentional nonverbal behaviors that may reveal deceptive communication. Three types of nonverbal cues can help you *detect* a lie. By minimizing these behaviors, you can also *avoid* detection when bending the truth.

1. *Displays of nervousness*: More blinking, higher pitched speech, vocal tension, less gesturing, more fidgety movements, longer pauses, fewer facial changes
2. *Signs of negative emotions*: Reduced eye contact, fewer pleasant facial expressions, agitated vocal tone
3. *Incompetent communication*: More speech errors, physical rigidity, hesitations, exaggerated movements, lack of spontaneity[11]

Keep in mind that leakage cues are not the same for everyone. Rather than reduce or eliminate eye contact, a skillful liar may look you in the eye. Some nonverbal behaviors, however, are better lie indicators than others. For instance, since facial muscles are generally easier to control than other muscles in the body, facial expressions can be managed and therefore don't necessarily reveal a liar. But, vocal pitch is less controllable, so any noticeable changes may give a liar away.

Mark Knapp, another prominent researcher in lying and deception, acknowledges that a small minority of people are highly skilled lie detectors. These human "lie detectors" pay close attention to what nonverbal communication tells them; they look for discrepancies between verbal and nonverbal behavior.[12] So pay attention to what people say as well as how they act. Likewise, pay attention to your own nonverbal behaviors when you know you're about to tell a lie, however "harmless" you may think it is. For example, researchers have noted that people telling the truth tend to add 20 to 30 percent more external detail to their stories and explanations than do those who are lying.[13]

communicating without words

THE NATURE OF NONVERBAL COMMUNICATION

MORE CONVINCING

Nonverbal communication is more believable because it seems spontaneous and revealing. **CAUTION:** Perceptions can deceive. Think of the times you've heard, "He *seemed* so honest when I met him," or "She acted like she really cared."

HIGHLY CONTEXTUAL

The meaning of nonverbal messages depends on a situation's psychosocial, logistical, and interactional context. **CAUTION:** Depending on the context, a laugh can be interpreted as amusement, approval, contempt, scorn, or embarrassment.

CONTINUOUS

Whereas verbal communication may stop and start, nonverbal communication usually continues uninterrupted. **CAUTION:** People interpret your opinions and feelings even when you are not talking.

LESS STRUCTURED

Unlike verbal communication, nonverbal communication has few agreed-upon rules. **CAUTION:** Nonverbal behavior can communicate multiple and ambiguous meanings, and can be difficult to interpret.

LEARNED INFORMALLY

You learn to communicate nonverbally by watching others and interpreting feedback about your nonverbal behavior. **CAUTION:** Failure to learn appropriate nonverbal behavior can embarrass you and result in misunderstanding and confusion.

Linking Verbal and Nonverbal Communication

Verbal communication and nonverbal communication often rely on each other to generate and interpret the meaning of a message. When you verbally congratulate someone, you may smile, shake hands, or hug that person. When you verbally express anger, you may frown, stand farther away, or use a harsh voice. In *Nonverbal Communication in Human Interaction*, communication scholar Mark Knapp and his colleagues express this notion eloquently:

> . . . like words, nonverbal signals can and do have multiple uses and meanings; like words, nonverbal signals have denotative and connotative meanings; and like words, nonverbal signals play an active role in communicating liking, power, and responsiveness.[14]

In the 1960s, psychologist Paul Ekman examined the relationship between language and nonverbal communication. He wrote that nonverbal behavior:

> serves to repeat, contradict, or substitute for a verbal message, as well as accent certain words, maintain the communicative flow, and indicate a person's feelings about his verbal statements.[15]

In his summary, Ekman concludes that nonverbal behaviors can repeat, complement, accent, regulate, substitute for, and/or contradict verbal messages.[16]

Repeat **Repetitive nonverbal behaviors** visually repeats the meaning of a verbal message. For example, when a waiter asks if anyone is interested in dessert, Miranda nods as she says, "Yes." She then points at a selection on the dessert tray and says, "I want the cheesecake." Luke says he would like the same, so Miranda holds up two fingers and says, "Make it two pieces."

Complement **Complementary nonverbal behaviors** are consistent with the verbal message. During a job interview, your words tell the interviewer that you are a confident professional, but what you say will be more believable if nonverbal elements such as posture, facial expressions, and vocal quality send the same message. Even the meaning of a simple *hello* can be strengthened if your facial expression and tone of voice communicate genuine interest and pleasure in greeting someone.

Accent **Accenting nonverbal behaviors** emphasize important elements in a message by highlighting its focus or emotional content. Saying the words *I'm angry* may fail to make the point, so you may couple this message with louder volume, forceful gestures, and piercing eye contact. Stressing a word or phrase in a sentence also focuses meaning.

Regulate We use **regulating nonverbal behaviors** to manage the flow of a conversation. Nonverbal cues tell us when to start and stop talking, whose turn it is to speak, how to interrupt other speakers, and how to encourage others to talk more. If you lean forward and open your mouth as if to speak, you are signaling that you want a turn in the conversation. In a classroom or large meeting, you may raise your hand when you want to speak. When your friend nods her head as you speak, you may interpret her nod as a sign to continue talking.

Substitute Nonverbal behavior can take the place of verbal language. This is called **substituting nonverbal behaviors**. When we wave hello or good-bye, the meaning is usually clear even in the absence of words. Without saying anything, a mother may send a message to a misbehaving child by pursing her lips, narrowing her eyes, and moving a single finger to signal "stop."

Contradict **Contradictory nonverbal behaviors** conflict with the meaning of spoken words. On receiving a birthday gift from a coworker, Sherry says, "It's lovely. Thank you." However, her forced smile, flat vocal expression, and lack of eye contact suggest that Sherry does not appreciate the gift. This is a classic example of a **mixed message**: a contradiction between verbal and nonverbal meanings. When nonverbal behavior contradicts spoken words, messages are confusing and difficult to interpret. Because nonverbal channels can carry more information than verbal ones, we usually rely on the nonverbal cues to determine the true meaning of a message.

Types of Nonverbal Communication

6.2 *Explain how your physical characteristics and movement generate meaning.*

Nonverbal communication is undeniably complex. To interpret nonverbal meaning accurately, you must pay attention to a multitude of nonverbal dimensions. To be an effective communicator you must consider the totality of your own and others' nonverbal behavior.

Physical Appearance

When you first meet someone, you automatically analyze that person's physical appearance to form an impression. Although it seems unfair to judge a person's personality and character based on physical characteristics such as attractiveness, clothing, hairstyle, weight, and personal accessories, these factors strongly influence your opinion of others and how you subsequently interact with them.

For better or worse, we perceive attractive people as kinder, more interesting, more sociable, more successful, and sexier than those considered less attractive. One study found that good-looking people tend to make more money and get promoted more often than those with average looks.[17]

Generally, taller people are viewed as more attractive, powerful, outgoing, and confident than shorter people. A 2009 study found a positive association between height and both income and education, both of which are positively linked to better lives.[18]

Certainly the images of attractive men and women in the media influence how we see others and ourselves. Many of us strive to achieve what are largely unrealistic standards of "beauty." For example, in the quest to communicate an impression of ideal beauty, approximately 75 to 80 percent

Expectancy Violation Theory

The following two scenarios are quite similar but may produce significantly different reactions.

Scenario 1. You stop at a local convenience store for a cup of coffee on your way to work, and you notice a poorly dressed man looking at you as you walk into the store. You've never seen him before. While you are preparing your coffee, he approaches and stands right next to you, smiling. As he reaches for a cup, his hand brushes against your arm. You turn to leave. Now he is standing directly behind you to pay for the coffee—and smiles again. As you leave, he follows you out the door.

Scenario 2. You stop at the office snack bar to get a cup of coffee, and you notice a well-dressed man looking at you. He's a valued friend and colleague you've worked with for many years. While you are preparing your coffee, he approaches and stands right next to you, smiling. As he reaches for a cup, his hand brushes against your arm. You turn to leave. Now he is standing directly behind you to pay for the coffee— and smiles again. As you leave, he follows you out the door.

Both scenarios are similar. Yet in the first case, you may react with suspicion and disapproval, whereas in the second case you feel more relaxed and positive. According to **Expectancy Violation Theory**, your expectations about nonverbal behavior have a significant effect on how you interact with others and how you interpret the meaning of nonverbal messages. When you enter an elevator, you probably conform to nonverbal expectations: you turn around and face front, avoid eye contact with others, avoid movement, refrain from talking or touching others, and stare at the numbers as they go up or down. But how would you react if someone entered a cramped elevator with three unruly dogs and lit a cigar? You'd most likely object or get off at the next floor because this is not the kind of behavior you'd expect in a confined public space.

At least three characteristics influence your expectations and reactions to the nonverbal behavior of another person.[19] Think of the previous two scenarios as you consider these characteristics.

1. *Communicator characteristics.* Similarities and differences in physical and demographic characteristics, such as age, gender, ethnicity, and physical appearance, as well as personality and reputation

2. *Relational characteristics.* Level of familiarity, past experiences, relative status, and type of relationship with others, such as close friend, romantic partner, business associate, service provider, or stranger

3. *Contextual characteristics.* Physical, social, psychological, cultural, and professional settings and occasions, such as football games, upscale shopping malls, religious services, classes, or business meetings

Clearly, the first scenario highlights differences in communicator, relational, and contextual characteristics, whereas the second scenario highlights similarities. In the first scenario, the man violates a number of nonverbal expectations: don't stare, follow, or touch strangers. In the second scenario, the man is "allowed" to violate the same nonverbal "rules" because you know him well.

When someone "violates" your nonverbal expectations, you may react negatively or even positively if the violation comes from someone you know, like, or admire. Likewise, your decision to "violate" a nonverbal expectation should be based on a careful analysis of your personal goals, the other people involved, and the potential outcomes.

of women in the United States either diet or have dieted in the past because they feel unhappy about their weight and want to be thinner. Some of these women develop eating disorders and become fatally thin.[20] The resulting appearance ends up conveying an impression quite different from what was likely intended.

Not surprisingly, your physical appearance plays a significant role in selecting romantic partners, getting and succeeding in a job, persuading others, and maintaining high self-esteem. For example, a person wearing a stylish suit, a high-end watch, and carrying an expensive leather briefcase suggests a higher income, a college education, and more status within a company than a person wearing a uniform and carrying a toolbox. Accessories such as a college ring, a wedding band, or a religious necklace communicate a great deal about another person.

Hair is another example and something of an obsession in the United States. In *Reading People*, jury consultant Jo-Ellan Dimitrius and attorney Mark Mazzarella use hair as a predictor of people's self-image and lifestyle. They claim that your hairstyle can reveal "how you feel about aging, how extravagant or practical you are, how much importance you attach to impressing others, your socioeconomic background, your overall emotional maturity, and sometimes even the part of the country where you were raised or now live."[21]

In his documentary, *Good Hair*, comedian Chris Rock took a serious look at the high price that black women pay (in harsh chemical treatments, hours of tight braiding, and dollars) to have *good hair*, a colloquial phrase in the African American community that describes the straight or soft-curly hair of non-black women. Rock exposed a $90 billion (that's right, billion dollar) industry that profits by transforming "nappy" hair into hair more like that of European women or into elaborate weaves.[22] In an attempt to combat this negative view of "good hair" *Sesame Street* writer Joey Mazzarino, the white parent of an adopted Ethiopian girl, wrote "I Really Love My Hair," a celebration of natural hair sung by a brown-skinned Muppet. Here's a short excerpt:

> Don't need a trip to the
> beauty shop,
> 'cause I love what I got
> on top.
> It's curly and it's brown and
> it's right up there!
> You know what I love?
> That's right, my hair![23]

Body Movement and Gestures

Jamal points to his watch to let the chairperson know that the meeting time is running short. Robin gives a thumbs-up gesture to signal that her friend's speech went well. Shenaz stands at attention as the American flag is raised. How you sit, stand, position the body, or move your hands generates nonverbal messages. Even your posture can convey moods and emotions. Slouching back in your chair may be perceived as lack of interest or dislike, whereas sitting upright and leaning forward communicates interest and signifies active listening.

Gestures are body movements that communicate an idea or emotion. They can emphasize or stress parts of a message, reveal discomfort with a situation, or convey a message without the use of words. The hands and arms are used most frequently for gesturing, although so can the head.[24]

Many people have difficulty expressing their thoughts without using gestures. Why else would we gesture when speaking to someone on the phone? Gesturing can also ease the mental effort required when communication is difficult. For example, we tend to gesture more when using a language that is less familiar or when describing a picture that a listener cannot see. Paul Ekman and Wallace Friesen classify hand gestures as **emblems**, **illustrators**, and **adaptors** as shown on page 103.[25]

Keep in mind that the examples of emblems, illustrators, and adaptors discussed in this chapter are gestures commonly used in the United States and have very specific meanings. Therefore, before interacting with people from other countries and cultures, think before you gesture. For example, the emblem that means "OK" to most Americans (forming a circle with the thumb and index finger) is considered an obscene gesture to Brazilians and signifies money to the Japanese.[26] When describing the height of a person, we may hold an arm out, palm down, and say, "My friend is this tall." In some South American countries, this same gesture is fine for describing a dog but would not be used for describing a person. To designate a person's height, a South American would hold her arm out with her palm sideways. Even putting your hands in your pockets can offend others, as a professor friend of ours learned when he spent a year teaching in Indonesia.

Physical Characteristics and Movement

Physical Appearance

Body Movement and Gestures

Touch

Facial Expressions

Eye Behavior

Vocal Expressiveness

WHAT MESSAGES DOES TATTOOING SEND TO OTHERS?

In many cultures, both past and present, people have tattooed their bodies. These markings often commemorated a rite of passage such as puberty, marriage, or a successful hunt. For example, traditional Maori tattooing in New Zealand—often on the face—is sacred. Each tattoo depicts "ancestral/tribal messages specific to the wearer. These messages tell the story of the wearer's family and tribal affiliations, and their place in these social structures."[27]

In Western cultures, tattoos have been associated with people of lower social status, gangs, prisoners, "bikers," and lower-ranked military personnel. That is no longer true, as tattooing has become more popular and acceptable, particularly among today's younger population for both men and women in all socio-economic classes.[28]

Today there are more than 1,500 tattoo parlors in the United States earning $2.3 billion a year.[29] In 2012, for the first time, the percentage of U.S. women with tattoos—23 percent—surpassed that of men at 19 percent.[30] Another 2012 survey reported that 21 percent of Americans have a tattoo as do 36 percent of eighteen to twenty-five year olds and 38 percent of thirty to thirty-nine year olds.

Despite the increasing popularity of tattoos, the Pew Research Center notes, "the public is divided about the impact of more people getting tattoos: 45 percent say it has not made much of a difference, 40 percent think it has been a change for the worse, and only 7 percent say this has been a change for the better." In one interesting study, about 30 percent of Americans with tattoos report it makes them feel sexier. On the other hand, about 50 percent of those *without* tattoos report that it makes the tattooed person less attractive to them.[31]

Not surprisingly, 64 percent of those ages sixty-five and older and 51 percent of those ages fifty to sixty-four say that the increase in tattoos is a change for the worse.[32]

Interestingly and perhaps more surprising, a study at Texas State University found, "individuals of age 18–24, the age group with more body art than any other, tend to consider *visible* tattoos unacceptable at work, particularly when face-to-face customer contact or commission sharing goes with the job."

> Contrary to what many people believe, it is not generally illegal for employers to ban visible body art in their dress code policies.[33]

David Brooks, political and cultural commentator for *The New York Times*, observes, "a cadre of fashion-forward types thought they were doing something to separate themselves from the vanilla middle class but are now discovering that the signs etched into their skins are absolutely mainstream."[34] Even so, some cities and public school systems force "employees to cover up tattoos if they want to keep their jobs."[35] Regardless of whether *you* like or dislike them, the popularity of tattoos has made it more difficult and unfair to negatively stereotype those who tattoo their bodies.

TYPES OF **GESTURES**

TYPE OF GESTURE	CHARACTERISTICS	EXAMPLES
EMBLEM 	Expresses the same meaning as a word in a particular group or culture	• Forming a V with your index and middle finger as a sign of victory or peace • Raising your hand in class to indicate "I want to speak" • Placing your index finger over your lips to mean "be quiet" • Extending the middle finger to offend someone or declare "up yours"
ILLUSTRATOR	Used with a verbal message that would lack meaning without the words	• Pointing as a way of identifying an object or person. • Holding your hands two feet apart and saying, "The fish I caught was this big" • Counting out the steps of a procedure with your hand while orally describing each step • Snapping your fingers while saying, "It happened just like that," to indicate that an event occurred quickly
ADAPTOR	Habitual gestures that help manage and express emotions	• Scratching your head to signify confusion or an inability to answer • Chewing your nails because you are worried or anxious • Drumming your fingers on a table because you are impatient • Wringing your hands because you are distressed • Playing with your hair or an object to relieve stress or impatience

Touch

Touch is one of the most potent forms of human expression. It not only has the power to send strong messages, but it can also affect your physical and psychological health. For example, babies need human touch to survive and develop. When new parents and hospital nurses engage in more touching behavior, infant death rates decrease.[36]

Many people have difficulty expressing their thoughts without touching someone. A reassuring pat on the shoulder from a coworker or a lover's embrace can convey encouragement, appreciation, affection, empathy, or sexual interest. Playful touches tend to lighten the mood without expressing a high degree of emotion. Lightly punching a friend in the arm or covering another's eyes and asking, "Guess who?" are forms of playful touch.

Psychologist Dacher Keltner writes that touch "is the first language we

When shaking hands with President Park Geun-hye of Korea, Bill Gates did not realize that putting his other hand in his pocket is considered a rude gesture in Korea and other Asian countries. It signifies that one person is purposely expressing superiority to the other. Some Korean newspapers media cropped the photo so it didn't show his hand in his pocket.

learn" and that it "remains [the] richest means of emotional expression" throughout our life.[37] In a series of experiments, psychologist Matthew Hertenstein, asked volunteers to try to communicate a list of emotions by touching blindfolded strangers. The result was surprising. The researchers found that touch "can signal at least six emotions: anger, fear, disgust, love, gratitude, and sympathy." Equally important, the accuracy rates for identifying these emotions ranged from 48 to 83 percent, which is about the same as our ability to identify emotions from observing facial expressions and listening to vocal expression.[38] Even so, other researchers have claimed that most adults only interpret touch as either positive or negative.

We also use touch to express control or dominance. In some instances, only a minor level of control is needed, such as when we tap someone on the shoulder to get her or his attention. In other cases, touch sends very clear messages about status or dominance. Research shows that individuals with more power and status are more likely to touch someone of lesser status and subordinates rarely initiate touch with a person of higher status.[39]

Touch approaches are comfortable with touch and often initiate touch with others. A touch approacher is more likely to initiate a hug or a kiss when greeting a friend. Some touch approaches even touch or hug people they don't know very well. At the extreme end of the continuum are touch approaches who touch too much and violate nonverbal expectations.

Touch avoiders are less comfortable initiating touch or being touched. They are also more conscious of when, how, and by whom they are touched. Extreme touch avoiders avoid any physical contact even with loved ones. Most of us are somewhere in the middle of the continuum. Obviously, misunderstandings can result when touch approaches and avoiders meet. Approaches may view avoiders as cold and unfriendly, and avoiders may perceive approaches as invasive and rude.

Not surprisingly, norms for touch depend on the context. For example, violating touch norms in the workplace can result in misunderstandings or allegations of sexual harassment. Norms for touch also vary according to gender and culture. Most North American men tend to avoid same-sex touch except for the hugging, chest bumping, and high-fiving we see on sports teams.

Facial Expressions

Your face is composed of complex muscles capable of displaying well over a thousand different expressions. Facial expressions let you know if others are interested in, agree with, or understand what you have said. Women tend to be more facially expressive and smile more often than men. But although men are more likely to limit the amount of emotion they reveal, everyone relies on facial expressions to comprehend the full meaning of a message.

At the beginning of this chapter, we reported that researchers have confirmed the power of eye contact, but that without at least the hint of a smile, eye contact will not make you more attractive. The thought of a grim face staring at us is more frightening than attracting.

Smiling can make you and others feel better because smiles are contagious. If someone smiles at you, mirror neurons in your brain trigger a smile response in you. Smiling is also good for your health because smiles "translate into lower heart rates and stress levels."[41] The prescription is obvious—smile more, be happy, get healthy.

Researchers have also found that people who do not smile can learn to smile and smile more often. There's even a smile coach ready to help you. Patti Wood, a body-language expert, coaches politicians, business executives, applicants preparing for critical job interviews, and people who are dating on how to smile effectively. Before signing up, consider her rates: She charges "$1,200 for a 3½–hour body-language training package."[42]

Know Thy Self

Are You Touchy?[40]

How touchy are you? Indicate the degree to which each statement below applies to you using the following rating scale: (5) strongly agree, (4) agree, (3) undecided or neutral, (2) disagree, or (1) strongly disagree.

_____ 1. I don't mind if I am hugged as a sign of friendship.
_____ 2. I enjoy touching others.
_____ 3. I seldom put my arms around others.
_____ 4. When I see people hugging, it bothers me.
_____ 5. People should not be uncomfortable about being touched.
_____ 6. I really like being touched by others.
_____ 7. I wish I were free to show my emotions by touching others.
_____ 8. I do not like touching other people.
_____ 9. I do not like being touched by others.
_____10. I find it enjoyable to be touched by others.
_____11. I dislike having to hug others.
_____12. Hugging and touching should be outlawed.
_____13. Touching others is a very important part of my personality.
_____14. Being touched by others makes me uncomfortable.

Scoring:

_____ 1. Add up the responses you put next to the following items: 1, 2, 5, 6, 7, 10, and 13. Your Step 1 score = _____.
_____ 2. Add up the responses you put next to the following items: 3, 4, 8, 9, 11, 12, and 14. Your Step 2 score = _____
_____ 3. Complete the following formula: 42 + Total of Step 1 – Total of Step 2 = _____.

Your score should be between 14 and 70 points. A score of more than 53 points suggests that you are a touch approacher. A score of less than 31 points indicates that you tend to avoid touch.

ADAPTING FACIAL EXPRESSIONS

TECHNIQUE	CHARACTERISTICS	EXAMPLES
Masking	Conceals true emotions by displaying expressions considered more appropriate in a particular situation	• Smiling and congratulating a colleague for getting a promotion you wanted • Looking stern when reprimanding a toddler who has dumped a bowl of spaghetti on his head
Neutralization	Eliminates displays of emotions	• Avoiding any display of emotion when serving as a juror during a trial • Displaying a "poker face" during a card game
Intensification	Exaggerates expressions to meet other people's needs or to express strong feelings	• Hugging someone a few more seconds than usual to communicate how much you care • Pouting dramatically when you do not get your way
Deintensification	Reduces or downplays emotional displays to accommodate others	• Looking mildly disapproving when a committee member rudely interrupts another speaker during a meeting • Subduing smiles of happiness after defeating a highly competitive friend in a tennis match

Facial expressions tell us a lot about what other people think, how they feel, and whether they're holding a winning poker hand. As a result, most of us learn to manage our facial expressions in order to convey or conceal an emotion and to adapt our facial expressions to particular situations. The most common techniques for adapting facial expressions are **masking**, **neutralization**, **intensification**, and **deintensification**.[43]

MEDIATED COMMUNICATION IN ACTION

Expressing Emotions Online

As you now know, as much as 60 to 70 percent, or about two-thirds, of the meaning you generate when communicating face-to-face with others may be conveyed through nonverbal behaviors.

The Internet adds another element to the mix of verbal and nonverbal communication. How do you express emotions online? At first the answer seems simple: You just tell them. You write "I'm angry" or "I love you" or "Shut up" or "I'm thrilled." Unfortunately, and as you now know, meanings are in people, not in words. What does "I'm angry" mean? Does it mean you're annoyed, furious, or just joking? When you write "Shut up" are you asking someone to stop "talking" online or are you using the phrase to indicate surprise or doubt as in "You're kidding?" or "You'd never do that!"

Never at a loss for ideas, Internet users developed **emoticons**, text symbols for expressing emotions. The most common emoticon is the smiley face, so common that when you try to create the original :-) or :), your device may change it into ☺. You also can show you are sad :(, stick out your tongue :P, kiss someone on the lips :-x, wink ;), or laugh :-D. But, no matter how many emoticons you know, there's a problem. Just like words, emoticons can be misinterpreted and easily ignored.

Some researchers suggest that emoticons have little or no effect on the interpretation of an online text message.[44] Other research argues that a happy, smiling emoticon increased the "positivity" of a positive text message more than a negative, frowning emoticon increased the negativity of a negative message.[45]

It's hard to know which studies to believe because what's true for you may not be true for others in online situations. The person you are e-mailing or texting may rely more on your words than on your emoticons when interpreting the intended meaning of your message. If you overuse such symbols, they may just ignore them. In their book *Rules of the Net*, Thomas Mandel and Gerard Van der Leun offer the following suggestion: "Nothing—especially the symbols on the top row of your keyboard—can substitute for a clear idea simply expressed. Avoid :-) and all associated emoticons as you would avoid clichés—for example, like the plague."[46] Generally, we advise you to avoid using a lot of emoticons, particularly if you are communicating in a business or professional situation. However, if you and your online friends like using creative emoticons, ☺ away. Our best advice is to use emoticons wisely depending on your purpose, the people you're sending them to, and the nature of the occasion.

Eye Behavior

Eye behavior may be the most revealing and complex of all your facial features. They can express social position, both positive and negative emotion, and indicate a willingness to relate.[47] When we try to understand what someone else is saying, most of us will look at a speaker more than 80 percent of the time. A group member who wants to be viewed as a leader may choose a seat at the head of the table to gain more visual attention. We tend to increase our gaze in response to positive emotions, such as surprise, and avert our eyes in response to negative experiences, such as disgust or horror. We use eye contact to get a server's attention in a restaurant and avert our eyes when we don't want the instructor to call on us in class.

Recall the introduction to this chapter. We explained that when you smile and maintain eye contact with someone else, it makes you more attractive to that person.[48] We like a French proverb that captures the same idea: "The first love letters are written with the eyes."[49]

As with all nonverbal behavior, norms for eye contact vary according to gender and culture. Women tend to engage in more eye contact when listening than men. In North America, lack of eye contact is frequently perceived as rudeness, indifference, nervousness, or dishonesty. This is not true across all cultures. For example, "direct eye contact is a taboo or an insult in many Asian cultures. Cambodians consider direct eye contact an invasion of one's privacy."[50]

After reviewing and conducting significant research on eye behavior, Virginia Richmond and her colleagues offer a summary that answers the question "What do we know about eye behavior?"[51]

1. We look at people and things we like.
2. We avoid looking at people and things we do not like.
3. Our eyes can express sadness, contempt, anger, disgust, fear, interest, surprise, and happiness.
4. We look more at another person when seeking approval or wanting to be liked.
5. The type of gaze we use tells another person about our intentions.
6. When we avert our gaze from someone, it's an intentional act.

7. Deception can rarely be detected by looking solely at another person's eye behavior.
8. Our pupils dilate when we look at someone or something that is appealing or interesting to us.
9. Our pupils constrict when we look at someone or something that is not appealing or interesting to us.
10. Women often look longer at their conversational partners than men do.

Vocal Expressiveness

How you *say* a word significantly influences its meaning. Your vocal quality also affects how others perceive you. For example, it can be difficult to listen to a person with a very high-pitched or monotone voice.

Some of the most important vocal characteristics are volume, pitch, and word stress. **Volume** refers to the loudness of your voice. Whispering can indicate that information is confidential; yelling suggests urgency or anger. **Pitch** refers to how high or low your voice sounds. In the United States, Americans seem to prefer low-pitched voices. Men and women with deeper voices are seen as more authoritative and effective. Men with a naturally high pitch may be labeled effeminate or weak, and women with very high pitches may be labeled as childish, silly, or anxious.

Rate is the speed at which you speak. A speaking rate that is too fast makes it difficult for others to understand your message. On the other hand, we become bored by or stop listening to a person who speaks too slowly.

When volume, pitch, and rate are combined, they can be used to vary the stress you give to a word or phrase. **Word stress** refers to the "degree of prominence given to a syllable within a word or words within a phrase or sentence."[52] Notice the differences in meaning as you stress the italicized words in the following sentences:

Is *that* the report you want me to read?
Is that the report you want *me* to read?
Is that the report you want me to *read*?

Although the same words are used in all three sentences, the meaning of each question is quite different. In Chapter 14, "Language and Delivery," we will take a closer look at these and other vocal characteristics and see how they contribute to a speaker's success.

ETHICAL COMMUNICATION

The Dark Side of Nonverbal Behavior

Just as a smile or a pat on the back can communicate, so too can an angry shove or a slap. Unfortunately, some people use violent nonverbal communication to express negative emotions or exert power over others.

Each year, approximately 1.5 million women and more than 800,000 men are victims of violence from an intimate partner such as a husband, wife, boyfriend, girlfriend, or date.[53] Although female victims are more likely to need medical attention, research reveals that women hit men as often as men hit women.[54] Violence also occurs in the workplace between coworkers and by frustrated customers.

Physical intimidation and violence includes acts such as hitting, restraining, and shoving as well as behavior that stops short of physical contact, such as throwing objects, pounding on a desk, or destroying property. Intimidating nonverbal communication can also take more subtle forms, such as physically blocking another's path, moving aggressively and too close, or creating a threatening presence. The use of unjustified physical aggression violates the National Communication Association's Credo for Ethical Communication, which specifically condemns communication that is intimidating, coercive, or violent.[56]

Fifteen percent of homicides in the workplace are committed by coworkers.[55]

Silence

The well-known phrase "silence is golden" may be based on a Swiss saying, "*Sprechen ist silbern; Swchweigen ist golden,*" which means "speech is silver; silence is golden." This metaphor contrasts the value of speech and silence. Although speech is important, silence may be even more significant in certain contexts.

Understanding the value of silence is important because we use silence to communicate many things: to establish interpersonal distance, to put our thoughts together, to show respect for another person, or to modify others' behaviors.[57]

Silence is also speech. (African proverb)

A loud voice shows an empty head. (Finnish proverb)

Those who know, do not speak. Those who speak, do not know. (Lao Tzu, *Tao Te Ching*)

Silence is a friend who will not betray. (Confucius)

The quieter you become, the more you can hear. (Baba Ram Dass, contemporary American spiritual teacher)

Time, Place, and Space As Nonverbal Communication

6.3 *Explain how time, place, and space generate meaning.*

The functions and forms of nonverbal communication extend beyond the borders of your physical characteristics, vocal tone, and movements. In this section we look at the ways in which time, place, and space affect how we communicate nonverbally in three significant contexts.

Time

In Chapter 3, "Adapting to Others," we introduced the cultural dimension of time orientation, which focuses on how and when people from different cultures achieve goals: short-term or long-term. People with a short-term time orientation want things to run on schedule because time is valuable. They can become impatient with people who take a long-term perspective in which they tolerate interruptions and look for future rather than immediate outcomes.

Although many researchers study how we make use of and respond to time, making rules about it proves difficult. For example, it's unforgivable to be late for a job interview but okay to be late for an informal party. According to some researchers, students walking into the classroom after the class has begun are seen by most U.S. students as disruptive.[58] As you pay attention and observe others' nonverbal behavior, try to learn what their attitudes are about time and punctuality, compare it to yours, and do your best to understand, respect, and adapt to the differences.

Place

Do you behave the same way in the classroom as you do at home? Probably not. The place in which you communicate does more than influence nonverbal communication; it *is* a form of nonverbal communication. In other words, the characteristics of an environment can communicate a message. For example, an office with unorganized stacks of papers, a stale smell, uncomfortable chairs, and ugly orange walls may create a negative impression of the occupant. It may also affect how comfortably you interact in that space. Environmental elements, such as furniture arrangement, lighting, color, temperature, and smell, communicate.

Most environments are designed with a purpose in mind. An expensive restaurant may separate tables at some distance to offer diners privacy. The restaurant's atmosphere may be comfortable, quiet, and subject to only the mouth-watering aroma of good food. How does this differ from the environment of your local fast-food restaurant?

The table below presents Mark Knapp's six nonverbal dimensions that affect how you are likely to behave in different nonverbal environments. For example, a weekly staff meeting may be informal, warm, usually private, familiar, regularly scheduled, and set in a room where people are physically close to one another. At a courtroom trial, however, you may find yourself in an environment that is more formal, less comfortable, open or private (depending on your role), unusual, temporary, and set in a place where people are more physically separated from one another.[59]

You can ask questions about all six dimensions in most nonverbal contexts. For example, think of the environment

Environmental Analysis Dimensions of the Nonverbal Context

Environmental Feature	Dimensions of Communication Environments	
Formality	Informal ←	→ Formal
Warmth	Comfortable ←	→ Uncomfortable
Privacy	Open ←	→ Private
Familiarity	Unusual ←	→ Usual
Constraint	Temporary ←	→ Permanent
Distance of Others	Others Close ←	→ Others Far

you are in right now—or your classroom environment. How would you rate your environment in terms of the six dimensions? Now consider another environment and do the same. If the two environments have been designed for the same purpose, they may have similar "ratings." If not, you may find yourself communicating quite differently in the that context.[60]

Space

The ways in which we claim, use, and interpret space and distance are significant dimensions of nonverbal communication.

In nonverbal terms, **territoriality** is the sense of personal ownership attached to a particular space. For instance, most classroom students sit in the same place every day. If you have ever walked into a classroom to find another person in *your* seat, you may have felt that your territory had been violated. Ownership of territory is often designated by objects acting as **markers** of territory. Placing a coat on a chair or books on a table can send a clear message that a seat is taken or saved.

Anthropologist Edward T. Hall uses the term **proxemics** to refer to the study of spatial relationships and how the distance between people communicates information about their relationship. Hall maintains that we have our own personal portable "air bubble" that we carry around with us. This personal space is culturally determined. For example, the Japanese, who are accustomed to crowding, need less space around them, whereas North Americans need "wide open spaces" around them to feel comfortable.[61]

According to Hall and as the table below illustrates, most Americans interact within four spatial zones or distances: **intimate**, **personal**, **social**, and **public**.[62]

Not surprisingly, we reduce the distance between ourselves and others as our relationships become more personal. Intimate distance is usually associated with affection and increased physical contact. In most situations, you encounter a mixture of distances. You may feel comfortable using a personal distance with a good friend at work but use social distance with other colleagues.

Hall's FOUR U.S. Spatial Zones

Zone	Distance	Purpose and Context	Communication Characteristics
Intimate Distance	0 to 18 inches	Loving; comforting; protecting; fighting	Minimal talk; can smell and touch one another; little eye contact
Personal Distance	18 inches to 4 feet	Conversations with intimates; friends; acquaintances	Touch possible; more eye contact and visual details seen
Social Distance	4 feet to 12 feet	Impersonal; business settings; social gatherings	More formal tone; loses some visual detail; eye contact likely
Public Distance	More than 12 feet	Lectures; concerts; plays; speeches; ceremonies	Subtle details lost, only obvious details noticed

THE TEENAGE BRAIN

For decades, parents, teachers, and psychologists "threw up their hands and cried, 'Hormones!' when asked why children become so nutty around the time of adolescence."[63] Scientists now claim that hormones are only part of the answer.

Using neuroimaging, neuropsychologist Deborah Yurgelun-Todd and her colleagues found that teenage brains work differently than adult brains when processing nonverbal emotional information.[64] Before explaining more about this research, look at the image of the young person in the inset. What emotion do you see on her face?

The answer is: fear. While most of the adults who were shown this photo guessed this woman's emotion correctly, only 50 percent of teenagers got it right. Many teens identified the emotion as shock, confusion, or sadness.[65] It turns out that teens and adults use different parts of their brains to identify emotions.

The results of these studies are significant for communicators of all ages. It means that what we see as teenage indifference to emotions is, in fact, an inability to recognize emotions correctly, particularly the feelings expressed in an adult's face. According to Dr. Yurgelun-Todd, [teenagers] see anger when there isn't anger, or sadness when there isn't sadness. And if that's the case, then clearly their own behavior is not going to match that of the adult. This results in miscommunication, both in terms of what they think the adult is feeling, but also what the response should be.

In Chapter 2, "Understanding Your Self," we explained how effective self-monitoring helps you identify your own feelings and the feelings of others, particularly when they're expressed nonverbally. People who are high self-monitors astutely watch other people; correctly interpret the meaning of their facial expressions, body language, and tone of voice; and then appropriately respond to their behavior. Research on the teenage brain helps us understand why many teenage brains need to "grow up" and physically mature in order to develop and practice self-monitoring skills.

Improving Nonverbal Communication

6.4 *Practice effective nonverbal communication strategies and skills.*

Most people learn to communicate nonverbally by imitating others and by paying attention to and adapting to feedback. Thus, when someone responds positively to a particular nonverbal behavior, you tend to keep using it. If you receive negative reactions, you may choose a more effective behavior next time. Training and practice can help you develop more effective nonverbal communication skills.

Be Other Oriented

Other-oriented people are effective self-monitors and sensitive to others. They give serious, undivided attention to, feel genuine concern for, and focus on the needs of other communicators.

For example, during a casual phone conversation, note whether your friend's tone of voice communicates more than the words you hear. During face-to-face encounters, observe and "listen" to the nonverbal messages—that is, *look* while you listen. The more of your five senses you use, the more nonverbal cues you will notice.

As you make your own observations of people as they communicate, ask yourself some of these questions:

- Does their nonverbal behavior repeat, complement, accent, regulate, or substitute for what they say, or does it contradict their verbal messages?

- How does the use of emblems, illustrators, or adaptors affect the meaning of their messages?

- Do facial expressions mask, neutralize, intensify, or deintensify their thoughts and feelings?

- Do they maintain or avoid eye contact?

- Do they display leakage cues that may reveal a lie or deceptive communication?

- Do they ignore or adapt to your time orientation?

- Do they use an appropriate intimate, personal, social, or public distances from you and others?

Nodding your head, leaning forward, and engaging in direct eye contact are just some of the nonverbal cues that indicate to others that you are paying attention and interested. Your nonverbal feedback lets another communicator sense your response to a message. For example, if your nonverbal behaviors suggest you don't understand or that you disagree with what is being said, the other person may try to clarify information or present a better argument.

If, as you listen, you have difficulty interpreting the meaning of nonverbal behavior, ask for help. Describe the message as you understand it. For example, if someone tells you about a tragic event while smiling, you might say, "George, you don't seem very upset by this. Maybe your smile is just a sign of nervousness?" If you are having trouble setting up a meeting with someone and sense a problem, ask the person, "You seem to be avoiding me—or is it just my imagination?" In Chapter 7, "Understanding Interpersonal Relationships," we discuss several techniques for ensuring that you understand the meaning of verbal and nonverbal messages.

> Not only should you look at someone *while* you are listening, but you should also look as though you are listening.

Use Immediacy Strategies

Generally, we avoid people who seem cold, unfriendly, or hostile. Similarly, we tend to feel more comfortable and want to approach people who seem warm and friendly. **Immediacy** is the degree to which a person appears more open, likeable, and approachable.[66] In addition to how you appear and move, immediacy includes nonverbal cues such as touch, vocal quality, and physical closeness as well as verbal cues in the form of messages that communicate an open, likeable, and approachable attitude.

Not surprisingly, patients respond better to health professionals who communicate immediacy through their body "stance, eye contact, facial expressions, gestures, and touch."[67] Think about the many physicians you've seen. Would you agree with the following research findings? When physicians show more nonverbal immediacy, patients are more likely to trust them, to talk to them about their symptoms and concerns, to understand and remember what the doctor tells them, to be more motivated to follow medical advice, and to be more satisfied with the visit to their doctor.[68] Interestingly, doctors are becoming highly motivated to use immediacy strategies because "under new Medicare rules, providers won't get as much money if they rack up poor patient satisfaction scores."[69]

In another study, researchers focused on how e-mail can build strong student–teacher ties. Students who believed that e-mail messages from their professors were high in immediacy, were more likely to perceive future rewards for developing a student–teacher relationship. Online immediacy strategies can range from "using emoticons such as smiley faces, signing off using the professor's first name, incorporating pronouns like 'we' and 'our' when referencing the class, and encouraging a response or further interaction with the student."[70]

A variety of nonverbal behaviors can promote immediacy.[71] Neat, clean, and pleasant-smelling people are, understandably, more approachable than those who are dirty, sloppy, and smelly. The degree to which you are perceived as likable and approachable may be the difference between a smile and a frown, leaning toward rather than away from another person, direct eye contact versus looking away, a relaxed rather than a rigid body posture, or animated instead of neutral vocal tones.

Researchers have found, "immediacy is the overriding factor in a teacher's overall effectiveness."[72] Think about some of the most effective and least effective teachers you've had, and the extent to which they demonstrated the following nonverbal immediacy behaviors:

- consistent and direct eye contact
- a warm voice
- approving head nod
- expressive hand gestures
- smiles
- appropriate and natural body movement
- vocal variety
- direct eye contact
- relaxed body posture
- closer physical distance[73]

Whether at home with friends and family members or with colleagues at work, other people are more likely to want to communicate with you when you use nonverbal immediacy behaviors.

Conversational Skills Rating Scale[74]

Read the items on Brian Spitzberg's *Conversational Skills Rating Scale*. Check the items that describe verbal communication and those that describe nonverbal communication in face-to-face conversations. (Although most of the items depict either verbal or nonverbal communication, a few may warrant a check mark for both.)

Verbal or Nonverbal	Communication Behavior
_____ Verbal _____ Nonverbal	1. Speaking rate (neither too slow nor too fast)
_____ Verbal _____ Nonverbal	2. Speaking fluency (pauses, silences, frequent "uhs")
_____ Verbal _____ Nonverbal	3. Vocal confidence (neither too tense/nervous nor overly confident-sounding)
_____ Verbal _____ Nonverbal	4. Articulation (clarity of individual sounds and words)
_____ Verbal _____ Nonverbal	5. Vocal variety (neither overly monotone nor dramatic voice)
_____ Verbal _____ Nonverbal	6. Volume (neither too loud nor too soft)
_____ Verbal _____ Nonverbal	7. Posture (neither too closed/formal nor too open/informal)
_____ Verbal _____ Nonverbal	8. Leaning toward partner (neither too forward nor too far back)
_____ Verbal _____ Nonverbal	9. Shaking or nervous twitches (not noticeable or distracting)
_____ Verbal _____ Nonverbal	10. Unmotivated movements (tapping feet, fingers, hair-twirling)
_____ Verbal _____ Nonverbal	11. Facial expressiveness (neither neutral/blank nor exaggerated)
_____ Verbal _____ Nonverbal	12. Nodding of head in response to partner statements
_____ Verbal _____ Nonverbal	13. Using gestures to emphasize what is being said
_____ Verbal _____ Nonverbal	14. Using humor and/or stories
_____ Verbal _____ Nonverbal	15. Smiling and/or laughing
_____ Verbal _____ Nonverbal	16. Using eye contact
_____ Verbal _____ Nonverbal	17. Asking questions
_____ Verbal _____ Nonverbal	18. Speaking about partner (involvement of partner as a topic of conversation)
_____ Verbal _____ Nonverbal	19. Speaking about self (neither too much nor too little)
_____ Verbal _____ Nonverbal	20. Encouragement or agreement (encouragement of partner to talk)
_____ Verbal _____ Nonverbal	21. Personal opinion expression (neither too passive nor too aggressive)
_____ Verbal _____ Nonverbal	22. Initiating new topics
_____ Verbal _____ Nonverbal	23. Maintenance of topics and follow-up comments
_____ Verbal _____ Nonverbal	24. Interrupting partner
_____ Verbal _____ Nonverbal	25. Using more time speaking relative to partner

When you are finished, add up the number of items you checked as verbal and those you checked as nonverbal. Which category received the most checks? What does this tell you about the role of nonverbal communication in everyday interactions? To what extent do you skillfully employ these nonverbal communication behaviors when you are having a conversation with someone?

Communicating Without Words

6.1 Describe the nature and scope of nonverbal communication.

- Nonverbal communication refers to message components other than words you use to generate and respond to meaning.

- Nonverbal communication accounts for between 60 and 70 percent of the meaning in a face-to-face message.

- In everyday life, you use nonverbal communication to express emotions, define relationships, establish power and influence, interpret verbal messages, deceive and detect deception.

- Nonverbal communication differs from verbal communication in that it is more convincing, highly contextual, learned informally, less structured, and continuous.

- Nonverbal behavior can repeat, complement, accent, regulate, substitute, and/or contradict verbal messages.

- Expectancy violation theory demonstrates how your expectations about nonverbal behavior significantly affect how you interact with others and how you interpret the meaning of nonverbal messages.

Types of Nonverbal Communication

6.2 Explain how your physical characteristics and movement generate meaning.

- Your body's characteristics and movements have many dimensions, including physical appearance, body movement and gestures, touch, facial expressions, eye behavior, and vocal expressiveness.

- Physical appearance includes nonverbal elements such as attractiveness, clothing and accessories, body tattooing, and hairstyles.

- Hand movements can be classified as emblems, illustrators, and adaptors.

- Facial expressions can function to mask, neutralize, intensify, or deintensify an emotion.

Time, Place, and Space As Nonverbal Communication

6.3 Explain how time, place, and space generate meaning?

- Nonverbal communication dimensions include the timing of events and perspectives about the use of time.

- *Proxemics* is the study of how the distance between people communicates information about the nature of their relationship.

- Edward Hall's four spatial zones—intimate, personal, social, and public distances—are culturally determined.

- The dimensions of a nonverbal environment include the degree of formality, warmth, privacy, familiarity, predictable scheduling, and the physical closeness of people to one another.

Improving Nonverbal Communication

6.4 Practice effective nonverbal communication strategies and skills.

- By observing others' nonverbal behavior and confirming your interpretation of its meaning, you can become more other-oriented.

- What seems like teenage indifference to emotions may be an inability to recognize emotions correctly, particularly the feelings in an adult's face.

- Nonverbal immediacy strategies such as maintaining eye contact, smiling, using vocal variety and appropriate body movements, and maintaining close physical distance can enhance your interactions with others.

Key Terms

Accenting nonverbal behaviors	Immediacy	Public distance
Adaptors	Intensification	Rate
Complementary nonverbal behaviors	Intimate distance	Regulating nonverbal behaviors
Contradictory nonverbal behaviors	Leakage cues	Repetitive nonverbal behaviors
Deintensification	Markers	Social distance
Emblems	Masking	Substituting nonverbal behavior
Emoticons	Metamessage	Territoriality
Expectancy Violation Theory	Mixed message	Touch approachers
Gestures	Neutralization	Touch avoiders
Illustrators	Nonverbal communication	Volume
	Other-oriented	Word stress
	Personal distance	
	Pitch	
	Proxemics	

TEST YOUR KNOWLEDGE

6.1 *Describe the nature and scope of nonverbal communication.*

1 The textbook defines *nonverbal communication* behaviors that generate meaning without using words. Which of the following answers is *not* an example of nonverbal communication?

   a. using :-) in an e-mail to highlight your feelings

   b. reading an old letter from a good friend who was living abroad

   c. putting on perfume or cologne before going to a party

   d. brightening up your apartment with flowers before your parents come over for dinner

2 Even though Fiona has nothing but good things to say about her boyfriend, her family can tell she's angry at him. Which nonverbal characteristic best explains this experience?

   a. Nonverbal communication is more convincing.

   b. Nonverbal communication is highly contextual.

   c. Nonverbal communication is learned informally.

   d. Nonverbal communication is less structured.

6.2 *Explain how your physical characteristics and movement generate meaning.*

3 If one of your coworkers tells you that she got the promotion that both of you applied for, you may smile at the news even though you feel awful. Which technique for adapting facial expressions are you using?

   a. masking

   b. neutralizing

   c. intensification

   d. unmasking

4 If a speaker stresses the word indicated in italics, which of the following statements means "I was born in New Jersey, not in New York as you seem to think."

   a. "*I* was born in New Jersey."

   b. "I *was* born in New Jersey."

   c. "I was *born* in New Jersey."

   d. "I was born in *New Jersey*."

6.3 *Explain how time, place, and space generate meaning.*

5 According to anthropologist Edward Hall, how close to a business or class acquaintance does the average person in the United States stand?

   a. 0 to 6 inches

   b. 6 to 18 inches

   c. 18 inches to 4 feet

   d. 4 feet to 12 feet

6 Which of the following nonverbal hand movements is an example of an illustrator?

   a. Making a circle with your thumb and index finger to indicate "OK."

   b. Holding your thumb and fingers about two inches apart as you describe how much shorter your hair was after your last haircut.

   c. Putting your face in the palms of your hands when you realize that you've forgotten to buy your spouse a Valentine's present.

   d. Raising your hand in class so the instructor will call on you.

6.4 *Practice effective nonverbal communication strategies and skills.*

7 Recent studies have found that teenage brains work differently than adult brains when processing nonverbal emotional information. Which answer identifies the conclusion of these studies?

   a. Teenagers do not dress appropriately for serious or sad occasions.

   b. Teenagers do not maintain the appropriate distance from others in public settings.

   c. Teenagers do not accurately identify nonverbal expressions of emotions.

   d. Teenagers do not recognize the characteristics of immediacy.

8 _____ refers to the degree to which you seem approachable and likable.

   a. Other oriented

   b. Immediacy

   c. Observant

   d. Confirming

Answers found on page 368.

Understanding
Interpersonal Relationships **7**

The 2010 film *Social Network* tells the story of Mark Zuckerberg, the undergraduate Harvard student who developed Facebook. Even if you didn't see the film, you certainly know that Facebook is huge with half a billion subscribers and would be absolutely right in guessing that Zuckerberg is the youngest billionaire in history.[1]

There is, however, an enormous irony in this story. Although Facebook helps us make and communicate with friends, Zuckerberg wasn't very good at either skill. To put it mildly, Zuckerberg's interpersonal skills were dreadful as was his ethical behavior. One reviewer describes Zuckerberg as portrayed in the film:

> Mark exists in his own world. He dresses like he just rolled out of bed and doesn't relate to people half as well as he does to computers, algorithms and user databases. He finds people, at best, helpful to his creations or, at worst, annoying. He cannot speak civilly to anyone yet has the verbal skills to hone in on sore points with his acquaintances.[2]

If you're thinking that this story proves that a lousy communicator can become a billionaire, think again. Rather, the story tells us that a more skilled and more ethical communicator could have become a billionaire *and* avoided the personal and legal problems that have plagued and continue to plague Mark Zuckerberg today.

Despite his exceptional technical intelligence, Zuckerberg would have benefited from interpersonal and emotional intelligence. In this chapter we look at the nature of interpersonal communication in many forms: in daily conversations and in close relationships with friends, romantic partners, and family members. We also recommend communication strategies and skills that can help you develop, strengthen, and maintain meaningful relationships with others in a wide variety of situations and circumstances.

Understanding Interpersonal Relationships

7.1 *Identify the characteristics and benefits of effective interpersonal communication.*

Forming positive and lasting relationships is a human instinct. Communication scholar Malcolm R. Parks writes, "We humans are social animals down to our very cells. Nature did not make us noble loners."[3]

Unlike some animals that live most of their lives on their own except when mating, we cannot survive on our own. Newborn babies and infants cannot stand up and run from predators. Our ancestors formed hunting-and-gathering relationships long before bows and arrows, let alone guns, made solo hunts possible. Even as humans advanced and developed more modern means of survival, one thing has always remained the same: the need for interpersonal relationships. No person on this earth will do well or even survive if deprived of contact with others.

Developing interpersonal relationships "gives meaning and purpose to our lives like no other activity or endeavor can."[4] Your ability to communicate effectively in close personal relationships affects your mental and physical health, your identity and happiness, your social and moral development, your ability to cope with stress and misfortunes, and the quality and meaning of your life.[5]

Interpersonal Communication and Relationship Building

When we use the phrase **interpersonal communication**, we are referring to what happens when a limited number of people, usually two, interact and generate meaning using verbal and nonverbal messages. This interaction typically results in sharing information, achieving a mutual goal, and/or maintaining a relationship. When we use the word **relationship** in this textbook, we are referring to a continuing and meaningful attachment or connection to another person.

There are many types of interpersonal relationships—perhaps as many as there are people you know. In addition to the emotional connections and commitments you have in close **personal relationships** with friends, romantic partners, and family members, you also have work-based relationships. **Professional relationships** involve connections with people you associate and work with to accomplish a goal or perform a task. Many relationships fall into both categories. A best friend may also be a colleague at work.

John Gottman, who studies the value and consequences of close personal relationships and strong

> Medical researchers have found "a link between relationships and physical health.... People with rich personal networks—who are married, have close family and friends, are active in social and religious groups—recover more quickly from disease and live longer."
>
> Daniel Goleman[6]

What Types of Relationships Are Shown in These Photos?

marriages, offers several conclusions drawn from his own and others' research:

- People with good friends usually have less stress and live longer.
- Longevity is determined far more by the state of people's closest relationships than by genetics.
- People who have good marriages live longer than those who don't.
- Loners are twice as likely to die from all causes over a five-year period as those who enjoy close friendships.[7]

Some people mistakenly believe that Gottman is urging us to make as many friends (including Facebook "friends") as possible and (if not already married) to get married as soon as we can in order to live longer. This is not what Gottman recommends. Rather, he claims that *meaningful* and lasting personal relationships lead to happy, healthy lives. Quality relationships do not just happen. *You* make them happen, and the success of those relationships depends largely on how well you communicate.

The Need for Interpersonal Relationships

We form interpersonal relationships for many reasons. One motive should be obvious: we develop relationships with other people because we are attracted to them. What isn't as easy to answer is *why*? Why are we attracted to some people and not the least bit attracted to others? And before you think we're only describing physical attraction, think again.

Sometimes we're attracted to another person for social reasons ("I think

MEDIATED COMMUNICATION IN *ACTION*

How Many Friends Do You Need?

For some people, building a network of online friends and followers has become an obsession. Others avoid this type of social media because they worry that they won't attract any friends or followers. When former president Bill Clinton appeared on *The Colbert Report* in 2013, Clinton revealed that he wasn't on Twitter. When asked why, he said he felt "sort of insecure" because "There's nothing worse than a friendless Twitter, right?" Right then and there, Mr. Colbert set up @PrezBillyJeff and asked Clinton to write his first tweet. Within an hour after *The Colbert Report* aired, Mr. Clinton "had 20,000 followers."[8]

There's no question that social media fulfills the promise of connecting you to people with whom you can interact and track. There is, however, a downside to what some have labeled an obsession for more and more online relationships as well as an addiction to social media.

Oxford University professor Robin Dunbar has studied social communities throughout the centuries—from human ancestors who lived in caves or led nomadic lives to those living in the twenty-first century. He concludes that the part of our brain "used for conscious thought and language . . . limits us to managing 150 friends, no matter how sociable we are."[9] In terms of online "friends," Dunbar "declares that all of those extra 'friends' don't really count as true

friends." However, he acknowledges that Facebook does help preserve and maintain "long-standing and long-distance friendships that might otherwise decay."[10]

Path, a recent social media app embraced Dunbar's 150-friends concept. Launched in 2010, Path limits you to a social network of no more than 150 people and is "designed with the people you love, your close friends and family, in mind."[11] One reviewer noted that you get "the sociability of Facebook without the nagging obligation to accept those pesky friend requests from high school acquaintances you haven't seen since the senior prom."[12] If you doubt the appeal of Path, it now has more than 12 million users.[13]

Unfortunately, an obsession with the number of social media friends or an addiction to online communication

"interferes with everyday life and becomes detrimental to daily functioning at work or at school."[14] If you doubt this conclusion, look around you. You may know people who are always on some form of social media: their heads are down and their fingers are texting and scrolling the screen. They seem oblivious to the world around them. Taking their hardware and online access away from them would be a catastrophe. One study concluded that quitting Facebook, Twitter, and other social media is more difficult than quitting smoking or giving up alcohol. In another study, students who gave up access to social media for twenty-four hours reported that they felt "fretful, confused, anxious, irritable, insecure, nervous, restless . . . [and even] depressed, jittery, and paranoid."[15]

she'd fit in very well with my friends."), physical reasons ("He is so good-looking!"), and task reasons ("Virginia and Jim are great leaders; I'd love to work for either of them").[16]

Psychologist William Schutz's **Fundamental Interpersonal Relationship Orientation (FIRO) Theory** contends that people interact with others in order to satisfy three basic interpersonal needs: the need for inclusion, the need for control, and the need for affection.[17]

The **inclusion need** represents a desire to belong, to be involved, and to be accepted. When your inclusion needs are met, you enjoy being with others but are also comfortable being alone. If,

however, your inclusion needs are not met, you may feel unworthy or undervalued. As a result, you may withdraw and become a loner or try to compensate by attracting attention and impressing others with what and whom you know.

The **control need** refers to whether you feel competent and confident. When control needs are met, you have no problem with power and feel just

as comfortable giving orders as taking them. Unmet control needs can make a person desperate to control everything and everyone by dominating others. Or it can make them passive and submissive.

The **affection need** is your desire to feel liked by others.[18] When your affection needs are met, you easily develop close friendships and intimate relationships, but are also secure enough to function in situations where affection is not forthcoming. When affection needs are not met, people believe they are not liked and establish only superficial relationships with others or they try to get close to everyone by seeking intimate relationships despite the disinterest of others.

Conversing with Others

7.2 *Describe strategies and skills that enhance conversation competencies.*

Let's begin our look at relationships with one of the most basic forms of interpersonal interaction: conversations. A **conversation** is an interaction, often informal, in which we exchange speaking and listening roles with another person. In his book *A Good Talk*, Daniel Menakar regards conversation as a human art of great importance produced by all people everywhere.[19]

On any given day, you may have a conversation with a close friend on the phone, a classmate in the hallway, a coworker at the next desk, or someone you've just met at a party. Conversations differ depending on where they take place and the type of relationship. For example, you may wait until others aren't around or until a championship game on television is over to have a serious and private conversation with a close friend. You may discuss highly personal issues with your life partner, but you probably won't share as much with someone you've just met.

Starting a Conversation

Introducing yourself and sharing superficial information is the most obvious way to begin a conversation with someone you do not know: "I'm Ahmad; my family and I are here on vacation from Michigan." The other person will usually reciprocate by

We negotiate conversational turn-taking primarily through our nonverbal behavior.

offering similar information or following up on what you've shared: "I have cousins in Michigan and visited them one summer when I was a kid." A second approach to opening a conversation is to ask simple questions: "Do you know anything about this movie?"

Maintaining a Conversation

One of the best ways to keep a conversation going is to ask **open-ended questions** that encourage specific or detailed responses. "What do you think of Dr. Pearson's course and assignments?" invites someone to share an observation or opinion. A **closed-ended question**, "Is this class required

for your major?" requires only a short and direct response and can generally be answered with a yes or no.

When you answer questions during a conversation, give a response that provides the other person information about your thoughts or experiences. An engaging conversation requires the commitment of two people. Without such effort, a conversation can quickly deteriorate into an awkward silence.

Finally, make sure you balance talking with listening. A successful conversationalist takes turns listening and speaking. Watch for nonverbal cues to find out when it's your turn to listen or speak. **Turn-requesting cues** are

Smartphone Etiquette

"One of the oldest forms of social media is the telephone. That's right, the phone. Person to person, speedy, and affordable, the phone is a key building block in how we do business." So writes Cory Huff, in "The Telephone Is Social Media."[20] What makes today's phones different from the telephones of yesteryear is that we use them in public places. This change in place also has changed the way we use and observe others on the phone.

Cell phone etiquette has been the subject of countless newspaper and magazine articles—and for good reasons. There is almost nothing as annoying and even embarrassing as being forced to listen in on someone else's cell phone conversation.[21] We're sure you have heard people complain to their spouses and colleagues or listened to boyfriends and girlfriends express their puppy love for one another. Surveys indicate that the majority of cell phone users believe that loud or private calls made in public settings are inappropriate. However, "that same majority indulges in such calls themselves."[22]

To avoid embarrassing yourself and annoying others nearby, follow a few simple rules when talking on a cell phone:[23]

- Do not make or take personal calls or text during business meetings, family celebrations, or class sessions.
- Maintain a distance from others of at least ten feet when talking on the phone.
- Avoid cell phone conversations in enclosed public spaces, such as elevators, waiting rooms, or buses and trains.
- Avoid cell phone conversations and texting in public places where side talk is considered bad manners, such as libraries, museums, theaters, restaurants, and places of worship.
- Control the volume of your voice. Tilt your chin downward so that you're speaking toward the floor. That way, your voice won't carry as far.
- Avoid cell phone conversations and texting when engaged in other tasks, such as driving, eating, or shopping.
- Do not talk on the phone or text someone while engaged in a face-to-face conversation or interaction with another person.
- Take advantage of your phone's features, such as vibrate mode and voice mail. When you step into your workplace or a classroom, put your cell phone on vibrate and let your calls roll to your voice mail.

---

verbal and nonverbal messages that signal a desire to speak, such as leaning forward, providing direct eye contact, and lifting one hand as if beginning to gesture. **Turn-yielding cues** are verbal and nonverbal messages, which signal that you are completing your comments and are preparing to listen, such as slowing down your speaking rate, relaxing your posture or gestures, and leaning slightly away. Good conversationalists are sensitive to turn-taking cues.

Effective listening promotes a genuine conversation rather than a one-way speech. In Chapter 4, "Listening," we introduced the Golden Listening Rule: Listen to others as you would have them listen to you. That rule is of utmost importance in every conversation.

Daniel Menaker explains that both parties in a conversation must "listen very closely, not only to the loud notes, but to the quiet one . . . as well—to what seems as though it's being downplayed or skipped over. Such attention is, for one thing, flattering, but it also yields insights that the people we're talking to sometimes don't even know they have."[24] Review Chapter 4 to make sure that you listen to understand, remember, interpret, evaluate, and appropriately respond to what you hear and see during a conversation.

Ending a Conversation

Ending a conversation abruptly can send a rude message to the other person. Look for a moment in the conversation where an ending seems natural—either when the topic seems fully exhausted or when someone shifts to the edge of a chair, stands up, looks away, leans away, or picks up personal belongings.[25] Try to end every conversation on a positive and courteous note. If, however, your companion is ignoring your attempts to end the conversation, you may need to be direct but firm: "I hate to cut our conversation short, but I have to get going."

Strengthening Personal Relationships

7.3 *Discuss specific strategies for improving interpersonal relationships with friends, romantic partners, and family members.*

Everyone has a multitude of personal relationships—with family members and friends, with teachers and students, with business associates and service providers, and with that special person who is your beloved partner or spouse. Unfortunately, we lack the space in this chapter and textbook to examine all of these relationships in detail. Instead, we focus on three of the most significant personal relationships you develop in your lifetime: friends, romantic partners, and family members. The distinct context and importance of these relationships require distinct communication strategies and skills to enhance their quality and longevity.

Friend Relationships

Although just about everyone has close friends, not all friendships are alike. Several factors influence the kind of friendship you have with another person. For example, for very young children, a friend is simply someone with whom they share toys and play; when these activities are absent, so is the friendship.[26]

In adolescence and young adulthood, we often establish enduring and intimate relationships with best friends. **Intimacy**, the feeling or state of knowing someone deeply, occurs in many forms. For example, in most romantic relationships, physical intimacy is a way of expressing affection and love. In friend and romantic relationships, intimacy can take on a variety of forms. It can be emotional (sharing private thoughts and feelings), intellectual (sharing attitudes, beliefs, and interests), and/or collaborative (sharing and achieving a common goal).[27]

Close friends learn that it's okay to share personal thoughts, secrets, hopes, and fears, but whether we do so depends on our ability (1) to disclose personal information in a way that maintains the relationship; (2) to recognize that most of these disclosures center on mundane, everyday issues;

COMMUNICATION&CULTURE

GIRL-FRIENDS AND BOY-FRIENDS DIFFER

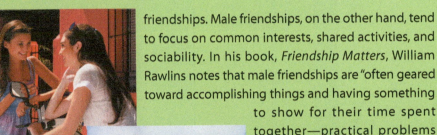

In adolescence as well as in young, middle, and older adulthood, men report less intimacy, less complexity, and less contact with same-gender friends. In contrast, women report greater continuity in their long-term, same-sex friendships than men and see these friends as important in their lives over time. One interesting study notes that throughout middle and older adulthood, women often value talk with their friends more than talk with their husbands.[28]

Mutual and confirming talk is both the substance and central feature of many women's

friendships. Male friendships, on the other hand, tend to focus on common interests, shared activities, and sociability. In his book, *Friendship Matters*, William Rawlins notes that male friendships are "often geared toward accomplishing things and having something to show for their time spent together—practical problems solved, the house painted or deck completed . . . cars washed or tuned, poker, or music played, and so on."[29]

Despite these differences, both adult men and women view close friendship as a mutually dependent, accepting, confidential, and trusting relationship.

strengthening personal relationships

119

and (3) to respect that some topics are taboo, such as negative life events and some serious personal issues.[30]

During late adolescence and young adulthood, most of us leave home—to work, to go to college, or to marry and raise a family. The dual tasks of developing new friendships while adapting to a new job, new living conditions, or new academic settings can take its toll. Although adolescents and young adults have more opportunities to make friends than any other age-group, this stage, more than at any other life stage, proves to be one of their loneliest times.[31]

Romantic Relationships

Learning how to develop and strengthen loving relationships is both a communicative art and skill. Researchers confirm that people who need others, and can admit to this, are the lucky ones.

How do you let another person know that you "like" her or him? How do you find out whether that person likes you? The process of romancing another person begins with generating and assessing *liking*, which can be

ROMANTIC RELATIONSHIP **STAGES**[32]

Bonding. The couple makes a public commitment to one another. The couple enjoys a stable relationship.

"I want to be with you always."

5

Integrating. Personalities, opinions, and behaviors join together. Individuals become a couple.

"What happens to you happens to me."

4

Intensifying. There is more intimate physical contact, more talk, and more self-disclosure.

"I . . . I think I love you."

3

Experimenting. The two people look for and learn about similarities and common interests. There is pleasant and casual small talk.

"Oh, so you like to ski . . . so do I."

2

Initiating. There is a cautious assessment of the other person and polite communication.

"Hi, how ya doin'?"

1

Coming Together

Differentiating. Each person becomes distinct and different in character. More use of "I" and "you" than "we" and "our." There is more conflict.

"I don't like big social gatherings."

6

Circumscribing. There is a decrease in communication. Personal and important topics are no longer discussed.

"Did you have a good time on your trip?"

7

Stagnating. Communication shuts down. More time and attention is devoted to work and other friends.

"What's there to talk about?"

8

Avoiding. There is a lack of desire to spend time together. Communication may become antagonistic or unfriendly.

"I may not be around when you call."

9

Terminating. Psychological and physical barriers are created. Each person is more concerned about self.

"I'm leaving you . . . and don't bother trying to contact me."

10

Coming Apart

communicated both nonverbally and verbally. In Chapter 6, "Nonverbal Communication," we introduced the concept of immediacy. Nonverbal cues, such as increased eye contact, touch, standing closer, and leaning forward, can signal romantic interest. When it comes to expressing interest verbally, most people don't take the direct route. We don't walk up to someone and say, "I like you." Instead, we tend to use more subtle strategies, such as inviting the other person to social activities; asking questions that encourage the other person to share personal information while also sharing our own when appropriate; presenting ourselves as positive, interesting, and dynamic; doing favors for or assisting the other person; and seeking and demonstrating similarities in tastes, interests, and attitudes.[33] Taken one at a time, these strategies may not seem significant or romantic, but when combined, they let the other person see that the relationship is becoming closer and has the potential for future development.

Romantic relationships do not happen by chance, nor do they magically come into being. Rather, we start, develop, maintain, strengthen, and end romantic relationships. Communication scholars Mark Knapp and Anita Vangelisti describe ten predictable stages in intimate relationships as shown on the previous page.[34] Their model is heavily oriented toward male–female romantic couples, yet it certainly accounts for same-sex relationships as well as many close friendships and work relationships. Knapp

"People who are in loving relationships with another adult have better hormonal balance and better health, and are of course happier."

British Economist, Richard Layard[35]

and Vangelisti divide relationship stages into two major processes: coming together and coming apart. The figure on the previous page uses a romantic relationship to illustrate the five interaction stages of each of these processes.

Knapp and Vangelisti's model only scratches the surface of each stage in

a relationship. Just because your partner doesn't like big social gatherings as much as you does not mean your relationship will come apart. "It is not necessarily 'bad' to terminate a relationship nor is it necessarily 'good' to become more intimate with someone. The model is descriptive of what often seems to happen—not necessarily what should happen."[36]

Family Relationships

Not that long ago, the ideal nuclear family was a mother, father, and their biological children. In 1960, about 45 percent of U.S. families were nuclear families. According to the 2010 U.S. Census, that number has dropped to 23 percent. In some major cities, "fewer than 10 percent of households are made up of married couples and their children. In the city of Baltimore, only 8.6 percent of households are such nuclear families."[37]

So what *is* a family? In their book on family communication, Lynn Turner and Richard West define a **family** as "a self-defined group of intimates who create and maintain themselves through their own interactions and their interactions with others."[38] A family may include both involuntary relationships (you don't get to choose your biological parents) and voluntary relationships (you choose your spouse). More family types are explained in the table below, "Types of Families."

All of us face the challenge of understanding family communication patterns and developing communication strategies and skills that meet our own

Types of Families[39]

Family Type	Description
Nuclear Family	Wife, husband, and their biological children
Extended Family	Biological: Family includes other relatives such as grandparents, aunts and uncles, cousins, etc. Communal: Family includes close friends
Stepfamily	Two adults and children who are not the biological offspring of both parents
Adopted Family	One or two adults and an adopted child or children
Single-Parent Family	One adult with a child or children
Gay or Lesbian Family	Two people of the same gender in an intimate relationship (who may have a child or children—as biological offspring or adopted)
Couples	Two adults living together in a romantic relationship with no children
Unmarried with Children	Unmarried couple with a biological child or children

and our family's needs. Here we examine two communication variables that affect all types of families: (1) family roles and rules, and (2) parenting skills.

Family Roles and Rules When you watch children play "house," they take on roles—mother, father, and children. Even at an early age, children learn that certain patterns of behavior and expectations are characteristic of each family member.

Family roles are often linked to family rules. For example, "Dad deals with car problems" may be interpreted as a rule, which in turn suggests that dad's role is vehicle caretaker. Family rules are contextual: they vary according to the situation and family culture. In some cultures, a daughter may not date until her

COMMUNICATION IN *ACTION*

Do Parents Really Matter?

Do parents make a major difference in the way children behave outside the home—and the way they grow up? Developmental psychologist Judith Rich Harris believes that parenting has almost no long-term effects on a child's personality, intelligence, or mental health. Instead she claims that children are most influenced by two other factors: their genes and their peers.[40] Harris points out that the children of immigrant parents (who speak English poorly) quickly learn to speak Standard English. They learn this from their peers, who have more influence on how they speak and sound.[41]

Same-age peers show children how to fit in and behave—in the classroom, on the ball field, or at parties. Children adopt certain behaviors in social settings to win acceptance from their peers, and it's those behaviors outside the home that remain steadfast through adulthood. Blame your peers, Harris says, not your parents.[42]

Judith Harris's research raises many questions and has created considerable controversy and debate among psychologists, communication scholars, and family members.[43]

Now consider the uproar over the 2011 book *Battle Hymn of the Tiger Mother* written by Amy Chua, a Yale University professor and mother of two daughters. Chua uses the phrase "Chinese mother" to mean "driven, snobbish and hell-bent on raising certifiably Grade A children."[44] Detractors argue that Chua has deprived her daughters of many things young girls enjoy—texting and hanging out with girlfriends (rather than practicing the piano or violin for hours under Mom's stern gaze), staying up all night at sleep-overs, going through phases with different clothing styles, and creating a "cool" Facebook page.

David Brooks, a columnist for *The New York Times*, claims that Chua's daughters have not learned hard, but critical lessons about deciding whom to trust beyond the family circle and about accurately interpreting and appropriately responding to nonverbal feedback.[45] In other words, they have not learned how to communicate interpersonally with skill and confidence.

More recently, we've read stories about "helicopter parents" who hover over their children and frequently intervene in all aspects of their children's lives—from who their friends are, how well or poorly their schools and teachers are performing, and even whether their doctor knows enough about their unique and precious child to make an accurate diagnosis. Even college students have had difficulty separating from "Velcro parents" who call to wake them up for class, complain to their colleges and professors about non-A grades, and review their major assignments and papers before giving their child "permission" to turn them in. Certainly all of these parents love their children and seek what is, in their opinion, best for them. Unfortunately, conclude some educators and psychologists, we are setting up such students for "long-term failure" because they haven't learned how to handle anything but parent-ensured success.[46]

What do you think? Do parents really matter? Did your childhood friends teach you more about getting along with others than your parents? Perhaps, when it comes to defining good parenting, there are more questions than answers.

parents meet the young man and approve her choice. In other cultures, grandparents are revered as the wisest members of the family, and their advice and approval are sought by all family members.[47]

The following examples of communication rules may be characteristic of your family:

- Tell the truth.
- Say "please" and "thank you."
- Share your toys.
- Don't talk back to your parents or grandparents.
- Say your prayers before going to bed.[48]

Family rules serve an important purpose: they allow family members to make sense out of family episodes. Rules also help family members understand one another's behavior. Although some family rules may seem unfair or arbitrary, they do help families define and maintain themselves.[49]

Parenting Skills In supportive, healthy families, parents give children love, values, and social skills. Socially skilled children are better at understanding and appropriately reacting to the emotions of others, understand how their behavior impacts others in interpersonal situations, and communicate more effectively.[50] Not surprisingly, the key

to acquiring these social skills is effective communication. One recent study found that the most important factor in a child's "early learning is talking—specifically, the greater a child's exposure to language spoken by parents and caretakers from birth to age 3, the better." Even silly-sounding "parent-to-child baby talk is very, very important. (So put those smartphones away!)"[51] Apparently, "the greater the number of words children heard from their parents and caregivers before they were 3, the higher their IQ and the better they did in school. TV talk not only didn't help, it was detrimental." In short, when children are young, we should talk and talk and talk to them.

Sharing Your Self with Others

7.4 *Explain how appropriate self-disclosure and sensitivity to feedback can strengthen interpersonal communication.*

Sharing your self with others is essential for developing meaningful relationships. Whether you are talking about your favorite apps with a new acquaintance or revealing your deepest fears to someone you love, both of you must be able and willing to share personal information and feelings.

Self-disclosure is the process of sharing with others personal information, opinions, and emotions that would not otherwise be known to them. This is *not* to say you should reveal the most intimate details of your life to everyone you meet. Rather, you must judge if and when sharing is appropriate by understanding and adapting to the other person's attitudes, beliefs, and values.[52] Deciding what, where, when, how, and with whom to self-disclose is one of the most difficult communication challenges you face in a personal relationship.

The Johari Window Model

Psychologists Joseph Luft and Harrington Ingham provide a useful

model for understanding how the connections between self-disclosure and feedback affect relationship development and growth.[53] They use the metaphor of a window, calling their model the **Johari Window** (the name is a combination of their first names).[54] The model looks at two interpersonal communication dimensions: willingness to self-disclose and receptivity to feedback. *Willingness to self-disclose* describes the extent to which you are prepared to disclose personal information and feelings to other people. *Receptivity to feedback* describes your awareness, interpretation, and response to someone else's self-disclosure about you.[55] When these two dimensions are graphed against one another, the result is a figure that resembles a four-paned window as shown on the next page.

Each pane means something different, and each pane can vary in size.

Four Different Panes The *open area* of your Johari Window contains information you are willing to share with others as well as information you have learned about yourself by accurately interpreting others' feedback. For example, suppose you wonder whether it's okay to tell an embarrassing but funny personal story to a group of new colleagues. You decide to take the risk. If your listeners laugh and seem to appreciate your sense of humor, you've learned two things: that it's safe to share personal stories with this group and that you are, in fact, funny.

The *hidden area* represents your private self, which includes information you know about yourself ("I am attracted to that person," "I was once arrested") but that you are not yet willing to share with others. The hidden area contains your secrets. Some people retain a lot of personal information in this area that could enhance their personal relationships and likability if that information were shared.

The *blind area* contains information others know about you but that you do *not* know about yourself because you don't pay attention to or correctly interpret feedback from others. If you don't notice that someone disapproves of your behaviors or wants your praise for a job well done, you may not develop or maintain a close relationship with that person.

Information unknown to *both* you and others exists in the *unknown area*. For example, suppose you have always avoided doing any writing at work because you don't think you're a good writer. And yet, when working with a group of colleagues on an interesting project, you

RECEPTIVITY TO FEEDBACK

Known to Self   Unknown to Self

Open area   Blind area

Hidden area   Unknown

WILLINGNESS TO SELF-DISCLOSE (Known to Others / Unknown to Others)

The Johari Window[56]

level of self-awareness. As a relationship develops, you should disclose more, which enlarges your open area and reduces the amount of information in your hidden area. As you become more receptive to feedback, you reduce your blind area and enlarge your open area.[57] And as your open area expands, your unknown area gets smaller.

Effective self-disclosure and receptivity feedback improve your self-awareness and the overall quality of your personal relationships. Social Penetration Theory (see page 125) and the Johari Window Model focus on the specific communication strategies and skills you need to express yourself appropriately and thereby strengthen and preserve your relationships with others.

Effective Self-Disclosure

When you self-disclose, you reveal how you are reacting to a situation while sharing relevant information about yourself and your experiences. Successful self-disclosure is not a solo activity. If the other person does not self-disclose or respond to your self-disclosures, you may want to rethink the relationship or stop sharing your thoughts and feelings.[58]

Effective Feedback

Effective interpersonal communication relies on giving and receiving feedback from others. No matter where or when you provide feedback, it should not be threatening

> Although it can be painful and risky, when the emotional stakes are high, self-disclosure can benefit a relationship in significant ways.

end up doing most of the writing. As time passes, you and your coworkers recognize and appreciate your writing talent. This "discovery" about yourself now moves from your unknown area to your open area.

Varying Size of Panes Depending on how willing you are to self-disclose and how receptive you are to feedback, each of the four panes in the Johari Window differs in size. Although this makes a very unusual-looking window, it does a good job of reflecting your

STRATEGIES FOR **EFFECTIVE SELF DISCLOSURE**

STRATEGY	RATIONALE
Focus on the present, not the past.	Obsessing about past problems may not help or enlighten either person.
Be descriptive, not judgmental.	Criticizing someone's behavior can lead to a hostile argument.
Disclose your feelings, not just the facts.	Explaining how you feel about what is happening clarifies and justifies your reactions.
Adapt to the person and context.	Revealing intimate personal information to the wrong person at the wrong time in the wrong place benefits no one.
Be sensitive to others' reactions.	Modifying or discontinuing self-disclosure is essential if the other person's reaction is extreme (rage, crying, hysteria).
Engage in reciprocal self-disclosure.	Modifying or discontinuing self-disclosure is appropriate if the other person does not respond in kind.
Gradually move disclosure to a deeper level.	Increasing the breadth, depth, and frequency of your self-disclosure should occur as your level of comfort with the other person increases.

Social Penetration Theory

Social Penetration Theory, developed by Irwin Altman and Dalmas Taylor, describes the process of relationship bonding in which individuals move from superficial communication to deeper, more intimate communication.[59] According to Altman and Taylor, the process of developing an intimate relationship is similar to peeling an onion. The outer skin of the onion represents superficial and mostly public information about yourself. The inner layers—those closest to the core—represent intimate information.

Social Penetration Theory explains that self-disclosure has three interconnected dimensions: depth, breadth, and frequency.[60] Deep self-disclosure is intimate and near the core of the onion—for example, there's a big difference between telling someone "You're OK" and telling someone "I love you." When self-disclosure is broad, it covers many topic areas, some very personal, some impersonal. In addition to sharing information about your hobbies and job, you may also share your strong beliefs and values about family and religion. Self-disclosure becomes more frequent as both the depth and breadth of your relationship expand. For example, blurting out a personal secret or pent-up emotions may seem odd if it's not part of an ongoing pattern of self-disclosure.

The animated film *Shrek* captures the underlying premise of Social Penetration Theory. As Shrek, the large, lumbering, green ogre, and his hyperactive companion, Donkey, trek through fields and forests, Shrek tries to enlighten Donkey by explaining that theres a lot more to ogres than most people realize. He compares himself to an onion with multiple layers. You have to go deeper than the superficial appearances of the outer layer to appreciate the good character and heart of an ogre. Or a Donkey. Or you and me.

Social Penetration Theory contends that as two people get to know each other better, they reveal personal information, feelings, and experiences below the public image layer. Relationships develop when this process is reciprocal—that is, one person's openness leads to another's openness, and so on.

The Social Penetration Process

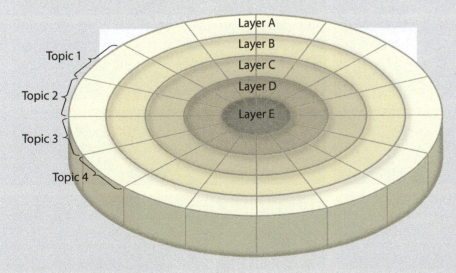

Topic 1
Topic 2
Topic 3
Topic 4

Layer A
Layer B
Layer C
Layer D
Layer E

EXAMPLES OF LAYERS

Layer A: Most impersonal layer (music, clothing, food preferences)

Layer B: Impersonal layer (job, education, home town, hobbies)

Layer C: Middle layer (religious beliefs, social attitudes, political views)

Layer D: Personal layer (personal goals, fears, hopes, secrets)

Layer E: Most personal layer (inner core, self-concept)

EXAMPLES OF TOPICS

Topic 1: Leisure activities
Topic 2: Career
Topic 3: Family
Topic 4: Health

or demanding. At the same time, remember that there is only so much that you and another person can comprehend and process at one time. Too much personal information can overwhelm and overload the best of listeners.

Defensive and Supportive Messages

In 1961, Jack Gibb identified six pairs of behaviors that create either a defensive or supportive climate for communication.[63] **Defensive behaviors** reflect our instinct to protect ourselves when we are being physically or verbally attacked by someone. Even though such reactions are natural, they also discourage reciprocal self-disclosure. On the other hand, **supportive behaviors** create a climate in which self-disclosure and responsiveness to feedback benefit both parties.

To a large extent we disagree with Gibb's either/or approach, as does recent research. The paired communication behaviors in Gibb's model are not necessarily "good" or "bad" behaviors. For example, you may behave strategically when you have important and strong personal motives. You may behave with certainty when your expertise is well recognized and a critical decision must be made. And you may respond neutrally when the issue is of little consequence to you or others.[64]

DEFENSIVE BEHAVIORS

EVALUATION: Judges another person's behavior. Makes critical statements. "Why did you insult Sharon like that? Explain yourself!" "What you did was terrible."

CONTROL: Imposes your solution on someone else. Seeks control of the situation. "Give me that report and I'll make it better." "Since I'm paying for the vacation, we're going to the resort I like rather than the spa you like."

STRATEGY: Manipulates others. Hides or disguises personal motives. Withholds information. "Frankie's going to Florida over spring break." "Remember when I helped you rearrange your office?"

NEUTRALITY: Appears withdrawn, detached, indifferent. Won't take sides. "You can't win them all." "Life's a gamble." "It doesn't matter to me." "Whatever."

SUPERIORITY: Implies that you and your opinions are better than others. Promotes resentment and jealousy. "Hey—I've done this a million times—let me have it. I'll finish in no time." "Is this the best you could do?"

CERTAINTY: Believes that your opinion is the only correct one. Refuses to consider the ideas and opinions of others. Takes inflexible positions. "I can't see any other way of doing this that makes sense." "There's no point in discussing this any further."

SUPPORTIVE BEHAVIORS

DESCRIPTION: Describes another person's behavior. Makes understanding statements. Uses more I and we language. "When we heard what you said to Sharon, we were really embarrassed for her." "I'm sorry about that."

PROBLEM ORIENTATION: Seeks a mutually agreeable solution. "Okay. Let's see what we can do to get that report finished to specifications." "Let's figure out how both of us can enjoy our vacation."

SPONTANEITY: Makes straightforward, direct, open, honest, and helpful comments. "I'd like to go to Florida with Frankie over spring break." "Would you help me move some heavy boxes?"

EMPATHY: Accepts and understands another person's feelings. "I can't believe she did that. No wonder you're upset." "It sounds as though you're having a hard time deciding."

EQUALITY: Suggests that everyone can make a useful contribution. "If you don't mind, I'd like to explain how I've handled this before. It may help." "Let's tackle this problem together."

PROVISIONALISM: Offers ideas and accepts suggestions from others. "We have a lot of options here—which one makes the most sense?" "I feel strongly about this, but I would like to hear what you think."

Gibb's Defensive and Supportive Behaviors[65]

Expressing Emotions Appropriately

7.5 *Practice emotional intelligence and providing emotional support to others.*

Emotions play a major role in all relationships. An **emotion** is the feeling you experience when reacting to a situation that is often accompanied by physical changes. Emotions are fundamental to effective and ethical communication. They also play a significant role in how you develop, maintain, and strengthen interpersonal relationships.

The Basic Emotions

Everyone experiences basic, primary emotions, although researchers disagree on the number of such emotions. Robert Plutchik's **Psychoevolutionary Emotion Theory** illuminates the development and meaning of emotions.[66] According to this theory, each basic emotion has a range of feelings (from mild to intense). Plutchik further explains that some emotions blend two or more emotions. As the figure below shows, love is a combination of joy and acceptance.

Contempt is a combination of anger and disgust.

Emotional Intelligence

Science writer Daniel Goleman defines **emotional intelligence** as "the capacity for recognizing our own feelings and those of others, for motivating ourselves, and for managing emotions well in ourselves and in our relationships."[68] His influential book *Emotional Intelligence: Why It Can Matter More Than IQ* credits two psychologists, Peter Salovey and John Mayer, who coined the term *emotional intelligence* in 1990.[69] You can examine emotional intelligence as a set of interpersonal communication competencies summarized and described in the figure, "Emotionally Intelligent Communication" on page 128.[70]

What happens when people cannot make emotions work for them? Neurologist Antonio Damasio, who studies patients with physical damage to

> ** " ... feelings are indispensable for rational decision making. "**
> —Antonio Damasio, Neurologist[71]

the emotional center of their brains, reports that these patients make terrible decisions even though their IQ scores stay the same. Even though they test as "smart," they "make disastrous choices in business and in their personal lives, and can even obsess endlessly over a decision as simple as when to make an appointment." Their decision-making skills are poor because they have lost access to their emotions. Damasio's claims make sense when you consider whether you could answer any of the following questions without taking emotions into account: Whom should I marry? What career should I pursue? Should I buy this house? What should I say to a bereaved friend or relative?[72]

Emotions and Jealousy

Jealousy, an intense feeling caused by a perceived threat to a relationship, comes in two very common forms: reactive jealousy and suspicious jealousy. This distinction is important, because almost everybody feels **reactive jealousy**, which occurs when a person becomes aware of a real, threatening danger to the relationship, such as learning that a romantic partner has, in fact, been unfaithful.

Suspicious jealousy is just what the word *suspicious* implies—you suspect that your partner has done something that threatens the future of the relationship.[73] "For example, you are seated at a bar and notice that an attractive stranger across the way is

Plutchik's Primary and Compound Emotions[67]

Communication Strategies	As an Emotionally Intelligent Communicator, You . . .
Intrapersonal Communication Strategies	
Develop Self-Awareness	Monitor and identify your feelings in order to guide your decision making. <u>Example:</u> Noticing whether you have raised your voice because you are angry or surprised.
Manage Your Emotions	Restrain or release your emotions when the situation is appropriate. Practice relaxation to recover from emotional distress. <u>Example:</u> Deciding whether expressing strong emotions will facilitate or interfere with your goals.
Motivate Yourself	Persevere in the face of disappointments and setbacks. Seek the support of friends, colleagues, and family members to stay motivated, improve your mood, and bolster your confidence. <u>Example:</u> Seeking help from a trusted mentor.
Interpersonal Communication Strategies	
Listen to Others	Engage effective listening skills to ensure you understand what another person means. Use effective, empathic listening. <u>Example:</u> Paraphrasing what you hear to make sure you understand someone before responding.
Develop Interpersonal Skills	Use self-disclosure, assertiveness, and appropriate verbal and nonverbal communication. Try to resolve conflicts. <u>Example:</u> Deciding whether and how to share your emotions with a close friend.
Help Others Help Themselves	Help others become more aware of their emotions. Help them speak and listen more effectively. <u>Example:</u> Providing emotional support to a distressed friend.

Emotionally Intelligent Communication

smiling at your partner. A victim of suspicious jealousy might perceive such a gesture as a threat to his or her stature in the relationship and get angry at the partner for flirting with the stranger."[74]

Interestingly, some researchers believe that extreme jealousy may be hardwired in the brains of some people. They claim that obsessively suspicious, jealous people mistrust innocent behavior and believe the potential loss of a loved one as a likely, life-shattering experience. This in turn can lead to extreme anger and violent behavior.[75]

People express jealousy in a variety of ways: through accusations and sarcasm or depression and physical withdrawal (the "silent treatment"). Extremely jealous people are often aggressive, manipulative, or violent. Pathologically jealous individuals are highly sensitive to "every nuance in [their] environment that may hint of

unfaithfulness." Jealousy taken to extremes can destroy relationships and lead to stronger feelings of resentment and inferiority.[76] (See the list of strategies for Coping with Jealousy in the feature on the next page.)

However, if someone's jealousy becomes extreme or is based on unfounded beliefs, none of these discussed strategies may help. When jealous people become cruelly aggressive, manipulative, or violent, professional counseling may be necessary.

Emotional Support

Have you ever felt at a loss for words when someone needed emotional support and comfort? A colleague's home is destroyed by a fire or storm. Your partner fails to get a "sure-thing" job. Your cousin's spouse or child dies. What do you say or do? As a concerned and compassionate person, you probably wanted to comfort your

friend, colleague, partner, or family member. Unfortunately, many of us feel inadequate to this task. We worry about saying the wrong thing. We search through racks of greeting cards to find a card that can "say it" better than we can.

As much as we may want to support and comfort a person in distress, many of us lack an understanding of the basic nature of emotional support as well as the communication skills needed to achieve its purpose. Communication scholar Brant Burleson defines **emotional support** as "specific lines of communicative behavior enacted by one party with the intent of helping another cope effectively with emotional distress." The distress can be acute (disappointment over not winning a contest or anxiety over an upcoming exam) or chronic (grief over the loss of a loved one or lingering depression over poor health) and may be mild or intense in character.[77]

Coping with Jealousy

In the eyes of a jealous partner, the perceived threat to a relationship can come from a boyfriend spending time with his friends, a wife being honored for achievements at work, a child seeming to get more love and attention from a parent than another sibling does, or a romantic partner hugging an old friend at a party. Highly jealous people may interpret an innocent look or a conversation with another person as signs of sexual unfaithfulness and may see other people as potential rivals, whether they are or not.

In a study of couples married twenty-five or more years, none (0 percent) of the couples that described themselves as happy were

concerned that their spouse was attracted to other people. By contrast, nearly 20 percent of the unhappy couples said they "often" or "sometimes" felt worried or mistrustful.[78]

The following communication strategies can help minimize the negative effects of jealousy in a relationship, particularly if you are highly motivated to maintain the relationship:

Communication Strategies	. . . for addressing jealousy
Stay Calm, Cool, and Collected	Provide direct but nonaggressive communication about jealousy in an effort to work things out. In other words, talk about it calmly and compassionately.
Defuse Jealous Feelings	Work to improve the relationship or make yourself more desirable. Strategies such as sending flowers, giving a gift, demonstrating affection, and being extra nice can reduce or counteract jealous feelings.
Show How It Hurts	Express yourself nonverbally so the jealous person can see how it affects you (e.g., appearing hurt, distressed, or crying).[79]
Be Honest	If there is good reason for your partner to be jealous, it may be time for a heart-to-heart conversation about the future of the relationship.
Listen Comprehensively and Empathically	Don't dismiss your partner's feelings and fears. It probably wasn't easy for your partner to fess up and express jealous concerns or worries.
Build Your Partner's Self-Confidence	Realize that jealousy may have nothing to do with you or your behavior. In situations where there is no factual basis for your partner to be jealous, the existence of jealous feelings suggests that your partner may be suffering from a lack of confidence.[80]

expressing emotions appropriately

Emotionally supportive communication strategies can help you comfort and support others. These strategies include being clear about your intentions, protecting the other person's self-esteem, and centering your messages on the other person.

Communicate Your Intentions Clearly When someone is in great distress, you may think this person knows you want to be helpful and supportive. You may assume that just "being there" tells the other person that you care. In some cases, your assumptions are correct. In other situations, a person in distress needs to know that you *want* to help or provide assistance.

You can enhance the clarity of your supportive messages by stating them directly ("I want to help you") and by making it clear you care ("I'm here for you"). You can also intensify the perceived sincerity of your response by emphasizing your desire to help ("I really want to help in any way I can"), by reminding the person of the personal history you share ("You know we've always been there for each other"), and by indicating what you feel ("Helping you is important to me; I'd feel terrible if I weren't here to help").[83]

Protect the Other Person's Self-Esteem Make sure that your offer of help does not imply that the other person is incapable of solving the problem or dealing with the situation. Otherwise, you may damage someone's self-esteem. Even with the best of intentions, expressions of sympathy ("Oh, you poor thing . . .") can convey judgments about the person's lack of competence and lack of independence. Try to encourage and praise the other person.[84]

Offer Person-Centered Messages Messages that reflect "the degree to which a helper validates [a] distressed person's feelings and encourages him or her to talk about the upsetting event" are **person-centered messages**.[85] Rather than focusing on helping someone feel better, your goal is helping the person develop a deeper understanding of the problem so that they may take on the task of solving or coping with it. You can help someone in distress understand the problem by encouraging her or him to tell an

Know Thy Self

Are You an Active-Empathic Listener?

Expressing a supportive message is only half of the emotional support process. Listening actively and empathically forms the other half. Characteristics of active-empathic listening include:

- being sensitive to what another person is not saying,
- listening for more than spoken words,
- being aware of what the other person means or implies, and
- being open to the other person's ideas and feelings.[81]

Unless you actively listen to another person and communicate your understanding and concern for that person, your verbal response may be meaningless or inappropriate. Listening scholar Graham Bodie and his colleagues suggest assessing your ability to engage in active-empathic listening. On a scale from 1 to 7 in which 1 stands for "never or almost never true of me" and 7 stands for " always or almost always true of me," assign a number to each statement below:[82]

1. _____ I am aware of what others imply but do not say.
2. _____ I understand how others feel.
3. _____ I assure others that I will remember what they say.
4. _____ I keep track of the points others make.
5. _____ I ask questions to show my understanding of the other person's positions.
6. _____ I show that I am listening by my body language (e.g., head nods, leaning forward, touching).

As you might guess, the higher your score, the more active and empathic a listener you are. Take another look at the six statements. They also represent the critical skills of a listener committed to helping another person cope effectively with emotional distress.

Strategies for Encouraging Coping Through Storytelling

- Ask for your friend's version of the situation. ("What happened here?")
- Create a supportive environment and provide enough time for the person to talk. ("Take your time. I want to hear the whole story.")
- Ask about the person's feelings, not just the events. ("How did you feel when that happened?" "What was your reaction when she said that?")
- Legitimize the expression of feelings. ("I certainly understand why you'd feel that way.")
- Indicate that you connect with what the other person is saying. ("If that happened to me, I'd be furious too.")[86]

extended, personal story about the problem or upsetting event. People in need of emotional support may want nothing more than to share the details with a trusted friend.

While these communication strategies express your willingness to help, your supportive feelings, and your personal commitment, take care to avoid counterproductive strategies. Do not focus on or share *your* emotional experiences—for example, "I know exactly how you feel. Last year, I went through a similar kind of problem. It all started when . . ." Not only does this stop the other person from sharing, but it also shifts the focus to yourself. You should also avoid messages that criticize or negatively evaluate another person because these can hurt more than help. Do not tell others that their feelings are wrong, inappropriate, immature, or embarrassing. Consider using some of the behaviors Gibb recommends for creating a support climate for communication such as describing, not evaluating; being empathic, not neutral; express equality, not superiority.

ETHICAL COMMUNICATION

The Ethics of Caring

The NCA Credo for Ethical Communication includes a principle that speaks directly to interpersonal relationships: "We promote communication climates of caring and mutual understanding that respect the unique needs and characteristics of individual communicators."[87] The ethical value of caring focuses on the responsibilities we have for others in our interpersonal relationships.[88]

Philosopher and educator Nel Noddings believes we make moral choices based on an ethic of caring. For example, a mother picks up a crying baby, not because of a sense of duty or because she is worried about what others will say if she doesn't but because she cares about the baby. Relationship theorists emphasize that this is not a gender-based ethic. Rather, it is based on a way of thinking that honors two fundamental characteristics of ethical behavior: avoiding harm and providing mutual aid.[89]

In what way does this scene depict an ethic of caring, and how does such behavior promote supportive communication?

COMMUNICATION IN ACTION

The Comforting Touch

As a child you experienced nonverbal comforting well before you understood and communicated with language. "Not surprisingly, the nonverbal behaviors first used in infancy continue as expressions of emotional support throughout a lifetime. Hugs, touches and pats, hand-holding, focused looks and soothing sounds can be remarkably effective ways of expressing reassurance, love, warmth, and acceptance."[90] In terms of physical health, researchers note that a hospital patient's family and friends help just by visiting, regardless of whether they know what to say.[91] According to another study, a five-second touch can convey specific emotions, such as sympathy and sadness.[92]

Touch plays a significant role in comforting others. "Skin-on-skin touch

Touch can be worth a thousand words.

is particularly soothing because it primes oxytocin," a neurotransmitter that causes our body to undergo many healthy changes. Blood pressure lowers and we relax. Our pain threshold increases so that we are less sensitive to discomforts. Even wounds heal faster.[93]

How would you react nonverbally if a close same-sex friend told you that she or he had just ended a serious romantic relationship? In one study, most college students ranked hugging as their number one response. Other high-ranking responses included being attentive, moving closer to the other person, using certain facial expressions, increasing touch, and making eye contact. Not surprisingly, men and women suggested different nonverbal responses. Men were less likely than women to hug their troubled friend; they were more likely to pat their friend on the arm or shoulder and to suggest going out and doing something to take their minds off the problem. Women were more likely to cry with their friend and to use a variety of comforting touches.[94]

expressing emotions appropriately

How Emotionally Intelligent Are You?[95]

Earlier in this chapter, we examined emotional intelligence as a set of six interpersonal communication competencies. Here we present these competencies as questions. Use the rating scale that follows to assess your level of competence for each question:

5 = Always 4 = Usually 3 = Sometimes 2 = Rarely 1 = Never

Develop Self-Awareness

_____ 1. Can you accurately identify the emotions you experience and why you experience them?

_____ 2. Are you aware of your strengths and limitations?

_____ 3. Are your inclusion, control, and affection needs met in most relationships?

Manage Your Emotions

_____ 4. Can you keep disruptive emotions under control?

_____ 5. Do you take responsibility for your emotions and resulting actions?

_____ 6. Are you open-minded and flexible in handling difficult situations?

Motivate Yourself

_____ 7. Do you strive to improve or meet high standards of excellence?

_____ 8. Do you persist in the face of obstacles and setbacks?

_____ 9. Can you postpone gratification and regulate your moods?

Listen to Others

_____ 10. Do you accurately listen to and understand others?

_____ 11. Do you engage in active-empathic listening?

_____ 12. Are your responses appropriate in various contexts?

Help Others Help Themselves

_____ 13. Do you accurately interpret others' feelings and needs?

_____ 14. Do you provide appropriate emotional support to others?

_____ 15. Do you clearly communicate that you want to help or provide assistance to others?

Demonstrate Interpersonal Skills

_____ 16. Are you effective and comfortable in conversations with others?

_____ 17. Do you effectively manage and help resolve emotional disagreements?

_____ 18. Do you self-disclose appropriately as well as give and ask for feedback?

Scoring: Add up your ratings. The higher your score, the more "emotionally intelligent" you are. Keep in mind that your ratings are only your *perceptions* about your feelings and behaviors. For example, despite what you think, you may not interpret others' feelings and needs accurately or persist in the face of obstacles. On the other hand, you may not recognize that you provide appropriate emotional support to others, even though your friends often turn to you when they need an empathetic ear.

Interpersonal Communication and Relationships

7.1 Identify the characteristics and benefits of effective interpersonal relationships.

- Good personal relationships positively affect your psychological and physical health, your happiness, your social and moral development, and your ability to cope with stress.
- William Schutz's Fundamental Interpersonal Relationship Orientation (FIRO) Theory identifies three interpersonal needs: inclusion, control, and affection.

Conversing With Others

7.2 Describe strategies and skills that enhance conversation competencies.

- Good conversations occur when both communicators ask one another questions, listen and respond appropriately, and conclude naturally.
- We negotiate turn-taking in face-to-face conversations primarily through nonverbal behavior.

Strengthening Personal Relationships

7.3 Discuss specific strategies for improving interpersonal relationships with friends, romantic partners, and family members.

- Strong friendships increase life satisfaction and help increase your life expectancy.
- There are ten common stages in most romantic relationships, divided into five coming-together steps and five coming-apart steps.
- Two significant variables that affect communication in all types of families are (1) family roles and rules and (2) parenting skills and peer influence.

Sharing Your Self With Others

7.4 Explain how appropriate self-disclosure and sensitivity to feedback can strengthen interpersonal communication.

- Self-disclosure is the process of sharing personal information, opinions, and emotions.
- The Johari Window displays the extent to which you are willing to self-disclose and are receptive to feedback from others.
- Social Penetration Theory describes the process in which individuals move from superficial communication to deeper, more intimate communication.
- Effective self-disclosure focuses on the present, is descriptive and understanding, respects and adapts to others, reciprocates self-disclosure, and moves toward intimacy.
- Effective feedback requires giving and asking for information about behavior, actions, perceptions, and feelings that you and others can change.
- Gibb's defensive-supportive communication behaviors are evaluation-description, control-problem orientation, strategy-spontaneity, neutrality-empathy, superiority-equality, and certainty-provisionalism.

Expressing Emotions Appropriately

7.5 Practice emotional intelligence and providing emotional support to others.

- Robert Plutchik's eight basic emotions are fear, acceptance, anger, disgust, joy, expectancy, sadness, and surprise.
- Emotional intelligence is the capacity for recognizing your own feelings and those of others, for motivating yourself, and for effectively managing your emotions in relationships.
- Reactive and suspicious jealousy are intense feelings caused by a perceived threat to a relationship.
- Active-empathic listening and comforting touch can provide emotional support to others.
- When comforting another person, make your intentions clear, protect the person's self-esteem, and center your message on the other person.

Key Terms

Affection need	**Inclusion need**	**Psychoevolutionary**
Control need	**Interpersonal**	**Emotion Theory**
Conversation	**communication**	**Reactive jealousy**
Defensive behaviors	**Intimacy**	**Relationship**
Emotion	**Jealousy**	**Self-disclosure**
Emotional intelligence	**Johari Window**	**Social Penetration Theory**
Emotional support	**Personal relationships**	**Supportive behaviors**
Fundamental Interpersonal	**Person-centered messages**	**Suspicious jealousy**
Relationship Orientation	**Professional**	**Turn-requesting cues**
(FIRO) Theory	**relationships**	**Turn-yielding cues**

TEST YOUR KNOWLEDGE

7.1 *Identify the characteristics and benefits of effective interpersonal relationships.*

1 Research by Robin Dunbar has been used as the basis for Path, a new social media app that limits you to no more than
   a. 50 friends.
   b. 150 friends.
   c. 500 friends.
   d. 1,500 friends.

2 According to Schutz's FIRO Theory, people whose inclusion needs are met
   a. may withdraw and become a loner because they don't need the company of others.
   b. may try attracting attention and impressing others with what and who they know.
   c. may enjoy being with others but are also comfortable being alone.
   d. may have no problems with power and feel just as comfortable giving orders as taking them.

7.2 *Describe strategies and skills that enhance conversation competencies.*

3 When, in a face-to-face conversation, you lean forward, establish direct eye contact, and lift a hand as if beginning to gesture, you are signalling
   a. a desire to exert power and significant influence over the other person.
   b. a desire for inclusion, control, and affection.
   c. a desire to complete your comments and listen.
   d. a desire to speak.

7.3 *Discuss specific strategies for improving interpersonal relationships with friends, romantic partners, and family members.*

4 According to Knapp and Vangelisti's Model of Relationship Stages, in which stage do the personalities, opinions, and behaviors of two people join together so that they become a couple rather than two separate individuals?
   a. Intensifying
   b. Differentiating
   c. Integrating
   d. Circumscribing

7.4 *Explain how appropriate self-disclosure and sensitivity to feedback can strengthen interpersonal communication.*

5 In the Johari Window Model, the more receptive and adaptive you are to feedback from others, your _____ area becomes larger.
   a. open
   b. hidden
   c. blind
   d. private

6 In terms of Gibb's categories of behavior for creating a supportive communication climate, how would you classify the following statement? "Let's find a way for both of us to go where we want on our vacation."
   a. Description
   b. Strategy
   c. Empathy
   d. Problem orientation

7 All of the following are effective ways to give and respond to feedback except
   a. using "you" rather than "I" statements.
   b. making your statements specific, not general or abstract.
   c. focusing on what was said and done, not on why it was said and done.
   d. focusing on current rather than past behavior.

8 All of the following behaviors are characteristics of effective self-disclosure except _____.
   a. focusing on the past, not on the present.
   b. disclosing your feelings as well as facts.
   c. adapting to the person and context.
   d. describing rather than judging.

7.5 *Practice emotional intelligence and providing emotional support to others.*

9 In Plutchik's Psychoevolutionary Emotion Theory, which two basic emotions combine to create the emotion of love?
   a. Submission and surprise
   b. Anticipation and awe
   c. Acceptance and joy
   d. Awe and envy

10 Which of the following statements communicates your desire to help and support a person dealing with emotional distress?
   a. You need to buck up.
   b. I had the same thing happen to me.
   c. Are you sure it was as bad as you say?
   d. I'd feel terrible if I weren't here to help.

Answers found on page 368.

Improving **Interpersonal Communication** 8

Can you predict a couple's breakup or divorce? Diane Vaughan, author of *Uncoupling: How Relationships Come Apart*, says that she can. Her research concludes that a couple's break up usually begins with a secret. One of the partners starts to feel uncomfortable in the relationship and keeps those thoughts, feelings, or actions to themselves. The world the two of them have built together no longer "fits."[1]

Marriage psychologist, John Gottman claims he can predict a divorce without digging up any secrets. After charting the amount of time couples spent arguing negatively and interacting positively by touching, smiling, paying compliments, and laughing, Gottman found a consistent ratio between the number of positive and negative interactions. His "magic" ratio is 5:1. As long as there are five times as many positive interactions between partners as there are negative, the relationship is likely to be stable and permanent. When the percent of negative interaction increases, Dr. Gottman predicts a divorce.[2]

Media outlets thrive on public and celebrity breakups. Stories about married state governors Arnold Schwarzenegger of California (love child with the maid) and Mark Stanford of South Carolina (lover in Argentina), competed for media space with the celebrity breakups of Jennifer Lopez and Mark Anthony, Kristin Stewart and Robert Pattinson and whoever was George Clooney's girlfriend that year.

Most breakups are not newsworthy or open for public scrutiny. They affect millions of people in all walks of life. However, millions more continue to live in loving and lasting relationships.

In this chapter, we examine how interpersonal tensions affect relationships—be they between lovers, friends, family members, colleagues, neighbors, and brief acquaintances. Then we recommend communication-based strategies that can help you resolve such tensions as you develop and maintain healthy and satisfying interpersonal relationships.

Balancing Interpersonal Tensions

8.1 *Explain how to balance contrary tensions in interpersonal relationships.*

All interpersonal relationships experience tensions. Romantic and married couples may experience tension when one person wants a quiet evening at home while the other person wants to go out. Work colleagues may experience tension when one coworker completes a project ahead of schedule or on time, while another coworker leaves it to the last minute or ends up behind schedule. If left unresolved and allowed to escalate, these kinds of tensions can damage relationships beyond repair. If, however, you know how to analyze and resolve such tensions, your chances of strengthening a relationship significantly improve.

In this section, we describe two approaches that will help you recognize, respect, and appropriately respond to contradictory tensions in interpersonal relationships. These two approaches focus on relational dialectics and personality types.

Relational Dialectics

The following pairs of common sayings illustrate several contradictory beliefs about personal relationships:

"Opposites attract" *but* "Birds of a feather flock together."

"To know him is to love him" *but* "Familiarity breeds contempt."

"Out of sight, out of mind" *but* "Absence makes the heart grow fonder."

These contradictory folk sayings do not require an "either/or" verdict to determine which one is true or false. Rather, they demonstrate why these sayings survive: All of them can be true depending on the circumstances, on the people involved, and on the nature of the interpersonal relationship.

Relational Dialectics Theory makes a strong case for a "both/and" focus when communicating with others rather than an either/or approach. Although the theory does not offer surefire guidelines for improving

interpersonal relationships, it does help explain your experiences in new as well as ongoing relationships. It also suggests several strategies for negotiating tensions in close personal relationships.[3]

The integration-separation dialectic often surfaces when a child leaves home for college.

Relational Dialectics Theory

Leslie Baxter and Barbara Montgomery's Relational Dialectics Theory claims that personal relationships are characterized by **dialectics**, the interplay of opposing or contradictory forces. **Relational Dialectics Theory** focuses on the ongoing tensions between contradictory impulses in personal relationships.[4]

Rather than an "either/or" response to opposing tensions, relational

Integration — Separation

Stability — Change

Expression — Privacy

dialectics takes a "both/and" approach. For example, two people in a romantic relationship seek togetherness, but they also need time to be alone, time to think about personal needs, to escape the daily routine, and to engage in personal interests not shared by the other person.

In many close relationships, you want *both* intimacy *and* independence.

You want *both* the comfort of a stable relationship *and* the excitement of change. You can hear these dialectic tensions in the words a student wrote about her three-month romantic relationship: "Every relationship is a meeting of two people and however hard you try, you're not gonna form one sort of unified whole; you need the unity but there also has to be individuality for a relationship to be really close."[5]

Leslie Baxter and her colleagues identify three major dialectics in personal relationships: integration-separation, stability-change, and expression-privacy.[6]

---

1 The Integration-Separation Dialectic.

Interpersonal relationships survive when we successfully negotiate our desire for *both* connection *and* independence. Generally, most of us want to be close to others without having to give up our separate selves. For example, as you grow up, you may want to remain closely connected to your parents but still live an independent life free from their intrusion. Or let's say you want to build a life with your partner, but you also want to build your career. As much as you want to be close to others, you also need to be an independent person.

2 The Stability-Change Dialectic.

Most of us want the security of a stable relationship *and* the novelty and excitement of change, the predictability of day-to-day interactions *and* an occasional change in routine. For example, an engaged couple might decide to follow several wedding traditions—formal invitations, a wedding reception, flowers and traditional wedding music, and even the bride in white—but also decide to hold the wedding in a riding stable with the bride, groom, and presiding official on horseback. Another couple may share a permanent home in a city but go wilderness camping every summer.[7]

3 The Expression-Privacy Dialectic.

Like most people, you may be open and honest with another person while also protecting your privacy. Do your best friends, romantic partner, and close family members know every secret you have? Should they? This dialectic addresses your conflicting urges to tell your secrets *and* to keep them hidden.[8] For example, when Jane tells Jack she'd like to rent an apartment in a building closer to where she works, he may say he wants to stay in the suburbs. In truth, he doesn't want to move to a building where a former girlfriend lives.

Strategies for Negotiating Dialectic Tensions

Strategy	Example
Choose different options at different points in your life.	You may be close to siblings when you're young but less close when you're married and/or raising your own family.
Choose different options in different contexts.	You may be less connected and open when interacting with a close friend in a work environment.
Choose one option and ignore the other.	You may decide that being close to your family is more important at certain times than socializing with nonfamily friends.
Choose a compromise between opposite options.	You can invite relatives to join you on a vacation rather than only visiting them in their home.
Choose a new point of view that doesn't *appear* so opposite.	You may decide you can be close to someone if you occasionally put a little time and distance between you.
Choose to avoid the topic in order to avoid the tension.	You may decide to be totally open with coworkers about all topics except sex, finances, and highly personal problems.

The above strategies are not a To-Do list for resolving dialectic tensions. Rather, they illustrate a range of options, the success of which depends on how your choice best meets the interpersonal needs of both communicators.

> **Meaningful and lasting interpersonal relationships do not just happen. *You* make them happen.**

The Myers-Briggs Type Indicator

The psychological concept of **personality** represents the style in which we interact with the world around us and particularly with other people.[9] Understanding *and* appreciating your own and others' personality traits are central to improving the quality of interpersonal communication.

Isabel Briggs Myers and her mother, Katharine Briggs, developed the **Myers-Briggs Type Indicator**, a personality type assessment that examines the ways in which we perceive the world around us as well as how we reach conclusions and make decisions.[10] Thousands of corporations, including most Fortune 100 companies use the Myers-Briggs Type Indicator "to identify potential job applicants whose skills match those of their top performers," while others use it "to develop communication skills and promote teamwork among current employees."[11]

According to Myers-Briggs, all of us have preferred ways of thinking and behaving that can be divided into four categories, with two opposite preferences in each category, as indicated in the figure on the next page. As you read about these types and their traits, ask yourself which preferences best describe how you communicate.[12]

Extrovert or Introvert Extrovert and introvert are two traits that describe where you focus your attention: outward or inward. **Extroverts** are outgoing; they talk more and frequently gesture when they speak. They get their energy by being with people and enjoy solving problems in groups. They also have a tendency to dominate conversations without listening to others.

Introverts think before they speak and usually are not as talkative as extroverts. They prefer socializing with one or two close friends rather than spending time with a large group of people. Introverts recharge by being alone and often prefer to work by themselves.

"Extroverts complain that introverts don't speak up at the right time in meetings. Introverts criticize extroverts for talking too much and not listening well."[13] In classrooms, extroverts like to participate in heated discussions, whereas introverts dislike being put on the spot.

Sensor or Intuitive How do you look at the world around you? Do you see the forest (the big picture) or the

> **The Myers-Briggs Type Indicator tells us a great deal about how and why we get along with some people and have difficulty interacting with others.**

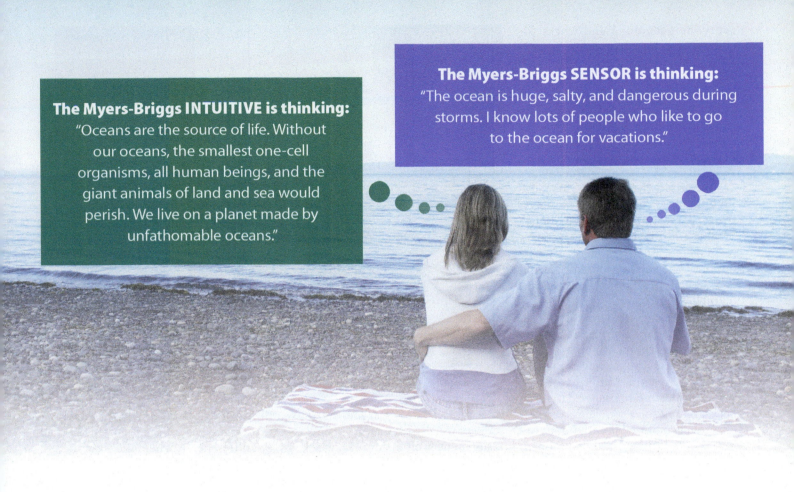

The Myers-Briggs INTUITIVE is thinking:
"Oceans are the source of life. Without our oceans, the smallest one-cell organisms, all human beings, and the giant animals of land and sea would perish. We live on a planet made by unfathomable oceans."

The Myers-Briggs SENSOR is thinking:
"The ocean is huge, salty, and dangerous during storms. I know lots of people who like to go to the ocean for vacations."

trees (the details)? **Sensors** focus on details and prefer to concentrate on one task at a time. They may uncover minor flaws in an idea and like having detailed instructions for doing a task. **Intuitives** look for connections and concepts rather than rules and flaws. They come up with big ideas but are bored with details. Sensors focus on regulations, step-by-step explanations, and facts, whereas intuitives focus on outwitting regulations, supplying theoretical explanations, and skipping details.

Both personality types are needed in the workplace. Management communication experts Carl Larson and Frank LaFasto emphasize the importance of having a balance between the "nuts and bolts types" and those individuals who are capable of being creative and conceptual.[14]

Thinker or Feeler Thinker and feeler are two traits that explain how you go about making decisions. **Thinkers** are analytical and task-oriented people who take pride in their ability to make difficult decisions. They want to get the job done, even at the cost of others' feelings. **Feelers** are more people oriented. They want everyone to get along. Feelers spend time and effort helping others.

Thinkers may appear unemotional and aggressive, whereas feelers may annoy others by "wasting time" with social chitchat. Although the thinker makes decisions and moves things forward, the feeler makes sure

The Myers-Briggs Personality Preferences

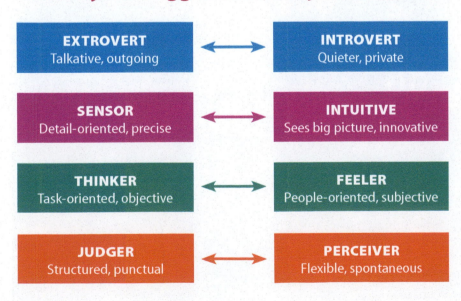

EXTROVERT Talkative, outgoing	**INTROVERT** Quieter, private
SENSOR Detail-oriented, precise	**INTUITIVE** Sees big picture, innovative
THINKER Task-oriented, objective	**FEELER** People-oriented, subjective
JUDGER Structured, punctual	**PERCEIVER** Flexible, spontaneous

balancing interpersonal tensions

everyone gets along and works together harmoniously.

Judger or Perceiver Do you approach the world and its challenges in a structured and organized way? If so, you are most likely a judger. **Judgers** are highly structured people who plan ahead, are punctual, and become impatient with people who show up late or waste time. **Perceivers** are less rigid than judgers. Because they like open-endedness, being on time is less important than being flexible and adaptable. Perceivers are risk takers who are willing to try new options. They often procrastinate and end up in a frenzy to complete a task on time.

Judgers and perceivers often have difficulty understanding each other. To a judger, a perceiver may appear scatterbrained. To a perceiver, a judger may appear rigid and controlling. Whereas judgers are prepared to make decisions and solve problems, perceivers "aren't comfortable with things being 'decided'; [they] want to reopen, discuss, rework, argue for the sake of arguing."[15] In classroom settings, judgers usually plan and finish class assignments well in advance, whereas perceivers may pull all-nighters to get their work done. It's important to note that both types get their work done— the difference is when and how they go about doing it.

The Myers-Briggs THINKER type: "I like this guy because he's smart, analytical, well organized, and takes a firm, but fair approach to grading."

The Myers-Briggs FEELER type: "I like this teacher because he takes an interest in every student, cares whether we learn or not, and never puts down anyone in class."

Each of the characters on the TV series *Modern Family* has a distinct personality. Which Myers-Briggs traits would you assign to each of them?

What Is Your Personality Type?

Read the *pairs* of descriptions for each personality type and put a check mark next to the *one* phrase in each pair that *best* describes you.[16] For example, do you usually work now and play later **or** play now and work later? You should only check *one* of these options. When you have finished, add up the check marks in each column and note the personality type with the most check marks.

1. Are you an extrovert or an introvert?

_____ I am outgoing, sociable, and expressive.	**OR**	_____ I am reserved and private.
_____ I enjoy groups and discussions.	**OR**	_____ I prefer one-to-one interactions.
_____ I often talk first, think later.	**OR**	_____ I usually think first, then talk.
_____ I think out loud.	**OR**	_____ I think to myself.
_____ Other people give me energy.	**OR**	_____ Other people often exhaust me.

_____ **Total** (Extrovert)   _____ **Total** (Introvert)

2. Are you a sensor or an intuitive?

_____ I focus on details.	**OR**	_____ I focus on the big picture.
_____ I am practical and realistic.	**OR**	_____ I am theoretical.
_____ I like facts.	**OR**	_____ I get bored with facts and details.
_____ I trust experience.	**OR**	_____ I trust inspiration and intuition.
_____ I want clear, realistic goals.	**OR**	_____ I want to pursue a vision.

_____ **Total** (Sensor)   _____ **Total** (Intuitive)

3. Are you a thinker or a feeler?

_____ I am task oriented.	**OR**	_____ I am people oriented.
_____ I am objective, firm, analytical.	**OR**	_____ I am subjective, caring, appreciative.
_____ I value competence, reason, justice.	**OR**	_____ I value relationships and harmony.
_____ I am direct and firm-minded.	**OR**	_____ I am tactful and tenderhearted.
_____ I think with my head.	**OR**	_____ I think with my heart.

_____ **Total** (Thinker)   _____ **Total** (Feeler)

4. Are you a judger or a perceiver?

_____ I value organization and structure.	**OR**	_____ I value flexibility and spontaneity.
_____ I like having deadlines.	**OR**	_____ I dislike deadlines.
_____ I will work now, play later.	**OR**	_____ I will play now, work later.
_____ I adjust my schedule to complete work.	**OR**	_____ I do work at the last minute.
_____ I plan ahead.	**OR**	_____ I adapt as I go.

_____ **Total** (Judger)   _____ **Total** (Perceiver)

Summarize your decisions by indicating the letter that best describes your personality traits and preferences:

_____	_____	_____	_____
Extrovert (E)	Senor (S)	Thinker (T)	Judger (J)
or	or	or	or
Introvert (I)	Intuitive (N)	Feeler (F)	Perceiver (P)

balancing interpersonal tensions

Resolving Interpersonal Conflict

8.2 *Practice strategies for resolving interpersonal conflicts.*

Conflict occurs in relationships when disagreements are expressed. All healthy relationships, no matter how important or well managed, face interpersonal conflict. Unfortunately, conflict is often associated with quarreling, fighting, anger, and hostility. Although these elements can be present, conflict does not have to involve negative emotions. As Dudley Weeks writes in his book on conflict resolution, "Conflict is an outgrowth of the diversity that characterizes our thoughts, our attitudes, our beliefs, our perceptions, and our social systems and structures."[17]

Many people avoid conflict because they do not understand the differences between destructive and constructive conflict. **Destructive conflict** is the result of behaviors that create hostility or prevent problem solving. Constant complaining, personal insults, conflict avoidance, and loud arguments or threats all contribute to destructive conflict.[18] This kind of conflict has the potential to permanently harm a relationship.

In contrast, **constructive conflict** occurs when you express disagreement in a way that respects others' perspectives and promotes problem solving. Kenneth Cloke and Joan Goldsmith of the Center for Dispute Resolution explain that all of us have a choice about how to deal with conflict. We can treat conflict as experiences "that imprison us or lead us on a journey, as a battle that embitters us or as an opportunity for learning. Our choices between these contrasting attitudes and approaches will shape the way the conflict unfolds."[19]

Conflict Styles

When you are involved in a personal conflict, do you jump into the fray or run the other way? Do you marshal your forces and play to win, or do you work with everyone to find a mutually agreeable solution? Psychologists Kenneth Thomas and Ralph Kilmann claim that we primarily use one or two of five conflict styles in most situations: avoidance, accommodation,

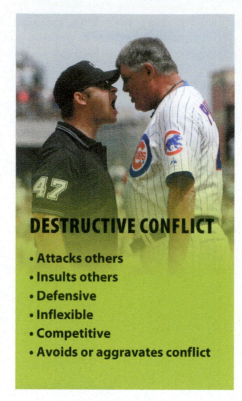

DESTRUCTIVE CONFLICT

- Attacks others
- Insults others
- Defensive
- Inflexible
- Competitive
- Avoids or aggravates conflict

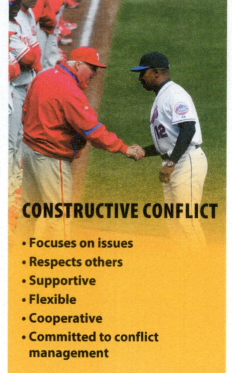

CONSTRUCTIVE CONFLICT

- Focuses on issues
- Respects others
- Supportive
- Flexible
- Cooperative
- Committed to conflict management

competition, compromise, and collaboration.[20] These five styles represent the extent to which you focus on achieving personal needs and/or mutual needs. The *Communication Assessment* "How Do You Respond to Conflict?" on page 153 will help identify *your* primary conflict style or styles.

People who are motivated to fulfill their own needs tend to choose more competitive approaches, whereas collaborative people are more concerned with achieving mutual goals. The Conflict Styles figure below illustrates the relationship of each conflict style to an individual's motivation.[21]

Conflict Styles

Assertiveness and Concern for Self

High — **COMPETITION** I win, you lose. / **COLLABORATION** We both win!

Moderate — **COMPROMISE** Give a little, get a little.

Low — **AVOIDANCE** Leave me alone. / **ACCOMMODATION** I give in.

Cooperativeness and Concern for Others — Low / Moderate / High

Avoidance If you are unable or unwilling to stand up for your own needs or the needs of others, you may rely on the **avoidance conflict style**. People who use this style often change the subject, sidestep a controversial issue, or deny that a conflict exists. Avoiding conflict can be counterproductive because you fail to address a problem and can increase tension in a relationship.

Ignoring or avoiding conflict does not make it go away.

However, in some circumstances, avoiding conflict is an appropriate response. Consider avoiding conflict when the issue is not important to you, when you need time to collect your thoughts or control your emotions, when the consequences of confrontation are too risky, or when the chances of resolution are unlikely.

Accommodation Do you give in to others during a conflict at the expense of meeting your own needs? If so, you use the **accommodating conflict style**. You may believe that giving in to others preserves peace and harmony, but frequently dealing with conflict by accommodating others can make you less influential in personal or professional relationships.

On the other hand, when the issue is very important to the other person but not very important to you, an accommodating conflict style may be appropriate and effective. Accommodation is also appropriate when it is more important to preserve harmony in a relationship than to resolve a particular issue, when you realize you are wrong, or if you have changed your mind.

Competition If you are more concerned with fulfilling your own needs than with meeting the needs of others, you are using a **competitive conflict style**. Quite simply, you want to win because you believe that your ideas are better than anyone else's. When used inappropriately, the competitive style may result in hostility, ridicule, and personal attacks against others. Approaching conflict competitively tends to reduce people to winners or losers.

In certain situations, however, the competitive approach may be the most appropriate style. Approach conflict competitively when you have strong beliefs about an important issue or when immediate action is needed in an urgent situation. The competitive approach is particularly appropriate when the consequences of a bad decision may be harmful, unethical, or illegal.

Compromise The **compromising conflict style** is a "middle-ground" approach that involves conceding some goals to achieve others. Many people believe that compromise is an effective and fair method of resolving problems because, in theory, everyone loses and wins equally. However, if you are dissatisfied with the outcome or believe it is unfair, you may not do much to implement the solution or course of action.

The compromise approach should be used when you are unable to reach a unanimous decision or resolve a problem. Consider compromising when other methods of conflict resolution are not effective, when you have reached an impasse, or if there is not enough time to explore more creative options.

Collaboration The **collaborative conflict style** is a *win-win* approach that searches for new solutions that will achieve both your goals and the goals of others. Instead of arguing about whose ideas are superior, the parties collaborate and look for creative solutions that satisfy everyone.

A couple disagree about how to get from here to there, but are not having a hostile argument.

Friends disagree about something, but are not threatening or insulting one another.

resolving interpersonal conflict

UNDERSTANDING DIVERSITY AND CONFLICT

Cultural values tell us a great deal about how people feel about conflict and the methods they use to resolve conflict. For example, collectivist cultures place a high value on "face." From a cultural perspective, **face** is the positive image you wish to create or preserve.

Cultures that place a great deal of value on "saving face" discourage personal attacks and outcomes in which one person "loses." The table below summarizes individualistic and collectivist perspectives about conflict.[22]

Cultural Perspective About Conflict

INDIVIDUALISTIC CULTURES

- Conflict is closely related to individual goals.
- Conflict should be dealt with openly and honestly.
- Conflict should result in a specific solution or plan of action.
- Conflict is addressed appropriately in terms of the situation and timing.

COLLECTIVIST CULTURES

- Conflict is understood within the context of relationships and the need to preserve face.
- Conflict resolution requires that face issues be mutually managed before a discussion of other issues.
- Conflict resolution is considered successful when both parties save face and when both can claim they have won.
- Conflict resolution requires attention to verbal and nonverbal communication as well as the nature of the relationship.

Cultural differences also affect whether disagreements should occur and who should or should not express those differences. People in conformist cultures such as those in Japan, Germany, Mexico, and Brazil are less likely to express disagreement than individualistic cultures such as those in the United States, Sweden and France.[23] In cultures that honor their elders, a young person arguing with an older adult would be disrespectful. Among several Native American and African cultures, older adults are considered wiser and more knowledgeable, and young people are expected to accept the views of elders rather than challenge or rebel against them.

There are two potential drawbacks to the collaborative approach. First, collaboration requires a lot of time and energy, and some issues may not be important enough to justify the extra time and effort. Second, in order for collaboration to be successful, everyone—even the avoiders and accommodators—must fully participate in the process. Collaboration works best when both parties welcome new and creative ideas and are committed to the resulting decision.

Conflict Resolution Strategies

Effective communicators are flexible and use a variety of styles and strategies to resolve conflicts. There is no "best" way to manage or resolve conflict because no two conflict situations are exactly alike. In this section, we present two strategies for resolving or moderating conflicts: application of step-by-step models and strategies of managing emotions.

The AEIOU Model of Conflict Resolution

Assume the other person means well and wants to resolve the conflict. "I know that both of us want to do a good job and complete this project on time."

Express your feelings. "I'm frustrated when you ask me to spend time working on a less important project."

Identify what you would like to happen. "I want to share the responsibility and the work with you."

Outcomes you expect should be made clear. "If both of us don't make a commitment to working on this full time, we won't do a good job or get it done on time."

Understanding on a mutual basis is achieved. "Could we divide up the tasks and set deadlines for completion or bring in another person to help us?"

Apply Step-by-Step Models

When you're not sure how to resolve a conflict, consider using a step-by-step conflict resolution method such as the A-E-I-O-U Model and the Six-Step Model. The **A-E-I-O-U Model of Conflict Resolution** focuses on communicating personal concerns and suggesting alternative actions to resolve a conflict.[24] Of utmost importance in this model is that you try to understand the attitudes, beliefs, and values of those with whom you are involved in conflict.

The **Six-Step Model of Conflict Resolution** offers a series of steps to help you move a conflict toward successful resolution. The six steps illustrated below are neither simple, nor easy. They do, however, tell you "what to do and what not to do when confronting someone" in a conflict situation.[25]

The Six-Step Model of Conflict Resolution

	Step	Task	Strategies
1	**Preparation**	Identify the problem, issues, and causes of the conflict.	Analyze the conflict by asking yourself: Who is involved? What happened? Where, when, and why did the conflict occur. **Example:** "Why and how did things go wrong?"
2	**Initiation**	Tell the person: "We need to talk."	Ask the other person to meet and talk about the problem. Provide some information about the subject. **Example:** "Can we get together for lunch and talk about the late report?"
3	**Confrontation**	Talk to the other person about the conflict and the need to resolve it.	Express your feelings constructively and describe, specifically, what you see as a solution. **Example:** "I want you to come to the family reunion with us."
4	**Consideration**	Consider the other person's point of view.	Listen, empathize, paraphrase, and respond with understanding. **Example:** "I didn't realize your mother was sick when I asked you to work so late."
5	**Resolution**	Come to a mutual understanding and reach an agreement.	Specify the outcome that both parties accept. **Example:** "Okay. I'll make sure I call you if they want us to work later than 6 P.M."
6	**Reevaluation**	Follow up on the solution.	Set a date for seeing whether the solution is working as hoped. **Example:** "Let's meet for lunch in two weeks to see if this is working as we hope it will."

resolving interpersonal conflict

How Argumentative Are You?[26]

Argumentativeness, your "willingness to debate controversial issues with others," is a positive trait that does not promote hostility or anxiety.[27] Argumentative people tend to focus on the most important issues and have no desire to make personal attacks.[28] This questionnaire assesses how you feel about arguing with others. Use the following ratings to respond to each statement:

1 =almost never true   **2** =rarely true   **3** =occasionally true
4 =often true   **5** =almost always true

1. _____While in an argument, I worry that the person I am arguing with will form a negative impression of me.

2. _____Arguing over controversial issues improves my intelligence.

3. _____I enjoy avoiding arguments.

4. _____I am energetic and enthusiastic when I argue.

5. _____After I finish an argument, I promise myself that I will not get into another.

6. _____Arguing with a person creates more problems for me than it solves.

7. _____I have a pleasant, good feeling when I win a point in an argument.

8. _____When I finish arguing with someone, I feel nervous and upset.

9. _____I enjoy a good argument over a controversial issue.

10. _____I get an unpleasant feeling when I realize I am about to get into an argument.

11. _____I enjoy defending my point of view on an issue.

12. _____I am happy when I keep an argument from happening.

13. _____I do not like to miss the opportunity to argue a controversial issue.

14. _____I prefer being with people who rarely disagree with me.

15. _____I consider an argument an exciting intellectual challenge.

16. _____I find myself unable to think of effective points during an argument.

17. _____I feel refreshed after an argument on a controversial issue.

18. _____I have the ability to do well in an argument.

19. _____I try to avoid getting into arguments.

20. _____I feel excitement when I expect that a conversation I am in is leading to an argument.

Scoring:

1. Add your scores on items 2, 4, 7, 9, 11, 13, 15, 17, 18, and 20.

2. Add 60 to the sum obtained in step 1.

3. Add your scores on items 1, 3, 5, 6, 8, 10, 12, 14, 16, and 19.

4. To calculate your argumentativeness score, subtract the total obtained in step 3 from the total obtained in step 2.

Score Interpretation:

73–100 points = highly argumentative

56–72 points = Moderately argumentative

20–55 points = Not or mildly argumentative

Resolving Online Conflicts

Regardless of whether you use e-mail or online social media such as Facebook, Twitter, or Google Hangouts, face-to-face interaction still "wins" as the best medium for conflict resolution. Professor Kathleen Valley's research finds that 50 percent of negotiations conducted by email end in an unsuccessful stalemate whereas only 19 percent of face-to-face interactions do so. She explains these results as follows:

> With e-mail, negotiations are considerably more likely to degenerate into an unpleasant exchange. In face-to-face encounters, if the conversation gets a little nasty, someone will back down. You'll hear, "I'm sorry, I didn't mean it that way," or, "I don't think you understood what I was trying to say. Let me try to explain it a different way. What I meant was . . ."When the interaction is purely electronic, people are more willing to escalate conflict—to get downright rude, even. There's a reason that flaming has become so common on the Internet.[29]

Valley also notes that people are more likely to lie on e-mail and may be unwilling to say what they really believe because the discussion is captured in writing for all to see—now and in the future. As a result, users may be "less flexible, less willing to get involved in the kind of give and take that's normal in more personal communications."[30]

These results are not surprising. The lack of nonverbal communication—both physical and vocal—in most e-mail and social media interactions acts as a barrier to effective conflict resolution. If you can't see someone's facial expressions or hear the individual's tone of voice, you may end up misunderstanding its meaning. In addition, "conflict can get blown out of proportion online. What may begin as a small difference of opinion, or misunderstanding, becomes a major issue very quickly."[31]

The following strategies may help overcome some of the online obstacles to resolving conflicts, assuming you also take into account the nature and importance of the issues, the characteristics and attitudes of the people involved, and the particular type of media you're using:

1. Take a deep breath. Do not respond immediately. Read and process the posts several times before responding.
2. Assume that most other people mean well unless you have a history of difficulties with the other person or persons.
3. If you don't understand what others mean, ask for clarification. Paraphrase what you think they mean and ask for confirmation.
4. Use "I" statements rather than accusatory "you" statements (see Chapter 5, "Verbal Communication," page 91 on how to use *I* and *you* wisely).
5. Try not to take the messages personally. Focus on the task or problem, not on yourself.
6. Try to find something to agree with or something you have in common with the other person or group of people.
7. Use the Six-Step Model of Conflict Resolution to coordinate conflict resolution interactions: prepare, initiate, confront, consider, resolve, and re-evaluate.

Manage Your Emotions In Chapter 7, "Understanding Interpersonal Relationships," you learned that emotional intelligence is the ability to recognize and manage your emotions in interpersonal relationships. In a conflict situation, you want to be as emotionally intelligent as possible. Two critical skills can help you create an emotional climate conducive to conflict resolution. First, try to "quickly reduce your own stress." Second try to "remain comfortable enough with your emotions to react in constructive ways even in the midst of an argument or a perceived attack."[32]

Take a moment to think about whether you experience any of the following stressful symptoms during a conflict: Are your muscles or stomach tight? Are your hands clenched? Is your breath shallow or your heart beating faster than normal?[33] If you feel any of these symptoms, try to relax physically. Some of these strategies also help reduce communication apprehension.

Try the Silent Reee-Laaax

As you face a conflict or feel your emotions taking control of you and your thoughts, repeat a two-syllable word or phrase quietly to yourself, syllable by syllable, deeply inhaling and exhaling each time. Use, for example, the word *relax*. Breathe in slowly through your nose while saying the sound *re* (ree) silently to yourself, holding the long *e* sound all the while you are inhaling. This should take just about two to three seconds. Then breathe out slowly, also for about two to three seconds, as you say the sound *lax* (laks) silently to yourself. Hold the *a* sound while exhaling. Inhale and exhale, thinking "REEE-LAAAX" four or five times. By the time you finish this thirty-second relaxation exercise, your pulse should be slower, and ideally, you will also feel calmer. A word of caution, though: avoid inhaling and exhaling too deeply for too long, lest you end up feeling lightheaded or faint.

- Silently tell yourself you need to calm down. Remind yourself that if you are calm and in control of your emotions, the more likely you will be able to communicate effectively and resolve the conflict.
- Try to control your facial expressions and appearance so you seem open for discussion rather than tense, anxious, or hostile.

Use a quick relaxation technique such as deep breathing, sighing, clenching and unclenching your stomach muscles. The Silent Reeee-Laaax technique on the previous page has helped many of our students calm down and focus.

When you succeed in regulating your emotional response to conflict, you will have more energy and time to understand someone else's or a group's points of view. This kind of awareness helps you understand the real problem. Regulating your emotions also help "you stay motivated until the conflict is resolved. It enhances your ability to communicate clearly and effectively. And, with good preparation, increase the likelihood you will influence others."[34]

Managing Anger

8.3 *Manage and respond appropriately to your own anger and the anger of others.*

Anger is a natural, human emotion. Everyone feels angry at some time. In many instances, anger may be fully justified. If a friend lies to you, a coworker takes credit for your work, or an intimate partner betrays you, **anger**—an emotional response to unmet expectations that ranges from minor irritation to intense rage—is a natural response. Effective anger management requires that you know how to communicate your angry feelings appropriately while treating others with respect.

Understanding *Your* Anger

Everyone experiences anger. That's not the problem. The problem occurs when anger becomes so out-of-control that it hurts you and others. As Jeanne Segal and Melinda Smith write in their *Help Guide*, "Learning to control your anger and express it appropriately can help you build better relationships, achieve your goals and lead a healthier, more satisfying life."[35]

Before examining how to manage your anger, consider some of the common misconceptions many people have about this normal emotion as show in the box on Three Anger Misconceptions.

If you are quick to anger, we strongly recommend that you take time to analyze why you are angry. Remember that anger is a reaction to unmet expectations. You expect others to be honest—and they're not. You expect others to treat you with respect—and they don't. You expect a candidate

> The issue is not whether you are angry but how well you understand and manage your anger.

THREE ANGER MISCONCEPTIONS[36]

1. **Anger and aggression are human instincts.** There is *no* scientific evidence to support the claim that humans are innately aggressive. Our survival depends on cooperation, not destructive conflict and aggression.[37]

2. **Anger is always helpful.** Anger can be beneficial when it warns you of danger or prepares your body for a fight-or-flight response. However, anger fueled by hostility to others (as opposed to anger that serves as a warning) is bad for your health, particularly for your heart.[38]

3. **Anger is caused by others.** When you're angry, you may say, "She made me angry when she didn't show up" or "The boss made me angry when he didn't give me credit for writing the report." By blaming others for your anger, you don't have to change your own behavior in any way. As a result, you stay angry.[39]

who, in your opinion is much better than the other candidate whom you dislike, to win—and the candidate loses. You expect to get a good grade/job/promotion/award—and you don't get it. As a result, you're angry. Or perhaps, as Segal and Smith suggest, your anger is "masking other feelings such as embarrassment, insecurity, hurt, shame, or vulnerability?"[40]

Expressing Anger

What's the best way to deal with your anger—hold it in or let it out? Some people see anger as a destructive emotion that should always be suppressed. However, when you suppress justified anger, it can fester or build while recurring problems go unresolved. Psychotherapist Bill DeFoore compares suppressed anger with a pressure cooker. "We can only suppress or apply pressure against our anger for so long before it erupts. Periodic eruptions can cause all kinds of problems."[41]

Other people believe in fully expressing their anger, regardless of how intense or potentially damaging it is. They also believe that angry outbursts release tension and calm them down. Psychologists explain that venting anger to let off steam "is really worse than useless. Expressing anger does not reduce anger. Instead it functions to make you even angrier."[42] Moreover, people on the receiving end of angry outbursts usually get angry right back—which only makes the problem worse.

Both of these extreme views about anger can be counterproductive. Not only can they damage interpersonal relationships, but they may contribute to serious health problems, such as hypertension and heart disease.[43]

In late fourth century B.C., Aristotle famously wrote that anyone can become angry—that is easy. But to be angry at the right things, with the right people, to the right degree, at the right time, for the right purpose, and in the right way—is worthy of praise.[44] Here we provide some strategies for expressing your anger constructively:[45]

- State that you are angry.
- Do not vent or suppress it.
- Avoid expressing your anger in personal attacks.
- Identify the source of your anger.

Shouting may let others know you are angry, but calmly and clearly stating "I am angry" will let them know how you feel *and* pave the way for resolving conflict constructively. Furthermore, although you have a right to your feelings, screaming angrily at someone is disruptive and disrespectful and rarely solves anything.

Try to avoid making personal attacks; these only escalate a conflict. Use "I" statements ("I expected you to . . .") instead of "you" statements ("You messed up when you …"). Finally, help

Tony Soprano's often uncontrollable anger hurt himself, his family, and his victims.

others understand why you are angry: "Because the report isn't finished, I'm now in a bind with my supervisor." Social psychologist Carol Tavris writes that anger "requires an awareness of choice and an embrace of reason. It is knowing when to become angry—'this is wrong, this I will protest'—and when to make peace; when to take action, and when to keep silent; knowing

the likely cause of one's anger and not berating the blameless."[46]

Understanding Others' Anger

Even if you succeed in understanding your anger and expressing it appropriately, you have only resolved your own feelings, not those of others. Although we'd recommend avoiding people and situations that "make" you angry, we

COMMUNICATION IN *ACTION*

Apologize

An apology can go a long way toward diffusing anger and opening the door to constructive conflict resolution. Yet, despite the importance and simplicity of an apology, many people find it difficult to say the words *I'm sorry*. Although you may "lose" a conflict or sacrifice some of your pride, an effective apology can earn the respect of others and help build trusting relationships. Consider the following guidelines for making an effective apology:[47]

- *Take responsibility for your actions with "I" statements.* "I paid the bills late."
- *Clearly identify the behavior that was wrong.* "I made a major commitment without talking to you about it first."
- *Acknowledge how the other person might feel.* "I understand that you are probably annoyed with me."
- *Acknowledge that you could have acted differently.* "I should have asked if you wanted to work together on this project."
- *Express regret.* "I'm upset with myself for not thinking ahead."
- *Follow through on any promises to*

correct the situation. "I'll send an e-mail message today acknowledging that your name should have been included on the report."
- *Request, but don't demand, forgiveness.* "I value our relationship and hope that you will forgive me."

When you say you are sorry, you take responsibility for your behavior and actions.

know that this is an impossible dream. Learning how to respond to others' anger is the other half of the anger management equation.

If someone expresses anger toward you, consider using any or all of the following strategies.[48]

- Acknowledge the other person's feelings of anger. *"I understand how angry you are." "I can see how upset you are."*

- Identify the issue or behavior that is the source of the anger. *"I don't believe I promised to work both your shifts next weekend, but you seem to think we made this agreement."*

- Assess the intensity of the anger and the importance of the issue. *"I know it's important for you to find someone to cover your shifts so you can attend your friend's wedding."*

- Encourage collaborative approaches to resolving the conflict. *"I can only cover one of your shifts this weekend. Why don't we work together to find someone else who will take the second shift?"*

- Make a positive statement about the relationship. *"I enjoy working with you and hope we can sort this out together."*

Developing Assertiveness

8.4 *Practice assertiveness while respecting the rights and needs of others.*

So far we've looked at the inevitable tensions that affect interpersonal relationships and how these tensions influence your ability to get along with others. We also examined how well you manage and respond to conflict and anger. In this section we focus on assertiveness, a communication strategy that does more than help you achieve your communication goals: it also helps you minimize and even avoid harmful conflict and emotional reactions.

Consider the following hypothetical examples: What should you do if your boss wants you to work longer hours, but you want more time with your family? What if your friend wants to go to a party, but you need to stay home and study? How do you balance these competing needs and resolve potential conflicts? The answer may lie in whether you know how to be assertive.

Assertiveness is the ability to stand up for your own needs and rights while also respecting the needs and rights of others. When you are assertive, you are equally concerned about your own needs as well as those of others. You can express and communicate your feelings accurately, appropriately, and respectfully. You can also ask for help. You can ask for things you want, and say no to things you don't want. You can take responsibility for your own thoughts, feelings, and behaviors.[49]

Passivity and Aggression

Assertiveness is best understood by considering three alternatives to

assertiveness: passivity, aggression, and passive aggression.

Passivity is characterized by giving in to others at the expense of your own needs in order to avoid conflict and disagreement. For example, Emile's boss asks him to work over the weekend. Emile agrees and says nothing about his plans to attend an important family event. Not surprisingly, passive individuals often feel taken advantage of by others and blame them for their unhappiness. As a result, they fail to take responsibility for their own actions and the consequences of those actions.[50] If you are a passive communicator, you tend to give in to others even when it's not in your own best

THE BENEFITS OF ASSERTING YOURSELF

- Expressing your feelings appropriately
- Accepting compliments graciously
- Speaking up for your rights when appropriate
- Enhancing your self-esteem and self-confidence
- Expressing disagreement on important issues
- Asking others to change their inappropriate or offensive behavior[51]

interest, have difficulty saying no to people, have a hard time making decisions and maintaining eye contact with others, and avoid confrontations at all costs.[52]

The opposite of passive behavior is **aggression**, in which communicators put their personal needs first while violating someone else's needs and rights. Aggressive individuals demand compliance from others. Although aggressive behavior can be violent, it is usually displayed in more subtle behavior, such as a raised voice, rolled eyes, or a withering glance.[53] Aggressive communicators look out for themselves and only themselves. They tend to lose their tempers, shout or bully others to get their way, call others names or use obscenities when angry, openly criticize and find fault with others, and continue to argue long after everyone else has had enough.[54]

Sometimes people may *seem* passive when, in fact, their intentions are aggressive. Although **passive-aggressive** individuals may *appear* cooperative and willing to accommodate others and their needs, their behavior is a subtle form of aggressive behavior. Passive-aggressive communicators manipulate others to get what they want. For example, when you refuse to do a favor for your brother, he mopes around the house until you finally give in to his request. You may have difficulty recognizing passive-aggressive individuals at first. They may appear pleasant, but hide inner resentments. They may procrastinate in order to frustrate others, claim to forget something they promised to do, and if they think they can get away with it, harm others.[55]

While aggressive, passive, and passive-aggressive behavior may initially seem effective, in the long run, they damage interpersonal and professional relationships.

Assertiveness Skills

Assertiveness can be difficult to learn, particularly if you are likely to become passive or aggressive when challenged or if you primarily rely on an avoiding, accommodating, competing, or compromising conflict style.

Being assertive may involve breaking old communication habits while recognizing that in some contexts those styles may be appropriate. Initially, assertive behavior may feel strange or uncomfortable because asserting your rights can open the door to conflict.

COMMUNICATION

Principles of Interpersonal Ethics

Ethical communication decisions can be challenging on a daily basis. When, however, conflict, anger, aggression, and passivity join the mix, the challenge of responding ethically may seem impossible. Are you more likely to want an eye for an eye and a tooth for a tooth rather than turning the other cheek? During a heated argument, are you more likely to flee or fight? If you're extremely angry, are you tempted to use words that hurt the other person so they feel as badly as you do? These dilemmas are more than communication challenges. They are ethical challenges as well.

In her book *Practicing Communication Ethics*, Paula Tompkins offers four principles for evaluating the ethical challenges you face in interpersonal encounters.[56]

1. **The Golden Rule:** Do unto others as you would have them do unto you. Is the communication response you want to use fair, honest, and caring?

2. **The Platinum Rule:** Do unto others as they wish to have done to themselves. Do you really know what others want or think, without asking or listening to them? Have you considered their age, culture, ethnicity, gender, status, education, and so on? In other words, what "you would have them do unto you" may well not be what they want done to themselves.

3. **The Principle of Generalizability:** Distinguish between what is momentary or limited and what is more enduring or broadly applicable. Are you using a different ethical value or principle with this particular person or in this particular situation? For example, would you let your best friend get away with an unethical act that you would condemn in others?

4. **The Test of Publicity:** Can you convince others that your communicative response is ethical and justified? What would a friend or colleague say? What would someone you don't know but who could ultimately be affected by your behavior say?[57]

An unresolved conflict or uncontrollable anger between two people can have far-reaching consequences. Unmanaged anger can escalate into violence. Failure to assert your own needs and rights can also compromise the needs and rights of others. Use the above principles to evaluate your own and others' ethical behavior.

Sharon and Gordon Bower, the authors of *Asserting Yourself*, have developed what they call a **DESC script**—a four-step process that relies on communication skills for becoming more assertive. DESC is an acronym for **D**escribe, **E**xpress, **S**pecify, and **C**onsequences. This scripting method can be used in both personal and professional relationships.[58] In some cases, you may want to write out your DESC script in advance and practice it before you have to confront someone.

Assertive behavior can improve your self-esteem, your ability to resolve conflict, and the quality of your relationships.

DESC Script

Steps	Example
D: Describe. Describe the unwanted situation or offensive behavior as completely and objectively as you can. Describe the other person's action, not his or her perceived motive.	"The last time we had to do a group project in this class, I did most of the work."
E: Express. Express your feelings clearly and calmly. Use "I" and not "you" in order to avoid eliciting a defensive reaction.	"As a result, I was exhausted and angry."
S: Specify. Specify what you want to happen or the behavior you want from the other person. Take into account whether the other person can do what you request and what changes you're willing to make.	"For this next project, I would like us to share the work more equally."
C: Consequences. Specify the consequences (both positive and negative) of accepting or denying your request. Ask yourself: What rewarding consequences can I provide?	"If we work together on this project, we will do a better job, get it done sooner, and hopefully earn a good grade."

COMMUNICATION IN *ACTION*

Just Say No

Saying "no" to someone can be difficult—even scary. In his book *The Anxiety and Phobia Workbook*, Edmund Bourne writes, "an important aspect of being assertive is your ability to say no to requests you don't want to meet. Saying no means that you set limits on other people's demands for your time and energy when such demands conflict with your own needs and desires. It also means you can do this without feeling guilty."[59]

In some cases, you may need to say no to a family member, good friend, or close colleague. Here are the four steps Bourne recommends:

1. Acknowledge the other person's request by repeating it. "I'd love to have lunch with you tomorrow."
2. Explain your reason for declining. "But, I have a deadline on Friday, so I have lots of work to do and can't take the time this week."
3. Say no. "So I'll have to say no."
4. (Optional) Suggest an alternative proposal in which both of your and the other person's needs will be met. "I'd love to do this another time. How about next Tuesday or Wednesday?"[60]

When there isn't a reasonable alternative proposal that works for both parties, leave out the fourth step. Bourne offers this example:

I hear that you need help with moving (acknowledgement). I'd like to help out but I promised my boyfriend we would go away this weekend (explanation), so I'm not going to be around (saying no). I hope you can find someone else.[61]

Saying no means setting limits.

There are times, however, when you must say no to a person you don't want to be friends with, don't like, or who seems "unsafe." In such cases, simply say "No" or "No thank you" in a polite and firm manner. If the other person persists, say no again without apologizing.

How Do *You* Respond to Conflict?[62]

The following twenty statements represent remarks made by a person in a conflict situation. Consider each message separately and decide how closely it resembles your attitudes and behavior in a conflict situation, even if the language does not represent the exact way you express yourself. Use the following numerical scale to rate the statements. Choose only one rating for each message.

5 = I always do this   4 = I usually do this   3 = I sometimes do this
2 = I rarely do this   1 = I never do this

When I'm involved in a conflict …

_____ 1. I try to change the subject when I face a conflict.

_____ 2. I play down differences so conflicts don't become too serious.

_____ 3. I don't hold back in a conflict, particularly when there is something I really want.

_____ 4. I try to find a trade-off that everyone can agree to.

_____ 5. I try to look at a conflict objectively rather than taking it personally.

_____ 6. I avoid contact with the people when I know there's a serious conflict brewing.

_____ 7. I'm willing to change my position to resolve a conflict and let others have what they want.

_____ 8. I fight hard when an issue is very important to me and others are unlikely to agree.

_____ 9. I understand that I can't get everything I want when resolving a conflict.

_____ 10. I try to minimize status differences and defensiveness in order to resolve a conflict.

_____ 11. I put off or delay dealing with the conflict.

_____ 12. I rarely disclose much about how I feel during a conflict, particularly if it's negative.

_____ 13. I like having enough power to control a conflict situation.

_____ 14. I like to work on hammering out a deal among conflicting parties.

_____ 15. I believe that all conflicts have potential for positive resolution.

_____ 16. I give in to the other person's demands in most cases.

_____ 17. I'd rather keep a friend than win an argument.

_____ 18. I don't like wasting time in arguments when I know what we should do.

_____ 19. I'm willing to give in on some issues, but not on others.

_____ 20. I look for solutions that meet everyone's needs.

Conflict Style	Avoid	Accommodate	Compete	Compromise	Collaborate
Item Scores	1 = _____	2 = _____	3 = _____	4 = _____	5 = _____
	6 = _____	7 = _____	8 = _____	9 = _____	10 = _____
	11 = _____	12 = _____	13 = _____	14 = _____	15 = _____
	16 = _____	17 = _____	18 = _____	19 = _____	20 = _____
Total Scores	_____	_____	_____	_____	_____

Your scores identify which conflict style(s) you use most often. There are, however, no right or wrong responses. Your conflict style may differ depending on the issues, the people involved, and the situation.

Balancing Interpersonal Tensions

8.1 Explain how to balance contrary tensions in interpersonal relationships.

- Relational Dialectics Theory explains how the interplay of contradictory forces affects interpersonal relationships in three domains: integration-separate, stability-change, and expression-privacy.

- The Myers-Briggs Type Indicator helps you balance interpersonal tensions by understanding the extent to which you and others are extroverts or introverts, sensors or intuitives, thinkers or feelers, and judgers or perceivers.

Resolving Interpersonal Conflicts

8.2 Practice strategies for resolving interpersonal conflicts.

- Conflict can be constructive or destructive depending on your intentions and how well you communicate.

- The cultural dimensions of individualism-collectivism can affect how people approach and resolve interpersonal conflicts.

- There are five conflict styles: avoidance, accommodation, competition, compromise, and collaboration.

- The A-E-I-O-U Model and the Six-Step Model can help you resolve conflicts.

- Determine how argumentative you are and how it affects the way you handle an interpersonal conflict.

- Additional conflict resolution strategies include learning how to manage your emotions and apologizing.

Managing Anger

8.3 Manage and respond appropriately to your own anger and the anger of others.

- Anger is a natural, emotional response to unmet expectations.

- There are several common myths about anger: anger is a human instinct, anger is always helpful, and my anger is caused by others.

- You can express anger appropriately by stating that you are angry without venting or exploding, by avoiding personal attacks, and by identifying the source of your anger.

Developing Assertiveness

8.4 Practice assertiveness while respecting the rights and needs of others.

- Assertive communicators promote their own needs and rights while respecting the needs and rights of others.

- Passivity is characterized by giving in to others at the expense of your own needs; aggression involves putting your own needs first often at the expenses of someone else's needs; passive aggression may appear to accommodate others but is a subtle form of aggressive behavior.

- DESC scripting is a four-step process (describe, express, specify, and consequences) for becoming more assertive.

- Assertive communicators say "no" to requests they can't or don't want to meet.

Key Terms

Accommodating conflict style	**Conflict**	**Judgers**
A-E-I-O-U Model of Conflict Resolution	**Constructive conflict**	**Myers-Briggs Type Indicator**
Aggression	**DESC script**	**Passive aggressive**
Anger	**Destructive conflict**	**Passivity**
Argumentativeness	**Dialectics**	**Perceivers**
Assertiveness	**Expression-privacy dialectic**	**Personality**
Avoidance conflict style	**Extroverts**	**Relational Dialectics Theory**
Collaborative conflict style	**Face**	**Sensors**
Competitive conflict style	**Feelers**	**Six-Step Model of Conflict Resolution**
Compromising conflict style	**Integration-separation dialectic**	**Stability-change dialectic**
	Introverts	**Thinkers**
	Intuitives	

TEST YOUR KNOWLEDGE

Explain how to balance contradictory tensions in interpersonal relationships.

1   Which relational dialectic is involved when you're looking for some new excitement in your life while your partner is content to stay home, work on hobbies, and interact with lifelong friends?

   a. Integration versus separation

   b. Expression versus privacy

   c. Stability versus change

   d. Individualism versus collectivism

2   Which Myers-Briggs personality trait is evident in the following description? "Sarita is a risk taker who is willing to try new options. But she often procrastinates and end ups in a frenzy to complete a project task on time."

   a. Introvert

   b. Sensor

   c. Intuitive

   d. Perceiver

8.2 *Practice strategies for resolving interpersonal conflicts.*

3   In which of the following conflict styles do people respond by giving in to others at the expense of meeting their own needs?

   a. Avoidance

   b. Accommodation

   c. Compromise

   d. Collaboration

4   Which word does the *I* in the A-E-I-O-U Model of Conflict Resolution stands for?

   a. Intimidate

   b. Identify

   c. Intuitive

   d. Initiation

8.3 *Manage and respond appropriately to your own anger and the anger of others.*

5   All of the following are common misconceptions about anger except

   _____.

   a. anger is a natural, human emotion

   b. anger and aggression are human instincts

   c. anger is always helpful

   d. anger is caused by what others do to you

6   Which of the following ethical principles asks the question: What would friends or colleagues say if I responded angrily?

   a. The Golden Rule

   b. The Platinum Rule

   c. The Principle of Generalizability

   d. The Test of Publicity

8.4 *Practice assertiveness while respecting the rights and needs of others.*

7   Which of the following characterizes passive-aggressive behavior?

   a. You advance your own needs and rights while also respecting the needs and rights of others.

   b. You give in to others at the expense of your own needs in order to avoid conflict and disagreement.

   c. You put your personal needs first often at the expense of someone else.

   d. You appear to go along with others but sabotage their plans behind their backs.

8   The letters in DESC scripting are an acronym for

   a. Describe, Express, Specify, Consequence.

   b. Decide, Empathize, Self-Disclose, and Conflict.

   c. Dialectic, Expression, Separation, and Change.

   d. Decider, Extrovert, Sensor, and Controller.

Answers found on page 368.

This *Communication Currents* article has been slightly edited and shortened with permission from the National Communication Association.

Communication Currents

Knowledge for Communicating Well

N C A

A Publication of the National Communication Association

Volume 7, Issue 1 - February 2012

Coping with Hurtful Events

Comment. *Dr. Laura Guerrero, a highly respected interpersonal communication scholar, effectively summarizes decades of her research focusing on the "dark side" of interpersonal communication.*

Even in the best of relationships, couples encounter problems that lead them to feel negative emotions, such as jealousy, anger, and frustration, and to communicate in destructive ways. Managing these types of situations effectively by using constructive forms of communication is one key to maintaining a healthy and happy relationship.

One method for coping with relationship problems is to use *integrative communication*. This style of communication focuses on problem solving, negotiation, and social support and is effective when people are experiencing negative emotions such as anger, jealousy, and hurt. Integrative communication strategies include calmly questioning the partner about her or his actions and feelings, explaining one's own feelings, validating the partner's position by noting areas of agreement, reassuring one another, and discussing what can be done to prevent a similar problem from occurring in the future (e.g., "I understand why you feel that way" and "You know that I will always love you").

Comment. *In addition to encompassing communication principles related to providing social support and dealing with conflict, anger, and jealousy, Guerrero's concept of integrative communication also addresses other topics in Chapter 7 and 8, such as appropriate self-disclosure and receptivity to feedback, strategies for comforting others, and developing assertiveness.*

Another strategy involves using effective remedial strategies. After people engage in hurtful acts, such as cheating, lying, making an especially cruel remark, or betraying a confidence, they often use remedial strategies, such as sincere apology, appeasement, and relationship invocation.

Sincere apology involves saying "I'm sorry" while also expressing remorse for one's actions.

For example, a wife might tell her husband, "I'm sorry I lied to you. I feel really bad about it. If I had it to do over again, I would have told you the truth in the first place." Apologies are more likely to be accepted if they are perceived to be heartfelt.

Appeasement involves doing something to try and make it up to the partner. Sending flowers, planning a special evening out, and doing extra favors for the partner are all classic examples of appeasement strategies.

Finally, when people use *relationship invocation* they talk about the hurtful event within the context of the broader relationship. For example, Spencer might tell his girlfriend, "I know we can get through this because we love each other so much." This type of statement reinforces the positive qualities of the relationship.

Other remedial strategies are not so successful. Sometimes people try to justify or minimize their actions by saying things like "Someone else made me do it," or "It's not that big of a deal." This type of communication often infuriates the hurt person who is looking for an apology and an acknowledgement of wrongdoing rather than an excuse. Of course, some explanations are valid and can be effective. For example, Sophie might explain that she only had lunch with her ex-boyfriend because he seemed depressed and she wanted to help him, not because she is still attracted to him. This type

Assessment. *In Chapter 7, we recommend strategies for romancing another person. How does Dr. Guerrero's appeasement strategy compare to the behaviors we use for beginning romantic relationships?*

Assessment. *How do these less successful strategies illustrate one or more conflict styles or the myths about anger?*

Assessment. *In Chapter 8, we wrote "When you say you are sorry, you take responsibility for your behavior and action." Explain why the act of apologizing can help couples cope with hurtful events. What guidelines should you follow when apologizing?*

Assessment. *In Chapter 7, we discuss the nature of jealous and recommend strategies for reducing its harmful effects. For example, "Stay Calm, Cool, and Collected," and "Defuse Jealous Feelings." Can you name and explain additional jealousy-reducing strategies?*

of explanation showcases that Sophie is a good person and that her ex-boyfriend is not a threat. In general, explanations are more effective when they provide this type of reassurance.

Perhaps the least effective remedial strategy is a refusal. *Refusals* occur when people refuse to acknowledge that they did anything wrong. In the classic television series *Friends*, Ross and Rachel have a big fight and decided to "take a break." That same night, Ross hooks up with someone else. When Rachel finds out, Ross tries to defend himself by saying that he didn't do anything wrong because they were "on a break." This only made matters worse. The first step toward forgiveness and relationship repair is acknowledging wrongdoing.

Forgiveness plays an essential role in maintaining and repairing relationships after hurtful events have occurred. People report more forgiveness if they perceive themselves to have used integrative communication and their partner to have apologized sincerely and engaged in appeasement behavior. There are times, however, when communication cannot repair the situation.

Forgiveness is likely to be forthcoming, and people are more likely to communicate forgiveness by using methods such as being nonverbally affectionate (e.g., giving the offender a hug) or discussing issues related to the hurtful event. People may also be more likely to forgive when they have put a lot of investment (in terms of time, energy, and other resources) into their relationship. In short, hurtful events should be considered in the context of the shared. The same hurtful event is more forgivable in an otherwise good relationship than it would be in a relationship that is plagued with other problems.

There are ups and downs in every relationship as well as bumps that come when partners hurt one another. The saying "we always hurt the ones we love" rings true, but if a couple's relationship is built on a solid foundation and partners employ constructive rather than destructive communication, they are well equipped to weather the storms that can cloud even the best relationships.

ABOUT THE AUTHOR

Laura K. Guerrero is a Professor of Communication at Arizona State University, Tempe. This essay is based on her program of research examining "the dark side" of interpersonal communication. See Laura K. Guerrero, Peter A. Andersen, and Walid A. Afifi. (2014). *Close Encounters: Communication in Relationships* (4th ed.). Thousand Oaks, CA: Sage. *Communication Currents* is a publication of the National Communication Association.

Comment. *Learn to accurately assess the nature and severity of a hurtful event as well as your reactions. Avoid the blame game: "Something's wrong (I'm hurt). You did this to me, so I'll punish you until you fix it." This is no way to live in or save a close relationship.*

Assessment. *Do you agree that "we always hurt the ones we love"? Why or why not?*

Assessment. *Analyze other television shows or films in which characters refused or accepted that they'd done something wrong, something that hurt another character. What were the consequences of these actions?*

Comment. *Remember that jealousy comes in two forms: reactive jealousy (when a person becomes aware of a real danger to the relationship, such as an affair) and suspicious jealousy (an unverified or unjustified belief that a partner has done something that threatens the relationship).*

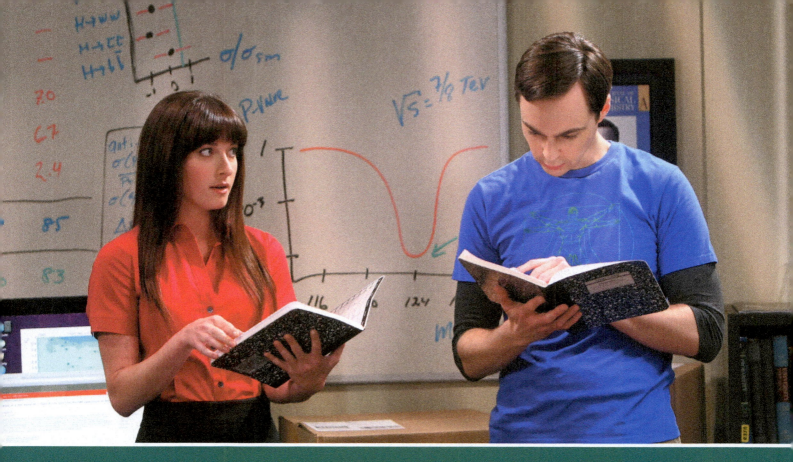

Professional Relationships 9

If you were born between 1982 and 2000, you are a member of the millennial generation. Members of this generation are described positively (confident, connected, open to change, better educated) and negatively (selfish, highly individualistic, and less involved in civic and community issues). According to a Pew Research study, almost 40 percent of "18- to 29-year-olds are unemployed or out of the workforce, the highest share among this age group in more than three decades."[1] Since the Great Recession of 2008, the tasks of finding, keeping, and prospering in a job have become much more difficult for millennials, particularly when coupled with competition from other unemployed Americans.

Even though career success depends, in large part, on how well you communicate in professional settings, millennials often "perform poorly and exhibit oddball behavior."[2] As we noted in Chapter 1, "Human Communication," business executives report that the recent college graduates need better communication skills to secure a job and succeed in the workforce.

This chapter focuses on professional relationships and the communication strategies and skills needed to succeed—regardless of your generation—in the twenty-first century's workforce and job market.

The Nature of Professional Relationships

9.1 *Describe the qualities that exemplify productive and satisfying professional relationships.*

There was a time when the word *professional* only referred to lofty and lucrative occupations such as doctor, engineer, and lawyer. Today the term *professional* is used more broadly to describe anyone whose job requires expert knowledge, specialized skills, and diligence. Put another way, a professional sets high standards for doing skillful work. You can be a professional athlete, chef, financial analyst, or musician as well as a professional nurse, soldier, manicurist, or landscaper.

According to a 2013 study, *Professionalism in the Workplace*, true professionals work until a task is completed competently. They also exemplify the following qualities"[3]

- Interpersonal skills including civility
- Appropriate appearance
- Punctuality and regular attendance
- Communication skills

Can you tell who the supervisor is and who the subordinates are in this photo? What nonverbal cues might help you decide?

All of these qualities reflect how well you use verbal and nonverbal communication in professional relationships. In a recent survey of 400,000 students and employers worldwide on job-related issues, researchers identified the top personality traits employers are looking for in job candidates. Professionalism topped the list and was identified as the most important trait by 86 percent of the respondents.[4]

The quality and success of your professional relationships depend on how well you communicate with your boss, your coworkers, and your customers or clients. For example, a corporate attorney may communicate differently when interacting with a paralegal or assistant (superior–subordinate relationship), when discussing a case with a colleague (coworker relationship), or when counseling a client (customer relationship). Your professional relationships also extend beyond traditional workplace settings. For example, you may have professional interactions with the members of a labor union, an academic association, a community organization, or a volunteer group.

Researchers who study the nature of professional relationships report a host of depressing statistics related to our interactions at work: 55 percent of managers are seen as unfit for their jobs,[5] 60 percent of employees consider dealing with a supervisor the most stressful part of their jobs,[6] and 85 percent of workers who quit their jobs report doing so because they are unhappy with their boss.[7] Recent surveys report that most U.S. workers feel worse about their jobs than ever before. The cost of such employee disengagement is $300 billion a year in lost productivity.[8]

Despite these distressing numbers, there is good news: Effective and ethical communication can create a more positive, productive, and (yes) happy work environment, reduce interpersonal conflicts, and help employees deal with work-related problems more effectively.

Superior–Subordinate Relationships

In **superior–subordinate relationships**, the superior (supervisor) has formal authority over the productivity and behavior of subordinates (workers).[9] Superiors direct activities, authorize projects, interpret policies, and assess subordinates' performance. Subordinates provide information about themselves, about coworkers, and about the progress of their work as well as "what needs to be done and how it can be done" to supervisors.[11]

Poor superior–subordinate relationships negatively affect productivity, job satisfaction, and employee retention. Recall some of the statistics presented on the previous page. In addition to considering interactions with a supervisor the most stressful part of their jobs, the majority of employees who quit their jobs do so because they are unhappy with their boss.

For supervisors, success largely depends on their ability to establish trust with subordinates, convey immediacy and caring, and give useful feedback about work and progress.[12] Not surprisingly, organizations that

Criteria for a
SATISFYING
Coworker Relationship[13]

have happy employees, strong organizational health, empathetic leaders, and even a social mission, outperform their peers.[14] Thus some superior–subordinate relationships are formal and distant while others flourish in informal, friendly, and nonthreatening interactions without sacrificing respect and productivity.

Coworker Relationships

Interactions among people who have little or no official authority over one another but who must work together to accomplish the goals of an organization are known as **coworker relationships**.

A coworker who won't share important information or who has a different work style can derail *your* performance. A colleague who does a poor job or is uncooperative won't be respected. How you would answer the questions in the box "Criteria for Satisfying Coworker Relationships" on this page? Satisfying coworker relationships make the difference between looking forward to and dreading another day at work.

Customer Relationships

The success of any business or organization depends on effective and ethical communication with customers and clients, particularly in the United States, where the average company loses half its customers within five years.[15] **Customer relationships** are interactions between someone communicating on behalf of an organization and an individual who is external to the organization. This category of relationships includes the way colleges treat students, the way medical professionals take care of patients, the way police officers respond to crime victims, and the way corporations communicate with shareholders.

Unfortunately, some employees lack appropriate training or have inaccurate assumptions about customer service. One study checked thousands of applications for grocery store workers and identified several false assumptions about customer service.[16] Almost half the applicants

> **"Good relationships with coworkers are the primary source of most job satisfaction."**
> Robert Longely[17]

Does *customer relationship* describe the interaction between teachers and students? Or are these relationships more like *superior–subordinate* or *coworker relationships*?

Organizational Culture Theory

Most workplaces are organized in a structured hierarchy that establishes levels of authority and decision-making power. That hierarchy may influence who talks to whom, about what, and in what manner. In large organizations, employees are often expected to convey information and voice concerns to their immediate supervisor. Only when a problem cannot be remedied at that level do employees have the "right" to speak to the next person up the hierarchy.

In general, the more levels within an organization's structure, the more likely it is that information will be distorted as communication goes up or down the "chain of command." The accuracy of information can be reduced by up to 20 percent every time a message passes through a different level.[18]

In addition to an organizational structure, every organization has a unique culture that influences member communication. According to Michael Pacanowsky and Nick O'Donnell-Trujillo, **Organizational Culture Theory** describes the ways in which shared symbols, beliefs, values, and norms affect the behavior of people working in and with an organization.[19] For example, one company may expect their employees to wear suits, spend much of their time working silently in their offices, arrive and leave promptly, and get together in small groups to socialize only after hours.

Another company may encourage a less formal climate in which employee interaction is highly encouraged.

Just as cultural beliefs, norms, and traditions change when you travel from one country to another, organizational culture can vary from job to job. Customs in an organizational culture include personal, celebratory, and ritual behaviors (responding promptly to e-mail, celebrating birthdays, attending department meetings), social behaviors (politeness, thanking customers, supporting worried colleagues), and communication behaviors (retelling legendary stories, using in-house-only jargon, giving colleagues nicknames).

Organizations also have subcultures. An **organizational subculture** consists of a group of people who engage in behaviors and share values that are, in part, different from that of the larger organizational culture. For example, the marketing department in an organization may develop different customs than the accounting department across the hall. The regional sales office in Texas may have different traditions than the Chicago office.

How would you describe the organizational culture being depicted in this photo of Google employees?

Classic Organizational Hierarchy

BOARD OF DIRECTORS
Makes policy and key decisions

UPPER MANAGEMENT
Senior executives who implement board policies and decisions

MIDDLE MANAGEMENT
Managers who link upper management to supervisors and their workers

LOWER MANAGEMENT
Supervisors or team leaders who have regular and direct contact with workers

SUPPORT STAFF
Secretaries, administrative assistants, project directors

FRONTLINE WORKERS
People who do the fundamental tasks of the organization

believed that customers should follow company policies if they want help and should be told when they are wrong. Approximately 10 percent of would-be employees would not help a customer if it was not part of their jobs and would not volunteer to assist a customer unless the customer asked for help.

Effective employees understand that, in a typical customer relationship, the customer has several basic communication needs.[20] First, the customer or client needs to feel welcome. Many retail staff members are trained to greet customers the moment they enter a store or business. Second, customers need enough information to make a decision or solve a problem regarding a service or product. Thus, sales and customer service representatives must be product experts who offer information and ask insightful questions. Finally, customers need to be treated with respect, especially because they have the power to take their business elsewhere and may tell others to do the same.

COMMUNICATION IN *ACTION*

Is the Customer Always Right?

Dealing with dissatisfied and angry customers can be difficult and stressful, especially when customers with legitimate complaints behave in inappropriate ways. When a customer is rude or disrespectful, you may become angry. Expressing your anger, however, may only escalate the conflict. The Better Business Bureau points out that even when a customer isn't happy with the solution, an employee who listens and attempts to help will be perceived as cooperative.[21] The following strategies can help calm an unruly customer and promote effective problem solving:[22]

- Don't take a complaint personally.
- Listen attentively and ask questions.
- Try to separate the issues from the emotions. A rude customer may have legitimate complaints and may only be expressing well-founded frustrations inappropriately.
- Make statements that show you empathize: "I can understand why you're upset."
- Share information or explain the reasons for a decision but do not argue with a customer.
- If the company is at fault, acknowledge it and apologize.
- Ask the customer how she or he would like the problem to be resolved.

Professional Communication Challenges

9.2 *Apply appropriate strategies for dealing with office rumors and gossip, workplace romances, sexual harassment, working with friends, and leaving a job.*

Nigel didn't want anyone at work to know that he was dating Jin, his coworker. Unfortunately, his officemate overheard him talking with Jin on the phone and told several other people in the office about the relationship. Soon there was a buzz about it. Nigel was worried that their boss would disapprove and that their coworkers would tease or harass them.

In this section, we discuss several of the tensions you may experience in the workplace that can limit advancement opportunities and affect your overall satisfaction with a job. Specifically, we examine office rumors and gossip, workplace romances, sexual harassment, working with friends, and quitting or losing a job. But before doing that, assess how well you usually communicate on-the-job in the Know Thy Self feature on the next page.

Office Rumors and Gossip

Whereas a **rumor** is an unverified story or statement about the facts of a situation, **gossip** is a type of rumor that focuses on the private, personal, or even scandalous affairs of other people. Nicholas DiFonzo of the Rochester Institute of Technology describes gossip as a rumor that is "more social in nature, usually personal and usually derogatory." When spreading "gossip, truth is beside the point. Spreading gossip is about fun."[23]

Most of us listen to rumors because we want to have as much information as everyone else. Typically, we spread gossip because we want to be perceived as "in the know."[24] In one survey of office workers, more than 90 percent of employees admitted to engaging in gossip.[25] The same study also found that after learning information about a colleague that was intended to be secret, 75 percent of employees revealed that secret to at least two other employees that same day.

The Quality of On-the-Job Communication

In previous sections of this chapter we recommended strategies for effective, on-the-job communication at three different levels: supervisor, colleague, and customer/client. Review these strategies again in terms of your current or a previous job. Keep in mind that a "job" can be paid or volunteer work, can be full-time or part-time, and can be as significant as a major career opportunity or as short-lived as a summer or after-school job.

Rate the Quality of Communication on the Job

	Always	Often	Sometimes	Rarely	Never
Boss: Does your boss (or you as the boss)_____					
1. behave in a consistent and predictable manner?					
2. keep promises and tell the truth?					
3. share and/or explain decision-making?					
4. demonstrate concern for employees?					
Colleagues: When interacting with colleagues, do you _____					
1. work well with your colleagues?					
2. devote time and resources to help them?					
3. share information openly with colleagues?					
4. treat each colleague with respect?					
Customers/Clients: When interacting with customers or clients, do you _____					
1. listen attentively and ask questions?					
2. show that you care and empathize?					
3. share accurate information?					
4. apologize (if appropriate)?					

Review your responses in each of the three areas. Are most of them in the Always or Often boxes? Or are more of them in the other three columns? Depending on your answers, you may find that you work very well with colleagues, but not as well with your boss. You may have a good relationship with your boss but only a fair relationship with customers or clients. Or you may work in a highly competitive environment where colleague cooperation is rare. Based on your answers, develop a plan for improving how you interact with others that will also improve your overall productivity and job satisfaction.

While rumors and gossip have the potential to be harmful, they can also serve an important social function. Consultant Annette Simmons observes, "a certain amount of small talk—sharing small details of your life—helps people feel closer to co-workers. It is what humanizes the workplace and helps people bond."[26] However, unchecked or malicious gossip can have serious consequences. Private and potentially embarrassing information, even if untrue, can damage your professional credibility. Divulging company secrets can get you fired. Time spent gossiping is time not spent doing your job.

An organization can take measures that prevent the *need* for gossip by keeping employees well informed.[27] For example, when a company is purchased by a larger corporation, many employees worry about losing their jobs and spend hours talking about who will stay and who will be asked to leave. If no personnel cutbacks are planned, employees should be told. When cutbacks are anticipated, an organization should inform everyone about how and when those decisions will be made—this way, everyone will have more accurate information.

Strategies for MANAGING OFFICE GOSSIP

▶ Do not spread malicious rumors. If you don't know if the information is accurate or if someone else will be hurt if the information is shared, don't repeat it.

▶ Evaluate the reliability of a rumor or gossip by asking questions and checking facts.

▶ When others gossip, change the subject, tell them you prefer not to discuss certain topics, or say that you're too busy to talk at the moment.

▶ Consider the potential consequences of divulging confidential information or spreading a rumor.

▶ Before self-disclosing to a co-worker, assume that your secret will be told to others.

▶ If you believe that gossip has created a serious problem, talk to someone with more power or influence.[28]

When organizations learn that misinformation is making its way through the rumor mill, they should address and correct it quickly before any more harm is done.

In some workplaces, malicious gossip infects the workplace and creates a climate of hostility and distrust.

Workplace Romances

Workplace romances occur "between two members of an organization where sexual attraction is present, affection is communicated, and both members recognize the relationship to be something more than just professional and platonic."[29] Most of us have heard about, seen, or personally experienced a romance that began and blossomed at work. Not surprisingly the statistics vary (some folks won't kiss and tell). They indicate that about 40 to 60 percent of employees have been involved in at least one workplace romance.[30]

Although some workplace romances result in long-lasting relationships and marriages, it can be difficult to manage the blurred distinction between private and professional lives. On the other hand, the successful marriages of Melinda and Bill Gates, Ellen DeGeneres and Portia de Rossi, as well as Michelle and Barack Obama began as workplace romances.

> **Approximately one-third of all romantic relationships begin in the workplace.**
>
> Bill Leonard[31]

A public display of affection in the workplace may be viewed as unprofessional and may make other colleagues feel uncomfortable. Coworkers may also suspect that a romantic partner receives preferential treatment. Romantically involved couples may find it difficult to separate issues at work from personal issues that arise after work. And if a romantic relationship ends, the professional relationship may become strained or awkward.

President Barack Obama and First Lady Michelle Obama demonstrate how professional relationships can evolve into workplace romances that eventually become long-lasting marriages. In this photo, President Obama puts on a scary face to mimic a character in the book he is reading to a group of children. Mrs. Obama laughs with pleasure.

MEDIATED COMMUNICATION IN *ACTION*

Are You Tweeting Away Your Career?

Do you send and respond to personal e-mails at work? Do you tweet, text, or visit friends on Facebook while being paid to do a job? If your answer is *yes*, check the rules where you work before doing it again.

According to a study commissioned by Robert Half Technology, an information technology staffing firm, "54% of companies ban workers from using social networking sites like Twitter, Facebook, LinkedIn and others while on the job. . . . Only 10 percent of the 1,400 surveyed companies said they allowed employees full access to social networks during work hours."[32]

Why such strict rules? Nucleus Research, an IT research firm, provides part of the answer: "nearly half of all online workers use Facebook at the office and one in every 33 employees has built their entire profile during work hours." The firm also reports that companies allowing unlimited employee "access to Facebook in the workplace lose an average of 1.5% in total employee productivity."[33]

The problem of on-the-job social networking involves more than concerns about employee productivity. What if employees use social media to send discriminatory statements, racial slurs, or sexually explicit messages to coworkers or clients? What if employees reveal, either intentionally or unintentionally, confidential company information? What should a company do if an information technology worker reports finding child pornography on a company computer they're servicing? Employees and corporate officers may be fired, the company may be sued, and/or law enforcement officials may prosecute.[34]

> Before deciding to redesign your Facebook page or get involved in a controversial political debate online, make sure you know the "rules."

Most companies and organizations have policies or guidelines to restrain social networking at work. At the same time, they may permit certain employees—depending on their job—to use social media during work hours. In either case, more and more companies are monitoring how you use computers at work.

Half the romantic relationships begun in the workplace also end there.[35] Yet, attitudes about workplace romances are changing, particularly for millennial employees. In a Workplace Options survey, 84 percent of millennials said they'd date a coworker compared to 46 percent of Generation X (thirty to forty-six) and only 29 percent of baby boomers (forty-seven to sixty-six).[36]

Sexual Harassment

Workplace romances should not be confused with sexual harassment. Romance in the workplace involves two individuals who communicate a desire for a close, personal relationship, whereas **sexual harassment** is characterized by unwanted sexual advances for sexual favors, inappropriate verbal or physical conduct of a sexual nature, or an intimidating, hostile, or offensive work environment.[37]

Sexual harassment is rarely an isolated incident. Usually, it is a pattern of offensive or unwelcome behavior that takes place over a period of time. In many instances, sexual harassment involves a supervisor or colleague using power to demand sexual favors—from coercing a subordinate to perform sexually in order to guarantee her or his job to making sex a prerequisite for securing a promotion, a higher salary, or extra time off. Sexual harassment may also include offensive communication in the form of e-mails containing sexually explicit messages and jokes or inappropriate comments made directly to a coworker.

In some cases, office romances that end badly result in sexual harassment. For example, the slighted or rejected person might seek "revenge" against the "ex" by posting compromising photographs on Instagram, Facebook, or even via attachment through company e-mail. The victim will likely end up too humiliated and offended to work productively with colleagues. The victim may also end up with grounds for a sexual harassment suit against the other person.

Consider, for instance, the recently exposed cases of sexual harassment in the U.S. military: In 2013 "the Pentagon released a report estimating that 26,000 service members were sexually assaulted last year, up from 19,000 in 2010." The three premier military academies (Army, Navy, and Air Force) reported 89 cases of sexual assault in 2012, a 23 percent increase from the year before. More than 60 percent of the assaults were reported at the Air Force Academy in Colorado Springs.[38]

Victims of sexual harassment often experience "decreased work performance, anxiety, depression, self-blame, anger, feelings of helplessness, fear of further or escalating harassment, and fear of reporting the incident."[39] Most

---

COMMUNICATION&CULTURE

DIFFERING VIEWS ON SEXUAL HARASSMENT

Identifying sexual harassment is complicated by the fact that men and women perceive similar behavior differently. Thus, women may regard a sexually explicit joke in the office as harassment, whereas men may view the joke as harmless. However, both men and women judge overt behavior, such as demands for sexual favors, as harassment. According to the Equal Employment Opportunity Commission, approximately 15,000 complaints of sexual harassment are filed every year.[40] Thirteen percent of these are filed by men.[41]

Have you or someone you know experienced the following behaviors in the workplace?

- touching, leaning over, cornering, or pinching
- sexually suggestive looks or comments
- letters, telephone calls, or materials of a sexual nature
- pressure for dates
- sexual teasing, jokes, remarks, or questions

Now ask yourself this question: Are any of these experiences examples of sexual harassment? A large study asked these same questions to more than 8,000 federal government employees; the results indicated that women are more likely than males to view all of these behaviors as sexually harassing. Regardless, no one should have to tolerate a sexually hostile work environment.[42]

employees claim that they would immediately address or report harassment to Human Resources or other appropriate groups within the company. However, research reveals that, when confronted with this situation, many people feel uncomfortable and fail to report the behavior.[43]

To encourage victims to come forth, most organizations have established policies against sexual harassment as well as grievance procedures for reporting such behavior—if for no other reason than to avoid costly lawsuits. If you believe that you are the victim of sexual harassment, keep in mind that complaints are taken more seriously when brought to the attention of management immediately.[44]

Workplace Friendships

Coworker friendships may be both personal as well as professional. Mixing personal and professional relationships, however, can be difficult: You want your friend to like you, but you also need coworkers, superiors, and subordinates to respect you; you want approval from your friend, but you also must make objective decisions in the workplace; you hope for professional success but not at the expense of your friends' advancement.

STRAINS on FRIENDSHIPS[45]

- Equal status in a friendship may be compromised by inequality at work.
- The need to withhold confidential work information may clash with the need for openness in a friendship.
- Collaboration may be impossible when one friend has more decision-making power at work.
- The friendship may be damaged by negative feedback given at work.
- Public expressions of friendship may need to be minimized in the workplace.

STRAINS on PROFESSIONAL RELATIONSHIPS

- A friendship may make it difficult to manage unequal levels of power at work.
- It may be difficult to handle sensitive work information with discretion.
- Personal knowledge and feelings about a friend may compromise objectivity at work.
- A friend may be held to a higher performance standard at work.
- Socializing may adversely affect productivity and the quality of performance at work.

In *Organizational Communication*, communication scholar Daniel Modaff and his colleagues recommend that you seek your most important relationships outside the workplace and that, if you do have a friend relationship at work, you should be prepared to manage the consequences.[46] Telling a best friend that he has not met expectations on a work team can be difficult and even impossible if you want to preserve the friendship. At the same time, letting a friend get away with less-than-excellent work can destroy the morale of a group and put your reputation and leadership at risk.

Leaving a Job

According to the Bureau of Labor Statistics, before the age of thirty-two, the average American has had nine jobs and one-third of workers predict that they will probably change jobs again within five years.[47] There are many reasons for leaving a job or changing careers. Whatever your reason, try to depart on as good terms as possible and handle your resignation or exit with professionalism and courtesy. Just as you want to make a good first impression when interviewing and beginning a new job, it is equally important to leave a positive impression when leaving a job.

Even when a resignation is the result of dissatisfaction with the job or a poor relationship with a boss or coworkers, leaving on good terms is important. After you resign, a

LEAVING YOUR JOB
Best Practices[48]

- Follow company policies and procedures when resigning.
- Inform your immediate supervisor of your plans first.
- Resign in person but also write a brief resignation letter.
- Give the appropriate advance notice.
- Phrase explanations positively.

Difficult Behavior at Work

Supervisors and coworkers who are difficult to work with can have a negative impact on your ability to do your job and make it difficult to enjoy what you're doing. They engage in counterproductive behaviors, such as chronic lateness, poor performance, derogatory e-mailing, persistent negativity, resisting needed change, shooting down new ideas, complaining constantly, and neglecting commitments, as well as more serious forms of behavior, such as harassment, work sabotage, and even physical abuse.[49]

Failure to minimize or remedy such behaviors can create a work environment that takes its toll on everyone. In his book *Dealing with Difficult People*, Hal Plotkin recommends a six-step approach for providing feedback to such people and helping them realize their full potential:[50]

1. *Identify specific successes and failures.* Rather than saying, "You're always late," state the exact number of times the person has been late during a defined period of time. Be equally specific when offering praise.
2. *Stop talking and start listening.* Use all types of listening—hear, understand, remember, interpret, evaluate, and appropriately respond—to make sure you fully grasp the other person's point of view.
3. *Discuss the implications of behavior.* Help others understand the consequences of their behavior—in both organizational and personal terms.
4. *Link past accomplishments to needed change.* Point out how the traits that have led to past successes can be applied to areas that need improvement.
5. *Agree on an action plan.* Work *together* to come up with a plan that has specific ideas or steps, clear timetables, and realistic standards for success.
6. *Follow up.* Stay engaged and set up times to meet often and regularly. Use follow-up sessions to help the other person deal with problems, provide personal support, and offer praise.

Finally, be aware of how you define the problem. If you refer to *people* as difficult, you are shifting attention from what they *do* to who they *are*. Rather, identify their *behavior* as the problem, and then maybe you can do something about it.[51]

supervisor or human resources manager may request an **exit interview**. Organizations gather information in exit interviews to develop strategies for retaining other employees and to improve the workplace for those who remain. Because you don't know how this information will be used or whether it will be treated confidentially, remain calm and communicate a positive attitude. Focus on issues, not people. An "exit interview is not the time to burn bridges. Most industries are small, and bad behavior is not something you want people remembering about you."[52]

Sometimes, leaving a job is not a decision you make by choice. As a stressful event, job loss ranks right up there with a death in your family, divorce, and serious illness. Job loss can have a profound effect on your emotional well-being. Typically, most people experience a resulting cycle of denial, anger, frustration, and eventually adaptation.[53] If you lose your job and your anxiety seems out of control, go back to the section on communication apprehension in Chapter 2, "Understanding Your Self". The relaxation strategies recommended there—cognitive restructuring, visualization, and systematic desensitization—can help you build confidence and reduce stress.

BE PROACTIVE

- [ ] Did you discuss the details of any unemployment benefits (e.g., severance, health insurance, life insurance) with a human resources officer?
- [ ] Did you honestly and objectively assess the reasons why you lost your job?
- [ ] Have you asked yourself whether you want to stay in the same field?
- [ ] Is it, perhaps, time for a career change?
- [ ] Is there a skill you need to learn to become an indispensable employee?

USE YOUR COMMUNICATION SKILLS

- [ ] Have you networked with family members, friends, and colleagues to connect with potential employers?
- [ ] Have you consulted employment agencies, checked the classifieds, and surfed the Internet for available jobs?
- [ ] Do you know the dos and don'ts of effective job interviewing?

CRAFT A PERSUASIVE MESSAGE

- [ ] Does your résumé highlight your marketable skills?
- [ ] Does your résumé reflect your knowledge of recent economic and industry trends?
- [ ] Does your cover letter express how ready, willing, and able you are to give 100 percent to a new position?

Workplace and Job Interviews

9.3 *Practice effective strategies and skills to prepare for, participate in, and follow up after workplace and job interviews.*

When you hear the phrase "job interview," what comes to mind? Most people think of a job interview as one of the last steps in the job application process. However, interviews do not end once you get a job.

Types of Workplace Interviews

You will encounter several types of interviews in the workplace, including selection interviews, appraisal interviews, information-gathering interviews, disciplinary interviews, and exit interviews. (To learn more about the purpose and unique function of each type of work place interview, review the table on the next page.)

In the world of work, an **interview** is an interpersonal interaction between two parties in which at least one party has a predetermined purpose and uses questions and answers to share or obtain information, to solve a problem, and/or to influence the other.[54]

Although a traditional job interview (a form of selection interview) can be a stressful communication situation, a good interview can land you the job of your dreams. Unfortunately, a poor interview can result in a major disappointment and the loss of a promising career opportunity.

In terms of specific communication skills, how is this television interview similar or different from other types of workplace interviews?

In the following sections, we focus on the communication skills needed to prepare for, participate in, and follow up on a job interview.

Before the Job Interview

In *What Color Is Your Parachute?*, the best-selling annual guidebook for career changers and job seekers, Richard

The saying that you never get a *second* chance to make a first impression is especially true in job interviews.

Bolles recounts the story of an interview between an IBM recruiter and a college senior. The recruiter asked the student, "What does IBM stand for?" The student didn't know and thus ended the interview.[55]

As with any important communication situation, a successful job interview requires careful preparation. In a survey of the most pre-interview mistakes, senior executives identified three major errors: (1) having little or no knowledge of the company, (2) being unprepared to discuss relevant skills and experiences, and (3) being unprepared to discuss career plans and goals.[56] Before going to an interview, make sure you research the organization, assess your own strengths and weaknesses, and practice interviewing.

Research the Organization Learn as much as you can about the organization. Begin with a thorough search of the organization's website; it will tell you a great deal about the organization's mission, products and services, financial status, and achievements. If the website includes information about key employees, read about their backgrounds and job responsibilities. See if there's information about the person who will be interviewing you. Look for stories about the company or organization on news websites.

Given that other good candidates will be researching relevant websites, go one step further. Contact the company or organization directly and request or download documents that they make available to the public, such as brochures, catalogs, newsletters, and annual reports. If you know current or former employees, ask them about the organization. The more you know, the easier it is to explain how you can make a positive contribution. Research may also uncover reasons

Types of Workplace Interviews	Purpose	Process
Selection interview	To evaluate and choose a candidate for a job or promotion	Potential employers assess whether your knowledge, maturity, personality, attitude, communication skills, and work record match the job.
Appraisal interview	To evaluate an employee's job performance	Employers assess an employee's job performance, identify training needs, and provide motivation through constructive feedback.
Information-Gathering Interview	To obtain facts, opinions, data, feelings, attitudes, and reactions	Employer and employee analyze important issues and try to solve identified problems.
Disciplinary interview	To identify, discuss, and/or correct problematic behaviors	Employer assesses why problems are occurring and how, if at all, the employee can change behavior and resolve the problem.
Exit interviews	To learn why an employee is leaving and whether problems contributed to that decision	Employer provides closure for the departing employee and identifies ways to improve other employees' satisfaction and retention.

you don't want to work for that organization, ranging from a company's policy on unions or political issues to its health benefits or pension options.

Assess Your Strengths and Weaknesses Ron, a thirty-two-year-old man with sales experience, was preparing to interview for a sales director position at a midsized company. He found a story on the Internet reporting that the company was restructuring its product pricing. Although the job description did not mention needing experience in this area, Ron decided to make a point of saying that his last job involved

reevaluating product pricing. Using the information he unearthed about the organization helped Ron demonstrate why he was the best candidate for the position.

Be prepared to explain your weaknesses as well as your strengths. Plan how to explain any employment gaps on your résumé, several jobs in a short period of time, or the lack of a skill specifically mentioned in the job description. The time to develop an acceptable answer to such reasonable concerns is not in the middle of an interview.

For example, Luke quit his computer animation job when his first child was

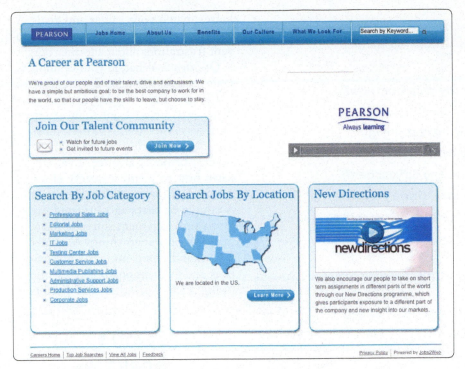

In addition to telling you about an organization's mission, products, services, financial status, and achievements, a website gives you a feel for the company's organizational culture and career opportunities.

born and chose to be a stay-at-home father. When he decided, four years later, to reenter the workplace, he knew he would have to demonstrate knowledge of current trends in his field. After careful consideration, he developed an answer to satisfy interviewers who might question the four-year gap on his résumé. He would tell potential employers that he'd kept up with industry trends by taking online animation courses regularly, and doing freelance animation work for the marketing departments of several not-for-profit organizations. He would also say that his experience as a father and as a freelance animator has helped his "design eye" mature and grow more sophisticated. The bottom line is, whatever your weakness might be, don't assume that the interviewer hasn't noticed it on the application or résumé. If the interviewer asks you about it, be ready with a thoughtful response.

Practice Interviewing A job interview can be a stressful communication situation, and you have limited time to make a good impression. Doing a mock interview *before* the real thing will make a difference. In addition to the list of

> ## Identify what you can bring to the job that will promote the organization's goals.

common and standard interview questions presented in this section, create an additional list comprising questions you might be asked about your own expertise. Then practice answering them.

Because the interview will probably take place in a meeting room or an office, sit at your desk or a table and practice reciting your answers out loud and confidently. Then, ask a few friends or family members to interview you. They can give you feedback on the quality of your answers and may suggest some additional questions to consider.

During the Job Interview

An interview is a golden opportunity for both you and the interviewer. The interviewer wants to learn more about

you, and you can learn more about the job and the organization while creating a positive impression. The extent to which you accomplish these goals depends on how well you respond to questions and present yourself.

Standard Interview Questions Interviewers often ask one or more of five standard types of questions listed in the figure on the next page. As we explained in Chapter 7 "Understanding Interpersonal Relationships," a closed-ended question requires only a short answer, such as *yes* or *no*. An open-ended question requires or encourages a more detailed answer. A **hypothetical question** describes a set of circumstances and asks how you would respond to those circumstances. A **leading question** suggests or implies the response the questioner wants to hear or is posed as a challenge to see if and why you disagree. A **probing question** is used to follow up another question and/or a previous response by encouraging clarification and elaboration.

Answering Interview Questions Regardless of the type of question, you must know how to formulate an appropriate response for every question asked of you. Consider, for example, how the following answers to two commonly asked interview questions illustrate the differences between an effective and an inappropriate response.

Question 1: Why did you leave your last job?

Inappropriate Response: My boss and I just didn't get along. She expected me to do work that was really her responsibility. They didn't pay me enough to do my job and someone else's. When I complained, nobody did anything about it.

Analysis: While honest, this is not a very effective or flattering response. Interviewers often ask questions like these to determine whether you had problems with a former employer and whether you will be just as troublesome in a new job. In this example, the interviewer could conclude that the applicant doesn't work well with others, resists doing required work, complains a lot, and evaluates work only in terms of a paycheck. A better approach is to focus on why a new job would offer more desirable opportunities and

COMMON Interview Questions[57]

1. Briefly, tell me about yourself.
2. What do you hope to be doing five years from now?
3. Where do you hope to be in ten years?
4. In terms of this job, what is your greatest strength?
5. What, in your opinion, is your greatest weakness?
6. What motivates you to work hard and do your best?
7. How well do you deal with pressure? Give an example.
8. What are the two or three characteristics you are seeking in a job?
9. Describe a major problem you encountered in a previous job. How did you deal with it?
10. What kind of relationship should be established between a supervisor and subordinates?
11. Why did you choose to pursue this particular career?
12. Why did you leave your last job(s)?
13. How can you contribute to our company?
14. How do you evaluate or determine success?
15. Given the fact that we have other applicants, why should we hire you?

STANDARD Interview Questions and Examples

Closed-ended question.	Are you able to work on weekends?
Open-ended question.	What do you view as the most significant challenges facing this industry over the next few years?
Hypothetical question.	How would you handle an employee who does good work, but even after being warned, continues to arrive late?
Leading question.	Why is the ability to work well in a group is just as important as the ability to perform routine technical tasks?
Probing question.	Could you explain what you mean by a "difficult client"?

better match your values and goals. A job interview is not the time or place to vent frustrations about a former boss.

Question 2: What, in your opinion, is your greatest job-related weakness?

Effective Response: My natural tendency is to focus on one thing at a time until it's completed. However, most of my jobs have required me to manage several projects at once. I've had to learn how to juggle a variety of tasks, particularly when things get hectic. A couple of years ago I started using project management software to track projects and keep things organized. This has helped me shift attention back and forth among projects without losing track of priorities and deadlines.

Don't hesitate to ask for clarification of a question before responding to it.

Analysis: This answer is effective and strategic. When answering a question about a weakness, figure out how to acknowledge it while simultaneously demonstrating how you learned to deal with or overcome it. As a result, you transform the weakness into an example of your problem-solving abilities. But, don't exaggerate. When asked about your weakness, don't say, "I work too hard." We all do that. Working hard is usually considered a strength.

Addressing Inappropriate Interview Questions Federal and state laws prohibit discrimination in hiring. Therefore, most interviewers take care not to ask questions about race or ethnicity, gender, marital status, religion, sexual orientation, or disabilities. If you are asked such questions, however, consider the context in which they are asked, what information you feel comfortable revealing, and what your personal communication style is. These

ETHICAL COMMUNICATION

Tell No Lies

Approximately 20 to 45 percent of applicants lie on a résumé or in a job interview.[58] Another study reports that 11 percent of applicants do not tell the truth about why they left a previous job, and 9 percent lie about their education and responsibilities in previous jobs.[59] Not only is lying to a prospective employer unethical, but it can backfire and have serious personal consequences.

Most organizations have become much more rigorous when screening applicants. Private detective Fay Faron explains that many organizations conduct extensive background checks to avoid a lawsuit and ensure the safety of customers.[60] Count on being carefully screened, having your references checked, and being investigated for a criminal background. Furthermore, if your lie is discovered, your application will be rejected or, if you're already hired, you will be fired. A survey conducted by an executive search firm revealed that 95 percent of employers would reject applicants who lied about a college degree and that 80 percent would not hire someone who falsified previous job titles.[61]

Your goal is more than getting a job, it is getting a job that is right for you.[62] If you have to falsify your credentials or work experience, you are probably not qualified for the job. Moreover, the consequences of lying can be long lasting. If your lie is discovered, it can ruin your reputation for years to come.

For instance, a hiring manager who asks whether you plan to have children may simply want to talk about the company's excellent parenting and child care benefits or brag about his or her own newborn child. These types of questions are often asked out of simple curiosity or an effort to engage in social conversation.

The last recommendation to consider during an interview: in addition to preparing to answer questions, prepare to ask some questions as well (see the list of sample questions below). Many interviewers assess your knowledge, interest, and communication skills based on the kinds of questions you ask. Use this opportunity to enhance your credibility and to learn more about the job, its employees, and the organization.

Remember that interviews help employers decide whether you are the right person for a job, not just from your answers but also from the way you speak, ask questions, and behave during the interview. You are being observed from the moment you arrive until the time you leave the building. In fact, it's not unusual for an interviewer to ask receptionists or office administrators for their impressions of you.

considerations can help you determine the most effective approach to fielding such questions. Review the following list of questions that might be asked during an interview. Which ones are inappropriate and why?

- Are you single or married?
- What does your partner do?
- Do you plan to have children?
- How many more years do you plan to work before retiring?
- Are there religious holidays you will want to take off from work?
- Do you have any disabilities?
- What country are your parents or grandparents from?

All of the above questions are inappropriate for a job interview.[63]

Recognize that you have the right to refuse to answer any question you believe is inappropriate. But, before assuming the question is inappropriate, assess its purpose. Then respond to as tactfully as possible so as not to embarrass the interviewer, and redirect the interview to a discussion of your qualifications. For example, "Do you have children?" may reflect the interviewer's concern that a busy parent won't work the number of hours necessary to demonstrate a full commitment to the job. An appropriate response might be, "If you're asking whether I can balance a demanding job with family obligations, I have always effectively done so in the past."

Furthermore, don't assume that the interviewer intends to discriminate.

Questions TO ASK
During an Interview:[64]

- Can you tell me more about the specific, everyday responsibilities of this position?

- What, in your opinion, are the major challenges facing the organization?

- What is the most important characteristic you are looking for in an employee for this position?

- How would you describe the culture of your organization?

- How will success be measured for this position?

- What other people or departments will I be working with?

workplace and job interviews

173

Interviewing Pitfalls and Best Practices Just about every book, article, website, counseling session, and seminar addressing job-interviewing skills provides a list of dos and don'ts. Each list is based on survey responses from company executives, human resource directors, and professional interviewers. In this section we organize and present the most common dos and don'ts from among these lists.

Suppose you get an interview for a job you especially want. You're well prepared and are sure you aced the interview. Yet, you're not called back for a follow-up meeting. You don't get the job. Before blaming the interviewer, remember that there may have been other very well qualified candidates, that someone may have had an inside track, or that there was too much distance between your salary expectations and theirs.

In a survey conducted by Northwestern University, 153 companies were asked why they rejected job applicants.[65] Of the 50 reasons identified, almost half were related to lack of communication skills and failure to create a positive impression. One of the most common mistakes made by applicants is talking too much. If you talk *too* much, you may bore your listeners or may appear insensitive to the time limits of an interview.

According to Richard Bolles, when it is your turn to speak or answer a question in an interview, try "not to speak any longer than two minutes at a time if you want to make the best impression."[66] Generally, it's better to leave interviewers hungry for more information about you rather than to overwhelm them with information.

Certainly we could conclude this chapter by listing dozens of Do-Not-Do interviewing commandments. Instead we decided to flip the coin and make lemonade out of lemons. The table to the left presents *best* interviewing practices in four competency categories: (1) Appearance (2) Attitude, (3) Expression, (4) Behavior.[67]

After the Job Interview

When you walk out of an interview, the job application process isn't over. Now it's time for follow up. As one counselor put it, "Lack of follow up = Lack of interest." Send a brief note thanking the interviewer for her or his time and consideration. The note should refer to the key issues discussed in the interview. Re-emphasize that you can perform the job and help the organization meet its goals. A brief but well-written letter or, if appropriate, an e-mail or text message, reinforces that you have a professional approach to and enthusiasm for the job.

Keep in mind that you can make an excellent impression during an interview and still not be hired because you may have been one of several outstanding candidates. Regardless of whether you are selected or not, view each interview as an opportunity to practice your communication skills.

Interviewing Competencies	Effective Interviewing Practices
1. **Appearance:** You appear professional, likable, and appropriate for the interview and job 	• Wear business-appropriate attire, dress up, not down • Make sure you are well groomed • Wear conservative jewelry, make-up, and accessories • Carry an appropriate purse and/or briefcase • Stand and sit tall without being stiff
2. **Attitude:** You communicate a positive, confident, and professional demeanor and temperament 	• Pay attention and actively listen • Show genuine interest and enthusiasm • Demonstrate confidence and good character • Do not blame or criticize former employers • Be polite and well mannered • Focus on the job, not yourself • Do not appear evasive or make excuses
3. **Expression:** You convey your ideas and opinions clearly and persuasively 	• Establish and maintain direct eye contact • Answer questions directly and succinctly • Use grammatically correct language • Use a pleasant and expressive voice • Use job-related terminology • Ask an appropriate number of questions • Do not talk too much • Smile!
4. **Behavior:** Your actions and mannerisms are appropriate and professional 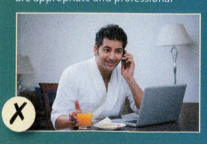	• Be on time; get there early • Do not bring a drink or food with you to the interview • Turn off your cell phone • Shake hands firmly and with confidence • Avoid frequent glances at your watch or a clock • Sit in an alert, forward-leaning posture • Behave and dress professionally for a video interview using technology such as Skype or Facetime.

What *Not* to Do During Job Interviews

The "digi-sphere" has made it possible to interview job candidates anywhere and anytime and to send and receive a résumé or a cover letter swiftly. But it has also caused a generation of people to nearly abandon formality in language and self-presentation. Just because "tweeting" or "Facebooking" speech such as "How u? Whatevs, and LOL" is so commonly spoken by so many—in class, on the road, or in bedtime pajamas—does not mean such speech should be used in formal situations, least of all in a job interview.

In a recent poll surveying hiring managers, about 75 percent reported that many job candidates, mainly of the millennial generation, fail to wear appropriate interview attire. Even if the interview is conducted via Skype or Facetime, the interviewer can still see you. Business attire is expected. Other reports describe two additional blunders: failing to remove "compromising content" from a job candidate's social media sites before the interview and failing to research the prospective position adequately.[68]

There have also been reports of interviewees overusing slang and laid-back language; some have even engaged in nontraditional interviewing behaviors such as:

- bringing a parent, friend, or spouse to the job interview
- having a parent or spouse call the company after the interview to negotiate a higher salary
- answering and chatting to someone in a non-emergency phone call during the interview
- bringing a pet to an interview

When one job candidate set a crate-housed cat on the interviewer's desk and periodically played with it, the interviewer reported: "It hit me like—why would you think that's OK? She cut herself off before she had a chance." Jaime Fall, vice president of the HR Policy Association, warns: "Behavior that may be completely appropriate outside the interview may not be acceptable. Most interviews are still conducted in a traditional environment."[69]

In an article written for *Forbes* magazine, J. Maureen Henderson offers several recommendations for millennials, which we've modified and then added our own advice.[70]

1. *The Interview Is Not About You.* Employers are thinking about you only in terms of what you can do for them. That goal is foremost in their minds as they listen to what you say and watch your behavior. Make sure you let an interviewer know how your skills and accomplishments help them meet their objectives.
2. *Put Tech in Its Rightful Place.* In addition to making sure you've turned off your cell phone, do not exaggerate or brag about your "digital footprint."[71] Don't brag that you use MS Office or that you have lots of social media friends and followers. So does just about everyone else. Instead, explain how your technical skills can help the organization achieve its goals and mission. Equally important, remember that many employers will check your social media sites and Twitter feeds. As one corporate president wrote, "I know it's informal, but a stream littered with Us and LUVs makes you look 12-years-old—definitely not hiring material."[72]
3. *Interview Without a Safety Net.* As obvious as this should be, we have to say it: don't let your parents write your résumé. Do it yourself. Certainly you can ask family members and friends to review it. Also do not let your parents or a friend accompany you to the interview. Even being seen saying goodbye to your best friend, spouse, or parents at the door can make you look as if you don't have the nerve to be there on your own.[73] If you feel anxious about the job interview, talk to a career counselor or read up on interviewing strategies.

Certainly, millennials are not the only job seekers who do "odd" things during interviews. Whatever your generation, make sure you are as well-prepared for an interview as you would be for a make-or-break presentation.

Evaluating Your Job Interview Performance[74]

Use this instrument to evaluate your performance in a past job interview, a classroom interview assignment, or a practice interview to help you prepare for an upcoming interview. Using criteria based on the seven key competencies of effective communication discussed in Chapter 1 "Human Communication," rate yourself as an interviewee with the following scores:

E = excellent; **G** = good; **A** = average; **W** = weak; **P** = Poor or **N/A** = not applicable.

Job Interview Competencies	E	G	A	W	P	N/A
Self: I was well prepared and confident.						
Others: I researched and knew a lot about the organization; I listened carefully and adapted to the interview questions.						
Purpose: I could explain how hiring me would promote my personal and professional goals as well as the organization's mission.						
Context: I adapted to the logistics and psychosocial climate of the interview.						
Content: I included ideas and information relevant to and needed in the job or assignment; I asked good questions; I knew a great deal about the organization and its challenges.						
Structure: I organized the content of my answers in a clear and memorable way. I asked questions at appropriate points in the interview.						
Expression: I used verbal and nonverbal behavior appropriately and effectively. I was dressed appropriately and professionally.						
Overall Assessment:						

Additional Assessment Questions:

1. Which questions did I answer best? What made my answers effective?

2. Which questions were the most difficult? Are these questions likely to be asked in future interviews? How could I answer such questions more effectively in the future?

3. Did I miss opportunities to emphasize particular strengths? How might I have incorporated those into my other answers?

4. What additional questions should I have asked?

5. What should I do differently in a future job interview?

The Nature of Professional Relationships

9.1 Describe the qualities that exemplify productive and satisfying professional relationships.

- The term *professional* describes a person whose job requires expert knowledge, specialized skills, and diligence; Professionals set high standards for doing skilful work.

- Organizational culture describes the ways in which shared symbols, beliefs, values, and norms affect the behavior of people working in and with an organization.

- Superiors request work, supervise projects, and assess a subordinate's performance; subordinates provide information about themselves and coworkers as well as information about the progress of work, what needs to be done, and how to do it.

- Satisfying coworker relationships are characterized by individual excellence, interdependence, investment, information, integration, and integrity.

- Customers have three basic communication needs: to feel welcome, to have enough good information to make a decision, and to be treated with respect.

Professional Communication Challenges

9.2 Apply appropriate strategies for dealing with office rumors and gossip, workplace romances, sexual harassment, working with friends, and leaving a job.

- Although rumors and gossip serve several social functions in an organization, self-serving rumors and malicious gossip can embarrass others, damage your credibility, waste time, and create a hostile and distrustful work environment.

- Many organizations disapprove of office romances because they can decrease productivity, make other colleagues feel uncomfortable, create suspicions that a romantic partner receives preferential treatment, and eventually end badly.

- Sexual harassment is characterized by unwanted sexual advances, inappropriate verbal or physical conduct of a sexual nature, or a hostile, or offensive work environment.

- Working with a close friend at work can put strains on both the friendship and the professional relationship.

- When dealing with someone's difficult behavior at work, identify specific successes and failures, listen actively, explain the consequences of the behavior, call on the person's strengths, and mutually agree and follow up on an action plan.

- Leaving a job—either voluntarily or involuntarily—requires communication strategies that leave a good impression with your former employer and create an equally good impression with your new or potential employer.

Job Interviews

9.3 Practice effective strategies and skills to prepare for, participate in, and follow up after workplace and job interviews.

- Workplace interviews serve several purposes and come in many forms such as selection, appraisal, information-gathering, disciplinary, and exit interviews.

- Before going to a job interview, research the organization, assess your own strengths and weaknesses, and practice answering probable questions.

- During an interview, answer questions directly and concisely while presenting yourself and your skills positively.

- Effective interviews require candidates to demonstrate four key competencies in terms of their appearance, attitude, expression, and behavior.

- In addition to sending a follow-up note to the interviewer after an interview, assess your own performance and how you can do better in future interviews.

Key Terms

Coworker relationship	Interview	Probing question
Customer relationship	Leading question	Rumor
Exit interview	Organizational Culture	Sexual harassment
Gossip	Theory	Superior–subordinate
Hypothetical question	Organizational subculture	relationships

TEST YOUR KNOWLEDGE

9.1 *Describe the qualities that exemplify productive and satisfying professional relationships.*

1 In a superior–subordinate relationship at work, effective subordinates provide all of the following to the manager except _____.

   a. information about themselves and coworkers

   b. information on the progress of work

   c. information on what needs to be done

   d. information on how the manager should help more

2 According to Organizational Culture Theory, the practice of giving colleagues nicknames is an example of a _____ behavior.

   a. ritual

   b. impersonal

   c. communication

   d. celebratory

9.2 *Apply appropriate strategies for dealing with office rumors and gossip, workplace romances, sexual harassment, working with friends, and leaving a job.*

3 Which of the following is an effective strategy for managing office gossip during a meeting?

   a. Share the gossip with your manager, even if you are uncertain of its reliability.

   b. Ask questions about the gossip to find out how many others have heard about it.

   c. Let your colleagues know you would prefer not to discuss the matter, but instead, focus on the task at hand.

   d. Request an quick end to the meeting so there's more time to talk about the gossip.

4 Which of the following behaviors could be *misinterpreted* as sexual harassment?

   a. a supervisor demands sexual favors from a subordinate as a guarantee of keeping a job

   b. a supervisor demands sexual favors from a subordinate in order to earn a promotion

   c. a colleague shares a gender-specific joke during lunch

   d. a coworker makes sexually demeaning comments about another coworker

9.3 *Practice effective strategies and skills to prepare for, participate in, and follow up after workplace and job interviews.*

5 Which type of interview is conducted for the purpose of evaluating an employee's job performance?

   a. Selection interview

   b. Appraisal interview

   c. Information-gathering interview

   d. Disciplinary interview

6 "What are the most significant challenges facing this industry in the current economic climate?" is what type of interview question?

   a. Closed-ended question

   b. Leading question

   c. Probing question

   d. Open-ended question

Answers found on page 368.

Working in **Groups 10**

Cirque du Soleil (French for Circus of the Sun) is a unique and enormously successful entertainment company. If you've never seen Cirque du Soleil in action, we urge you to check out their official website as well as clips from their shows on YouTube.[1] Once you've seen Cirque du Soleil perform—either live or mediated—you'll understand why the most frequently asked question after a show is, "How do they *do* that?"

Cirque du Soleil also demonstrates the power of working in groups. Lyn Heward, former creative director and executive producer of special events for Cirque, explains that the most essential ingredient in their productions is group creativity. "Creativity," she says "is fostered in work groups where people first get to know each other and then learn to trust one another. And in this playground we recognize that a good idea can emerge from anywhere in the organization or from within a team. We make our shows from this collective creativity."[2]

Compared to Cirque du Soleil, a staff meeting, pre-exam study group, and pickup basketball game may seem light years away. Not so. If you work well in groups, you know that good ideas, solutions to a problem, and strategies for resolving conflicts can emerge from anyone. And like Cirque, you also know that group members' complementary abilities, diverse perspectives, and commitment to shared goals can ensure group success beyond expectations.

In this chapter, we look at the nature of groups: how they form, and the communication challenges they face as they develop into productive teams.

The Challenges of Working in Groups

10.1 *Describe the advantages and disadvantages of working in groups.*

All of us work in groups. We work in groups at home, in school, and on the job; with family members, friends, colleagues, and volunteers; in diverse situations, from sports fields and battlefields to courtrooms and classrooms. Whereas individual accomplishments were once the measure of personal success, notable achievements in today's complex world depend on the ability to work in groups. Researchers Steve Kozlowski and Daniel Ilgen describe our profound dependence on groups:

> Teams of people working together for a common cause touch all of our lives. From everyday activities like air travel, fire fighting, and running the United Way drive to amazing feats of human accomplishments like climbing Mt. Everest and reaching for the stars, teams are at the center of how work gets done in modern times.[3]

Working in groups may be one of the most important skills you learn in college. A comprehensive study commissioned by the Association of American Colleges and Universities asked employers to rank essential learning outcomes for college graduates entering the workplace. In two of the four major categories—*intellectual and practical skills* and *personal and social responsibility*—the number one learning outcome was "teamwork skills and the ability to collaborate with others in diverse group settings." Recent graduates ranked the same learning outcome as a top priority.[4]

The Nature of Group Communication

In 2009, the Educational Testing Service unveiled the Personal Potential Index, an evaluation instrument professors can use to rate students on their potential for success in graduate school. The instrument includes six critical traits, two of which are *communication skills* and *teamwork*. The teamwork trait specifies skills such as the abilities to work well in group settings, to behave in an open and friendly manner, to support the efforts of others, and to share ideas easily.[5] The

American Management Association's "2010 Critical Skills Survey" found that 72 percent of top corporate managers rated the ability to work with others in groups as critical for career advancement.[6] These critical skills characterize the nature of effective **group communication**—the interaction of three or more interdependent people working to achieve a common goal.[7]

Group Size The phrase "two's company; three's a crowd" recognizes that an interaction between two people is quite different from a three-person discussion. The ideal size for a problem-solving group is five to seven members. To avoid ties when making a decision, an odd number of members works better than an even number. Groups larger than seven tend to divide into subgroups; talkative members may dominate or drown out quiet members.

Interaction and Interdependence Next time you're in a group, observe the ways members behave toward one another. A group member raises a

controversial issue. In response, everyone starts talking at the same time. Later, the group listens intently to a member explain an important concept or advocate a possible action plan. When tensions arise, a funny comment eases the strain. Members exchange good cheer as they conclude their meeting or finalize a course of action. What you have just observed is group *interaction*—a necessity for effective group communication in both face-to-face and virtual meetings.

Group members are *interdependent*—that is, the actions of each group

Members of a curling team depend on one another to achieve a common goal. The curler and two sweepers become a well-coordinated team that charts a strategic path for placement of the "stone" as it moves toward a specific target.

member affects every other member. For example, if a member fails to provide needed background information, the group as a whole will suffer when it attempts to make an important decision or solve a significant problem.

Without a common goal, groups wonder: why are we meeting? why should we care or work hard?

Common Goal Group members come together for a reason: a collective purpose or goal that defines and unifies the group. A classic study by Carl Larson and Frank LaFasto concludes, "in every case, without exception, where an effectively functioning team was identified, it was described . . . as having a clear understanding of its objective."[9]

While some groups have the freedom to develop their own goals, other groups are assigned a goal. For example, a gathering of neighbors may meet to discuss ways of reducing crime in the neighborhood. Students may form a study group to prepare for an upcoming exam. On the other hand, a marketing instructor may assign a semester-long project to student groups in which they must research, develop, and present a marketing campaign. A manufacturing company may assemble a group of employees from various departments and ask them to develop recommendations for safer storage of hazardous chemicals. Whatever the circumstances, effective groups work to accomplish a common goal.

Advantages and Disadvantages of Working in Groups

If you're like most people, you have had to sit through some long and boring meetings. You may have lost patience (or your temper) in a group that couldn't accomplish a simple task you could have done better and more quickly by yourself. In the long run, however, the advantages of working in groups usually outweigh the disadvantages.

Advantages In *The Wisdom of Teams*, Jon Katzenbach and Douglas Smith note that groups "outperform individuals acting alone . . . especially when performance requires multiple

Working in groups often leads to friendships, enhanced learning, and member satisfaction.

skills, judgments, and experiences."[10] In general, the "approaches and outcomes of cooperating groups are not just better than those of the average group member, but are better than even the group's best problem solver functioning alone." Furthermore, the lone problem solver can't match the diversity of knowledge and perspectives of a group.[11]

Many of us also belong to and work in groups because we can make friends, socialize, and feel part of a successful team. Moreover, working in groups can enhance learning when members share information, stimulate critical thinking, challenge assumptions, and establish high standards of achievement.

Disadvantages Working in groups requires time, energy, and resources. For example, when 3M Corporation researchers calculated the hourly wages and overhead costs of workplace meetings, they concluded that meetings cost the company $78.8 million annually.[12] A similar study by Xerox estimated direct meeting costs at $100.4 million a year.[13] In addition to financial costs, there is also the potential for irreparable conflict among members.

As much as we may want everyone in a group to cooperate and work hard, the behavior of some members may create problems. They may talk too much, arrive late for meetings, and argue aggressively. However, these same members may also be excellent researchers, effective critical thinkers, and good friends.

Types of Groups

Groups are as diverse as the people in them and the goals they seek. Yet there are common characteristics that can be used to separate groups into several categories. These categories range from the most personal and informal types of groups to more professional and formal types. You can identify each type of group by noting its purpose (why the group meets) and by its membership (who is in the group).

The first six types of groups described in the figure below serve your personal needs and interests. In Chapter 7, "Understanding Interpersonal Relationships," we examined the importance of effective communication with family members, friends, and romantic partners—the people who belong to family and social groups. Self-help, learning, service, and civic groups are groups you join by choice because they offer support and encouragement, help you gain knowledge, and assist others. There are two types of groups—work groups and public groups—that serve the diverse interests of organizations and public audiences. Understanding your role in these types of groups requires more detailed information about their various forms, functions, and goals.

Work Groups Labor crews, sales staff, faculty, management groups, and research teams are all **work groups**—groups that are responsible for making decisions, solving problems, implementing projects, or performing assigned duties in an organization. Committees and work teams are both types of work groups. **Committees** (social committees, budget committees, and awards committees) are created by a larger group or by a person

TYPES OF GROUP

	PURPOSE	MEMBERSHIP
Primary	To provide members with affection, support, and a sense of belonging	Family members, best friends
Social	To share common interests in a friendly setting or participate in social activities	Athletic team members, hobbyists, sorority and fraternity members
Self-Help	To support and encourage members who want or need help with personal problems	Therapy group members, participants in programs such as Weight Watchers and Alcoholics Anonymous
Learning	To help members gain knowledge and develop skills	Classmates, book group members, participants in a ceramic workshop
Service	To assist worthy causes that help other people outside the group	Members of Kiwanis, Police Athletic League, charity groups
Civic	To support worthy causes that help people within the group or community	Members of a PTA, labor unions, veterans' groups, neighborhood associations
Work	To achieve specific goals on behalf of a business or organization	Committee members, employees, task force members, management teams
Public	To discuss important issues in front of or for the benefit of the public	Participants in public panel discussions, symposiums, forums, governance groups

Working in Virtual Groups

A **virtual group** uses technology to communicate, often across time, distance, and organizational boundaries. Communication may take the form of text messages, blogs, wikis, e-mails, webinars, and teleconferences. Multimedia conferencing tools such as Skype or WebEx allow participants to hear one another, see one another, and instant message privately or publicly to group members. Other tools such as digital white boards and Google docs make virtual brainstorming, information sharing, editing, and group decision-making possible.

As Linda Stewart notes in her *Forbes* magazine article: "Virtual teams are a fact of business life for most of us and running them effectively is fast becoming a major challenge." According to surveys of large companies, this "challenge is only getting bigger." More than half of those surveyed (56 percent) "expect virtual teams to increase over the next couple of years. An almost equal number (57 percent) said earning trust is a key hurdle for managers of virtual teams."[14]

Virtual groups are complex. Members may come from different organizations, cultures, time zones, and geographic locations—not to mention the many technological variables they may encounter. For example, group members may have different levels of experience using the virtual medium; they may also have computer systems with different capabilities, such as an older or newer version of the software being used for group communication. As a result, virtual groups

develop a different group dynamic from those meeting face to face.[15]

Unfortunately, when some members participate in virtual groups, they mistakenly believe it will be easier than meeting face-to-face. As a result, they underestimate the time needed to prepare, coordinate, and collaborate.[16] They also may think they can "hide" during remote conferences. Although you may not be in the same room or even on the same continent as the other members of a virtual group, you are just as responsible for being fully prepared to contribute to the group's work.

When conducting or participating in a virtual team meeting, group members should assume the following responsibilities:

- Prepare for the meeting by reading the background material and becoming familiar with the technology.
- Make sure you know the group's goal and fully understand why you are involved as well as what is expected of you.[17]
- Check your understanding by paraphrasing: "Are you saying that _____?" Get verbal agreements on any decisions—don't assume agreement from silent team members.[18]
- Speak out (orally or in writing) during the meeting.
- Read and/or listen to others. Ensure comprehension before evaluation.
- Follow up on meeting actions.[19]

---

in a position of authority to take on specific tasks. **Work teams** are usually given full responsibility and resources for their performance. Unlike committees, work teams are relatively permanent. They don't take time *from* work to meet—they unite *to* work.

Public Groups Panel discussions, symposiums, forums, and governance groups are types of **public groups** that discuss issues in front of or for the benefit of the public. Their meetings usually occur in unrestricted public settings in front of public audiences. During a **panel discussion**, several people interact about a common topic to educate, influence, or entertain an audience.

In a **symposium**, group members present short, uninterrupted presentations on different aspects of a topic for the benefit of an audience. Very often, a panel or symposium is followed by a **forum**, which provides an opportunity for audience members to comment or ask questions. A strong moderator is needed in a forum to make sure that audience members have an equal opportunity to speak and that the meeting is orderly and civil.

Governance groups such as state legislatures, city and county councils, and governing boards of public agencies and educational institutions make policy decisions in public settings.

Balancing Group Development Tensions

10.2 *Select appropriate strategies for managing individual and group tensions in various group development stages.*

As groups form and develop, effective members learn how to manage a variety of individual and group goals. In the best of groups, your personal goals support the group's common goal. This balancing act, however, requires an understanding of several roadblocks to success: primary and secondary tensions, hidden agendas, and the tension between group conflict and cohesion.

Primary Tension

Group communication scholar Ernest G. Bormann describes **primary tension** as the social unease and inhibitions that accompany the getting-acquainted period in a new group.[20] Because most new group members want to create a good first impression, they tend to be overly polite with one another.

In most groups, primary tension decreases as members feel more comfortable with one another. But if a group is bogged down in primary tension, you can and should intervene by talking about it and discussing how to break the cycle. Urge members to stick to the group's agenda and express opinions about relevant issues. When your group meets, be positive, energetic, patient, open-minded, and well-prepared.

Secondary Tension

When a group members become comfortable interacting with one another, a different kind of tension develops. Confident members begin to compete with one another. They openly disagree on substantive issues. It is still too early in the group's existence to predict the outcome of such competition. At this point, secondary tension may arise. **Secondary tension** describes the frustrations and personality conflicts experienced by group members as they compete for social acceptance, status, and achievement.[21] Regardless of the causes, a group cannot hope to achieve its goals if secondary tension is not managed effectively.

If you sense that your group cannot resolve its secondary tension, it is time to intervene. One strategy is to joke about the tension. The resulting laughter can ease individual and group stress. Another option is to work outside the group setting to discuss any personal difficulties and anxieties with individual group members.

Successful groups learn that a little bit of tension can motivate a group toward action and increase a group's sensitivity to feedback. As Donald Ellis and Aubrey Fisher point out, "The successful and socially healthy group is not characterized by an absence of social tension, but by successful management of social tension."[22]

Hidden Agendas

Many (if not most) of us have personal goals we want to achieve in a group. As long as our personal goals support the group's goal, all is well. A **hidden agenda**, however, occurs when a member's private goals conflict with the group's goals. Hidden agendas represent what people *really* want rather than what they *say* they want. When hidden agendas become more important than a group's agenda or goal, the result can be group frustration, unresolved conflicts, and failure.

Even when a group recognizes the existence of hidden agendas, some of them cannot and should not be shared because they may create an atmosphere of distrust. For instance, not many people would want to deal with the following revelation during a group discussion: "The reason I don't want to be here is that I don't want to work with Kenneth, who is untrustworthy and incompetent."

Sociologists Rodney Napier and Matti Gershenfeld suggest that discussing hidden agendas during the early stages of group development can counteract their disruptive power.[23] Initial discussion could include some of the following questions:

- What are the group's goals?
- Do any members have any personal concerns or goals that differ from these?
- What outcomes do members expect?

Unrecognized and unresolved hidden agendas can permeate and infect *all* stages of group development.

> ### Characteristics of SECONDARY TENSION
> - Energy and alertness levels are high.
> - The group is noisy and dynamic; members are loud and emphatic.
> - Several members may speak at the same time.
> - Members sit up, lean forward, and squirm in their seats.

> ### Characteristics of PRIMARY TENSION
> - Members rarely interrupt one another.
> - Long, awkward pauses often come between comments.
> - Members are soft-spoken and very polite.
> - Members avoid expressing strong opinions and emotions.

A little bit of tension can motivate a group to work harder and better.

Tuckman's Group Development Model

Most groups experience recognizable milestones. A "newborn" group behaves differently from an "adult" group that has worked together for a long time. In 1965, Bruce Tuckman, an educational psychologist, identified four discrete stages in the life cycle of groups—forming, storming, norming, and performing.[24] Since introducing **Tuckman's Group Development Model**, more than 100 theoretical models have described how a group moves through several "passages" during its lifetime.[25] Here we focus on Tuckman's original model because it is a highly comprehensive and relevant to all types of groups.[26]

Stage 1: **FORMING**

During the **forming stage**, group members may be more worried about themselves ("Will I be accepted and liked?") than about the group as a whole. Primary tension may thrive. Understandably, members are hesitant to express strong opinions or assert their personal needs during this stage until they know more about how other members think and feel about the task and about one another. Although little gets done during this stage, members need time to become acquainted with one another and define group goals.

Stage 2: **STORMING**

During the **storming stage**, group members become more argumentative and emotional as they discuss important issues and compete for leadership and status. Some groups are tempted to suppress the secondary tension and conflict experienced in this stage. However, conflict can help members develop relationships, decide who's in charge and who can be trusted, and clarify the group's common goal.

Stage 3: **NORMING**

During the **norming stage**, members define roles and establish norms. The group begins to work harmoniously as a cohesive team and makes decisions about the best ways to achieve a common goal. At this point in group development, members feel more comfortable with one another and are willing to disagree and express their opinions. "Communication becomes more open and task oriented" as "members solidify positive working relationships with each other."[27]

Stage 4: **PERFORMING**

During the **performing stage**, members focus their energy on working harmoniously to achieve group goals. Roles and responsibilities change according to group needs. Decisions are reached, problems are solved, and ideas are implemented. When the performing stage is going well, members are highly energized, loyal to one another, and willing to accept every challenge that arises.

Tuckman's group development theory helps explain why and how groups and their members behave at different stages in their development. Understanding the natural development of a group can help explain, predict, and improve group productivity and member satisfaction.

Like people, groups move through stages as they develop and mature.

Conflict and Cohesion in Groups in Groups

As groups develop and begin discussing important issues, members may become more argumentative and emotional. Many groups are tempted to discourage or avoid this kind of behavior because they fear or want to minimize conflict. However, when conflict is accepted as normal and beneficial, it helps establish a climate in which members feel free to disagree with one another.[28]

Group researchers have categorized the conflicts that occur in groups as one of three types: task conflict, relationship conflict, and process conflict.

1. Task conflict occurs when members have different or contradictory ideas and opinions about the group's task.
2. Relationship conflict occurs when there is hostility, nervous tension, and anxiety among members.
3. Process conflict occurs when there are "disagreements about assignments of duties and resources" including logistics and the coordination of decisions.[29]

In Chapter 8, "Improving Interpersonal Communication," we focused on the first two types of conflict. Here, we highlight the characteristics and potential impact of unresolved process conflicts. If your group is facing any of the following problems, look to the process and procedures you are using when choosing an appropriate conflict resolution strategy:

- One person causes friction and frequently derails the group's progress.
- Members are reluctant and/or uncomfortable expressing themselves.
- The distribution of work assignments is unfair.
- Time management is poor: deadlines are unrealistic and too difficult to meet.
- Members communicate in a disrespectful or ineffective manner. They may interrupt one another, misuse time, or complain rather than trying to solve a problem.
- Members cannot agree on a procedure for addressing an issue or problem.
- Members cannot resolve differences of opinion on how to structure a discussion, analyze a situation, accommodate differences, or make a decision.[30]

Effective groups learn to balance conflict and cohesion as they interact to achieve a common goal.

Certainly task, relationship, and process conflict are related—ineffective procedures or unfair task assignments may provoke frustration and anger. Conflict resolution in such circumstances may require an initial focus on processes rather than the emotions generated by those processes.

Group **cohesion** is the mutual attraction that holds the members of a group together as expressed in the saying,

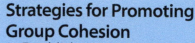

"All for one and one for all!" Cohesive groups are united and committed to a common goal, have high levels of interaction, and enjoy a supportive communication climate. Their members also share a sense of teamwork and pride in the group, want to conform to group expectations, and are willing to use creative approaches to achieve the group's goals.[31] Several decades of research confirm that when a group's task requires "coordination, communication, and mutual performance monitoring among group members," cohesion has a significant and positive effect on the group's ability to achieve its common goal.[32]

We recommend four general strategies for developing the kind of group cohesion that makes group happier and more productive:[33]

- **Establish group identity and traditions.** Refer to the group by using pronouns such as *we* and *our* rather than *I* and *my*. Develop rituals and ceremonies to reinforce group traditions and values.
- **Emphasize teamwork.** Emphasize group rather than individual accomplishments. Members should feel responsible for and take pride in both the work they do and the work of other members. Rather than taking personal credit for success, members emphasize the group's accomplishments.
- **Recognize and reward contributions.** Create a supportive, encouraging climate that rewards praiseworthy contributions. Some groups use celebration dinners, letters of appreciation, certificates, and gifts to reward individual effort and initiative, although a simple compliment can make a group member feel appreciated.
- **Respect group members.** Treat everyone with respect by showing concern for their personal needs, promoting a feeling of acceptance, and appreciating the value of diversity.

Cohesive group members feel responsible for and take pride in their own work as well as the work of other members.

Balancing Group and Member Dimensions

10.3 *Explain how group norms and member roles affect group productivity and member satisfaction.*

During the norming stage of group development, members define their roles and determine how the group will do its work. Effective groups learn to balance a commitment to group customs, rules, and standards (conformity) with a willingness to differ and change (nonconformity). They also learn to appreciate and further develop the positive roles members assume and as they work together to achieve a common goal.

Balancing Conformity and Nonconformity

Communication scholar Patricia Andrews defines **norms** as "sets of expectations held by group members concerning what kinds of behavior or opinions are acceptable or unacceptable, good or bad, right or wrong, appropriate or inappropriate."[34] Group norms express the values of a group, help the group to function smoothly, define appropriate and inappropriate behavior, and facilitate group success.[35] Norms are the group's rules of behavior; they determine how members dress, speak, listen, and work. For example, one group may discourage interruptions, whereas another group may view interruptions and overlapping conversations as acceptable forms of interaction. Without norms, a group lacks agreed-on ways to organize and perform a task.

Group norms can have positive or negative effects on member behavior and group success. For example, if your group's norms place a premium on pleasant and peaceful discussions, members may be reluctant to voice disagreement or share bad news. If group norms permit members to arrive late and leave early, you may not have enough members to do the job. Norms that don't support your group's goals can prevent the group from succeeding. When this is the case, you are perfectly within your rights (in fact, it may be your duty) to engage in nonconforming behavior. **Constructive nonconformity** occurs when a member resists a norm while still working to promote the group goal.

> "I know we always have our annual retreat at a golf resort, but many of our new staff members don't play golf and feel pressured to play or feel totally left out."

There are times when constructive nonconformity is needed and valued. Movies, television shows, and books champion the holdout juror, the stubbornly honest politician, and the principled but disobedient soldier or crew member. Sometimes there is so much pressure for group members to conform that they need a nonconformist to shake up the process, to provide critical feedback, and to create doubt about what had been a group-sanctioned but poor decision. Nonconformity can serve a group well *if it* prevents members from ignoring important information or making poor decisions.

Constructive nonconformity contributes to effective group decisions and more creative solutions because it

> ## Group norms function only to the extent that members conform to them.

allows members to voice serious and well-justified objections without fear of personal criticism or exclusion for taking a different position. In contrast, **destructive nonconformity** occurs when a member resists conformity without regard for the best interests of the group and its goal, such as by showing up late to attract attention or interrupting others to exert power.

When members do not conform to norms, a group may have to discuss the value of a particular norm and then decide to change, clarify, or continue to accept it. At the very least, nonconforming behavior helps members recognize and understand the norms of the group. For instance, if a member is reprimanded for leaving

How does this parade of Marine Corps soldiers demonstrate the importance and value of group norms?

Effective groups appreciate constructive nonconformity.

early, other members learn it is not acceptable to leave before a meeting is adjourned.

Balancing Group Roles

Every member brings unique talents, preferences, and perspectives to a group. As a result, group members assume different roles depending on the nature of the group, its membership, and its goal. A **group role** is a pattern of behaviors associated with an expected function within a particular group context. For example, when someone asks, "Who will get the information we need for our next meeting?" all eyes turn to Zhu because researching and sharing information are tasks he performs well. If a disagreement between two group members becomes heated, the group may look to Alicia for help because she has a talent for resolving conflicts and mediating differences.

Know Thy Self

Can You Name Your Norms?

The left-hand column in the following table describes several types of group norms. In the middle column, list related group norms in your classroom. In the right column, list related group norms in a current or former job, be it full-time, part-time, paid, or volunteer. Examine all these norms with a critical eye. Do they help the group achieve its common goal? If not, are you willing to challenge these norms for the good of the group?

Types of Group Norms	Classroom	Workplace
Verbal (formal or informal style; use of jargon, slang, obscenities, profanity)		
Nonverbal (formal or informal attire, physical arrangements, activity level, touching, eye contact)		
Interactional (use of first or last names, nicknames, speaking turns, listening behavior, playful or unruly behavior)		
Content (discussion is serious, work related, social, intimate, humorous)		
Status (who makes decisions, who has influence, is disagreement allowed)		
Rewards (how success is measured, how achievement is rewarded)		

Group Task and Maintenance Roles

Key group member roles are divided into two functional categories: task roles and maintenance roles. Group **task roles** focus on communication behaviors that help manage a task and complete a job. When members assume task roles, they provide useful information, ask important questions, explain procedures, analyze issues, and solve problems.

Group **maintenance roles** influence how well group members get along with one another while pursuing a common goal. Members who assume maintenance roles help to create a supportive communication climate, resolve conflicts, and encourage members or praise good work.

In addition to assuming roles on your own, analyze the group to determine whether important roles are missing. For example, if members are

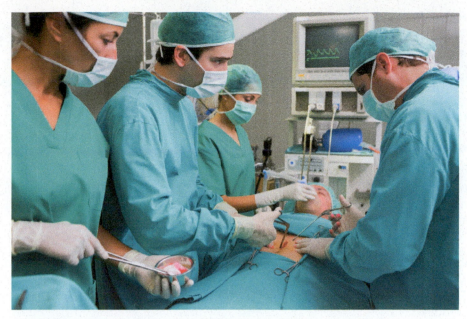

What task roles are critical to the success of a surgical team? Is there an appropriate place for maintenance roles in this group?

GROUP **TASK** ROLES[36]

ROLE	DESCRIPTION	EXAMPLE
INITIATOR/ CONTRIBUTOR	Proposes ideas; provides direction; gets the group started	"Let's begin by considering the client's point of view."
INFORMATION SEEKER	Asks for relevant information; requests explanations; points out information gaps	"How can we decide on a policy without knowing more about the cost and the legal requirements?"
INFORMATION GIVER	Researches, organizes, and presents relevant information	"I checked with human resources and they said . . ."
OPINION SEEKER	Asks for opinions; tests for agreement and disagreement	"Lyle, what do you think? Will it work?"
OPINION GIVER	States personal belief; shares feelings; offers analysis and arguments	"I don't agree that he's guilty. He may be annoying, but that doesn't constitute harassment."
CLARIFIER/ SUMMARIZER	Explains ideas and their consequences; reduces confusion; summarizes	"We've been trying to analyze this problem for two hours. Here's what I think we've agreed on."
EVALUATOR/ CRITIC	Assesses the value of ideas and arguments; diagnoses problems	"These figures don't consider monthly operating costs."
ENERGIZER	Motivates members; creates enthusiasm, and if needed, a sense of urgency	"This is incredible! We've come up with a unique and workable solution to the problem."
PROCEDURAL TECHNICIAN	Helps prepare meetings; makes room arrangements; provides materials and equipment	"Before our next meeting, let me know if you will need a flip chart again."
RECORDER/ SECRETARY	Keeps accurate written records of group recommendations and decisions	"Maggie, please repeat the two deadline dates so I can get them into the minutes."

balancing group and member dimensions

GROUP MAINTENANCE ROLES[37]

ROLE	DESCRIPTION	EXAMPLE
ENCOURAGER/ SUPPORTER	Praises and encourages group members; listens empathically	"Thanks for taking all that time to find the information we needed."
HARMONIZER	Helps resolve conflicts; mediates differences; encourages teamwork and group harmony	"I know we're becoming edgy, but we're almost done. Let's focus on the task, not our frustrations."
COMPROMISER	Offers suggestions that minimize differences; helps the group reach consensus	"Maybe we can improve the old system rather than adopting a brand-new way of doing it."
TENSION RELEASER	Uses friendly humor to alleviate tensions, tempers, and stress	"Can Karen and I arm-wrestle to decide who gets the assignment?"
GATEKEEPER	Monitors and regulates the flow of communication; encourages productive participation	"I think we've heard from everyone except Michelle, who has strong feelings about this issue."
STANDARD MONITOR	Reminds group of norms and rules; tests ideas against group-established standards	"We all agreed we'd start at 10 A.M. Now we sit around waiting for latecomers until 10:30 A.M."
OBSERVER/ INTERPRETER	Monitors and interprets feelings and nonverbal communication; paraphrases member comments	"Maybe we're not really disagreeing. I think we're in agreement that . . ."
FOLLOWER	Supports the group and its members; willingly accepts others' ideas and assignments	"That's fine with me. Just tell me when it's due."

when the member's positive contributions far outweigh the inconvenience or annoyance of putting up with the negative behavior. For example, a "clown" may be disruptive on occasion but may also be the group's best report writer or a valued harmonizer.

When it becomes impossible to accept or ignore self-centered behavior, the group should take action. For instance, members can confront a member by making it clear that the group will progress despite that person's non-productive behavior. "Ron, I think we fully understand your strong objections, but ultimately this is a group decision." In a moment of extreme frustration, one member may say what everyone is thinking—"Lisa, please let me finish my sentence!" Although such an outburst may make everyone uncomfortable, it can put a stop to disruptive behavior.

When all else fails, a group may ask disruptive members to leave the group and bar them from meetings; this is a humiliating experience that all but the most stubborn members would prefer to avoid.

Common Self-Centered Roles:[38]

- **Aggressor.** Puts down other members, is sarcastic and critical; takes credit for someone else's work or ideas
- **Blocker.** Stands in the way of progress, presents uncompromising positions; uses delay tactics to derail an idea or proposal
- **Dominator.** Prevents others from participating, interrupts others; tries to manipulate others
- **Recognition Seeker.** Boasts about personal accomplishments, tries to be the center of attention; pouts if not getting enough attention
- **Clown.** Injects inappropriate humor, seems more interested in goofing off than working, distracts the group from its task
- **Deserter.** Withdraws from the group, appears "above it all" and annoyed or bored with the discussion, stops contributing
- **Confessor.** Shares very personal feelings and problems, uses the group for emotional support in ways that inappropriately distract members from the group's task

becoming frustrated because one or two people are doing all the talking, you might suggest that someone serve as a gatekeeper. If the group has trouble tracking its progress, suggest that someone take on the role of recorder/ secretary. In highly effective groups, all the task and maintenance roles are available to mobilize a group toward achieving its common goal.

Self-Centered Roles

Sometimes group members assume **self-centered roles** in which they put

their own goals ahead of the group's goal and other member needs. Self-centered roles can disrupt the work of a group, adversely affect member relationships, and prevent the group from achieving its goals.

Three strategies can help you and your group deal with self-centered members: accept, confront, or even exclude the troublesome member. Acceptance is not the same as approval. A group may allow disruptive behavior to continue when it's not detrimental to the group's ultimate success or

Do You Disrupt Group Work?

Disruptive group behavior comes in all varieties. Do any of the following types describe the way you communicate in groups?[39] For each item, indicate how frequently you behave like the description: (1) usually, (2) often, (3) sometimes, (4) rarely, or (5) never.

—— 1. *The Put-Downer.* Do you assume that members are wrong until they're proven right? Do you make negative remarks such as, "That will never work," "Been there, done it, forget it," or "I don't like it" before the group has had time to discuss the issue in detail?

—— 2. *The Interrupter.* Do you start talking before others are finished? Do you interrupt because you're impatient or annoyed?

—— 3. *The Nonverbal Negative Naybobber.* Do you disagree nonverbally in a dramatic or disruptive manner? Do you frown or scowl, shake your head, roll your eyes, squirm in your seat, audibly sigh or groan, or madly scribble notes after someone has said something?

—— 4. *The Laggard.* Are you late to meetings? Do you ask or demand to be told what happened before you arrived? Are you usually late in completing assigned tasks?

—— 5. *The Chronic Talkaholic.* Talkaholics are compulsive communicators who have great difficulty (and often little desire for) being quiet in groups. Chronic talkaholics talk so much, they disrupt the group and annoy or anger other members. Do you ever talk when you know it would be much smarter to keep quiet? Do other group members often tell you that you talk too much?[40]

Developing Group Leadership

10.4 *Practice appropriate leadership strategies and skills.*

If you enter the word *leadership* into the Amazon book search engine, you will find thousands of books. And if you review these offerings, you'll see that most of them are written by highly respected scholars and well-regarded business leaders. Some unusual titles, however, demonstrate the range of leadership books. Here are just a few:

- *Lincoln on Leadership*
- *Leadership Secrets of Hillary Clinton*
- *Leadership Secrets of Colin Powell*
- *Jesus on Leadership*
- *Leadership Secrets of Attila the Hun*
- *The Leadership Secrets of Santa Claus*

Before you chuckle too much over *The Leadership Secrets of Santa Claus*, consider how you could translate some of his "secrets" into useful leadership tips: choose your reindeer wisely, make a list and check it twice, listen to the elves, find out who's naughty and nice, and be good for goodness' sake.[41]

Leadership is the ability to make strategic decisions and use communication to mobilize group members toward achieving a common goal. Even though just about everyone recognizes the importance of leadership, it is not always easy to practice effectively.

One review of leadership studies estimates that leadership incompetence is "as high as 60 to 75 percent—and that our hiring practices are so flawed that more than 50 percent of leaders hired by organizations are doomed to fail."[42]

In his book on leadership, Antony Bell describes communication as the mortar or glue that connects all leadership competencies. The abilities to think and act while remaining self-aware and self-disciplined are critical building blocks to leadership competency, but it takes communication to bind these blocks together.[43]

Three Approaches to Leadership

Leadership is a quality that defies precise measurement. However, three theories can help you understand your own and others' approaches to leadership: Trait Theory, Styles Theory, and Situational Theory.

Trait Theory Based on the belief that leaders are born, not made, the **Trait Theory of Leadership** identifies specific characteristics associated with leadership. Most of us can come up with a list of desirable leadership traits: intelligence, confidence, enthusiasm, organizational talent, trustworthiness, humility, humor, assertiveness, emotional stability, extroversion, and good listening skills. The weakness of Trait Theory is that many effective and great leaders only exhibit a few of these traits. For example, Harriet Tubman, an illiterate slave, did little talking but led hundreds of people from bondage in the South to freedom in the North. Bill Gates, an introverted computer geek, became the richest man in the world as head of Microsoft, a company that all but dictates how we use personal computers.

Styles Theory The **Styles Theory of Leadership** examines a collection of specific behaviors that constitute three distinct leadership styles: autocratic, democratic, and laissez-faire. **Autocratic leaders** seek power and authority by controlling the direction and outcome of a discussion, making many of the group's decisions, giving orders, and expecting followers to carry out those orders, and taking credit for successful results. An autocratic style is often appropriate during a serious crisis when there may not be time to discuss issues or consider the wishes of all members. In an emergency, the group may want its leader to take total responsibility. However, too much control can lower group morale and sacrifice long-term productivity.

A **democratic leader** promotes the social equality and interests of group members. This type of leader shares decision making with the group, helps the group plan a course of action, focuses on the group's morale as well as on the task, and gives the entire group credit for success. In groups with democratic leadership, members are often more satisfied with the group experience, more loyal to the leader, and more productive in the long run.

Laissez-faire is a French phrase that means "to let people do as they choose." A **laissez-faire leader** lets the group take charge of all decisions and actions. Such a leader may be a perfect match for mature and highly productive groups because a laid-back leadership style can generate a climate in which communication is encouraged and rewarded. Unfortunately, laissez-faire leaders may do little or nothing to help a group when it needs decisive leadership.

Situational Leadership Theory Rather than describing traits or styles, **Situational Leadership Theory** claims that effective leaders use different leadership strategies and style depending on the situation. This theory seeks an ideal fit between leaders and leadership roles.[44] The situational approach explains how leaders can become more effective by analyzing themselves, their group, and the situation.

Situational Theory identifies two leadership styles: task motivated and relationship motivated. **Task-motivated leaders** want to get the job done. They gain satisfaction from completing a task even if it results in bad feelings between the leader and group members. As a result, task-motivated leaders are often criticized for being too focused on the job and overlooking group morale. **Relationship-motivated leaders** gain satisfaction from working well with other people even if the cost is failing to complete a task. Not surprisingly, they are sometimes criticized for paying too much attention to how members feel and for tolerating disruptive behavior.

Situational Theory requires you to match your leadership style to the situation in terms of three important dimensions: leader–member relations, task structure, and power. **Leader–member relations** can be positive, neutral, or negative. Are group members friendly and loyal to the leader and the rest of the group? Are they cooperative and supportive? **Task structure** can range from disorganized and chaotic to highly organized and rule driven. Are the goals and task clear? The third situational factor is the amount of power and control the leader possesses.

> Without leadership, a group may be nothing more than a collection of individuals lacking the coordination and will to achieve a goal.

Three THEORETICAL Approaches to Leadership

1 TRAIT THEORY ▶ You Have It or You Don't

2 STYLES THEORY ▶ Are Democracies Always Best?

3 SITUATIONAL THEORY ▶ Matching Leaders and Jobs

Relationship between leadership style and situational factors

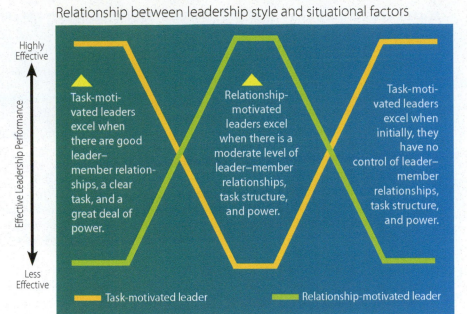

Highly Effective

Effective Leadership Performance

Task-motivated leaders excel when there are good leader–member relationships, a clear task, and a great deal of power.

Relationship-motivated leaders excel when there is a moderate level of leader–member relationships, task structure, and power.

Task-motivated leaders excel when initially, they have no control of leader–member relationships, task structure, and power.

Less Effective

▬ Task-motivated leader ▬ Relationship-motivated leader

Low control of leader–member relationships, task structure, and power

High control of leader–member relationships, task structure, and power

Situational Factors

The figure to the left shows the relationship between leadership style and situational factors. Task-motivated leaders perform best in extremes, such as when the situation requires high levels of leader control or when it is almost out of control. They excel when there are good or poor leader–member relationships, a clear or unclear task, and a great deal of or no power. Relationship-motivated leaders do well when in the middle ground where there is a mix of conditions, such as a semistructured task or a group of interested but not eager followers.

By identifying your leadership style, Situational Leadership Theory helps you understand when and why you are most likely succeed as a leader. And rather than changing your leadership style, you may find it easier to change the leadership situation.

COMMUNICATION IN *ACTION*

Becoming a Leader

Just about anyone can become a leader. Abraham Lincoln, Harry S. Truman, and Barack Obama rose from humble beginnings and hardship to become U.S. presidents. Corporate executives have worked their way up from the sales force and the secretarial pool to become chief executive officers.[45]

- Verizon chief executive officer (CEO) Ivan Seidenberg, the son of an electrical supply shop owner, started his business career as a telephone cable splicer's assistant.[46]

The strategies for becoming a leader are *not* necessarily the same strategies for successful leadership.

- Oprah Winfrey, born to an unwed teenager and raised on her grandmother's farm in Kosciusko, Mississippi, became a CEO and the richest self-made woman in the United States.[47]
- John Boehner, one of twelve children who worked in and then ran his father's bar, Andy's Café, in Cincinnati, became speaker of the U.S. House of Representatives.[48]

The path to a leadership position can be as easy as being in the right place at the right time or being the only person willing to take on a difficult job.[49] Although there is no foolproof method, there are ways to improve your chances of becoming a group's leader.

- *Talk early and often (and listen).* The person who speaks first and most often is more likely to emerge as the group's leader.[50] How frequently you talk is even more important than

what you say. The quality of your contributions becomes more significant *after* you become a leader.

- *Know more (and share it).* Leaders often are seen as experts. A potential leader can often explain ideas and information more clearly than other group members, and therefore be perceived as knowing more. While groups need well-informed leaders, they do not need know-it-alls who see their own comments as most important; effective leaders value everyone's contributions.
- *Offer your opinion (and welcome disagreement).* Groups appreciate someone who offers valuable ideas and informed opinions. However, this is not the same as having your ideas accepted without question. If you are unwilling to compromise or listen to alternatives, the group may be unwilling to follow you. Effective leaders welcome constructive disagreement and discourage hostile confrontations.

After you become a leader, you may find it necessary to listen more than talk, welcome and reward better-informed members, and challenge the opinions of others. Your focus should shift from *becoming* the leader to *serving* the group you lead.

developing group leadership

The 5-M Model of Leadership Effectiveness

As we noted earlier in this chapter, thousands of books and articles have been published about leadership. To help you understand contributions made by these many approaches, we offer the **5-M Model of Leadership Effectiveness**, an integrated model of leadership effectiveness that emphasizes specific communication strategies and skills applicable to five interdependent leadership functions: modeling, motivating, managing, making decisions, and mentoring.[51]

Model Leadership Behavior Model leaders project an image of confidence, competence, and trustworthiness. Model leaders publicly champion the group and its goals rather than their own accomplishments and ego needs. They speak and listen effectively, behave consistently and assertively, confront problems head-on, and work to find solutions.

No matter how much you may want to be a model leader, only your followers can grant you that honor. In *The Leadership Secrets of Colin Powell*, the author quotes Powell's view on modeling behavior:

> The leader sets an example. Whether in the Army or in civilian life, the other people in an organization take their cue from the leader— not from what the leader says but what the leader does.[52]

Motivate Members

Motivating others is a critical task for leaders. Effective leaders guide, develop, support, defend, and inspire group members. They develop relationships that meet the personal needs and expectations of followers. Motivational strategies include supporting and rewarding deserving members, helping members solve interpersonal problems, and adapting tasks and assignments to member abilities and expectations. Most important of all, motivating leaders give members the authority to make decisions about doing the group's work.

Mike Krzyzewski (Coach K), the highly successful men's basketball coach at Duke University, believes that motivating team members is the key to his success. "As a coach, leader, and teacher, my primary task is motivation. How do I get a group motivated, not only to be their individual best but also to become better as a team?"[53]

Manage Group Processes From the perspective of group survival, managing group processes may be the most important function of leadership.[54] If a group is disorganized, lacks sufficient information to solve problems, or is unable to make important decisions when necessary, the group cannot be effective. Effective leaders are well organized and fully

To what extent did Martin Luther King, Jr., exemplify the 5-M Model of Leadership Effectiveness? How well, if at all, did he model leadership, motivate members, manage group processes, make decisions, and mentor members?

prepared for all group meetings and work sessions. They adapt to member strengths and weaknesses and help solve task-related and procedural problems. They also know when to monitor and intervene to improve group performance.

Make Decisions An effective leader is willing and able to make appropriate, timely, and responsible decisions. When you assume or are appointed to a leadership role, you should accept the fact that some of your decisions may be unpopular, and some may even turn out to be wrong. But you still have to make them. It's often better for a group leader to make a bad decision than no decision at all, "for if you are seen as chronically indecisive, people won't let you lead them."[55]

In "Building the 21st Century Leader," Carol Tice reviews the evolution of corporate leadership, claiming that today's leaders must be able to do *both*—collaborate with others *and* be decisive.[56]

Several strategies can help a leader make decisions that support a group

> **"** The desire to reach consensus or get buy-in from all parties has to be curtailed at some point, and the leader has to make a decision. **"**
> —Carol Tice [57]

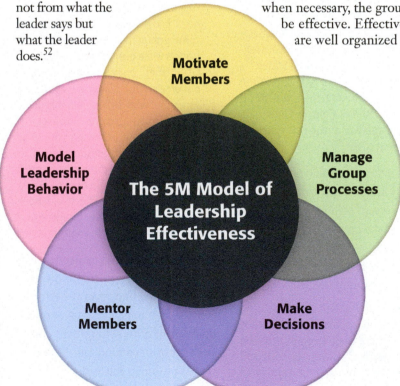

Motivate Members

Model Leadership Behavior

The 5M Model of Leadership Effectiveness

Manage Group Processes

Mentor Members

Make Decisions

and its goal. First, make sure everyone has and shares the information needed to make a quality decision. If appropriate, discuss your pending decision and solicit feedback from members. Listen to members' opinions, arguments, and suggestions *before* making a decision. When you make a decision, explain your reasons for doing so and communicate your decision to everyone.

Effective leaders intervene and tell members what to do when a group lacks the confidence, willingness, or ability to make decisions. However, when group members are confident, willing, and skilled, a leader can usually turn full responsibility over to the group and focus on helping members implement the group's decision.

Mentor Members Good leaders are very busy people, particularly if they model leadership, motivate members, manage group process, and make decisions. Even so, great leaders find the time and energy to mentor others. They know that effective mentoring does more than teach someone how to do a job—it also motivates that person to set high standards, seek advice when needed, and develop the skills characteristic of an excellent leader.

We, your authors, credit exceptional mentors for helping us to succeed in high school and college, to take on challenging tasks as college professors, and for guiding us toward becoming professional leaders. Our mentors were teachers, debate team coaches, senior professors, distinguished researchers, and esteemed colleagues.

In his book *Great Leadership*, Anthony Bell urges would-be leaders to find a mentor because a good "mentor will challenge you to ask (and answer) the tough questions."[58] The following strategies can help leaders decide when and how to mentor group members:

1. *Be ready and willing to mentor every group member.* Although you cannot be a full-time mentor for everyone, you should be open to requests for advice. Eventually, you may develop a close relationship with a few mentees (that is, the people being mentored) who share your vision.

2. *Encourage and invite others to lead.* Look for situations in which group members can assume leadership responsibilities. Ask them to chair a meeting, take full responsibility for a group project, or implement a group's decision. And make sure they know you're there as backup.

3. *Inspire optimism.* When problems or setbacks occur, do not blame the group or its members. Instead, convert the situation into a teachable moment and encourage members to accept personal responsibility for a problem and its consequences.[59]

4. *Balance responsibilities.* Effective mentors create appropriate balance and boundaries. They know when to intervene and when to back off. A mentor is neither a psychiatric counselor nor a group member's best friend. At some point, even the best mentors must let their mentees succeed or fail on their own.

COMMUNICATION&CULTURE

DIVERSITY AND LEADERSHIP

In the early studies of leadership, there was an unwritten but additional prerequisite for becoming a leader: Be a man. Despite the achievements of exceptional female leaders, some people still question the ability of women to serve in leadership positions.

A summary of the research on leadership and gender concludes, "women are still less likely to be preselected as leaders, and the same leadership behavior is often evaluated more positively when attributed to a male than a female."[60]

Developing a leadership style is a challenge for most young managers but particularly for young women. If their behavior is similar to that of male leaders, they are perceived as unfeminine, but if they act "like a lady," they are viewed as weak or ineffective. One professional woman described this dilemma as follows:

I was thrilled when my boss evaluated me as "articulate, hard-working, mature in her judgment, and a skillful diplomat." What disturbed me were some of the evaluation comments from those I supervise or work with as colleagues. Although they had a lot of good things to say, a few of them described me as "pushy," "impatient," "disregards social niceties," and "hard driving." What am I supposed to do? My boss thinks I'm energetic and creative while other people see the same behavior as pushy and aggressive.

Cultural differences also affect whether members become and succeed as leaders. For example, individualistic Western cultures (United States, Australia, Great Britain) assume that members are motivated by personal growth and achievement. However, a collectivist member might desire a close relationship with the leader and other group members rather than personal advancement. The same member may act out of loyalty to the leader and the group rather than for personal achievement or material gain.[61]

Group Member Participation and Leadership Evaluation

Evaluate the quantity and quality of participation by members of a group to which you belong or have belonged by circling the number that describes its performance.

1. *Task Functions.* Members provide or ask for information and opinions, initiate discussion, clarify, summarize, evaluate, energize, and so on.

5	4	3	2	1
Excellent		Average		Poor

2. *Maintenance Functions.* One or more members serve as encourager, harmonizer, compromiser, tension releaser, gatekeeper, standard monitor, observer, follower, and so on.

5	4	3	2	1
Excellent		Average		Poor

3. *Group Processes.* Members avoid disruptive behavior, follow the agenda, and adapt to group development stages and group norms.

5	4	3	2	1
Excellent		Average		Poor

4. *Manage Difficulties.* Members are ready, willing, and able to deal with difficult behavior and overall group problems.

5	4	3	2	1
Excellent		Average		Poor

5. *Leadership.* One or more members model leadership behavior, motivate others, help manage group processes, make necessary decisions, and mentor others.

5	4	3	2	1
Excellent		Average		Poor

6. *Group's Overall Effectiveness.*

5	4	3	2	1
Excellent		Average		Poor

COMMENTS:

SUMMARY

The Challenges of Working in Groups

10.1 Describe the advantages and disadvantages of working in groups.

- Group communication refers to the interaction of three or more interdependent people working to achieve a common goal.
- In general, the advantages of working in groups far outweigh the disadvantages.
- Groups differ in terms of whether they are meeting personal goals, work goals, or public goals.
- Virtual groups use technology to communicate, often across time, distance, and organizational boundaries.

Balancing Group Development Tensions

10.2 Select appropriate strategies for managing individual and group tensions in various group development stages.

- Bruce Tuckman's Group Development stages include forming, storming, norming, and performing.
- During the forming stage of group development, most groups experience primary tension, the social unease and inhibitions that accompany the getting-acquainted period in a new group.
- During the storming stage of group development, groups must resolve secondary tensions and personality conflicts in order to achieve cohesion.
- Hidden agendas occur when a member's private goals conflict with the group's goals.
- Most conflicts that occur in groups are one or more of three types: task conflict, relationships conflict, and process conflict.
- Cohesive groups share a sense of teamwork and pride.

Balancing Group and Member Dimensions

10.3 Explain how group norms and member roles affect group productivity and member satisfaction.

- Whereas constructive nonconformity is appropriate and helps a group achieve its goal, destructive nonconformity has little regard for the best interests of the group and its goal.
- Group task roles help a group achieve its goals. Group maintenance roles affect how group members get along.
- Self-centered roles adversely affect task and social goals.

Developing Group Leadership

10.4 Practice appropriate leadership strategies and skills.

- Leadership is the ability to make strategic decisions and use communication to mobilize group members toward achieving a common goal.
- The Trait Theory of Leadership identifies individual leadership characteristics.
- The Styles Theory of Leadership examines autocratic, democratic, and laissez-faire leadership.
- Situational Leadership Theory seeks an ideal fit between a leader's style and the leadership situation.
- People become leaders by talking more, knowing more, and offering their opinions.
- The 5-M Model of Leadership Effectiveness identifies five critical leadership tasks: (1) model leadership behavior, (2) motivate members, (3) manage group processes, (4) make decisions, and (5) mentor members.
- Female and nonmajority group members are less likely to be preselected as leaders and are often evaluated less positively than are male leaders.

Key Terms

Autocratic leader	Hidden agenda	Situational Leadership Theory
Cohesion	Laissez-faire leader	
Committee	Leader–member relations	Storming stage
Constructive nonconformity	Leadership	Styles Theory of Leadership
Democratic leader	Maintenance role	Symposium
Destructive nonconformity	Norming stage	Task role
	Norms	Task structure
5-M Model of Leadership Effectiveness	Panel discussion	Task-motivated leader
	Performing stage	Trait Theory of Leadership
Forming stage	Primary tension	Tuckman's Group Development Model
Forum	Public group	
Governance group	Relationship-motivated leader	Virtual group
Group communication	Secondary tension	Work group
Group role	Self-centered role	Work team

TEST YOUR KNOWLEDGE

10.1 *Describe the advantages and disadvantages of working in groups.*

1 The ideal size for a problem-solving group is _____ members.
   a. 2–4
   b. 3–5
   c. 5–7
   d. 7–12

2 Which of the following best describes a forum?
   a. Several people interact about a common topic in front of an audience.
   b. Group members present short, uninterrupted presentations on different aspects of a topic for the benefit of an audience.
   c. Audience members comment or ask questions to a speaker or group of speakers.
   d. Elected officials and governing boards of public agencies conduct their meetings in public.

10.2 *Select appropriate strategies for managing individual and group tensions in various group development stages.*

3 Which is the correct order for Tuckman's group development stages?
   a. Forming, storming, norming, performing
   b. Storming, forming, performing, norming
   c. Forming, norming, storming, performing
   d. Norming, forming, performing, storming

4 Which of the following is *not* a characteristic of secondary tension in groups?
   a. The group becomes more argumentative and emotional.
   b. Group members compete for acceptance and achievement.
   c. The social unease and inhibitions that accompany the getting-acquainted period in a new group.
   d. The social unease and anxieties that accompany the process of competing for status.

10.3 *Explain how group norms and member roles affect group productivity and member satisfaction.*

5 Which answer best completes the following statement: Nonconformity _____.
   a. will always undermine group performance.
   b. can improve group performance.
   c. occurs only when stubborn members are present.
   d. occurs under poor leadership.

6 Which of the following represents a group task role?
   a. Tension releaser
   b. Gatekeeper
   c. Encourager/supporter
   d. Clarifier/summarizer

10.4 *Practice appropriate leadership strategies and skills.*

7 Which leadership theory or model can be summarized as "either you have it or you don't"?
   a. Trait Theory
   b. Styles Theory
   c. The 5-M Model of Leadership
   d. The Styles and Situational Theories

8 Which of the following strategies is most likely to help you *become* a leader?
   a. Talk early and often
   b. Know more
   c. Offer your opinion
   d. All of the above

Answers found on page 368.

Group Decision Making and Problem Solving **11**

KEY OBJECTIVES

11.1 Justify the prerequisites that enhance group deliberation.

11.2 Compare the advantages and disadvantages of decision-making methods in groups.

11.3 Analyze the nature and value of problem-solving methods in groups.

11.4 Practice effective meeting strategies and skills.

The decisions of three significant groups led to the death of Osama bin Laden on May 2, 2011.

In 2010 and early 2011, a CIA intelligence team—the first group—had been gathering information about bin Laden's whereabouts and reported a 60 percent chance that he was in a Pakistani compound.[1] The National Security Council—the second group—met with President Obama to review the CIA report and discuss possible military action. Although several military officers expressed doubts about whether bin Laden was in the compound and whether a commando raid was worth the risk, Obama ordered the military to develop a set of mission options.[2]

Numerous meetings, deliberations, and CIA updates later, the Council proposed three specific plans of action from which the principal decision makers had to choose: to raid, to launch a missile strike, or to do nothing. Despite major dissenters, Vice President Biden being one of them, they recommended the raid.[3] President Obama agreed. Ultimately, he issued the order for the helicopter raid to take place. Although the final decision was his to make, Obama did so only after engaging in extended discussions with his advisors.

When the go-ahead for the mission was ordered, an already-prepared Navy SEAL team—the third group—moved into action. Without sustaining any major injuries, the military team located and killed Osama bin Laden. After securing and verifying the identity of his body, it was secretly buried at sea.

In an article written for *The Atlantic*, American foreign policy writer John A. Gans, Jr. hailed the mission as "a textbook example of complex national security decision-making."[4] Yet, the story of the bin Laden raid also demonstrates the power of effective decision making and problem solving in groups—especially those that have a significant impact on our lives.

Prerequisites for Group Decision Making and Problem Solving

11.1 *Justify the prerequisites that enhance group deliberation.*

You make hundreds of decisions every day. You decide when to get up in the morning, what to wear, when to leave for class or work, and with whom to spend your leisure time. Many factors influence how you make these decisions—your culture, age, family, education, social status, and religion, as well as your dreams, fears, beliefs, values, interpersonal needs, and personal preferences.[5] Now take five people, put them in a room, and ask them to make a *group* decision. As difficult as it can be to make personal decisions, the challenge is multiplied many times over in groups.

Fortunately and in large part because of the many differences among members, effective groups have the potential to make excellent decisions because more minds are at work on the problem. As we noted in Chapter 10, "Working in Groups," groups have the potential to accomplish more and perform better than individuals working alone. So, while the road may be paved with challenges, group decision making and problem solving can be highly creative, effective, and satisfying.

Although the terms *decision making* and *problem solving* are often used interchangeably, their meanings differ. **Decision making** refers to making a judgment, reaching a conclusion, or making up your mind. In a group setting, decision making results in a position, opinion, judgment, or action. For example, hiring committees, juries, and families decide which applicant is best, whether the accused is guilty, and whom they should invite to the wedding, respectively. Management expert Peter Drucker put it simply: "A decision is a judgment. It is a choice between alternatives."[6]

Most groups make decisions, but not all groups solve problems. **Problem solving** is a complex *process* in which groups make *multiple* decisions as they analyze a problem and develop a plan for solving the problem or reducing its harmful effects. For

> ## As difficult as it can be to make personal decisions, the challenge is multiplied many times over in groups.

instance, if student enrollment has significantly declined, a college faces a serious problem that must be analyzed and dealt with if the institution hopes to survive. Fortunately, there are decision-making and problem-solving strategies that can help a group "make up its mind" and resolve a problem.

However, before a group takes on such challenges, four prerequisites should be in place: a clear goal, quality content, structured procedures, and a commitment to effective deliberation.

A Clear Goal

As we noted in Chapter 10, "Working in Groups," the first and most important task for all groups is to have a shared goal that everyone understands and supports. One strategy for developing and understanding the group's goal is to word it as a question. The question format helps a group decide whether it should accept, reject, modify, or suspend judgment about an idea, belief, or proposal.

A group may ask four types of questions to achieve its goal. **Questions of fact** investigate the truth, reliability, and cause of something using the best information available. **Questions of conjecture** examine the possibility of something happening in the future using valid facts and expert opinions to reach the most probable conclusion. **Questions of value** consider the worth or significance of something, and **questions of policy** investigate a course of action for implementing a plan.

Group members understand that the answers to each type of question will shape the nature of their discussions. In some group contexts, an outside group or authority may dictate assignments. For example, a work group may be asked to find timesaving ways to process an order or contact a customer. A research group may be asked to test the durability of a new product. Even so, wording assignments as questions can help a group understand and structure its task.

Can You Identify the Type of Discussion Question?

Each of the following examples represents a question of fact, conjecture, value, or policy. Can you correctly identify each type?

1. What causes global warming?
2. Are community colleges a better place than a prestigious university to begin higher education?
3. Will company sales increase next quarter?
4. Which candidate should we support for president of the student government association?
5. For how many more years will Americans feel the negative effects of the 2008 Recession?
6. Does cold beer soothe the burn of hot peppers?

Answers:
1. fact, 2. value, 3. conjecture, 4. policy, 5. conjecture, 6. fact

Quality Content

Well-informed groups are more likely to make good decisions. The amount and accuracy of information available to a group are critical factors in predicting its success.

The key to becoming a well-informed group lies in the ability of members to collect, share, and analyze the information needed to achieve the group's goal. The reading on pages 218–219 emphasizes the importance of sharing new information with members in order to make a sound collaborative decision.

When a group lacks relevant and valid information, effective decision making and problem solving become difficult, even impossible. During an initial meeting, a group should discuss how to become better informed.

Structured Procedures

Groups need clear procedures that specify how they will make decisions and solve problems. Group communication scholar Marshall Scott Poole claims that structured procedures are "the heart of group work [and] the most powerful tools we have to improve the conduct of meetings."[7]

"Tribe" members on *Survivor* make strategic group decisions in order to win a team "challenge."

> ❝ The ability of a group to gather and retain a wide range of information is the single most important determinant of high-quality decision making. ❞
> —Randy Hirokawa, group communication scholar [8]

GROUP RESEARCH STRATEGIES

- Assess the group's current knowledge.
- Identify areas needing research.
- Assign research responsibilities.
- Set research deadlines.
- Determine how to share and analyze information effectively.

There are, however, many different kinds of procedures, including complex, theory-based problem-solving models designed to tackle the overall problem as well as decision-making methods designed for tasks such as idea generation, assessing options, and solution implementation. The remainder of this chapter describes how various procedures can and should be used to improve group decision making and problem solving.

Commitment to Deliberation

The fourth prerequisite for effective decision making and problem solving requires a commitment by all members to be well prepared and willing to tackle challenging tasks, to meet the needs of members, and to balance competing tensions. Put another way, group members are committed to engaging in productive **deliberation**, a collective, critical thinking process that enlists the values of democracy and puts them in a communication context. John Gastil explains that constructive deliberation calls for thoughtful arguments, critical listening, and earnest decision making.[9]

Before your group embarks upon a decision-making and problem-solving journey, make sure that all members are ready, willing, and able to deliberate. Your group should share a strong commitment to:

- weighing ideas, information, and opinions carefully and fairly;
- discussing personal and emotional experiences;
- giving equitable speaking opportunities to all participants;
- encouraging active listening by all participants, particularly when there is disagreement;
- sharing new information and opinions;
- understanding, discussing, respecting, and adapting to differences among participants' diverse ways of thinking, speaking, and listening.[10]

Knowing what deliberation is and what it should do may not accomplish anything unless group members accept and apply its principles. Although most juries deliberate fairly and intelligently, other juries seem unable to evaluate evidence and argue judiciously, to listen to one another comprehensively and analytically, and to bridge differences among jurors. Even a small, self-contained work group can spend hours talking, but fail to accomplish anything because they do not understand and are not committed to constructive deliberation.

The rest of this chapter goes beyond these basic prerequisites and offers theories, strategies, and skills that enhance the efficiency and effectiveness of group deliberation, especially in the face of decision-making and problem-solving challenges.

Groupthink

In his book *Group Genius*, Keith Sawyer retells a story about a group of twelve heavy smokers who signed up for a stop-smoking group at a local health clinic. One heavy smoker revealed that he had stopped smoking right after joining the group. His comment infuriated the other eleven members. They ganged up on him so fiercely that at the beginning of the next meeting, he announced that he'd gone back to smoking two packs a day. The entire group cheered. "Keep in mind," writes Sawyer, "that the whole point of the group was to reduce smoking!"[11]

What happened in the stop-smoking group is not unusual.

Although conforming to group norms and promoting group cohesiveness benefit groups in many ways, too much of either is a bad thing. They can result in a phenomenon that Yale University psychologist Irving Janis identified as **groupthink**—the deterioration of group effectiveness as a consequence of in-group pressure.[12] It is "a mode of thinking that people engage in when they are deeply involved in a cohesive in-group, when the members' striving for unanimity overrides their motivation to realistically appraise alternative courses of action."[13]

Groupthink stifles the free flow of information, suppresses constructive disagreement, and erects nearly impenetrable barriers to effective decision making and problem solving.

Janis's groupthink theory focuses on patterns of behavior in policy-making fiascos, such as the failed Bay of Pigs invasion in Cuba, decision errors during the Korean and Vietnam wars, the tragic *Challenger* space shuttle disaster, and the decision to invade Iraq in 2003, to name a few.

Groupthink tends to occur when one or more of three preconditions or causes are present in a group:

- *The group is highly cohesive.* Members overestimate their competence and perceptions of rightness. In order to maintain cohesiveness, the group may discourage disagreement in order to achieve total consensus.

- *There are structural flaws in the group process.* Structural flaws—such as insulating the group from other groups or an inappropriate leadership style—can "inhibit the flow of information and promote carelessness in the application of decision-making procedures."[15] For example, a leader or one member may have too much influence, or the group's procedures may limit access to outside or contrary information.

- *The situation is volatile.* When a group must make a high-stakes decision, stress levels are high. Members may rush to make a decision that turns out to be flawed, and they may shut out other reasonable options.

Fortunately, there are ways to minimize the potential for groupthink. Every member should assume the role of critical evaluator and should ask questions, offer reasons for their positions, express disagreement, and evaluate one another's ideas.

Consider inviting an expert to your meeting and encourage constructive criticism. If nothing else, the group should discuss the potential negative consequences of any decision or action. Finally, before finalizing a decision, give members a second chance to express any lingering doubts.

Effective groups avoid groupthink by spending time and energy working through differences without sacrificing group cohesiveness in pursuit of responsible decisions. As an added and positive consequence, taking such "procedural steps can turn a dysfunctional group into a highly competent one."[16]

SYMPTOMS of Groupthink[14]

Irving Janis identified eight symptoms of groupthink. Each one can cause or be an indicator of flawed decision making.

SYMPTOMS	DESCRIPTION	EXAMPLE
Invulnerability	Group is overconfident; willing to take big risks	"We're right. We've done this before and nothing's gone wrong."
Rationalization	Group makes excuses; discounts warnings	"What does he know? He's only been here three weeks."
Morality	Group ignores ethical and moral consequences	"Sometimes the end justifies the means. Only results count."
Stereotyping Outsiders	Members believe opponents are too weak or unintelligent to make trouble	"Let's not worry about them—they can't get their act together."
Self-Censorship	Members doubt their own reservations; are unwilling to disagree	"I guess it's okay if I'm the only one who disagrees."
Pressure on Dissent	Members are pressured to agree	"Why are you holding this up? You'll ruin the project."
Illusion of Unanimity	Most members erroneously believe that everyone agrees	"Hearing no objections, the motion passes."
Mindguarding	Group shields members from adverse information or opposition	"Tamela wanted to come to this meeting, but I told her that it wasn't necessary."

Effective Group Decision Making

11.2 *Compare the advantages and disadvantages of decision-making methods in groups.*

All groups make decisions. Some decisions are simple and easy; others are complex and consequential. Regardless of the issue, effective groups look for the best way to reach a decision, one that considers the group's common goal and the characteristics and preferences of its members.

As a decision-making group, the Supreme Court has the power to determine the constitutionality of laws in areas such as school desegregation, abortion rights, the separation of church and state, and freedom of speech.

Decision-Making Methods

Although there are many ways to make decisions, certain methods work best for groups. Groups can let the majority have its way by voting, by striving to reach consensus, or by leaving the final decision to a person in a position of authority. Each approach has its strengths and weaknesses. An appropriate approach should be selected to match the needs and purpose of the group and its task.

Voting When a quick decision is needed, there is nothing more efficient and decisive than voting. Sometimes, though, voting may not be the best way to make important decisions. When a group votes, some members win, but others lose.

A **majority vote** requires that more than half the members vote in favor of a proposal. However, if a group is making a major decision, there may not be enough support if only 51 percent of the members vote in favor of the project because the 49 percent who lose may resent working on a project they dislike. To avoid such problems, some groups opt for a two-thirds vote rather than majority rule. In a **two-thirds vote**, at least twice as many group members vote for a proposal as against it.

Consensus Because voting has built-in disadvantages, many groups rely on consensus to make decisions.

Consensus represent group agreement "which all members have a part in shaping, and that all find at least minimally acceptable as a means of accomplishing some mutual goals."[17] Consensus does not work for all groups. Imagine how difficult it would be to achieve *genuine* consensus among pro-life and pro-choice or pro–gun control and anti–gun control group members. If your group seeks consensus when making decisions, follow the guidelines to the left.

Before choosing consensus as a decision-making method, make sure that group members trust one another and expect honesty, directness, and candor. Avoid rushing to achieve consensus—make sure that everyone's opinion is heard. Finally, be wary of a dominant leader or

Guidelines for ACHIEVING GROUP CONSENSUS

DO THIS:

- Listen carefully to and respect other members' points of view.
- Try to be logical rather than emotional.
- If there is a deadlock, work to find the next best alternative that is acceptable to all.
- Make sure that members not only agree but also will be committed to the final decision.
- Get everyone involved in the discussion.
- Welcome differences of opinion.

DON'T DO THIS:

- Don't be stubborn and argue only for your own position.
- Don't change your mind to avoid conflict or reach a quick decision.
- Don't give in, especially if you have a crucial piece of information or insight to share.
- Don't agree to a decision or solution you can't possibly support.
- Don't use "easy" or arbitrary ways to reach a solution such as flipping a coin, letting the majority rule, or trading one decision for another.

False Consensus

Many groups fall short of achieving their common goals because they have complete faith in the virtues of achieving consensus. As a result, they believe the group *must* reach consensus on *all* decisions. The problem of false consensus haunts most decision-making groups. **False consensus** occurs when members reluctantly give in to group pressures or an external authority. Rather than achieving consensus, the group agrees to a decision masquerading as consensus.[18]

In addition, the all-or-nothing approach to consensus "gives each member veto power over the progress of the whole group." In order to avoid an impasse, members may "give up and give in" or seek a flawed compromise. This is much like the "illusion of unanimity" symptom of groupthink; members work hard to achieve total agreement even though the outcome may be a flawed decision. When this happens, the group will fall short of success as "it mindlessly pursues 100% agreement."[19]

In *The Discipline of Teams*, John Katzenbach and Douglas Smith observe that members who pursue complete consensus often act as though disagreement and conflict are bad for the group.

> One powerful but misguided member can be responsible for the poor quality of a group's decision.

Nothing, they claim, could be further from the reality of effective group performance. "Without disagreement, teams rarely generate the best, most creative

The limited time and format of the television show *Top Chef* requires judges to reach consensus—even if it's false consensus.

solutions to the challenges at hand. They compromise . . . rather than developing a solution that incorporates the best of two or more opposing views. . . . The challenge for teams is to learn from disagreement and find energy in constructive conflict, not get ruined by it."[20]

---

member who can make true consensus impossible. Sociologists Rodney Napier and Matti Gershenfeld put it this way: "A group that wants to use a consensual approach to decision making must be willing to develop the skills and discipline to take the time necessary to make it work. Without these, the group becomes highly vulnerable to domination or intimidation by a few and to psychological game playing by individuals unwilling to 'let go.'"[21]

Authority Rule Sometimes a single person or someone outside the group makes the final decision. When **authority rule** is used, groups may be asked to gather information for and recommend decisions to another person or larger group. For example, an association's nominating committee considers potential candidates and recommends a slate of officers to the association. Or a hiring committee screens dozens of job applications and submits a top-three list to the person or persons making the hiring decision.

If a leader or outside authority ignores or reverses group recommendations, members may become demoralized, resentful, and unproductive on future

ETHICAL COMMUNICATION

Ethical Group Decision Making

Regardless of how contentious the discussion or controversial an issue, group members should always apply ethical standards to decision making. These standards include the following ethical responsibilities:[22]

1. ***Research***. Ethical group members are well informed and use what they know honestly.
   - Do not distort, suppress, or make up information.
   - Reveal the sources of information so others can evaluate them.

2. ***Common Good***. Ethical group members are committed to achieving the group goal rather than winning a personal argument.
   - Consider the interests of those affected by group decisions.
   - Promote the group's goal ahead of personal goals.

3. ***Reasoning***. Ethical group members avoid presenting faulty arguments; they build valid arguments and recognize fallacies.
   - Do not misrepresent the views of others.
   - Use sound critical thinking supported by valid evidence.
   - Avoid making fallacious arguments.

4. ***The Social Code***. Ethical group members promote an open, supportive, and group-centered climate for discussion.
   - Treat other group members as equals.
   - Do not insult or attack the character of group members.
   - Respect established group norms.

assignments. Even within a group, a strong leader or authority figure may use a group and its members to give the appearance of collaborative decision making. The group thus becomes a "rubber stamp" and surrenders its will to authority rule. Group scholars Randy Hirokawa and Roger Pace warn, "influential members [can] convince the group to accept invalid facts and assumptions, introduce poor ideas and suggestions, lead the group to misinterpret information presented to them, or lead the group off on tangents and irrelevant discussion."[23]

Decision-Making Styles

In Chapter 8, "Improving Interpersonal Communication," we described the Myers-Briggs Type Indicator. Two traits—thinking and feeling—focus on how we make decisions. Thinkers are task-oriented members who prefer to use logic in making decisions. Feelers, on the other hand, are people-oriented members who want everyone to get along, even if it means taking on another group member's responsibilities rather than risking a confrontation or interpersonal problems with that member. Each of the two Myers-Briggs decision making traits impacts a group's choice of decision-making methods and their outcomes.

Here we present five decision-making styles, each of which has the potential to improve or impair member interaction and group outcomes.[24]

Rational decision makers carefully weigh information and options before making a decision. They focus on "creating a sense or order and structure to deal with information" by using logical reasoning to justify their final decisions.[25] They claim, "I've carefully considered all the issues," and make decisions systematically. This type of person must be careful not to analyze a problem for so long that she or he never makes a decision. **Intuitive decision makers** make decisions based on instincts, feelings, impressions, or hunches. They tend to say, "It just feels like the right thing to do." They may not always be able to explain the reasons for their decisions but know that their decisions "feel" right.

Dependent decision makers solicit the advice and opinions of others before making a decision: "If you think it's okay, then I'll do it." They feel uncomfortable making decisions that others disapprove of or oppose. They may even make a decision they aren't happy with just to please others. **Avoidant decision makers** feel uncomfortable making decisions. As a result, they may not think about a problem at all or will make a final decision at the very last minute: "I just can't deal with this right now."

Know Thy Self

What Is Your Decision-Making Style?[26]

Indicate the degree to which you agree or disagree with each of the following statements by circling the appropriate number: (1) strongly disagree, (2) disagree, (3) undecided (neither agree nor disagree), (4) agree, or (5) strongly agree. There are no right or wrong answers; answer as honestly as you can. Think carefully before choosing option 3 (undecided)—it may suggest you cannot make decisions.

1. When I have to make an important decision, I usually seek the opinions of others.	1	2	3	4	5
2. I tend to put off decisions on issues that make me uncomfortable.	1	2	3	4	5
3. I make decisions in a logical and systematic way.	1	2	3	4	5
4. When making a decision, I usually trust feelings or gut instincts.	1	2	3	4	5
5. When making a decision, I generally consider the advantages and disadvantages of many alternatives.	1	2	3	4	5
6. I often avoid making important decisions until I absolutely have to.	1	2	3	4	5
7. I often make impulsive decisions.	1	2	3	4	5
8. When making a decision, I rely on my instincts.	1	2	3	4	5
9. It is easier for me to make important decisions when I know others approve or support them.	1	2	3	4	5
10. I make decisions very quickly.	1	2	3	4	5

Scoring: To determine your score for each type of decision making, add the total of your responses to specific items as indicated. Your higher scores identify your preferred decision-making styles.

Answers to items 3 and 5 = _____ rational decision maker
Answers to items 4 and 8 = _____ intuitive decision maker
Answers to items 1 and 9 = _____ dependent decision maker

Answers to items 2 and 6 = _____ avoidant decision maker
Answers to items 7 and 10 = _____ spontaneous decision maker

Spontaneous decision makers tend to be impulsive and make quick decisions on the spur of the moment: "Let's do it now and worry about the consequences later." As a result, they often make decisions they later regret.

Now consider what would happen if you had a group where half the members were rational decision makers and the other half were intuitive decision makers. Or what would happen if the group included *only* dependent or avoidant decision makers? Different decision-making styles can disrupt a group, but having only one type also has its pitfalls. The key is learning to recognize and adapt to different decision-making styles while pursuing a common goal.

Effective Group Problem Solving

11.3 *Analyze the nature and value of problem-solving methods in groups.*

Although there are many problem-solving methods, there is no "best" model or magic formula that ensures effective problem solving. However, as groups gain experience and succeed as problem solvers, they learn that some procedures work better than others depending on the problem, the context, and the characteristics and talents of members. In other cases, groups modify problem-solving procedures to meet their tasks and social needs. Here we present four problem-solving methods: Brainstorming, Nominal Group Technique (NGT), the Decreasing Options

Brainstorming Guidelines[27]

Sharpen the focus	• Start with a clear question or statement of the problem. • Give members a few minutes to think about possible ideas before brainstorming begins.
Display ideas for all to see	• Assign someone to write down the group's ideas. • Post the ideas where everyone can see them.
Number the ideas	• Numbering can motivate a group: for example, "Let's try to list 20 or 30 ideas." • Numbering makes it easier to jump back and forth among ideas.
Encourage creativity	• Announce that wild and crazy ideas are welcome. • Announce that quantity is more important than quality.
Emphasize input, prohibit put-downs	• Keep the ideas coming. • Evaluate ideas only *after* brainstorming is over.
Build and jump	• Build on, modify, or combine ideas offered by others to create new ideas.

WHEN NOT TO BRAINSTORM

• **In a crisis.** If the group needs to make decisions quickly or follow a leader's directions.

• **To repair.** If the group knows what went wrong and how to fix it, organize a repair team.

• **For planning.** If the group knows exactly what it has to do to reach its goal, hold a planning session to map out implementation details.

Technique (DOT), and the Standard Agenda along with advice about when to use them and when to avoid them.

Brainstorming

In 1953, Alex Osborn introduced the concept of brainstorming in *Applied Imagination*.[28] **Brainstorming**, a fairly simple and popular method, is used for generating as many ideas as possible in a short period of time. It assumes that postponing the evaluation of ideas increases the quantity of participants' input. It also assumes that the quantity of ideas breeds quality, based on the notion that creative ideas will come only after we have gotten the obvious suggestions out.[29] More than 70 percent of businesspeople claim that brainstorming is used in their organizations.[30] Unfortunately, many groups fail to use brainstorming effectively.

Brainstorming is a great way to tackle open-ended, unclear, or broad problems. If you're looking for lots of ideas, it is a very useful technique. But if you need a formal plan of action or you have a critical problem to solve that requires a single "right" answer, you may be better off trying another method.

There are several surefire ways to derail a productive brainstorming session.[31] If, for example, leaders or dominant members speak first and at length, they may influence and limit the direction and content of subsequent input and ideas. In an effort to be more democratic, some brainstorming groups require members to speak in turn. However, this approach prevents a group from building momentum and will probably result in fewer ideas. Finally, members who try to write down all of the group's ideas may end up being so focused on note taking that they rarely contribute ideas. It is better to have one person record all the ideas contributed by group members.

Although many groups use brainstorming, their success depends on the nature of the group and the characteristics of its members. If a group is self-conscious and sensitive to implied criticism, brainstorming can fail. However, if a group is comfortable with such a freewheeling process, brainstorming can enhance creativity and produce numerous ideas and suggestions.

Nominal Group Technique (NGT)

Andre L. Delbecq and Andrew H. Van de Ven developed the **Nominal Group Technique (NGT)** as a way of maximizing participation in problem solving while minimizing some of the interpersonal problems associated with group interaction.[32] The term *nominal* means "existing in name only." Thus, a nominal group is a collection of people who, at first, work individually rather than collectively. NGT combines aspects of silent voting with limited discussion to help a group build consensus and arrive at a decision.[33]

A Nominal Group Technique session has two phases: an idea-generation phase and an evaluation/voting phase. During Phase 1, the idea-generation phase, group members assemble and write down their ideas without interacting with one another. During Phase 2, the evaluative phase, group members share, record, and discuss their ideas and then vote for the ideas they like the best. By tabulating the

votes, the group can rank the ideas in order of preference.

Nominal Group Technique works particularly well when individual judgments and expertise are valued. Groups use NGT to rank job applicants, to determine which of many possible solutions receives the most support, to establish budget priorities, and to reach consensus on the causes

of a problem. The highly structured NGT process guarantees equal participation during the idea-generation phase and provides opportunities for discussion and critical evaluation in the second phase. NGT can also be useful when dealing with a sensitive or controversial topic on which contrary opinions or a myriad of details could paralyze the discussion.[34]

The Phases of NGT
Phase 1: Idea Generation

1. Each member writes his or her ideas on a piece of paper.
2. At the end of five to ten minutes, each member, in turn, presents one idea from her or his private list.
3. A recorder writes the ideas on a flip chart (or posts ideas using computer projections) in full view of other members. There is no discussion at this point—only the recording of members' ideas.
4. Round-robin listing continues until all members have no further ideas to share.[35]

Phase 2: Idea Evaluation and Voting

1. Members discuss each idea before independent voting.
2. Members clarify or state their support or nonsupport for each item.
3. Members vote by ranking or rating ideas privately, in writing.
4. The group analyzes the mathematically pooled outcome of the individual votes.[36]
5. The group makes a decision.

Brainstorming Versus Nominal Group Technique

Researchers comparing the effectiveness of brainstorming and Nominal Group Technique conclude that when it comes to generating numerous and creative ideas, NGT often works best. An article in the *Encyclopedia of Creativity* claims that the number of ideas generated in a period of time using NGT almost always exceeds the number generated from group brainstorming; furthermore, the quality of ideas resulting from brainstorming usually fail to match the quality of ideas resulting from NGT.[37] Such conclusions may be explained in several ways:[38]

- Because each member of a brainstorming group must wait his or her turn before speaking (rather than write down ideas simultaneously in advance), thinking becomes disrupted and idea production slows.
- Due to the fear of being evaluated by others, members may withhold their ideas, even though the group has been told to defer judgment.
- Not all brainstorming group members will perform equally. Some may loaf or coast along, letting others do all the thinking and talking.
- Typically, when one group member contributes more to a brainstorming session, the higher in status that member becomes, which tends to discourage others from speaking.
- Extroverted group members will produce significantly more unique and diverse ideas than introverted group members—this seems to be the case regardless of whether members engage in face-to-face or mediated communication.[39]

Nominal Group Technique avoids most of these problems because members have time to think and write during the idea-generating process. For brainstorming group members who want to avoid such problems, the group may decide to work at networked computers to generate a master list of ideas simultaneously *and* anonymously.[40]

Although NGT may be more effective in generating high-quantity and high-quality ideas, brainstorming does have its advantages. For one thing, it helps to improve group morale; for another, it can create an enjoyable and supportive communication climate.

Decreasing Options Technique (DOT)

The **Decreasing Options Technique (DOT)** helps groups reduce and refine a large number of suggestions and ideas into a manageable set of options.[41] In our work as professional facilitators, we have used this technique to assist small and large groups facing a variety of complex tasks, such as creating an ethics credo for a professional association and drafting a vision statement for a college. The DOT method works best when a group needs to sort through multiple ideas and options. In addition to what we call the DOT method, there are other versions with names such as Dot Voting, Multi-Voting, and the cleverly named Dotmocracy.[42] All of these methods have similar goals: to measure levels of agreement among a large number of people.

Generate Individual Ideas At the beginning of the DOT process, group members generate ideas or suggestions related to a specific topic. Ideas can be single words or full-sentence suggestions. For example, when creating a professional association's ethics credo, participants contributed words such as *honesty*, *respect*, and *truth*.[43]

Post Ideas for All to See Each idea should be written on a separate sheet of thick paper in large, easy-to-read letters—only one idea per page. These pages are posted on the meeting room's walls for all to see and consider. Postings should be displayed only after all members have finished writing their ideas on separate sheets of paper.

Sort Ideas Not surprisingly, many group members will contribute similar or overlapping ideas. When this happens, sort the ideas and post similar ideas close to one another. For example, when facilitating the development of a college's vision statement, phrases such as *academic excellence*, *quality education*, and *high-quality instruction* were posted near one another. After everyone is comfortable with how the postings are sorted, give a title to each grouping of ideas. In the vision statement session, for instance, the term *quality education* was used as an umbrella phrase for nearly a dozen similar concepts.

Prioritize Ideas At this point, individual members decide which of the displayed ideas are most important: Which words *best* reflect the vision we have for our college? Which concepts *must* be included in our association's ethics credo?

In order to prioritize ideas efficiently, every member receives a limited number of colored sticker dots. They use their stickers to "dot" the most important ideas or options. In our example, each member of the vision statement group was given ten dots and asked to "dot" the most important concepts from among the

When to Use the DOT METHOD

- When the group is so large that the open discussion of individual ideas is unworkable.
- When a significant number of competing ideas are generated that must be evaluated.
- When members want equal opportunities for input.
- When dominant members do not exert too much influence.
- When there is not enough time to discuss all the ideas.

twenty-five phrases posted on the walls. After everyone has finished walking around the room and posting dots, the most important ideas are usually very apparent. Some ideas will be covered with dots, others will be speckled with only three or four, and some will remain blank. After a brief review of the outcome, the group can eliminate some ideas, decide whether marginal ideas should be kept or combined, and end up with a limited and manageable number of options to consider and discuss.

Advantages of the DOT Method When a group generates dozens of ideas, valuable meeting time can be consumed by discussing every idea, regardless of its merit or relevance. The DOT method reduces the quantity of ideas to a manageable number. Despite its advantages, the DOT may not be appropriate in some circumstances. A group may decide to generate ideas in an extended brainstorming or NGT session to improve the quantity and quality of ideas.

When a simple dot does not provide enough information about why it was affixed to a particular idea, you can attach a sheet to the idea display that allow participants to check whether they strongly agree, agree, neutral, disagree, or strongly disagree. Members may also write additional suggestions on the posted sheets or explain why they did or did not dot an idea.

Although the DOT examples discussed here focus on face-to-face interaction, this strategy works very well in virtual settings. A virtual group can follow the same steps by using e-mail or group software designed for interactive work.

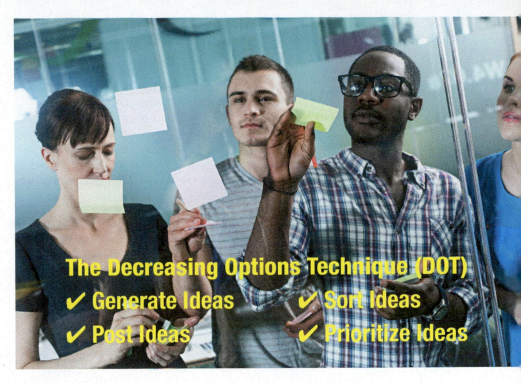

The Decreasing Options Technique (DOT)
✔ Generate Ideas ✔ Sort Ideas
✔ Post Ideas ✔ Prioritize Ideas

The Standard Agenda

The founding father of problem-solving procedures is a U.S. philosopher and educator named John Dewey. In 1910, Dewey wrote a book titled *How We Think* in which he described a set of practical steps that a rational person should follow when solving a problem.[44] These guidelines have come to be known as Dewey's *reflective thinking process*.

Dewey's step-by-step guidelines have been adapted for group problem solving. They begin with a focus on the problem itself and then move to a systematic consideration of possible solutions. In this section, we offer one version of this process: the **Standard Agenda** involves clarifying the task at hand, understanding and analyzing the problem, assessing possible solutions, and implementing the decision or plan.[45]

Task Clarification: Make Sure That Everyone Understands the Group's Assignment The primary purpose of a group's first meeting is to determine what the group wants or needs to accomplish so that everyone is working to achieve an agreed-upon common goal. During this phase, group members should ask questions about their roles and responsibilities in the problem-solving process.

Problem Identification: Avoid Sending the Group in the Wrong Direction Once a group understands and supports a common goal, members should focus on understanding the problem and developing a set of key questions. Identifying questions of fact, value, conjecture, and/or policy can help focus and aim the group in the right direction.

Fact-Finding and Analysis: Ask Questions of Fact and Value The following questions require research and critical thinking about the facts, causes, and seriousness of a problem, as well as an analysis of the barriers that prevent a solution:

- What are the facts of the situation?
- What additional information or expert opinion do we need?
- How serious or widespread is the problem?

The Seven Basic Steps in the Standard Agenda

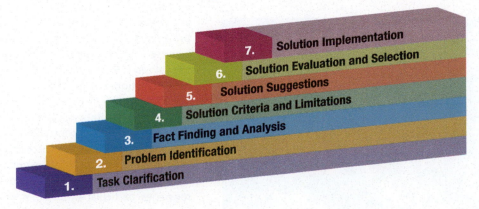

7. Solution Implementation
6. Solution Evaluation and Selection
5. Solution Suggestions
4. Solution Criteria and Limitations
3. Fact Finding and Analysis
2. Problem Identification
1. Task Clarification

Decision Making and Problem Solving in Virtual Groups

Although the group decision-making and problem-solving methods described in this chapter were designed for face-to-face meetings, they also work well in virtual groups. Additionally, specialized computer software, or groupware, can facilitate group collaboration, decision making, and problem solving.

Different types of mediated technology, however, are not equally suited to all types of virtual group meetings. In *Mastering Virtual Teams*, Deborah Duarte and Nancy Tennant Snyder offer a matrix that rates the effectiveness of different types of technology in relation to meeting goals.[46]

In this matrix below, *Product Production* refers to a meeting in which group members work on a collaborative project such as analyzing complex data, developing a design, or drafting a policy. Electronic Meeting Systems used in face-to-face settings allow members to use a laptop computer to input comments and analyses into a central display screen. [47]

Technology Matrix for Virtual Groups Meetings

Type of Technology	PURPOSE OF MEETING			
	Information Sharing	Discussion and Brainstorming	Decision Making	Product Production
Telephone or Computer Audioconference	Effective	Somewhat effective	Somewhat effective	Not effective
Email and Texting	Effective	Somewhat effective	Not effective	Not effective
Bulletin Board, Restricted Blog	Somewhat effective	Somewhat effective	Not effective	Not effective
Videoconference Without Shared Documents	Effective	Somewhat effective	Effective	Not effective
Videoconference with Text and Graphics	Effective	Effective	Effective	Effective
Electronic Meeting System with Audio, Video, and Graphics	Effective	Highly effective	Highly effective	Effective
Collaborative Writing with Audio and Video	Effective	Effective	Somewhat effective	Highly effective

The members of virtual groups have the potential to generate more ideas and enhance overall productivity with fewer blocking behaviors. Researchers claim that mediated idea generation and consolidation can be more productive and satisfying than face-to-face efforts.[48] On the other hand, most computer-linked groups require more time to complete certain tasks; while waiting, group members may become frustrated or bored. So, before you exclaim "Let's not have any more face-to-face meetings," consider these additional research findings:

- In mediated discussions, demographic differences in age and nationality initially make it more difficult for group members collaborate and can reduce the group's overall creativity and participation.[49]
- Virtual groups benefit from planning and attending an initial, face-to-face meeting before going virtual, especially if members "do not know each other and the project or work is complex and requires a high degree" of coordination, open mindedness, and individual expertise.[50]

- When groups go online, two opposite phenomena may arise. The first is a high degree of writing apprehension by poor writers or members who are not fluent English speakers. The second is that that some members may feel *more* confident when communicating virtually because they are good writers and prefer that medium to face-to-face interactions.[51]
- Some members need additional time to construct suitable replies when using a text-only medium. They want to make sure they send something that won't embarrass or be used against them later.
- Virtual groups benefit from shared leadership. A virtual group leader has additional management duties such as providing technical training, arranging when and how the group will meet use specialized software, establishing rules for interaction, and criteria for group decision making. This burden can be offset if other members assume some of these leadership responsibilities.
- Virtual groups will be more successful if they continuously check that members understand the meaning of shared messages, particularly those that have an emotional component.[52]

- What are the causes of the problem?
- What prevents or inhibits us from solving the problem?

Although carefully evaluating facts and opinions is critical to effective problem solving, groups must also avoid analysis paralysis.

Analysis paralysis occurs when groups are so focused on analyzing a problem that they fail to make a decision.[53] "Chances are you've been in [situations where] good ideas have been presented, but by the time enough people consider and reconsider the situation, it seems more complex, or not as great an idea as you originally thought. As a result, a conclusion about how to act is never reached."[54]

Rather than spending too much time arguing about the issue or giving up on finding the correct answer, a group may have to move on and begin its search for solutions.

Solution Criteria and Limitations: Set Standards for an Ideal Resolution Solution criteria are standards that should be met in order to achieve an ideal resolution of a problem. A group can establish criteria by asking questions such as: Is the solution reasonable and realistic? Is it affordable? Do we have the staff, resources, and time to implement it? The development of solution criteria should also include an understanding of solution limitations, which may be financial, institutional, practical, political, and legal in scope.

Solution Suggestions: Consider Multiple Solutions Without Judgment At this point in a group's deliberations, some solutions are probably obvious. Even so, the group should suggest or engage in a brainstorming or an NGT session to identify as many solutions as possible without criticizing them. Having spent time analyzing the problem and establishing solution criteria, members should be able to offer numerous solutions.

Solution Evaluation and Selection: Discuss the Pros and Cons of Each Suggestion During this phase, a group should return to the solution criteria and use them to evaluate the strengths and weaknesses of each suggested solution. This stage of the Standard Agenda may be the most difficult and controversial. Discussion may become heated, and disagreements may grow fierce. Consider using a modified DOT method to sort and prioritize potential solutions.

If, however, the group has been conscientious in analyzing the problem and establishing criteria for solutions, some solutions will be rejected quickly, whereas others will swiftly rise to the top of the list.

Solution Implementation: Decide on a Plan of Action After selecting a solution, a group faces one more challenge: How should the decision be implemented? For all the time a group spends trying to solve a problem, it may take even more time organizing the task of implementing the solution. Brilliant solutions can fail if no one takes responsibility or has the authority to implement a group's decision.

Effective Group Meetings

11.4 *Practice effective meeting strategies and skills.*

Millions of business meetings occur daily in the United States. "Employees and managers attend approximately 3.2 meetings per week. However, the quality of these meetings is evaluated as poor in 41.9 percent of the cases."[55] How bad is this problem? The *Business Management Daily* reports that "too many meetings" is the second biggest employee complaint, with "too much work" being the first.[56] The amount of time people spend in meetings has even been "linked to decreased well-being and increased fatigue."[57] Even so, abolishing all of these meetings is highly unlikely.

Yet, when meetings are well planned and conducted, they build strong alliances and confer a sense of control. Members are more motivated to implement group ideas and actions when they have a real voice in the decision-making process.[58] Fortunately, the solution to the "big, bad, boring" meeting problem is *not* more meetings.

Before looking at how to plan and conduct meetings, we should specify what we mean by the word. A random gathering of people in one place does not constitute a meeting. Rather, a **meeting** is a scheduled gathering of group members for a structured discussion guided by a designated chairperson. The leader designated as a meeting's chairperson has a tremendous amount of influence over and responsibility for its success.

Planning the Meeting

Proper planning largely determines the success or failure of a meeting. To help make your meeting more efficient and effective and to decide whether one is even necessary, ask and answer the five W questions (see the "5 Ws of Planning a Meeting" feature on the next page): Why are we meeting? Who should attend? When should we meet? Where should we meet? and What materials do we need?

> **"Careful planning can prevent at least twenty minutes of wasted time for each hour of a group's meeting."**
> —Karen Anderson, *Making Meetings Work*[59]

Preparing the Agenda

The most important item to prepare and distribute to a group prior to a meeting is an **agenda**, an outline that puts the meeting topics in the order they will be discussed. A well-prepared agenda serves many purposes. First and foremost, the agenda is an organizational tool—a road map for the discussion that helps a group focus on its task and goal.

In *Meetings: Do's, Don'ts, and Donuts*, Sharon Lippincott uses a simile to explain why a well-planned agenda

5 Ws of Planning a Meeting

Why Are We Meeting? The most important step in planning a meeting is defining its purpose and setting clear goals. Merely asking what a meeting is about only identifies the topic of discussion: "employer-provided day care." Asking *why* this topic is being discussed will lead you to the purpose: "to determine whether our employer-provided day care system needs to be expanded." If your group cannot achieve its purpose in a single meeting, focus on a more specific outcome. If many cases, you'll need a series of meetings to achieve group goals.

Who Should Attend? Most group membership is predetermined. However, if a task requires input only from certain people, only invite those participants who can make a significant contribution. Select participants with special expertise, diverse opinions and approaches, and the power to implement decisions.

When Should We Meet? Seek input and decide on the best day and time for the meeting, as well as when a meeting should begin and end. Schedule the meeting when the most essential and productive members are free.

Where Should We Meet? Choose an appropriate location for the purpose and size of the meeting. Try to find a comfortable setting, making sure that the meeting room is free of distractions such as ringing phones and noisy conversations. An attractive and quiet meeting room can help your group stay motivated and focused.

What Materials Do We Need? The most important item to prepare and distribute to the group is the meeting's agenda. You may also need to distribute reports or other reading material for review well before the meeting. Also make sure that supplies and equipment such as pens, paper, or computers and screens are available.

is essential for conducting effective meetings:

> Starting a meeting without an agenda is like setting out on a journey over unfamiliar roads with no map and only a general idea of the route to your destination. You may get there, but only after lengthy detours. A good agenda defines the destination of the meeting, draws a map of the most direct route, and provides checkpoints along the way.[60]

When used properly, an agenda identifies what participants should expect and prepare for in a meeting. After a meeting, the agenda can be used to assess a meeting's success by determining the extent to which all items were addressed.

The following guidelines for agenda preparation can improve meeting productivity:

- Note the amount of time it should take to complete a discussion item

SAMPLE AGENDAS

Sample Meeting Agenda

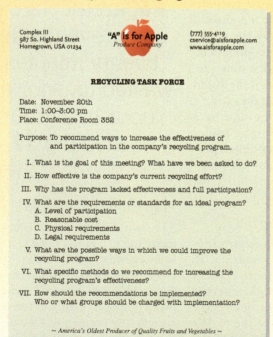

Sample discussion agenda for a group examining a specific issue: ways to improve a company's recycling program.

Standard Business Agenda

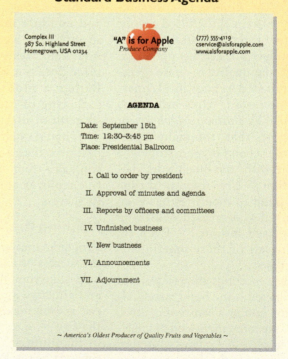

Basic components of a standard business agenda that follows a traditional format for formal business meetings.

> **An agenda ... is a road map for the discussion that helps a group focus on its task and goal.**

or action. This lets the group see the relative importance of the item and help to manage the time available for discussion.

- Identify how the group will deal with each item. Will the group share information, discuss an issue, and/or make a decision? Consider putting the phrases *For Information*, *For Discussion*, and *For Decision* next to appropriate agenda items.

- Include the names of members responsible for reporting information on a particular item or facilitating a portion of the discussion. Such assignments remind members to prepare for participation.

After selecting the agenda items, carefully consider the order for discussing each topic. When a group must discuss several topics during a single meeting, put them in an order that will maximize productivity and group satisfaction:

- Begin the meeting with simple business items and easy-to-discuss issues.
- Reserve important and difficult items for the middle portion of the meeting.
- Use the last third of the meeting for easy discussion items that do not require difficult decisions.

Taking Minutes

Most business and professional meetings require or benefit from a record

CLOSE TO HOME JOHN McPHERSON

© 1994 John McPherson/Dist. by Universal Press Syndicate

McPHERSON   12-5

As soon as Mrs. Felster began to read the minutes of the last meeting, the board members knew she was not going to work out as the new secretary.

of group progress and decision making. Responsible group leaders assign the important task of taking **minutes**—the written record of a group's discussion and activities—to a recorder, secretary, or a volunteer. The minutes cover discussion issues and decisions for those who attend the meeting and provide a way to communicate with those who do not attend. Most important, minutes help prevent disagreement about what was said or decided in a meeting and what tasks individual members agreed to or were assigned to do.

Well-prepared minutes are brief and accurate. They are not a word-for-word record of everything that members say. Instead, they summarize arguments, key ideas, actions, and votes. Immediately after a meeting, minutes should be prepared for distribution to group members. The longer the delay, the more difficult it will be for members to recall the details of the meeting and the individual task assignments made at the meeting.

Chairing a Meeting

The responsibilities of planning a meeting, preparing an agenda, and making sure that accurate and useful minutes are recorded belong to the person with the title of *chair*. The person who chairs a meeting may be the

---

Information to Include While Taking Minutes

✔ Name of the group.

✔ Date and place of the meeting.

✔ Names of those attending and absent.

✔ Name of the person chairing the meeting.

✔ Exact times the meeting was called to order and adjourned.

✔ Name of the person preparing the minutes.

✔ Summary of the group's discussion and decisions, using agenda items as headings.

✔ Specific action items or tasks that individual members have been assigned to do after the meeting.

Guidelines for CHAIRING A MEETING

- Always begin on time. Discourage chronic or inconsiderate late arrivals.
- Don't waste time explaining what's already been discussed prior to the late-comer's arrival.
- Create a positive climate in which members feel comfortable contributing to the discussion as well as disagreeing with it, or aspects of it.
- Establish ground rules for member behavior.
- Delegate someone to take the minutes. Make sure the minutes are distributed to members soon after the meeting.
- Develop and follow an agenda. Keep the group on track and aware of its progress. If needed, place a time limit on each agenda item.
- Ensure that all views are heard. Intervene when members ramble or discuss irrelevant topics.
- Summarize ideas and suggestions.
- Do not let anyone (including yourself) dominate the meeting.
- Provide closure and stop on time.[61]

group leader, a designated facilitator, or a group member who usually assumes that role.

The 3M Meeting Management Team describes the critical role of the chair as "a delicate balancing act" in which chairpersons must:

...influence the group's thinking—not dictate it. They must encourage participation but discourage domination of the discussion by any single member. They must welcome ideas but also question them, challenge them, and insist on evidence to back them up. They must control the meeting but take care not to overcontrol it.[62]

In the conclusion of an article on supervisor-led group meetings at work, researchers identified three distinct ways to promote effective task achievement and member satisfaction. The authors urge leaders to pay special attention to "the meeting process, fair interpersonal treatment of meeting participants, and fair explanations regarding decisions and procedures."[63] We believe that practicing the Guidelines for Chairing a Meeting on the previous page can help you achieve these important goals.

COMMUNICATION&CULTURE

MOTIVATING MULTICULTURAL GROUP MEMBERS

In Chapter 3, "Adapting to Others," we described a number of cultural dimensions, all of which have implications for motivating group members to fully participate in group decision making and problem solving meetings.

- *Individualism–collectivism.* Individualistic members may need praise and seek public recognition for their personal contributions. Collectivistic members may be embarrassed by public praise and prefer being honored as a member of an outstanding group.
- *High power distance–low power distance.* Members from high-power-distance cultures value recognition by a leader and take pride in following instructions accurately and efficiently. Members from low-power-distance cultures prefer compliments from other group members and enjoy working in a collaborative environment.
- *Gender orientation.* Members—both male and female—who hold masculine values are motivated by competition, opportunities for leadership, and tasks that require assertive behavior. Members with more feminine values may be extremely effective and supportive of group goals but have some difficulty achieving a respected voice or influence in the group. Such members are motivated by taking on group maintenance roles, such as encourager/supporter, harmonizer, or compromiser.
- *High context–low context.* Group members from high-context cultures do not need to *hear* someone praise their work—they are highly skilled at detecting admiration and approval because they are more sensitive to nonverbal cues. Members from low-context cultures often complain that they never receive praise or rewards when, in fact, other members respect them and value their contributions. Low-context members need to hear words of praise and receive tangible rewards.
- *Short-term—long-term time orientation.* Members from cultures with short-term time orientations are motivated in groups that concentrate their energy and effort on a specific task, meeting deadlines, and immediate rewards. Members from cultures with long-term time orientations often find the single-mindedness of short-term time members stifling rather than motivating. They prefer to work on multiple tasks with flexible deadlines. The prospect of future rewards can motivate long-term time members to work more effectively.

Group Problem-Solving Competencies[64]

Use this assessment instrument to evaluate how well you or another group member participates in a problem-solving discussion. Rate yourself or another group member on each item by placing a check mark in the appropriate column, using the following scale:

1 = excellent   **2** = satisfactory   **3** = unsatisfactory

Group Problem-Solving Competencies	1	2	3
1. *Clarifies the task.* Helps clarify the group's overall goal as well as member roles and responsibilities.			
2. *Identifies the problem.* Helps the group define the nature of the problem and the group's responsibilities.			
3. *Analyzes the issues.* Identifies and analyzes issues that arise during the discussion. Contributes relevant and valid information.			
4. *Establishes solution criteria.* Suggests criteria for assessing the workability, effectiveness, and value of a solution.			
5. *Generates solutions.* Identifies possible solutions that meet the solution criteria.			
6. *Evaluates solutions.* Evaluates potential solutions.			
7. *Plans solution implementation.* Helps the group develop a workable implementation plan that includes necessary resources.			
8. *Maintains task focus.* Stays on task and follows the agreed-on agenda. If responsible for taking or distributing minutes, makes sure the minutes are accurate.			
9. *Maintains supportive climate.* Collaborates with and appropriately supports other group members.			
10. *Facilitates interaction.* Communicates appropriately, manages interaction, and encourages others to participate.			

What makes this group effective or ineffective? _____

_____

_____

_____

How could this group improve its problem-solving strategies and skills? _____

_____

_____

_____

Prerequisites For Group Decision Making and Problem Solving

11.1 Justify the prerequisites that enhance group deliberation.

- Whereas *decision making* refers to the passing of judgment or making up your mind, *problem solving* is a complex process in which groups make multiple decisions while trying to solve a problem.

- Before a group takes on decision-making and problem-solving challenges, four prerequisites should be in place: a clear goal, quality content, structured procedures, and a commitment to effective deliberation.

- Groups should take steps to prevent groupthink, which results in the deterioration of group effectiveness as a consequence of in-group pressure.

- A group's most important task is making sure that all members understand and support the group's common goal. Group members should determine whether they are trying to answer a question of fact, conjecture, value, or policy.

- In addition to being well-informed, groups need clear procedures that specify how they will make decisions and solve problems.

- Constructive deliberation requires thoughtful arguments, critical listening, concern for others, and earnest decision making.

Effective Group Decision Making

11.2 Compare the advantages and disadvantages of decision-making methods in groups.

- Although voting is the easiest way to make a group decision, some members win while others lose when a vote is taken.

- Consensus requires that all members agree to support a decision. Groups should look for and prevent false consensus.

- Authority rule occurs when a single person or someone outside the group makes the final decision.

- Different decision-making styles—rational, intuitive, dependent, avoidant, and spontaneous—can improve or impair group decision making.

Effective Group Problem Solving

11.3 Analyze the nature and value of problem-solving methods in groups.

- Brainstorming, a group technique for generating as many ideas as possible in a short period of time, works well when members are comfortable with the rules.

- Nominal Group Technique (NGT) maximizes participation in problem-solving while minimizing some of the interpersonal problems associated with group interaction because it separates idea generation and evaluation/voting phases of problem-solving.

- The Decreasing Options Technique (DOT) helps groups reduce and refine a large number of suggestions or ideas into a manageable set of options.

- The Standard Agenda is based on Dewey's reflective thinking process and divides problem solving into a series of ordered steps: task clarification, problem identification, fact-finding and analysis, solution criteria and limitations, solution suggestions, solution evaluation and selection, and solution implementation.

Effective Group Meetings

11.4 Practice effective meeting strategies and skills.

- Before calling a meeting, make sure you decide or know why the group is meeting, who should attend, when and where the group should meet, and what materials are needed.

- An agenda—the outline of items to be discussed and the tasks to be accomplished at a meeting—should be prepared and delivered to all group members in advance of a meeting.

- The minutes of a meeting are the written record of a group's discussion, actions, and decisions.

- When chairing a meeting, begin and end on time, create a positive climate, delegate someone to take minutes, follow the agenda, and facilitate the discussion.

Key Terms

TEST YOUR KNOWLEDGE

11.1 *Justify the prerequisites that enhance group deliberation.*

1 Which of the following groups is *primarily* responsible for solving a problem?
   a. A jury
   b. A hiring committee
   c. A department's social committee
   d. A toxic waste disaster team

2 Which of the following symptoms of groupthink is expressed by a member who says, "Let's not worry about how the other departments feel about this—they're all so dumb they don't even know there's a problem"?
   a. Invulnerability
   b. Stereotyping others
   c. Rationalization
   d. Mindguarding

11.2 *Compare the advantages and disadvantages of decision-making methods in groups.*

3 All of the following answers are guidelines for achieving consensus except:
   a. use stress-free ways of achieving consensus, such as flipping a coin or letting the majority make the decision.
   b. try to be logical rather than highly emotional.
   c. welcome differences of opinion.
   d. listen carefully to and respect other members' points of view even if they are very different from your point of view.

4 Which ethical responsibility are you assuming in a group if you treat other group members as equals and give everyone, including those who disagree, the opportunity to respond to an issue?
   a. The research responsibility
   b. The common good responsibility
   c. The social code responsibility
   d. The moral responsibility

11.3 *Analyze the nature and value of problem-solving methods in groups.*

5 Under which circumstances is brainstorming useful as a problem-solving method?
   a. If there is a crisis in which the group needs rapid decisions and clear leadership.
   b. If you need to correct something and know how to fix the problem.
   c. If your group knows its goal and how to achieve it but needs a planning session to map out details.
   d. If your group needs to generate as many ideas as possible in a short period of time.

6 Unlike brainstorming, Nominal Group Technique (NGT)
   a. gives members the opportunity to generate a significant number of ideas.
   b. gives members time to think and write in private during the idea-generating process.
   c. postpones discussion and criticism of ideas as they are shared.
   d. improves morale by letting members have fun as they listen to one another generate creative ideas.

7 Use the Decreasing Options Technique (DOT) when
   a. the group is small and can discuss individual ideas openly.
   b. the group wants to prevent a dominant member from dictating ideas or solutions.
   c. the group does not want to take a position on or discuss controversial ideas.
   d. the group wants to ensure that everyone's suggestions are considered and approved.

8 Which of the following answers presents the correct order for the first three steps in the Standard Agenda model of problem solving?
   a. Task clarification, problem identification, fact-finding and analysis.
   b. Fact-finding and analysis, problem identification, solution suggestions.
   c. Solution suggestions, solution evaluation and selection, solution implementation.
   d. Problem identification, fact-finding and analysis, solution criteria and limitations.

11.4 *Practice effective meeting strategies and skills.*

9 Before calling a meeting, ask all questions except the following:
   a. why are we meeting?
   b. who should attend?
   c. when and where should we meet?
   d. who will implement decisions?

10 All of the following responsibilities are essential for chairing an effective meeting except the following:
   a. begin on time.
   b. create a positive communication climate and ground rules for member behavior.
   c. take the minutes.
   d. follow the agenda.

Answers found on page 368.

THINK
COMMUNICATION

This *Communication Currents* article has been slightly edited and shortened with permission from the National Communication Association.

Communication *Currents*

A Publication of the National Communication Association

Volume 4, Issue 2 - April 2009

Why Can't Groups Focus on New Information?

In discussions, groups often fail to adequately use the unique information of their members. Rather, groups focus upon and repeat information that all group members know, even before the discussion began. That is, group members repeat what they know and every other group member knows, and fail to share new information with others. When this happens, the group cannot take advantage of the diverse informational perspectives available from its members. However, recent research has found that structuring group members into the roles of decision maker and advisor may increase the focus on unique information.

Imagine a group of three members (member A, member B, and member C) discussing whether to hire a job applicant. Assume all members of the hiring team have read the applicant's resume. This would be shared information. However, from individual interviews with the applicant, each learned information that the other two did not. For example, A may have had knowledge about the applicant's educational history that B and C did not have, and C may have talked to the applicant about a mutual professional interest, but A and B did not. According to research on the discussion of information in groups, members of the hiring team would probably mention and repeat more information about the applicant's resume—the shared information—in their discussion and

fail to integrate the unshared information that each member has.

One reason shared information is mentioned more is that all group members have access to it. However, once shared information is mentioned, groups often keep repeating the same shared information.

When unshared information is mentioned, groups often fail to repeat and integrate the unshared information into discussion. Thus, an opportunity to gain a new perspective is lost. Research by Gwen Whittenbaum on *mutual enhancement* has helped shed light on why groups continue to focus on shared information. When shared information is first mentioned, other members can validate this information because they too are aware of it. They might respond by nodding their head or making comments affirming the information, such as "Yes, yes, I know." Group members observe this positive response to the shared information and may be more likely to then repeat that information later in the discussion. However, when unshared information is mentioned, other group members may not be able to respond to the information and cannot validate it. They may not completely trust the information since they are learning about it secondhand from another person. This can cause the member who mentioned the unique information to not repeat it. In support of mutual enhancement, it

Assessment. The roles of decision maker and advisor are not included in the list of positive group member roles in Chapter 10. After reading this article, do you think these roles should be added, or do the listed roles capture the functions of a decision maker and advisor? Which of the roles in Chapter 10—if any—encompass these functions?

Assessment. Does this conclusion seem warranted to you? Would you withhold information you know about a job applicant? Does this example support Gwen Whittenbaum's conclusions about mutual enhancement in the next column?

Assessment. To what extent can the tendency of members to keep repeating the same shared information increase the chance of groupthink?

Comment. Gwen Whittenbaum (Michigan State University) explains that group members experience mutual enhancement when they evaluate one another's contributions and competencies more positively because they are discussing shared rather than unshared information.

Assessment. Why, in your opinion, would group members fail to respond to unshared information? Have you experienced this phenomenon in a group to which you belong or have belonged? What was the outcome of that behavior?

Assessment. Think of the groups to which you now belong or have belonged. Did this tendency to focus on shared information occur when there was one decision maker or multiple advisors? If so, how did it affect group decision making?

Assessment. The discussion of consensus in Chapter 11 explains that when group members reluctantly give in to group pressures, they may achieve a false consensus. To what extent—if at all—would Van Swol's recommendation to assign members the roles of advisor and decision maker help avoid this problem?

has been found that members who mention shared information are more influential and viewed as more competent in the group discussion.

Would the same pattern of information sharing hold true in groups that have differences in status and roles? What if one group member holds the decision-making power for the group? Imagine a group in which a cancer patient is meeting with a medical team to discuss treatment options, a congresswoman is meeting with constituents to get feedback about upcoming legislation that she needs to vote on, or a manager is meeting with subordinates to discuss reducing the budget. In each case there is a group discussion, but only one person will ultimately make the decision.

Research by Lyn Van Swol has found that in structured groups with one decision maker and multiple advisors, there is greater focus on unshared information. Moreover, members are more likely to repeat unshared information. Several studies have found that decision makers prefer to receive advice from group members who have more unshared information than those with shared information. Decision makers perceive group members with more unshared information as more competent. This is the opposite of studies about unstructured groups. In unstructured groups, members who shared information were more influential and perceived as more competent.

There are several reasons why structured groups may focus more on unshared information.

Unstructured groups need to reach a group consensus. Because shared information influences everyone's opinion, it validates everyone's opinion and facilitates reaching consensus. When one person is the decision maker in a group, consensus is not necessary, so group members may be more open to new information and viewpoints and do not have to worry about the new information upsetting group agreement. Also, when put in the role of advisor, a group member may feel more responsible for providing a unique perspective than when a group member is in an unstructured group and has no assigned role. Decision makers may also try to pool more unique perspectives from their advisors and may expect advisors to provide new information as part of their role. These expectations may not exist for members of unstructured groups.

In conclusion, if your goal is to encourage your group or team members to share information that is unknown to others, then assigning members the roles of advisor and decision maker may help.

ABOUT THE AUTHOR

Lyn M. Van Swol is an Assistant Professor of Communication Arts at University of Wisconsin–Madison. This article is based on Lyn M. Van Swol. (2009). "Discussion and Perception of Information in Groups and Judge Advisor Systems." *Communication Monographs:* 75: 99–120. *Communication Currents* and *Communication Monographs* are publications of the National Communication Association.

Assessment. Why would a group's decision makers conclude that members with more unshared information are more competent? And why wouldn't that be true in groups without a designated decision maker?

Comment. When members serve as an advisor and decision make, they help a group meet the prerequisites for group work: a clear goal, quality content, structured procedures, and a commitment to effective deliberation.

Planning Your Presentation **12**

KEY OBJECTIVES

12.1 Identify key competencies for beginning the speech preparation process.

12.2 Explain the importance of and differences between a presentation's purpose and topic.

12.3 Analyze the characteristics and attitudes of an audience and adapt your presentation accordingly.

12.4 Adapt to the logistics and occasion of a presentation.

12.5 Practice strategies and skills that can enhance your credibility as a speaker.

It was a four-minute speech. A speech that you will never read or see. The speaker was Cardinal Jorge Mario Bergoglio. He had already purchased his return airplane ticket to Argentina, refused the chauffeured limousines used by other Cardinals, and stayed in a modest room at a Jesuit college. And yet . . . in only four minutes the future Pope Francis captured the attention and support of the College of Cardinals.

On March 7, 2013, Cardinal Bergoglio addressed the General Congregation of Cardinals. He "took out a sheet of white paper bearing notes written in tiny tight script. They were bullet-pointed." The notes were written in Spanish, but he "spoke in Italian, the language most commonly used in Vatican City and the native tongue of Italy's 28 voting-age Cardinals." Unlike other speakers, Bergoglio spoke about issues no one else had addressed: "the long-term future of the church and its recent history of failure."

Rather than speaking about strengthening and promoting the Catholic Church, Bergoglio spoke about "justice, human dignity. And it was simple, clear, refreshing." Rather than focusing on the inner workings, politics, and scandals of the church, the man who became Pope focused on the church's outreach to those in need.[1]

Regardless of your religious beliefs or opinions about Catholicism and other religions, the story of Cardinal Bergoglio's ascendancy to Pope demonstrates the power of speech. Famous speeches—President Abraham Lincoln's *Gettysburg Address* and Martin Luther King Jr.'s *I Have a Dream*—have shaped the world we live in. Responsible speakers employ the power of speech to make the world a better place. Unethical speakers use the same power to impose tyranny and suffering on millions. In this chapter and those that follow, we examine the theories, strategies, and skills that personify effective and ethical speaking.

The Speech Preparation Process

12.1 *Identify key competencies for beginning the speech preparation process.*

Martin McDermott, author of *Speak with Courage*, writes, "A successful speech is not a matter of luck; it's a matter of preparation." He then describes watching *unprepared* students deliver speeches in class. "It's like watching a deer in the headlights of an oncoming tractor trailer . . . in slow motion. Both speakers and audience feel grueling pain." To prevent such torment, he offers three important pieces of advice: "prepare, prepare, prepare."[2]

Research conducted by John Daly and his colleagues conclude that anxious speakers are less likely to prepare effectively because, in short, they don't know *how*.[3] Rather than making orderly decisions about their purpose, audience, content, organization, language, and delivery, they become "lost" in the process.[4]

McDermott also observes that we often put off what we don't like doing; we procrastinate about going to the dentist, tax preparation, and speechmaking. Although you don't have much control of what happens in the dentist's office or during encounters with the IRS, you can control how well you prepare and deliver presentations. "Being prepared," writes McDermott, "will reduce your anxiety and increase the likelihood of a positive outcome. . . . Inadequate preparation often leads to a self-fulfilling prophecy: Speakers who don't prepare well don't do well and then 'hate' public speaking. Your fate is in your own hands."[5]

When discussing the wide range of speaking opportunities and occasions, we use the phrase **presentation speaking** to describe the process of using verbal and nonverbal messages to generate meaning with audience members. Presentation speaking encompasses oral reports, informal talks, and business briefings in private settings as well as public speeches to small and large audiences. Regardless of its purpose, audience, or place, if you know how to effectively plan and deliver a strong presentation, you are more likely to be noticed, believed, respected, and remembered.

A few years ago, two national surveys—one administered to working professionals and the other to students in college-level public speaking courses—asked respondents to identify the *most* important

TOP-RANKED SPEAKING SKILLS[6]

WORKING PROFESSIONALS

1. Keeping your audience interested
2. Beginning and ending your presentation
3. Organizing your presentation
4. Selecting ideas and information for your presentation
5. Deciding what to say; choosing a topic or an approach
6. Understanding and adapting to your audience
7. Determining the purpose of your presentation
8. Choosing appropriate and effective words
9. Enhancing your credibility
10. Using your voice effectively

COLLEGE STUDENTS

1. Keeping your audience interested
2. Organizing your presentation
3. Deciding what to say; choosing a topic or approach to your presentation
4. Using your voice effectively
5. Selecting ideas and information for your presentation
6. Determining the purpose of your presentation
7. Overcoming/reducing nervousness/stage fright
8. Understanding and adapting to your audience
9. Beginning and ending your presentation
10. Choosing appropriate and effective words

Myanmar democracy leader and Nobel Peace Prize winner Aung San Suu Kyi speaks at the 2013 World Economic Forum where she declared her intention to run for president.

skills for effective presentations.[7] Student responses were similar to those of the working professionals (see the previous page), with two exceptions, which we'll discuss later in this and subsequent chapters.[8]

Knowing how to prepare a presentation is an indispensable step toward mastering the top-ranked speaking skills the survey respondents identified. Effective preparation can also reduce your anxiety and increase your likelihood of success. The key competencies for initiating the preparation process focus on determining your purpose, analyzing and adapting to your audience, adapting to the context, and enhancing your credibility.

Determine Your Purpose and Topic

12.2 *Explain the importance of and differences between a presentation's purpose and topic.*

When inexperienced speakers are given a speaking assignment, the first question that often comes to mind is: What should I talk about? You may have asked yourself or your professor the same question. However, years of teaching *and* speaking have taught us that the first and most crucial step in developing an effective presentation is to determine your purpose.

Begin with Your Purpose

Purpose asks, *What do I want my audience to know, think, feel, or do as a result of my presentation?* rather than *What should I talk about?* Purpose focuses on *why: Why am I speaking, and what outcome do I want?* You must know *why* you are speaking before you can select or develop an appropriate topic.

Professional speakers and communication consultants fully understand and endorse the need to determine a purpose. Dorothy Leeds, author of *Power Speak*, writes: "Have you ever sat in an audience and asked yourself when the speaker was going to get to the point? Or heard a speech just drift—along with the audience? The subject may be compelling, the speaker even charismatic, but without . . . a clear purpose," the presentation may fail.[9]

Nancy Duarte, a respected communication trainer and speaker, insists that first and foremost, you must figure out "where your audience is starting," and where you want them to end up. "This," she writes, "is the most critical step in planning your presentation, because that desired endpoint is the whole reason you're presenting in the first place, and people won't get there on their own."[10] In other words, begin the preparation process by determining your overall goal. Then you can "build up to it with strong, powerful ideas and words."[11]

Determining your purpose does not guarantee you will achieve it. But without a clear purpose, you will have difficulty deciding what to say, what materials to include, and how to deliver your presentation.

Identify the Type of Presentation

As you develop your purpose, consider which kind of presentation will best convey your intended message. Do you plan to inform, persuade, entertain, inspire, or do all four?

Speaking to Inform An **informative presentation** is designed to report new information, clarify difficult terms, explain scientific phenomena, and/or overcome confusion and misunderstanding. Teachers spend most of their lecture time informing students.

Informative presentations may take the form of oral reports in a classroom or boardroom, project updates, how-to demonstrations, financial account explanations, research summaries, and formal lectures. (See Chapter 15, "Speaking to Inform.")

Speaking to Persuade A **persuasive presentation** seeks to change or influence audience opinions and/or behavior. Advertisements persuade customers to buy products. Political candidates persuade voters to elect them. Persuasive presentations occur in courtrooms and classrooms, as well

Without a purpose, it is difficult to decide what to say, what materials to include, and how to deliver your presentation.

EXAMPLES OF PERSUASIVE TOPICS

IDEA
Anger is *not* caused by others.

PEOPLE
Susan B. Anthony was the most influential advocate for women's rights in the U.S.

OBJECT
Bike helmets save lives!

ACTION
Protect the planet. Recycle.

as at college fairs, in car dealerships, around the dinner table, and in daily conversations. (See Chapter 16, "Speaking to Persuade.")

Speaking to Entertain

Entertainment speaking amuses, interests, delights, or "warms up" an audience. Stand-up comedy is a form of entertainment speaking. After-dinner speakers amuse audiences too full to move or absorb serious ideas and complex information. At a retirement party, friends may "roast" a retiree. (For more details on when and how to use humor in presentations, see Chapter 15, "Speaking to Inform.")

Speaking to Inspire

Inspirational speaking brings like-minded people together, creates social unity, builds goodwill, or celebrates by arousing audience emotions. Inspirational speaking occurs in special contexts, takes many forms, and can tap a wide range of emotions by appealing to societal and cultural values. Inspirational speaking is also more common than you may think. Examples include motivational speeches, sermons, toasts at weddings and anniversaries, eulogies to honor the dead and comfort the grieving, commencement addresses, dedications, and tributes, as well as award presentations and acceptances. (For more on inspiring an audience, see Chapter 16, "Speaking to Persuade.")

Inform, Persuade, Entertain, *and* Inspire

Presentations that only inform, persuade, entertain, or inspire are rare. You can make your presentation more compelling by doing all four. A professor's lecture may inform students about intercultural communication theories as well as persuade students that understanding cultural differences will improve communication in their daily lives and careers. To entertain them, the professor might use humorous examples of cultural misunderstandings and include captivating stories about other cultures to inspire students to travel abroad.

Choose an Appropriate Topic

Your **topic** is the subject matter of your presentation. A topic is often a simple word or phrase: *Egypt*. Yet two presentations on the same topic can have very different purposes. Look at the differences between these two informative purpose statements:

"I want my audience to appreciate the profound achievements and contributions of ancient Egypt to Western Civilization."

"I want my audience to understand the differences between the 2011 and 2013 revolutionary uprisings in Egypt."

When looking for a good topic, start with these questions: (1) What interests you? (2) What do you value? (3) What do you and your audience have in common?

What Interests You? If you are called on to make a presentation, but find it difficult to decide on a topic, consider talking about your personal interests, special expertise, unusual jobs, unique experiences, or worthy causes you support. Or create a chart in which you list potential topics under broad headings—sports, food, hobbies, places, famous people, music, major events, personal goals, community issues, and so on.

What Do You Value? **Values** are beliefs that guide your ideas about what is right or wrong, good or bad, just or unjust, and correct or incorrect. If you examine the values that are most important to you, you may find a speech topic that's right and appropriate for you and your audience.

❝Values trigger emotions and guide your actions.❞
The Institute for Global Ethics[12]

Be cautious when you review your personal values for a topic; they may not align with those of your audience. For example, you may strongly support gun control, but audience members may consider gun ownership a basic freedom. Also, cultures often differ in terms of what they value. Although most Americans value individualism, other cultures place greater value on community and group goals.

The Daily Show is a satirical television show that does more than entertain. Jon Stewart informs, persuades, and inspires as well. In 2008 and 2009, he was rated as one of the most trusted and influential people in the U.S.

Interesting Speech Topics Chosen by Your Peers

Afro-Cuban jazz
Alternative energy sources
Beer brewing
Big data
Body piercing
Christmas in April
Church of the Latter Day Saints
Cleopatra myths
Clogging
Closing a sale
Dream interpretation
Exercise and long life
Filibuster fury
Flash dance mobs
Genealogy and your family tree
Guantanamo
Gun laws
Hair braiding
Homework hardships
Immigration reform
Insects for lunch
Internet addiction
Investment strategies
Neanderthal genes in us
Prezi software
Privacy versus national security
Stilettos shoes
Therapeutic massage
U.S. Post Office
Vaccine safety
Vitamin myths
Vuzix smart glasses
Weight lifting

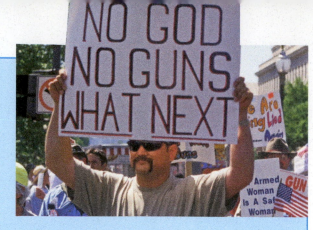

What Do You Value?

Regardless of culture or upbringing, all of us have a set of core values. The Institute for Global Ethics identifies eight universal values: love, truthfulness, fairness, freedom, unity, tolerance, responsibility, and respect for life.[13] What issues come to mind when you think about these values? Carefully consider the value-issue combinations that follow. Decide upon a presentation topic for each and think about how your topic choice reflects your personal interests and values. We provide an example for the first value.

- *Love* + Marital infidelity = Presentation topic: <u>How to save a marriage if your spouse has been unfaithful</u>.

- *Truthfulness* + Plagiarism = Presentation topic: _____

- *Fairness* + Gender biases = Presentation topic: _____

- *Freedom* + Gun control = Presentation topic: _____

- *Unity* + Labor unions = Presentation topic: _____

- *Tolerance* + Hate speech = Presentation topic: _____

- *Responsibility* + Parental accountability = Presentation topic: _____

- *Respect for life* + Human cloning = Presentation topic: _____

What Do You and Your Audience Have in Common? Nancy Duarte urges presenters to "Think about what's inside them that's also inside you." That way you're not imposing something on your audience. Instead, "you're into something they already believe."[14] Here are some questions to help you discover what you and your audience have in common:

- What characteristics, experiences, backgrounds, and interests do you have in common?

- What historic events have you and most audience members lived through or witnessed?

- What goals for your family, your community, your career, your hopes for peace, medical care, and safety do you have in common?

- What do you know and what have you learned from common challenges and even failures that will benefit your audience?

Narrow Your Topic

Make sure that you appropriately narrow or modify your topic to achieve your purpose and adapt to

listeners' needs and interests. Select the most important and interesting ideas and information for your presentation rather than telling your audience everything you know about a topic.

Although *you* may be an expert on your topic, your audience may be hearing about it for the first time. Don't bury them under mounds of information. Ask yourself, "If I only have time to tell them one thing about my topic, what would it be?" Chances are that conveying a single important idea is enough to achieve your purpose.

Develop Your Purpose Statement

When you know *why* you are speaking (your purpose) and *what* you are speaking about (your topic), develop a clear **purpose statement**, a specific, achievable, and relevant sentence that identifies the purpose and main ideas of your presentation. It is not enough to say, "My purpose is to tell my audience about my job as a phone solicitor." This statement is too general and probably an impossible goal to achieve in a time-limited presentation. Instead,

NARROW YOUR TOPIC

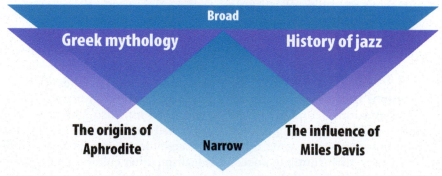

Broad

Greek mythology   History of jazz

The origins of Aphrodite   Narrow   The influence of Miles Davis

Characteristics of an EFFECTIVE PURPOSE STATEMENT

PURPOSE STATEMENTS	EFFECTIVE	NOT EFFECTIVE
SPECIFIC Narrows a topic to content appropriate for your purpose and audience.	Use the government's new food group recommendations as your personalized diet guide.	The benefits of good health.
ACHIEVABLE Purpose can be achieved in the given time limit.	Two effective treatments for depression can help you or someone you know.	Identify the causes, symptoms, treatments, and preventions of mental depression.
RELEVANT Topic is related to specific audience needs and interests.	Next time you witness an accident, you'll know what to do and how to help.	Next time you encounter an Ecuadorian poison dart frog, you'll appreciate its morphology.

your purpose statement must convey the specific focus of your presentation, such as "I want my audience to recognize two common strategies used by effective phone solicitors to overcome listener objections."

A purpose statement is similar to a writer's thesis statement, which identifies the main idea you want to communicate to your reader.

Notice how the purpose statements examples in the above table include more than *your* perspective on the topic. They also indicate why audience members should care about or be interested in your presentation. Using the word *you* in a purpose statement calls attention to "what you can do for them, not what they must do for you."[15]

In *Advocacy*, John Daly urges you to figure out WIIFT (What's In It For Them?) WIIFT answers audience questions such as, "Why should I care?" and "What's in it for me." When you create your purpose statement, consider how achieving your purpose will also benefit audience members in terms of, for example, their health, finances, career success, family and social relationships, security, status, enjoyment, abilities, and emotional well-being.[16]

> A purpose statement guides how you research, create, organize, and present your message.

Analyze and Adapt to Your Audience

12.3 *Analyze the characteristics and attitudes of an audience and adapt your presentation accordingly.*

Audience analysis is the process you use to understand, respect, and adapt to audience members before and during a presentation. It involves researching your audience, interpreting those findings, and selecting appropriate strategies to achieve your purpose.

Know Your Audience

Knowing your audience means asking questions about audience members' characteristics, attitudes, values, backgrounds, and needs as well as what they may and may not know about your topic. The answers to the following questions will help you understand your audience and decide what to include in your presentation.

Who Are They? Gather as much general **demographic information** (information about audience characteristics such as age, gender, marital status, race, religion, place of residence, ethnicity, occupation, education, and income) as you can about the people who will be watching and listening to you. If the audience is composed of a particular group or is meeting for a special reason, gather more specific demographic information as well. See the audience demographics figure on the next page.

Avoid "one-size-fits-all" conclusions about audience members based on visible or obvious characteristics, such as age, race, gender, occupation, nationality, or religion. As you know from Chapter 3, "Adapting to Others," oversimplified conclusions are stereotypes that can distort your perceptions. In addition, remember that *your* age, nationality, race, gender, educational level, and socioeconomic background may be just as critical in determining how well an audience listens to you.

Why Are They Here? Audience members attend presentations for

> The examples in your presentation, the words you choose, and even your delivery style should be adapted to your audience's interests and needs.

many reasons. They may attend course lectures in order to pass a course or because they've heard about the professor's famous and funny talk on Cleopatra. They may attend because they are interested in the speaker, for example, a candidate running for office or a celebrity giving a public talk.

Audience members who are interested in your topic or who stand to benefit from attending a presentation will be different from those who don't know why they are there or who are required to attend. Each type of audience presents unique challenges. A highly interested and well-informed audience demands a compelling, knowledgeable, well-prepared speaker. An audience required or reluctant to attend may be pleasantly surprised and influenced by a dynamic speaker who gives them a good reason to listen. Entire audiences rarely fit into one type or group. Your audience may include people with many diverse reasons for attending.

Age	Cultural background	Place of residence	Education
Race	Marital status	Income level	Parental status
Occupation	Religion	Gender	Disabilities

GENERAL

AUDIENCE DEMOGRAPHICS

SPECIFIC

Political affiliations	Professional memberships
Employment positions	Career goals
Military experience	Individual and group achievements

What do you know about your audience?

What Do They Know? Almost nothing is more boring than listening to a speaker talk about a subject about which you know more. Just as frustrating is listening to a speaker talk over your head. When considering your own audience, ask questions such as: How much do they know about this topic? How much background material should I cover? Will they understand topic-related terms or jargon?

What Are Their Interests? Find out if audience members have interests that match your purpose and topic. Consider two types of interests: self-centered interests and topic-centered interests.

Self-centered interests are aroused when a presentation can result in personal gain. Some audience members are enthralled by a speaker who advises them how to earn or save money. Others will be riveted by a talk about ways to improve their appearance or health. In all these cases, the listener stands to gain something as a result of the presentation and its outcome.

Audiences also have **topic-centered interests**—subjects they enjoy hearing and learning about. Topic-centered interests include hobbies, favorite sports or pastimes, or subjects loaded with intrigue and mystery. Topic-centered interests tend to be personal. A detailed description of a Civil War battle may captivate Civil War history buffs but bore other audience members. Whether self-centered or topic-centered, listener interests have a significant effect on how well an audience pays attention to you and your message.[18]

What Are Their Attitudes? When assessing **audience attitudes**, you are asking whether they agree or disagree with you as well as how strongly they agree or disagree. Some audience members will already agree with you, others will disagree no matter what you say, and others will be undecided or have no opinion. (See Chapter 16, "Speaking to Persuade," for strategies that adapt to specific audience attitudes.)

> There can be as many opinions in your audience as there are people.

Modifying Your Purpose to Suit the Audience

Preliminary Purpose: To describe journalism in the twenty-first century.

Who Are They? They are twelve women and six men; most are eighteen to twenty-one years old; the rest are in their thirties, early forties.

Why Are They Here? They are students in a mass communication course.

What Do They Know? They already know that the face of journalism is changing—that most people get their news from online sources; they also know that many print-only newspapers are in financial trouble.

What Are Their Interests? Some are more interested in public relations; others want to know more about journalism careers in online sources (blogs, corporate newsletter and reports, newspaper and magazine websites).

What Are Their Attitudes? Some think that, armed with a smartphone camera, Internet access, and writing ability, anyone can become a journalist.

Revised Purpose. To explain recent trends in journalism—backpack journalism, citizen journalism, industry-based online journalism—and their potential as career paths.

Adapt to Your Audience

Everything you learn about your audience tells you something about how to prepare and deliver your presentation. Depending on the amount of audience research and analysis you do, you can adapt your presentation to your audience as you prepare it. In other cases, you may use audience feedback to modify your presentation as you speak.

Pre-presentation Adaptation After researching and analyzing information about your audience's characteristics and attitudes, go back to your purpose statement and apply what you've learned. Answers to the above five audience questions can help you modify your preliminary purpose into one that better suits your audience.

Mid-presentation Adaptation No matter how well you prepare a presentation, you should expect the unexpected. What if audience members seem restless or hostile? How can you adjust? What if you must shorten your twenty-minute presentation to ten minutes to accommodate another speaker?

Adapting to your audience *during* a presentation requires doing three things at once: deliver your

How do park rangers adapt to the demographics, interests, and attitudes of their listeners?

COMMUNICATION & CULTURE

ADAPT TO NONNATIVE SPEAKERS OF ENGLISH

Did you take any foreign language courses in high school, college, or in an adult education program? If so, what happens when you listened to native speakers of that language? Did you understand every word? Were you able to talk to them with ease? Probably not. Such an experience can be challenging and frustrating. Imagine what it must be like for a nonnative speaker of English to understand a normally paced presentation in English. The following guidelines are derived from general intercultural research and from our observations of international audiences, both at home and abroad.[19]

- *Speak slowly and clearly.* Nonnative speakers of English often need more time because they translate your words into their own language as you speak. But don't shout at them; they are not hard of hearing.
- *Use visual aids.* Most nonnative speakers of English are better readers than listeners. Use slides or provide handouts for important information. Give the audience time to read and take notes.
- *Be more formal.* In general, use a more formal style and dress professionally when speaking to international audiences.
- *Adapt to contextual perspectives.* If you are addressing an audience from a high-context culture (see Chapter 3, "Adapting to Others"), be less direct. Let them draw their own conclusions. Give them time to get to know and trust you.
- *Avoid humor and clichés.* Humor rarely translates into another language and can backfire if misunderstood. Avoid clichés—overused expressions familiar to a particular culture—or common idioms. Will a nonnative speaker of English understand "A penny for your thoughts," "He opened a can of worms," or "She went cold turkey"?

---

presentation, correctly interpret audience feedback as you speak, and skillfully modify your message, the logistics, and/or delivery. Interpreting audience responses involves looking at individual audience members, interpreting their nonverbal messages, and sensing their moods. If audience feedback suggests that you're not getting through to them, don't be afraid to stop and ask comprehension questions such as, "Would you like more detail on this point before I go on to the next one?"

Think about adjusting your presentation in the same way you adjust your conversation with a friend. If your friend looks confused, you might ask what's unclear. If your friend interrupts with a question, you probably will answer it or ask if you can finish your thought before answering. If your friend tells you that he has a pressing appointment, you are likely to shorten what you have to say. The same adaptations work just as well when speaking to an audience.

Adapt to Cultural Differences

Respecting and adapting to a diverse audience begins with understanding the nature and characteristics of various cultures. Two of the cultural dimensions we examined in Chapter 3, "Adapting to Others," are especially critical for presentations: power distance and individualism–collectivism.

Power Distance As we indicated in Chapter 3, "Adapting to Others," *power distance* refers to varying levels of equality and status among the members of a culture. In the United States, a low-power-distance culture, authority figures often play down status differences. U.S. presidents are often photographed wearing casual clothes, corporate executives may promote an open-door policy, and college students and full professors may interact on a first-name basis.

If most audience members are from a low-power-distance culture, encourage them to challenge authority and make independent decisions.

However, if most audience members come from high-power-distance culture *and* if you also command authority and influence, you may be able to tell them what you want them to do—and expect compliance.

Individualism and Collectivism When speaking to individualistic audiences (e.g., listeners from the United States, Australia, and Great Britain), appeal to their sense of adventure, their desire to achieve personal goals, and their defense of individual rights. When speaking to a collectivist audience (e.g., listeners from most Asian and Latin American countries), demonstrate how a particular course of action will benefit their company, family, or community. If you are an individualistic American who feels comfortable drawing attention to your own or your organization's accomplishments in your presentation, a collectivist audience may dislike what they see as your seeming arrogance and lack of concern for others.

Adapt to the Context

12.4 *Adapt to the logistics and occasion of a presentation.*

Whether you are preparing a presentation for a public speaking course, formal banquet, prayer meeting, retirement celebration, or awards ceremony, take time to analyze the context of the situation.

Analyze and Adapt to the Logistics

Adapting to the place where you will be speaking requires you to think critically about logistics. The term **logistics** describes the strategic planning, arranging, and use of people, facilities, time, and materials relevant to your presentation, such as the audience's size, the facilities, the equipment, and the amount of time you have.[20]

Audience Size Knowing the size of your audience helps you choose appropriate audio and visual aids. For example, if there are hundreds of people in your audience, plan to use a microphone and make sure it's supported by a good sound system. If you expect 500 people in your audience, projecting images onto a large screen is more effective than using a small chart or demonstrating a detailed procedure.

Facilities Make sure you know as much as you can about where you will be speaking. Will audience members be seated in a theater-style auditorium, around a long conference table, or at round tables scattered throughout a seminar room? If you are in an auditorium that seats 800 people and you expect only 100 listeners to attend, consider closing off the balcony or side sections so that the audience will sit in front of you.

Equipment Computer-generated slide presentations are the norm in many speaking situations. Wireless microphones and sophisticated sound systems enable speakers to address large audiences with ease. Make sure you know in advance what is—and what is not—available at the location where you will be speaking.

Here's a story that could have had a better ending if the speaker had not made the wrong assumptions about her presentation's logistics.[21] When invited to speak to seventy people at a major corporation, she prepared a formal presentation for a room with traditional rows of chairs. But when she got there, she was taken to a tiny conference room with twenty people crammed into it—and with the small faces of webcam participants projected on wall screens. A question-and-answer session or a more conversational approach would have been a better choice than a scripted, formal presentation. Instead, she faced a series of unanticipated questions: Where should she stand? Where should she focus her eyes? Will the webcam participants be able to see the slides? An e-mail or phone call in advance could have avoided a lot of problems.

When possible, arrive at least forty-five minutes before you speak. Make sure that everything you need is in the room, that the equipment works, and that you know how to dim or brighten the lights if needed. Allow enough time to find equipment if something is missing or to make last-minute changes.

Time The most important thing to consider about the logistic of time is how long you are *scheduled* to speak. Plan your presentation so that it fits well within your time limit. Put a watch next to you when you speak or ask someone to give you a signal when it's time to begin your conclusion. And when that signal comes, don't ignore it, even if it means skipping major sections of your presentation. Audiences rarely like, appreciate, or return to hear a long-winded speaker.

Consider the following questions in relationship to your time limit: At what hour will you be speaking? For how long are you scheduled to speak? What comes before or after your presentation (other speakers, lunch, entertainment, a question-and-answer session)?

ASSESS the Facilities

- **What is the size, shape, and decor of the room?**

- **Does the room have good ventilation, comfortable seating, distracting sights or sounds?**

- **What are the seating arrangements (rows, tables)?**

- **What kind of lighting will be there? Can it be adjusted for the presentation?**

- **Will you speak from a stage or platform?**

- **Is there a good sound system?**

ASSESS the Equipment

- **What equipment, if any, do you need to be seen and/or heard?**

- **What equipment, if any, do you need for your audio or visual aids?**

- **Is there a lectern (adjustable, with a built-in light or microphone, space enough to hold your notes)?**

- **Do you need to make any special arrangements (a timer, water, special lighting, wireless microphone, a media technician)?**

Remember, your presentation should be the center of an audience's attention. If something in your appearance could distract listeners, FIX IT.

Analyze and Adapt to the Occasion

What's the occasion of your presentation? Will you be speaking at a celebration? Or is the occasion an oral class assignment, a memorial service, a convention keynote address, or testimony before a government agency? Make sure that your presentation suits the **occasion**—the reason an audience has assembled at a particular place and time. As is the case with logistics, there are important questions to respond to as you prepare a presentation.

What Does the Audience Expect? The nature of an occasion creates audience expectations about the way a presentation should be prepared and delivered. Business audiences may expect well-qualified speakers to pepper their presentations with sophisticated, computer-generated graphics. Audiences at political events are accustomed to sound bites on television and expect to hear short, crisp phrases. Audiences expect an uplifting tone at a graduation ceremony and a more raucous tone at a football pep rally. At a funeral, a eulogy may be touching or funny, but it's almost always very respectful and short. Do your best

---

MEDIATED COMMUNICATION IN *ACTION*

Web-Based Presentations

Web-based presentations come in many forms. For example, YouTube provides a place for creating your own biographical video and for sharing your video presentations with others. On many campuses, students enroll in online courses in which they access online lectures by their professors. More imaginative instructors use virtual worlds such as Second Life in which "to hold distance-education classes." They claim that communication among students actually gets livelier when they assume "digital identities."[22] Some of our colleagues in communication studies have created a special place in Second Life where students can deliver and evaluate one another's presentations.

Imagine the challenge confronting speakers (as was the case with your authors) making their first WebEx presentation. WebEx allows speakers to use computer-generated slides and their voices to address a geographically dispersed audience sitting at their computers or a collected audiences watching computer projections. Although videoconferencing is available via WebEx, many of these meetings are commonly done without it. In such cases, not only can't the audience see you, you cannot see them or their reactions.

After a harrowing experience doing his first WebEx presentation, Gene Zelazny realized that there were some new rules at work. He learned that, in general, "the medium works best for conveying information that requires visual illustrations and involves a small amount of audience interaction, such as questions and answers."[23] We also recommend, regardless of the medium, that you get as much technical support as you can from experts who understand and know how to make the most of the technology.

Online presentations usually require significantly more preparation than a traditional speaker facing an audience. Here's one speaker's recollection of an online presentation, which she had to prepare and deliver on behalf of a major computer company:

Once I had to deliver the keynote address to a conference of five hundred senior military and government officials in Singapore. To make matters more interesting, I was in New York at the time delivering the address online. I had to select a mix of learning activities and supporting technologies to make this a high-energy, distance-learning experience. I wanted to have a different visual every three minutes and to vary the format of my presentation several times. I combined slides, live camera shots of myself and audience members (we had a camera in the conference room in Singapore that fed to a monitor in New York), and still pictures. I also reserved about fifteen minutes after the speech for audience questions, which really made it feel as if we were in the same room. I built a website for the presentation with hundreds of links and resources so audience members could also follow up at their leisure.

I was struck by how much energy it took to prepare the presentation. I had to produce my own presentation as I was giving it by pointing and clicking the mouse on my laptop. Yet it paid off. I saved twenty-eight hours of travel for a forty-minute presentation. I saved our hosts a lot of money. Most important, though, the online format drove home the message about the power of technology-assisted learning.[24]

How Long *Should* You Speak?

We often hear two questions about the time limit for a presentation: "What if I'm not given a time limit?" and "What if I have something *really* important to say and I have to talk longer?"

If you are not given a time limit, we recommend keeping your presentation under twenty minutes. Peggy Noonan, one of President Reagan's speechwriters, recommends a twenty-minute limit.[25] Granville Toogood, author of *The Articulate Executive*, reports the results of a study conducted by the U.S. Navy in which they tried to determine how long people can listen and retain information. The answer: eighteen minutes.[26]

If you have ever seen and/or listened to a TED (Technology, Entertainment, Design) talk, you'll notice that each talk takes no longer than eighteen minutes. TED is a nonprofit organization that sponsors high-powered speaking contests, which "bring together the world's most fascinating thinkers and doers, who are challenged to give the talk of their lives." So why the eighteen-minute time limit? According to TED, "It's long enough to be serious and short enough to hold people's attention." It forces speakers "to really think about what they want to say. What is the key point they want to communicate? It has a clarifying effect. It brings

discipline." Google TED talks and you'll find many videos of these award-winning presentations.[27]

Of course, there are times when the circumstances or content requires that you speak longer than eighteen or twenty minutes. In such cases, you have several options. You can cover the basics in twenty minutes and then set aside time for a question-and-answer session. You can use presentation aids or videos to break up your talk. You may also want to insert short personal stories or anecdotes to help drive home your point and give the audience a pleasant respite.[28]

Regardless of the time limit, don't fall into the ego trap of thinking that what you have to say is *so* important that it deserves more time. Your audience may not share this belief—no matter how long you take to convince them. Demonstrate respect for your audience's time and they will appreciate your self-discipline and consideration.

---

to match your speaking style and message to audience expectations.

What Should You Wear? Long before an audience hears what you say, they will see you, so wear something that matches the purpose and tone of your presentation. Your clothes don't have to be expensive or make a fashion statement. What matters is that they are appropriate for the situation. Common sense dictates our number-one piece of advice: wear comfortable, attractive, and appropriate clothes. Presentations are stressful enough without worrying about your clothing. When selecting clothes for a presentation, dress as key members of your audience would.

Nothing on your body (clothes, grooming, accessories) should draw attention to itself. Clanging bracelets or ties featuring big patterns or cartoon characters may not be appropriate. Take items out of your pockets, whether they're pens in your shirt pocket or the change and keys in your pants pockets.

Enhance your Credibility

12.5 *Practice strategies and skills that can enhance your credibility as a speaker.*

Speaker credibility represents the extent to which an audience believes a speaker and the speaker's message. The more credible you are in the eyes of your audience, the more likely it is that you will achieve the purpose of your presentation. If your audience rates you as highly credible, they may excuse poor delivery. They are so ready to believe you that the presentation doesn't have to be perfect.[29]

Components of Speaker Credibility

Three significant factors contribute to a speaker's credibility: character, competence, and charisma.[30] The speaker credibility chart on the next page summarizes the distinct characteristics that personify each of these components.

Character Of the three components of speaker credibility, **character**—a speaker's perceived honesty and goodwill—is the most important. A speaker of good character is seen as a good person—trustworthy, sincere, and fair. Is your evidence valid and

The more credible you are in the eyes of your audience, the more likely it is that you will achieve the purpose of your presentation.

your claims warranted? Are you doing what is right and ethical? If an audience doesn't trust you, it won't matter if you are an expert speaker or an electrifying performer.

Competence Competence refers to a speaker's perceived expertise and abilities. Proving that you are competent can be as simple as mentioning your credentials and experience. An audience is unlikely to question a recognized brain surgeon, a professional baseball player, or famous fashion designer as long as they stick to brain surgery, baseball, and fashion, respectively. A skilled auto mechanic, waitress, parent of six children, nurse, and government employee can be experts in their own right. Such speakers rely on their

expertise, life experiences, and opinions to demonstrate competence.

But what happens when you are not an expert? How can you demonstrate that you know what you're talking about? The answer lies in one word: *research*. If you don't have firsthand experience or cannot claim to be an expert, let your audience know how well prepared you are: "I conducted a phone survey of more than thirty individuals and found . . ." or "After reviewing the top ten textbooks on this subject, I was surprised that only one author includes information about. . . ."

Charisma Your perceived level of energy, enthusiasm, vigor, and commitment reflects your **charisma**. A speaker with charisma is seen as dynamic, forceful, powerful, assertive, and intense. Among U.S. presidents, John F. Kennedy, Ronald Reagan, and Bill Clinton were charismatic. Charisma has more to do with how you deliver a presentation than with what you have to say; in that regard, Adolf Hitler was also a charismatic speaker.

Speakers with strong and expressive voices are seen as more charismatic than speakers with hesitant or unexpressive voices. Speakers who gesture naturally and move gracefully are viewed as more charismatic than those who look uncomfortable and awkward in front of an audience. Speakers who look their audiences in the eye are thought of as more charismatic

than those who avoid eye contact with audience members. Practicing and developing your performance skills enhances your charisma in the same way that preparation helps you to be seen as a competent speaker.

Developing Speaker Credibility

Credibility does not exist in an absolute sense; it is solely based on the attitudes and perceptions of the audience. Thus, even if you are the world's greatest expert on your topic and deliver your presentation with skill, the ultimate decision about your credibility lies with your audience. Credibility is "like the process of getting a grade in school. Only the teacher (or audience) can assign the grade to the student (or

Researching and sharing up-to-date information helps establish your competence as a conscientious and knowledgeable speaker.

speaker), but the student can do all sorts of things—turn in homework, prepare for class, follow the rules—to influence what grade is assigned."[31]

Nathan Crick, author of *Rhetorical Public Speaking*, cautions, "Establishing ethos is a complex process that involves more than simply offering an audience a list of accomplishments and admirable characteristics."[32] A more subtle approach is needed in which you strategically build a positive personal image (see impression management in Chapter 2, "Understanding Your Self,") and effectively identify with your audience.

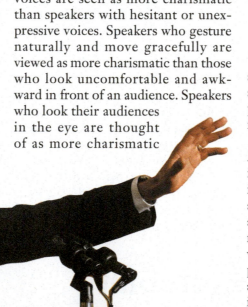

In light of his general approval ratings, how would you assess President Obama's ethos? In your opinion, which of the three components of speaker credibility is his strongest asset? Which is the weakest?

COMPONENTS OF SPEAKER CREDIBILITY

Character	Competence	Charisma
Honest	Experienced	Active
Kind	Well prepared	Enthusiastic
Friendly	Qualified	Energetic
Fair	Up to date	Confident
Respectful	Informed	Stimulating
Caring	Intelligent	Dynamic

Aristotle's Ethos

The concept of speaker credibility is more than 2,000 years old. Aristotle's *Rhetoric*, written during the late fourth century B.C., established many of the public-speaking strategies we use today. His definition of **rhetoric** as the ability to discover "in the particular case what are the available means of persuasion"[33] focuses on strategies for selecting the most appropriate persuasive arguments for a particular audience in a particular circumstance. His division of proof into logical arguments (*logos*), emotional arguments (*pathos*), and arguments based on speaker credibility (*ethos*) remains a basic model for teaching the principles of persuasive speaking. (See Chapter 16, "Speaking to Persuade.")

Here we focus on Aristotle's **ethos**, the Greek word for *character* that encompasses what we refer to as speaker credibility. Aristotle wrote, "The character [ethos] of the speaker is a cause of persuasion when the speech is so uttered as to make him worthy of belief. . . . His character [ethos] is the most potent of all the means to persuasion."[34]

> Aristotle's concept of ethos evolved into what we now call speaker credibility.

A speaker's ethos is not a permanent, personal trait. It varies with each audience and over time. Thus, you may have high, positive ethos with one audience and negative ethos with another. For example, when campaigning for public office, a Republican candidate has higher ethos when speaking to conservative audiences than to liberal audiences. Moreover "a speaker who is highly regarded at one time may be considered a has-been ten years later."[35] After losing an election by a wide margin, the same candidate's ethos may decrease among once loyal followers.

Several strategies can influence your audience's positive opinion of you and your presentation. Share your accomplishments and evidence of your devotion to a worthy cause. Prepare an engaging presentation and show your audience why you're uniquely motivated and qualified to deliver it.

Share Your Accomplishments

Each of us can do or has done something that sets us apart from most other people. It's just a matter of discovering what that something is. Take time to pinpoint your unique gifts, accomplishments, and contributions to worthy causes that can strengthen your credibility. An experience that seems routine to you may be a new experience for your listeners. Consider how you might answer the following questions: Have you lived or worked in another town, city, state, or country? Do you have or have you had an unusual job? Are you a volunteer for or sponsor of a worthy cause? What experiences or people have had a major impact on your life (childbirth, a visit to a foreign country,

> Credibility does not exist in an absolute sense; it is solely based on the attitudes and perceptions of the audience.

a life-changing mentor, a natural disaster, competition on a team, combat experience)? What can you do that most of your peers cannot (play the cello, write a song or short story, speak Turkish)?

A presentation lets you show an audience that your ideas and opinions are based on more than good preparation. They are based on personal experiences, accomplishments, and special skills. There is nothing wrong with using words such as *I* and *my* and *me* if they are appropriate; overuse, however, can sound boastful. Instead, tell the audience: "In my ten years of leading . . ." or "When my partner and I won the state's debate championship. . . ." In neither case would you be exaggerating or boasting. Rather, you would be explaining how and why you know what you're talking about.

Identify with Your Audience

Identification is a communication strategy for "creating a common bond with an audience by drawing parallels between the characteristics of the speaker and audience."[36] Put another way, identification is demonstrating that you and your audience are *we* as opposed to *me* and *you*. If, when developing your purpose and choosing a topic, you consider what you and your audience have in common, you are well on your way to identifying with your audience and establishing your ethos.

The Ethical Speaker

The words *ethos* comes from the Greek word meaning *character*. As we noted in our discussion of character, the apparent "goodness" of a speaker is

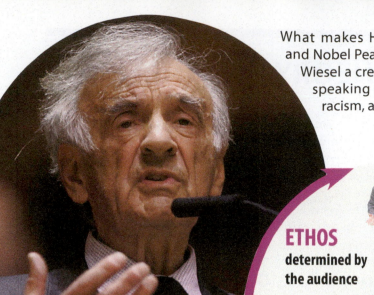

What makes Holocaust survivor and Nobel Peace Prize winner Elie Wiesel a credible speaker when speaking out against hatred, racism, and genocide?

ETHOS determined by the audience

ETHICS determined by the speaker

important in determining whether an audience believes that speaker. Audiences are also more likely to believe you if they see you as an ethical speaker. *Ethos* and *ethics*, however, are not the same. Ethos, or speaker credibility, relies on the perceived character, competence, and charisma of the speaker. The audience determines a speaker's ethos, but a speaker's beliefs about what is right or wrong, moral or immoral, good or bad determine her or his *ethics*. Only *you* can determine and demonstrate how ethical you are.

The Ethical Audience

The 2012 U.S. presidential election could also be called the Public Booing Extravaganza. In addition to the candidates' sharp attacks and condemnations of one another, recurring booing by audience members displayed a lack of civility and respect for speakers:

- At Clemson University, during a ceremony in which President Obama inducted ROTC cadets into the military, audience members booed during the section of the traditional oath taken by all military cadets in which they pledge to obey the President of the United States.
- During one of the Republican primary debates, the audience applauded and shouted "Yeah!" to the idea of letting an uninsured thirty-year-old man die without

care. In another debate, some audience members booed a gay soldier stationed in Iraq who asked a question through YouTube's video-sharing site.
- At an NAACP convention, the members of a predominantly black

audience booed when Mitt Romney explained his economic and educational proposals.
- At a convention of the American Association of Retired People (AARP), audience members booed Republican vice presidential nominee Paul Ryan for advocating the repeal of President Obama's Affordable Care Act.[37]

As much as we may complain about negative campaigns, we also have an obligation to behave ethically and to respect freedom of speech. Ethical audience members listen for ideas and information with open minds. They withhold evaluation until they comprehend what a speaker means. Ethical audiences are active listeners; they listen to understand, to empathize, to evaluate, and to appreciate. They think critically about a speaker's message.

Unfortunately and in day-to-day presentations, some audience members lack these skills. Even worse, they may not listen at all because they have decided, even before the presentation begins, that they don't like the message or the speaker. Audience members with open, unprejudiced minds is essential for a genuine transaction to occur between speakers and listeners.

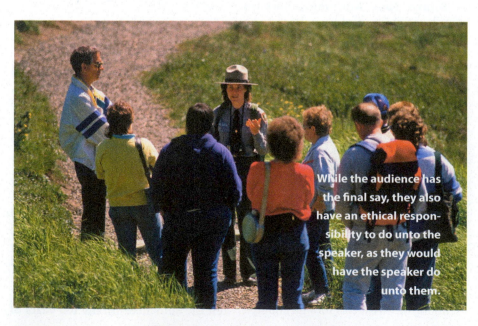

While the audience has the final say, they also have an ethical responsibility to do unto the speaker, as they would have the speaker do unto them.

COMMUNICATION

The Perils of Plagiarism

Plagiarism is dishonest, unethical, and in many cases, illegal. The word **plagiarism** comes from the Latin, *plagium*, which means "kidnapping." Simply put, if you include a quotation or idea from another source and claim it's your idea and words, you are plagiarizing.

> When you plagiarize, you are stealing or kidnapping something that belongs to someone else.

Some speakers believe that plagiarism rules don't apply to them. Others think they can get away with it. Still others plagiarize without knowing they are doing it. Ignorance, however, is no excuse. All of the examples in the following list are considered plagiarism:

- turning in someone else's work as your own
- copying words or ideas from someone else without giving credit
- failing to put a quotation in quotation marks
- giving incorrect information about the source of a quotation
- changing words but copying the sentence structure of a source without giving credit
- copying so many words or ideas from a source that it makes up the majority of your work, whether you give credit or not[38]
- downloading photographs, graphics, and PowerPoint slides from the web and treating them as your original work[39]

In a survey of college presidents, more than half report that they have seen a significant increase in plagiarism, claiming "computers and the Internet have played a major role in the rise in stealing other's work and claiming it as their own."[40] Other studies of plagiarism confirm this alarming rise, with more than 50 percent of students admitting to plagiarizing off the Internet for their class assignments.[41] Regardless of whether individuals plagiarize material for a book, article, classroom writing assignment, or a presentation, the result is the same: they are stealing something that belongs to someone else.

Although most speakers don't intend to kidnap or steal another person's work, plagiarism occurs more frequently than it should, often with serious consequences. Students have failed classes, been denied college degrees, and been expelled from academic programs and institutions of higher education. In the publishing business, authors have been sued by other writers who claim that their ideas and words were plagiarized. The careers of well-respected scientists, politicians, university officials, and civic leaders have been tarnished and even ruined by acts of plagiarism.

> Plagiarism is not just unethical; IT IS ILLEGAL.

- **High school student Blair Hornstine's** admission to Harvard University was revoked when it was discovered that she had passed off speeches and writings by famous people as her own in articles she wrote as a student journalist for a local newspaper.[42]
- **The Beatles' George Harrison** was successfully challenged in a prolonged suit for plagiarizing the Chiffons' "He's So Fine" for the melody of his own "My Sweet Lord."[43]

College instructors use a variety of techniques to catch students "kidnappers" of someone else's intellectual property. "The first thing I do," wrote one instructor, "when I want to check a student's work for plagiarism is to do a quick search on Google. . . . Put the suspected phrase inside quotation marks and search."[44] Faculty members also have access to websites that detect plagiarism, such as PlagScan, CheckForPlagiarism, iThenticate, PlagiarismDetection, Turnitin, and many more.[45]

The key to avoid plagiarism and its consequences is acknowledging the sources of your information in your presentation. Changing a few words of someone else's work is not enough to avoid plagiarism. Some of our students have told us that plagiarism occurs only if they use an entire article or someone else's written presentation. Others believe that it's okay to "borrow" a few phrases or someone else's idea. We immediately tell such students that this behavior is plagiarism—no matter how small the amount you are stealing, it is still stealing. If they're not your original ideas, designs, or words, you are ethically obligated to tell your audience who wrote, said, or designed the material and where it came from.

Use the following guidelines to help you avoid plagiarism:

- If you include key phrases or an idea that appears in someone else's work, always acknowledge and document your source.
- Do not use someone else's sequence of ideas and organizational pattern without acknowledging and citing the similarities in structure.
- Tell an audience exactly when you are citing someone else's exact words or ideas in your presentation.
- Never buy or use someone else's speech or writing and claim it as your own work.

enhance your credibility

What's Your Preparation Plan?[46]

Before you determine the content and structure of your message or practice your delivery, make sure you have made appropriate decisions about the four competencies involved in presentation planning: purpose, audience analysis, context, and speaker credibility. The following checklist can help you determine whether you are ready to take the next steps in preparing a presentation.

Purpose and Topic

_____1. I know whether my purpose will inform, persuade, entertain, and/or inspire.

_____2. I have a specific, achievable, and relevant purpose statement.

_____3. My topic reflects my interests, values, knowledge, and areas of commonality with my audience.

Audience Analysis

_____1. I have researched, analyzed, and planned ways of adapting to audience characteristics, motives, knowledge, and interests.

_____2. I have researched, analyzed, and planned ways of adapting to audience attitudes.

_____3. I have researched, analyzed, and planned ways of adapting to cultural differences in my audience.

Context

_____1. I have researched, analyzed, and planned ways of adapting to the logistics of the presentation (audience size, facilities, equipment, time).

_____2. I have researched, analyzed, and planned ways of adapting to the psychosocial context and occasion.

_____3. I have researched, analyzed, and planned ways of adapting to the cultural context.

Speaker Credibility

_____1. I have assessed my potential credibility by identifying my strengths, talents, achievements, and positive character traits.

_____2. I have planned how to demonstrate my competence and good character.

_____3. I have made ethical decisions about the purpose, audience, and context of my presentation.

Preparation Notes:

Ways to Improve My Preparation

_____

_____

_____

_____

_____

_____

_____

_____

_____

_____

_____

_____

The Speech Preparation Process

12.1 Identify key competencies for beginning the speech preparation process.

- Being well prepared for a presentation can reduce your anxiety and increase the likelihood of a positive outcome.

- Many speakers identify "keeping your audience interested" as the *most* important speaking skill.

- Preparation competencies include determining your purpose, analyzing and adapting to your audience, adapting to the logistics, and enhancing your credibility.

Determine Your Purpose and Topic

12.2 Explain the importance of and differences between a presentation's purpose and topic.

- Determining the purpose of a presentation helps you decide what you want your audience to know, think, feel, or do.

- Decide whether you want to inform, persuade, entertain, inspire, or a combination of all four goals.

- Choose a presentation topic that suits you and your purpose, consider your interests, values, knowledge, and what you and your audience have in common.

- Develop a specific, achievable, and relevant purpose statement to guide your preparation and narrow your topic appropriately.

Analyze and Adapt to Your Audience

12.3 Analyze the characteristics and attitudes of an audience and adapt your presentation accordingly.

- Audience analysis requires that you understand, respect, and adapt to listeners before and during a presentation.

- Answer the following questions about your audience: (1) Who are they? (2) Why are they here? (3) What do they know? (4) What are their interests? and (5) What are their attitudes?

- Adapt your presentation to what you know about your audience as you prepare it and use audience feedback to modify your presentation as you speak.

- As a speaker, honor the Audience's Bill of Rights. As an audience member, defend and stand up for your rights.

Adapting to the Context

12.4 Adapt to the logistics and occasion of a presentation.

- Adapt to the logistics of a presentation by analyzing and adjusting to the audience's size, the facilities, the equipment, and the time (time of day and length) of the presentation.

- Stay well within your time limit and generally limit your presentation to no more than twenty minutes if you do not have a time limit.

- Adapt to the occasion of the presentation by clarifying your relationship to the situation and by identifying and adapting to audience expectations.

- Dress comfortably and appropriately for the logistics and occasion of a presentation.

Enhancing Your Credibility

12.5 Practice strategies and skills that can enhance your credibility as a speaker.

- Speaker credibility (Aristotle's *ethos*) represents the extent to which an audience believes you and your message.

- The three major components of speaker credibility are character, competence, and charisma.

- A speaker's credibility is solely based on the attitudes and perceptions of the audience.

- You can improve your credibility by sharing your accomplishments, demonstrating good will, and identifying with your audience.

- Whereas the *audience* determines your credibility (*ethos*), *you* determine your ethics—your beliefs about what is right or wrong, moral or immoral, good or bad.

- Audience members have an ethical responsibility to listen with an open, unprejudiced mind and respect freedom of speech.

- Avoid plagiarism and its consequences by accurately identifying the sources of your information in your presentation.

Key Terms

Audience analysis	Identification	Purpose statement
Audience attitudes	Informative presentation	Rhetoric
Character	Inspirational speaking	Self-centered interests
Charisma	Logistics	Speaker credibility
Competence	Occasion	Topic
Demographic information	Persuasive presentation	Topic-centered interests
Entertainment speaking	Plagiarism	Values
Ethos	Presentation speaking	

TEST YOUR KNOWLEDGE

12.1 *Identify key competencies for beginning the speech preparation process.*

1 Research by John Daly and colleagues concludes that anxious speakers are less likely to prepare effectively for making a presentation because
   a. they don't know *how* to prepare an effective presentation.
   b. they worry more about choosing a topic than achieving their purpose.
   c. they confuse ethics and ethos.
   d. they already know what they want to say.

2 Which of the following answers was ranked first in a survey of college students asking them to identify the speaking skills most important for improving their presentations?
   a. Selecting good ideas and information.
   b. Keeping your audience interested.
   c. Deciding what to say; choosing a good topic.
   d. Reducing nervousness and stage fright.

12.2 *Explain the importance of and differences between a presentation's purpose and topic.*

3 Which type of presentation seeks to change or influence audience opinions and behavior?
   a. Informative presentation
   b. Persuasive presentation
   c. Entertainment presentation
   d. Inspirational presentation

12.3 *Analyze the characteristics and attitudes of an audience and adapt your presentation accordingly.*

4 "My audience wants to hear *me* speak because of my work in Darfur with Doctors Without Borders"? This answer is in response to which of the following audience analysis questions?
   a. Who are they?
   b. Why are they here?
   c. What are their demographics?
   d. What are their attitudes?

5 Which principle in the Audience's Bill of Rights is addressed when speakers clearly state their purpose statement at the beginning and/or end of a presentation?
   a. The right to receive value for the time you spend listening to a speaker.
   b. The right to know what the speaker wants you to do or think as the result of listening to a presentation.
   c. The right to know where the speaker is going and how the presentation will progress.
   d. The right to hear and see a speaker from anywhere in a room.

12.4 *Adapt to the logistics and occasion of a presentation.*

6 Logistical questions about a presentation's physical context focus on all of the following items *except*:
   a. the number of people in the audience.
   b. facilities and equipment.
   c. the nature of the occasion.
   d. time.

7 According to researchers and experienced speakers, most audience members cannot effectively listen to and retain information from an uninterrupted speech that is more than
   a. four to seven minutes long.
   b. eight to ten minutes long.
   c. eighteen to twenty minutes long.
   d. thirty to forty-five minutes long.

12.5 *Practice strategies and skills that can enhance your credibility as a speaker.*

8 The Institute for Global Ethics identifies eight universal values. Which value would be addressed in a presentation explaining how to avoid the pitfalls of plagiarism?
   a. Freedom
   b. Unity
   c. Love
   d. Truthfulness

9 Which component of speaker credibility (*ethos*) is reflected in a speaker's level of energy, enthusiasm, vigor, and commitment?
   a. Character
   b. Competence
   c. Charisma
   d. Charity

10 Whereas ethos is determined by the audience, ethics is determined by the
   a. content.
   b. speaker.
   c. others.
   d. structure.

Answers found on page 368.

Content and **Organization** 13

When asked how long it typically took him to prepare for a speech, President Woodrow Wilson offered the following formula:

"If I am to speak for ten minutes, I need a week for preparation; if fifteen minutes, three days; if half an hour, two days; if an hour, I am ready now."[1]

There are two important points to remember about Wilson's much-quoted statement. The first is that a well-crafted presentation requires a great deal of preparation time. Almost anyone can chatter at length about a bunch of topics with little attention to the presentation's purpose or structure. It is much more difficult, however, to develop and deliver a well-organized five or ten-minute presentation. You have to decide what to include (and exclude), how to organize that content in a meaningful way, and how to apply communication strategies appropriate for a particular audience. The second point is that for a short presentation, spending a week or more to prepare is both realistic and reasonable.

Nancy Duarte, CEO of Duarte, Inc., a company that applies visual storytelling principles to create compelling and persuasive presentations, confirms the importance of President Wilson's observation:

We live in a first-draft culture. Type an email. Send. Write a blog entry. Post. Whip up some slides. Speak. But it's in the crafting and recrafting—in iterations and rehearsal—that excellence emerges.[2]

In order to "craft and recraft" a message, you must have a clear purpose and topic in mind, adapt appropriately to your audience and the presentation's context, enhance your credibility, and—most importantly—know what you want to say. To describe the speaker's attempt "to find out what he should say," the great Roman senator and orator Cicero used the Latin word *inventio*. He also identified a subsequent step, *dispositio*, as the task of arranging ideas and information for a presentation in an orderly sequence.[3] In this chapter, we examine these two competencies and their vital role in developing an effective presentation.

Researching and Selecting Your Content

13.1 *Examine, analyze, and select appropriate ideas and supporting material for your presentation.*

The **content** of your presentation consists of the ideas, information, and opinions you include in your message. As soon as you know you will be speaking, you should begin searching for and collecting **supporting material** that explains and/or advances your presentation's purpose. Even if you are an expert, have a unique background, or life experience related to your topic, extensive research can help you better support and reinforce your message and your credibility.

Gather Supporting Material

Supporting material comes in many different forms from many different sources: definitions in dictionaries, background and historical information in encyclopedias, facts and figures online and in almanacs, true-life stories in magazines and on personal websites, and editorial opinions in newspapers, newsletters, and a host of online resources. The best presenters use a mix of supporting material; they don't rely on just one type. Why? Different types of material have different strengths and weaknesses. Most audiences find an unending list of statistics boring. A speaker who tells story after story frustrates listeners if there's no clear reason for telling the stories.

Different types of information give a presentation added life and vitality.

Facts A **fact** is a verifiable observation, experience, or event known to be true. For example, the statement "*Argo* won the 2013 Academy Award for Best Picture" is a fact, but the statement "I think *Les Misérables* should have won" is an opinion. Facts can be personal ("I went to the 2013 Super Bowl") or the official record of an event ("The Baltimore Ravens won

Types of Supporting Material

Facts	Descriptions
Statistics	Analogies
Testimony	Examples
Definitions	Stories

the 2013 Super Bowl"). Facts appear in news headlines around the world:

> The U.S. Center for Disease Control has issued warnings about a new, deadly Middle East Respiratory Virus (MERV). Cases are reported in Saudi Arabia, Qatar, Jordan, and the United Arab Emirates as well as Europe in Europeans who recently traveled in the Middle East.[4]

Sometimes, an unknown or unusual fact can spark audience interest: "By testing water from a city's sewage-treatment plant, researchers can determine what illicit drugs are being used by the population of a specific city on a daily basis."[5] Regardless of their purpose, most presentations are supported by facts, which inform, remind, illustrate, demonstrate, and clarify.

Statistics **Statistics** is a branch of mathematics concerned with collecting, summarizing, analyzing, and interpreting numerical data. Statistics are used for many purposes—from describing the characteristics of a specific population to predicting events ranging from economic trends to the outcomes of football games.

In a 2010 speech to UNESCO (the United Nations Educational, Scientific, and Cultural Organization), Secretary of Education Arne Duncan used statistics to highlight the plight of failing high schools in the United States.[6]

> Fewer than 2,000 high schools in the United States—a manageable number—produce half of all its dropouts. These "dropout factories" produce almost 75 percent—three-fourths—of our dropouts from the minority community, our African American and Latino boys and girls.

Although audiences often equate statistics with facts, statistics are factual only if they are collected and analyzed fairly.

Testimony **Testimony** refers to statements or opinions that someone has spoken or written. You can support a presentation with testimony from books, speeches, plays, magazine articles, radio or television, courtrooms, interviews, or web pages. The believability of testimony depends on the credibility of the speaker or writer. Here's an excerpt from a student presentation:

> In her book, *Mommy, I'm Scared*, Professor Joanne Cantor writes: "From my 15 years of research on mass media and children's fear, I am convinced that TV programs and movies are the number-one preventable cause of nightmares and anxiety in children."

Definitions **Definitions** explain or clarify the meaning of a word, phrase, or concept. A definition can explain what *you* mean when you use a particular word or be as detailed as an encyclopedia definition. In the following example, a speaker explained the differences between jazz and the blues by using two types of definitions:

> The technical definition of the blues is a vocal and instrumental music style that uses a three-line stanza and, typically, a 12-measure form in which expressive inflections—blues notes—are combined with uniquely African American tonal qualities. Or according to an old bluesman's definition: The blues ain't nothin' but the facts of life.

Use definitions if your presentation includes words or phrases that your audience may not know or may misunderstand.

MEDIATED COMMUNICATION IN ACTION

Be Wise About Wikipedia

In his 2007 article "A Stand Against Wikipedia," Scott Jaschik, editor and cofounder of *Inside Higher Education*, described faculty complaints about Wikipedia's "lack of accuracy or completeness of entries" and how, as a result, faculty members and departments were prohibiting students from using it as source in their papers and presentations. A spokesperson for Wikipedia responded to such criticism as follows:

Wikipedia is the ideal place to start your research and get a global picture of a topic, however, it is not an authoritative source. In fact, we recommend that students check the facts they find in Wikipedia against other sources. Additionally, it is generally good research practice to cite an original source when writing a paper, or completing an exam. It's usually not advisable, particularly at the university level, to cite an encyclopedia.[7]

Less than a decade later, opinions about Wikipedia and its content have changed—for the better. Expert-led investigations report that Wikipedia's content is highly accurate and certainly more current than the information published in several prestigious encyclopedias.[8] As a demonstration of its commitment to improving its quality, Wikipedia developed the following content-assessment criteria:[9]

1. The lead section is understandable.
2. The structure is clear.
3. Various aspects of the topic are well balanced; all aspects and relevant viewpoints are included.
4. Coverage is neutral; articles must be written without bias.
5. Footnote references are numerous and reliable.[10]

Warning banners now appear atop any article that does not meet these criteria. For example, when we looked up "Criticism of Wikipedia," *on* Wikipedia, we found a symbol of the earth with a clock superimposed on it followed by: "This article is outdated. Please update this article to reflect recent events or newly available information. (August 2012)"[11] Within a few months, the article had been updated and the warning banner was gone.

The increasing quality of Wikipedia content is also the result of more individuals becoming editors. If you are surfing a page and find an error or a biased statement, you can go into it and fix or modify the questionable content. More ambitious individuals become *Wikipedians*—writing articles in collaboration with other writers and checking each other's work. Many thousands of contributors do their best to make sure that Wikipedia's web pages are clear, relevant, accurate, balanced, politically neutral, up-to-date, and reliable. However, this does make it acceptable for you to rely on Wikipedia as your *only* source of research. You should always refer to more than one source.

Furthermore and because information on Wikipedia has become more accurate and reliable, some students may feel justified in simply cutting and pasting what they find on their topic into their speeches, and then later presenting that material as if it were their own. Such behavior is not justified; in fact, it is blatant plagiarism, as is copying Wikipedia's outline of topics and organizational scheme. Plagiarizing in any form is a serious offense, but plagiarizing off Wikipedia is especially unwise.

Remember, your instructors can also use Wikipedia and know how to look up the same topics you did. Without much effort, they can figure out if you've done honest work, or if you've copied the ideas and words of others.

Descriptions **Descriptions** create mental images for your listeners. They provide more details than definitions by offering causes, effects, historical background information, and characteristics. In an address about the Civil Rights Memorial in Atlanta, Carole Blair describes the architecture of the memorial. Here is an excerpt from that description:

Immediately in front of the wall . . . is an off-centred, black granite pedestal . . . the top of which forms a circle of about 12 feet in diameter. Water bubbles up from a well near the center of the structure and flows slowly and smoothly across its surface. Around the circumference of the tabletop is a . . . time line, marking 53 events of the civil rights movement, beginning with the *Brown* v. *Board of Education* decision in 1954 and ending with the assassination of Dr. King in 1968.[12]

Analogies **Analogies** compare two things in order to highlight some point of similarity. They can identify the similarities in things that function in different contexts—for example, "If a copilot must be qualified to fly a plane, a U.S. vice president should be qualified to govern the country." Analogies are a useful way of describing a complex process or relating a new concept to something that the audience understands well.

Poets use analogies—for example, "Memory is to love what the saucer is to the cup" (Elizabeth Bowen, *The*

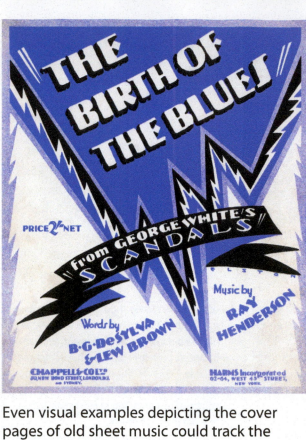

Even visual examples depicting the cover pages of old sheet music could track the "birth," development, and popularity of early blues music.

House in Paris, 1949). Comedians use analogies, such as "MTV is to music as KFC is to chicken" (Lewis Black). So do good speakers.

Use analogies to explain a complex process or to relate a new concept to something the audience already understands. The following analogy compares research on student success to predictions on racehorse success:

A horse's track record is like a student's high school academic record: those with better records tend to be more successful. The jockey and trainer are like faculty advisors and professors: those with talented assistance are more likely to succeed. Horses bred from winning stallions and mares are like students with college-educated parents: those with "winning" parents are more likely to "win."[13]

Examples An **example** refers to a specific case or instance. Examples make a large or abstract idea concrete and understandable; they can be facts, brief descriptions, or detailed stories. When

someone says, "Give me an example," it's natural to reply with an illustration or instance that explains your idea. When asked for examples of individualistic cultures, you might list the United States, Australia, Great Britain, and Canada. Or, if you were making a presentation on female blues singers from the 1920s, you might name Ma Rainey, Bessie Smith, Victoria Spivey, and Alberta Hunter.[14]

Stories Real stories about real people in the real world can arouse attention, create an appropriate mood, and reinforce important ideas. **Stories** are accounts or reports about something that happened.

In the following example, a successful attorney with an incapacitating physical disability used her personal story to emphasize the importance of hope, hard work, and determination:

I was in an automobile accident just after high school, which left me in a wheelchair for life. I was trying to deal with that, a new marriage, and other personal problems, not the least of which was uncertainty about what I could do—about the extent of my own potential.[15]

> **Audiences often remember a good story even when they can't remember much else about a presentation.**

> Documentation enhances your credibility as a speaker while assuring listeners of the validity of your content.

In Chapter 15, "Speaking to Inform," we devote an entire section to finding, developing, and telling good stories. As Abraham Lincoln, one of the greatest speakers of all time, is quoted as saying:

They say I tell a great many stories. I reckon I do; but I have learned from long experience that plain people . . . are more easily influenced through the medium of a broad and humorous illustration than in any other way.[16]

Document Your Sources

Documentation is citing the sources of your supporting material. You should document all supporting material (including information from Internet sources and interviews) in writing and then orally in your presentation.

Unlike writers, speakers rarely cite complete footnotes during a presentation. In speaking situations, documentation must be oral. Your spoken citation—sometimes called an **oral footnote**—should include enough information to allow an interested listener to find the original sources. Generally, it's a good idea to provide the name of the person (or people) whose work you are citing, to say a word or two about that person's credentials, and to mention the source of the information. If you want the audience to have permanent access to the information you use, provide a handout listing your references with complete citations.

In a delicious speech about the benefits of drinking chocolate milk after strenuous exercise a student provided all the information anyone would need to find and verify his statement:

According to a 2011 press release from the University of Texas, a study led by Dr. John Ivy found that "serious and amateur athletes

Don't Take It Out of Context

When you "take words out of context," you select isolated statements from a source and distort or contradict the speaker or writer's intended meaning. When you take words out of context, you do harm to the writer, the audience, and eventually yourself.

Words taken out of context resulted in a political uproar in 2010. Shirley Sherrod, an African American, was fired from her position as Georgia state director of rural development for the U.S. Department of Agriculture (USDA) after Andrew Breitbart, a politically conservative blogger, posted a two-and-a-half-minute video excerpt of a speech she gave. The short clip showed Sherrod admitting that race made her question whether she should help a white farmer. On his cable television show, Bill O'Reilly called for Sherrod's resignation in response to the blog posting. The National Association for the Advancement of Colored People (NAACP) condemned her comments.

But Breitbart's chosen clip took Sherrod's words out of context. The comments that Sherrod made immediately after the statement excerpted in the clip explained that it was not so much about white and black but "about poor versus those who have." She talked about the white farmer and said, "I didn't let [race] get in the way of trying to help" him and that "in the end, we became very good friends, and that friendship has lasted for some time."[17] In a subsequent interview, Roger Spooner, the farmer in question, said that Sherrod did everything she could for his family.

Unfortunately, those who read about or watched Breitbart's video excerpt failed to get a copy of the speech in its entirety. When it was discovered that her remarks were taken out of context, White House officials, the NAACP, and the secretary of agriculture apologized. The USDA offered Sherrod her job back. She refused it. When Bill O'Reilly learned about the rest of the speech, he said, "I owe Ms. Sherrod an apology for not doing my homework, for not putting her remarks into the proper context."[18]

Unethical speakers, audience members, and reporters often take testimony out of context in order to attack an author, discredit an idea, or gain credibility for something that is not supported by the full context.[19]

> ❝ When context is misplaced, so is the truth. ❞
> —Dan Le Batard, columnist for the *Miami Herald*[20]

alike enjoyed physical recovery benefits when they drank low-fat chocolate milk after a vigorous workout."

Imagine how cumbersome it would have been to say, "According to a June 22, 2011 press release from the University of Texas Office of the President titled 'Chocolate Milk Gives Athletes Leg-up After Exercises, Says University of Texas at Austin study,' posted on http://www.utexas.edu/news/2011/06/22/milk_studies, Dr. John Ivy. . . ."

Evaluate Your Supporting Material

Many successful speakers rely on researched information to support their claims and enhance their credibility. So should you, but only if you evaluate every piece of supporting material before you use it. Make sure your information is **valid**—that the ideas, information, and opinions you include are well founded, justified, and accurate. The questions described in the sections that follow will help you test the validity of your supporting material.

Is the Source Identified and Credible? Are the author and publisher identified? Are they reputable? For example, the sensational and often bizarre articles in the *National Enquirer* may be fun to read, but *The New York Times* and *The Wall Street Journal* are more likely to contain reliable information because their worldwide

In 2003, Hillary Clinton appeared on the "Tonight Show" with then host, Jay Leno. Together they chuckled over a bold headline that appeared in *Weekly World News*: "My Steamy Nights with Hillary in UFO Love Nest." We wonder how anyone could believe such an absurd claim.

■OMMUNICATION&■ULTURE

LINEAR VERSUS SPIRAL THINKING

Low-context cultures, such as the United States tend to use a linear style of thinking when developing a message—moving from facts, evidence, and proof to drawing logical conclusions. Other cultures use a more spiral style of thinking when developing a message—moving from dramatic supporting material to subtle conclusions. For example, members of many Arab and African cultures use detailed metaphors, similes, stories, and parables to reinforce or dramatize a point. The final message may be quite subtle or even elusive. It's up to the audience to draw the intended conclusion.[21]

Because this textbook is primarily written for U.S. speakers and audiences, we recommend a linear thinking style in which you use clear supporting material to back up your claims and outlines to map the content of your messages. However, when speaking to an audience that prefers a more spiral style of thinking, consider using supporting material more dramatically and presenting your conclusions in a less direct style.

---

reputations depend on publishing accurate information. Ask yourself whether the source you are quoting is a recognized expert, a firsthand observer, a respected journalist, or an informed blogger.

Is the Source Primary or Secondary? When researching and selecting supporting material, determine whether you are using a primary or secondary source of information. A **primary source** is the document, testimony, or publication in which information first appears. For example, an academic journal article that contains the results of an author's original research is a primary source. And don't overlook the most obvious primary source of all—you. If you interview several experts or conduct a survey, you are the primary source when reporting the results.

A **secondary source**, such as a news summary or encyclopedia article, reports, repeats, or summarizes information from many sources. Look carefully at secondary sources of information to uncover, if possible, the primary source of the information.

Is the Source Biased? A source is **biased** when it states an opinion so slanted in one direction that it may not be objective or fair. If the source has a very strong opinion or will benefit from your agreement, be cautious. For years, tobacco companies publicly denied that cigarette smoking was harmful, even though their own research confirmed that it was. Even not-for-profit special-interest groups, such as the National Rifle Association, pro-choice or pro-life groups, or the American Association of Retired Persons have biases. The information they publish may be true, but the conclusions they draw from that information may be biased.

Is the Information Recent? Always note the date of the information you want to use. When was the information collected? When was it published? In this age of rapidly changing information and events, your supporting material can become old

Criteria for Evaluating Online Information

Specialized questions to assess the validity and reliability of online supporting material:[22]

Criteria #1: Source Credibility

1. Is the author's/sponsor's identity and qualifications clearly identified on the site?
2. Are the sources of data on charts and graphs identified and credible?
3. If needed, have you checked other sources to assess the author's/sponsor's legitimacy and objectivity?
4. Does the author/sponsor provide a contact e-mail or address/phone number?

Criteria #2: Accuracy

1. Can you find and verify the information in other credible sources?
2. Is the information free of grammatical, spelling, and typographical errors that would indicate a lack of quality control?

Criteria #3: Objectivity

1. Is information represented as fact really an advertisement or biased opinion?
2. Is the point of view expressed clearly as a well-supported argument?

Criteria #4: Currency

1. When was the information produced and/or updated?
2. Is the material recent enough to be accurate and relevant?

news in a matter of hours. For current events or scientific breakthroughs, use respected magazines, journals, newspapers, and websites.

Is the Information Consistent? Check whether the information you want to use reports facts and findings similar to information in other reputable sources. Does the information make sense based on what you know about the topic? For example, if most doctors and medical experts agree that penicillin will *not* cure a common viral cold, why believe an obscure source that recommends it as a treatment?

Are the Statistics Valid? Good statistics can be informative, dramatic, and convincing. But statistics also can mislead, distort, and confuse. Make sure your statistics are well founded, justified, and accurate. Consider whether the statistics are believable and whether the researcher who collected and analyzed the data is an unbiased expert. Confirm who is reporting the statistics as well—is it the primary researcher or a secondary reporter?

Organizing Your Content

13.2 *Identify the central idea and key points of your presentation.*

Michael Kepper, a marketing communication specialist, compares the need for organizing a presentation's content with the needs of a human body:

> A speech without structure is like a human body without a skeleton. It won't stand up. Spineless. Like a jellyfish. . . . Having structure won't make the speech a great one, but lacking structure will surely kill all the inspired thoughts . . . because listeners are too busy trying to find out where they are to pay attention.[23]

Organization refers to the way you arrange the content of your presentation into a clear and orderly sequence. Organization helps you focus on the purpose of your presentation while deciding what to include and how to maximize the impact of your message.

Research confirms that audiences react positively to well-organized presentations and negatively to poorly organized ones.[24]

As an audience member, you know that organization matters. It is difficult to understand and remember the words of a speaker who rambles and doesn't connect ideas. In fact, you may never want to hear that speaker again.

Determine Your Central Idea

The **central idea** is a sentence that summarizes the key points of your presentation. Your central idea provides a brief preview of the organizational pattern you will follow to achieve your purpose.

The following example illustrates how topic area, purpose, and central idea are different but closely linked to one another:

Topic area Traveling abroad

Purpose To prepare travelers for a trip abroad

Central idea Before visiting a foreign country, research the culture and the places you will visit, make sure you have the required travel documents, and get any immunizations and medicines you might need.

Establish Your Key Points

Begin organizing your presentation by determining your key points. **Key points** represent the most important issues or the main ideas you want your audience to understand and remember about your message.

Look for a pattern or natural groupings of ideas and information as the basis for key points. Depending on your purpose and topic area, this can be an easy task or a daunting puzzle. Inexperienced speakers often feel overwhelmed by what seems to be mountains of unrelated facts and figures. Don't give up!

Before creating an outline, consider using two other techniques to identify your key points and build a preliminary structure for your message: mind mapping and the Speech Framer.

Mind Mapping **Mind mapping** is a method for organizing and recording potential ideas and information by brainstorming alone. It encourages the free flow of ideas and lets you define

Determining the key points of your presentation is like fitting together the pieces of a puzzle—if one point doesn't fit or follow, the rest may not work.

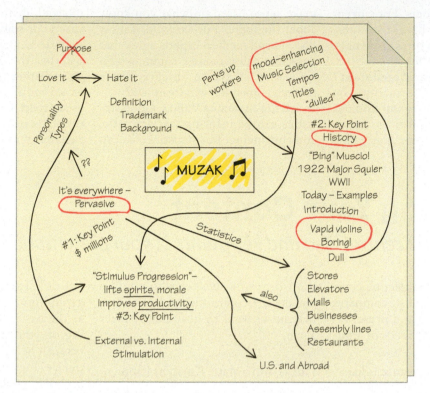

This mind map for a speech on Muzak demonstrates one method of determining key points and establishing relationships among ideas.

relationships among those ideas. It also harnesses the potential of your whole brain while it's in a highly creative mode of thought to generate ideas.[25] Take a look at the mind map on this page that one student created for a presentation on Muzak, that background music you often hear in stores, elevators, and offices.[26]

Harvard Business Review writer Nancy Duarte acknowledges, "It's intimidating to approach a blank piece of paper or whiteboard, but you have to start somewhere. Write down a key word and riff on that. Let your mind move in random directions. Then draw connections with lines."[27] The resulting mind map will be a hodgepodge of words, phrases, lists, circles, and arrows. Certainly it contains more concepts than should be included in a single presentation. After completing a mind map, you can label circled ideas as key points and put them in a logical order.

Mind maps allow you to see your ideas without superimposing a predetermined organizational pattern on them. They let you postpone the need to arrange your ideas in a pattern until you collect enough information to organize the content. Use mind mapping when you have lots of ideas and

information but are having trouble deciding how to select and arrange the materials for a presentation.

In addition to the hand-drawn mind map example in this chapter, consider other similar methods. Post-It Notes or 3-by-5 index cards let you put a single idea on each note, post them, and then sort them into similar categories—much like the steps in the DOT Method of group problem solving described in Chapter 11, "Group Decision Making and Problem Solving." If you want to mind map on a computer screen, look for software products such as *Inspiration*, *MindManager*, *Mindmapper*, and *Mindmup*.[28]

In his discussion of mind mapping, speech consultant Jerry Weissman writes that regardless of the mind map method you use, resist the temptation "to impose structure during your free flow. If you impose structure too soon, you impose censorship and could lose a fresh idea. Save the structuring for *after* the brainstorming is done."[29]

The Speech Framer The **Speech Framer** is a visual model for organizing presentation content that provides a place for every component of a presentation while encouraging

experimentation and creativity.[30] The Speech Framer example on the next page is based on student Camille Dunlap's class presentation on the dangers of driving while sleep deprived.[31]

The Speech Framer lets you experiment with a variety of organizational formats. For example, if you have four key points, you merely add a column to the frame. If you think you have three key points but find that you don't have good supporting material for the second key point, you might consider deleting that point. If you have only three types of supporting material for one key point and two for the others, that's okay—just make sure all the supporting material is strong. If you notice that several pieces of supporting material apply to two key points, you can combine them into a new key point. And if you must have five or more key points, use only one or two pieces of supporting material for each point to control the length of your presentation.

In addition to helping you organize the content of your presentation, you can use the single-page Speech Framer as your speaking notes. It allows you to see the presentation laid out entirely as you practice or deliver it.

THE SPEECH FRAMER: ASLEEP AT THE WHEEL

Introduction: Story about my best friend's death in a car accident.

Central Idea: Falling asleep accounts for 100,000 car accidents and 1,500 deaths every year. Everyone knows about the dangers of drunk driving, but very few of us know about the dangers of sleep deprivation—and what to do about it.

Key Points	#1 Why we need sleep. *Transition:* What happens when you don't get enough sleep?	#2 Sleep deprivation affects your health, well-being, and safety. *Transition:* So how can you ease your tired body and mind?	#3 Three steps can help you get a good night's sleep.
Support	Would you drive home from class drunk? 14 hours w/o sleep = 0.1 blood alcohol level. Very long day = 0.05 blood alcohol level	Lack of sleep affects your attitude and mood (results of study)	1 Decide how much sleep is right for you: a Keep a sleep log. b Most people need 8 or more hours a night.
Support	Circadian clock controls sleep and also regulates hormones, heart rate, body temperature, etc.	Lack of sleep affects your health. Most important sleep is between 7th and 8th hour of sleep.	2 Create a comfy sleep environment. a Don't sleep on a full or empty stomach. b Cut back on fluids. c No alcohol or caffeine before sleep.
Support	Things that rob you of sleep: 24-hour stores; Internet; television; studying; homework; a good book	Symptoms: • Crave naps or doze off? • Hit snooze button a lot? • Hard to solve problems? • Feel groggy, lethargic?	3 Don't take your troubles to bed. a Can't sleep, get up. b Soothing music. c Read.

Conclusion: Summarize the Three Key Points. Final line: There is so much in life to enjoy. Sleep longer, live longer.

Applying an Organizational Pattern

13.3 *Describe commonly used organizational patterns for arranging presentation content.*

Even the most experienced speakers may find it difficult to see how their ideas and information fall into a clear structure. Fortunately, there are several commonly used organizational patterns that can help you clarify your central idea and find an effective format for your presentation.[32]

Arrange by Subtopics

Topical arrangement involves dividing a large topic into smaller subtopics. Subtopics can describe reasons, characteristics, or techniques. Use a topical arrangement if your ideas and information can be divided into discrete categories of relatively equal importance.

Topic area Facial expressions in different cultures

Purpose To appreciate that some facial expressions may not translate between cultures

Central idea Americans and native Japanese often misinterpret facial expressions depicting fear, sadness, and disgust.

Key points
A Fear
B Sadness
C Disgust

Arrange by Sequence in Time

Time arrangement orders information according to time or calendar dates. Most step-by-step procedures begin with the first step and continue chronologically through the last step. Use a time arrangement when your key points occur in time relative to each other, as in recipes, assembly instructions, technical procedures, and historical events.

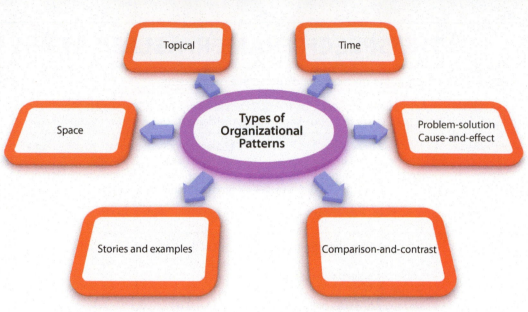

Topic area Making vanilla ice cream

Purpose To explain how to make custard-based vanilla ice cream

Central idea To make homemade, custard-based vanilla ice cream, make sure that you combine and heat the ingredients properly, know when the custard is thick enough, and correctly churn the ice cream.

Key points

A Warm up and whisk in the first ingredients.

B Cook the custard slowly.

C Cool and add final ingredients.

D Refrigerate before churning.

Arrange by Position in Space

Use a **space arrangement** if your key points can be arranged in terms of their location or physical relationship to one another. A proposed highway system is hard to describe unless you can show where it will go and what it will displace. You can also use space arrangement to discuss unusual laws in different U.S. states or unique holidays in different countries.

Topic area Brain structure

Purpose To explain how major sections of the brain are responsible for different functions

Central idea A guided tour of the brain begins in the hindbrain, moves through the midbrain, and ends in the forebrain, with side trips to the right and left hemispheres.

Key points

A The hindbrain

B The midbrain

C The forebrain

D The right and left hemispheres

Present a Problem and a Solution

Use a **problem–solution arrangement** to describe a harmful or difficult situation (the problem) and then offer a plan to solve the problem (the solution). Problems can be as simple as a squeaky door or as significant as world hunger.

Topic area Behavioral problems in groups

Purpose To provide strategies for solving common behavioral problems that occur in group discussions and meetings

Central idea Learning how to deal with three common behavioral problems will improve group performance.

Key points

A Dealing with nonparticipants

B Dealing with disruptive behavior

C Dealing with latecomers and early leavers

For a presentation about facial expressions in different cultures, a topical arrangement works well.

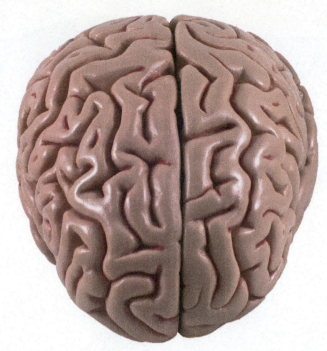

For a presentation that discusses the various parts of the brain, a space arrangement works well.

Show Cause and Effect

Use a **cause-and-effect arrangement** either to present a cause and its resulting effects or to detail the effects that result from a specific cause.

Topic area Young adults and video games

Purpose To describe the harmful effects that playing video games can have on young adults

Central idea Excessive video gaming negatively affects young adults and their families because it uses time that could be spent on more important activities.

Key points

A Video games have a negative effect on young adults' physical fitness.

B Video games have a negative effect on young adults' school achievement.

C Video gaming may become a serious addiction.

In cause-and-effect presentations, speakers may claim that eating red meat causes disease or that lower taxes stimulate the economy. In effect-to-cause presentations, speakers may claim that sleepiness or lack of energy can be caused by an iron deficiency or that a decrease in lake fish is caused by global warming. Be careful with cause-and-effect arrangements. Just because one thing follows another does not mean that the first causes the second. Lack of sleep, not lack of iron, can be a cause of sleepiness. This kind of conclusion is a classic example of a faulty cause fallacy (see Chapter 16, "Speaking to Persuade").

Tell Stories and Share Examples

A series of well-told stories or dramatic examples can be so compelling and interesting that they become the organizational pattern for a presentation.

Topic area Leaders and adversity

Purpose To convince listeners that disabilities are not barriers to success

Central idea Many noteworthy leaders have lived with disabilities.

Key points

A Franklin D. Roosevelt, president of the United States, had polio

B Jan Scruggs, disabled soldier and Vietnam Memorial founder

C Helen Keller, deaf and blind advocate

Compare and Contrast

Use a **comparison–contrast arrangement** to demonstrate how two things are similar or different. This pattern works well in two situations: (1) when an unfamiliar concept can be explained by comparing it with a familiar concept or (2) when you are demonstrating the advantages of one alternative over

For a presentation about the advantages of fuel-efficient vehicles, consider using the comparison–contrast arrangement.

How Creative Are You?

If you want your presentation to be interesting and memorable, think creatively about its structure. Lee Towe, president of Innovators International, defines creativity as consisting of two parts: creative thinking and creative output.[33] *Creative output* consists of connecting and combining previously unrelated elements. For example, the circles and arrows you draw on a mind map allow you to combine ideas from various places on the page. In this spirit, Patricia Phillips, a customer service expert, used excerpts from popular songs to begin each major section of her training seminar in a creative way: "I Can't Get No Satisfaction" by the Rolling Stones, "Help" by the Beatles, "Respect" by Aretha Franklin, and "Don't You Come Back No More" by Ray Charles.

Creativity, however, runs some risks. Some audience members may be unfamiliar with the songs Patricia chose. Or, the audience may have expected or wanted a more technical presentation. If you want to use creative patterns, make sure your audience will understand and appreciate your creativity.

So how creative are you? Try the following exercise: In three minutes, list all of the uses you can imagine for a balloon. When you finish your three minutes of thinking, rate the creativity of your answers based on the following criteria:[34]

Quantity: Did you come up with more than twenty-four ideas?

• **Variety:** Did you come up with at least five categories of answers? For example, birthday decorations and prom decorations would be the same category—decorations.
• **Uniqueness:** Did you have unusual items on your list? For example, most people would say that a balloon can be used as a party decoration. A more creative person might suggest using blown-up balloons to fill empty space when packing a box.

---

another. Comparisons can be real (comparing products or contrasting medical treatments) or fanciful (comparing student success to racehorse success).

Topic area   Gas-powered cars versus gas–electric hybrid cars

Purpose   To recommend ways of evaluating gas-powered and gas–electric hybrid cars

Central idea   Comparing performance, fuel economy, and reliability can help you decide whether to purchase a gas-powered or gas–electric hybrid car.

Key points
A Performance
B Fuel economy
C Predicted reliability and battery life

Outlining Your Presentation

13.4 *Describe and apply different outlining methods for organizing a presentation.*

Outlines—just like presentations and speakers—come in many shapes and forms. Here we look at three types of outlines and how they can help you organize the content of a presentation.

Preliminary Outlines

Outlines begin in a preliminary form with a few basic building blocks. You can use a **preliminary outline** to put the major pieces of almost any presentation in order, modifying it on the basis of the number of key points and the types and amount of supporting material. Aim for at least two pieces of supporting material under each key point—facts, statistics, testimony, definitions, descriptions, analogies, examples, or stories.

After you identify the key points that will support your central idea and choose an organizational pattern to structure your message, determine which key points go first, second, or last. In many cases, the organizational pattern dictates the order. For example, if you use time arrangement, the first step in a procedure comes first. If

Topic Area

I **Introduction**

  A Purpose/topic

  B Central idea

  C Brief preview of key points

    1 Key point #1

    2 Key point #2

    3 Key point #3

II **Body of the presentation**

  A Key point #1

    1 Supporting material

    2 Supporting material

  B Key point #2

    1 Supporting material

    2 Supporting material

  C Key point #3

    1 Supporting material

    2 Supporting material

III **Conclusion**

Asleep at THE WHEEL

Brief Outline

I Introduction: Story of Best Friend's Death in Car Accident

II Central idea: Sleep Longer, Drive Safer, Live Longer

III Key Points

  A Importance and Need for Sleep

    1 Lack of sleep = alcohol-impaired effects

    2 Things that rob our sleep: media, work hours, study and homework, etc.

    3 Circadian clock regulates body functions

  B Sleep Deprivation

    1 Influences attitudes and moods

    2 Symptoms of sleep deprivation: dozing, groggy, flawed thinking, etc.

  C How to Get a Good Night's Sleep

    1 Decide how much sleep you need

    2 Create a comfy sleep environment

    3 Don't take trouble to bed

IV Conclusion: Recognize the symptoms. Alter your habits. Sleep Longer, Live Longer

your format does not dictate the order of key points, place your best ideas in strategic positions.

If you use mind mapping or the Speech Framer to generate key points, you have everything you need to develop a preliminary outline for your presentation. Take another look at the student Speech Framer for the student speech *Asleep at the Wheel* on page 247. Notice how easily it serves as the basis for the outline to the right.

Comprehensive Outline

A **comprehensive outline** is an all-inclusive presentation framework that follows established outlining rules. A preliminary outline helps you plan your presentation; a comprehensive outline creates the first draft of your presentation. There are two very basic rules for comprehensive outlining: (1) use numbers, letters, *and* indentations and (2) divide your subpoints logically.

Use Numbers, Letters, and Indentations Like most good outlines, a comprehensive outline uses a system of indenting and numbers and letters. Roman numerals (I, II, III) signify the major divisions such as the introduction, body, and conclusion. Indented capital letters (A, B, C) are used for key points. Additional indents use Arabic numbers (1, 2, 3) for more specific points and supporting material. If you need a fourth level,

indent again and use lowercase letters (a, b, c).

Divide Your Subpoints Logically Each major point should include at least two subpoints indented under it, or none at all. If there is an A, there must be a B; for every 1, there must be a 2.

Wrong: I.

              A.

        II.

Right: I.

              A.

              B.

        II.

As much as possible, try to keep your key points consistent in terms of grammar and format—for example, if you begin each subpoint with a verb, then each subpoint that follows should also begin with a verb and so forth. The comprehensive outline on the next page for "What's Fair Is Fair," by Regina Smith, was developed for her class presentation on affirmative action and college admissions.

Speaking Outline

When delivering your presentation, you may create a separate **speaking outline**—either a short outline that includes little more than a list of key points and reminders of supporting material or a more complex and detailed outline that includes quotations, statistics, or other data. Some speaking outlines may also include notes on when to introduce and remove a visual aid or provide a handout.

Strategies for ORDERING KEY POINTS[35]

■ **STRENGTH AND FAMILIARITY.** Place your strongest points first and last and your weakest or least familiar idea in the middle position so that you start and end with strength.

■ **AUDIENCE NEEDS.** If your audience needs current information, satisfy that need early. Background information can come later. If you are speaking about a controversial topic, begin with a point that focuses on the background of an issue or on the reasons for a change.

■ **LOGISTICS.** If you're one of a series of presenters, you may end up with less time to speak than was originally scheduled. Plan your presentation so that the strongest key points come first in case you need to cut your presentation short.

COMPREHENSIVE OUTLINE

"What's Fair Is Fair" by Regina Smith

I Introduction

  A Americans love fairness.

  B Many Americans oppose affirmative action for minority students because it seems unfair.

  C There are other preferences for college admission that are just as unfair.

(*Transition*: Let's start with the oldest type of preference.)

II Body

  A Legacy Admissions

    1 Legacy admissions began in the 1920s to give the children of wealthy white alumni preference over the children of Jews and immigrants.

    2 Legacy students' SATs and GPAs are lower than nonlegacy students.

    3 Percent of legacy students: U. of Penn, 41%; U. of Virginia, 52%; Notre Dame U., 57%.

  B Athletic Scholarships

    1 National Collegiate Athletic Association college admissions standards:

      a Combined SAT score of 1010 with a 2.0 high school GPA.

      b Combined SAT score of 850 with a 2.5 high school GPA.

    2 Athletes get special treatment: special advisors, paid tutors, easier classes.

    3 Poor graduation rates:

      a Division I football players: 51% rate.

      b Division I basketball players: 40% rate.

      c Of 3,700 athletes, only 50% earn degrees.

      d Exception at Duke University: 90% graduation rate for scholarship athletes.

    4 Reason for athletic preferences is money:

      a $6 billion for NCAA television contracts.

      b $187 million to Division I schools.

      c Low-income scholarships.

  C Affirmative Action

    1 Why is affirmative action singled out as unfair?

    2 Universities relax standards for alumni children and athletes, why not African American and other underrepresented groups?

    3 Quote from Ron Wilson, African American representative from Texas.

III Conclusion

  A Either stop giving preferences to legacy students and athletes or continue affirmative action programs.

  B Do what is fair.

Connecting Your Key Points

An outline shows the structure, key points, and supporting material of your presentation, but it's missing the "glue" that connects these elements to one another and makes your presentation a coherent whole. **Connectives** constitute this glue. In this feature we discuss four types: internal previews, internal summaries, transitions, and signposts.[36]

Internal preview identifies, in advance, the key points of a presentation or section in a specific order. It tells audience members what you are going to cover and in what order.

Example: How do researchers and doctors explain obesity? Some offer genetic explanations; others psychological ones. Either or both factors can be responsible for your never-ending battle with the bathroom scale.

Internal summaries are a useful way to end a major section and to reinforce important ideas. They are also an opportunity to repeat critical ideas or information.

Example: So remember, before spending hundreds of dollars on diet books and exercise toys, make sure that your weight problem is not influenced by the number and size of your fat cells, your hormone level, your metabolism, or the amount of glucose in your bloodstream.

Transitions are the most common type of connective—a word, number, brief phrase, or sentence that helps you move from one key point or section to another. Transitions act like lubricating oil to keep a presentation moving smoothly. In the following examples, the transitions are underlined:

Yet it's important to remember . . .
In addition to metabolism, there is . . .
On the other hand, some people believe . . .
Finally, a responsible parent should . . .

Transitions also function as mini-previews and minisummaries that link the conclusion of one section to the beginning of another.

Example: After you've eliminated these four genetic explanations for weight gain, it's time to consider several psychological factors.

Signposts are the fourth type of connective, short phrases that—like signs on the highway—tell or remind listeners where you are in the organizational structure of a presentation. If you are discussing four genetic explanations for weight gain, begin each explanation with numbers—first, second, third, and fourth: "Fourth and finally, make sure your glucose level has been tested and is within normal levels."

Example: Even if you can't remember all of the genetic explanations for weight gain, please remember one thing: Consult your doctor before embarking on a strict diet.

Beginning Your Presentation

13.5 *Practice effective strategies for creating dynamic introductions.*

Introductions capitalize on the power of first impressions—if you manage to create a positive first impression, you've paved the way for a successful presentation. Likewise, a weak introduction creates a poor first impression, giving audience members a reason to tune out or question your credibility. An effective introduction captures audience attention and gives them time to adjust, to block out distractions, and to focus attention on you and your message.[37] It establishes a critical relationship among three elements: you, your message, and your audience by demonstrating why you are qualified to discuss the topic, what the main points of your topic will be, and what you hope your audience will gain by listening to your presentation.

Review the following introduction to "Asleep at the Wheel," a persuasive presentation by Camille Dunlap. To what extent does the introduction achieve its goals?

On June 23, 2001, at 7:43 P.M., a smoldering car was found twisted around a tree. Two dead bodies. One adult. One baby. Why did this happen? Was it drunk driving? No. Adverse road conditions? No. A defect in the car? No. Something else took the life of my best friend and her baby brother. Something quite simple, quite common, and deadly: my best friend fell asleep at the wheel. "Fall asleep crashes" account for 100,000 car accidents and 1,500 deaths every year. Everyone knows about the dangers of drunk driving, but very few of us know about the dangers of sleep deprivation.[38]

Camille's introduction meets all of the standard criteria: She successfully links herself, her message, and her audience; she clarifies her purpose; and she effectively captures the audience attention by starting out with a compelling story.

You can begin your presentation with a variety of effective strategies—telling a story is just one way. There are many effective methods that can be used separately or in combination:

beginning your presentation

GOALS OF THE INTRODUCTION

Focus Audience Attention and Interest
Gain audience attention by using compelling supporting material, involving them actively, and speaking expressively.

Connect to Your Audience
Find a way to connect your message to audience interests, attitudes, beliefs, and values.

Put You in Your Presentation
Link your expertise, experiences, and personal feelings to your topic or purpose. Personalize your message.

Set the Emotional Tone
Make sure the introduction sets an appropriate emotional tone that matches its purpose. Use appropriate language, delivery styles, and supporting material.

Preview the Message
Give your audience a sneak preview about the subject. State your central idea and *briefly* list the key points you will cover.

statistics and examples; quotations; stories; questions; references to places; occasions; incidents and events; and addressing audience needs.

Use a Statistic or an Example

Sometimes, your research turns up a statistic or an example that is unusual or dramatic. If you anticipate a problem in gaining and keeping audience attention, an interesting statistic or example can do it for you:

> The statistics are appalling: On average, the annual U.S. firearm homicide rate is 20 times higher than the combined rates of 22 countries that are comparable in wealth and population."[39] Equally, if not more horrifying, in the six months following the Newtown elementary school massacre in 2012 "the number of gun deaths in the U.S., . . . exceeded the total number of U.S. troops killed in the Iraq war."[40]

Effective introductions establish a relationship among three elements: you, your message, and your audience.

Quote Someone

A dramatic statement or eloquent phrase written by someone else can make an ideal beginning. A good quotation from a highly respected writer, speaker, or a topic expert helps listeners overcome doubts they may have about you and your message. Remember to give the writer or speaker of the quotation full credit.

> We need more money, high-quality instruction, and better equipment in all of our science classes. Here is how Arne Duncan, the secretary of education—respected by both Democrats and Republicans in Congress—put it in a 2009 address to the National Science Teachers Association: "America won the space race but, in many ways, American education lost the science race. A decade ago . . . our best districts could compete with anyone in the world, but our worst districts—which, of course, were in low-income communities—were on a par with third-world countries."[41]

TEST THINK ABOUT THEORY
FACTS IDEA PLAN EXPERIMENT METHOD

The Primacy and Recency Effects

As predicted by Hermann Ebbinghaus, a German psychologist who conducted early research on memory and recall, the parts of a presentation that audiences best remember are the beginning and the end. Ebbinghaus, who is known for his discovery of the *forgetting curve* and the *learning curve*, also identified the *serial position effect*, which explains "for information learned in a sequence, recall is better for items at the beginning (**primacy effect**) and the end (**recency effect**) than for items in the middle of the sequence."[42]

Interestingly, the primacy and recency effects link up with what we know about listening and memory. We are more likely to recall the last thing we hear because the information is still in our short-term memory. In contrast, we are likely to remember the first thing we hear because the information has had time to become part of our long-term memory. The poorest recall of information is in the middle of a sequence "because the information is no longer in short-term memory and has not yet been placed in long-term memory."[43]

Originally, the primacy and recency effects evolved from studies of what people remember after hearing a list of words or numbers. Today, it has been applied to studying how first and last impressions affect the way we react to and feel about other people as well as the critical importance of a presentation's introduction and conclusion.

Tell a Story

Audiences will give you their undivided attention if you tell a good story and tell it well. Consider using a story about a personal hardship, a triumph, or even an embarrassment. Remember that a good story can highlight and illustrate an idea, concept, or opinion. The following example is from a student presentation:

> When I was 15, I was operated on to remove the deadliest form of skin cancer, a melanoma carcinoma. My doctors injected 10 shots of steroids into each scar every three weeks to stop the scars from spreading. I now know that it wasn't worth a couple of summers of being tan to go through all that pain and suffering. Take steps now to protect yourself from the harmful effects of the sun.

Ask a Question

Asking a question attracts your audience's attention because it challenges them to think. One of the best kinds of questions elicits a response such as, "I had no idea!" A student speaker used this technique in a series of questions:

> What do China, Iran, Saudi Arabia, and the United States have in common? Nuclear weapons? No. Abundant oil resources?

No. What we have in common is this: Last year, these four countries accounted for nearly all the executions in the world.[44]

Refer to the Current Place or Occasion

A simple way to begin a presentation is to refer to the place in which you are speaking or the occasion for the gathering. Your audience's memories and feelings about a specific place or occasion conjure up the emotions needed to capture their attention and interest.

When Dr. Martin Luther King Jr. made his famous "I Have a Dream" speech on the steps of the Lincoln Memorial, his first few words echoed Abraham Lincoln's famous Gettysburg Address ("Four score and seven years ago"): Five score years ago, a great American, in whose symbolic shadow we stand, signed the Emancipation Proclamation.[45]

Address Audience Needs

When there is a crisis, address the problem directly and immediately. If budget cuts require salary reductions, audience members are not interested in clever questions or dramatic statistics:

> As you know, the state has reduced our operating budget by

2.7 million dollars. It is also just as important that you know this: All of you will have a job here next year—and the year after. There will be no layoffs. Instead, there will be cutbacks on nonpersonnel budget lines, downsizing of programs, and possibly short furloughs.

TIPS FOR STARTING STRONG

- **PLAN THE BEGINNING AT THE END.** Don't plan your introduction until you have developed the content of your presentation.

- **DON'T APOLOGIZE.** Don't use your introduction to offer excuses or apologize for poor preparation, weak delivery, or nervousness.

- **AVOID JOKES.** Don't open with a joke unless it "is very brief, utterly hilarious, and directly related to your topic."[46] A botched or offensive joke can make you look like a fool.

- **AVOID BEGINNING WITH "MY SPEECH IS ABOUT . . ."** Boring beginnings do not capture audience attention or enhance a speaker's credibility. Be original and creative.

Concluding Your Presentation

13.6 *Practice effective strategies for creating dynamic conclusions.*

Just as audiences remember things that are presented first (primacy effect), they also remember information that comes last (recency effect). Your final words have a powerful and lasting effect on your audience members and determine how they think and feel about you and your presentation.[47] Like the introduction, a conclusion establishes a relationship among you, your topic, and your audience.

Some methods of concluding your presentation reinforce your message; others strengthen the audience's final impression of you. Use any of the following

approaches separately or in combination: summarize, quote someone, tell a story, call for action, or refer to the beginning.

Summarize

One of the best and most direct ways of concluding a presentation is to provide a succinct summary that reinforces your key points. Summaries should be memorable, clear, and brief. Here, a student speaker uses questions to emphasize his central idea and key points:

> Now, if you hear someone ask whether *more* women should serve

in the U.S. Congress, ask and then answer the two questions I discussed today: Can women and their issues attract big donors? And, are women too nice to be "tough" in politics? Now that you know how to answer these questions, don't let doubters stand in the way of making a woman's place in the House.

Summarizing your key points is an effective way of concluding most presentations. If, however, your key points have been laid out clearly *and* you want to conclude by motivating, inspiring, arousing emotions, or moving

GOALS of the Conclusion

Be Memorable
Give the audience a reason to remember you and your presentation. Show how your message affected you and how it affects them.

Be Clear
Repeat the one thing you want your audience to remember at the end of your presentation.

Be Brief
The announced ending of a presentation should never go beyond one or two minutes.

your audience to action, you will need to consider other or additional concluding strategies.

Quote Someone

Concluding a presentation with a quotation can be as effective and appealing as quoting someone in your introduction. Well-chosen quotations can be memorable, clear, and brief. For example, in the conclusion of his tribute to those who died on 9/11, the then-mayor of New York City Rudolph Giuliani quoted the final words of Abraham Lincoln's Gettysburg Address:

"... that we here highly resolve that these dead shall not have died in vain—that this nation, under God, shall have a new birth of freedom—and that the government of the people, by the people, and for the people, shall not perish from this earth." God bless New York and God bless America.

Tell a Story

End with a story when you want the audience to visualize the central idea of your presentation. Marge Anderson, chief executive of the Mille Lacs Band of Ojibwe Indians, concluded a presentation with a story. (See the complete speech in Chapter 16, "Speaking to Persuade.")

Years ago, white settlers came to this area and built the first European-style homes. When Indian People walked by these homes and saw [windows], they looked through them to see what the strangers inside were doing. The settlers were shocked, but it made sense when you think about it: Windows are made to be looked

through from both sides. Since then, my People have spent many years looking at the world through your window. I hope today I've given you a reason to look at it through ours.[48]

Call for Action

A challenging but effective way to end a presentation is to call for action. "Presentations," writes Nancy Duarte, "move people to act—but only if you explicitly state what actions you want them to take."[49] The call to "do something" can rally an audience to sign a petition, make a donation, change their eating habits, or vote for a political candidate. In can also ask an audience to remember a set of shocking statistics, to think about the relevance of a story you told, or to take up an intellectual challenge.

Dr. Robert M. Franklin, president of Morehouse College, concludes with an eloquent call for action in remarks delivered at a town hall meeting of students on his campus:

Morehouse is your house. You must take responsibility for its excellence. . . . If you want to be part of something rare and noble, something that the world has not often seen—a community of educated, ethical, disciplined black men more powerful than a standing army—then you've come to the right place. . . . Up, you mighty men of Morehouse, you aristocrats of spirit, you can accomplish what you will![50]

Refer to the Beginning

Consider ending your presentation with the same technique you used to begin it. If you began with a quotation, end with the same or a similar

quotation. If you began with a story, refer back to that story. Audiences like this concluding method because it returns to something familiar and "bookends" the content of your presentation:

Remember the story I told you about two-year-old Joey, a hole in his throat so he can breathe, a tube jutting out of his stomach so he can be fed. For Joey, an accidental poisoning was an excruciatingly painful and horrifying experience. For Joey's parents, it was a time of fear, panic, and helplessness. Thus, it is a time to be prepared for, and even better, a time to prevent.

TIPS FOR ENDING STRONG

Make Sure the Mood and Style Are Consistent.
Don't tack on an irrelevant or inappropriate ending.

Have Realistic Expectations.
Most audience members will not act when called on unless the request is carefully worded, reasonable, and possible.

Don't Read It.
Remember the recency effect: Reading your conclusion is anticlimactic and takes your eyes away from the people you want to inform, persuade, entertain, and/or inspire. Practice your conclusion repeatedly "until you can deliver it confidently and emphatically."[51]

Be Brief, Be Memorable, Be Seated.

Don't end by demanding something from your audience unless you are reasonably sure you can get it.

COMMUNICATION ASSESSMENT

Can You Identify the Organizational Pattern?

Each of the following examples demonstrates one (or more) of the organizational patterns discussed in this chapter. Try to match each outline with a pattern.

Organizational Patterns

A Topical arrangement

B Time arrangement

C Space arrangement

D Problem–solution

E Causes and effects

F Stories and examples

G Comparison–contrast

Outline Examples

_____ 1. The Three Stages of Pregnancy
First trimester
Second trimester
Third trimester

_____ 2. Four Basic Techniques Used to Play Volleyball
Setting
Bumping
Spiking
Serving

_____ 3. The Richest Sources of Diamonds
South Africa
Tanzania
Murfreesboro, Arkansas

_____ 4. Attending a two-year college rather than a university
Low cost versus high cost
Small freshmen classes versus large lecture classes
Individual attention versus lost in the crowd

_____ 5. The Legacies of Presidents Reagan, Bush Sr., Clinton, and Bush Jr.
Domestic politics
International politics
Party politics

_____ 6. The dangers of hydraulic fracking for natural gas
Poor air quality
Ground water contamination
Earthquakes

_____ 7. Homeless Shelters and Homeless Families
The Khoo family
The Taylor family
The Arias family

_____ 8. Aspirin and Heart Attacks
Does research verify that aspirin prevents heart attacks?
Who should follow the aspirin prescription?
Are there potential, dangerous side effects of aspirin therapy?

_____ 9. Running out of drinkable water
Severe droughts
Industrial water pollution
Poor sanitation
Overuse and waste

Researching and Selecting Your Content

13.1 Examine, analyze, and select appropriate ideas and supporting material for your presentation.

- Effective speakers use several forms of supporting material: facts, statistics, testimony, definitions, descriptions, analogies, examples, and stories.

- Document your supporting material in writing and then orally in your presentation.

- Make sure your source is identified, credible, and unbiased.

- Test the validity of your supporting material by determining whether the information comes from a primary or secondary source and whether it's recent and consistent.

- Evaluate the validity of statistics by making sure they are well founded, justified, and accurate.

Organizing Your Content

13.2 Identify the central idea and key points of your presentation.

- The first step in organizing the content of a presentation is to determine your central idea and your key points. Make sure your key points reflect your central idea.

- Mind mapping and the Speech Framer can help you identify key points and organize your message.

Applying an Organizational Pattern

13.3 Describe commonly used organizational patterns for arranging presentation content.

- Common organizational patterns include topical, time, space, problem–solution, causes and effects, stories and examples, and comparison–contrast arrangements.

- Use creative organizational methods that go beyond common patterns in order to make your presentation more interesting and memorable.

Outlining Your Presentation

13.4 Describe and apply different outlining methods for organizing a presentation.

- Use a preliminary outline to identify the basic building blocks of a presentation.

- When preparing a comprehensive outline, use numbers, letters, and indentation; divide your subpoints logically; and keep the outline consistent in style.

- Connective phrases (internal previews and summaries, transitions, signposts) are the "glue" that links the key points to one another and makes your presentation a coherent whole.

Beginning Your Presentation

13.5 Practice effective strategies for creating dynamic introductions.

- The primacy effect explains our tendency to recall the introduction of a presentation better than the middle.

- Presentation introductions should focus attention and interest, connect with the audience, enhance your credibility, set the emotional tone, and preview the message.

- Methods of beginning a presentation include using a statistic or example, quoting someone, telling a story, asking a question, referring to the current place or occasion, and addressing audience needs.

- Your introduction will be more effective if you plan the beginning at the end, do not apologize, and avoid beginning with "*My speech is about . . .*"

Concluding Your Presentation

13.6 Practice effective strategies for creating dynamic conclusions.

- The recency effect explains our tendency to recall the conclusion of a presentation.

- Presentation conclusions should be memorable, clear, and brief.

- Methods of concluding a presentation include summarizing, quoting someone, telling a story, calling for action, and referring back to your beginning.

- Your conclusion will be more effective if its mood and style are consistent with the presentation's purpose and realistic about audience expectations and attitudes.

Key Terms

Analogy	Fact	Signpost
Biased	Internal preview	Space arrangement
Cause-and-effect arrangement	Internal summary	Speaking outline
Central idea	Key points	Speech Framer
Comparison–contrast arrangement	Mind mapping	Statistics
Comprehensive outline	Oral footnote	Story
Connectives	Organization	Supporting material
Content	Preliminary outline	Testimony
Definition	Primacy effect	Time arrangement
Description	Primary source	Topical arrangement
Documentation	Problem–solution arrangement	Transition
Example	Recency effect	Valid
	Secondary source	

TEST YOUR KNOWLEDGE

13.1 *Examine, analyze, and select appropriate ideas and supporting material for your presentation.*

1 What kind of supporting material is used in the following excerpt from a student's presentation? *Ron Wilson, an African American representative in Texas, stated "it's a great hypocrisy when courts allow selective universities to relax their academic standards for athletes and children of alumni but not for African Americans."*

   a. Fact

   b. Statistics

   c. Testimony

   d. Description

2 What kind of supporting material is used in the following example? *One way to understand neuroplasticity (how the brain creates mind-sets) is by comparing it to snow skiing. Plasticity is like snow on a hill in winter. Because it is pliable we can take many paths if we choose to ski down that hill. But because it is pliable, if we keep taking the same path, we develop tracks, and then ruts, and get stuck in them.*

   a. Description

   b. Analogy

   c. Example

   d. Story

3 Ask all of the questions that test supporting material for the following example except one. Which test is not needed for this example? *Joseph Farah, editor of* World News Daily, *the politically conservative, conspiracy-theory website, writes "Obama is choreographing a top-down revolution in America—one from which it may take generations to extricate ourselves. It will be a shame if we learn he was ineligible to serve in the office of president only after he's gone."*

   a. Is the source credible?

   b. Is the source biased?

   c. Is the source identified?

   d. Is the information valid?

13.2 *Identify the central idea and key points of your presentation.*

4 Which of the following answers constitutes the best example of a central idea for a presentation on the different meanings of facial expressions in other cultures?

   a. Facial expressions differ across cultures.

   b. The meaning of some facial expressions differs from culture to culture.

   c. Facial expressions for fear, sadness, and disgust are the same across cultures.

   d. Although many facial expressions are the same in different cultures—such as smiling—other facial expressions differ.

13.3 *Describe commonly used organizational patterns for arranging presentation content.*

5 Which organizational pattern works best for explaining to an audience how to bake a cake?

   a. Time

   b. Topical

   c. Space

   d. Causes and effects

13.4 *Describe and apply different outlining methods for organizing a presentation.*

6 All of the following answers are good rules for outlining a presentation except:

   a. use numbers and letters.

   b. leave the introduction and conclusion out of the outline.

   c. divide subpoints logically.

   d. keep the outline consistent in design and grammatical structure.

7 Which kind of connective is used in the following example? *Once you've collected all of your ingredients, you can begin the process of putting the recipe together.*

   a. Internal preview

   b. Signpost

   c. Internal summary

   d. Transition

13.5 *Practice effective strategies for creating dynamic introductions.*

8 What introductory technique did Abraham Lincoln use when he started the Gettysburg Address with these words? *Four score and seven years ago, our fathers brought forth on this continent, a new nation, conceived in liberty, and dedicated to the proposition that all men are created equal.*

   a. Refer to a current place or occasion.

   b. Refer to a well-known incident or event.

   c. Quote someone.

   d. Address audience needs.

9 The primacy effect explains why

   a. an effective introduction is so important at the beginning of a presentation.

   b. an effective conclusion is so important at the end of a presentation.

   c. transitions are so important in the middle of a presentation.

   d. presentations should "end with a bang."

13.6 *Practice effective strategies for creating dynamic conclusions.*

10 What concluding technique did a student use when he ended a classroom presentation on Cliffs Notes as follows: ". . . at least now you know that, unlike Ronald McDonald or Homer Simpson, Cliff was a real person who began a major industry and who did not dodge the issues. *CliffsNotes* and its competitors will continue explaining the finer points of literature to students around the globe. Because as long as teachers assign the classics of literature, the study guides will continue to grow and prosper.

   a. Summarize

   b. Quote someone

   c. Tell a story

   d. Call to action

Answers found on page 368.

Language and Delivery 14

KEY OBJECTIVES

14.1 Explain how each of the CORE language styles can enhance the power of a presentation.

14.2 Identify and manage the causes and effects of presentation anxiety.

14.3 Compare the advantages and disadvantages of the four delivery modes.

14.4 Describe the components of effective vocal delivery.

14.5 Describe the components of effective physical delivery.

14.6 Apply effective strategies for designing and displaying presentation aids.

14.7 Practice using effective language and skilled delivery.

In Chapter 12, "Planning Your Presentation," we described a study that asked professional speakers and college students to identify the presentation skills that are *most* important for improving their success as speakers. Both groups identified "choosing appropriate and effective words" and "using your voice effectively" in the top-ten list of speaking skills.

Language and delivery skills can make the difference between an average and a superb presentation, between a meaningless and a meaningful talk; between a forgettable and a motivational speech.

Unlike speakers, actors do not write the words they speak. They also go through years of training learning how to use their voices and bodies to deliver their lines with meaning and artfulness. Good actors know how to modify their voices, appearance, and behavior for a particular role. But when some actors are stripped of these roles and asked to speak as themselves in their own words, many find it very difficult to do so. Their language may not be as eloquent and their delivery may not be as polished as that of the characters they play on screen or stage. As speakers, we do more than "play" a character. We write our own "scripts" and we portray ourselves.

In his book *President Reagan: The Role of a Lifetime*, Lou Cannon quotes Ronald Reagan's response to criticism that he was nothing more than "an actor who knew how to give a good speech."

I suppose that's not too far wrong. Because an actor knows two or three important things—to be honest in what he's doing and to be in touch with the audience. That's not bad advice for a politician either. My actor's instincts simply told me to speak the truth as I saw it.[1]

In this chapter, we demonstrate that every speaker can learn to engage (as in "to use") effective language and delivery skills as well as to become engaging (as in "compelling, interesting, and convincing") speakers.

The CORE Language Styles

14.1 *Explain how each of the CORE language styles can enhance the power of a presentation.*

Carefully chosen words add power and authority to a presentation and transform good speeches into great ones. Your language style can add a distinct flavor, excitement, and clarity to every presentation.

Language style refers to how you use vocabulary, sentence structure and length, grammar and syntax, and rhetorical devices to express a message.[2] In this section, we describe the four **CORE language styles**: **c**lear style, **o**ral style, **r**hetorical style, and **e**loquent style. Your task is to decide which style or styles suit you, your purpose, your audience, the setting and occasion of your presentation, and your message.[3]

The four CORE language styles are often most effective when used in combination. Once you are skilled and comfortable using the clear and oral styles, you are on "firm ground" to use the rhetorical and eloquent styles to persuade and inspire your audience. In short, use the styles that best match you and your message.

Clear Style

Clarity always comes first. If you aren't clear, your audience won't understand you or your message. The **clear style** uses short, simple, direct words and phrases as well as concrete words, and plain language. Don't let long, fancy words get in the way of your message. When speakers express themselves clearly and simply, they "are viewed as more credible, and their ideas are judged more positively."[5]

Oral Style

In Chapter 5, "Verbal Communication," we emphasized the importance of using oral language when interacting with others. Recall the features of the **oral style**: short, familiar words; succinct, simple, and even incomplete sentences; and more personal pronouns and informal colloquial expressions. The oral style resembles the way we talk in most conversations. Rather than worrying about what you may *think* is expected—formal language, perfect grammar, impressive vocabulary—remember your purpose and what you want to achieve. For an example of both clear and oral styles, see John Sullivan's informative presentation, "Cliff's Notes" on pages 294–297.

> **"Nobody has time to try and figure out what you're trying to say, so you need to be direct. Most great advertising is direct. That's how people talk. That's the style they read. That's what sells products and services or ideas."**
>
> —Jerry Della Femina, marketing expert[4]

The **CORE** Language Styles

The CORE language styles build on a strong foundation that uses clear and oral styles as firm ground for enlisting the rhetorical and eloquent language styles.

When using an oral style, say what you mean by speaking the way you talk, not the way you write.

Rhetorical Style

The **rhetorical style** uses language designed to influence, persuade, and/or inspire. Vivid and powerful words enhance the intensity of a persuasive presentation. **Language intensity** refers to the degree to which your language deviates from bland, neutral terms.[6] For example, instead of using a word like *nice*, try *delightful* or *captivating*. *Disaster* is a much more intense word than *mistake*. A *vile* meal

Differences in Written and Oral Styles[7]

Ann Raimes, *Keys for Writers: A Brief Handbook*, 3rd ed. (Boston: Houghton Mifflin, 2004), pp. 152–158.

EXCERPTS FROM AN ESSAY ON NEUROMUSICOLOGY

"I haven't understood a bar of music in my entire life, but I have felt it" (quoted in Peter, page 350). These words were spoken by Igor Stravinsky, who composed some of the most complex and sophisticated music of his century. If the great Stravinsky can accept the elusive nature of music, and still love it, why can't we? Why are we analyzing it to try to make it useful?

Ours is an age of information—an age that wishes to conquer all the mysteries of the human brain. Today there is a growing trend to study music's effects on our emotions, behavior, health, and intelligence. Journalist Alex Ross reports how the relatively new field of neuromusicology (the science of the nervous system and its response to music) has been developed to experiment with music as a tool and to shape it to the needs of society. Observations like these let us know that we are on the threshold of seeing music in a whole new way and using music to achieve measurable changes in behavior. However, this new approach carries dangers, and once we go in this direction, there can be no turning back. How far do we want to go in our study of musical science? What effects will it have on our listening pleasures?

A short history lesson reveals that there has been an awareness that music affects us, even if the reasons are not clear. Around 900 B.C., the Bible's King David played the harp "to cure Saul's derangement" (Gonzalez-Crussi, page 69).

EXCERPTS FROM A PRESENTATION ON NEUROMUSICOLOGY

[Note: As an opening, the speaker plays an excerpt from "God Bless America" followed by an excerpt from *Sesame Street*'s theme music.]

What did you think of or feel when you heard "God Bless America"? What about the *Sesame Street* theme? I'm sure that you're not surprised to learn that "God Bless America" reminds many people of the September 11th tragedy, the War in Afghanistan, and patriotism. And the theme from *Sesame Street* probably put a smile on your face as you revisited the world of Kermit the Frog, Miss Piggy, and Big Bird.

Why were your responses so predictable and so emotional? The answer lies in a new brain science—a science that threatens to control you by controlling the music you hear. Is resistance futile?

In the next few minutes, we'll take a close look at the field of neuromusicology. What? Neuro, meaning related to our brain and nervous system. And musicology—the historic and scientific study of music.

Journalist Alex Ross put it this way: By understanding the nervous system and its response to music, neuromusicologists study music as a tool and shape it to the needs of society.

As New Age as all this may sound, there's plenty of history to back up the claims of neuromusicologists. For example, those of you who know your Bible know that King David played the harp to "cure Saul's derangement."

---

sounds much worse than a *bad* meal. In Chapter 5, "Verbal Communication," we devoted a section to Powerful and Powerless Language. Powerful language is direct, assertive, confident, and persuasive. It also increases the perceived credibility of the speaker.

The rhetorical style often relies on **rhetorical devices**, word strategies designed to enhance a presentation's impact and persuasiveness. Two rhetorical devices work particularly well in presentations: repetition and metaphors.

Repetition Because your listeners can't rewind and immediately re-hear what you've just said, use repetition to highlight the sounds, words, ideas, and phrases you want your audience to remember. Repetition can be as simple as beginning a series of words (or words placed closely together) with the same sound. This type of repetition is called **alliteration**. For example, the first part of Lincoln's Gettysburg Address—"*Four score and seven years ago our fathers brought forth*"—includes three words beginning with the letter *f*.

Repetition can be extended to a word, a phrase, or an entire sentence. Dr. Martin Luther King Jr. used the phrase "I have a dream" nine times in his famous 1963 speech in Washington, DC. He used "let freedom ring" ten times. Repetition can drive home an idea and provoke action. Audience members anticipate and remember repeated phrases.

George Lakoff, a highly respected professor of Cognitive Science and Linguistics writes, "When a word or phrase is repeated over and over for a long period of time," it "physically changes your brain."[8] Negative connotations for "Obamacare" and positive connotations for "tax relief" have become ingrained and difficult to change in political discussions.

Metaphors Metaphors and their cousins—similes and analogies—are powerful rhetorical devices. A **metaphor** makes a comparison between two unrelated things or ideas. Shakespeare's famous line "All the world's a stage" is a classic metaphor. The world is not a theatrical stage, but we do assume many roles during a lifetime. Author Isabel Allende's colorful description of art is another potent metaphor: "Art is a rebellious child, a wild animal that will not be tamed." Metaphors leave it to the audience to get the point for themselves.[9] In Chapter 13, "Content and Organization," we explained how a sentence in Shirley Sherrod's speech was taken out of context. Her speech should also be known for its grace and use of a metaphor in her conclusion: "Life is a grindstone, but whether it grinds us down or polishes us up depends on us."[10]

Many linguists claim that metaphors are windows into the workings of the human mind.[11] Metaphors are so deeply embedded in our language that we often use them without realizing it. For example, you've probably tried something new by "getting your feet wet." Or, you may have described an object using a body part, such as *mouth* of a river or *foot* of a mountain.[12] When Steve Jobs introduced the 2007 iPhone, he compared Apple's switch to Intel processors as a "huge heart transplant."[13]

Metaphors are powerful, but don't overdo it. The word *war* is often used by political candidates and elected officials: from former President Lyndon Johnson's "War on Poverty," to President Ronald Reagan's "War on Drugs," to the 2012 U.S. presidential election's "War on Women," and "War on Families."

Eloquent Style

The **eloquent style** uses poetic and expressive language in a way that makes thoughts and feelings clear, inspiring, *and* memorable. Eloquent language does not have to be flowery or grand; it can use an oral style, personal pronouns, and repetition or metaphors. You don't have to be a famous orator, an Abraham Lincoln, or a Martin Luther King, Jr. to speak eloquently. In his comments on being inducted into the Pro Football Hall of Fame in 2010, Oakland 49er Jerry Rice uses an oral style and repetition: "There are no more routes to run, no more touchdowns to score, no more records to set. That young boy from Mississippi has finally stopped running. Let me stand here and catch my breath."[14]

In *Eloquence in an Electronic Age: The Transformation of Political Speechmaking*, Kathleen Jamieson notes that eloquent speakers comfortably disclose personal experiences and feelings. Rather than explaining the lessons of the past or creating a public sense of ethics, today's most eloquent speakers often call on their own past or their own sense of ethics to inspire an audience.[15] Consider the words of Malala Yousafzai, the Pakistani teenager who was nearly killed by Taliban gunmen for advocating that girls should have the right to go to school. She gave her first public speech at the United Nations General Assembly, July 12, 2013.[16]

Dear friends, on 9 October 2012, the Taliban shot me on the left side of my forehead. They shot my friends, too. They thought that the bullets would silence us, but they failed. And out of that silence came thousands of voices. The terrorists thought they would change my aims and stop my ambitions. But nothing changed in my life except this: weakness, fear and hopelessness died. Strength, power and courage was born. I am the same Malala. My ambitions are the same. My hopes are the same. And my dreams are the same.

> The eloquent style is like poetry: It has the remarkable ability to capture profound ideas and feelings in a few simple words.

Confident Delivery

14.2 *Identify and manage the causes and effects of presentation anxiety.*

At the beginning of our courses or units on presentation speaking, we often ask students to complete the sentence: "Giving a speech makes me feel . . ." Their responses range from feelings of empowerment to total terror. Here are some examples:

- "Giving a speech makes me feel powerful. Although nervousness enters the picture, so does a feeling of power. The thought of having everybody's full attention and being able to convey my point of view makes me feel as though I'm in charge."

- "Giving a speech makes me feel uncomfortable. I'm very quiet and shy in front of most people, especially people I don't know. Because I'm a quiet person, I'm not comfortable with just coming out and speaking to someone—which is just like giving a speech because you are speaking to people you've never met."

- "Giving a speech makes me feel like I'm going to lose control—my heart starts to race, my body starts to tremble. I've tried taking deep breaths to calm myself down when I feel this way."

All three of these students did quite well in their presentations, especially after realizing they were not alone in their fears. Nervousness is inevitable but certainly not fatal. In fact, a little bit of anxiety can keep you on your toes and motivate you to spend the time and effort needed to both develop and deliver an effective presentation.

In Chapter 2, "Understanding Your Self," we described communication apprehension as the fear or anxiety associated with communicating in group discussions, meetings, interpersonal conversations, and public speaking. If you haven't completed and scored the Personal Report of Communication Apprehension (PRCA) on page 38, do so now. You can compare the score for the public speaking section to the average score for most people. You may find that you are not alone in your level of apprehension.

Will the Audience Know I'm Nervous?

Many speakers fear that audience members can see and therefore know that they're anxious. Use the following table to make a list of your own symptoms of speaking anxiety or symptoms you have seen or heard in others. In the left-hand column, list symptoms the audience *can* see or hear. In the right-hand column, list symptoms the audience *cannot* see or hear. An example of each has been provided.

In most cases, speaking anxiety is invisible. Audiences cannot see a pounding heart, an upset stomach, cold hands, or worried thoughts. They do not notice small changes in your vocal quality or remember occasional mistakes. Although you may feel as though your legs are visibly quivering and quaking uncontrollably, the audience will rarely see any movement.

Most speakers who describe themselves as being very nervous appear confident and calm to their audiences. Even experienced communication instructors, when asked about how anxious a speaker is, seldom accurately estimate the speaker's level of anxiety.[18]

Symptoms the audience *can* see or hear	Symptoms the audience *cannot* see or hear
Example: Shaking hands	*Example:* Upset stomach
1.	1.
2.	2.
3.	3.
4.	4.
5.	5.

Yet, when American adults were asked what they feared the most, 51 percent chose snakes. Public speaking came in second (40 percent), and heights earned third place (36 percent).[17]

In terms of coping with any form of anxiety, we often fear things we don't understand. Here, we use contemporary research to correct two common misconceptions about speaking anxiety:

- "I am more nervous than most people."
- "Reading about speaking anxiety will make me more nervous."

Are You More Nervous Than Most People?

When we ask students about their presentation speaking goals, they tell us that they want to "gain confidence," "overcome anxiety," "stop being nervous," "get rid of the jitters," and "calm down." No other answer comes close in terms of frequency. Most of these students also believe they are more nervous than other speakers are.

Successful presenters know two very important facts about speaking anxiety: they know that it's very common and that it's usually invisible. As speakers—experienced or otherwise—we all share many of the same worried thoughts, physical discomforts, and psychological anxieties. This means that most audience members understand your feelings, don't want to trade places with you, and may even admire your courage for being up there.

If you still believe that you are more nervous than anyone else is, make an appointment with your instructor to discuss your concerns. Many colleges and communication departments offer special assistance to students who feel disabled by their level of fear and anxiety associated with speaking to others.

> Despite most people's worst fears, audiences are usually kind to speakers. They are willing to forgive and forget an honest mistake.

Will Reading About Speaking Anxiety Make You *More* Nervous?

You may think that the more you learn about speaking anxiety, the more nervous you'll become. Just the opposite is true: the more accurate information and sound advice you read about speaking anxiety, the more likely you will build confidence. In his study on reading about public speaking apprehension, Michael Motley had one group of college students read a booklet that discussed the nature and causes of, as well as strategies for minimizing, speaking anxiety. A second group viewed relaxation videos, read an excerpt from a popular self-help book on reducing fears, or received no treatment at all. The greatest decrease in speaking anxiety occurred in the group that read the booklet on speaking anxiety.[19] Similarly, reading this textbook can help you understand why you become anxious when you have to make a presentation, teach you techniques for managing those fears, and increase your speaking confidence.

Modes of Delivery

14.3 *Compare the advantages and disadvantages of the four delivery modes.*

The term **delivery** describes the ways in which you use your voice, body, and presentation aids to express your message. You should begin planning how to deliver your presentation by deciding which delivery mode to use: impromptu, extemporaneous, manuscript, memorized, or a combination of forms. But, before you do, decide which of these modes best suits you and your purpose.[20]

Impromptu

Impromptu speaking occurs when you speak without advanced preparation or practice. For example, you may be called on in class or at work to answer a question or share an opinion. You may be inspired to get up and speak on an important issue at a public meeting. Even in those instances when you don't have a lot of time to prepare, you can quickly think of a purpose and a way to organize and adapt your message to the audience.

Extemporaneous

Extemporaneous speaking is the most common form of delivery and occurs when you use a set of notes or an outline to guide you through a well-prepared presentation. Your notes can be a few words on a card or a detailed, full-sentence outline.

Classroom lectures, business briefings, and courtroom arguments are usually delivered extemporaneously.

Extemporaneous speaking is easiest for beginners to do well and the method preferred by professionals. No other form of delivery gives you as much freedom and flexibility with preplanned material. A well-practiced extemporaneous presentation seems spontaneous and has an ease to it that makes the audience and speaker feel comfortable.

Manuscript

Manuscript speaking involves writing your presentation in advance and reading it out loud. For very nervous speakers, a manuscript may *seem* like a lifesaving document, keeping them afloat when they feel as though they're drowning. However, manuscript speeches are difficult to deliver for all but the most skilled speakers, and we strongly discourage speakers from using manuscript delivery. When, however, an occasion is a major public event after which your words will be published word for word, you may have no choice but to use a manuscript for at least part of your presentation. And if an occasion is highly emotional—such as delivering a eulogy—you may need the support of a manuscript.

Using a manuscript allows you to choose each word carefully. You can plan and practice every detail. It also ensures that your presentation will fit within your allotted speaking time.

If you must use a manuscript, focus on maintaining an oral style when you write your presentation: *Write as though you are speaking.*

Memorized

Memorized speaking requires a speaker to deliver a presentation from recall with very few or no notes. A memorized presentation offers one major advantage and one major disadvantage. The major advantage is physical freedom. You can gesture freely and look at your audience 100 percent of the time. The disadvantage, however, outweighs any and all advantages. If you forget the words you memorized, it is more difficult to recover your thoughts without creating an awkward moment for both you and your audience.

Speakers rarely memorize an entire presentation. However, there's nothing wrong with memorizing your introduction or a few key sections as long as you have your notes to fall back on.

ADVANTAGES AND DISADVANTAGES OF IMPROMPTU DELIVERY	
ADVANTAGES	**DISADVANTAGES**
• Natural and conversational speaking • Maximum eye contact • Demonstrates speaker's knowledge and skill	• Limited time to make basic decisions about purpose, audience adaptation, content, and organization • Speaker anxiety can be high • Speaker may be at a "loss for words" • Delivery may be awkward and ineffective • Difficult to gauge speaking time • Limited or no supporting material • Speaker may have nothing to say on such short notice

Today's Lesson

ADVANTAGES AND DISADVANTAGES OF EXTEMPORANEOUS DELIVERY

ADVANTAGES

- More preparation time than impromptu delivery
- Seems spontaneous but is actually well prepared
- Speaker can monitor and adapt to audience feedback
- Allows more eye contact and audience interaction than manuscript delivery
- Audiences typically respond positively to speakers who use extemporaneous delivery
- Speaker can choose concise language for the central idea and key points
- With practice, it becomes the most powerful form of delivery

DISADVANTAGES

- Speaker anxiety can increase for content not covered by notes
- Language may not be well chosen or stylistically appropriate
- Can be difficult to estimate speaking time

Mix and Match Modes of Delivery

Learning to mix and match modes of delivery appropriately lets you select the method that works best for you and your purpose. An impromptu speaker may recite a memorized statistic or a rehearsed argument in the same way that a politician responds to press questions. An extemporaneous speaker may read a lengthy quotation or a series of statistics and then deliver a memorized ending.

Speaking Notes

Effective speakers use their notes efficiently. Even when your presentation is impromptu, you may use a few quick words jotted down just before you speak. Speaking notes may appear on index cards and outlines or as a manuscript.

Index Cards and Outlines A single card can be used for each component of your presentation—for example, you can use one card for the introduction, another card for each key point, and one card for your conclusion. Record key words rather than complete sentences; use only one side of each index card. To help you organize your presentation and rearrange key points at the last minute, number each of the cards. If you have too many notes for a few index cards, use an outline on a full sheet of paper.

Manuscript When preparing a speech manuscript, double space each page and use a fourteen- to sixteen-point font size. Use only the top two-thirds of the page to avoid having to bend your head to see the bottom of each page and lose eye contact with your audience or constrict your windpipe. Set wide margins so that

ADVANTAGES AND DISADVANTAGES OF MANUSCRIPT DELIVERY

ADVANTAGES

- Speaker can pay careful attention to all the basic principles of effective speaking
- Speaker can choose concise and stylistically appropriate language
- Speaker anxiety may be eased by having a "script"
- Speaker can rehearse the same presentation over and over
- Ensures accurate reporting of presentation content
- Speaker can stay within time limit

DISADVANTAGES

- Delivery can be dull
- Difficult to maintain sufficient eye contact
- Gestures and movement are limited
- Language can be too formal, lacking oral style
- Difficult to modify or adapt to the audience or situation

you have space on the page to add any last-minute changes. Remember to number each page so that you can keep everything in order and do not staple your pages together. Instead, place your manuscript to one side of the lectern and slide the pages to the other side when it's time to go on to the next page. Some speakers put their manuscripts in a three-ring notebook so they can quickly flip each page over without losing their place.

Bruce Springsteen uses a lectern and manuscript during his tribute to U2 at the Rock and Roll Hall of Fame Induction Ceremony.

Vocal Delivery

14.4 *Describe the components of effective vocal delivery.*

Developing an effective speaking voice requires the same time and effort that you would devote to mastering any skill. You can't become an accomplished carpenter, pianist, swimmer, writer, or speaker overnight. Because only a few lucky speakers are born with beautiful voices, the majority of us must work at sounding clear and expressive. Fortunately, there are ways to improve the characteristics and quality of your voice. Begin by focusing on the basics: breathing, volume, rate, pitch, articulation, and pronunciation.[21]

Breathing

Effective breath control enables you to speak more loudly, say more in a single breath, and reduce the likelihood of vocal problems such as harshness or breathiness. Thus, the first step in learning how to breathe for presentation speaking is to note the differences between the shallow, unconscious breathing you do all the time and the deeper breathing that produces strong, sustained sound quality. Many speech coaches recommend the exercise on the next page to learn deep, abdominal breathing.

Volume

Volume measures the loudness level of your voice. The key to producing adequate volume is adapting to the size of the audience and the dimensions of the room in which you will be speaking. If there are only five people in an audience and they are sitting close to you, speak at a normal, everyday volume. If there are fifty people in your audience, you need more energy and force to support your voice. When your audience exceeds fifty, you may be more comfortable with a microphone. However, a strong speaking voice can project to an audience of a 1,000 people without electronic amplification. Opera singers, for example, do it all the time. "We can blast through a 100 piece orchestra and about the same number of the chorus members with just the natural power of our bodies. . . . 100% completely natural, pure physical force. Body building for the voice."[22]

Practice your presentation in a room about the same size as the one in which you will speak, or, at least, imagine speaking in such a room. Ask a friend to sit in a far corner and report back on your volume and clarity. Also note that a room full of people absorbs sound; you will have to turn up your volume another notch when your audience is present. Speakers who cannot be heard are a common problem. It's very rare, though, for a speaker to be too loud.

Exercise for Deep Breathing

1. Lie flat on your back. Support the back of your knees with a pillow.

2. Place a moderately heavy, hardbound book on your stomach, right over your navel.

3. Begin breathing through your mouth. The book should move up when you breathe in and sink down when you breathe out.

4. Place one of your hands on the upper part of your chest in a "Pledge of Allegiance" position. As you inhale and exhale, this area should not move in and out or up and down.

5. Take the book away and replace it with your other hand. Your abdominal area should continue to move up when you breathe in and sink down when you breathe out.

6. After you're comfortable with step 5, try doing the same kind of breathing while sitting up or standing.

7. Add sound. Try sighing and sustaining the vowel *ahh* for five seconds with each exhalation. Then try counting or reciting the alphabet.

> **Remember that audiences can listen faster than you talk, so it's better to keep the pace up than speak at a crawl.**

Rate

Your speaking **rate** refers to the number of words you say per minute (wpm). Generally, a rate less than 125 wpm is too slow, 125 to 150 wpm is acceptable, 150 to 180 wpm is better, and 180 wpm or more exceeds the speed limit. But these guidelines are not carved in stone. Your preferred rate depends on you, the nature and mood of your message, and your audience. If you are explaining a highly technical process or expressing personal sorrow, your rate may slow to 125 wpm. On the other hand, if you are telling an exciting, amusing, or infuriating story, your rate may hit 200 wpm. For maximum effectiveness, speakers vary their rate. Martin Luther King Jr.'s "I Have a Dream" speech opened at a slow 90 wpm but ended at 150 wpm.[23]

Listeners perceive presenters who speak quickly *and* clearly as energized, motivated, and interested as well as more competent and credible.[24] Given the choice, we'd rather be accused of speaking too quickly than run the risk of boring an audience. Too slow a rate suggests that you are unsure of yourself or, even worse, that you are not very bright.

Pitch

Pitch is how high or low your voice sounds—just like the notes on a musical scale. Anatomy determines pitch (most men speak at a lower pitch than women and children). Your **optimum pitch** is the pitch at which you speak most easily and expressively. If you speak at your optimum pitch, you will not tire as easily; your voice will sound stronger and will be less likely to fade at the end of sentences. It will also be less likely to sound harsh, hoarse, or breathy.

To find your optimum pitch, sing up the musical scale from the lowest note

Most opera singers do not need or like using microphones.

you can sing. By the fifth or sixth note, you should have reached your optimum pitch. Test your optimum pitch to see if your voice is clear and whether you can increase its volume with minimal effort. Finding your optimum pitch does *not* mean using that pitch for everything you say in your presentation. Think of your optimum pitch as "neutral" and use it as your baseline to raise or lower your pitch for emphasis and variety.

Articulation

A strong, well-paced, optimally pitched voice that is also expressive may not be enough to ensure the successful delivery of a presentation. Proper **articulation**—clearly making the sounds in the words of a language—is just as important. Poor articulation is often described as sloppy speech, poor diction, or mumbling. Fortunately, you can improve and practice your articulation by speaking more slowly, speaking with a bit more volume, and opening your mouth wider when you speak.

CHAPTER 14 | language and delivery

268

Mastering the Microphone

Do you or someone you know suffer from "microphonobia" (a term we made up just for this feature)? It's not the same as communication apprehension or speaking anxiety. Rather it's the fear and apprehension associated with using a very common, simple, and useful amplifying device. We cannot explain this fear, but we can suggest ways to use a microphone effectively and confidently.

Microphones benefit both the audience *and* you. Without it, audience members may strain to hear you, may misinterpret what they manage to hear, may not hear you at all, and may leave doubting your competence. As one speech trainer put it, "If you've gone to all that trouble to put together a speech, . . . you need the right people to hear you, and the right equipment to make sure they hear it loud and clear. Otherwise, what a waste of your time and effort. . . ."[25]

When a speaking situation requires a microphone, make the most out of this technology. Unless a sound technician is monitoring the presentation, your microphone will be preset for one volume. If you speak with too much volume, it may sound as though you are shouting at your audience. If you speak too softly, the microphone may not pick up everything you have to say. The trick is to go against your instincts. If you want to project a soft tone, speak closer to the microphone and lower your volume. Your voice will sound more intimate and will convey subtle emotions. If you want to be more forceful, speak farther away from the microphone and project your voice.

Experienced speakers make the adjustments they need during the first few seconds that they hear their own voices projected through an amplification system.

Most important, familiarize yourself with the specific microphone and system you will be using. For example, when placed on a lapel, a microphone faces outward rather than upward. As a result, it receives and sends a less direct sound than a handheld microphone.[26] Here are some tips to follow for all microphones:

- Test the microphone ahead of time.
- Determine whether the microphone is sophisticated enough to capture your voice from several angles and distances or whether you will need to keep your mouth close to it.
- Place the microphone about five to ten inches from your mouth. If you are using a handheld microphone, hold it below your mouth at chin level.

- Focus on your audience, not the microphone. Stay near the mike but don't tap it, lean over it, keep readjusting it, or make the p-p-p-p-p "motorboat sounds" as a test.
- Keep in mind that a microphone will do more than amplify your voice; it will also amplify other sounds—coughing, clearing your throat, shuffling papers, or tapping a pen.
- If your microphone is well adjusted, speak in a natural, conversational voice.

Certain sounds account for most articulation problems: combined words, "-ing" endings, and final consonants. Many speakers combine words—"what's the matter" becomes "watsumata." Some speakers shorten the "ing" sound to an "in" sound: "sayin" instead of "saying." The final consonants that get left off most often are the ones that pop out of your mouth. Because these consonants—*p, b, t, d, k,* and *g*—cannot be hummed like an "m" or hissed like an "s," it's easy to lose them at the end of a word. Usually you can hear the difference between "Rome" and "rose," but poor articulation can make it difficult to hear the difference between "hit" and "hid" or "tap" and "tab."

Pronunciation

Proper **pronunciation** involves putting all the correct sounds of a word in the correct order with the correct stress. In a presentation speaking situation, poor pronunciation can result in misunderstanding and embarrassment. For example, we once heard a speaker undermine her credibility in a talk about effective communication when she repeatedly said the word "pro*noun*ciation" instead of "pro*nun*ciation."

Pronunciations can and do change. According to most dictionaries, the word *often* should be pronounced "aw-fen," but many people now put the "t" sound in the middle and pronounce it the way it's spelled. The word *a* should be pronounced "uh," not rhymed with *hay*, but many people now use both versions. Even the word *the* is often mispronounced. When *the* appears before the sound of a consonant as in "the dog" or "the paper," it should be pronounced "thuh." When *the* comes before the sound of a vowel as in "the alligator" or "the article," it should be pronounced "thee."

Expressing Yourself Expressively

If you are excited about your message and truly interested in sharing it with your audience, you are well on your way to being an expressive speaker. **Expressiveness** is the vitality, variety, and sincerity that speakers put into their delivery.

Expressive speakers are not only mindful of what they say, they are also mindful of how varying their vocal quality helps communicate their intended meaning. To enhance the expressiveness to your voice, vary your **inflection**—the changing pitch, stress, and volume within a syllable, word, or group of words. Lack of inflection results in a monotone voice. A slight change, however, even just a fraction, can change the entire meaning of a sentence:

I was born in New Jersey. (You, on the other hand, were born in Texas.)
I *was* born in New Jersey. (No doubt about it!)
I was *born* in New Jersey. (So I know my way around.)
I was born in New *Jersey*. (Not in New York.)

Expressive speakers demonstrate **fluency**. They speak smoothly without tripping over words or pausing at awkward moments. The more you practice your presentation, the more fluent you will become. Practice will alert you to words, phrases, and sentences that may look good in your notes but sound awkward or choppy when spoken.

Listen for **filler phrases**—*you know, uh, um, okay,* and *like*—that can break up your fluency and annoy your audience. There is nothing wrong with an occasional filler phrase, particularly when you're speaking informally or impromptu. In fact, the much-feared "um" and "uh" is a universal speech filler woven into the fabric of every language on earth.[27] In Michael Erard's book *Um*, he notes that "um" and "uh" demonstrate "thinking, not, as had been previously thought, lack of thinking."[28]

If you're trying to reduce an *excessive* number of fillers, such as "really," "you know," "like," or even "um," record your practice sessions and listen for filler phrases as you play back the recording. To break the filler-phrase habit, slow down and listen to the words you use. You will have to work on breaking this habit all the time, not just when you are speaking in front of an audience.

Expressiveness is more than enthusiasm, energy, inflection, and fluency. When these four delivery elements effectively interact with one another, your expressiveness becomes an extension of your personality, attitudes, and desire to communicate effectively.

Physical Delivery

14.5 *Describe the components of effective physical delivery.*

The key to effective physical delivery is naturalness. However, being natural doesn't mean "letting it all hang out." Rather, it means being so well prepared and well practiced that your presentation is an authentic reflection of you.

Audiences jump to conclusions about speakers based on first impressions of their appearance and behavior. The way you stand, move, gesture, and make eye contact has a significant impact on your presentation.[29]

Eye Contact

Eye contact, establishing and maintaining direct, visual links with individual audience members, may be the most important component of effective physical delivery. Generally, the more eye contact you have with your audience, the better. Try to maintain eye contact during *most* of your presentation. If you are using detailed notes or a manuscript, use a technique called *eye scan*. **Eye scan** involves glancing at a specific section of your notes or manuscript and then looking up at your audience to speak. Begin by placing your thumb and index finger on one side of the page to frame the section of the notes you are using. Then, as you approach the end of a phrase or sentence within that section, glance down again and visually grasp the next phrase to be spoken. This allows you to maintain maximum eye contact without losing your place.

Eye contact does more than ensure that you are looking in the direction of your audience. It also helps you to initiate and control communication, enhance your credibility, and interpret valuable audience feedback.

Your physical delivery tells an audience a great deal about who you are and how much you care about reaching them.

Control Have you ever noticed a teacher "catch the eye" of a student or "give the eye" to an inattentive student? When you establish initial eye contact with your audience, you indicate that you are ready to begin speaking and that they should get ready to listen. Lack of eye contact communicates a message, too: It says that you don't care to connect with your audience.

Credibility Direct eye contact says, "I'm talking to *you*; I want *you* to hear this." In Western cultures, such directness positively affects your credibility.[30] It says, "I'm of good character (I care enough to share this important message with you)," "I'm competent (I know this subject so well I can leave my notes and look at you)," and "I'm charismatic (I want to energize and connect with everyone in this room)."

> After all, if you don't look at your audience, why should they look at you?

Feedback Eye contact is the best way to gauge audience feedback during a presentation. At first, making eye contact with individual audience members may distract you. Some people smile, others may look bored or confused, and some may be looking around the room or whispering to friends. With all this going on in the audience, it's easy to become sidetracked. However, these different responses are also the very reason you must establish and maintain eye contact. Speakers who don't look directly at audience members rarely have a clue about why their presentations succeed or fail.

Facial Expression

Your face reflects your attitudes and emotional states, provides nonverbal feedback, and, next to the words you speak, is the primary source of information about you.[31]

Despite the importance of facial expressions, they are difficult to control. Most of us tend to display a particular style of facial expression. Some people show little expression—they have

a stoic, poker face most of the time. Others are as open as a book—you have little doubt about how they feel. It's very difficult to change a "poker face" into an "open book" or vice versa. A nervous speaker may be too distracted to smile, too frightened to stop smiling, or too agitated to register displeasure or anger when appropriate.

Audiences will direct their eyes at your face, so unless your topic is very solemn or serious, try to smile. A smile shows your listeners that you are comfortable and eager to share your ideas and information. Audience members are more likely to smile if you smile. However, if you do not feel comfortable smiling, don't force it. Let your face communicate your feelings; let your face do what comes naturally. If you speak honestly and sincerely, your facial expression will be appropriate and effective.

Gestures

As Chapter 6, "Nonverbal Communication," explains, a gesture is a body movement that conveys or reinforces a thought or an emotion. Most gestures are made with your hands and arms, but shrugging a shoulder, bending a knee, and tapping a foot are gestures, too. Gestures can clarify and support your words, relieve nervous tension, and arouse audience attention.

Repetitive movements such as constantly pushing up your eyeglasses, tapping on a lectern, or jingling change or keys in your pocket can distract and eventually annoy an audience. One of the best ways to eliminate unwanted gestures is to video and then watch a practice session. Once you see how often you fidget, you'll work even harder to correct your behavior.

When students ask us "What should I do with my hands?" our answer is always the same: Do what you normally do with your hands. If you gesture a lot in conversations with other people, keep doing what comes naturally. If you rarely gesture, don't try to invent new and unnatural hand movements.

Peggy Noonan, a former speechwriter for President Ronald Reagan, describes a whole industry that exists to tell people how to move their hands when giving a presentation. It's one of the reasons, she maintains, why so many politicians and television journalists look and gesture alike. "You don't have to be smooth; your audience is composed of Americans, and they've seen smooth. Instead, be you. They haven't seen that yet."[32]

"Your face . . .

. . . is the primary source of [nonverbal] information about you."

—Mark Knapp and Judith Hall

In other words, effective gestures are a natural outgrowth of what you feel and what you have to say. Rather than thinking about your hands, think about your audience and your message. In all likelihood, your gestures will join forces with your emotions in a spontaneous mixture of verbal and nonverbal communication.

Posture and Movement

Posture and movement involve how you stand and move and whether your movements add or detract from your presentation. If you stand comfortably and confidently, you will radiate alertness and control. If you stoop or look unsure on your feet, you will communicate anxiety or disinterest. Try to stand straight but not rigid. Your feet should be about a foot apart. If you stand tall, lean forward, and keep your chin up, you will open your airways and help make your voice clear and your volume appropriate.

In general, a purposeful movement can attract attention, channel nervous energy, or support and emphasize a point you are making. Movement allows for short pauses during which

you can collect your thoughts or give the audience time to ponder what you have said.

If your presentation is formal or your audience large, you will probably have a lectern. Learn how to take advantage of a lectern without allowing it to act as a barrier. First, don't lean over your lectern. It may look as though you and the lectern are about to come crashing down into the audience. Second, avoid hitting the lectern or

tapping it with a pen or pointer while you speak. Given that a microphone is often attached to the lectern, the tapping can become a deafening noise.

Lecterns provide a place to put your notes, a spot to focus audience attention, and even an electrical outlet for a light and microphone. When possible *and* appropriate, come out from behind the lectern and speak at its side. In this way, you can remain close to your notes but also get closer to the audience.

COMMUNICATION&CULTURE

ADAPT YOUR GESTURES FOR DIFFERENT CULTURES

People all over the world "talk" with their hands. The meanings of gestures, however, may be quite different in different cultures and cultural contexts—both domestic and international. Everett Rogers and Thomas Steinfatt share a story about a U.S. professor teaching at a university in Thailand. The professor frequently put his hands in his pockets or held them behind his back while lecturing to his class. At the end of the semester, his polite Thai students gently informed him that he should hold his hands in front of himself. They had been embarrassed and distracted when he broke the cultural norm of keeping your hands visible when communicating.[33]

Most of our hand gestures are culturally determined. One of the best examples is a gesture in which you touch the tips of your thumb to your index finger to form a circle. In the United States, this gesture

usually means that everything is "A-okay." The same gesture, however, can be a sign for the sex act in some Latin American countries. To the French, the sign may indicate that someone is a "zero," and to people in Malta, it is an invitation to have homosexual sex.[34]

In most speaking situations—both inside and outside the United States—certain gestures can trigger negative responses from an audience. Pointing or wagging your index finger at an audience, for example, may be seen as rude and offensive because it is associated with parental scolding. Instead of pointing your index finger at your audience, try gesturing with an open hand—fingers together, palm and inner wrist turned slightly toward the audience, and forearm slightly bent and extended at about a 45-degree angle to the side (not aimed directly *at* the audience).[35] The photo on page 267 shows a speaker in this position.

Presentation Aids

14.6 *Apply effective strategies for designing and displaying presentation aids.*

We use the term **presentation aids** to refer to the many supplementary resources—most often visual—for presenting and highlighting key ideas and supporting material.

Although it's tempting to use computer-generated slides for every presentation, remember that you and your presentation come first. Prepare visuals only after deciding what you want to say and what you want audience members to understand and remember.[36]

Functions and Types of Presentation Aids

Presentation aids are more than pretty pictures or a set of colorful computer graphics. They serve specific functions, namely, to attract audience attention and to enhance the comprehension and impact of your message. Presentation

> Don't let your presentation aids and their technical razzle-dazzle steal the show.

aids can also save you time and help audiences remember your message.

There are as many different types of presentation aids as there are people to imagine them. The key to selecting an appropriate type requires a thoughtful answer to the following question: Which type of aid will help you achieve your purpose? Review the different types of presentation aids and their functions on page 275 to decide which ones best support your message. But first, make sure you choose appropriate

media and use effective design principles to support your message.

Choosing the Media

When selecting media for a presentation, consider your purpose, the audience, the setting, and the logistics of the situation. You may want to do a multimedia presentation, but the place where you're scheduled to speak cannot be darkened or the facility doesn't have the equipment you need. Writing detailed notes on a board or flip chart for an audience of hundreds will frustrate listeners in the back rows.

Using Design Principles

Even with the best intentions, equipment, and cutting-edge software, presentation aids can fail to have an impact. They can be dull, distracting, and difficult to follow.

> **" It's about design, not software. "**
> —Janet Bozarth, *Better Than Bullet Points*[37]

Regardless of what type of supporting materials or how you decide to display them, the basic visual design principles on the next page can help you create aids that inform and please the eye without distracting or detracting from your presentation.

Because strict design principles may not apply in every situation, in

---

STRATEGIES FOR USING PRESENTATION AIDS

- **Begin with you, not your visual.** Establish rapport with your audience before you start using presentation aids.

- **Touch, turn, talk.** Touch your aid (or refer to it with your hand or a pointer), turn to your audience, then talk.

- **Pick the right time to display your aids.** Display aids for at least the length of time it takes an average reader to read them twice. When you're finished talking about a presentation aid, remove it.

- **Be prepared to do without.** Can you deliver your presentation without your presentation aids? It's always a good idea to have a "plan B" in case something goes wrong.

- **Practice before you present.** Rehearse as you would in an actual presentation. Don't sit at your computer mouthing the words as you scroll through your visuals.

In light of the above strategies for using presentation aids and the guidelines for designing and handling presentation aids on the next page, evaluate the design and presentation of the slide as well as the speaker in the photo.

DESIGN PRINCIPLES FOR PRESENTATION AIDS

Preview and Highlight	Presentation aids should preview your key points and highlight important facts and features.
Headline Your Visuals	Clear headlines reduce the risk that readers will misunderstand your message.
Exercise Restraint	Avoid using too many graphics, fonts, colors, and other visual elements and effects.
Choose Readable Type and Suitable Colors	Don't use more than two different fonts on a slide, a font size smaller than 24 points, or illegible colors.
Use Appropriate Graphics	Make sure your graphics are essential and support your purpose.

some cases, you may need to break the "rules." For example, we are reluctant to give you a rule for the maximum number bullet points on a slide and the number of words per bullet point. Different sources advocate different ideal numbers: three words, five words, and seven words per line. But there are times when you should use more than seven words and times when you should highlight only one word. In general, there's nothing wrong with following a reasonable standard—such as the "six-by-six" rule (six bullets per slide and six words per bullet)—to make sure that you don't end up with too many bullet points or full paragraphs on your slides. However, in *The Non-Designer's Presentation Book*, Robin Williams cautions us to be skeptical about most of the slide rules we hear or read. She offers more reasonable advice: Although "it's okay to put five bullet points on every slide," you're much better off putting the right number of lines and words on slides based on the needs of your speech.[38] To that she adds, "Make every word count, be as succinct as possible, but don't arbitrarily limit the number of words because of [a] rule. Be clear."[39]

Handling Presentation Aids

After you invest time, effort, and significant resources to plan and prepare presentation aids, make sure you handle your aids smoothly and professionally by following several guidelines: Don't turn your back to the audience or stand in front of your screen or flip chart while speaking. Decide when to introduce your aids, how long to leave them up, and when to remove them. Even if you have numerous presentation aids to display, always start and end your presentation by making direct and personal contact with your audience.

> Remember that presentation aids are not the presentation; they are only there to assist you. You and your message should always come first.

ETHICAL COMMUNICATION

Plagiarism Plagues Presentation Aids

When the creation of visuals or audio is a person's livelihood, the uncompensated use of such works raises ethical and legal questions about violating copyright laws.

In response to this concern, companies such as Microsoft have developed online banks of clip art, clip video, and clip audio for fair use. For instance, Microsoft's Design Gallery Live and Google Images offer more than hundreds of thousands of free images. The U.S. Library of Congress's own online catalog offers more than seven million images, many of which are in the public domain and no longer protected by copyright. If you purchase a graphics package, you have the right to make copies of the images and use them in your presentations.

If, however, you use a photo scanned from a photographer's portfolio, an audio or video clip copied from a CD or iPod, or a graph downloaded from the Internet without identifying the source, you are plagiarizing.

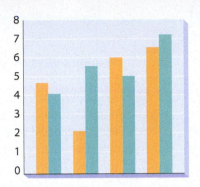

Graphs show *how much* by demonstrating comparisons. They can illustrate trends and show increases or decreases by using bars or lines to represent countable things.

Media	Small Audience (50 or fewer)	Medium Audience (50–150)	Large Audience (150 or more)
Chalk/white board	✓		
Flip chart	✓		
Hand held object	✓	✓	
Overhead transparencies	✓	✓	✓
Presentation software slides	✓	✓	✓
Videotapes/DVDs	✓	✓	✓
Multimedia	✓	✓	✓

Tables *summarize and compare* data. When graphs aren't detailed enough and descriptions require too many words, tables are an effective alternative for showing numeric values. Tables also summarize and compare key features.

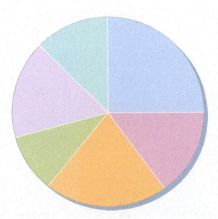

Pie charts show *how much* by identifying proportions in relation to a whole. Each wedge of the pie usually represents a percentage. Most audiences comprehend pie charts quickly and easily.

Maps show *where* by translating data into spatial patterns. Maps give directions, compare locations, or link statistical data to population characteristics.

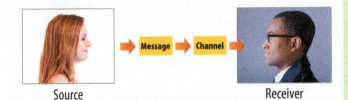

Source   Receiver

Diagrams and illustrations show *how things work*. They take many forms: flowcharts, organizational diagrams, time lines, floor plans, and even enlargements of physical objects so that you can see the inside of an engine, a heart, or a flower.

Group Advantages	Group Disadvantages
• Groups generally accomplish more and perform better than individuals working alone. • Groups provide members with an opportunity to socialize and create a sense of belonging. • Collaborative group work promotes learning.	• Group work requires a lot of time, energy, and resources. • Conflict among group members can be frustrating and difficult to resolve. • Working with members who are unprepared, unwilling to work, or have difficult personalities can be aggravating.

Text charts *list ideas or key phrases*, often under a title or headline. They depict goals, functions, types of formats, recommendations, and guidelines. Items listed on a text chart may be numbered, bulleted, or set apart on separate lines.

Photographs *portray reality*—a real face or place is easily recognized and can capture emotions.

Note: Other forms of presentation aids include audio and video recordings, objects, handouts, and physical demonstrations.

presentation aids

Cognitive Science Meets Presentation Aids

Cognitive science, the interdisciplinary study of the mind and intelligence, can help you design visuals that adapt to your audience members' perception, thinking, and learning.

Here we present two significant cognitive science principles based on a synthesis of Stephen Kosslyn's study of PowerPoint presentations and Richard Mayer's broader research on multimedia learning using both verbal forms (written and spoken words) and images (illustrations, graphs, photos, maps, and animation or video).[40] These two principles—coherence and contrast—are described in the table to the right.

Cognitive science also explains why emotionally interesting but irrelevant pictures *reduce* learning and comprehension. The term **seductive details** describes elements that attract audience attention but do not support a speaker's key points. Instead of learning, audience members are "seduced," distracted, and confused by seductive details, such as interesting scenes,

dramatic graphics, vivid colors, and engaging motion.[41]

When you design or view a computer-generated slide, ask yourself: Is the slide coherent and does it use contrast to focus audience attention? Look at the two slides shown below. Which is the most coherent and which uses contrast more effectively? We hope you choose the slide on the right.

Cognitive Principle	Research Finding	Practical Application
Coherence	Irrelevant words, pictures, sounds, and music compete for cognitive resources in our working memory *and* divert our attention.	Cut or exclude extraneous material. Focus on and highlight only essential ideas and items. Scrap the fancy stuff and focus on the message.
Contrast	Contrast reduces extraneous processing and directs audience attention to important information.	Use visual contrast to guide audience attention to key elements and the connections between them.

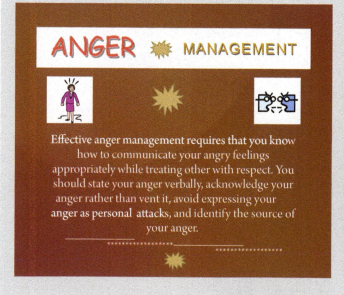

Strategies for Rehearsing a Presentation

14.7 *Practice using effective language and skilled delivery.*

In *Present Like a Pro*, Cyndi Maxey and Kevin E. O'Connor describe a study of the National Speakers Association's nearly 4,000 professional members who were asked to identify their top tips for a successful speech. *Practice* received more than 35 percent of the vote, making it first in importance.[42]

Effective rehearsals require more than repeating your presentation over and over again. Practice lets you know whether there are words you have trouble pronouncing or sentences that are too long to say in one breath. In addition, you may discover when you practice that what you thought was a ten-minute talk takes thirty minutes to deliver. Practicing with presentation aids is critical, as anyone can tell you who has seen the embarrassing results that befall speakers who don't have their visuals in order. Rehearsing is the only way to make sure that you sound and look good in a presentation.[43]

To put it another way, "give your speech before you give it."[44]

Practice can take many forms. It can be as simple as closing your door and rehearsing your presentation out loud in private or as complex as an onstage, videotaped dress rehearsal in front of a volunteer audience.

At the same time, don't get carried away with excessive practicing. Too much practice can make you sound *canned*, a term used to describe speakers who have practiced so much or given the same speech so many times that they no longer sound spontaneous, sincere, or natural. Our advice: keep practicing until you feel satisfied. Then, practice with the goal of improving the fine points of your presentation. Practice until you feel confident. Then, stop.

As you practice and deliver a presentation, remember that there are very few "must do" rules for effective speaking. Although this book is filled with good advice, successful speakers adapt that advice to their purpose, their audience, and the situation. Is it sometimes all right to put your hands in your pockets while speaking? Yes. Is it acceptable, in some situations, to sit down rather than to stand when speaking? Sure. Will the audience protest if you occasionally say "um" or "uh"? Nope.

Delivery and practice "rules" are guidelines, not commandments. Sometimes breaking a commonly accepted rule can make your presentation more interesting and memorable. Smart speakers use rules when they improve their presentations and dismiss them when they get in the way. If there is one cardinal rule, it's this: rules only work when they help you achieve your purpose.

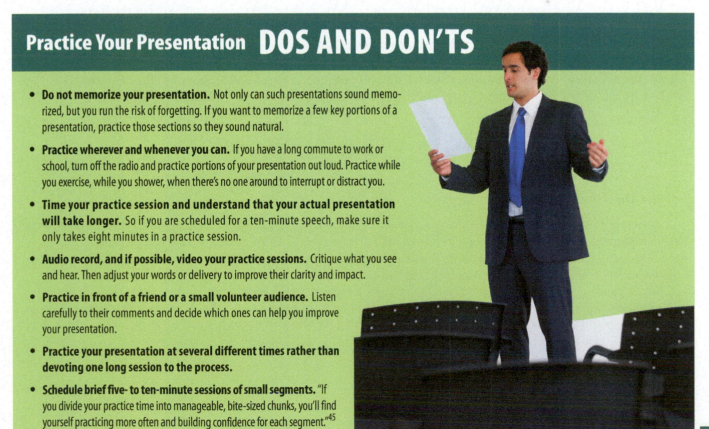

Practice Your Presentation DOS AND DON'TS

- **Do not memorize your presentation.** Not only can such presentations sound memorized, but you run the risk of forgetting. If you want to memorize a few key portions of a presentation, practice those sections so they sound natural.

- **Practice wherever and whenever you can.** If you have a long commute to work or school, turn off the radio and practice portions of your presentation out loud. Practice while you exercise, while you shower, when there's no one around to interrupt or distract you.

- **Time your practice session and understand that your actual presentation will take longer.** So if you are scheduled for a ten-minute speech, make sure it only takes eight minutes in a practice session.

- **Audio record, and if possible, video your practice sessions.** Critique what you see and hear. Then adjust your words or delivery to improve their clarity and impact.

- **Practice in front of a friend or a small volunteer audience.** Listen carefully to their comments and decide which ones can help you improve your presentation.

- **Practice your presentation at several different times rather than devoting one long session to the process.**

- **Schedule brief five- to ten-minute sessions of small segments.** "If you divide your practice time into manageable, bite-sized chunks, you'll find yourself practicing more often and building confidence for each segment."[45]

COMMUNICATION ASSESSMENT

Assess *Their* Language Style and *Your* Delivery

Read the brief excerpts from the following presentations:

1. **President Barack Obama's Remarks at a Memorial Service for the Victims of the Shooting in Tucson, Arizona, January 12, 2011.**[46]

Imagine—imagine for a moment, here was a young girl who was just becoming aware of our democracy; just beginning to understand the obligations of citizens; just starting to glimpse the fact that some day she, too, might play a part in shaping her nation's future. She had been elected to her student council. She saw public service as something exciting and hopeful. She was off to meet her Congresswoman, someone she was sure was good and important and might be a role model. She saw all this through the eyes of a child, undimmed by the cynicism or vitriol that we adults all too often just take for granted. I want to live up to her expectations.

2. **Nick Jonas's speech on "Diabetes Awareness" at the National Press Club, August 24, 2009.**[47]

I was diagnosed with type I diabetes in November, 2005. My brothers were the first to notice that I'd lost a significant amount of weight, 15 pounds in three weeks. I was thirsty all the time, and my attitude had changed. I'm a really positive person, and it had changed during these few weeks. It would have been easy to blame my symptoms on a hectic schedule, but my family knew I had to get to a doctor. The normal range of a blood sugar is between 70 to 120. When we got to the doctor's office, we learned that my blood sugar was over 700. The doctor said that I had type I diabetes, but I had no idea what that meant. The first thing I asked was, "Am I going to die?"

3. **Aung Sang Suu Kyi,** *Freedom from Fear,* **delivered 1990.**[48]

Aung San Suu Kyi is the daughter of Burmese nationalist hero Aung San. In 1989, the government placed Suu Kyi under house arrest, and she spent fifteen of the next twenty-one years in custody. In 1991, her ongoing efforts won her the Nobel Prize for Peace, and she was finally released from house arrest in November 2010.

It is not power that corrupts but fear. Fear of losing power corrupts those who wield it and fear of the scourge of power corrupts those who are subject to it. . . . Within a system which denies the existence of basic human rights, fear tends to be the order of the day. Fear of imprisonment, fear of torture, fear of death, fear of losing friends, family, property or means of livelihood, fear of poverty, fear of isolation, fear of failure. A most insidious form of fear is that which masquerades as common sense or even wisdom, condemning as foolish, reckless, insignificant, or futile the small, daily acts of courage which help to preserve man's self-respect and inherent human dignity.

****

Further Directions:

Review each speaker's style and language strategies. Which CORE language style or styles predominate? What language strategies do these speakers use? How well do they use them? What are the similarities and differences in these speakers' styles? Then be prepared to read each excerpt out loud in a way that expresses the speaker's intentions, mood, and message most effectively. You may find this task difficult until you have practiced them at length.

When you listen to other class members read these excerpts, note the ways in which they use their voices and bodies to emphasize words and phrases. Also note how reading from a manuscript affects each speaker's delivery. You also can watch and listen to the original speeches by searching for them on the web.

The CORE Language Styles

14.1 Explain how each of the four CORE language styles can enhance the power of a presentation.

- Choose an appropriate language style from among the CORE language styles: **c**lear style, **o**ral style, **r**hetorical style, and **e**loquent style.
- The clear style uses short, simple, and direct words.
- The oral style employs familiar words; short sentences, personal pronouns, and colloquial expressions.
- The rhetorical style features vivid and powerful language.
- The eloquent style includes poetic and persuasive language in inspiring and memorable ways.

Confident Delivery

14.2 Identify and manage the causes and effects of presentation anxiety.

- Although all speakers experience speaking anxiety, it is usually invisible. Audiences can rarely see or hear your fear.
- When you read accurate information about speaking anxiety, you build confidence rather than increase your fear.

Modes of Delivery

14.3 Compare the advantages and disadvantages of the four delivery modes.

- Impromptu speaking occurs without advance preparation or practice.
- Extemporaneous speaking involves using an outline or a set of notes.
- Manuscript speaking involves reading a written presentation out loud.
- Memorized speaking is recalling a presentation without notes.
- A mix of all four styles is appropriate and effective in most presentations.

Vocal Delivery

14.4 Describe the components of effective vocal delivery.

- Effective breath control enables you to speak more loudly and say more in a single breath.
- Adapt your volume to the size of the audience and the dimensions of the room.
- Your speaking rate depends on your speaking style, the nature of your message, and your audience.
- Optimum pitch is the pitch at which you speak most easily and expressively.
- Develop expressiveness by putting vitality, variety, inflection, fluency, and sincerity into your delivery.
- Articulation involves clearly making the sounds in words; *pronunciation* refers to whether you say a word correctly.

Physical Delivery

14.5 Describe the components of effective physical delivery.

- Direct effective eye contact helps you control communication, enhance your credibility, and interpret audience feedback.
- Speak naturally to ensure that your facial expressions and gestures support your message.
- Speakers who stand and move confidently radiate alertness and control.

Presentation Aids

14.6 Apply effective strategies for designing and displaying presentation aids.

- Choose media and presentation aids appropriate for your purpose, context, audience, and content.
- Five basic design principles for creating presentation aids include (1) preview and highlight, (2) headline your visuals, (3) exercise restraint, (4) choose readable type and suitable colors, and (5) use appropriate graphics.
- When handling presentation aids, focus on your audience (not the aids or yourself); begin with you, not your aids, and be prepared to do without your aids.

Strategies for Rehearsing a Presentation

14.7 Practice using effective language and skilled delivery.

- Rehearsing a presentation ensures that you sound and look good.
- Practice your entire presentation several times by dividing each practice session into bite-sized chunks.

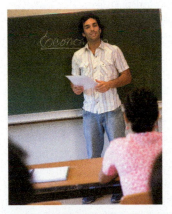

Key Terms

Alliteration	**Eye scan**	**Pitch**
Articulation	**Filler phrases**	**Presentation aids**
Clear style	**Fluency**	**Pronunciation**
Cognitive science	**Impromptu speaking**	**Rate**
CORE language styles	**Inflection**	**Rhetorical devices**
Delivery	**Language intensity**	**Rhetorical style**
Eloquent style	**Manuscript speaking**	**Seductive details**
Expressiveness	**Memorized speaking**	**Volume**
Extemporaneous speaking	**Metaphor**	
Eye contact	**Optimum pitch**	

TEST YOUR KNOWLEDGE

14.1 *Explain how each of the four CORE language styles can enhance the power of a presentation.*

1 In a speech on "Diabetes Awareness" at the National Press Club in Washington, DC, Nick Jonas said: *And at times . . . it would be a lot easier to throw in the towel and say, "Enough's enough, I'm done, and I'd like to just have a day off from having diabetes." But it just doesn't work like that.* Which answer best identifies Jonas's language style?

a. Clear and Oral style

b. Rhetorical style

c. Eloquent style

d. Academic style

2 In Abraham Lincoln's first inauguration address (1861), he concluded by imploring his mostly Southern audience not to go to war: *"The mystic chords of memory, stretching from every battlefield and patriot grave to every living hearth and hearth stone all over this broad land, will yet swell the chorus of the Union when again touched, as surely they will be by the better angels of our nature."* Which answer best identifies Lincoln's language style?

a. Clear and Oral style

b. Rhetorical style

c. Eloquent style

d. Academic style

14.2 *Identify and manage the causes and effects of presentation anxiety.*

3 Which of the following statements is *NOT* a myth about speaking anxiety?

a. Reading about speaking anxiety will make you more nervous.

b. Americans are more afraid of public speaking than they are of snakes.

c. Speaking anxiety is usually invisible to audience members.

d. All of the above are myths about public speaking.

14.3 *Compare the advantages and disadvantages of the four delivery modes.*

4 Which is the most common mode of presentation delivery?

a. Impromptu

b. Extemporaneous

c. Manuscript

d. Memorized

14.4 *Describe the components of effective vocal delivery.*

5 What, in general, is the most effective rate of delivery?

a. 100–125 words per minute

b. 125–150 words per minute

c. 150–180 words per minute

d. 180–200 words per minute

14.5 *Describe the components of effective physical delivery.*

6 Which component of physical delivery is the most important for a successful presentation?

a. Eye contact

b. Facial expression

c. Gestures

d. Posture and movement

14.6 *Apply effective strategies for designing and displaying presentation aids.*

7 The phrase *seductive details* refers to

a. the tendency of some speakers to focus on the personal details of their lives.

b. a presentation that uses very vivid and intense language.

c. using PowerPoint slides when other media would be more successful for sharing visual aids with an audience.

d. elements in presentation aids that attract audience attention but do not support a speaker's key points.

8 Which presentation aid design principle advises speakers to avoid using too many graphics, fonts, colors, and other visual elements and effects?

a. Use appropriate graphics

b. Headline your visuals

c. Exercise restraint

d. Select appropriate media

9 Which presentation aid design principle advises speakers to avoid more than two different fonts on a slide as well as font sizes smaller than twenty-four points?

a. Preview and highlight

b. Exercise restraint

c. Choose readable type and suitable colors

d. Use appropriate graphics

14.7 *Practice using effective language and skilled delivery in presentations.*

10 All of the following recommendations for practicing a presentation can help improve your delivery and confidence when speaking except:

a. practicing until you have memorized your presentation.

b. practicing sections of and the entire presentation several times.

c. practicing using a voice or video recorder.

d. practicing in front of someone and ask for feedback.

Answers found on page 368.

Speaking to Inform 15

The informative presentation heard most often by college students is the classroom lecture—either on campus or online.[1] In recent years, however, traditional lectures have fallen out of favor. Researchers claim that if a professor speaks 150 words per minute, students hear only about 50 of them.[2] Furthermore, most students tune out of a 50-minute lecture around 40 percent of the time.[3]

Is there anything professors can do to ensure that students listen to and learn from their lectures? In *Teaching Tips*, Wilbert McKeachie provides the answer. Like other researchers, he notes that the typical attention span of students peaks within the first ten minutes of a class session and then decreases after that point.[4] As a result, you might expect McKeachie to recommend abandoning lectures in favor of other teaching methods. Not so. Rather, he sees lectures as a very efficient and effective teaching method *if* the instructor knows how to gain and maintain attention, *if* the lecture is well-planned and well-organized, *if* the body of the lecture includes various types of supporting material and clear transitions, and *if* the instructor speaks well and actively involves students.[5] Here's the point: McKeachie's description of a successful lecture also describes the characteristics of a successful informative presentation.

Unlike persuasive speakers, who can gain and maintain audience attention and interest by addressing a controversial issue, informative speakers face a more difficult challenge. Whether presenting information to third graders or to corporate executives, you must know how to interest and enlighten your audience if you want them to value, understand, and remember your message. This chapter focuses on the strategies and skills needed to achieve these informative speaking goals.

The Purpose of Informative Speaking

15.1 *Describe the goals of informative presentations.*

Informative speaking is the most common type of presentation. Students use informative speaking to present oral reports, to share research with classmates, and to explain group projects. Beyond the classroom, businesses use informative presentations to orient new employees, to present company reports, and to explain new policies.

Informative presentations report new information, clarify difficult terms, explain scientific phenomena, and/or overcome confusion and misunderstanding. They do so by instructing, defining enlightening, describing, correcting, reminding, and/or demonstrating.

You will be asked to prepare and deliver many informative presentations throughout your lifetime, so learning how to do it well will ensure audience attention, comprehension, and interest.[6]

Sometimes it's difficult to determine where an informative presentation ends and a persuasive presentation begins. Most informative presentations contain an element of persuasion. For example, an informative presentation explaining the effects of global warming may convince an audience to support stricter controls on air pollution. Even demonstrating how to sew on a button properly can persuade some listeners to change the way they've been doing it or to do it themselves rather than giving it to mom or paying to have it done at the cleaner.

Your purpose signifies the difference between informative and persuasive presentations. When you ask listeners to change their opinions or behavior, your presentation becomes persuasive.

Informative Communication Strategies

15.2 *Identify specific communication strategies most applicable to different types of informative messages.*

In her **Theory of Informatory and Explanatory Communication**, Katherine Rowan explains how to make strategic decisions about the content and structure of an informative presentation. Her two-part theory focuses on the differences between what Rowan labels *informatory communication* and *explanatory communication*.

Informatory communication seeks to *create* or *increase audience awareness* by reporting the latest new information—much like news reporting. **Explanatory communication** seeks to *deepen audience understanding* of complex ideas and information by clarifying difficult terms, explaining quasi-scientific phenomena, or overcoming confusion and misunderstanding. Not surprisingly, different types of informative messages have different purposes and require different communication strategies. Rowan offers one set of strategies for informatory communication and then further divides explanatory communication into three different types of explanatory functions, each with its own set of communication strategies. Good explanatory presentations answer such questions as "Why?" or "What does that mean?"[7]

(See the figure on classifications and examples of informative and explanatory communication on page 284.)

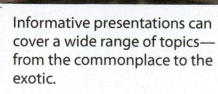

Informative presentations can cover a wide range of topics—from the commonplace to the exotic.

COMMUNICATION IN *ACTION*

Including a Value Step to Capture Audience Attention

Just because *you* love banjo music, bowling, or bidding on eBay doesn't mean audience members share your enthusiasm. How, then, do you give them a reason to listen? The answer is: include a value step in your introduction to capture their attention. A **value step** explains how the information can enhance their personal well-being and success. While this step may not be necessary in every informative presentation, there is no harm in using a value step to boost and reinforce audience interest.

When looking for a value step, ask yourself whether your presentation will benefit an audience in any of the following ways:

- *Socially.* Will your presentation help listeners interact with others, become more popular, or throw a great party?
- *Physically.* Will your presentation offer advice about treating common ailments, getting a good haircut, or exercising productively?
- *Psychologically.* Will your presentation help audience members feel better about themselves or help them cope with psychological problems?
- *Intellectually.* Will your presentation explain intriguing and novel discoveries in science? Will it satisfy listeners' intellectual curiosity?
- *Financially.* Will your presentation help audience members make, save, invest, or spend money wisely?
- *Professionally.* Will your presentation help audience members succeed and prosper in a career or profession?

> If there's a good reason for you to make a presentation, there should be a good reason for your audience to listen.

In informative presentations, inexperienced speakers often spend too much time talking about features and functions rather than benefits. John Daly, the author of *Advocacy: Championing Ideas and Influencing Others*, explains that *features* are the characteristics of an item or idea, *functions* are what those features do, and *benefits* are what the functions offer us. "Because a bottle is cylindrical (feature), it is easy for us to hold (function), which means we can carry it as we walk and talk (benefit)."[8] What would you rather hear: a presentation on the technology used to bottle water or an analysis of how bottled water products benefit you? In other words, if audience members do not value your message, they may see no reason to listen to or care about what you say. Also recall the concept of WIIFT in Chapter 12, "Planning Your Presentation." A value step tells audience members *what's in it for them*.

The table below provides two examples of a topic, related value categories, and a value step for an informative presentation. Fill in the second and third columns for the four remaining topics. Make sure that the value step reflects an *informative* purpose.

Determine the Value Step (Why Should Audience Members Listen to or Care About Your Presentation?)		
Topic	**Value Categories**	**Value Step**
The Middle East Respiratory Syndrome (MERS)	Physical	Follow the route of this deadly disease as it moved from the Middle East to Europe and how it can affect United States.
Geographic Literacy	Financial	Learn how the depleted fresh water resources in our state explain the increasing cost of water in your home.
Math Apprehension		
The Millennial Generation		
Good Bacteria		
Job Interviews		

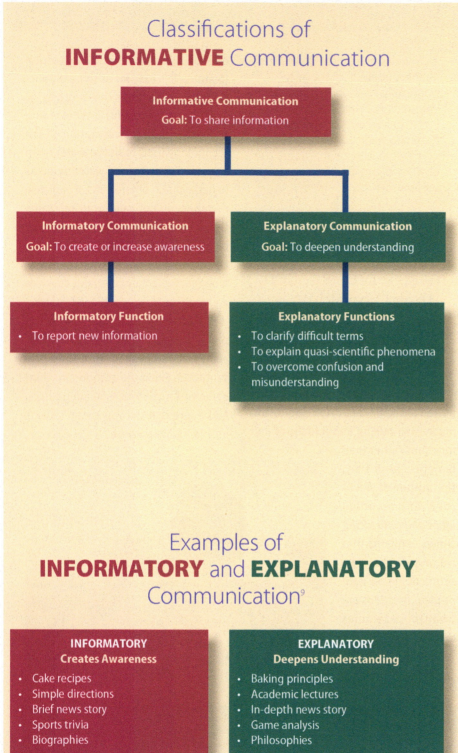

Classifications of INFORMATIVE Communication

Informative Communication
Goal: To share information

Informatory Communication
Goal: To create or increase awareness

Explanatory Communication
Goal: To deepen understanding

Informatory Function
- To report new information

Explanatory Functions
- To clarify difficult terms
- To explain quasi-scientific phenomena
- To overcome confusion and misunderstanding

Examples of INFORMATORY and EXPLANATORY Communication[9]

INFORMATORY
Creates Awareness
- Cake recipes
- Simple directions
- Brief news story
- Sports trivia
- Biographies

EXPLANATORY
Deepens Understanding
- Baking principles
- Academic lectures
- In-depth news story
- Game analysis
- Philosophies

it must be presented clearly and in a well-organized manner. Second, you may need to give audience members a reason to listen, learn, and remember. Rowan recommends four strategies for reporting new information, as shown below.

Informatory strategies work best when reporting new, uncomplicated information about objects, people, procedures, and events. Keep in mind, however, that your topic is not a purpose statement or central idea, so you need to develop one, as the example on fire ants shows on the next page.

When informing an audience about a procedure or how something works, consider demonstrating the process. Through a series of well-ordered steps, **demonstration speeches** show an audience how to do something and/or how something functions. These presentations can range from creating PowerPoint templates or washing clothes properly to making guacamole or doing a magic trick. Organizational patterns for such presentations include topical, time, and space arrangement, often accompanied by effective visual aids.

When informing about an event such as the race to the moon or a presidential campaign, remember that the *purpose* of your presentation will determine how you will talk about that event—regardless of the date, size, or significance of the event.

Strategies for REPORTING NEW INFORMATION

- Include a value step in the introduction.
- Use a clear, organizational pattern.
- Use a variety of supporting materials.
- Relate the information to audience interests and needs.

Report New Information

Reporting new information is what most journalists do when they answer *who*, *what*, *where*, *when*, *why*, and *how* questions. New information is published in newspapers, popular magazines, and online.

You face two challenges when a presentation is informatory. First, when information is new to an audience,

Clarify Difficult Terms

Understanding a difficult term is just that—difficult. Unlike an object, person, procedure, or event, a difficult term is usually abstract—rarely can you touch it, demonstrate it, or explain it with a short and simple definition.

Clarifying a difficult term requires more than reporting. It requires explanatory communication in which you help audience members understand and separate essential characteristics from nonessential features. For example, what is the difference between *validity* and *reliability* or *ethos* and *ethics*? Why are corals classified as *animals* and not *plants*?[10]

In the outline on the next page, the meaning of *heuristics* is explained using the above four strategies that Rowan recommends for clarifying difficult terms.

MEDIATED COMMUNICATION IN *ACTION*

Fact and Fiction Go Viral

All of us rely on news media for information about current events, pop culture exposés, and tips for living better lives—be it from television, radio, newspapers, magazines, or the multitude of online sites and sources. These media sources are competing with one another for your attention. It never stops: twenty-four hours a day; seven days a week.

As a result, the lines between fact and fiction easily become blurred. Our computers and social media devices bombard us with instant news—sometimes before anyone has had a chance to review whether the information is true or false. Unfortunately and because it takes longer to verify a news item, false information, half truths, and hoaxes often reach us before the truth comes out.

The respected Poynter Institute laments the fact that major breaking news events—such as the Boston Marathon bombing in the spring of 2013—"unleashed a torrent of rumors, hoaxes, reporting errors and misinformation.... It will happen over and over again, whether it be related to a hurricane, a mass shooting, a Supreme Court decision, a bombing, and on and on."[11] For example, in the immediate aftermath of the Boston Marathon bombing, CNN reported that a suspect had been arrested—it turned out to be untrue. Then the *New York Post* refused to acknowledge its mistake of reporting that twelve people had been killed in the bombing.[12]

Further blurring of the line between fact and fiction occurs when misinformation goes viral on social media. Certainly going viral about Gangnam Style, Charlie Bit My Finger, and cat videos (LOL Cats, The Keyboard Cat, Ninja Cat) are fun. Harmless. What's not fun and devastating are false news stories. When photos of the Boston Marathon bombing suspects were released, Twitter and Reddit ran stories identifying one of the bombers as missing Brown student, Sunil Tripathi.[13] The story went viral. The initial tweet was retweeted thousands of times. Shortly thereafter, "there was a full-on frenzy as thousands upon thousands of tweets poured out, many celebrating new media's victory in trouncing old media."[14] Sadly and as we now know, Sunil Tripathi, who'd been missing since mid-March, was not one of the bombers. About a week after the bombing, his body was found in a river near his university.

When the truth came out, Reddit users were quick to condemn: ". . . it has done more harm than good." "And worst of all the mainstream media leapt on the information here like hungry hyenas." "Unreliable crowd-sourced material plus the media's ravenous desire for fresh information has proved a disgusting mix. Let's never ever do this again."[15]

We know that many of you rely on the web and social media as your primary source of news. Please remember that what you read in a tweet, blog, or website article may not be true. When in doubt, check other news sources and wait for confirmation or until numerous news sources agree.

The *Independent*, a newspaper in England summed up our call for caution: "The story surrounding the false identification of Sunil Tripathi is a cautionary reminder of how the pervasive reach of social media can be used for both good and bad."[16]

PRESENTATION OUTLINE: Clarifying Difficult Terms

Topic area Heuristics

Purpose To explain how heuristics affect persuasion.

Central idea Understanding heuristics will help you analyze the validity of persuasive arguments.

Value step Understanding heuristics can improve your ability to persuade others and to reject invalid arguments.

Organization Topical plus questions to audience

Key points

A. The essential features of heuristic messages.

B. Common heuristics
   1 Longer messages are stronger.
   2 Confident speakers are more trustworthy.
   3 Celebrity endorsements sell products.

C. Contrast heuristic messages with valid messages.

D. Quiz the audience about the characteristics and uses of heuristic messages.

Celebrity endorsements can accelerate the potential for a brand to reach the conscious mind of consumers. Pop music star Beyonce's $50 million deal with Pepsi relies on using heuristics to grab viewer attention and to create a positive impression.

Explain Quasi-Scientific Phenomena

The phrase *quasi-scientific phenomena* requires clarification. The key word here is *quasi*. Quasi (pronounced *kwah-zee*) means to resemble or be similar to something. When you explain a **quasi-scientific phenomenon**, you look for a way to enhance audience understanding of scientific concepts without using complicated scientific terminology, data, and statistical methodologies.

Unlike difficult terms, quasi-scientific phenomena are complex, multidimensional processes. You are asking audience members to unravel something that is complicated, and that may require specialized knowledge to understand. The biggest challenge when making this kind of explanatory presentation is identifying the key components of the phenomenon.

The presentation outline for "Breathing for speech" is designed to teach audience members how to improve the quality of their voices. By comparing something well known (breathing for life) with something less well known (breathing for speech), the speaker helps the audience understand this anatomical process. Rowan recommends four strategies for explaining quasi-scientific phenomena as shown below.

Strategies for EXPLAINING QUASI-SCIENTIFIC PHENOMENA

- Provide clear key points.
- Use analogies and metaphors.
- Use presentation aids.
- Use clear and frequent transitions, previews, summaries, and signposts.

PRESENTATION OUTLINE: Explaining Quasi-Scientific Phenomena

Topic area Breathing for speech

Purpose To explain how to breathe correctly for speech.

Central idea The ability to produce a strong and expressive voice requires an understanding and control of the inhalation/exhalation process.

Value step Learning to breathe for speech will make you a more effective, expressive, and confident speaker.

Organization Compare and contrast three components of the breathing process.

Key points

A. Active versus passive exhalation

B. Deep diaphragmatic versus shallow clavicular breathing

C. Quick versus equal time for inhalation

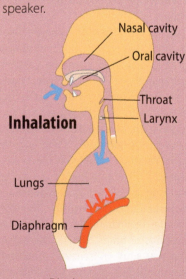

Diaphragm contracts and flattens during inhalation.

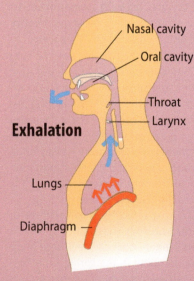

Diaphragm relaxes and moves upward during exhalation.

COMMUNICATION

Trust Me . . . I'm Just Informing You

The long infomercials on television are not presented solely for your enjoyment. They have only one purpose: to persuade you to buy a product. When a salesperson or infomercial star says, "I'm not here to sell you anything. I just want to give you some information about this amazing product." we know the opposite is true.

One of today's most successful infomercial "stars" is Debby Boone, originally known for her hit song "You Light Up My Life." Today, she is better known as the spokesperson for Lifestyle Lift® and the company's short commercials and long infomercials. Lifestyle Lift® is the largest medical practice of facial rejuvenating plastic surgeons in the country.[17] Not surprisingly, Debby Boone's unwrinkled, happy smile is a profitable one.

Then there are the numerous infomercials for workout DVDs and their must-have fitness packages. For two payments of $29.95 plus shipping and handling, you can get Tony Horton's amazing *10 Minute Trainer® Base Kit—Over $500 Value!* or save 25 percent off his P90X Ultimate kit, which includes everything in the base kit and more! There's Shaun T's *Miracle 14-Minute Workout* ranging from *Insanity* for as little as $29.97 to *Beachbody* for $119.85 plus, of course, shipping and handling. What actual *information* is being emphasized here, other than the *price* discounts? And the promises of a "beach body"? In reality these workouts often look easier than they are when you try them.

Whether you love or hate infomercials, never doubt that the "information" in them is designed to persuade you.

And like many aspiring beachbody hopefuls, you're likely to abandon them.[18]

When considering the purpose of any informative presentation, remember the first principle in the National Communication Association's Credo for Ethical Communication: "We advocate truthfulness, accuracy, honesty, and reason as essential to the integrity of communication."[19] Claiming to inform when your real purpose is to persuade violates this ethical principle.

Overcome Confusion and Misunderstanding

Audience members sometimes cling to strong beliefs, even when those beliefs have been proved false. As a result, informative speakers often face the challenge of replacing old, erroneous beliefs with new, more accurate ones. As long as your overriding purpose is to instruct, explain, clarify, or correct—rather than persuade—your presentation is informative. Rowan recommends four strategies for overcoming confusion and misunderstanding as shown below.

The presentation outline below dispels misconceptions about the fat content in our diets.

PRESENTATION OUTLINE: Overcome Confusion and Misunderstanding

Topic area Fat in food

Purpose To explain that fat is an important element in everyone's diet

Central idea Our health-conscious society has all but declared an unwinnable and unwise war on food containing fat.

Value step Eliminating all fat from your diet can hurt you rather than help you lose weight.

Organization Problem (misinformation)—solution (accurate information)

Key points

A. Many people believe that eliminating all fat from their diet will make them thinner and healthier.

B. This belief is understandable given that fat is the very thing dieters are trying to reduce in their bodies.

C. Fat is an essential nutrient.

D. Fats are naturally occurring components in all foods that, in appropriate quantities, make food tastier and bodies stronger.

Strategies for OVERCOMING CONFUSION AND MISUNDERSTANDING

1. State the belief or theory.

2. Acknowledge its believability and the reason(s) it is believed.

3. Create dissatisfaction with the misconception or explain the misconception by providing contrary evidence.

4. State and explain the more acceptable or accurate belief or theory.

informative communication strategies

At first, an explanatory presentation designed to overcome confusion and misunderstanding may seem more persuasive than informative. Yet, it clearly seeks to instruct, define, enlighten, describe, correct, remind, and/or demonstrate. If it's successful, a presentation about fat in the diet will encourage listeners to rethink what they believe. The primary purpose of such presentations is to provide accurate information in the hope that a misunderstanding will be corrected. To that end, instructors correct mistaken beliefs about theories, physicians explain why penicillin doesn't cure the common cold, and nutritionists enlighten dieters about the need for fat in their diet.

Generating Audience Interest

15.3 *Use appropriate stories, humor, and involvement strategies to generate audience interest.*

In Chapter 12, "Planning Your Presentation," we described two surveys that identified the most important skills for becoming a better speaker according to working adults and college students. In both cases, the top-rated skill was "keeping your audience interested."[20] Thus, it's not surprising that many of our students ask, "How can I make sure I'm not boring?" Novice speakers often *assume* they're not interesting; they can't imagine why an audience would want to listen to them. Or they have heard lots of boring presentations and fear they are doomed to the same fate. Rarely is either assumption true. Fortunately, three strategies can help keep your audience interested: tell stories, use humor, and involve your audience.[21]

Tell Stories

Throughout history, storytellers have acted as the keepers of tradition and held honored places in their societies.[22] All of us respond to stories, whether they are depicted in prehistoric cave paintings, read to us, or chronicled in films.[23]

Stories are accounts of real or imagined events. They can be success stories, personal stories, humorous stories, and even startling stories. Members of the clergy use parables, or stories with a lesson or moral, to apply religious teachings to everyday life. "Politicians, lawyers, salespeople, motivational speakers all have stories of success, truth, strength, will, heart, and human endurance."[24]

The power of storytelling is much more than reliving the warm memories of hearing stories as a child. Stories have the ability to grab and hold our attention for several reasons. The first is the most obvious: they entertain and engage us. "When someone says, 'Let me tell you a story,' we perk up and lean close . . . our minds don't wander . . . listening feels effortless."[25] Good stories make complex ideas and abstract concepts easier to understand. Skilled storytellers "can boil a complex idea into a coherent whole that makes sense. . . ." Finally, listeners vividly remember good stories and "the messages that derive from them."[26]

Storytelling also benefits speakers. If you're anxious, it can reduce your nervousness. Stories are easy to remember and usually easy to tell, particularly when they relate to events that you experienced personally.

Where to Find Stories Stories are everywhere, from your favorite children's book to your local news sources. To find the "right" story for your presentation, consider three excellent sources: you, your audience, and other people.

You are a living, breathing collection of stories. The origin of your name, for example, might produce a fascinating narrative. Personal incidents or events that changed your life can lead to a good story. Or consider your family's roots, a place that holds significant meaning for you, your successes or failures, and your values.[27]

Your *audience* is also a rich source of stories. Tap into their interests, beliefs, and values. If your audience is deeply religious, you may share a story about a neighbor who gave up her worldly goods to work on a mission. If your audience loves sports, you may share a story about your own triumphs or trials as an athlete. If your audience is culturally diverse, you may share a story about how you, a friend, or colleagues succeeded in bridging cultural differences.

Finally, stories about *other people* can help you connect with your audience.

STORYTELLING
Best Practices

- **Use a simple story line.** Long stories with complex themes are hard to follow and difficult to tell. If you can't summarize your story in less than twenty-five words, don't tell it.[28]

- **Limit the number of characters.** Unless you're an accomplished actor or storyteller, limit the number of characters in your story. If your story has more than three or four characters, look for another story.

- **Connect to the audience.** Make sure that your story is appropriate for your audience.

- **Exaggerate effectively.** You can exaggerate both content and delivery when telling a story. Exaggeration makes a story more vivid and helps you highlight its message. The tone of your voice, the sweep of your gestures, and your facial expression add a layer of meaning and emphasis to your story.

- **Share the Moral.** Every good story has a moral—a lesson you want the audience to understand, appreciate, and remember. Keep that moral in mind as you develop and tell a story.[29]

- **Practice.** Practice telling your story to others—your friends, colleagues, or family members. Practice until you can tell a planned story without notes.

This Tlingit storyteller of Haines, Alaska, wears the traditional story-telling regalia to enhance his credibility and audience interest as he tells his tale.

Regardless of the type, stories must have a point that relates to your purpose, a reason for being told; otherwise, you run the risk of annoying your audience. [30]

Think about people you know or people you have read about. Consider interviewing friends or family to uncover relevant stories about their life and knowledge. If you are going to tell a story about someone you know, make sure you have that person's permission. Don't embarrass a good friend or colleague by divulging a private story.

The Structure of a Story Most good stories, no matter how short or how simple, follow the structure illustrated by the Story-Building Chart on page 290. Not only can this chart help you develop a good, original story, it can also help you analyze the stories you hear and read.

FACTS TEST **THINK** ABOUT THEORY
IDEA PLAN
EXPERIMENT
METHOD

Narrative Theory

Walter R. Fisher, a respected communication scholar, studies the nature of **narratives**, a term that encompasses the process, art, and techniques of storytelling. Fisher's **Narrative Theory** examines storytelling as an essential aspect of being human. We experience life "as an ongoing narrative, as conflict, characters, beginnings, middles, and ends."[31] Good stories, he claims, have two essential qualities: probability (coherence) and fidelity (truthfulness).[32]

Story probability refers to whether the elements of a story, such as the consistency of characters and actions, hang together and make sense. In terms of a question, story probability asks "Could this possibly happen given the characters, events, and timing of the story?" Would it, for example, seem right if Catniss Everdeen were not the "Girl on Fire" during the Hunger Games? Would she have killed fellow District 12 tribute Peeta Mellark in order to win? Stories that make sense have a clear and coherent structure—one event leads logically to another. When trying to assess a story's probability, ask yourself the following questions:

- **Does the story make sense?** Can you follow the events as they unfold?
- **Do events logically follow one another?** Could these events have occurred in the order and the time allotted to them?
- **Do the characters behave in a consistent manner?** Do you wonder "Why did he do that?" or "How could she do that given everything else she's said and done?"

- **Is the plot plausible?** Do you find yourself saying, "That just couldn't happen?"

Story fidelity refers to whether a story seems true and whether it resonates with listeners. Whereas story probability examines formal storytelling rules related to plot and characters, story fidelity focuses on the story's relationships to the audience's values and knowledge.[33] Walter Fisher explains that when you evaluate a story's fidelity, you try to determine whether the audience's experience rings true "with the stories they know to be true in their lives."[34] To assess the fidelity of a story, ask the following questions:

- **Are events in the story consistent with experiences in your life?**[35]
- **Do the facts and incidents in the story seem realistic?**
- **Does the story reflect your personal values, beliefs, and experiences?**

STORY-BUILDING CHART [36]

STORY COMPONENTS	STORY-BUILDING GUIDELINES	STORY EXAMPLE
TITLE OF THE STORY	Title of the Story	The Three Little Pigs [37]
BACKGROUND INFORMATION	• Where and when does the story take place? What's going on? • Did anything important happen before the story began? • Provide an initial buildup to the story. • Use concrete details. • Create a vivid image of the time, place, and occasion of the story.	Once upon a time, three little pigs set off to seek their fortune. . . .
CHARACTER DEVELOPMENT	• Who is in the story? • What are their backgrounds? • What do they look and sound like? • How do you want the audience to feel about them? • Bring them to life with colorful and captivating words.	Each little pig built a home. One was made of straw and one was made of sticks. The most industrious pig built a house of bricks. . . .
ACTION OR CONFLICT	• What is happening? • What did you or a character see, hear, feel, smell, or taste? • How are the characters reacting to what's happening? • Let the action build as you tell the story.	Soon, a wolf came along. He blew down the houses made of straw and sticks, but both pigs ran to the house of bricks. At the house of bricks the wolf said, "Little pig, little pig, let me come in." All three pigs said, "No, no, not by the hair of our chinny chin chin." So the wolf huffed and puffed but could not blow the house in. . . .
HIGH POINT OR CLIMAX	• What's the culminating event or significant moment in the story? • What's the turning point in the action? • All action should lead to a discovery, decision, or outcome. • Show the audience how the character has grown or has responded to a situation or problem.	The wolf was very angry. "I'm going to climb down your chimney and eat all of you up," he laughed, "including your chinny chin chins." . . .
PUNCH LINE	• What's the punch line? • Is there a sentence or phrase that communicates the climax of the story? • The punch line pulls the other five elements together. • If you leave out the punch line, the story won't make any sense.	When the pigs heard the wolf on the roof, they hung a pot of boiling water in the fireplace over a blazing fire. . . .
CONCLUSION OR RESOLUTION	• How is the situation resolved? • How do the characters respond to the climax? • Make sure that you don't leave the audience wondering about the fate of a character. • In some cases, a story doesn't need a conclusion—the punch line may conclude it for you.	When the wolf jumped down the chimney, he landed in the pot of boiling water. The pigs quickly put the cover on it, boiled up the wolf, and ate him for dinner. And the three little pigs lived happily ever after.
THE CENTRAL POINT OF THE STORY	The Central Point of the Story	The time and energy you use to prepare for trouble will make you safe to live happily ever after.

Use Humor

Humor captures audience member attention and helps them remember you and your presentation. Audiences tend to remember humorous speakers positively, even if they are not enthusiastic about the speaker's message.

Typically, the best source of humor is *you*. **Self-effacing humor**—directing humor at yourself—is usually much more effective than funny stories you've made up or borrowed from a book. But be careful that you don't poke too much fun at yourself. If you begin to look foolish or less than competent, you will damage your credibility. President Ronald Reagan was well known for making fun of his age, an approach that also defused campaign controversy about

him being the oldest president in U.S. history:

> There was a very prominent Democrat who reportedly told a large group, "Don't worry. I've seen Ronald Reagan, and he looks like a million." He was talking about my age.[38]

There are, however, some approaches to humor that audiences will not and should not tolerate. Offensive humor—swearing, jokes that make fun of any group of people, references to private body functions—tops the list because it insults your audience and damages your credibility.

In addition to cautions about using humor when speaking to culturally diverse audience, we offer some additional advice. Avoid singling out audience members for ridicule, unless

> **❝ Humor can generate audience respect for the speaker,** hold listeners' attention, and help an audience remember your main points. ❞
>
> —Gene Perret, *Using Humor for Effective Business Speaking* [39]

you are speaking at a roast—an event at which a series of speakers warmheartedly tease an honored guest. And, although it should go without

---

COMMUNICATION&CULTURE

THE BOUNDARIES OF HUMOR—DON'T CROSS THE LINE

Humor is universal, but "what is considered funny in one culture many not be so in another culture."[40] A joke that evokes laughter in Louisiana may insult an audience in Lebanon—and vice versa.

In general, American humor is more aggressive and sexual than humor in other countries. Members of collectivist cultures—which represent the majority of world cultures—are often not amused by this kind of humor. For example, the "Chinese tend to use less aggressive humor.... [Their] jokes focus on social interaction."[41] In other words, because they put "greater emphasis on the importance of the group rather than the individual, [they] are less likely to engage in sarcastic or disparaging forms of humor, which would tend to impair group cohesion."[42] In conservative cultures and in U.S. co-cultures, sexually explicit humor may offend and shock an audience.

The nature of what is and is not funny also differs by gender. Generally, men are funnier than women are. Think about it: most stand-up comedians are men. Some researchers claim that humor evolved in men as a way to attract a mate. No joke. Here's how the argument goes: research verifies that a good sense of humor is also a good indicator of intelligence, a quality women seek in a mate. Additionally, humor is one of the top three traits found in surveys of women's mate preferences. "In personal dating ads for example, women requested dates with a sense of humor at least twice as

often as men did. . . . Women want a man that will make them laugh, while men prefer women that will laugh at their humor."[43] A perfect match! Unless, that is, the humor is offensive, crude, and demeaning to women.

Several years ago, one of us was hired to write a speech for a man who would be addressing a gathering of state legislators and their staff. After reading the draft, he asked whether it would be okay to begin with a joke about an old, rich man who'd married a sexy, young woman. "No" was the answer. On the day of the speech, he began by telling the audience that his speechwriter had warned him not to tell a joke he liked, but he was going to do it anyway. He told the joke with skill and most audience members laughed. But a significant group of female listeners—including several legislators—saw nothing funny about the joke. They stood stone-faced, rolled their eyes, or shook their heads in disagreement. Don't let this happen to you. Before using humor in a presentation, make sure it works and that it will not offend your audience or harm your credibility.

The research we've cited in this feature is clear: using humor can backfire when addressing a culturally diverse or opposite-gender audience. We urge you to heed this warning. At the same, we believe that humor is a powerful strategy for generating audience interest and enhancing your credibility *if* you engage in thoughtful audience analysis and adaptation.

saying, avoid ethnic or religious jokes. Even if everyone in the audience shares your ethnicity and religion, don't assume they will appreciate your humor. Don't let the prospect of arousing audience laughter distract you from your purpose. You are a presenter, not a comedian. Humor counts, but too much humor can be counterproductive.

To ensure you are using humor effectively, make sure that your humor is relevant—that it supports the central idea and key points of your presentation. Then use the kind of humor that comes naturally to you—be it jokes, stories, puns, imitations. Also remember that humorous speaking requires more than reciting witty content. It also requires effective delivery and comic timing—knowing when and how to say a line, when to pause, and when to look at the audience members for their reactions.

We thought the Cartoon Caption activity to the right was a wonderful and unique activity of ours until we discovered that psychologists have also used *The New Yorker* cartoons without captions to examine the relationships between gender, humor, and intelligence, using college students as subjects.[45] Our own observations are similar to the following research results:

- Humor is difficult. "Most of the submitted captions were not very funny."
- Men are funnier. "Men, on average, produced a larger number of captions, and more importantly, funnier ones. This might represent two things: men are funnier than women on average, and they also try harder to be funny."
- Humor requires intelligence. "Funny people were more intelligence on average, and this was true for both sexes."[46]

Like the researchers who conducted the study, we urge you to remember that humor can be a highly effective communication strategy, but also a risky strategy. As much as you may want to impress others by using humor, it may fall flat and hurt your reputation as well as your chances of achieving your presentation's goal.

Are You Funny?

Every month, *The New Yorker* magazine conducts its popular cartoon caption contest. The magazine displays the illustrated part of a cartoon and invites readers to write a funny caption.

Here we present a cartoon that one of us has used for many years as a way to discuss the challenge of developing and using humor. The cartoon comes from a 2001 drawing by Frank Cotham that asks the question, "Why would a man drive a car in circles in front of a couple of guys seated by a garage?"[44] Just to get you started, here's a sample caption submitted by a student: "That's not what we meant by rotate your tires."

What caption would you submit? The editors look for a caption that is simple, elegant, and of course, funny.

7 Tips for USING HUMOR in a Presentation[47]

1. Focus your humor on the message. Don't use a joke or one-liner or tell an embarrassing story just because you know how to tell it.
2. Make sure the humor suits you. Seasoned performers can get away with silly humor and humorous temper tantrums. Most speakers should stick to humor that reflects their taste, personality, and talents as well as audience attitudes.
3. Avoid offensive humor such as talking about body functions.
4. Don't tease anyone in your audience.
5. Avoid ethnic or religious humor, unless you are making fun of yourself in an inoffensive way.
6. Limit your funny content. It's a presentation, not a stand-up comedy routine.
7. Practice, practice, practice. Then practice some more.

Involve the Audience

One of the most powerful ways to keep audience members alert and interested is to ask them to participate actively in your presentation. You can involve the audience by using several strategies: ask questions, encourage interaction, do an exercise, ask for volunteers, and invite feedback.

Ask Questions Involve audience members by asking questions, posing riddles, or soliciting reactions during or at the end of your presentation. Even if your listeners do little more than nod their heads in response, they will be involved in your presentation. Audience members will be more alert and interested if they know that they will be quizzed or questioned during or after a presentation.

Encourage Interaction Something as simple as asking audience members to shake hands with one another or to introduce themselves to the people sitting on either side of them generates more audience attention and interest. If you are addressing a professional or business audience, ask them to exchange business cards. If you're addressing college students, ask them to tell each other their majors or career aspirations.

Do an Exercise Simple games or complex training exercises can involve audience members in your presentation and with one another. Bookstores sell training manuals describing ways to involve groups in games and exercises. Interrupting a presentation for a group exercise gives the audience and the speaker a break during which they can interact in a different but equally effective way.

Ask for Volunteers If you ask for volunteers from the audience, someone will usually offer to participate.

Volunteers can help you demonstrate how to perform a skill or how to use a piece of equipment. Some can even be persuaded to participate in a funny exercise or game. Most audiences love to watch a volunteer in action.

Invite Feedback Invite questions and comments from your audience. If audience members seem reluctant to participate, don't badger or embarrass them. If no one responds, continue your presentation. It takes a skillful presenter to encourage and respond to feedback without losing track of a prepared presentation. The more you speak, the easier and more useful feedback is.

Two-time Grammy award–winning comedian Lewis Black use strategies such as personal storytelling, self-effacing humor, and exaggerated delivery to involve and engage his audiences.

What does the raised hand in this photo reveal about the way the speaker has involved the audience in his presentation?

Informative Speaking in Action

15.4 *Practice the communication competencies that characterize effective informative presentations.*

"For all the trust I put in *Cliffs-Notes*, I don't know one thing about them" was the sentence that inspired an informative presentation on *CliffsNotes*.[48] John Sullivan, a former student who is now the director of information technology at a large nonprofit organization, translated his likable speaking style into a delightful and memorable presentation. The presentation included most types of supporting material: facts, statistics, testimony, descriptions, analogies, examples, and stories from a variety of sources. When John discovered that very little was written about the history of *CliffsNotes*, he phoned the company's headquarters and interviewed the then managing editor, Gary Carey.

The information in this presentation has been updated but has not changed the speaker's purpose, key points and organizational pattern, or personal and language style.

Use the *Preparation and Message Content* section of the Information Presentation Assessment instrument on page 299 to see how well this speech and the outline that follows meet the criteria for an effective informative presentation.

Cliff's Notes
John Sullivan

John's simple, opening *story* uses short sentences as well as grammatically incomplete sentences. His *clear* and *oral style* immediately engage listeners who can relate to pulling an all-nighter before an exam.

Eight o'clock Wednesday night. I have an English exam bright and early tomorrow morning. It's on Homer's *Iliad.* And I haven't read page one. I forgo tonight's beer drinking and try to read. Eight forty-five. I'm only on page 12. Only 482 more to go. Nine thirty, it hits me. Like a rock. I'm not going to make it.

Throughout this presentation, John uses *I, me,* and *my* to make his presentation personal, engaging, and enjoyable. In this paragraph he uses the word I nine times.

The way I see it I have three options. I can drop the class, cheat, or go ask Cliff. Because I'm not a quitter, and because I know that cheating is wrong, I borrow a copy of the *CliffsNotes* from my roommate. Yes, I know, I could have used *SparkNotes* or *Shmoop,* but at 9:30 at night, with a copy of *CliffsNotes* close at hand, I wasn't going to comparison shop online.

So I put my trust in *CliffsNotes* that night, even though I couldn't have told you one thing about the origins or quality of these yellow and black booklets. The time had come to learn more. After an exhaustive but not too productive search through sources as diverse as *People Magazine*, the *Omaha World-Herald*, and *Forbes Magazine* as well as almost a hundred websites, I turned to Cliff himself to get the real story. Yes, there is a Cliff behind *Cliffs-Notes* and no, his last name is not Notes. After two phone interviews with the managing editor of *CliffsNotes*, it became clear to me that *CliffsNotes* was truly an American success story. Whereas newcomers like *SparkNotes* and *Shmoop* keep the market humming, the history of *CliffsNotes* helps explain the long-term success of these study guides.

Humor helps the audience remember that there is a real person named Cliff behind *CliffsNotes*.

Conducting a personal interview with the editor of *CliffsNotes* demonstrates the speaker's success in finding credible *information* from a *primary source*. John's purpose is primarily *informatory* (creates awareness) rather than *explanatory* (deepens understanding).

At one time, the notes were nothing more than simple plot summaries. But today, they offer the reader much more in terms of character analysis and literary criticism. To better appreciate this unique publishing phenomenon, it is necessary to trace the history of *CliffsNotes* along with some of the changes the company has undergone, the growth of its competitors, and finally, to understand why study guides get put down by teachers and praised by students.

In the last sentence of this paragraph, John *previews* the three *key points* of his presentation. Notice how well he systematically covers each of these points in the body of the presentation.

The *descriptive story* of how *CliffsNotes* started includes details that humanize the founder and share relevant facts about the company.

Mr. Cliff Hillegass, owner and founder of *CliffsNotes*, literally started the business in 1958 with a loan of $4,000. Headquarters was in the basement of his home and functioned as a mail-order company. As an employee of the Nebraska Book Company, he met Jack Cole, the co-owner of a Canadian publishing company who had a full line of study guides. Upon returning home from a trip to Canada, he brought with him the notes to sixteen plays by Shakespeare and the rights to publish them in the United States. He immediately produced three thousand copies of each and sent them throughout the U.S. Bookstore managers were very receptive to the idea and quickly put the first *Notes* on sale.

When *CliffsNotes* first splashed onto the scene in 1958, 18,000 copies were sold. By 1960 sales had increased to 54,000 per year. By the mid-'60s, the magic number was two million and soon everyone wanted a piece of the action. By 1968, no less than thirteen other companies were in the market. Mr. Hillegass was confident through it all that none could overtake him. He told his sales staff not to worry. He said, "I believe most of our competitors are large publishers for whom the study guides would never be more than one item in their line." He couldn't have been more correct. By 1968, just two years later, only three competitors were left. And as the competition went down, sales figures for *CliffsNotes* went up.

Because *CliffsNotes* has been so successful for so long, it holds a rare honor: it's become a common noun and frequently used adjective. For example, when the Financial Crisis Inquiry Commission report was published in 2011, a *The New York Times* reporter began her summary of the study by writing "For those who might find the report's 633 pages a bit daunting . . . we offer a Cliff Notes version." A simple web search can put you in touch with "Health Care Reform: The Cliff's Notes Version," "Wikileaks: Cliff Notes Version," and my personal favorite, "Cliffs Notes Version: Seven Psychological Principles Con Artists Exploit."

Despite its long and profitable history, *CliffsNotes* now faces its greatest challenge from both print and online competitors. A review of what a *The New York Times* article calls "online cheat sheets" reports that *CliffsNotes* publishes 159 literature booklets and provides more than 250 study guides online. They also have free podcasts called *CramCasts*, the "literature light" versions with little more than three to five minute overviews and plot summaries. *SparkNotes*—who cleverly decided to substitute *Spark* for *Cliffs*— is the major competitor with similar booklets and online resources. The *SparkNotes* website claims they are "Today's Most Popular Study Guides." New online sites are emerging to join the competitive fray.

Even with hundreds of titles, a few dozen dominate most of *CliffsNotes* sales. Obviously certain titles have remained relatively constant through the years. Here are the top-ten *CliffsNotes* sold in 1992. As I list them in descending order, guess which book might be number one. And, as a hint, keep in mind that most *CliffsNotes* are sold to high school juniors and seniors.

10. *To Kill a Mockingbird*	5. *The Great Gatsby*
9. *The Scarlet Letter*	4. *Julius Caesar*
8. *Great Expectations*	3. *Macbeth*
7. *A Tale of Two Cities*	2. *The Adventures of Huckleberry Finn*
6. *Romeo and Juliet*	1. *Hamlet*

A direct *quotation* from Cliff Hillegass adds a personal touch and *credibility* to the *story*.

After explaining one example of how *CliffsNotes* has become a widely-used general term, John provides three short examples to demonstrate the extent of its use in this way.

This sentence concludes the first key points and makes a transition to the second key point.

Although John acknowledges that *SparkNotes* is the leading publisher of study guides— particularly for college students—he focuses on *CliffsNotes*, given its unique history and status as the founding study guide.

John encourages audience participation—challenging them to think critically about what book will end up number one by presenting the list in descending order.

Now let's jump ahead more than 20 years and look at the 2013 top-sellers in two categories: Shakespeare's plays and other literary classics. The top-three Shakespearean plays from *CliffsNotes* and *SparkNotes* are *Romeo and Juliet*, *Hamlet*, and *Macbeth*. Alas, poor Hamlet is no longer number one.

In terms of other classics, both *CliffsNotes* and SparkNotes include *To Kill a Mockingbird*, *Lord of the Flies*, *The Great Gatsby*, and *The Catcher in the Rye* in their list of the 10 best-sellers. Whereas *To Kill a Mockingbird* came in tenth on the best-seller list in 1992, it now rules the roost as number one for both study guides. I guess not much has changed in the list of books we read *and* the study guides we still rely on.

Although study guides—in a variety of formats—are here to stay, many educators are seriously concerned about their quality. There have also been claims of copyright infringements as well as questions about the ethics of using a study guide rather than reading the real thing.

Quality control issues abound even though study guide authors are PhDs, literature instructors, or graduate students who have experience with the literary work. Dr. Carl Fisher, chair of the comparative world literature and classics department at California State University, Long Beach, reviewed samples from a variety of study guide publishers to evaluate their quality. Much to my relief, *CliffsNotes* and *SparkNotes* got high grades. Although *Shmoop* claims their writers come from graduate students at top universities, their guides contain misspellings of authors' names and other errors. Three other guides—*Pink Monkey*, *Book Rags*, and *Bookwolf*—"did not make the grade at all." With those names, I'm not surprised.

In the early days, *CliffsNotes* saw its share of problems. In 1966 Random House filed suit against *CliffsNotes* for quoting too extensively from some of its copyrighted works by William Faulkner. Both sides had lawyers poised and ready to do combat. It could have become a landmark case. Instead Cliff and Random House solved their problems out of court. Cliff saw this as a turning point for both himself and his company. It forced them to take a fresh look at the notes. As a result, the classic guides were revamped to the point that they are now approximately 50 percent text summary and 50 percent critical analysis.

Although study guide publishers have learned lessons about quality control and copyright laws, academic critics are still at their door. I'm sure you have heard (or can easily imagine) teacher complaints that study guides allow students to avoid reading the original text.

Margin notes:

John is having fun with the members of his audience who know Shakespeare's *Hamlet*. Did you catch the literary reference in this short phrase? In the graveyard scene of Act 5, Scene 1, Hamlet holds the skull of the court jester, Yorick, and says: "Alas, poor Yorick! I knew him, Horatio, a fellow of infinite jest, of most excellent fancy."

This paragraph is a major *connective* in which John quickly summarizes his first two points and then provides a mini-preview of the third key point—a summary of the three primary criticisms of *CliffsNotes*-type study guides.

John provides Dr. Fisher's credentials to establish Fisher's credibility as a reviewer of study guides.

In several sections of his presentation, John adds an aside that is usually humorous and personal. In this way, he is a friendly and often amusing presence in the speech.

In your opinion, does the 50 percent summary and 50 percent analysis make it even easier or more difficult to use a study guide rather than reading an assigned book?

Gary Carey, a former managing editor for *CliffsNotes*, countered such criticism in the same article by stating: "Teachers' apprehensions concerning *CliffsNotes* may have been well founded many years ago when they were simple plot summaries. But, today, they are mainly composites of mainstream literary criticism that are of little value to students who have not read the book." An informal survey at Creighton University and the University of Nebraska found that Mr. Carey may be correct. Where students' older brothers and sisters may have used *CliffsNotes* in place of the real thing, more than 80 percent of those students interviewed said they never used *CliffsNotes* by themselves. They only used them to accompany the reading of the required text.

However, another survey, this time of students at the University of Missouri-Columbia found that "one-third of the respondents admitted reading the 'cliffs notes' rather than the actual work." As one educator said, "Reading *CliffsNotes* is like letting someone else eat your dinner. They deprive students of the pleasure of discovering literature for themselves."

As for me . . . I did pass my exam, and I have yet to read *The Iliad*. And I'm sure there are plenty of students out there who have missed the delights of *Huckleberry Finn* or the pathos of *The Grapes of Wrath*. And "To be or not to be," "Friends, Romans, countrymen," and "Out, damned spot" very well could be the only lines of Shakespeare that some students know despite their passing grades.

So the controversy continues. But at least now you know that, unlike Ronald McDonald, SpongeBob Squarepants, or Homer Simpson, Cliff was a real person who began a major industry and who did not dodge the issues. *CliffsNotes* and its competitors will continue explaining the finer points of literature to students around the globe. Because as long as teachers assign the classics of literature, the study guides will continue to grow and prosper.

Does Gary Carey's admission about the questionable quality of *CliffsNotes* 20 years ago help or hurt his credibility.

How would you explain the differences in survey results at different universities?

John returns to his *personal experience* and acknowledges that many students miss the delights of reading literature by solely relying on *CliffsNotes*.

Once again, John uses *humor*, this time as a way to effectively conclude his presentation.

Cliff's Notes: Basic Outline

I. Introduction	I. Introduction
	Eight o'clock Wednesday night. . . .
A. Purpose/Topic	A. Study guides help students understand great literature and succeed in literature courses.
B. Central Idea	B. Study guides are a unique publishing phenomenon often criticized by instructors and praised by students.
C. Brief Preview of Key Points	C. Preview
1. Key Point #1	1. History of *CliffsNotes*
2. Key Point #2	2. Competition and comparisons of study guides
3. Key Point #3	3. Criticism of study guides
II. Body of the Presentation	II. Body of the Presentation
A. Key Point #1	A. History of *CliffsNotes*
1. Supporting Material	1. Story of Cliff Hillegass, owner and founder of *CliffsNotes*
2. Supporting Material	2. Growth and success of *CliffsNotes*
3. Supporting Material	3. *CliffsNotes* becomes a common noun/adjective.
B. Key Point #2	B. Competition and Comparisons
1. Supporting Material	1. Competition of *CliffsNotes* and *SparkNotes*
2. Supporting Material	2. Comparisons of best-selling titles
C. Key Point #3	C. Criticism of Study Guides
1. Supporting Material	1. Questions about the quality of content
2. Supporting Material	2. Copyright issues
3. Supporting Material	3. Overreliance on Study Guides
III. Conclusion	III. Conclusion
	I passed the exam without reading *The Iliad*. . . .
	Study guides will continue to grow and prosper.

Informative Presentation Assessment

Use the following ratings to assess each of the competencies on this assessment instrument for a presentation you are preparing or for one you watch, listen to, and/or read.

E = excellent; G = good; A = average; W = weak; M = missing; N/A = not applicable.

COMPETENCIES	E	G	A	W	M	N/A
Preparation and Message Content						
Purpose and topic						
Audience adaptation						
Adaptation to context						
Introduction						
Organization						
Supporting material						
Transitions						
Conclusion						
Language						
Interest factors						
Informative strategies						
Delivery						
Extemporaneous mode						
Vocal delivery						
Physical delivery						
Presentation aids, if used						
Other Criteria						
Outline/written work						
Bibliography						
Other: _____						
Overall Assessment (circle one)	E	G	A	W	M	N/A
Comments:						

The Purpose of Informative Speaking

15.1 Describe the goals of informative presentations.

- Informative presentations report new information, clarify difficult terms, explain scientific phenomena, and/or overcome confusion and misunderstanding.

- An effective informative presentation can instruct, define, enlighten, describe, correct, remind, and/or demonstrate.

- The dividing line between informing and persuading is the speaker's purpose.

- When speaking to inform, include a value step that explains why the information is valuable to audience members and how it can enhance their success or well-being.

Informative Communication Strategies

15.2 Identify the specific communication strategies most applicable to different types of informative messages.

- Katherine Rowan's Theory of Informatory and Explanatory Communication explains how to make strategic decisions about the content and structure of different types of informative presentations.

- Classify your informative presentation in terms of whether its purpose is informatory (reports new information) or explanatory (clarifies difficult terms, explains quasi-scientific phenomena, or overcomes confusion and misunderstanding).

- Strategies for reporting new information include beginning with a value step, using a clear organizational pattern, including various types of supporting material, and relating the information to audience interests and needs.

- Strategies for clarifying difficult terms include defining the term's essential features, using various examples, discussing nonexamples,

and quizzing the audience to ensure comprehension.

- Strategies for explaining quasi-scientific phenomena include providing clear key points, using analogies and metaphors, using presentation aids, and using transitions, previews, summaries, and signposts to connect key points.

- Strategies for overcoming confusion and misinformation include stating the belief or theory, acknowledging its believability, creating dissatisfaction with the misconception, and stating and explaining the more acceptable belief or theory.

Generating Audience Interest

15.3 Use appropriate stories, humor, and involvement strategies to generate audience interest.

- In order to tell stories that captivate and educate your audience, look for good sources of stories, structure the story effectively, check the story for probability (coherence)

and fidelity (truthfulness), and use effective storytelling skills.

- In order to use humor to generate audience interest, avoid offensive humor, be prepared to direct humor at yourself, and avoid inappropriate humor.

- If you use humor, make sure it adapts to differences in culture and gender.

- Involve audience members in your presentation by asking questions, encouraging interaction, doing exercises, asking for volunteers, and inviting feedback.

Informative Speaking in Action

15.4 Practice the communication competencies that characterize effective informative presentations.

- Effective informative speakers use a clear and oral speaking style, adapt to audience experiences and needs, generate interest by using stories, humor, and audience involvement, and promote their own credibility.

Key Terms

Demonstration speeches	**Informatory and**	**Self-effacing humor**
Explanatory	**Explanatory**	**Story**
communication	**Communication Theory**	**Story fidelity**
Informative presentations	**Narratives**	**Story probability**
Informatory	**Narrative Theory**	**Value step**
communication	**Quasi-scientific phenomenon**	

TEST YOUR KNOWLEDGE

15.1 *Describe the goals of informative presentations.*

1 If you ask yourself, "Will my presentation explain intriguing and novel discoveries in science?" when searching for a value step, which audience benefit are you trying to achieve?

   a. Social benefit

   b. Psychological benefit

   c. Physical benefit

   d. Intellectual benefit

2 Which of the following constitutes a value step for a presentation on cooking hard-boiled eggs?

   a. Hard-boiled eggs are easy to make.

   b. I will teach you how to make foolproof hard-boiled eggs.

   c. There are four steps—cold-water start, stopping the boiling, the fifteen-minute stand, and cold-water rinse—for cooking perfect hard-boiled eggs.

   d. You won't have cracked or leaky eggs if you use this method for making perfect hard-boiled eggs.

15.2 *Identify the specific communication strategies most applicable to different types of informative messages.*

3 All of the following topics are appropriate for an *informatory* type of informative presentation except:

   a. learning how to take, edit, and print quality photographs.

   b. learning how to change gears on a bicycle.

   c. giving directions for sewing on a button.

   d. understanding the chemistry of yeast in bread baking.

4 When clarifying a difficult term in an informative presentation, which of the following strategies should you use?

   a. Use analogies and metaphors.

   b. Use various and typical examples.

   c. Use presentation aids.

   d. Quiz the audience.

5 When explaining a quasi-scientific phenomenon, which of the following strategies should you include?

   a. Use analogies and metaphors.

   b. Use various and typical examples.

   c. Use nonexamples.

   d. Create dissatisfaction with the theory.

15.3 *Use appropriate stories, humor, and involvement strategies to generate audience interest.*

6 According to Fisher's narrative theory, which of the following questions tests a story's probability?

   a. Do the facts and incidents in the story ring true?

   b. Do the characters behave in a consistent manner?

   c. Does the story reflect my personal values, beliefs, and experiences?

   d. Does the story address or support the speaker's point?

7 Which of the following is the third step in the story-building chart?

   a. High point or climax

   b. Action or conflict

   c. Background information

   d. Punch line

8 All of the following statements are good tips for using humor except:

   a. do not tease anyone in your audience.

   b. focus your humor on the message.

   c. do not direct humor at yourself.

   d. be wary of telling stories about body functions.

9 Which of the following strategies does your textbook recommend for involving the audience in your presentation?

   a. Ask questions

   b. Encourage interaction

   c. Invite feedback

   d. All of the above

15.4 *Practice the communication competencies that characterize effective informative presentations.*

10 What language styles did John Sullivan primarily use in his presentation, *Cliff's Notes*?

   a. Clear and rhetorical styles

   b. Oral and eloquent styles

   c. Clear and oral styles

   d. Oral and rhetorical styles

Answers found on page 368.

Speaking to Persuade 16

Businesses use persuasion to sell products and services. Attorneys use persuasion to influence judges and juries. Colleges use persuasion to recruit students and faculty. And children use persuasion to convince their parents to let them stay up past their bedtimes.

Persuasive presentations can do much more than sell products and recruit students. They can arouse strong emotions in both audience members *and* speakers. They can inspire and motivate others to change their attitudes and take action. For example, during her delivery of a speech to Chicago business leaders, First Lady Michele Obama held back tears as she talked about the death of Hadiya Pendleton. Ms. Pendleton was the fifteen-year old girl who performed in President Obama's inauguration festivities and was shot and killed in Chicago a few days later.[1] Here are three excerpts from Michelle Obama's speech:[2]

Thousands of children in this city live in neighborhoods where a funeral for a teenager is considered unfortunate, but not unusual; where wandering onto the wrong block or even just standing on your own front porch can mean putting yourself at risk. Those are the odds that so many young people are facing in this city—young people like Hadiya Pendleton, whose funeral I attended back in February.

. . . And as I visited with the Pendleton family at Hadiya's funeral, I couldn't get over how familiar they felt to me. Because what I realized was Hadiya's family was just like my family. Hadiya Pendleton was me, and I was her. But I got to grow up, and go to Princeton and Harvard Law School, and have a career and a family and the most blessed life I could ever imagine.

. . . Hadiya's family did everything right, but she still didn't have a chance. And that story—the story of Hadiya's life and death—we read that story day after day, month after month, year after year in this city and around this country.

In this chapter we explain why and how persuasion works in many different contexts. Then we show you how to apply audience-targeted strategies and skills to develop and deliver effective and inspiring persuasive presentations.

The Purpose of Persuasion

16.1 *Describe the goals of persuasive presentations.*

Persuasion seeks to change audience opinions (what they think) or behavior (what they do). Your purpose determines whether you will speak to inform or to persuade. Whereas informative presentations *tell* audiences something by *giving* them information or explanations, persuasive presentations *ask* for something *from* audiences—their agreement or a change in their opinions or behavior.

PERSUASIVE PRESENTATIONS ask for something from audience members—their agreement or a change in their opinions or behavior.

PERSUASION CHANGES OPINIONS AND BEHAVIOR

OPINIONS
- Your family is more important than your job.
- Japan still makes the best automobiles.
- Vegetarian diets are good for your body and good for the planet.

BEHAVIOR
- Eat dinner with your family at least five times a week.
- Buy a Japanese-made car.
- Stop eating meat.

Persuading Others

16.2 *Select persuasive strategies that adapt to audience attitudes.*

If you want to change audience members' opinions or behavior, you need to understand why they resist change. Why don't people vote for the first candidate who asks for their support? Why don't we run out and buy every product a celebrity or sports star recommends? Why don't most drivers pull to the side when their cell phone signals a call? All these questions have good answers—and that's the problem. Most audience members know why they *won't* vote, buy, pull over, or do any of the things you ask them to

do. It's up to you to determine what the reasons are and address them.

Classify Audience Attitudes

The more you know about audience members and their attitudes, the more effectively you can adapt your message to them. For example, an audience of homeowners may strongly agree that their property taxes are too high, but a group of local college students may support more taxes for higher education. If you're scheduled to talk to a group of avid gun owners, collectors,

and hunters, you can probably assume many of them will oppose strict gun control legislation.

Review what you know about your audience's demographic characteristics and attitudes. Then place your audience along a continuum (shown at the bottom of the next page) that measures the extent to which *most* members will agree or disagree with you. When you understand where audience members stand, you can begin the process of adapting your message to the people you want to persuade.

The Persuasive Power of Social Media

Social media has become one of the world's most powerful persuasive tools. Computer scientist James Caverlee's research concludes that social media "harness collective intelligence to perform tasks, to persuade and change minds, and maybe even to change the world." At the same time, he warns that social media have "become weapons of mass persuasion."[3]

In the few years since 2011, social media has played a significant role in igniting uprisings and revolutions around the world—from the Arab Spring in Tunisia, Egypt, and Libya to the Occupy Movements in New York City, Paris, and Cape Town, South Africa. Social media has also recruited donors and volunteers for disaster relief campaigns after the earthquake in Japan, the massive Philippine typhoon, Superstorm Sandy in New Jersey, as well as destructive tornados and floods in the U.S.

And as we were becoming a "fan" of web pages or "followers" on Facebook, marketing experts were crafting messages that influenced our buying decisions and habits. Well-known technology companies, attentive to customers' taste for all things visual, created accounts on sites such as Pinterest, a strictly visual, bulletin board site. If you go on to Pinterest, you'll see the colorful pins of Whole Foods Market, West Elm, Anthropologie, J Crew—just to name a few of the many corporations that have taken advantage of the persuasive power of images.

Robert Gass and John Seiter, the authors of *Persuasion, Social Influence, and Compliance Gaining*, write that today's generation of young college students "have been inundated with sophisticated marketing campaigns their entire lives." They are "*never not* being marketed to."[4] Persuasive marketing messages have instilled an unshakeable passion and desire for name-brand products ranging from almost anything with an *i* before its name (iPad, iPhone) to designer fashions and luxury hotels. Apparently, you don't mean a thing if you ain't got that bling.[5]

So what, you may ask, does this have to do with making a persuasive speech or presentation? Our answer: everything. All the theories, strategies, and skills in this chapter explain the success of social media as a persuasive tool.

Persuade Audience Members Who Agree with You

When audience members already agree with you, you don't have to *change* their way of thinking. Rather, your goal is to strengthen their attitudes and encourage them to act.

When you and your audience agree, consider giving them an **inoculation**. According to social psychologist William McGuire, protecting audience attitudes from counterpersuasion by the "other side" is like inoculating the body against disease.[6] You can build up audience resistance by exposing flaws in the arguments of the opposition *and* showing your audience how to refute them. This strategy creates a more enduring change in attitudes or behavior.

Inoculation works best when audience members are involved in and care about an issue; it makes them aware that their attitudes are vulnerable to attack and then provides ways to resist the attack.[7]

Persuade Audience Members Who Disagree with You

Disagreement does not mean that audience members will be hostile or rude. It *does* mean that changing their opinions can be difficult. In the face of audience disagreement, don't try to change the world. Focus on what can reasonably be changed. For example, you are unlikely to convince an audience full of avid red meat eaters to give up their steaks and become strict vegetarians. At best, you may be able to convince them that eating smaller portions of meat is healthier. That alone would be a great accomplishment. Every small step can add up to a big change over time.

Inoculation strategies can also work on audience members who disagree. The tactic, however, is slightly different.

CONTINUUM OF AUDIENCE ATTITUDES

| Strongly agree with me | Agree | Undecided | Disagree | Strongly disagree with me |

Give them a small dose of arguments against a particular idea or opinion and hope it takes hold. As sales experts like to say: put your foot in the door—to which we add—but not so far that they slam it in your face and break your toes.

Persuading Indecisive Audience Members

Some audience members may not have an opinion about your topic because they are uninformed, unconcerned, or undecided. Knowing which type of persuasive strategy to use in each case depends on audience members' reasons for indecision. In the following example, a college student begins her presentation on the importance of voting by getting the attention of the undecided students and giving them a reason to care:

How many of you applied for some form of financial aid for college?

With its humanitarian "One for One" campaign, new seasonal footwear, and overall efforts to make comfortable, affordable shoes for a good cause, TOMS devotees never tire of going back for more.

[More than half the class raised their hands.] How many of you got the full amount you applied for or needed? [Less than one-fourth of the class raised their hands.] I have some bad news for you. Financial aid may be even more difficult to get in the future. But the good news is that there's something you can do about it.

In the real world of persuasive speaking, you are likely to face audiences with some members who agree with your message, others who don't, and still others who are indecisive. In such cases, you can focus on just one group—the largest, most influential, or easiest to persuade—or appeal to all three types of audiences by gaining their attention and interest followed by providing new information from highly respected sources.

Persuasive Strategies FOR AUDIENCES THAT AGREE WITH YOU

- **Present new information.** New information reminds them why they agree and reinforces their agreement. After hearing or seeing evidence several times, its effectiveness decreases. "New evidence is more persuasive than old evidence."[8]

- **Strengthen audience resistance to opposing arguments.** Prepare them to answer questions asked by those who disagree. Inoculate them with arguments that refute opposing views.

- **Excite their emotions.** Use examples and stories that stimulate their feelings (joy, pride, fear, happiness). When appropriate, use intense language and expressive delivery.

- **Serve as a personal role model.** Tell them what you have seen or done. Enhance your credibility.

- **Advocate a course of action.** Explain why and how they should take action (such as sign a petition, vote, exercise). Call for action! It's a powerful form of persuasion.

Persuasive Strategies FOR AUDIENCES THAT DISAGREE WITH YOU

- **Set reasonable goals.** Do not expect audience members to change their opinions or behavior radically. Even a small step taken in your direction can eventually add up to a big change.

- **Find common ground.** Find a belief, value, attitude, or opinion that you and your audience have in common before moving on to areas of disagreement.

- **Accept and adapt to differences of opinion.** Acknowledge the legitimacy of audience opinions and give them credit for defending their principles. Demonstrate respect for their viewpoint.

- **Cite fair and respected evidence.** Make sure your supporting material is flawless. Choose evidence from respected, unbiased sources.

- **Build your personal credibility.** Present yourself as credible. Positive feelings about you enhance your persuasiveness.

Persuasive Strategies FOR INDECISIVE AUDIENCE MEMBERS

For the Uninformed
- Gain their attention and interest.
- Provide new, dramatic information.

For the Unconcerned
- Gain their attention and interest.
- Give them a reason to care.
- Present relevant information and evidence.

For the Adamantly Undecided
- Acknowledge the legitimacy of different viewpoints.
- Provide new, compelling information.
- Emphasize or reinforce the strength of arguments on your side of the issue.

Finding Common Ground

When you address an audience that disagrees with you, find **common ground**—a place where you and the audience can stand without disagreement. Sharing common ground is often the key to persuading an audience that disagrees with you. Skilled speakers identify and discuss a position or behavior that they share with the audience. For example, smokers and nonsmokers may both agree that smoking should be prohibited in and around schools.

> If you find common ground, your audience is more likely to listen to you when you move into less friendly territory.

Below you'll find two controversial topics that our students often choose for class presentations. Complete each sentence by stating an issue on which a speaker and audience might find common ground. For example, "Free speech advocates and anti-pornography groups would *probably* agree that . . . pornography should not be available to young children." Note that the word *probably* is written in italics. Audience members at extreme ends of any position or belief may not make exceptions and may not be willing to stand on common ground with you. If you anticipate audience disagreement, prepare for it by creating similar fill-in-the-blank statements that represent your position and your audience's opposing position.

1. Pro–capital punishment and anti–capital punishment groups would *probably* agree that _____

   _____

2. People who are for and against immigration reform would *probably* agree that _____

   _____

FACTS TEST THINK ABOUT THEORY
IDEA PLAN EXPERIMENT METHOD

Psychological Reactance Theory

Psychologist Jack W. Brehm explains why telling an audience what *not* to do can produce the exact opposite reaction. His **Psychological Reactance Theory** suggests that when you perceive a threat to your freedom to believe or behave as you wish, you may go out of your way to *do* the forbidden behavior or rebel against the prohibiting authority.[9]

Children react this way all the time. You tell them, "Don't snack before dinner!" or "Don't hit your brother!" or "Stop playing that video game!" so they hide their snacks, sneak in a few punches, and play their game on their computer instead of their Playstation. Consider this interesting fact: although legally designated "coffee shops" in Amsterdam sell marijuana, only about 15 percent of Dutch people older than twelve years have ever used marijuana, whereas 33 percent of Americans have used it illegally.[10]

> If you tell an audience "Do this" or "Don't believe that," you may run into strong resistance.

Because the drug is strictly prohibited by law in most states, it may be more attractive as an outlet of rebellion.[11]

If you believe that your audience may react negatively to your advice or directions, use the following strategies to reduce the likelihood of a reactance response:

- Avoid strong, direct commands such as "don't," "stop," and "you *must*."
- Avoid extreme statements depicting terrible consequences such as, "You will die," or "You will fail," or "You will be punished."
- Avoid finger-pointing—literally and figuratively. Don't single out specific audience members for condemnation or harsh criticism.
- Advocate a middle ground that preserves audience members' freedom and dignity while moving them toward attitude or behavior change.
- Use strategies that are appropriate for audience members who disagree with you.
- Respect your audience's perspectives, needs, and lifestyles.

Building Persuasive Arguments

16.3 *Describe the components and characteristics of valid persuasive arguments.*

Some people think of an *argument* as a dispute or hostile confrontation between two people. In this textbook, however, we define an **argument** as a claim supported by evidence and reasoning for or against that claim. For example, if a student speaker says, "The Latino/Latina Heritage Club should be given more funds next year," there is no argument because there is no evidence or reasons supporting the statement. To turn this statement into an argument, we would say, "The Latino/Latina Heritage Club should be given more funds next year because it has doubled in size; without an increase in funding, it cannot provide its members the same number or quality of programs." The statement now includes a claim supported by evidence and reasoning.

Use Toulmin's Model of an Argument

To help understand the essential structure of an argument, we turn to the **Toulmin Model of an Argument**, which was developed by Stephen Toulmin, a British philosopher. Toulmin's model maintains that a complete argument requires three essential components: a claim, evidence, and a warrant. In many speaking situations, three supplementary components—backing for the warrant, reservations, and qualifiers—are also necessary.[12] Regardless of whether you are putting together an argument for a presentation or you are an audience member listening to a speaker make an argument, you should think critically about all of Toulmin's components to determine whether the argument is worthy of belief.

Claim, Evidence, and Warrant A **claim** is the conclusion of an argument or the overall position you advocate in a presentation. Claims answer the question, *What is the argument trying to prove?* Stating a claim, however, is not an argument—it is only the starting point. "Where an argument starts is far

less important than where it finishes because the logic and evidence in between [are] crucial."[13]

In a complete argument, you support and prove the claim you advocate by providing relevant evidence. **Evidence** answers the question, *How do you know that?* A sound argument relies on strong evidence, which can range from statistics and multiple examples to the advice of experts and generally accepted audience beliefs.

In Chapter 13, "Content and Organization," we described how to gather and use supporting material to explain and/or advance your central idea and key points. The supporting material you choose and use in a presentation constitutes the evidence that justifies and strengthens your claim and choice of proof. Be strategic. Select your evidence based on the types of argument you are trying to prove and the attitudes and needs of your audience.

> Without the support of good evidence, your audience may be reluctant to accept your claims.

For example, if you claim that keeping a food-intake diary is the best way to monitor a diet, you might share the results of a study conducted at a major medical school, which concluded that food-intake diaries produce the best results. Alternatively, you might tell stories about how your attempts to lose weight failed until you spent two months keeping a food-intake diary. You might even distribute examples of food-intake diaries to the audience to show them how easy it is to surpass a 30-gram fat allowance during a "day of dieting."

The **warrant** explains why the evidence is relevant and why it supports the claim. For example, the warrant might say that the author of the article on food-intake diaries is one of the country's leading nutrition experts. Rather than asking, *How do you know that?* the warrant asks, *How did you get there? What gives you the right to draw that conclusion?* In their book *The Well-Crafted Argument*, Fred White and Simone Billings write, "compelling warrants are just as vital to the force of an argument as compelling evidence because they reinforce the validity and trustworthiness of both the claim and evidence."[14]

Figure 16.1 on the next page shows how the "Basic T" of the Toulmin Model represents the three components—claim, evidence, and warrant—of an argument. The argument advocating food diaries might sound something like this:

> Want to lose those extra pounds for good? Keep a food-intake diary. Dr. Nathan Carter, the lead researcher in a medical school study, reports that patients who kept food-intake diaries were twice as likely to lose weight as were patients who used other methods.

Backing, Reservation, and Qualifier In addition to the three essential elements of an argument, there are three supplementary components of the Toulmin Model: backing, reservation, and qualifier.

Backing provides support for the argument's warrant. Backing is not needed in all arguments, but it can be crucial if an audience questions why the warrant should be accepted as the link between the evidence and the claim. While the warrant answers the question, *How did you get there?* the backing answers the question, *Why is this the right way to get there?* Backing can be in the form of more information about the credibility of a source: "Dr. Nathan Carter and his colleagues received two national awards for their contributions to weight-loss research." Backing can also describe the

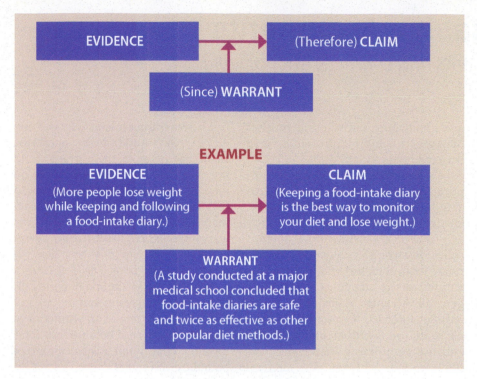

Figure 16.1 The Basic "T" of the Toulmin Model of Argument

a claim and therefore can make an argument more acceptable to a skeptical audience. Figure 16.2 below maps out a complete argument.

In the next section, we take a closer look at the strategies and skills needed to prove that your arguments are worthy of belief.

Choose Persuasive Claims

A good way to start building a persuasive argument is by listing all the possible claims you could use—all the reasons why the audience should agree with you. For example, a student speaker planning a presentation on hunting as a means of controlling the growing deer population listed several reasons:

The enormous deer population . . .

. . . is starving and dying of disease.

. . . is eating up crops, gardens, and forest seedlings.

. . . is carrying deer ticks that cause Lyme disease in people.

. . . is causing an increase in the number of highway accidents.

. . . is consuming the food needed by other forest animals.

Although there were many arguments for advocating hunting to reduce the deer population, the speaker

methodology used in the weight-loss study that determined the effectiveness of food-intake diaries.

Not all claims are true all the time. The **reservation** component of the Toulmin Model recognizes exceptions to an argument or indications that a claim may not be true under certain circumstances.

For example, a food-intake diary is only as good as the limits placed on daily food intake. Setting a limit of 4,000 calories and 100-gram fat a day for sedentary person whose ideal weight is 125 pounds won't result in weight loss. In addition, some people have weight problems with hormonal or genetic causes that do not respond to typical diets. The reservations could be stated this way: "Food-intake diaries must be well calibrated and may not work if there are genetic or hormonal causes of obesity. In such cases, keeping a standard food-intake diary may not be sufficient."

When an argument contains reservations, the speaker should qualify the claim. The **qualifier** states the degree to which a claim appears to be true. Qualifiers usually include the words *probably*, *possibly*, or *likely*. Consider this claim with a qualifier: "Unless there are medical reasons for seeking other therapies,

using and following a food-intake diary calibrated to your own dietary goals is *probably* the best way to lose weight."

Speakers need qualifiers when the evidence or warrant is less than certain and when audience members are likely to have doubts. Qualifiers soften

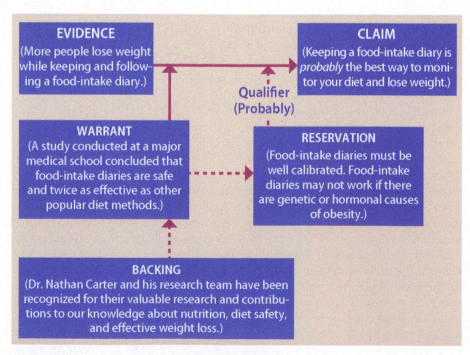

Figure 16.2 The Complete Toulmin Model of Argument

had to choose the arguments that, based on his analysis of the audience, were most likely to persuade his audience in the amount of time he was scheduled to speak.

There are, however, different types of claims. You might claim that something is true or false, probable or improbable, good or bad, reasonable or unreasonable, as shown below.

Many speakers use several types of claims in a single presentation. For example, in the presentation on deer hunting, the overall argument for reducing the deer population is a policy claim. The key points can be supported by claims of fact, conjecture, and/or value (see the box below).

Choose Persuasive Proof

Like lawyers before a jury, persuasive speakers must prove their case. Lawyers decide what evidence to use in court, but it's up to the jury or judge to determine whether the evidence is valid and persuasive. When trying to persuade an audience, your success depends on the quality and validity of your **proof**, the arguments and evidence you use to support and strengthen a persuasive claim. Because audiences and persuasive situations differ, so should your proof.[15]

Four Forms of PERSUASIVE PROOF

LOGOS	Logical Proof
PATHOS	Emotional Proof
ETHOS	Personal Proof
MYTHOS	Narrative Proof

During the early fourth century B.C., Aristotle developed a multidimensional theory of persuasion as we noted in Chapter 12, "Planning Your Presentation." Nearly 2,500 years later, his conclusions continue to influence the way we study persuasion. In *Rhetoric*, Aristotle identifies three major forms of proof. To that list we add a fourth type of proof—*mythos* (narrative proof).

Logos: Logical Proof Arguments that rely on reasoning and analysis are using **logos** or logical proof. Logical proof relies on an audience's ability to think critically and arrive at a justified conclusion or decision. Note how a student speaker shared the following facts and statistics to make an argument in favor of the Affordable Care Act:

Many hard-working Americans cannot afford the most basic forms of health care and health insurance. Some 50 million Americans—about 16.3 percent of the population—live without health insurance. In 2000, 64 percent received health insurance from their employers; today only 55 percent do.[16]

Pathos: Emotional Proof Pathos is aimed at deep-seated, emotional feelings about justice, generosity, courage, forgiveness, and wisdom.[17] Many television commercials succeed because they understand the power of emotional proof.

> ## Commercials succeed because they understand the power of emotional proof.

Notice, for instance, how this student speaker uses testimony as emotional proof to evoke the audience's sympathies and fears:

Kevin was 27 years old and only two months into a new job when he began to lose weight and feel ill. After weeks of testing and finally surgery, he was found to have colon cancer.

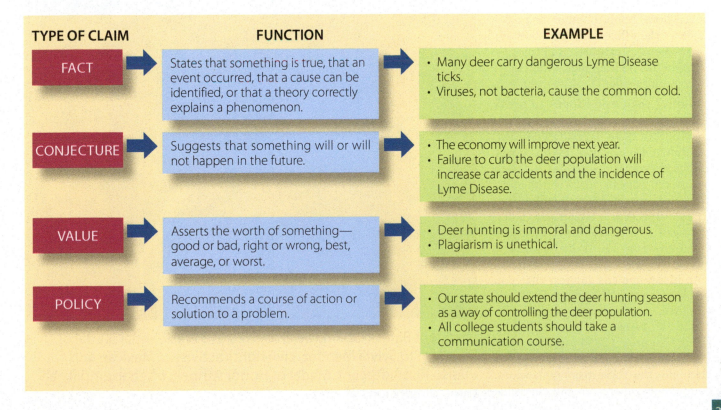

TYPE OF CLAIM	FUNCTION	EXAMPLE
FACT	States that something is true, that an event occurred, that a cause can be identified, or that a theory correctly explains a phenomenon.	• Many deer carry dangerous Lyme Disease ticks. • Viruses, not bacteria, cause the common cold.
CONJECTURE	Suggests that something will or will not happen in the future.	• The economy will improve next year. • Failure to curb the deer population will increase car accidents and the incidence of Lyme Disease.
VALUE	Asserts the worth of something—good or bad, right or wrong, best, average, or worst.	• Deer hunting is immoral and dangerous. • Plagiarism is unethical.
POLICY	Recommends a course of action or solution to a problem.	• Our state should extend the deer hunting season as a way of controlling the deer population. • All college students should take a communication course.

Do Fear Appeals Scare You?

Persuasion scholar Richard Perloff offers the following conclusions about using fear appeals to successfully persuade others:

- **Scare the heck out of listeners.** Describe the dangers in graphic details. Don't beat around the bush.

- **Discuss solutions as well as problems.** Offer them hope. Once you've scared audience members, tell them how to prevent the problem, avoid the danger, or minimize its consequences.

- **Emphasize the costs of *not* taking action *as well as* the benefits of taking action.** In other words, you must "get 'em well" after you "get them sick."

- **Make sure that what scares you also scares your audience.** Consider the values and needs of your audience when considering what frightens them.[18]

Now consider the following circumstances and assess whether fear appeals affect or have affected your attitudes, opinions, and behavior about each:

1. Your choice of locks or a security system to protect your home
2. Your decision to own a handgun for protection
3. Your willingness to travel abroad
4. Your decision to stop smoking or drinking
5. Your decision to use hand sanitizer and take vitamins to prevent or cure viral infections

The bills were more than $100,000. But soon after his release from the hospital, he found out that his insurance company denied his claim because he had what they considered "a pre-existing condition." Kevin's reaction: "At one point in the middle of the whole thing, I hit bottom; between having cancer and being told I had no insurance, I tried to commit suicide."[19]

Rather than using logos to prove that many Americans suffer because they do not have dependable health insurance, the speaker tries to evoke audience sympathies *and* fears. When emotional appeals adapt to the audience and context, are well crafted and well delivered, and tap strong values, they can change audience attitudes and behavior. Think of how many advertisements use this approach. Life insurance ads suggest that you invest not for yourself but for those you love.

Ethos: Personal Proof Recall from Chapter 12, "Planning Your Presentation," that **ethos** (speaker credibility) has three major dimensions: competence, character, and charisma.

Each of these dimensions can serve as a form of personal proof in a persuasive presentation. To demonstrate that you are a competent speaker of good character, deliver your presentation with conviction. Audiences are more likely to be persuaded when a speaker seems committed to the cause.

In his *Rhetoric*, Aristotle claims that the speaker's personal character "may almost be called the most effective means of persuasion he possesses."[20] Consider how ethos operates in your everyday life. Do you believe what your favorite professors tell you? If, in your opinion, they are of good character and are experts in their field of study, you probably do. Ethos is a powerful form of proof—but you have to *earn* it from your audience if you expect it to help you achieve your persuasive purpose.

Mythos: Narrative Proof During the second half of the twentieth century, *mythos*, or narrative proof, emerged as a fourth and significant form of persuasive proof. According to communication scholars Michael and Suzanne Osborn, **mythos** is a form of proof that addresses the values, faith, and feelings that make up our social character and is most often expressed in traditional stories, sayings, and symbols.[21]

Americans are raised on mythic stories that celebrate patriotism, freedom, honesty, and national pride. For instance,

President Barack Obama awards the 2013 Presidential Medal of Freedom to Sylvia Mendez, civil rights activist of Mexican and Puerto Rican descent. Medal of Honor winners often exemplify all three dimensions of *ethos*.

Lady Liberty's invitation from Emma Lazarus's poem, "Give me your tired, your poor ..." taps into the mythos that still draws thousands of immigrants to the United States in search of freedom and a better life.

President George Washington's statement "I cannot tell a lie" after cutting down the family's cherry tree may be a myth, but it has helped teach millions of young Americans about the value of honesty. The civil rights refrain "We shall overcome" also informs American beliefs and values. Speakers who tap into the *mythos* of an audience form a powerful identification with their listeners.

> **Mythos** can connect your message with your audience's social and cultural identity, and give them a reason to listen carefully to your ideas.[22]

One of the best ways to enlist mythos in persuasion is through storytelling. Religions, for example, teach many values through parables. (For more on storytelling, see Chapter 15, "Speaking to Inform.") In their book, *The Elements of Persuasion*, Richard Maxwell and Robert Dickman write: "Stories are facts wrapped in emotion. . . . [A] fact is twenty times more likely to be remembered if it is part of a story."[23]

Detect Fallacies

If you think critically about the content of conversations and quarrels, group discussions and meetings, speeches and presentations, mediated messages and mass communication, you will encounter valid and invalid arguments. One way to recognize invalid arguments is to look for fallacies. A **fallacy** is an error in thinking that has the potential to mislead or deceive others. Fallacies can be intentional or unintentional. When an unethical communicator misuses evidence or reasoning or when a well-meaning person misinterprets evidence or draws erroneous conclusions, the results are still the same—those who hear or read fallacious messages may be deceived, misled, confused, and reluctant to trust you.

After you've learned to identify a variety of fallacies, don't be surprised if you begin noticing them everywhere—in television commercials, in political campaigns, on talk radio, in tweets, and in everyday conversations. As you learn about fallacies, ask yourself what is fallacious about advertisers' claims that "no other aspirin is

---

COMMUNICATION IN *ACTION*

Watch Out for Heuristics

Heuristics help explain our susceptibility to claims that rely on questionable evidence and warrants. **Heuristics** are cognitive thinking shortcuts we use in decision making because they are correct often enough to be useful. Unfortunately, unethical persuaders sometimes use them to win agreement from their audiences even though their arguments are flawed.[24]

When audience members are not very interested or motivated to listen or when they are not thinking critically, they are more likely to believe arguments that lack valid evidence or that offer evidence unrelated to a speaker's claim. The following brief list includes common heuristics we see and hear in everyday life:

- The quality of an item correlates with its price.
- We should believe likable people.
- The behavior of others is a good guide as to how we should behave.
- Confident speakers know what they are talking about.

- Something that is scarce is also valuable.
- Longer messages are strong messages.

Successful salespeople often use heuristics. They appear confident, likable, and trustworthy. They also give you multiple reasons for purchasing expensive, high-quality, limited-edition products that are very popular with discerning customers. When you hear a message that is loaded with heuristics, be cautious. Analyze the arguments carefully before you succumb to their persuasive power.

more effective for pain than ours" and appeals to "buy America's best-selling pickup truck." Are fallacies involved when a political candidate talks about an opponent's past as an antiwar protester or a recovering alcoholic? Here we highlight six of the most common fallacies.

Attacking the Person The fallacy of **attacking the person** also has a Latin name—*ad hominem*—which means "against the man." An *ad hominem* argument makes irrelevant or false attacks against a person rather than against the content of that person's message. Responding to the claim "Property taxes should be increased" with "What would you know? You don't own a home!" attacks the person rather than the argument. Name-calling, labeling, and attacking a person rather than the substance of an argument are unethical, *ad hominem* fallacies. Political campaign ads are notorious for attacking candidates in personal ways rather than addressing their positions on important public issues. When, in an interview with *Huffington Post*, Senator John McCain referred to Tea Party Republicans

Rand Paul (Kentucky senator) and Ted Cruz (Texas senator) as "wacko birds," he brought down the wrath of Tea Party members and the conservative media. "Either way," wrote conservative blogger Andrew Breitbart, "McCain is single-handedly giving the media the exact narrative they need to attack conservatives' newest hero."[25]

Appeal to Authority So-called expert opinion is often used to support arguments. However, when the supposed expert has no relevant experience on the issues being discussed, the fallacy of **appeal to authority** occurs, as in "I'm not a doctor, but I play one on TV, and I recommend Nick's Cough Syrup." Unless the actor has expert credentials on medical issues, the argument is fallacious. You see television and magazine advertisements in which celebrities praise the medicines they use, the companies that insure them, and the beauty products that make them look young and attractive. Just because someone is a good actor or good looking does not make her or him an expert on these topics.

Appeal to Popularity An **appeal to popularity** claims that an action is acceptable or excusable because many people are doing it. "Most of your neighbors have agreed to support the rezoning proposal" is an appeal to popularity. Just because a lot of people hold a particular belief or engage in an action does not make it right. If most of your friends binge on alcohol, should you? If lots of people tell you that penicillin can cure a common cold, should you demand a prescription from your doctor? Unfortunately, appeals to popularity have also been used to justify discrimination, unscrupulous financial schemes, and dangerous behavior.

During the 2012 U.S. presidential campaign, Obama volunteers used a door-to-door, get-out-the-vote technique in which they informed potential Obama supporters that others in their neighborhood were planning to vote. In a very real sense, they were telling voters to do what was most popular where they lived.

Appeal to Tradition Claiming that a certain course of action should be followed because it was done that way

Common **FALLACIES**

FALLACY	DEFINITION	EXAMPLE
ATTACKING THE PERSON	Claiming that a person's opinion and arguments are wrong or untrue by attacking the person rather than their message.	Of course, she supports the Federal Government's so-called Affordable Care Action—she's a socialist!
APPEAL TO AUTHORITY	Basing a claim on the opinion of a supposed expert who has no relevant experience on the issues being discussed.	Look at all the celebrities who support him for governor. He must be the best candidate.
APPEAL TO POPULARITY	Claiming that an action is acceptable or excusable because many people are doing it.	The Kindle is much better than the Nook because more people buy Kindles.
APPEAL TO TRADITION	Claiming that a certain course of action should be followed because it has always been done that way in the past.	Grandma says that drinking brandy with a little honey is the best way to cure a cold.
FAULTY CAUSE	Claiming that a particular situation or event is the cause of another event before ruling out other possibilities.	In our family we rarely get sick because we drink brandy with honey when we feel a cold coming on.
HASTY GENERALIZATION	Claiming that something is true based on too little evidence or too few experiences.	My neighbor told me that vaccines cause autism and other disabilities in millions of children.

in the past is an **appeal to tradition**. "We must have our annual company picnic in August because that's when we always have it" appeals to tradition. Just because a course of action has been followed for a time does not mean it is the best option. Many people attend the church their parents attended and vote for the political party their parents voted for. When asked why they do that, their answer may have little justification other than "That's what my parents did."[26] Here are two more examples:

- The second amendment has always protected our right to own guns, therefore stricter gun control laws are unconstitutional and should not be permitted.
- My mother and her mother made chicken soup this way. Don't tell me how to make chicken soup.

Faulty Cause "We are losing sales because our sales team is not working hard enough." This statement may overlook other causes for low sales, such as a price increase that made the product less affordable or a competitor's superior product. The **faulty cause** fallacy occurs when you claim that a particular situation or event is the cause of another event before ruling out other possible causes. Will you catch a cold if you don't bundle up when you go outside? Will you have bad luck if you break a

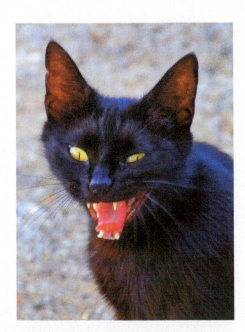

Superstitions are faulty cause fallacies.

Reject Fallacies

In this chapter we identified six common fallacies of argument. There are, in fact, hundreds of potential fallacies waiting to distort persuasive messages. Fallacies can mislead and misinform listeners, rob audiences of their precious time and well-founded convictions, and permanently damage your reputation and credibility.

Every communicator has an ethical obligation to recognize and reject the fallacies in persuasive arguments. Three factors lead to most mistakes in reasoning:[27]

- **Intentional and unintentional fallacies.** Unethical speakers may intentionally use fallacies to deceive or mislead audience members. Ethical, well-intentioned speakers may use fallacious reasoning without knowing it. Ignorance—as the old saying goes—is no excuse. Every speaker has an ethical obligation to avoid fallacies.

- **Careless listening and reasoning.** Inattentive listeners can fall prey to deceptive arguments and claims that evoke strong emotions. Poor critical thinking can lead speakers and listeners to accept fallacies as true.

- **Different worldviews.** Your worldview—developed over many years of life experiences—affects how you determine what you believe is reasonable and unreasonable. Prejudices may lead some people to see the questionable behavior of a few members of a particular demographic as typical of the behavior of everyone in that group. A politically conservative speaker or listener may automatically ignore or dismiss an argument made by a liberal speaker and vice versa. Ethical communicators consider how culture, language, gender, religion, politics, and social and economic status affect the way they and their audiences see the world.

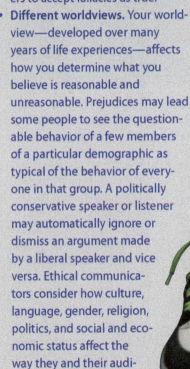

Is a fallacy operating when people assume that this particular style of dress reflects a rebellious or lazy life style? Or, is it merely the popular fashion of the times?

mirror? If you answer yes to either of these questions, you are not thinking critically. *Viruses* cause colds, although a chill can weaken your immune system. Beliefs about breaking a mirror or walking under a ladder or allowing a black cat to cross your path are nothing more than superstitions.

Hasty Generalizations You commit a **hasty generalization** fallacy when you jump to a conclusion based on too little evidence or too few experiences. The fallacy argues that if it is true for some, it must be true for all. "Don't go to that restaurant. I went once and the service was awful" is a hasty generalization. One negative experience does not mean that other visits to the restaurant would not be enjoyable. Here's another example: "My father smoked four packs of cigarettes a day since age fourteen, and lived until age eighty-five. Therefore, smoking really can't be that bad for me."

Persuasive Organizational Patterns

16.4 *Identify organizational patterns appropriate for persuasive presentations.*

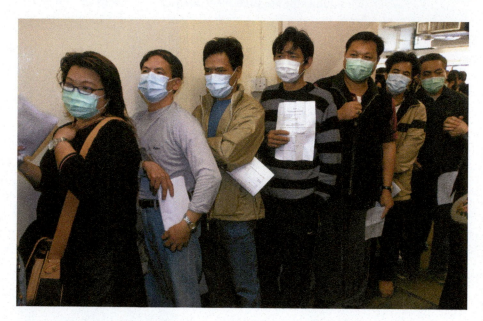

You have a topic you care about; a list of potential arguments; an understanding of how your arguments present claims of fact, conjecture, value, and policy; and good evidence and reasoning to support your arguments. You've reached a key decision-making point. It's time to put these elements together into an effective persuasive message. In addition to the organizational patterns discussed in Chapter 13, "Content and Organization," there are several strategic organizational patterns particularly suited to persuasive presentations.

Problem/Cause/Solution

As its name implies, the **problem/cause/solution pattern** describes a serious problem, explains why the problem continues (the cause), and offers a solution. This organizational pattern works best when you are proposing a specific course of action.

In the following outline, the speaker used a problem/cause/solution organizational pattern to support actions that would reduce and restrict the overuse of antibiotics:

A. Twenty-three thousand Americans die each year from antibiotic-resistant infections. (*Problem*)
  1. In addition to deaths, more than two million Americans are sickened each year by antibiotic-resistant infections.
  2. The Center for Disease Control reports that this problem has "potentially catastrophic consequences."
B. The overuse of antibiotic drugs is the strongest factor contributing to antibiotic resistance. (*Cause*)
C. Professional, personal, and government actions can reduce the number of serious illnesses and deaths resulting from the overuse of antibiotics. (*Solution*)
  1. Doctors should not prescribe antibiotics when they are unnecessary.
  2. Patients should not use prescribed antibiotics inappropriately.

3. People who are ill should not return to school or work if they have an infection.
4. The federal Food and Drug Administration should tightly regulate the use and amount of antibiotics fed to livestock.

Comparative Advantage

When your audience is aware of a problem and recognizes that a solution is necessary, the **comparative advantage pattern** may help you make your case. In this pattern, you present a plan that will improve a situation and help to solve a problem while acknowledging that a total solution may not be possible. In the following outline, the speaker contends that increased hunting is a more advantageous way of reducing the serious problems caused by the growing deer population.

A. There is a plan that will help reduce the deer population. (*Plan*)
  1. Extend the deer-hunting season.
  2. Permit hunters to kill more female than male deer.
B. This plan will reduce the severity of the problem. (*Comparative Advantages*)
  1. It will reduce the number of deer deaths from starvation and disease.
  2. It will reduce the number of ticks carrying Lyme disease.
  3. It will reduce the number of automobile deaths and injuries caused by deer crossing highways.

Refuting Objections Pattern

Sometimes, audience members agree that there is a problem and even know what should be done to solve it, yet they do not act because the solution is objectionable, frightening, expensive, or difficult to understand or implement. In other situations, an audience disagrees with a speaker and comes prepared to reject the message even before hearing it. With both types of audiences, try to overcome these objections by using appropriate forms of proof and persuasive evidence. The **refuting objections pattern** allows you to refute and disprove each point that stands in opposition to your own.

In the following outline, the speaker employs the refuting objections organizational pattern to encourage listeners to donate blood:

A. People should give blood but often don't. (*Problem*)
1. Most people approve of and support donations.
2. Most people don't give blood.

B. There are several reasons people don't give blood. (*Objections*)
1. They fear needles and pain.
2. They fear they could get a disease from giving blood.
3. They claim they don't have time or know where to give blood.

C. These objections are poor excuses. (*Refutation*)
1. There is little or no pain in giving blood.
2. In sanitary conditions, you can't get a disease by *giving* blood.
3. The Red Cross makes it easy and convenient to give the gift of life.

Monroe's Motivated Sequence

In the mid-1930s, communication professor Alan Monroe took the basic functions of a sales presentation (attention, interest, desire, and action) and transformed them into a step-by-step method for organizing persuasive speeches. This became known as **Monroe's Motivated Sequence**.[28]

The unique visualization step in Monroe's Motivated Sequence (D in the outline on the next page) makes this organizational pattern useful for audience members who are uninformed, unconcerned, and unmotivated to listen, or for listeners who are skeptical of or opposed to the proposed course of actions.

In the outline on the next page, note how the speaker uses Monroe's Motivated Sequence to organize a presentation on how to liberate women suffering from brutality and injustice in poor countries.[29]

COMMUNICATION&CULTURE

TALL POPPIES AND BIG BRITCHES

In a highly individualistic culture such as the United States, many audience members will value individual achievement and personal freedom. In collectivist cultures (Asian and Latin American countries as well as in co-cultures in the United States), audience members are more likely to value group identity, selflessness, and collective action. Audiences in collectivist cultures place less importance on the opinions and preferences of the individual than do audiences in individualistic cultures.[30] In the United States, appeals that benefit individuals—personal wealth, personal success, personal health and fitness—may be highly persuasive, while appeals that benefit society at large and other families may be less effective.

In low-context cultures such as those of the United States, England, and Germany, audiences expect messages to be clear, factual, and objective. In the United States, persuasive appeals are often direct—do this; buy that; avoid that; just do it! In advertising, this would be termed a *hard-sell* approach to persuasion.

In contrast, high-context cultures such as Chinese, Japanese, Native American, African American, and Latino American expect messages that are implied and situation specific. A soft-sell approach would be a better persuasive strategy. When addressing a high-context audience, encourage listeners to draw their own conclusions. Demonstrate benefits and advantages rather than advocating action.

Differences among cultures are very real. At the same time, be cautious about how you interpret and use this information. Are all Japanese collectivist and high-context? Many young Japanese business professionals are learning and embracing American ways that include a more direct and self-centered approach to communication. Are all Australians individualistic? Although Australians are very independent and value personal freedom, they also live in a culture in which power distance is minimal. Public displays of achievement or wealth are frowned upon.[31]

One of your authors lived in Australia for a year and was introduced to the tall poppy syndrome. If, in a field of poppies, one red blossom grows higher than the others, you chop it off. When people show off or try to rise above others, you cut them down to size, too. "He thinks he's a tall poppy," describes someone who—in American terms—is "too big for his britches."

A persuasive speech can motivate audience members to take actions such as joining the CARE Action Network to help women in countries such as Afghanistan.

A. The Attention Step. Stories about abused women in Pakistan and Rwanda.
   1. Saima Muhammad, Pakistan, was beaten and starved by her husband.
   2. Claudine Mukakarisa, Rwanda, was imprisoned in a rape house.
B. The Need Step
   1. Millions of women in poor countries are beaten, disfigured, raped, murdered, or sold into slavery or brothels.
   2. Millions of girls in poor countries are denied medical care, education, and civil rights.
   3. Countries that suppress women's rights are often poor and torn apart by religious fundamentalism and civil war.

C. The Satisfaction Step
   1. Focus private and government aid on women's health and education.
   2. Grant small microfinance loans to women.
   3. Advocate for women's rights through international organizations and government agencies.
D. The Visualization Step
   1. Saima Muhammad's embroidery business now supports her family and employs thirty other families.
   2. Claudine Mukakarisa was "adopted" by a U.S. woman who helped her start a business.
E. The Action Step
   1. Contribute to legitimate organizations dedicated to helping women in need.
   2. "Adopt" a woman by lending money to support a business.
   3. Become an advocate for change by joining the CARE Action Network.

The visualization step (D in the outline) intensifies the audience's motivation to believe, feel, or act. By encouraging listeners to "see" the result of taking or failing to take action, you can strengthen the impact of your message.

Persuasive Speaking in Action

16.5 *Practice the communication competencies that characterize effective persuasive presentations.*

"Looking Through Our Window" by Ms. Marge Anderson, chief executive of the Mille Lacs Band of Ojibwe Indians, includes both informative strategies for generating audience interest *and* persuasive strategies that use different types of proof.[32]

Chief Anderson's speech also shows the power of language as described in Chapter 14, "Language and Delivery," as well as the value of storytelling, humor, and audience involvement as described in Chapter 15, "Speaking to Inform." As you read Ms. Anderson's presentation, notice how she:

- adapts to her audience's interests, attitudes, and beliefs about Indian people;
- adapts to the audience's level of motivation and listening habits;
- uses clear, oral, rhetorical, and eloquent language;
- tells two stories—one real, one mythic;
- cites novel, believable, and dramatic evidence;
- relies on her competence, character, and charisma to enhance her credibility;

- uses informative speaking strategies to explain "what it means to be Indian" and "how my People experience the world" to help them understand why they "should care about all this;"
- uses the audience-centered example of St. Thomas Aquinas and the story of Jacob wrestling with the angel as a theme and a form of mythos (narrative proof);
- includes logical, emotional, personal, and narrative persuasive proof;
- acknowledges and respects differences between Indians and non-Indians;
- employs a modified version of Monroe's Motivated Sequence.

Looking Through Our Window: The Value of Indian Culture

Address by Marge Anderson, former Chief Executive, Mille Lacs Band of Ojibwe[33]

Delivered to the First Friday Club of the Twin Cities Sponsored by the St. Thomas Aquinas College Alumni Association in St. Paul, Minnesota.

Aaniin. Thank you for inviting me here today. When I was asked to speak to you, I was told you are interested in hearing about the improvements we are making on the Mille Lacs Reservation, and about our investment of casino dollars back into our community through schools, healthcare facilities, and other services. And I do want to talk to you about these things, because they are tremendously important, and I am very proud of them.

But before I do, I want to take a few minutes to talk to you about something else, something I'm not asked about very often. I want to talk to you about what it means to be Indian. About how my People experience the world. About the fundamental way in which our culture differs from yours. And about why you should care about all this.

The differences between Indians and non-Indians have created a lot of controversy lately. Casinos, treaty rights, tribal sovereignty—these issues have stirred such anger and bitterness.

I believe the accusations against us are made out of ignorance. The vast majority of non-Indians do not understand how my People view the world, what we value, what motivates us.

They do not know these things for one simple reason: they've never heard us talk about them. For many years the only stories that non-Indians heard about my People came from other non-Indians. As a result, the picture you got of us was fanciful or distorted or so shadowy it hardly existed at all.

It's time for *Indian* voices to tell *Indian* stories.

Now, I'm sure at least a few of you are wondering, "Why do I need to hear these stories? Why should I care about what Indian People think, and feel, and believe?"

I think the most eloquent answer I can give you comes from the namesake for this university, St. Thomas Aquinas. St. Thomas wrote that dialogue is the struggle to learn from each other. This struggle, he said, is like Jacob wrestling the angel—it leaves one wounded and blessed at the same time.

Indian People know this struggle very well. The wounds we've suffered in our dialogue with non-Indians are well documented; I don't need to give you a laundry list of complaints.

Anderson uses her introduction to warmly greets audience members and acknowledges their interests in Indian casino income.

Chief Anderson uses the word Indian to refer to herself and her People. Why doesn't she use the phrase Native American? Research both terms and decide which term you think is most appropriate.

Here, the speaker presents a need step by describing the misunderstandings about the Indian culture and practices that lead to problems and conflict.

Anderson attempts to overcome audience disagreement through identification with St. Thomas Aquinas, a European who is the namesake of the university alumni association she is addressing.

To counter audience expectations, she assures the audience that she will not read a long list of complaints about the mistreatment of Indians.

Anderson identifies her central idea: Non-Indians should care about what it means to be Indian in the United States. Note her effective oral style in this section—simple words, short sentences, active voice, personal pronouns, and repetition.

Anderson carefully chooses her words, using they to refer to people who do not understand Indians, rather than you. You would carry a more accusatory tone.

We also know some of the blessings of this struggle. As *American* Indians, we live in two worlds—ours and yours. In the 500 years since you first came to our lands, we have struggled to learn how to take the best of what your culture has to offer in arts, science, technology, and more, and then weave them into the fabric of our traditional ways.

But for non-Indians, the struggle is new. Now that our People have begun to achieve success, now that we are in business and in the headlines, you are starting to wrestle with understanding us.

Your wounds from this struggle are fresh, and the pain might make it hard for you to see beyond them. But if you try, you'll begin to see the blessings as well—the blessings of what a deepened knowledge of Indian culture can bring you. I'd like to share a few of those blessings with you today.

Earlier I mentioned that there is a fundamental difference between the way Indians and non-Indians experience the world. This difference goes all the way back to the Bible, and Genesis.

In Genesis, the first book of the Old Testament, God creates man in his own image. Then God says, "Be fruitful, multiply, fill the earth and conquer it. Be masters of the fish and the sea, the birds of the heaven, and all living animals on the earth."

Masters. Conquer. Nothing, *nothing* could be further from the way Indian People view the world and our place in it. Here are the words of the great nineteenth-century Chief Seattle: "You are a part of the earth, and the earth is a part of you. You did not weave the web of life, you are merely a strand in it. *Whatever you do to the web, you do to yourself.*" In our tradition, there is no mastery.

When you begin to see the world this way—through Indian eyes—you will begin to understand our view of land, and treaties, very differently. You will begin to understand that when we speak of Father Sun and Mother Earth, these are not New Age catchwords—they are very real terms of respect for very real beings.

And when you understand this, then you will understand that our fight for treaty rights is not just about hunting deer or catching fish. It is about teaching our children to honor Mother Earth and Father Sun. It is about teaching them to respectfully receive the gifts these loving parents offer us in return for the care we give them. And it is about teaching this generation and the generations yet to come about their place in the web of life. Our culture and the fish, our values and the deer, the lessons we learn and the rice we harvest—everything is tied together. You can no more separate one from the other than you can divide a person's spirit from his body.

When you understand how we view the world and our place in it, it's easy to appreciate why our casinos are so important to us. The reason we defend our businesses so fiercely isn't because we want to have something that others don't. The reason is because these businesses allow us to give back to others—to our People, our communities, and the Creator.

Here, she identifies the *visualization step by addressing her audience directly* and describing how casinos not only preserve the Indian way of life, but also give back to non-Indians.

I'd like to take a minute and mention just a few of the ways we've already given back:

Chief Anderson provides *multiple examples* (factual and statistical) of the benefits of casino income. She begins each example with the word *we*, a *stylistic device* that helps her focus on Indian contributions.

- We've opened new schools, new healthcare facilities, and new community centers where our children get a better education, where our elders get better medical care, and where our families can gather to socialize and keep our traditions alive.
- We've created programs to teach and preserve our language and cultural traditions.
- We've created a small Business Development Program to help band members start their own businesses.
- We've created more than 2,800 jobs for band members, People from other tribes, and non-Indians.
- We've generated more than $50 million in federal taxes, and more than $15 million in state taxes through wages paid to employees.
- And we've given back more than $2 million in charitable donations.

The list goes on and on. But rather than flood you with more numbers, I'll tell you a story that sums up how my People view business through the lens of our traditional values.

Anderson concludes her list with a factual story (*narrative proof/mythos*) that reflects Indian values such as caring for others and the environment in which they live.

Last year, the Woodlands National Bank, which is owned and operated by the Mille Lacs Band, was approached by the city of Onamia and asked to forgive a mortgage on a building in the downtown area. The building had been abandoned and was an eyesore on Main Street. The city planned to renovate and sell the building, and return it to the tax rolls.

Notice how Anderson acknowledges and respects the differences between Indians and non-Indian views of business practices and beliefs.

Although the bank would lose money by forgiving the mortgage, our business leaders could see the wisdom in improving the community. The opportunity to help our neighbors was an opportunity to strengthen the web of life. So we forgave the mortgage.

Now, I know this is not a decision everyone would agree with. Some people feel that in business, you have to look out for number one. But my People feel that in business—and in life—you have to look out for *every* one.

And this, I believe, is one of the blessings that Indian culture has to offer you and other non-Indians. We have a different perspective on so many things, from caring for the environment to healing the body, mind, and soul.

But if our culture disappears, if the Indian ways are swallowed up by the dominant American culture, no one will be able to learn from them. Not Indian children. Not your children. No one. All that knowledge, all that wisdom, will be lost forever.

The struggle of dialogue will be over. Yes, there will be no more wounds. But there will also be no more blessings.

There is still so much we have to learn from each other, and we have already wasted so much time. Our world grows smaller every day. And every day, more of our unsettling, surprising, wonderful differences vanish. And when that happens, part of each of us vanishes too.

I'd like to end with one of my favorite stories. It's a funny little story about Indians and non-Indians, but its message is serious: you can see something differently if you are willing to learn from those around you.

This is the story: Years ago, white settlers came to this area and built the first European-style homes. When Indian People walked by these homes and saw see-through things in the walls, they looked through them to see what the strangers inside were doing. The settlers were shocked, but it makes sense when you think about it: Windows are made to be looked through from both sides.

Since then, my People have spent many years looking at the world through your window. I hope today I've given you a reason to look at it through ours. *Mii gwetch.*

The speaker describes what will happen if the Indian culture disappears, and reuses words from the earlier cited Aquinas quote—*struggle, dialogue, wounds, blessing.*

Here Anderson's message becomes more urgent and *rhetorical in style.* She talks about wasting time, a world growing smaller, and the risk that Indian culture will vanish.

In this final *action step,* Chief Anderson relies on *metaphor* to ask the audience to continue a productive dialogue with the Indian people.

The Ojibwas word for thank you becomes a "bookend" conclusion to a speech that begins with *aaniin.*

Her final story is a good example of *mythos. She previews* the story's moral, which helps her return to her *central idea.*

Persuasive Presentation Assessment

Use the following ratings to assess each of the competencies on this assessment instrument for a presentation you are preparing or for one you watch, listen to, and/or read.

E = excellent;   G = good;   A = average;   W = weak;   M = missing;   N/A = not applicable.

Competencies	E	G	A	W	M	N/A
Preparation and Content						
Purpose and topic						
Audience adaptation						
Adaptation to the context						
Introduction						
Organization						
Supporting material						
Transitions						
Conclusion						
Language						
Persuasive strategies						
Delivery						
Delivery mode						
Vocal delivery						
Physical delivery						
Presentation aids, if used						
Other Criteria						
Outline or manuscript						
Bibliography						
Other: _____						
Overall Assessment (circle one)	E	G	A	W	M	N/A
Comments:						

The Purpose of Persuasion

16.1 Describe the goals of persuasive presentations.

- Persuasion seeks to change audience members' opinions (what they think) or behavior (what they do).
- Whereas informative presentations *give* audience members advice or explanations, persuasive presentations *ask* for their agreement or a change in their opinions or behavior.

Persuading Others

16.2 Select persuasive strategies that adapt to audience attitudes.

- When audience members agree with you, present new information, strengthen audience resistance to persuasion, excite emotions, provide a personal role model, and advocate a course of action.
- When audiences disagree with you, set reasonable goals, find common ground, adapt to differences of opinion, use evidence, and build your personal credibility.
- When audience members are (1) undecided: gain their attention and provide relevant information; (2) unconcerned: gain their attention, give them a reason to care, and use strong evidence; (3) adamantly undecided: acknowledge their opinions and strengthen the arguments on your side of the issue.
- Psychological Reactance Theory explains why telling an audience what *not* to do can produce the exact opposite reaction.

Building Persuasive Arguments

16.3 Describe the components and characteristics of valid persuasive arguments.

- Include persuasive claims that, based on audience analysis, will most likely persuade that audience.

- The Toulmin Model of an Argument requires three major components: a claim, evidence, and a warrant. In many speaking situations, three additional components—backing for the warrant, reservations, and qualifiers—are also necessary to build a strong argument.
- Whichever arguments you choose, make sure you know whether they are advocating claims of fact, conjecture, value, or policy.
- Effective persuaders often use logical proof (*logos*), emotional proof (*pathos*), personal proof (*ethos*), and narrative proof (*mythos*) in presentations.
- When fear appeals are well crafted and well delivered, they can influence audience attitudes.
- *Heuristics* (cognitive shortcuts that are correct often enough to be useful when we make decisions) help explain why we believe arguments that rely on questionable claims, evidence, and warrants.
- Detect and avoid common fallacies of argument such as attacking the person, appeal to authority, appeal to popularity, appeal to tradition, faulty cause, and hasty generalization.

Persuasive Organizational Patterns

16.4 Identify organizational patterns appropriate for persuasive presentations.

- Organizational patterns particularly suited for persuasive speaking include problem/cause/solution, comparative advantage, refuting objections, and Monroe's Motivated Sequence.

Persuasive Speaking in Action

16.5 Practice the communication competencies that characterize effective persuasive presentations.

- Effective persuasive speakers adapt their content to the characteristics and attitudes of audience members and to the context of the presentation.

Key Terms

Appeal to authority	Ethos (personal proof)	Problem/cause/solution
Appeal to popularity	Evidence	pattern
Appeal to tradition	Fallacy	Proof
Argument	Faulty cause	Psychological Reactance
Backing	Hasty generalization	Theory
Claim	Heuristics	Qualifier
Claim of conjecture	Logos (logical proof)	Refuting objections pattern
Claim of fact	Monroe's Motivated	Reservation
Claim of policy	Sequence	Toulmin Model of an
Claim of value	Mythos (narrative proof)	Argument
Common ground	Pathos	Warrant
Comparative advantage	Persuasion	
pattern		

TEST YOUR KNOWLEDGE

16.1 *Describe the goals of persuasive presentations.*

1 Given that persuasion seeks to change audience *opinions* and/or *behavior*, which of the following examples represents an appeal to audience opinions?

   a. Eat dinner with your family at least five times a week.

   b. Vegetarian diets are good for your health and the planet's health.

   c. Buy a gas–electric hybrid car.

   d. Vote!

16.2 *Select persuasive strategies that adapt to audience attitudes.*

2 Which persuasive strategy is likely to be more effective when speaking to an audience that disagrees with you?

   a. Excite audience emotions.

   b. Provide a personal role model.

   c. Set reasonable goals.

   d. Give them a reason to care.

3 You can reduce the likelihood of a reactance response to a persuasive presentation by heeding all of the following strategies except _____.

   a. avoid strong direct commands such as "you must" or "stop"

   b. advocate a middle ground that preserves audience freedom

   c. avoid extreme statements depicting horrible consequences such as "you will die"

   d. use fear appeals to scare them into action

16.3 *Describe the components and characteristics of valid persuasive arguments.*

4 Which form of proof relies on touching audience emotions—fear, anger, pride, love, jealousy, or envy?

   a. Mythos

   b. Ethos

   c. Logos

   d. Pathos

5 In terms of Toulmin's Model of an Argument, which statement is the claim of this argument? "John is coughing, has a lot of chest congestion, been throwing up and has had a temperature of 102 degrees for several days. Given that all of these symptoms are signs of the flu, he probably has the flu."

   a. John is coughing with a lot of chest congestion.

   b. John probably has the flu.

   c. John has had a temperature of 102 degrees for several days.

   d. John has been throwing up.

16.4 *Identify organizational patterns appropriate for persuasive presentations.*

6 Which persuasive organizational pattern features the following three sections? (1) People should do X, (2) People don't do X for several reasons, (3) These reasons should not stop you from doing X.

   a. Problem/cause/solution

   b. Comparative advantage

   c. Refuting objections

   d. Monroe's Motivated Sequence

7 Which step in Monroe's Motivated Sequence is most useful for audience members who are uninformed, unconcerned, skeptical, or opposed to the proposed course of action?

   a. Attention step

   b. Need step

   c. Satisfaction step

   d. Visualization step

16.5 *Practice the communication competencies that characterize effective persuasive presentations.*

8 What kind of audience was Chief Marge Anderson seeking to persuade when she said the following?

   Now, I'm sure at least a few of you are wondering, "Why do I need to hear these stories? Why should I care about what Indian People think, and feel, and believe?" I think the most eloquent answer I can give you comes from the namesake for this university, St. Thomas Aquinas. St. Thomas wrote that dialogue is the struggle to learn from each other. This struggle, he said, is like Jacob wrestling the angel—it leaves one wounded and blessed at the same time.

   a. An audience that agrees with her.

   b. An audience that disagrees with her.

   c. An audience that is adamantly undecided.

   d. An audience that is unconcerned.

Answers found on page 368.

This *Communication Currents* article has been slightly edited (based on the original article in the *Quarterly Journal of Speech*) and shortened with permission from the National Communication Association.

Communication
Currents
Knowledge for Communicating Well

A Publication of the National Communication Association

Volume 6, Issue 2 - April 2011

Muhammad Ali's Fighting Words for Justice

While Muhammad Ali has been the subject of countless articles and books written by sports historians and journalists . . . there is a great benefit from paying attention to Ali's influential eloquence as a world renowned celebrity espousing nonviolence. Muhammad Ali is commonly remembered through famous lines like, "float like a butterfly, sting like a bee," "I am the greatest," "No Viet Cong ever called me a [racial slur]," and "The fight is won or lost far away from witnesses—behind the lines, ion the gym, and out there on the road, long before I dance under those lights."

In the 1960s and beyond, Ali's rhetoric played a pivotal role in radicalizing the civil rights movement as it evolved into the twin forces of the Black Power and anti-Vietnam war movements. Ali's speeches and public actions invited audience members to make a connection between boxing ring violence and peaceful civil disobedience against racism and the War in Vietnam. He also provided a bridge that united the messages of Martin Luther King, Jr. and Malcolm X. Ali was a fighter, a man of violence inside the ring who has worked nonviolently for peace and justice outside of it.

Ali used his star power in a peaceful, nonviolent way to publicly expose and decry racism and militarism that he saw and critiqued in the United States. His celebrity status bolstered his ego, enhancing his ability to speak his own mind in public, rather than to perform the traditionally accepted second-class status that most whites at that time expected of African Americans.

By understanding the rhetoric of Ali, we are better able to understand civil rights leaders in American history, who are sometimes pitted as if they were opposites, when in reality they were all working together to achieve social justice by ridding the U.S. of racist attitudes and practices, including the conduct of wars against peoples of other races, such as the war in Vietnam. Muhammad Ali used his fame, gained from the violence and suffering he experienced from years slugging it out in the boxing ring, to fight a different kind of fight, a symbolic campaign against racism and militarism.

Ali's boxing ring exploits and often egotistical pronouncements in press conferences gave him a unique voice and social position to support the

---

Assessment.

In Chapter 14, we described the CORE language styles: **c**lear, **o**ral, **r**hetorical, and **e**loquent. Identify and analyze Muhammad Ali's language style(s) based on these short examples.

Assessment.

Analyze Muhammad Ali's speaker credibility in terms of the three characteristics of ethos, competence, and charisma. To what extent did he demonstrate any or all of these characteristics? To what extent did Ali's ethos affect audience perceptions of his messages and actions?

Assessment. What is Ali's message in the following statement? "Champions aren't made in the gym. Champions are made from something they have deep inside them—a desire, a dream, a vision. They have to have last-minute stamina, they have to be a little faster, they have to have the skill and the will. But the will must be stronger than the skill." Was he just talking about boxing? How could his statement be interpreted in other ways?

Comment.

Unlike other African American sports stars such as Michael Jordan and Tiger Woods who have refused to speak out about political and racial issues, Muhammad Ali stood up and decried what he saw as an unjustified war and discrimination and racism. When Michael Jordan was asked why he did not endorse worthy candidates or become an advocate for public causes, he reportedly told a friend, "Republicans buy sneakers too."

Muhammad Ali before a 1975 boxing match.

Assessment. *Analyze the effectiveness of statements Ali made about his belief in Islam. What communication strategies did he rely on to justify his conversion and beliefs?*

Comment. *Ali's use of analogies and metaphors demonstrates their power to engage and persuade others.*

civil rights activism of Dr. King and the anti-racism platforms of various leaders from the Nation of Islam, such as Malcolm X. As a result of Ali's unabashed, fearless tone in public venues, he took a lot of heat from the media, the wider public, and the U.S. Government. Ali's legal case to fight his conscription into the Army went all the way to the U.S. Supreme Court, a case he won in 1971.

"Rivers, ponds, lakes and streams—they all have different names, but they all contain water. Just as religions do—they all contain truth."

"People recognize me for being a boxer and a man of truth. I wouldn't be here representing Islam if it were terrorist . . . . I think all people should know the truth, come to recognize the truth. Islam is peace."

When he was banned from boxing for three years, Ali had lost most of what would have been his prime boxing years, while also facing financial ruin. During that time, he toured the U.S., giving over two hundred speeches at university campuses and other venues. The booming voice of Ali, as an outspoken orator, as a fighter for peace

and nonviolence, may have been quieted in recent years by Parkinson's disease, but those who seek out his words and deeds in the annals of civil rights and anti-war activism will find his voice rings as clearly and loudly as ever.

"This is the legend of Cassius Clay, The most beautiful fighter in the world today. He talks a great deal, and brags indeed-y, Of a muscular punch that's incredibly speed-y."

"Standin' against me is completely absurd. When Cassius says a mouse can outrun a horse,

Don't ask how; put your money where your mouse is! I AM THE GREATEST!"

Comment. *Many of Muhammad Ali's statements were written as poetry. What follows are some excerpts from his "I Am the Greatest" speech:*

ABOUT THE AUTHORS

Ellen W. Gorsevski and **Michael L. Butterworth** are Assistant Professors in the Department of Communication at Bowling Green State University in Bowling Green, Ohio. This essay is based on Ellen W. Gorsevski and Michael L. Butterworth, "Muhammad Ali's Fighting Words: The Paradox of Violence in Nonviolent Rhetoric." *Quarterly Journal of Speech 97* (2011): 50–73. *Communication Currents* and the *Quarterly Journal of Speech* are publications of the National Communication Association.

glossary

A

A-E-I-O-U Model of Conflict Resolution A model of conflict resolution that focuses on communicating personal concerns and suggesting alternative actions.

Abstract words Words that refer to ideas or concepts, which cannot be observed or touched and often require interpretation.

Accenting nonverbal behaviors Nonverbal behavior that emphasizes important elements in a message by highlighting its focus or emotional content.

Accommodating conflict style A conflict style in which people give in to others for the purpose of preserving peace and harmony.

Active voice A sentence in which the subject performs the action. Example: *Erin read the book.*

Adaptors Habitual gestures that help manage and express emotions.

Affection need The need to feel liked by others.

Agenda An outline that puts the meeting topics in the order they will be discussed.

Aggression Behavior in which communicators put their personal needs first and demand compliance of others, often at the expense of someone else's needs and rights.

Alliteration A type of repetition in which a series of words with the same sound are placed together or very near to one another.

Analogy A comparison of two things that highlights a point of similarity.

Analysis paralysis A situation in which group members are so focused on analyzing a situation that they fail to make a decision.

Anger An emotional response to unmet expectations that ranges from minor irritation to intense rage.

Appeal to authority A fallacy of argument that uses the opinion of a supposed expert who has no relevant experience on the issue or topic.

Appeal to popularity A fallacy of argument in which an action is deemed acceptable and excusable because many people are doing it.

Appeal to tradition A fallacy of argument in which a certain course of action is recommended because it has always been done that way in the past.

Argument A claim supported by evidence and reasoning for or against a claim.

Argumentativeness Willingness to argue controversial issues with others.

Articulation The process of clearly making the sounds in the words of a language.

Assertiveness The willingness and ability to stand up for your own needs and rights while also respecting the needs and rights of others.

Audience analysis The process of understanding, respecting, and adapting to audience members before and during a presentation.

Audience attitudes The degree or extent to which the audience agrees or disagrees with the speaker.

Authority rule A decision making method in which the leader or an authority outside the group makes the final decision.

Autocratic leader A type of leader who tries to control the direction and outcome of a discussion, makes many of the group's decisions, gives orders, expects people to obey orders, and takes credit for successful results.

Avoidance conflict style A conflict style in which people change the subject, sidestep a controversial issue, or deny that a conflict exists because they are unable or unwilling to stand up for their own needs or the needs of others.

Avoidant decision maker A person who is uncomfortable making decisions, may not think about a problem at all, or who makes a decision at the last minute.

B

Backing A component of the Toulmin Model of an Argument that provides support for the argument's warrant.

Basic terms General words that come to mind when you see an object, such as *car* or *cat.*

Biased When an opinion is so slanted in one direction that it may not be objective or fair.

Brainstorming A simple and popular problem solving method in which group members generate as many ideas as possible in a short period of time.

Bypassing A form of miscommunication that occurs when people "miss each other with their meanings."

C

Cause-and-effect arrangement An organizational pattern that presents a cause and its resulting effects or details the effects that result from a specific cause.

Central idea A sentence that summarizes the key points of a presentation.

Channels The various physical and electronic media through which we express messages.

Character A component of speaker credibility that focuses on the speaker's perceived honesty and goodwill.

Charisma A component of speaker credibility that focuses on the speaker's levels of energy, enthusiasm, vigor, and commitment.

Claim The conclusion of an argument or the overall position advocated in a presentation, group discussion, or conversation.

Claim of conjecture A claim that something will or will not happen in the future.

Claim of fact A claim that can be proved true or false.

Claim of policy A claim that recommends a course of action or solution to a problem.

Claim of value A claim that asserts the worth of something—good or bad, right or wrong, best, average, or worst.

Clear style A language style that features short, simple, and direct words and phrases as well as active verbs, concrete words, and plain language.

Closed-ended questions Questions that only require a short and direct response, such as yes or no.

Closure principle A perceptual tendency to fill in missing elements to form a more complete impression of an object, person, or event.

Co-cultures A group of people who coexist within the mainstream society yet remain connected to one another through their cultural heritage.

Code switching The process of modifying the use of verbal and nonverbal communication in different contexts.

Cognitive restructuring A method for reducing communication anxiety by replacing negative, irrational thoughts with more realistic, positive self-talk.

Cognitive science The interdisciplinary study of the mind and intelligence that focuses on how people process information.

Cohesion The mutual attraction that holds the members of a group together.

Collaborative conflict style A conflict style in which people search for new solutions that will achieve both personal goals and the goals of others.

Collectivism   A cultural dimension that emphasizes the views, needs, and goals of the group rather than focusing on the individual.

Committee   A group created by a larger group or by a person in a position of authority to take on specific tasks.

Common ground   A place where you and your audience can stand without disagreement, often in terms of shared interests, beliefs, values, attitudes, or opinions.

Communication   The process of using verbal and nonverbal messages to generate meaning within and across various contexts, cultures, and channels.

Communication Accommodation Theory   A theory claiming that when we believe others have more power or have desirable characteristics, we may adopt their accepted speech behaviors and norms.

Communication apprehension   An individual's level of fear or anxiety associated with real or anticipated communication with another person or persons.

Communication competencies   Measurable performance standards that require the knowledge, skills, attitudes, and personal qualities essential to the practice of effective and ethical communication

Communication models   Illustrations that simplify and present the basic elements and complex interaction patterns in the communication process.

Comparative advantage pattern   A persuasive organizational pattern that proposes a plan for improving a situation or helping solve a problem while acknowledging that a perfect solution is not available or possible.

Comparison–contrast arrangement   An organizational pattern that demonstrates how two things are similar or different.

Competence   A component of speaker credibility that focuses on the speaker's perceived expertise and abilities.

Competitive conflict style   A conflict style in which people are more concerned with fulfilling their own needs than with meeting the needs of others.

Complementary nonverbal behaviors   Nonverbal behavior that is consistent with the verbal message being expressed at the same time.

Comprehensive outline   An all-inclusive presentation framework that follows established outlining rules.

Compromising conflict style   A conflict style in which people seek a "middle ground" by conceding some goals to achieve others.

Computer-mediated communication   The way we interact with others using various technologies and software ranging from simple texting to multimedia communication.

Concrete words   Words that refer to specific things you can perceive with your senses—smell, taste, touch, sight, or hearing.

Conflict   A disagreement that occurs in relationships when differences are expressed.

Connectives   The internal previews, summaries, transitions, and signposts that help connect key components of a presentation.

Connotation   The emotional responses or personal thoughts connected to the meaning of a word.

Consensus   A group agreement, which all members have a part in shaping and that all find at least minimally acceptable as a means of accomplishing mutual goals.

Constructive conflict   A conflict style in which people express disagreement in a way that respects others' perspectives and promotes problem solving.

Constructive nonconformity   Occurs when someone resists a group norm while still working to promote the group goal.

Content   The ideas, information, and opinions included in a message.

Context   The circumstances and settings in which communication takes place.

Contradictory nonverbal behaviors   Nonverbal behavior that conflicts with the meaning of spoken words.

Control need   The need to feel influential, competent, and confident.

Conversation   An interaction, often informal, in which a person exchanges speaking and listening roles with another person.

CORE language styles   Four basic language styles—**c**lear style, **o**ral style, **r**hetorical style, and **e**loquent style—used to express a message.

Coworker relationship   A relationship characterized by interactions among people who have little or no official authority over one another but who must work together to accomplish the goals of an organization.

Critical Thinking   The reasonable reflective thinking that focuses on deciding what to believe, do, or say.

Culture   A learned set of shared interpretations about beliefs, values, norms, and social practices that affect the behaviors of a relatively large group of people.

Customer relationship   Professional interactions between someone communicating on behalf of an organization and an individual who is external to the organization.

D

Decision making   The process of making a judgment, reaching a conclusion, or making up your mind.

Decoding   The decision-making process used to interpret, evaluate, and respond to the meaning of verbal and nonverbal messages.

Decreasing Options Technique (DOT)   A problem-solving method, which helps groups reduce and refine a large number of suggestions or ideas into a manageable set of options.

Defamation   A false statement that damages a person's reputation.

Defensive behaviors   Behaviors that reflect our instinct to protect ourselves when we are being physically or verbally attacked by someone.

Definition   A statement that explains or clarifies the meaning of a word, phrase, or concept.

Deintensification   The process of displaying facial expressions that reduce or downplay emotional displays in an effort to accommodate others.

Deliberation   A critical thinking and collective process that enlists the values of democracy and calls for thoughtful arguments, critical listening, and earnest decision making.

Delivery   The various ways in which you use your voice, body, and presentation aids to express a message.

Democratic leader   A leader who promotes the social equality and interests of group members.

Demographic information   Information about audience characteristics such as age, gender, marital status, race, religion, place of residence, ethnicity, occupation, education, and income.

Demonstration speeches   Presentations that use a series of well-ordered steps to show an audience how to do something and/or how something functions.

Denotation   The specific and objective dictionary-based meaning of a word.

Dependent decision maker   A person who solicits the advice and opinions of others before making a decision.

DESC script   A four-step assertiveness process (describe, express, specify, consequences) that provides an appropriate way of addressing another person's objectionable behavior.

Description   An explanation that creates a mental image in the minds of listeners by providing details about causes, effects, historical background information, and characteristics.

Destructive conflict   The result of behaviors such as constant complaining, personal insults, conflict avoidance, and aggressive arguments that create hostility or prevent problem solving.

Destructive nonconformity   Occurs when a group member resists conformity without regard for the best interests of the group and its goal.

Dialectics   The interplay of opposing or contradictory forces.

Discrimination   Behavior that expresses prejudice and excludes others from opportunities granted to members of mainstream cultures.

Documentation   The practice of citing the sources of supporting material in writing or orally in a presentation.

E

Eloquent style   A language style that features poetic and expressive language used in a way that makes thoughts and feelings clear, inspiring, and memorable.

Emblems   Gestures that express the same meaning as a word in a particular group or culture.

Emoticons   Typographical characters such as :-) or :-(that serve as substitutes for expressing emotions verbally.

Emotion   The feeling you experience when reacting to a situation that is often accompanied by physical changes.

Emotional intelligence   The capacity for recognizing our own feelings and those of others, for motivating ourselves, and for managing emotions in ourselves and in our relationships.

Emotional support   Specific communication behaviors enacted by one person with the intent of helping another person cope effectively with emotional distress.

Empathic listening   The ability to understand and identify with someone's situation, feelings, or motives when you hear what they say.

Encoding   The decision-making process you use to create and send messages that generate meaning.

Entertainment speaking   A presentation designed to entertain, amuse, interest, drive, or warm-up an audience.

Ethics   Agreed-on standards of right and wrong.

Ethnocentrism   The mistaken belief that your culture is a superior culture with special rights and privileges that are or should be denied to others.

Ethos (personal proof)   A Greek word for speaker credibility that refers to the perceived character competence, and charisma of a speaker; also a form of persuasive proof.

Euphemism   A bland, mild, vague, or unobjectionable word or phrase that substitutes for indecent, harsh, offensive, or hurtful words.

Evidence   A component of the Toulmin Model of an Argument that answers the question—how do you know that? Evidence can include facts, statistics, testimony, definitions and descriptions, analogies, examples, stories, and generally accepted audience beliefs.

Example   A word or phrase that refers to a specific case or instance in order to make large or abstract ideas concrete and understandable.

Exclusionary language   Words that reinforce stereotypes, belittle other people, or exclude others from understanding an in-group's message.

Exemplification   An impression management strategy in which you offer yourself as a good example or a model of noteworthy behavior.

Exit Interview   An interview conducted after an employee resigns in order to learn why the employee is leaving and what factors contributed to the decision to leave.

Expectancy Violation Theory   A theory that explains how your expectations about nonverbal behavior significantly affect how you interact with others and how you interpret the meaning of nonverbal messages.

Explanatory communication   Communication that deepens audience understanding of complex ideas and information by clarifying difficult terms, explaining quasi-scientific phenomena, or overcoming confusion and misunderstanding.

Expression-privacy dialectic   The desire to be open and honest with another person while also protecting your privacy.

Expressiveness   The vitality, variety, inflection, fluency, and sincerity a speaker puts into the delivery of a presentation.

Extemporaneous speaking   The most common form of delivery, which occurs when you use an outline as a guide for delivering a prepared presentation.

External noise   Physical elements in the environment that interfere with effective communication.

Extroverts   A Myers-Briggs personality type; People who are outgoing who talk more and gesture when they speak and enjoy interacting with others and solving problems in groups.

Eye contact   The practice of establishing and maintaining direct, visual links with individual audience members.

Eye scan   The practice of glancing at a specific section of your speaking notes or manuscript and then looking at your audience.

F

Face   The positive image you wish to create or preserve when interacting with others.

Fact   A verifiable observation, experience, or event known to be true.

Fallacy   An error in thinking that leads to false and invalid claims and has the potential to mislead or deceive others.

False consensus   A state of agreement in a group when members reluctantly give in to group pressures or an external authority in order to make a decision masquerading as consensus.

Faulty cause   A fallacy of argument that claims a particular situation or event is the cause of another situation or event before ruling out other possible causes.

Feedback   Any verbal or nonverbal response you can see or hear from others.

Feelers   A Myers-Briggs personality type; People who want to get along with others and will spend time and effort helping others and creating a supportive communication climate.

Filler phrases   Frequently overused and usually unnecessary words, phrases, or sounds—such as *you know*, *uh*, *um*, *okay*, and *like*—that break up a speaker's fluency and that can also annoy listeners.

5-M Model of Leadership Effectiveness   An integrated model of leadership that emphasizes specific communication strategies and skills appropriate for five interdependent leadership functions: modeling, motivating, managing, making decisions, and mentoring.

Fluency   The ability to speak smoothly without tripping over words.

Forming stage   A group development stage in which group members are becoming acquainted with each other and may be more worried about themselves ("Will I be accepted and liked?") than about the group as a whole.

Forum   An opportunity for audience members to comment or ask questions after a public discussion or presentation.

Freedom of speech   The clause in the first amendment to the U.S. Constitution that states: "Congress shall make no law . . . abridging the freedom of speech . . ."

Fundamental Interpersonal Relationship Orientation (FIRO) Theory   A theory asserting that people interact with others to satisfy three basic interpersonal needs for inclusion, control, and affection.

G

Gender expectations dimension   A cultural dimension that includes both expectations about suitable role behaviors as well as expectations about the preferred similarities and differences in the behaviors of men and women.

Gestures   Body movements that communicate an idea or emotion.

Gobbledygook   The result of using many words in place of one or using a multisyllable word where a single-syllable word would suffice.

Golden Listening Rule   An ethical listening practice: "Listen to others as you would have them listen to you."

Gossip   A type of rumor that focuses on the private, personal, or even scandalous affairs of others.

Governance group   An elected or appointed group that makes public policy decisions in public settings.

Group communication   The interaction of three or more interdependent people who interact for the purpose of achieving a common goal.

Group communication   The interaction of three or more interdependent people who interact for the purpose of achieving a common goal.

Group role   A pattern of behaviors associated with an expected function within a particular group context.

Groupthink   The deterioration of group effectiveness as a consequence of in-group pressure.

H

Hasty generalization   A fallacy of argument that claims something is true based on too little evidence or too few experiences.

Heuristics   Cognitive thinking shortcuts we use in decision making because they are often correct to be useful.

Hidden agenda   Occurs when a member's private goals conflict with the group's goals.

High power distance   A cultural dimension in which people accept differences in power as normal.

High-context culture   A cultural dimension in which more of a message's meaning is expressed through nonverbal cues and an understanding of the relationship among communicator than it is through language.

Hypothetical question   A question that describes a set of circumstances and asks how you would respond to those circumstances.

I

I **Language**   Using the word *I* to take responsibility for your own feelings and actions, rather than using *you* language to judge, blame, or criticize others.

Identification   A communication strategy that creates a common bond with your audience by demonstrating that you and your audience are *we* as opposed to *me* and *you*.

Illustrators   Gestures used with a verbal message that would lack meaning without the words.

Immediacy   The degree to which a person seems approachable or likable.

Impression management   The strategies people use to shape and control the way other people see them.

Impromptu speaking   The practice of speaking without advanced preparation or practice.

Inclusion need   The need to belong, to be involved, and to be accepted.

Individualism   A cultural dimension that emphasizes the values of independence, personal achievement, and individual uniqueness.

Inflection   The changing pitch within a syllable, word, or group of words during a presentation that makes speech expressive.

Informative presentation   A presentation designed to report new information, clarify difficult terms, explain scientific phenomena, and/or overcome confusion and misunderstanding.

Informative presentations   Presentations that seek to report new information, clarify difficult terms, explain scientific phenomena, and/or overcome confusion and misunderstanding.

Informatory and Explanatory Communication Theory   A theory that explains how to make strategic decisions about the content and structure of an informative presentation depending on whether they are primarily informatory or explanatory in nature.

Informatory communication   Communication that creates or increases audience awareness by reporting the latest, new information—much like news reporting.

Ingratiation   An impression management strategy in which you try to be liked by others by giving complements, doing favors, and/or offering comfort.

Inspirational speaking   Presentations that bring like-minded people together, create social unity, build goodwill, or celebrate by arousing audience emotions.

Integration-separation dialectic   The desire for *both* connection *and* independence; to be close to others without having to give up your separate self.

Intensification   The process of exaggerating facial expressions in an effort to meet other people's needs or to express strong feelings.

Interactional context   Refers to whether communication interaction occurs between two people, among group members, or between a presenter and an audience.

Interactive communication model   This model includes the concepts of noise and feedback to show that communication is not an unobstructed or one-way street.

Intercultural dimension   An aspect of a culture that can be measured relative to other cultures.

Internal noise   Thoughts, feelings, and attitudes that interfere with your ability to communicate and understand a message as it was intended.

Internal preview   A connective that identifies, in advance, the key points of a presentation or section in a specific order.

Internal summary   A connective that signals the end of a major section of a presentation and reinforces important ideas.

Interpersonal communication   Communication that occurs when a limited number of people, usually two, interact for the purpose of sharing information, accomplishing a specific goal, and/or maintaining a relationship.

Interpersonal communication   Communication that occurs when a limited number of people, usually two, interact for the purpose of sharing information, accomplishing a specific goal, or maintaining a relationship.

Interview   An interpersonal interaction between two parties in which at least one party has a predetermined purpose and uses questions and answers to share information, solve a problem, or influence the other.

Intimacy   The feeling or state of knowing someone deeply in physical, psychological, emotional, intellectual, and/or collaborative ways because that person is significant in your life.

Intimate distance   One of four spatial zones or distances, intimate distance is usually 0 to 18 inches and is associated with love, comfort, protection, and increased physical contact.

Intimidation   An impression management in which you threaten and provoke fear in others as a way to establish power and authority or to protect yourself.

Introverts   A Myers-Briggs personality type; People who think before speaking, are not very talkative, and often prefer to work alone.

Intuitive decision maker   A person who makes decisions based on instincts, feelings, or hunches.

Intuitives   A Myers-Briggs personality type; People who look for connections, overall concepts, and basic assumptions rather than focusing on details and procedures.

J

Jargon   The specialized or technical language of a profession or homogeneous group that allows members to communicate with each other clearly, efficiently, and quickly.

Jealousy   An intense feeling caused by a perceived threat to a relationship.

Johari Window   A model for understanding the connections between willingness to self-disclose and receptivity to feedback.

Judgers   A Myers-Briggs personality type; People who are highly structured, plan ahead, are punctual, and become impatient with those who show up late or waste time.

K

Key points   Points that represent the most important issues or main ideas in a presentation.

L

Laissez-faire leader   A leader who lets the group take charge of all decisions and actions.

Language   A system of arbitrary signs and symbols used to communicate thoughts and feelings.

Language intensity   The degree to which one's language deviates from bland, neutral terms.

Leader–member relations   A situational leadership factor that assesses how well a leader gets along with group members and whether the group is cooperative and supportive.

Leadership   The ability to make strategic decisions and use communication to mobilize group members toward achieving a common goal.

Leading question   A question that suggests or implies the response the questioner wants to hear.

Leakage cues   Unintentional nonverbal behavior that may reveal deceptive communication.

Linear communication model   The earliest type of communication model, which addresses communication that functions in only one direction: a source creates a message and sends it through a channel to reach a receiver.

Listener-responsible language   A language in which speakers communicate their meaning indirectly in terms of what they want listeners to know or do.

Listening   The process of receiving, constructing meaning from, and responding to a spoken and/or nonverbal message.

Listening to evaluate   The ability to analyze and make judgments about the validity of someone's spoken and nonverbal messages.

Listening to hear   The ability to make clear, aural distinctions among the sounds and words in a language.

Listening to interpret   The ability to empathize with another person's feelings without judging the message.

Listening to remember   The ability to store, retain, and recall information you have heard.

Listening to respond   The ability to respond in a way that indicates you fully understand someone's meaning.

Listening to understand   The ability to accurately grasp the meaning of someone's spoken and nonverbal messages.

Logistical context   The physical characteristics of a particular communication situation—focuses on a specific time, place, setting, and occasion.

Logistics   The strategic planning and arranging of people, facilities, time, and materials relevant to a presentation.

Logos (logical proof)   A Greek word for a form of persuasive proof that relies on reasoning and analysis and an audience's ability to think critically and arrive at a valid and justified conclusion or decision.

Low power distance   A cultural dimension in which power distinctions are minimized: supervisors work with subordinates; professors work with students; elected officials work with constituents.

Low-context culture   A cultural dimension in which meaning is expressed primarily through language; low-context speakers talk more, speak directly, and may fail to notice or correctly interpret nonverbal messages.

M

Maintenance role   A member role that positively affects how group members get along with one another while pursuing a common goal.

Majority vote   A vote in which more than half the members of the group vote in favor of a proposal.

Manuscript speaking   A form of delivery in which a speaker writes a presentation in advance and reads it out loud.

Markers   The placement of an object to establish nonverbal "ownership" of an area or space.

Masking   The process of changing your facial expressions to conceal true emotions by displaying expressions considered more appropriate in a particular situation.

Mass communication   Forms of mediated communication that occur between a person and large, often remote audiences; radio, television, film, publications, and computer-based media are all forms of mass communication.

Media Richness Theory   A theory that examines how the qualities of different media affect communication and helps explain why your physical presence makes a significant difference in communication situations.

Mediated communication   Any form of communication in which something (usually technology) exists between communicators; for example, telephone, e-mail.

Meeting   A scheduled gathering of group members for a structured discussion guided by a designated chairperson.

Memorized speaking   The practice of delivering a presentation from recall with very few or no notes.

Messages   Communication that generates meaning.

Metamessage   A message about a message.

Metaphor   A comparison between two unrelated things or ideas.

Mind mapping   An organizing technique that uses a hodgepodge of words, phrases, lists, circles, and arrows in order to encourage the free flow of ideas and help define the relationships among ideas.

Mindfulness   The ability to be fully aware of the present moment without making hasty judgments.

Mindlessness   A state that occurs when people allow rigid categories and false distinctions to become habits of thought and behavior.

Minutes   The written record of a group's discussion and activities.

Mixed message   A contradiction between the verbal and nonverbal meanings of a message.

Mnemonic   A memory aid based on similarities in the beginning letters of words, acronyms, or rhyme.

Monroe's Motivated Sequence   An organizational pattern for persuasive presentations that follows five steps: attention, need, satisfaction, visualization, and action.

Muted Group Theory   A theory claiming that powerful, wealthy groups at the top of a society determine and control who will communicate and be listened to.

Myers-Briggs Type Indicator   A theory about personality types that examines the ways in which we perceive the world around us as well as how we reach conclusions and make decisions.

Mythos (narrative proof)   A Greek word for persuasive proof that addresses the values, faith, and feelings that make up our social character and is most often expressed in traditional stories, sayings, and symbols.

N

Narrative Theory   A theory claiming that storytelling—an essential aspect of human communication—has two essential qualities: probability (coherence) and fidelity (truthfulness).

Narratives   The process, art, and techniques of storytelling.

Netlingo   A variety of language forms used in Internet communication.

Netspeak   Typographic strategies used to achieve a sociable, oral, and interactive communication style on the Internet.

Neutralization   The process of controlling your facial expressions in order to eliminate all displays of emotions.

Noise   Internal and external obstacles that can prevent a message from reaching its receivers as intended.

Nominal Group Technique (NGT)   A way of maximizing participation in problem solving while minimizing some of the interpersonal problems associated with group interaction.

Nonverbal communication   Message components other than words that generate meaning; nonverbal communication encompasses physical appearance, body movement, facial expressions, touch, vocal characteristics, and the communication context.

Norming stage   A group development stage in which members define their roles, establish norms, and determine how the group will do its work.

Norms   Sets of expectations held by group members concerning what kinds of behavior or opinions are acceptable or unacceptable.

Occasion   The reason an audience has assembled at a particular place and time.

Open-ended questions   Questions that encourage specific and detailed responses.

Optimum pitch   The pitch at which you speak most easily and expressively.

Oral footnote   A spoken citation that includes enough information for listeners to find the original sources.

Oral style   A language style that uses short, familiar words; succinct, simple, and even incomplete sentences; and more personal pronouns and informal colloquial expressions.

Organization   The way you arrange the content of your presentation into a clear and orderly sequence.

Organizational Culture Theory   A theory that describes the ways in which shared symbols, beliefs, values, and norms affect the behavior of people working in and with an organization.

Organizational subculture   A group of people who engage in behaviors and share values that are, in part, different from that of the larger organizational culture.

Other-oriented   People who are effective self-monitors and who give serious, undivided attention to, feel genuine concern for, and focus on the needs of other communicators.

Panel discussion   A type of public discussion in which several people interact about a common topic to educate, influence, or entertain an audience.

Paraphrasing   The ability to restate what people say in a way that indicates you understand them.

Passive aggressive   Behavior that appears to accommodate another person's needs, but actually represents subtle aggressive behavior.

Passive voice   A sentence in which the subject receives the action. Example: *The book was read by Erin.*

Passivity   Behavior characterized by giving in to others at the expense of your own needs in order to avoid conflict and disagreement.

Pathos (emotional proof)   A Greek word for a form of persuasive proof that appeals to deep-seated feelings and emotions.

Perceivers   A Myers-Briggs personality type; People who are flexible and adaptable thinkers and are likely to take risks, act spontaneously, and procrastinate.

Perception   The process we use to select, organize, and interpret sensory stimuli in the world around us.

Perception checking   A method for improving the accuracy of your perceptual interpretations and subsequent behavior.

Performing stage   A group development stage in which members focus their energy on working harmoniously to achieve group goals.

Person-centered messages   Messages that reflect the degree to which a helper validates a distressed person's feelings and encourages the person to talk about the upsetting event.

Personal distance   One of four spatial zones or distances, personal distance is 18 inches to 4 feet and is used with close personal friends.

Personal integrity   Behaving in ways that are consistent with your values and beliefs while also understanding and respecting others.

Personal relationships   Relationships characterized by a high level of emotional connection and commitment.

Personality   The style in which each of us interacts with the world around us and particularly with other people.

Persuasion   Messages that seek to change audience members' opinions (what they think) or behavior (what they do).

Persuasive presentation   A presentation designed to change or influence audience members' opinions and/or behavior.

Pitch   How high or low your voice sounds in terms of the notes on a musical scale.

Pitch   How high or low your voice sounds in terms of the notes on a musical scale.

Plagiarism   Using ideas, information, visuals, or a series of words, from another source and passing them off as your own.

Power distance   A cultural dimension in which there is a large physical and psychological gap between those who have power and those who do not.

Powerful language   Language that is direct, assertive, and persuasive.

Powerless language   Language that conveys uncertainty and a lack of confidence, often by using filler phrases, tag questions, qualifiers, and disclaimers.

Prejudices   Positive or negative attitudes about an individual or cultural group based on little or no direct experience with that person or group.

Preliminary outline   A first-draft outline that puts the major pieces of a presentation in a clear and logical order.

Presentation aids   Supplementary aids—most often visual—used for presenting and highlighting key ideas and supporting material.

Presentation speaking   The process of using verbal and nonverbal messages to generate meaning with audience members.

Presentational communication   Communication that occurs between speakers and their audience members.

Primacy effect   Our tendency to recall the first item in a sequence; the reason why audiences often recall a presentation's introduction.

Primary source   The document, testimony, or publication in which new information first appears.

Primary tension   The social unease and inhibitions that accompany the getting-acquainted period in a new group.

Probing question   A question used to follow up another question or a response by encouraging clarification and elaboration.

Problem solving   A complex process in which groups make multiple decisions as they analyze a problem and develop a plan for solving the problem or reducing its harmful effects.

Problem–solution arrangement   An organizational pattern that describes a harmful or difficult situation (the problem) and then offers a plan (the solution) to solve the problem.

Problem/cause/solution pattern   An organizational pattern often used in persuasive presentations that describes a serious problem, explains why the problem continues (the cause) and offers a solution.

Professional relationships   Relationships characterized by connections with people with whom you associate and work to accomplish a goal or perform a task.

Pronunciation   The process of putting all the correct sounds of a word in the correct order with the correct stress.

Proof   The arguments and evidence used to support and strengthen a persuasive claim.

Proxemics   The study of spatial relationships and how the distance between people communicates information about the nature of their relationship.

Proximity principle   A perception principle that explains why objects, events, or people that are physically closer to one another are more likely to be perceived as belonging together.

Psychoevolutionary Emotion Theory   A theory that explains the development and meaning of basic and mixed emotions.

Psychological Reactance Theory   A theory claiming that when people perceive a threat to their freedom to believe or behave as they wish, they may go out of their way to do the forbidden behavior or rebel against the prohibiting authority.

Psychosocial context   The psychological and cultural environment in which you live and communicate.

Public distance   One of four spatial zones or distances, public distance is 12 plus feet and is used in lectures, speeches, and public events.

Public group   A group that discusses issues in front of or for the benefit of public audiences.

Purpose statement   A specific, achievable, and relevant sentence that identifies the purpose and main ideas of your presentation.

Q

Qualifier   A component of the Toulmin Model of an Argument that states the degree to which a claim appears to be true using terms such as *probably, possibility, certainly, likely,* and *unlikely.*

Quasi-scientific phenomenon   A phrase used to explain how an explanatory presentation about a complex scientific phenomenon can deepen audience understanding without using complicated scientific terminology, data, and statistical methodologies.

Questions of conjecture   Questions that ask whether something will or will not happen in the future.

Questions of fact   Questions that ask whether something is true or false.

Questions of policy   Questions that ask whether and/or how a specific course of action should be taken.

Questions of value   Questions that ask whether something is worthy—good or bad, right or wrong, ethical or unethical, best, average, or worst.

R

Race   A socially constructed concept (not a scientific classification) that is the outcome of ancient population shifts which left its mark in our genes.

Racism   The assumption that people with certain characteristics (usually superficial characteristics, such as skin color) have inherited negative traits that are inferior to those of other races; the culminating effect of ethnocentrism, stereotyping, prejudice, and discrimination.

Rate   The number of words a person says each minute (wpm).

Rational decision maker   A person who carefully weighs information and options before making a decision.

Reactive jealousy   Occurs when a person becomes aware of a real, threatening danger to the relationship, such as learning that a romantic partner has, in fact, been unfaithful.

Receiver   The person or group of people who interpret and evaluate messages.

Recency effect   Our tendency to recall the last item in a sequence; the reason why audiences often recall a presentation's conclusion.

Reference groups   Groups with whom you identify and who influence your self-concept.

Refuting objections pattern   An organizational pattern in a persuasive presentation in which you refute and/or disprove each point that stands in opposition to your own.

Regulating nonverbal behaviors   Nonverbal behaviors are used to manage the flow of a conversation.

Relational Dialectics Theory   A theory which explains how the interplay of contradictory forces affects interpersonal relationships in three domains: integration-separate, stability-change, and expression-privacy.

Relationship   A continuing and meaningful attachment or connection to another person.

Relationship-motivated leader   A leader who gets satisfaction from working well with other people even if the group's task or goal is neglected.

Religious literacy   It requires an accurate, objective, and respectful understanding of the history, beliefs, principles, and practices of world religions as well as those we encounter in our daily lives.

Repetitive nonverbal behaviors   Nonverbal behavior that visually repeats a verbal message.

Reservation   A component of the Toulmin Model of an Argument that recognizes exceptions to an argument or conceded that a claim may not be true under certain circumstances.

Rhetoric   The ability to discover the available means of persuasion appropriate for a particular audience in a particular circumstance or setting.

Rhetorical devices   Word strategies designed to enhance a presentation's impact and persuasiveness.

Rhetorical style   A language style designed to influence, persuade, and/or inspire.

Roles   Patterns of behaviors associated with an expected function in a specific context or relationship.

Rumor   An unverified story or statement about the facts of a situation.

S

Secondary source   A source that reports, repeats, or summarizes information from one or more other sources.

Secondary tension   The frustrations and personality conflicts experienced by group members as they compete for social acceptance, status, and achievement.

Seductive details   Elements in a visual text or presentation aid that attract audience attention but do not support a writer's or speaker's key points.

Selective attention   A perceptual tendency to pay attention to messages that are consistent with what we already believe.

Selective exposure   A perceptual tendency to only expose yourself to messages that are consistent with what you already believe.

Selective interpretation   A perceptual tendency to alter the meaning of messages so they become consistent with what you already believe.

Selective recall   A perceptual tendency to remember messages and experiences so they are consistent with what you already believe about yourself and your encounters with others.

Self-assertiveness   Your willingness and ability to stand up for yourself in appropriate ways to satisfy your needs and pursue your goals.

Self-centered interests   Audience interests that can result in personal gain.

Self-centered role   A role assumed by group members who put their own goals ahead of the group's goal; can adversely affect member relationships and prevent the group from achieving its goals.

Self-concept   The sum total of beliefs you have about yourself.

Self-disclosure   The process of sharing personal information, opinions, and emotions with others that would not otherwise be known to them.

Self-effacing humor Humor directed at yourself rather than others.

Self-esteem Your positive and negative judgments about yourself.

Self-fulfilling prophecy An impression formation process in which an initial impression elicits behavior that conforms to the impression; a self-prediction you make that you cause to happen or become true.

Self-identification The process of integrating your cultural affiliations, the various roles you assume, and your experiences into your self-concept.

Self-monitoring A sensitivity to your own behavior and others' reactions as well as the ability to modify how you present yourself.

Self-observation The process of interpreting your actual performance (how you look and act) and your behavior (how well you do something) as a basis for your self-concept.

Self-presentation The communication strategies and skills you use to shape and control how others perceive, evaluate, and treat you.

Self-promotion An impression management strategy in which you attempt to earn the respect of others by demonstrating your competences.

Self-talk The silent statements you make to yourself about yourself.

Sensors A Myers-Brigs personality type; People who focus on details and prefer to concentrate on one task at a time.

Sexual harassment Unwanted sexual advances or inappropriate verbal or physical conduct of a sexual nature, which creates an intimidating, hostile, or offensive work environment.

Short-term or long-term A cultural dimension that focuses on future rewards (long-term) or on past and present rewards (short-term).

Sign Something that stands for or represents a specific thing and often looks like the thing it represents.

Signpost A connective that consists of a short phrase that—like a sign on the highway—tells or reminds listeners where they are in the organizational structure of a presentation.

Similarity principle A perception principle that explains why similar items or people are more likely to be perceived as a group.

Simplicity principle A perception principle that explains why we tend to organize information in a way that provides the simplest interpretation.

Situational Leadership Theory A theory that explains how leaders can become more effective by analyzing themselves, their group, and the situation in order to find or create an ideal match between leaders and leadership roles.

Six-Step Model of Conflict Resolution A model which offers six steps (preparation, initiation, confrontation, consideration, resolution, and reevaluation) that help you move through a conflict toward successful resolution.

Skills Your acquired ability to accomplish communication goals when interacting with others.

Slang Informal, nonstandard, everchanging colloquial words and phrases that tend to originate in a society's various subcultures.

Social comparison The process of evaluating yourself in relation to others in your reference groups.

Social distance One of four spatial zones or distances, social distance is 4 to 12 feet and is used in business settings and social gatherings with acquaintances.

Social judgments The process of interpreting how other people's verbal and nonverbal reactions to you as a basis for your self-concept.

Social Penetration Theory A theory that describes the process of relationship bonding in which individuals move from superficial communication to deeper, more intimate communication.

Source A person or group of people who create a message intended to produce a particular response.

Space arrangement An organizational pattern in which key points are arranged in terms of their location or physical relationship to one another.

Speaker credibility (ethos) The characteristics of a speaker that determine the extent to which an audience believes the speaker and the speaker's message.

Speaker-responsible language A language in which speakers provide the specific meaning of a message—what they will talk about and exactly what they want listeners to know or do.

Speaking outline The outline used by a speaker to deliver a presentation; it may be short and simple or a complex and detailed outline including significant supporting material.

Speaking style The manner in which you use vocabulary, sentence structure and length, grammar and syntax, and rhetorical devices to express a message.

Speech Framer A visual model for organizing presentation content that provides a place for every component of a presentation while encouraging experimentation and creativity.

Spontaneous decision maker A person who tends to be impulsive and make quick decisions on the spur of the moment.

Stability-change dialectic The desire for both stable relationship *and* the novelty and excitement of change; the predictability of day-to-day interactions *and* an occasional change in routine.

Standard Agenda A procedure that guides a group through problem solving by using the following steps: clarify the task, understand and analyze the problem, assess and choose solutions, and implement the decision or plan.

Statistics The results from collecting, summarizing, analyzing, and interpreting numerical data.

Stereotypes Generalizations about a group of people that oversimplify the group's characteristics.

Storming stage A group development stage in which members become more argumentative and emotional as they discuss important issues and vie for leadership.

Story An account or report about something that happened.

Story fidelity Refers to whether a story seems true and whether it resonates with listeners.

Story probability Refers to whether elements of a story, such as the consistency of characters and actions, hang together and make sense.

Strategies Specific plans of action that help you achieve your communication goals.

Styles Theory of Leadership A theory that examines three distinct leadership styles: autocratic, democratic, and laissez-faire.

Subordinate terms The most concrete words that provide specific descriptions.

Substituting nonverbal behavior Nonverbal behavior that replaces verbal language; for example, waving hello instead of saying "hello."

Superior–subordinate relationships Professional relationships in which the superior (supervisor) has formal authority over the productivity and behavior of subordinates (workers).

Superordinate terms Words that group objects and ideas together very generally.

Supplication An impression management strategy in which you seek attention and compassion from others by making humble requests and asking for help from others.

Supporting material Ideas and information that help explain and/or advance a presentation's purpose and key points.

Supportive behaviors Actions that create an encouraging and caring climate in which self-disclosure and responsiveness to feedback benefit both communicators.

Suspicious jealousy Occurs when a person suspects, but cannot prove, that someone has done something that threatens the future of a relationship.

Swear words Words that are considered taboo or disapproved of in a culture, but that may *not* be meant literally, and are typically used to express strong emotions and attitudes.

Symbols   An arbitrary collection of sounds or letters that in certain combinations stands for a concept but does not have a direct relationship to the thing it represents.

Symposium   A public group in which group members present short, uninterrupted presentations on different aspects of a topic for the benefit of an audience.

Systematic desensitization   A relaxation and visualization technique that helps reduce communication apprehension.

T

Task role   A member role that positively affects the group's ability to manage a task and achieve its common goal.

Task structure   A situational leadership factor that assesses how a group organizes or plans a specific task.

Task-motivated leader   A leader who gains satisfaction from completing a task even at the expense of group relationships.

Territoriality   The sense of personal ownership attached to a particular space.

Testimony   Statements or opinions that someone has spoken or written.

Theories   Statements that explain how the world works; theories describe, explain, and predict events and behavior.

Thinkers   A Myers-Briggs personality type; People who are analytical, objective, and task-oriented and who take pride in making difficult decisions.

Thought speed   The speed (words per minute) at which most people can think compared with the speed at which they can speak.

Time arrangement   An organizational pattern that arranges key points and message content according to time or calendar dates.

Time orientation   A multifaceted cultural dimension that focuses on time variables such as short and long term; past, present, and future; one-thing-at-a-time and many-things-at-a-time; and the pace of activities.

Topic   The subject matter of your presentation.

Topic-centered interests   Audience interests that listeners enjoy hearing and learning about.

Topical arrangement   An organizational pattern that divides a large topic into smaller subtopics in order to describe specific reasons, characteristics, or techniques.

Touch approachers   People who are comfortable with touch and often initiate touch with others.

Touch avoiders   People who are not comfortable initiating touch or being touched.

Toulmin Model of an Argument   A model of an argument in which a complete argument requires three major components: a claim, evidence, and a warrant, and in some cases, backing, a reservation, and/or a qualifier.

Trait Theory of Leadership   A theory that identifies specific characteristics and behaviors associated with effective leadership.

Transactional communication model   A communication model that shows how we send and receive messages simultaneously within specific contexts.

Transition   A connective that uses a word, number, brief phrase, or sentence to help a speaker move from one key point or section of a presentation to another.

Tuckman's Group Development Model   A model that identifies four discrete stages in the life cycle of groups—forming, storming, norming, and performing.

Turn-requesting cues   Verbal and nonverbal messages that signal a desire to speak, such as leaning forward, providing direct eye contact, and lifting your hand as if beginning to gesture.

Turn-yielding cues   Verbal and nonverbal messages that signal that you are completing your comments and are prepared to listen—for example, you may slow down your speaking rate.

Two-thirds vote   A vote in which at least twice as many group members vote for a proposal as against it.

V

Valid   Well founded, justified, and accurate.

Value step   A step in an informative presentation that captures audience attention by explaining how the message can enhance their personal well-being and success.

Values   Beliefs that guide your ideas about what is right or wrong, good or bad, just or unjust, and correct or incorrect.

Verbal communication   The ways in which we use the words in a language to generate meaning.

Virtual group   A group that relies on technology to communicate across time, distance, and organizational boundaries.

Visualization   A method for reducing communication apprehension and for building confidence by imagining what it would be like to communicate successfully.

Volume   A measure of loudness in a person's voice.

W

Warrant   A component of the Toulmin Model of an Argument that explains how and why the evidence supports the claim.

Whorf Hypothesis   A hypothesis, which claims that language influences how we see, experience, and interpret the world around us.

Word stress   The degree of prominence given to a syllable within a word or words within a phrase or sentence.

Work group   Groups that are responsible for making decisions, solving problems, implementing projects, or performing routine duties in an organization.

Work team   A group given full responsibility and resources for its performance.

Writing apprehension   The fear or anxiety associated with writing situations and topic-specific writing.

Y

You **language**   Using the word *you* to judge, blame, or criticize others, rather than using *I* language to take responsibility for your own feelings and actions.

Chapter 1

[1] Gardiner Harris, "New for Aspiring Doctors, the People Skills Test," *The New York Times*, July 11, 2011, p. A1.

[2] Gardiner Harris, "New for Aspiring Doctors, the People Skills Test," *The New York Times*, July 11, 2011, p. A12.

[3] In association with the National Communication Association, the Association for Communication Administration's 1995 Conference on Defining the Field of Communication produced the following definition: "The field of communication focuses on how people use verbal and nonverbal messages to generate meanings within and across various contexts, cultures, channels, and media. The field promotes the effective and ethical practice of human communication." See http://www.natcom.org. The definition in this textbook is a more succinct version of the NCA definition.

[4] See Sherwyn P. Morreale, Michael M. Osborn, and Judy C. Pearson, "Why Communication Is Important: A Rationale for the Centrality of the Study of Communication," *Journal of the Association for Communication Administration* 29 (2000): 1–25. The authors of this article annotated nearly 100 articles, commentaries, and publications that call attention to the importance of studying communication.

[5] Robert M. Diamond, "Designing and Assessing Courses and Curricula," *Chronicle of Higher Education*, August 1, 1997, p. B7.

[6] Robert W. Pike, *High-Impact Presentations* (West Des Moines, IA: American Media, 1995), p. 9.

[7] Business-Higher Education Forum in affiliation with the American Council on Education, *Spanning the Chasm: Corporate and Academic Cooperation to Improve Work-Force Preparation* (Washington, DC: American Council on Education, 1997).

[8] "Graduates Are Not Prepared to Work in Business," *Association Trends* (June 1997): 4.

[9] American Management Association, *The AMA 2010 Critical Skills Survey*, http://www.p21.org/storage/documents/Critical%20Skills%20Survey%20Executive%20Summary.pdf, pp. 1-3. On p. 2, The *AMA 2010* report defines the four skill areas as follows:

- Critical thinking and problem solving—including the ability to make decisions, solve problems, and take action as appropriate;
- Effective communication—the ability to synthesize and transmit your ideas both in written and oral formats;
- Collaboration and team building—the ability to work effectively with others, including those from diverse groups and with opposing points of view;
- Creativity and innovation—the ability to see what's NOT there and make something happen.

[10] Rob Anderson and Veronica Ross, *Questions of Communication: A Practical Introduction to Theory*, 3rd ed. (New York: St. Martin's Press, 2002), p. 69.

[11] Pew Research Global Attitudes Project, *Arab Publics Most Likely to Express Political Views Online*, December 12, 2012, http://www.pewglobal.org/2012/12/12/social-networking-popular-across-globe.

[12] "Social Media Helped But Did Not Cause Arab Spring," *Homeland Security News Wire*, January 13, 2013, http://www.homelandsecuritynewswire.com/dr20130116-social-media-helped-but-did-not-cause-arab-spring.

[13] "After the Arab Spring, Signs of Chaos, Progress," *The Chicago Tribune*, January 30, 2013, http://articles.chicagotribune.com/2013-01-30/news/ct-edit-arab-0130-jm-20130130_1_morsi-civil-war-obama-administration.

[14] In this textbook, we prefer and use the broader term *presentational communication* rather than *public speaking* to describe the act of speaking before an audience. Public speaking is one type of presentational communication that occurs when a speaker addresses a public audience. See Isa N. Engleberg and John A. Daly, *Presentations in Everyday Life*, 3rd ed. (Boston: Pearson/Allyn and Bacon, 2009), p. 4; Isa N. Engleberg and John A. Daly, *Think Public Speaking* (Boston: Pearson, 2013), p. 5.

[15] See Richard L. Daft and Robert H. Lengel, "Information Richness: A New Approach to Managerial Behaviour and Organizational Design," in Barry M. Staw and Larry L. Cummings (Eds.), *Research in Organizational Behavior* (Greenwich, CT: JAI Press, 1984), pp. 355–366; Richard L. Daft, Robert H. Lengel, and Linda K. Trevino, "Message Equivocality, Media Selection, and Manager Performance: Implications for Information Systems," *MIS Quarters* 11 (1987): 355–366; Linda K. Trevino, Robert K. Lengel, and Richard L. Daft, "Media Symbolism, Media Richness, and Medic Choice in Organizations," *Communication Research* 14 (1987): 553–574.

[16] Corry Janssen, "Computer-Mediated Communication (CMC)," Technopedia, http://www.techopedia.com/definition/392/computer-mediated-communication-cmc.

[17] Erin M. Bryant, Jennifer Marmo, and Artemio Rimerez, Jr., "A Functional Approach to Social Networking Sites," in Kevin B. Wright and Lynne M. Webb (Eds.), *Computer-Mediated Communication in Personal Relationships* (New York, Peter Lang Publishing, 2011), p. 21.

[18] Geoffrey A. Fowler, "Facebook: One Billion and Counting," *The Wall Street Journal*, U.S. Edition, October 4, 2012, http://online.wsj.com/article/SB1000087

23963904436354045780361640273886112.html; Ingrid Lunden, "Analysis: Twitter Passed 500M Users In June 2012, 140M Of Them In US; Jakarta 'Biggest Tweeting' City, *TechCrunch*. July 30th, 2012, http://techcrunch.com/2012/07/30/analyst-twitter-passed-500m-users-in-june-2012-140m-of-them-in-us-jakarta-biggest-tweeting-city.

[19] "What's Happening?" *Twitter Blog*, November 19, 2009, http://blog.twitter.com/2009/11/whats-happening.html.

[20] Kevin B. Wright and Lynne M. Webb, "Preface," in Kevin B. Wright and Lynn M. Webb (Eds.), *Computer-Mediated Communication in Personal Relationships* (New York, Peter Lang Publishing, 2011), p. xvi.

[21] Charles Woodruffe, "What Is Meant by a Competency?" *Leadership and Organization Development Journal* 14 (1993): 29–36.

[22] Karl R. Popper, *The Logic of Scientific Discovery* (New York: Basic Books, 1959), p. 59.

[23] Mark A. Albanese et al., "Defining Characteristics of Educational Competencies." *Medical Education* 42 (2008): 248–255, http://www.personal.umich.edu/~rbrent/jc/albanese2008defining.pdf.

[24] Press Release, "Scientists Discover Why We Never Forget how to Ride a Bicycle," University of Aberdeen, King's College, July 17, 2009, http://www.abdn.ac.uk/news/archive-details-3980.php; Peer Wulff et al., "Synaptic Inhibition of Purkineje Cells Mediates Consolidation of Vestibulocerebeller Motor Learning," *Nature Neuroscience* 12 (2009): 1041–1049.

[25] Based on Robert H. Ennis, "Definitions of Critical Thinking," Robert H. Ennis's Academic Web Site, September 6, 2011, http://faculty.education.illinois.edu/rhennis/index.html. See also Brooke Noel Moore and Richard Parker, *Critical Thinking*, 5th ed. (Mountain View, CA: Mayfield, 1998); John Chaffee, *Thinking Critically*, 6th ed. (Boston: Houghton-Mifflin, 2000); Richard W. Paul, *Critical Thinking: How to Prepare Students for a Rapidly Changing World* (Santa Rosa, CA: Foundation for Critical Thinking, 1995); and Vincent Ryan Ruggero, *Becoming a Critical Thinker*, 4th ed. (Boston: Houghton Mifflin, 2002).

[26] Isa N. Engleberg and John A. Daly, *Presentations in Everyday Life*, 3rd ed. (Boston: Pearson/Allyn & Bacon, 2009), p. 59.

[27] John Chaffee, *Thinking Critically*, 7th ed. (Boston: Houghton Mifflin, 2003), p. 51.

[28] Robert H. Ennis, "Critical Thinking Assessment," *Theory into Practice* 32 (1993), p. 180.

[29] Based on Robert Ennis, "Critical Thinking: A Streamlined Conception," *Teaching Philosophy* 14 (1991): 8–9; Robert H. Ennis's Academic Web Site, September 6, 2011, http://faculty.education.illinois.edu/rhennis/index.html.

[30] Rob Anderson and Veronica Ross, *Questions of Communication: A Practical Introduction to Theory*, 3rd ed. (New York: St. Martin's Press, 2002), p. 301.

[31] Richard L. Johannesen, *Ethics in Human Communication*, 5th ed. (Prospect Heights, IL: Waveland Press, 2002), p. 1.

[32] National Communication Association Credo for Ethical Communication, http://www.natcom.org/aboutNCA/Policies/Platform.html.

[33] National Communication Association, http://www.natcom.org/uploadedFiles/About_NCA/Leadership_and_Governance/Public_Policy_Platform/PDF-PolicyPlatform-Credo_for_a_Free_and_Responsible_Communication_in_a_Democratic_Society.pdf. The Speech Association of America became the National Communication Association.

[34] Ryan Blethen, "Understand the Consequences of Free Speech," *The Seattle Times*, August 22, 2009, http://seattletimes.com/html/opinion/2009716909_ryan23.html. Note: *Defamation* is defined as a false statement communicated to another person that damages the person's reputation. Libel is communicating a defamatory statement by writing or picture, whereas slander is defamation by oral or spoken communication. See Oregon State Bar, "Libel and Slander," January 2012, http://www.osbar.org/public/legalinfo/1186_LibelSlander.htm.

Chapter 2

[1] Philippe Rochat, "Five Levels of Self-awareness as They Unfold Early in Life," *Consciousness and Cognition* 12 (2003): 717–731, http://psychology.emory.edu/cognition/rochat/Five%20levels%20.pdf.

[2] Sharon S. Brehm, Saul M. Kassin, and Steven Fein, *Social Psychology*, 6th ed. (Boston: Houghton Mifflin, 2005), p. 57.

[3] Nathaniel Branden, http://www.nathanielbranden.com.

[4] Leon Festinger, "A Theory of Social Comparison Processes," *Human Relations* 7 (1954): 117–140.

[5] Albert Bandura, *Social Foundations of Thought and Action: A Social Cognitive Theory* (Englewood Cliffs, NJ: Prentice Hall, 1986), pp. 399–408. Quoted in William Crain, *Theories of Development: Concepts and Applications*, 4th ed. (Upper Saddle River, NJ: Prentice Hall, 2000), p. 203.

[6] Min-Sun Kim, *Non-Western Perspectives on Human Communication* (Thousand Oaks, CA: Sage, 2002), p. 9.

[7]Sharon S. Brehm, Saul M. Kassin, and Steven Fein, *Social Psychology*, 6th ed. (Boston: Houghton Mifflin, 2005), p. 65.

[8]Monica T. Whitty and Adam N. Joinson, *Truth, Lies and Trust on the Internet* (New York: Routledge/Taylor & Fancis, 2009).

[9]Susan B. Barnes, *Online Connections: Internet Interpersonal Relationships* (Cresskill, NJ: Hampton Press, 2001), p. 234.

[10]Susan B. Barnes, *Online Connections: Internet Interpersonal Relationships* (Cresskill, NJ: Hampton Press, 2001), p. 91.

[11]Jeffrey Hall et al., "Strategic Misrepresentation in Online Dating: The Effects of Gender, Self-Monitoring, Personality, and Demographics," paper presented at the National Communication Association Convention, 2008; John R. Schafer, "Let Their Word Do the Talking: Verbal Cues to Detect Deception," November 3, 2011, http://www.psychologytoday.com/blog/let-their-words-do-the-talking/201111/detecting-deception-in-online-profiles.

[12]John R. Schafer, "Let Their Word Do the Talking: Verbal Cues to Detect Deception," November 3, 2011, http://www.psychologytoday.com/blog/let-their-words-do-the-talking/201111/detecting-deception-in-online-profiles.

[13]Avner Caspi and Paul Gorsky, "Online Deception: Prevalence, Motivation, and Emotion," *Cyber Psychology and Behavior* 9 (2009): 54.

[14]Reported by Robert Epstein in "The Truth About Online Dating," *Scientific American Mind*, January 30 2007, p. 31.

[15]Robert Epstein in "The Truth About Online Dating," *Scientific American Mind*, January 30, 2007, pp. 32–33.

[16]Robert Epstein in "The Truth About Online Dating," *Scientific American Mind*, January 30, 2007, p. 33.

[17]Nathaniel Branden, http://www.nathanielbranden.com.

[18]Roy F. Baumeister et al., "Exploding the Self-Esteem Myth," Scientific American.com, January 2005, http://www.papillonsartpalace.com/exSplodin.htm; http://cranepsych.edublogs.org/files/2099/06/Self_esteem_myth.pdf.

[19]Nathaniel Branden, *The Six Pillars of Self-Esteem* (New York: Bantam, 1994), pp. 117–128; Nathaniel Branden, *The Power of Self-Esteem* (Deerfield Beach, FL: Health Communications, 1992), pp. 168–169.

[20]Nathaniel Branden, *The Six Pillars of Self-Esteem* (New York: Bantam, 1994), p. 128.

[21]Nathaniel Branden, *The Six Pillars of Self-Esteem* (New York: Bantam, 1994), pp. 142–167; Nathaniel Branden, *The Power of Self-Esteem* (Deerfield Beach, FL: Health Communications, 1992), pp. 168–169.

[22]Based on Nathaniel Branden, *The Six Pillars of Self-Esteem* (New York: Bantam, 1994), pp. 144–145.

[23]Morris Rosenberg, *Society and the Adolescent Self-Image* (Princeton, NJ: Princeton University Press, 1965).

[24]Elizabeth Scott, "Reduce Stress and Improve Your Life with Positive Self-Talk," About.com, April 11, 2011, http://stress.about.com/od/optimismspirituality/a/positiveselftak.htm?p=1.

[25]Anthony G. Greenwald, "The Totalitarian Ego: Fabrication and Revision of Personal History," *American Psychologist* 35 (1980): 603–618.

[26]Richard E. Boyatzis, "Developing Emotional Intelligence Competencies," in Joseph Ciarrochi and John D. Mayer (Eds.), *Applying Emotional Intelligence: A Practitioner's Guide* (New York: Psychology Press, 2007), p. 42.

[27]Nathaniel Branden, http://www.nathanielbranden.com.

[28]Roy F. Baumeister et al., "Exploding the Self-Esteem Myth," Scientific American.com, January 2005, http://www.papillonsartpalace.com/exSplodin.htm; http://cranepsych.edublogs.org/files/2009/06/Self_esteem_myth.pdf.

[29]Nathaniel Branden, *The Art of Living Consciously: The Power of Awareness to Transform Everyday Life* (New York: Fireside Books/Simon and Schuster, 1999), pp. 168–169.

[30]"Women's Math Scores Affected by Suggestions," *The Washington Post*, October 20, 2006, p. A11. This article summarizes a study published in the October 2006 issue of *Science*.

[31]Sam Dillon, "Praise, Advice and Reminders of the Sour Economy for Graduates," *The New York Times*, June 14, 2009, p. A18.

[32]Mark R. Leary and Robin M. Kowalski, "Impression Management: A Literature Review and Two-Component Model," *Psychological Bulletin* 107 (1990): 34.

[33]See Erving Goffman, *The Presentation of Self in Everyday Life* (New York: Doubleday, 1959).

[34]Mark R. Leary and Robin M. Kowalski, "Impression Management: A Literature Review and Two-Component Model," *Psychological Bulletin* 107 (1990): 34.

[35]See Mark Snyder, "Self-Monitoring of Expressive Behavior," *Journal of Personality and Social Psychology* 30 (1974): 526–537; Mark Snyder and Steven Gangestad, "On the Nature of Self-Monitoring: Matters of Assessment, Matters of Validity," *Journal of Personality and Social Psychology* 51 (1986): 125–139; Steven W. Gangestad and Mark Snyder, "Self-Monitoring: Appraisal and Reappraisal," *Psychological Bulletin* 126 (2000): 530–555.

[36]Self-Monitoring, *SpringerReference*, http://www.springerreference.com/docs/html/chapterdbid/346016.html.

[37]Frederick Muench, "Self-Monitoring Made Easy," Published on *Psychology Today*'s web site, http:www.psychologytoday.com/print/47706, September 10, 2010, p. 1.

[38]Frederick Muench, "Self-Monitoring Made Easy," Published on *Psychology Today*'s web site, http:www.psychologytoday.com/print/47706), September 10, 2010, p. 1.

[39]"Self-Awareness," http://en.wikipedia.org/wiki/Self-awareness.

[40]William H. Turnley and Mark C. Bolino, "Achieving Desired Images While Avoiding Undesired Images: Exploring the Role of Self-Monitoring in Impression Management," *Journal of Applied Psychology* 80 (2001): 351.

[41]Derived from Edward E. Jones and Thane S. Pittman, "Toward a General Theory of Strategic Self-Presentation," in Jerry M. Suls (Ed.), *Psychological Perspectives on the Self, Vol 1* (Hillside, NJ: Erlbaum, 1982), pp. 231–262. See also Sandra Metts and Erica Grohskopf, "Impression Management: Goals, Strategies, and Skills," John O. Greene and Brant Burleson (Eds.), in *Handbook of Communication and Social Interaction Skills* (Mahwah, NJ: Lawrence Erlbaum, 2003), pp. 358–359. We have added parenthetical cautions to the list of strategies.

[42]Daniel Goleman, *Emotional Intelligence* (New York: Bantam, 1995), pp. 43, 47.

[43]Benjamin Weiser, "In New Jersey, Sweeping Shift on Witness IDs," *The New York Times*, August 25, 2011, p. A1.

[44]Adam Liptak, "Often Wrong but Rarely in Doubt: Eyewitnesses," *The New York Times*, August 23, 2011, p. A14.

[45]Brandon L Garrett, *Convicting the Innocent: Where Criminal Prosecutions Go Wrong* (Cambridge, MA: Harvard University Press, 2012); See also www.huffingtonpost.com/brandon-l-garrett.

[46]Adam Liptak, "Often Wrong but Rarely in Doubt: Eyewitnesses," *The New York Times*, August 23, 2011, p. A14.

[47]Yamiche Alcindor, "Differing Accounts Make Zimmerman Prosecution Tougher," *USA Today*, June 4, 2012, p. 2A.

[48]Yamiche Alcindor, "Differing Accounts Make Zimmerman Prosecution Tougher," *USA Today*, June 4, 2012, p. 2A.

[49]Note: There is a rich history of academic research on the "selectives" with foundations in psychology, attitude change, and mass media. Researchers include Leon Festinger, Melvin Lawrence DeFleur, Paul Lazarfeld, and Joseph Klapper and along with more contemporary scholarship that expands their work. In this chapter, we changed the phrase *selective perception* to *selective interpretation* because the use of the term *perception* in this phrase often confuses readers about the overall function of the selectives.

[50]Stanley J. Baran and Dennis K. Davis, *Mass Communication Theory: Foundations, Ferment, and Future*, 6th ed. (Boston: Wadsworth/Centage Learning, 2012), p. 154.

[51]Nate Silver, *The Signal and Noise* (New York: Penguin Press, 2012), p. 4.

[52]Ruth Marcus, "Inclined to Believe the Worst," *The Washington Post*, March 13, 2012, p. A17.

[53]Nate Silver, *The Signal and Noise* (New York: Penguin Press, 2012), p. 4.

[54]Douglas A. Bernstein et al., *Psychology*, 7th ed. (Boston: Houghton Mifflin, 2006), p. 162.

[55]Douglas A. Bernstein et al., *Psychology*, 7th ed. (Boston: Houghton Mifflin, 2006), p. 162.

[56]Richard E. Nisbett, *The Geography of Thought: How Asians and Westerners Think Differently … and Why* (New York: Free Press, 2003), p. 87.

[57]J. Richard Block and Harold Yuker, *Can You Believe Your Eyes?* (New York: Gardner Press, 1989), p. 239.

[58]Ronald B. Adler, Lawrence B. Rosenfeld, and Russell F. Proctor II, *Interplay: The Process of Interpersonal Communication*, 8th ed. (Fort Worth, TX: Harcourt Brace, 2001), p. 114.

[59]"The Golden Rule is found in the New Testament (Matthew 7:12, NIV) but is often confused with the related admonition to 'love your neighbor as yourself,' which appears repeatedly in both the Hebrew Bible and the New Testament. . . . The Golden Rule has also been attributed to other religious leaders, including Confucius, Muhammad, and the first-century rabbi Hillel." Stephen Prothero, *Religious Literacy: What Every American Needs to Know—And Doesn't* (New York: HarperCollins, 2007), pp. 182–183.

[60]George Bernard Shaw, *Maxims for a Revolutionist* (1903).

[61]The discussion of communication apprehension is based on Chapter 2 of Isa Engleberg and John Daly, *Presentations in Everyday Life*, 3rd ed. (Boston: Pearson/Allyn and Bacon, 2009), and Chapter 3 of Isa Engleberg and Dianna Wynn, *Working in Groups: Communication Principles and Strategies*, 6th ed. (Boston: Pearson, 2013).

[62]Virginia P. Richmond, Jason S. Wrench, and James C. McCroskey, *Communication: Apprehension, Avoidance, and Effectiveness*, 6th ed. (Boston: Pearson, 2013), p. 27.

[63]Sharon S. Brehm, Saul M. Kassin, and Steven Fein, *Social Psychology*, 6th ed. (Boston: Houghton Mifflin, 2005), p. 525.

[64]Virginia P. Richmond, Jason S. Wrench, and James C. McCroskey, *Communication: Apprehension, Avoidance, and Effectiveness*, 6th ed. (Boston: Pearson, 2013), p. 31.

[65]James C. McCroskey, "Oral Communication Apprehension: Summary of Recent Theory and Research," *Human Communication Research* 4 (1977): 80.

[66]Michael J. Beatty and James McCroskey with Kristin M. Valencic, *The Biology of Communication: A Communibiological Perspective* (Cresskill, NJ: Hampton, 2001), p. 80.

[67]Virginia P. Richmond, Jason S. Wrench, and James C. McCroskey, *Communication: Apprehension, Avoidance, and Effectiveness*, 6th ed. (Boston: Pearson, 2013), p. 106.

[68]Peter Desberg, *Speaking Scared, Sounding Good* (Garden City Park, NY: Square One Publishers, 2007), pp. 101–110. Desberg describes several effective relaxation exercises that readers can practice. Desberg notes, "Fortunately, it feels great to practice them." (p. 100).

[69]See John A. Daly and James C. McCroskey, (Eds.), *Avoiding Communication: Shyness, Reticence, and Communication Apprehension* (Thousand Oaks, CA: Sage, 1984); Virginia P. Richmond, Jason S. Wrench, and James C. McCroskey, *Communication: Apprehension, Avoidance, and Effectiveness*, 6th ed. (Boston: Pearson, 2013); Karen Kangas Dwyer, *Conquer Your Speechfright*, 2nd ed. (Belmont, CA: Thomson Wadsworth, 2005); Michael T. Motley, *Overcoming Your Fear of Public Speaking: A Proven Method* (Boston: Houghton Mifflin, 1997).

[70]Karen Kangas Dwyer, *Conquer Your Speechfright*, 2nd ed. (Belmont, CA: Thomson Wadsworth, 2005), p. 23.

[71]Peter Desberg, *Speaking Scared, Sounding Good* (Garden City Park, NY: Square One Publishers, 2007), p. 60.

[72]As cited in Virginia P. Richmond, Jason S. Wrench, and James C. McCroskey, *Communication: Apprehension, Avoidance, and Effectiveness*, 6th ed. (Boston: Pearson, 2013), pp. 95–99, 97–102; Karen Kangas Dwyer, *Conquer Your Speechfright*, 2nd ed. (Belmont, CA: Thomson Wadsworth, 2005), pp. 95–103, 137–41.

[73]Daniel Goleman, *Social Intelligence* (New York: Bantam, 2006), pp. 41–42.

[74]From Virginia P. Richmond and James C. McCroskey, *Communication: Apprehension, Avoidance, and Effectiveness*, 5th ed. (Boston: Allyn and Bacon, 1998). Copyright © 1998 by Pearson Education. Reprinted by permission of the publisher.

[75]Virginia P. Richmond and James C. McCroskey, *Communication: Apprehension, Avoidance, and Effectiveness*, 4th ed. (Scottsdale, AZ: Gorsuch, Scarisbrick, 1995), pp. 129–30. Reprinted by permission of the authors and publisher.

Chapter 3

[1]Derek Thompson, "2 Graphs That Should Accompany Every Discussion of the GOP's Demographics Problem," *The Atlantic*, November 9, 2012, http://www.theatlantic.com/politics/archive/2012/11/2-graphs-that-should-accompany-every-discussion-of-the-gops-demographics-problem/265032; Aaron Blanke, "Guess What? The Polls (and Nate Silver) Were Right," *The Washington Post*, November 7, 2012, http://www.washingtonpost.com/blogs/the-fix/wp/2012/11/07/guess-what-the-polls-and-nate-silver-were-right; Mark Hugo Lopez and Paul Taylor, "Latino Voters in the 2012 Election," *PewResearch Hispanic Center*, November 7, 2012, http://www.pewhispanic.org/2012/11/07/latino-voters-in-the-2012-election/#fn-16829-1; Laura Bassett, "Gender Gap in 2012 Election Aided Obama Win," *Huff Post*, November 7, 2012, http://www.huffingtonpost.com/2012/11/07/gender-gap-2012-election-obama_n_2086004.html; Kennedy Prewitt, "Fix the Census' Archaic Racial Categories," *The New York Times*, August 22, 2013, p. A23.

[2]Karen R. Humes, Nicholas A. Jones, and Roberto R. Ramirez, *Overview of Race and Hispanic Origin: 2010 Census Brief* (U.S. Census Bureau, March 2011), pp. 3, 4–5, 17, 22, http://www.census.gov/prod/cen2010/briefs/c2010br-02.pdf.

[3]U.S. Census Bureau, www.census.gov/population.

[4]Myron W. Lustig and Jolene Koester, *Intercultural Competence*, 7th ed. (Boston: Pearson, 2013), p. 25.

[5]Intercultural authors use a variety of terms (*co-cultures*, *microcultures*) to describe the cultural groups that coexist within a larger culture. Using either of these terms is preferable to using the older, somewhat derogatory term *subcultures*.

[6]Brenda J. Allen, *Difference Matters: Communicating Social Identity* (Long Grove, IL: Waveland Press, 2004), p. 10.

[7]Rita Hardiman, "White Racial Identity Development in the United States," in Elizabeth Pathy Salett and Dianne R. Koslow (Eds.), *Race, Ethnicity and Self: Identity in Multicultural Perspective* (Washington, DC: National MultiCultural Institute, 1994), pp. 130–131.

[8]Rita Hardiman, "White Racial Identity Development in the United States," in Elizabeth Pathy Salett and Dianne R. Koslow (Eds.), *Race, Ethnicity and Self: Identity in Multicultural Perspective* (Washington, DC: National MultiCultural Institute, 1994), pp. 130–131.

[9]J. Richard Hoel, "Developing Intercultural Competence," in Pamela J. Cooper, Carolyn Calloway-Thomas, and Cheri J. Simonds (Eds.), *Intercultural Communication with Readings* (Boston: Allyn and Bacon, 2007), p. 305.

[10]Stephen Prothero, *Religious Literacy: What Every American Needs to Know—And Doesn't* (New York: HarperCollins, 2007), p. 11. See also Prothero's religious literacy quiz, pp. 27–28, 235–239.

[11]Statements are based on three sources: Robert Pollock, *The Everything World's Religions Book* (Avon, MA: Adams Media, 2002); Leo Rosen (Ed.), *Religions of America: Fragment of Faith in an Age of Crisis* (New York: Touchstone, 1975); *Encyclopedia Britannica Almanac 2004* (Chicago: Encyclopedia Britannica, 2003).

[12]According to Richard L. Evans, a former member of the Council of Twelve of the Church of Jesus Christ of Latter-day Saints, "Strictly speaking, 'Mormon' is merely a nickname for a member of the Church of Jesus Christ of Latter-day Saints." When asked whether Mormons are Christians, he answered, "Unequivocally yes." See "What Is a Mormon?" in Leo Rosen (Ed.), *Religions of America: Fragment of Faith in an Age of Crisis* (New York: Touchstone, 1975), p. 187; Robert Pollock describes Mormonism as a "prevalent Christian faith" in Robert Pollock, *The Everything World's Religions Book* (Avon, MA: Adams Media, 2002), pp. 49–51.

[13]Data from Patricia G. Devine and A. J. Elliot, "Are Racial Stereotypes Really Fading? The Princeton Trilogy Revisited," *Personality and Social Psychology Bulletin* 21 (1995): 1139–1150.

[14]Stella Ting-Toomey and Leeva C. Chung, *Understanding Intercultural Communication* (Los Angeles: Roxbury, 2005), pp. 236–239.

[15]Based on Lustig and Koester, *Instructor's Manual to Accompany Intercultural Competence* (Boston: Pearson, 2013), p. 151.

[16]National Communication Association, "National Communication Association Policy Platform," http://www.natcom.org/index.asp?bid=510.

[17]See Brian A. Nosek, Anthony Greenwald, and Mahzarin R. Banaji, "Understanding and Using the Implicit Association Test: II. Method Variables and Construct Validity," *Personality and Social Psychology Bulletin* 31 (2005): 166–180; Anthony Greenwald, Debby E. McGhee, and Jordan L. K. Schwartz, "Measuring Individual Differences in Implicit Cognition: The Implicit Association Test," *Journal of Personality and Social Psychology* 74 (1998): 1464–1480; Patricia G. Devine, "Implicit Prejudice and Stereotyping: How Automatic Are They?," *Journal of Personality and Social Psychology* 81 (2001): 757–759.

[18]Patricia G. Devine, "Implicit Prejudice and Stereotyping: How Automatic Are They?," *Journal of Personality and Social Psychology* 81 (2001): 757–759; David M. Amodio and Patricia G. Devine, "Stereotyping and Evaluation in Implicit Race Biased: Evidence for Independent Constructs and Unique Effects on Behavior," *Journal of Personality and Social Psychology* 91 (2006): 642–661.

[19]Shankar Vedantam, "For Allen and Webb, Implicit Biases Would Be Better Confronted," *The Washington Post*, October 9, 2006, p. A2. See also http://www.washingtonpost.com/science; http://implicit.harvard.edu.

[20]Allan Johnson, *Privilege, Power, and Difference* (Mountain View, CA: Mayfield Publishing, 2006), pp. 104–105.

[21]Allan Johnson, *Privilege, Power, and Difference* (Mountain View, CA: Mayfield Publishing, 2006), p. 104.

[22]Jenna Johnson, "Obama Reelection Sparks Racially Charged Protest at Ole Miss," *The Washington Post*, November 7, 2012, http://www.washingtonpost.com/blogs/campus-overload/post/obamas-re-election-sparks-racially-charged-protest-at-Ole-Miss; Natash Lennard, "Ole Miss Student Start Racist Protest After Election Results," *Slate*, November 7, 2012, http://www.salon.com/2012/11/07/ole_miss_students_start_racist_protest_after_election_result; Kathy Lee, "Ole Miss Students Hold Candlelight March to Protest Racially-Fueled Anti-Obama Demonstration," *New York Daily News*, November 8, 2012, http://www.nydailynews.com/news/national/ole-students-hold-candlelight-march-counter-anti-obama-demonstration-article-1.1198946#ixzz2OO1M9AL8.

[23]Mark P. Orbe and Tina M. Harris, *Interracial Communication: Theory into Practice* (Belmont, CA: Wadsworth, 2001), p. 6.

[24]Mark P. Orbe and Tina M. Harris, *Interracial Communication: Theory into Practice* (Belmont, CA: Wadsworth, 2001), p. 28.

[25]Brenda J. Allen, *Difference Matters: Communication and Social Identity* (Long Grove, IL: Waveland, 2004), p. 67.

[26]Nicholas Wade, *Before the Dawn: Recovering the Lost History of Our Ancestors* (New York: Penguin, 2006), p. 188.

[27]Mark P. Orbe and Tina M. Harris, *Interracial Communication: Theory into Practice* (Belmont, CA: Wadsworth, 2001), p. 31.

[28]Nicholas Wade, *Before the Dawn: Recovering the Lost History of Our Ancestors* (New York: Penguin, 2006), p. 188.

[29]Geert Hofstede, Gert Jan Hofstede, and Michael Minkov, *Cultures and Organizations: Software of the Mind: Intercultural Cooperation and Its Importance for Survival*, 3rd ed. (New York: McGraw-Hill, 2010); Geert Hofstede, *Culture's Consequences: Comparing Values, Behaviors, Institutions, and Organizations Across Nation*, 2nd ed. (Thousand Oaks, CA: Sage, 2001); Edward T. Hall, *Beyond Culture* (Garden City, NY: Anchor, 1977); Florence Rockwood Kluckhohn and Frederick L. Strodtbeck, *Variations in Value Orientations.* (Evanston, IL: Row 1961); Shalom H. Schwartz, "A Theory of Cultural Value Orientations: Explication and Applications," *Comparative Sociology* 5 (2006): 137–182; Ronald Fischer et al., "Are Individual-Level and Country-Level Value Structures Different? Testing Hofstede's Legacy with the Schwartz Value Survey," *Journal of Cross-Cultural Psychology* 41 (2010): 135–151; Robert J. House et al., (Eds.), *Culture, Leadership, and Organizations: The GLOBE Study of 62 Societies* (Thousand Oaks, CA: Sage, 2004. Note: The "Global Leadership and Organizational Behavior Effectiveness" (GLOBE) Research Program was developed by Robert House of the Wharton School of Business, University of Pennsylvania; Jagdeep S. Chhokar, Felix C. Brodbeck, and Robert J. House (Eds.), *Culture and Leadership Across the World: The GLOBE Book of In-Depth Studies of 25 Societies* (New York: Taylor & Francis, 2008).

[30]Geert Hofstede, Gert Jan Hofstede, and Michael Minkov, *Cultures and Organizations: Software of the Mind* (New York: McGraw-Hill, 2010), p. 31. See also Geert Hofstede, *Culture's Consequences: Comparing Values, Behavior, Institutions and Organizations across Nations*, 2nd ed. (Thousand Oaks, CA: Sage, 2001), p. 29. In addition to the intercultural dimensions included in this chapter, Hofstede identifies two other dimensions: uncertainty avoidance and indulgence versus restraint. For other cultural patterns and taxonomies, see Myron W. Lustig and Jolene Koester, *Intercultural Competence*, 7th ed. (Boston: Pearson, 2013), pp. 100–128.

[31]Myron W. Lustig and Jolene Koester, *Intercultural Competence*, 7th ed. (Boston: Pearson, 2013), p. 123.

[32]William B. Gudykunst and Carmen M. Lee, "Cross-Cultural Communication Theories," in William B. Gudykunst and Bella Mody (Eds.), *Handbook of International and Intercultural Communication*, 2nd ed. (Thousand Oaks, CA: Sage, 2002), p. 27.

[33]Myron W. Lustig and Jolene Koester, *Intercultural Competence*, 7th ed. (Boston: Pearson, 2013), p.108.

[34]Harry C. Triandis, "The Self and Social Behavior in Different Cultural Contexts," *Psychological Review* 96 (1989): 506–520. See also Harry C. Triandis, *Individualism and Collectivism* (Boulder, CO: Westview, 1995), p. 29. Data from Geert Hofstede, *Cultural Consequences: Comparing Values, Behavior, Institutions and Organizations across Nations*, 2nd ed. (Thousand Oaks, CA: Sage, 2001), p. 215; Geert Hofstede, Gert Jan Hofstede, and Michael Minkov, *Cultures and Organizations: Software of the Mind: Intercultural Cooperation and Its Importance for Survival*, 3rd ed. (New York: McGraw-Hill, 2010), p. 90.

[35]Geert Hofstede, Gert Jan Hofstede, and Michael Minkov, *Cultures and Organizations: Software of the Mind: Intercultural Cooperation and Its Importance for Survival*, 3rd ed. (New York: McGraw-Hill, 2010), pp. 95–97.

[36]Peggy Nonnan, "About Those 2012 Political Predictions," *The Wall Street Journal*, December 29–30, 2012, p. A13.

[37]David Brooks, "What Our Words Tell Us," *The New York Times*, May 21, 2013, p. A21; Based on Jean M. Twenge, W. Keith Campbell, and Brittany Gentile, "Increases in Individualistic Words and Phrases in American Books," 1960–2008, *PLOS ONE*, July 10, 2012, http://www.plosone.org/article/info%3Adoi%2F10.1371%2Fjournal.pone.0040181.

[38]Geert Hofstede, *Cultural Consequences: Comparing Values, Behavior, Institutions and Organizations across Nations*, 2nd ed. (Thousand Oaks, CA: Sage, 2001), p. 53.

[39]Harry C. Triandis, *Individualism and Collectivism* (Boulder, CO: Westview, 1995).

[40]Harry C. Triandis, "Cross-Cultural Studies of Individualism and Collectivism," in J. J. Berman (Ed.), *Cross-Cultural Perspectives* (Lincoln: University of Nebraska Press, 1990), p. 52.

[41]Note: Whereas Geert Hofstede and The GLOBE Study use the phrase Power Distance, Shalom Schwartz uses Egalitarian-Hierarchical.

[42]Geert Hofstede, Gert Jan Hofstede, and Michael Minkov, *Cultures and Organizations: Software of the Mind* (New York: McGraw-Hill, 2010), p. 61.

[43]Geert Hofstede, Gert Jan Hofstede, and Michael Minkov, *Cultures and Organizations: Software of the Mind* (New York: McGraw-Hill, 2010), pp. 57–59.

[44]Myron W. Lustig and Jolene Koester, *Intercultural Competence*, 7th ed. (Boston: Pearson, 2013), pp. 123–124.

[45]Geert Hofstede, Gert Jan Hofstede, and Michael Minkov, *Cultures and Organizations: Software of the Mind* (New York: McGraw-Hill, 2010), p. 138.

[46]Myron W. Lustig and Jolene Koester, *Intercultural Competence*, 7th ed. (Boston: Pearson, 2013), p. 125.

[47]Geert Hofstede, Gert Jan Hofstede, and Michael Minkov, *Cultures and Organizations: Software of the Mind* (New York: McGraw-Hill, 2010), pp. 141–143.

[48]Geert Hofstede, Gert Jan Hofstede, and Michael Minkov, *Cultures and Organizations: Software of the Mind* (New York: McGraw-Hill, 2010), p. 43.

[49]Myron W. Lustig and Jolene Koester, *Intercultural Competence*, 7th ed. (Boston: Pearson, 2013), p. 120; See also Conveying Islamic Message Society, "Women's Rights in Islam: Respected, Honoured, Cherished," Alexandria, Egypt. www.islamicmessage.net: "God created men and women to be different, with unique roles, skills and responsibilities. . . . The man is responsible for the financial well being of the family while the woman contributes to the family's physical, education and emotional well being." Obtained by author while in Egypt, May 2013.

[50]The United Arab Emirates, "Traveling in a Muslim Country," http://www.uae-embassy.org/travel-culture/traveling-in-muslim-country.

[51]Richard West and Lynn H. Turner, *Introducing Communication Theory*, 3rd ed. (Boston: McGraw-Hill, 2007), pp. 515–532. See Cheris Kramarae, *Women and Men Speaking: Framework for Analysis* (Rowley, MA: Newbury House, 1981).

[52]Edward T. Hall, *The Silent Language* (Garden City, NY: Doubleday, 1959). See also Lustig and Koester, *Intercultural Competence* (Boston: Pearson, 2013), p. 226.

[53]Geert Hofstede, Gert Jan Hofstede, and Michael Minkov, *Cultures and Organizations: Software of the Mind* (New York: McGraw-Hill, 2010), p. 240.

[54]Edward T. Hall, *Beyond Culture* (Garden City, NY: Anchor, 1997).

[55]Peter Andersen et al. "Nonverbal Communication Across Cultures," in William B. Gudykunst and Bella Mody (Eds.), *Handbook of International and Intercultural Communication*, 2nd ed. (Thousand Oaks, CA: Sage, 2002), p. 99.

[56]Shirley van der Veur, "Africa: Communication and Cultural Patterns," in Larry A. Samovar and Richard E. Porter (Eds.), *Intercultural Communication: A Reader*, 10th ed., Larry A. Samovar and Richard E. Porter (Eds.) (Belmont, CA: Wadsworth, 2003), p. 84.

[57]Edward T. Hall, *Beyond Culture* (Garden City, NY: Anchor, 1997); Edward T. Hall, *The Silent Language* (Garden City, NY: Doubleday, 1959).

[58]Edward T. Hall, *Beyond Culture* (Garden City, NY: Anchor, 1997); Edward T. Hall, *The Silent Language* (Garden City, NY: Doubleday, 1959).

[59]Edward Wyatt, "Most of U.S. Is Wired, but Millions Aren't Plugged In," *The New York Times*, August 19, 2013, p. B1.

[60]Rich Karr, "Why Is European Broadband Faster and Cheaper? Blame the Government," *Engadget*, June 28, 2011, http://www.engadget.com/2011/06/28/why-is-european-broadband-faster-and-cheaper-blame-the-government.

[61]David Cay Johnston, "A Close Look at Your Bills 'Fine Print'," September 20, 2012, Fresh Air, *National Public Radio*, http://www.npr.org/2012/09/20/161477162/a-close-look-at-your-bills-fine-print.

[62]David Cay Johnston, "A Close Look at Your Bills 'Fine Print'," September 20, 2012, Fresh Air, *National Public Radio*, http://www.npr.org/2012/09/20/161477162/a-close-look-at-your-bills-fine-print.

[63]Gerald Smith, "Internet Speed in United States Lags Behind Many Countries, Highlighting Global Digital Divide," *The Huffington Report*, September 10, 2012, http://www.huffingtonpost.com/2012/09/05/internet-speed-united-states-digital-divide_n_1855054.html.

[64]Brian X. Chen "One on One: Susan P. Crawford, Author of 'Captive Audience'," Bits: The Business of Technology, *The New York Times*, February 13, 2013, http://bits.blogs.nytimnes.com/2013/02/19/one-on-one-susan-p-crawford.

[65]Brian X. Chen "One on One: Susan P. Crawford, Author of 'Captive Audience'," Bits: The Business of Technology, *The New York Times*, February 13, 2013, http://bits.blogs.nytimnes.com/2013/02/19/one-on-one-susan-p-crawford.

[66]Benedict Carey, "Lotus Therapy," *The New York Times*, May 27, 2008, http://www.nytimes.com/2008/05/27/health/research/27budd.html?pagewanted=all; Ellen J. Langer, *Mindfulness* (Cambridge, MA: Da Capo, 1989); Jonathan Landaw, Stephan Bodian, and Gudrun Buhnemann, *Buddhism for Dummies*, 2nd ed. (Hoboken, NJ: Wiley, 2011), pp. 59, 152–153.

[67]Ellen J. Langer, *Mindfulness* (Cambridge, MA: Da Capo, 1989), p. 11.

[68]Based on examples in Ellen J. Langer, *Mindfulness* (Cambridge, MA: Da Capo, 1989), p. 12.

[69]Benedict Carey, "Lotus Therapy," *The New York Times*, May 27, 2008, http://www.nytimes.com/2008/05/27/health/research/27budd.html?pagewanted=all; Ellen J. Langer, *Mindfulness* (Cambridge, MA: Da Capo, 1989); Jonathan Landaw, Stephan Bodian, and Gudrun Buhnemann, *Buddhism for Dummies*, 2nd ed. (Hoboken, NJ: Wiley, 2011), pp. 59, 152–153.

[70]Richard Boyatzis and Annie McKee, *Resonant Leadership* (Boston: Harvard Business School Press, 2005), p. 112.

[71]Richard Nisbett, *The Geography of Thought: How Asians and Westerners Think Differently ... and Why* (New York: Free Press, 2003), p. 13.

[72]Ellen J. Langer, *Mindfulness* (Cambridge, MA: Da Capo, 1989), p. 69.

[73]Marvin Harris, *Cows, Pigs, Wars, and Witches: The Riddles of Culture* (New York: Vintage Books, 1975), pp. 11–34.

[74]Marvin Harris, *Cows, Pigs, Wars, and Witches: The Riddles of Culture* (New York: Vintage Books, 1975), p. 30.

[75]Howard Giles et al., "Speech Accommodation Theory: The First Decade and Beyond," in Margaret L. McLaughlin (Ed.), *Communication Yearbook* (Newbury Park, CA: Sage, 1987), pp. 13–48; Howard Giles et al., "Accommodation Theory: Communication, Context, and Consequence," in Howard Giles et al. (Eds.), *Contexts of Accommodation: Developments in Applied Sociolinguistics* (Cambridge: Cambridge University Press, 1991), pp. 1–68.

[76]Mary M. Dwyer and Courtney K. Peters, "The Benefits of Study Abroad," http://www.transitionsabroad.com/publications/studyabroadmagazine/2007Spring/lasting_benefits_of_study_abroad.shtml.

[77]James Leigh, "Teaching Content and Skills for Intercultural Communication: A Mini Case Studies Approach," *The Edge: The E-Journal of Intercultural Relations* 2 (Winter 1999), http://www.interculturalrelations.com/v2ilWinter1999leigh.htm.

[78]James W. Neuliep and James C. McCroskey, "The Development of a U.S. and Generalized Ethnocentrism Scale," *Communication Research Reports*, 14 (1997): 385–398; James W. Neuliep, "Assessing the Reliability and Validity of the Generalized Ethnocentric Scale," *Journal of Intercultural Communication Research*, 31 (2002): 201–215; For additional information, see James W. Neuliep, *Intercultural Communication: A Contextual Approach*, 2nd ed. (Boston: Houghton Mifflin, 2003), pp. 29–30.

Chapter 4

[1]Spencer Morgan, "Hear Me Now?: The Verizon Guy Gets His Life Back," *The Atlantic*, April 2, 2011, http://www.theatlantic.com/magazine/archive/2011/05/hear-me-now/308449; Mark Cina, "Verizon Disconnects 'Can You Hear Me Now?' Guy," *Reuters*, April 14, 2011, http://www.reuters.com/article/2011/04/14/us-verizon-idUSTRE73D7TP20110414.

[2]Seth S. Horowitz, "The Science and Art of Listening," *The New York Times*, November 11, 2012, p. SR2.

[3]Phillip Emmert, "A Definition of Listening," *Listening Post* 51 (1995): 6.

[4]Seth S. Horowitz, "The Science and Art of Listening," *The New York Times*, November 11, 2012, p. SR2.

[5]Richard Emanuel et al., "How College Students Spend Their Time Communicating," *International Journal of Listening* 22 (2008): 13–28.

[6]Lynn O. Cooper and Trey Buchanan, "Listening Competency on Campus: A Psychometric Analysis of Student Learning," *The International Journal of Listening* 24 (2010): 141–163.

[7]Andrew D. Wolvin and Carolyn G. Coakley, *Listening*, 5th ed. (Madison, WI: Brown and Benchmark, 1996), p. 15.

[8]Reported in Sandra D. Collins, *Listening and Responding Managerial Communication Series* (Mason, OH: Thomson, 2006), p. 21.

[9]The numerical ranges in Figure 4.1 summarize research on communication and listening time studies. See Andrew Wolvin and Carolyn Gwynn Coakley, *Listening* (Madison, WI: Brown & Benchmark, 1996), pp. 13–15; Laura A. Janusik and Andrew D. Wolvin, "24 Hours in a Day: A Listening Update to the Time Studies," *The International Journal of Listening*, 23 (2009): 104–120; Richard Emanuel et al., "How College Students Spend Their Time Communicating," *International Journal of Listening* 22 (2008): 13-28.

[10]Graham D. Bodie, "Listening as Positive Communication," in Thomas J. Socha and Margaret J. Pitts (Eds.), *The Positive Side of Interpersonal Communication* (New York: Peter Lang, 2012), p. 109.

[11]Graham D. Bodie, "Listening as Positive Communication," in Thomas J. Socha and Margaret J. Pitts (Eds.), *The Positive Side of Interpersonal Communication* (New York: Peter Lang, 2012), pp. 109, 110, and 120.

[12]Michael P. Nichols, *The Lost Art of Listening* (New York: Guildford, 1995), p. 11.

[13]Ralph G. Nichols, "Listening Is a 10-Part Skill," *Nation's Business*, September 1987, p. 40.

[14]S. S. Benoit and J. W. Lee, "Listening: It Can Be Taught," *Journal of Education for Business* 63 (1986): 229–332.

[15]Florence I. Wolff and Nadine C. Marsnik, *Perceptive Listening*, 2nd ed. (Fort Worth, TX: Harcourt Brace Jovanovich, 1992), pp. 9–16.

[16]Michael P. Nichols, *The Lost Art of Listening* (New York: Guildford, 1995), pp. 196, 221.

[17]Graham D. et al., "Listening Competence in Initial Interactions I: Distinguishing Between What Listening Is and What Listeners Do," *The International Journal of Listening* 26 (2012): 1–28.

[18]Tony Alessandra and Phil Hunsaker, *Communicating at Work* (New York: Fireside, 1993), p. 55.

[19]Jim Collins, *Good to Great* (New York: HarperCollins, 2001), p. 14.

[20]Lynn O. Cooper and Trey Buchanan, "Listening Competency on Campus: A Psychometric Analysis of Students Listening," *The International Journal of Listening* 24 (2010): 157.

[21]Many sources substantiate this list of poor listening habits including Judi Brownell, *Listening: Attitudes, Principles, and Skills*, 4th ed. (Boston: Pearson/Allyn and Bacon, 2010); Madelyn Burley-Allen, *Listening: The Forgotten Skill*, 2nd ed. (New York: Wiley, 1995); Ralph G. Nichols, "Do We Know How to Listen? Practical Helps in a Modern Age," *The Speech Teacher* 10 (1961); Nichols, R. G., "Listening Is a 10-Part Skill," *Nation's Business*, September 1987; Andrew D. Wolvin and Carolyn G. Coakley, *Listening*, 5th ed. (Madison, WI: Brown and Benchmark, 1996).

[22]Judi Brownell, *Listening: Attitudes, Principles, and Skills*, 4th ed. (Boston: Pearson/Allyn and Bacon, 2010), p. 14.

[23]Judi Brownell, *Listening: Attitudes, Principles, and Skills*, 4th ed. (Boston: Pearson/Allyn and Bacon, 2010), p. 16.

[24]Judi Brownell, *Listening: Attitudes, Principles, and Skills*, 4th ed. (Boston: Pearson/Allyn and Bacon, 2010), pp. 16–17.

[25]Judi Brownell, *Listening: Attitudes, Principles, and Skills*, 4th ed. (Boston: Pearson/Allyn and Bacon, 2010), p. 73.

[26]Seth S. Horowitz, "The Science and Art of Listening," *The New York Times*, November 11, 2012, p. SR2.

[27]Seth S. Horowitz, "The Science and Art of Listening," *The New York Times*, November 11, 2012, p. SR2.

[28]National Institute on Deafness and Other Communication Disorders, "Quick Statistics," June 16, 2010, http://www.nidcd.nih.gov/health/statistics/quick.htm.

[29]Gallaudet Research Institute, Gallaudet University, "A Brief Summary of Estimates for the Size of the Deaf Population in the USA Based on Available Federal Data and Published Research," http://research.gallaudet.edu/Demographics/deaf-US.php, June 6, 2010.

[30]Based on Tony Alessandra and Phil Hunsaker, *Communicating at Work* (New York: Fireside, 1993), pp. 76–77.

[31]Don Gabor, *How to Start a Conversation and Make Friends* (New York: Fireside, 2001), pp. 66–68.

[32]Based on Don Gabor, *How to Start a Conversation and Make Friends* (New York: Fireside, 2001), pp. 66–68.

[33]Judi Brownell, *Listening: Attitudes, Principles, and Skills*, 4th ed. (Boston: Pearson/Allyn and Bacon, 2010), p. 168.

[34]Michael P. Nichols, *The Lost Art of Listening* (New York: Guildford, 1995), pp. 36–37.

[35]Based on Florence I. Wolff and Nadine C. Marsnik, *Perceptive Listening*, 2nd ed. (Fort Worth, TX: Harcourt Brace Jovanovich, 1992), p. 100.

[36]Florence I. Wolff and Nadine C. Marsnik, *Perceptive Listening*, 2nd ed. (Fort Worth, TX: Harcourt Brace Jovanovich, 1992), pp. 101–102.

[37]Isa Engleberg and Dianna Wynn, *Working in Groups: Communication Principles and Strategies*, 6th ed. (Boston: Pearson, 2013), pp. 160–161.

[38]National Communication Association Credo for Ethical Communication, http://www.natcom.org/aboutNCA/Policies/Platform.html.

[39]Michael P. Nichols, *The Lost Art of Listening* (New York: Guildford, 1995), pp. 42–43.

[40]Andrew D. Wolvin and Carolyn G. Coakley, *Listening*, 5th ed. (Madison, WI: Brown and Benchmark, 1996), pp. 135–138.

[41]Based on Florence I. Wolff and Nadine C. Marsnik, *Perceptive Listening*, 2nd ed. (Fort Worth, TX: Harcourt Brace Jovanovich, 1992), pp. 94–95.

[42]Michael P. Nichols, *The Lost Art of Listening* (New York: Guildford, 1995), p. 126.

[43]Based on David W. Johnson's Questionnaire on Listening and Response Alternatives in *Reaching Out: Interpersonal Effectiveness and Self-Actualization*, 7th ed. (Boston: Allyn and Bacon, 2000), pp. 234–239.

[44]Deborah Tannen, *You Just Don't Understand: Women and Men in Conversation* (New York: Ballantine Books, 1990), pp. 141–142.

[45]Deborah Tannen, *You Just Don't Understand: Women and Men in Conversation* (New York: Ballantine Books, 1990), pp. 142–143.

[46]See Deborah Tannen, *You Just Don't Understand: Women and Men in Conversation* (New York: Ballantine Books, 1990), pp. 123–48; Diana K. Ivy and Phil Backlund, *Exploring Gender Speak* (New York: McGraw-Hill, 1994), pp. 224–225.

[47]See Deborah Tannen, *You Just Don't Understand: Women and Men in Conversation* (New York: Ballantine Books, 1990), pp. 149–151; Diana K. Ivy and Phil Backlund, *Exploring Gender Speak* (New York: McGraw-Hill, 1994), pp. 206–208, 224–225; Teri Kwal Gamble and Michael W. Gamble, *The Gender Communication Connection* (Boston: Houghton Mifflin, 2003), pp. 122–128.

[48]John Hinds, "Reader Versus Writer Responsibility: A New Typology," in Ulla Connor and Robert B. Kaplan (Eds.) *Writing Across Languages: Analysis of L2 Written Text*, (Reading, MA: Addison-Wesley, 1987), pp. 141–152, as explained in Myron W. Lustig and Jolene Koester, *Intercultural Competence*, 7th ed. (Boston: Pearson, 2013), p. 208.

[49]Myron W. Lustig and Jolene Koester, *Intercultural Competence*, 7th ed. (Boston: Pearson, 2013), p. 208.

[50]Elizabeth A. Tuleja, *Intercultural Communication for Business* (Mason, OH: Thomson Higher Education, 2005), p. 43.

[51]Kittie W. Watson, Larry L. Barker, and James B. Weaver, "The Listening Styles Profile (LSP-16): Development and Validation of an Instrument to Assess Four Listening Styles," *The International Journal of Listening* 9 (1995): 1–13; See also Kittie W. Watson, Larry L. Barker, and James B. Weaver, *Listening Styles Profile*, http://www.flipkart.com/listening-styles-profile-combo-package-book.

[52]Graham Bodie and Debra Worthington, "Revisiting the Listening Styles Profile (LSP-16): A Confirmatory Factor Analytic Approach to Scale Validation and Reliability Estimation," *The International Journal of Listening* 24 (2010): 84; Debra Worthington, Graham D. Bodie, Christopher Gearhart, "The Listening Styles Profile Revised (LSP-R): A Scale Revision and Validation," paper presented at the Eastern Communication Convention, April 15, 2011; personal email exchanges with Bodie and Worthington in April 2011; Graham D. Bodie, Debra L. Worthington, and Christopher C. Gearhart, "The Listening Styles Profile—Revisited (LSP-R): A Scale Revision and Evidence of Validity," *Communication Quarterly* 61 (2013): 72–90.

[53]Graham D. Bodie, Debra L. Worthington, and Christopher C. Gearhart, "The Listening Styles Profile—Revisited (LSP-R): A Scale Revision and Evidence of Validity," *Communication Quarterly* 61 (2013): 86.

[54]Ralph G. Nichols, "Listening Is a 10-Part Skill," *Nation's Business*, September 1987, p. 40.

[55]Mark Knapp and Judith A. Hall, *Nonverbal Communication in Human Interaction*, 6th ed. (Belmont, CA: Thomson/Wadsworth, 2006), p. 296.

[56]Sindya N. Bhanoo, "Ability Seen in Toddlers to Judge Others' Intent," *The New York Times*, November 16, 2010, http://www.nytimes.com/2010/11/16/science/16obchildren.html?_r=1&sq=toddlers%20intention&st=cse&scp=1&page wanted=print.

[57]Ralph G. Nichols, "Do We Know How to Listen? Practical Helps in a Modern Age," *The Speech Teacher* 10 (1961): 121.

[58]Madelyn Burley-Allen, *Listening: The Forgotten Skill*, 2nd ed. (New York: Wiley, 1995), pp. 68–70.

[59]Paul J. Kaufmann, *Sensible Listening: The Key to Responsive Interaction*, 5th ed. (Dubuque, IA: Kendall/Hunt, 2006), p. 115.

[60]Ralph G. Nichols, "Do We Know How to Listen? Practical Helps in a Modern Age," *The Speech Teacher* 10 (1961): 122.

[61]Graham D. Bodie, "Listening as Positive Communication," in Thomas J. Socha and Margaret J. Pitts (Eds.), *The Positive Side of Interpersonal Communication* (New York: Peter Lang, 2012), p. 120.

[62]Based on Andrew Wolvin and Laura Janusik, "Janusik/Wolvin Student Listening Inventory," in Roy M. Berko, Andrew D. Wolvin, and Darlyn R. Wolvin, *Instructor's Manual for Communicating: A Social and Career Focus*, 9th ed. (Boston: Houghton Mifflin, 2004), pp. 129–131.

Chapter 5

[1]Geoffrey Finch, *Word of Mouth: A New Introduction to Language and Communication* (New York: Palgrave, 2003), p. 28.

[2]Permission granted by Lilian I. Eman, November 26, 1999.

[3]William O'Grady, Michael Dobrovolsky, and Mark Arnonoff, *Contemporary Linguistics: An Introduction*, 4th ed. (Boston: Bedford/St. Martin's, 2001), p. 659.

[4]Nicholas Wade, *Before the Dawn: Recovering the Lost History of Our Ancestors* (New York: Penguin, 2006), pp. 36–37.

[5]John H. McWhorter, *The Power of Babel: A Natural History of Language* (New York: Times Books/Henry Holt, 2001), pp. 4–5.

[6]Nicholas Wade, *Before the Dawn: Recovering the Lost History of Our Ancestors* (New York: Penguin, 2006), p. 226.

[7]Geoffrey Finch, *Word of Mouth: A New Introduction to Language and Communication* (New York: Palgrave, 2003), pp. 5–10; William O'Grady, Michael Dobrovolsky, and Mark Aronoff, *Contemporary Linguistics*, 2nd ed. (New York: St. Martin's Press, 1993), p. 9.

[8]Mark Twain, Letter to George Bainton, October 15, 1888, http://www.twainquotes.com/Lightning.html.

[9]Joann S. Lubin, "To Win Advancement, You Need to Clean Up Any Bad Speech Habits," *The Wall Street Journal*, October 5, 2004, p. B1.

[10]Victoria Fromkin and Robert Rodman, *An Introduction to Language*, 6th ed. (Fort Worth: Harcourt Brace, 1998), p. 3.

[11]Anne Donnellon, *Team Talk: The Power of Language in Team Dynamics* (Boston: Harvard Business School Press, 1996), p. 6.

[12]Gary Martin, "The Phrase Maker," 2013, http://www.phrases.org.uk/meanings/sticks-and-stones-may-break-my-bones.html.

[13]Donna Smith, "Bullying: When Words Hurt," *Disney Family.com*, http://family.go.com/parenting/pkg-teen/article-766446-bullying-when-words-hurt.

[14]Beverley Ireland-Symonds, "The Power of Words: Words That Hurt People," *Confidence Coaching*, April 24, 2011, http://bis-confidencecoaching.com/blog/2011/04/24/the-power-of-words-words-that-hurt-people.

[15]Jennifer Warner, "Study Shows Words Alone May Activate Pain Response in the Brain," *WebMD Health News*, April 2, 2010, http://www.webmd.com/pain-management/news/20100402/words-really-do-hurt.

[16]Nelson W. Francis, *The English Language: An Introduction* (London: English University Press, 1967), p. 119.

[17]Geoffrey Finch, *Word of Mouth: A New Introduction to Language and Communication* (New York: Palgrave, 2003), p. 1.

[18]Adapted from Charles Kay Ogden and Ivor Armstrong Richards, *The Meaning of Meaning* (New York: Harcourt Brace, 1936).

[19]Geoffrey Finch, *Word of Mouth: A New Introduction to Language and Communication* (New York: Palgrave, 2003), p. 11.

[20]S. I. Hayakawa and Alan R. Hayakawa, *Language and Thought in Action*, 5th ed. (San Diego, CA: Harcourt Brace Jovanovich, 1990), p. 39.

[21]S. I. Hayakawa and Alan R. Hayakawa, *Language and Thought in Action*, 5th ed. (San Diego, CA: Harcourt Brace Jovanovich, 1990), p. 43.

[22]Isa N. Engleberg and Dianna R. Wynn, *Working in Groups: Communication Principles and Strategies*, 6th ed. (Boston: Houghton Mifflin, 2013), p. 128.

[23]Vivian J. Cook, *Inside Language* (London: Arnold, 1997), p. 91.

[24]See Sally McConnell-Ginet, *Making Meaning, Making Lives: Gender, Sexuality, and Society* (Rowley, MA: Newbury, 2010), pp. 69–88; Diana K. Ivy, *GenderSpeak*, 5th ed. (Boston: Pearson, 2012), p. 173.

[25]Diana K. Ivy, *GenderSpeak*, 5th ed. (Boston: Pearson, 2012), p. 173.

[26]Kevin L. Blankenship and Thomas Holtgraves, "The Role of Different Markers of Linguistic Powerlessness in Persuasion," *Journal of Language and Social Psychology* 24 (2005): 3–24; Lawrence A. Hosman, Lawrence and Susan A. Siltanen, "Powerful and Powerless Language Forms: Their Consequences for Impression Formation, Attribution of Control of Self and Control of Others, Cognitive Responses, and Message Memory," *Journal of Language and Social Psychology* 25 (2006): 33–46; Brenda Russell, Jenna Perkins, and Heather Grinnel, "Interviewees' Overuse of the Word 'Like' and Hesitations: Effects in Simulated Hiring Decisions," *Psychological Reports* 102 (2008): 111–118.

[27]Mark Adkins and Dale E. Brashers, "The Power of Language in Computer-Mediated Groups," *Management Communication Quarterly* 8 (1995): 310.

[28]These descriptions and guidelines are based on several sources: James Price Dillard and Linda J. Marshall, "Persuasion as a Social Skill," in John O. Greene and Brant R. Burleson (Eds.), *Handbook of Communication and Social Interaction Skills* (Mahwah, NJ: Lawrence Erlbaum Associates, 2003), pp. 505–506; Richard M. Perloff, *The Dynamics of Persuasion* (New York: Lawrence Erlbaum Associates, 2008), pp. 283–285; Arthur Plotnik, *Spunk and Bite: A Writer's Guide to Bold Contemporary Style* (New York: Random House, 2007), pp. 120–126.

[29]Geoffrey Finch, *Word of Mouth: A New Introduction to Language and Communication* (New York: Palgrave, 2003), p. 2.

[30]Tony Hillerman, *The Wailing Wind* (New York: HarperTorch, 2002), p. 126.

[31]William O'Grady, Michael Dobrovolsky, and Mark Arnonoff, *Contemporary Linguistics: An Introduction*, 5th ed. (Boston: Bedford/St. Martin's, 2005), p. 509.

[32]See Geoffrey Finch, *Word of Mouth: A New Introduction to Language and Communication* (New York: Palgrave, 2003); http://www.aber.ac.uk/media/Documents/short/whorf.html; http://www.users.globalnet.co.uk/~skolyles/swh.htm.

[33]Marcel Danesi and Paul Perron, *Analyzing Cultures: An Introduction and Handbook* (Bloomington, IN: Indiana University Press, 1999), p. 61.

[34]Myron W. Lustig and Jolene Koester, *Intercultural Competence*, 7th ed. (Boston: Pearson, 2013), p. 167.

[35]Myron W. Lustig and Jolene Koester, *Intercultural Competence*, 7th ed. (Boston: Pearson, 2013), p. 167.

[36]Larry A. Samovar and Richard Porter, *Communication Between Cultures*, 5th ed. (Belmont, CA: Wadsworth, 2004), pp. 146–147.

[37]*The Washington Post*, April 6, 2002, p. A1, http://www.whitehouse.gov/news/release/2002/04/print/20020406-3.html.

[38]Geoffrey Finch, *Word of Mouth: A New Introduction to Language and Communication* (New York: Palgrave, 2003), p. 134.

[39]Geoffrey Finch, *Word of Mouth: A New Introduction to Language and Communication* (New York: Palgrave, 2003), p. 135.

[40]Nathalie Rothschild, "Sweden's New Gender-Neutral Pronoun: Hen," *Slate*, April 11, 2011, http://www.slate.com/articles/double_x/doublex/2012/04/hen_sweden_s_new_gender_neutral_pronoun_causes_controversy_html.

[41]John Tagliabue, "A School's Big Lesson Begins with Dropping Personal Pronouns," *The New York Times*, November 14, 2012, p. A8.

[42]Geoffrey Finch, *Word of Mouth: A New Introduction to Language and Communication* (New York: Palgrave, 2003), p. 136.

[43]Muriel Schultz, "The Semantic Derogation of Woman," in Barnie Thorne and Nancy Henley (Eds.), *Language and Sex: Difference and Dominance* (Rowley, MA: Newbury House, 1975), as quoted in Geoffrey Finch, *Word of Mouth: A New Introduction to Language and Communication* (New York: Palgrave, 2003), p. 137.

[44]Janet Holmes, "Myth 6: Women Talk Too Much," in Lauri Bauer and Peter Trudgill (Eds.), *Language Myths* (London: Penguin, 1998), p. 41.

[45]Janet Holmes, "Myth 6: Women Talk Too Much," in Lauri Bauer and Peter Trudgill (Eds.), *Language Myths* (London: Penguin, 1998), p. 41.

[46]David Brown, "Stereotypes of Quiet Men, Chatty Women Not Sound Science," *The Washington Post*, July 6, 2007, p. A2. See also Donald G. McNeill, "Yada, Yada, Yada. Him? Or Her?" *The New York Times*, July 6, 2007, p. A13.

[47]Janet Holmes, "Myth 6: Women Talk Too Much," in Lauri Bauer and Peter Trudgill (Eds.), *Language Myths* (London: Penguin, 1998), pp. 42–47.

[48]Janet Holmes, "Myth 6: Women Talk Too Much," in Lauri Bauer and Peter Trudgill (Eds.), *Language Myths* (London: Penguin, 1998), pp. 48–49.

[49]John McWhorter, *Word on the Street: Debunking the Myth of a "Pure" Standard English* (Cambridge, MA: Perseus, 1998), p. 143.

[50]John McWhorter, *Word on the Street: Debunking the Myth of a "Pure" Standard English* (Cambridge, MA: Perseus, 1998), pp. 145–146.

[51]Several news stories reported this story: Harvey Morris, "What's in a Name, Hurricane?" *IHT Rendezvous*, February 1, 2013, http://rendezvous.blogs.nytimes.com/2013/02/01/whats-in-a-name-hurricane/?pagewanted=print; Anna Andersen, "Teen Fights for Right to Her Name, Blaer, Which Is Banned in Iceland," *Huffington Post*, January 3, 2013, http://www.huffingtonpost.com/2013/01/03/blaer-banned-in-iceland; "Iceland: Court Says a Girl Can Finally Use Her Name," *The New York Times*, February 1, 2013, p. A5.

[52]Nathalie Rothschild, "Sweden's New Gender-Neutral Pronoun: Hen," *Slate*, April 11, 2011, http://www.slate.com/articles/double_x/doublex/2012/04/hen_sweden_s_new_gender_neutral_pronoun_causes_controversy_html.

[53]Harvey Morris, "What's in a Name, Hurricane?" *IHT Rendezvous*, February 1, 2013, http://rendezvous.blogs.nytimes.com/2013/02/01/whats-in-a-name-hurricane/?pagewanted=print.

[54]*The Week*, August 30, 2013, p. 6.

[55]William V. Haney, *Communication and Interpersonal Relations: Text and Cases*, 6th ed. (Homewood, IL: Irwin, 1992), p. 269.

[56]Randy Cohen, "The Ethicist," *The New York Times Magazine*, July 26, 2009, p. 17.

[57]William V. Haney, *Communication and Interpersonal Relations: Text and Cases*, 6th ed. (Homewood, IL: Irwin, 1992), p. 290.

[58]William O'Grady, Michael Dobrovolsky, and Mark Aronoff, *Contemporary Linguistics*, 2nd ed. (New York: St. Martin's Press, 1993), pp. 235–236.

[59]"The Leaked Memos: Did the White House Condone Torture?," *The Week*, June 25, 2004, p. 6.

[60]Tom Diemer, "West Virginia Democrat Strikes Back at GOP 'Hick' Ad: 'It's Insulting'," Politics Daily/*AOL News*, October 10, 2010, http://www.politicsdaily.com/2010/10/09/west-virginia-democrat-strikes-back-at-gop-hick-ad-its-insu/.

[61]Anna-Britta Stenstrom, "Slang to Language: A Description Based on Teenage Talk," in *i love english language*, http://aggslanguage.wordpress.com/slang-to-slanguage/.

[62]Shirley Johnson, "What Is Slang?" *Modern America, 1914–Present*, http://www.uncp.edu/home/canada/work/allam/1914-/language/slang.htm.

[63]Brian Jones, Jr., "Sir John Harrington—Inventor of 'The John'," *Ezine*, http://ezinearticles.com/?Sir-John-Harrington—Inventor-of-The-John&id=3570402.

[64]Kathryn Lindskoog, *Creating Writing: For People Who Can't Write* (Grand Rapids, MI: Zondervan Publishing, 1989), p. 66.

[65]Quoted in David Crystal, *The Cambridge Encyclopedia of the English Language* (NY: Cambridge University Press, 2003), p. 182.

[66]Alina Dizik, "Mastering the Finer Points of American Slang," *The Wall Street Journal*, May 30, 2012, p. D3; Jaymee Cuti, "Slang for English Learners," *Oregon Public Broadcasting*, June 12, 2012, http://www.opb.org/thinkoutloud/shows/slang-english-learners; www.englishbaby.com; http://learn-english-review.toptenreviews.com/english-baby-review-pg2.html.

[67]William Lutz, *Doublespeak* (New York: HarperPerennial, 1990), p. 3.

[68]Lyn Miller, "Quit Talking Like a Corporate Geek," *USA Today*, March 21, 2005, p. 7B.

[69]Stuart Chase, quoted in Richard Lederer, "Fowl Language: The Fine Art of the New Doublespeak," *AARP Bulletin* (March 2005), p. 27.

[70]Rudolf Flesch, *Say What You Mean* (New York: Harper and Row, 1972), p. 70.

[71]Excerpts from Jonathan Pitts, "At a D.C. Workshop, Participants in the Plain Language Conference Plead for End to Convoluted Communication," *The Baltimore Sun*, November 7, 2005, p. 1C, 6C; See also Roy Peter Clark, *How to Write Short* (New York: Little, Brown and Company, 2013).

[72]James V. O'Conner, *Cuss Control: The Complete Book on How to Curb Your Cursing* (New York: Three Rivers Press, 2000), p. 3.

[73]Natalie Angier, "Almost Before We Spoke, We Swore," Science Times in *The New York Times*, September 20, 2005, p. D6.

[74]Steven Poole, "Expletive Deleted," *The Wall Street Journal*, April 13–14, 2013, p. C6. Review of Melissa Mohr, *Holy Sh*t: A Brief History of Swearing* (New York: Oxford, 2013).

[75]Excerpts from Jonathan Pitts, "At a D.C. Workshop, Participants in the Plain Language Conference Plead for End to Convoluted Communication," *The Baltimore Sun*, November 7, 2005, pp. 1C, 6C.

[76]Lars Andersson and Peter Trudgill, "Swearing," in Leila Monaghan and Jane Goodman (Eds.), *A Cultural Approach to Interpersonal Communication: Essential Readings* (Malden, MA: Wiley-Blackwell, 2007), p. 195.

[77]Natalie Angier, "Almost Before We Spoke, We Swore," Science Times in *The New York Times*, September 20, 2005, p. D6.

[78]James V. O'Conner, *Cuss Control: The Complete Book on How to Curb Your Cursing* (New York: Three Rivers Press, 2000), pp. 18–27; Timothy Jay, *Why We Curse: A Neuro-Psycho-Social Theory of Speech* (Amsterdam/Philadelphia: John Benjamins Publishing, 2000), p. 328.

79 James V. O'Conner, *Cuss Control: The Complete Book on How to Curb Your Cursing* (New York: Three Rivers Press, 2000), pp. xvii, 18.

80 James V. O'Conner, *Cuss Control: The Complete Book on How to Curb Your Cursing* (New York: Three Rivers Press, 2000), pp. 18–27.

81 Steven Poole, "Expletive Deleted," *The Wall Street Journal*, April 13–14, 2013, p. C6. Review of Melissa Mohr, *Holy Sh*t: A Brief History of Swearing* (New York: Oxford, 2013).

82 Simon Critchley, "The Trauma of the Pink Shirt," *The New York Times*, April 14, 2013, p. SR9.

83 "Cleaning Up Potty-Mouths," *The Week*, August 18, 2006, p. 35.

84 Natalie Angier, "Almost Before We Spoke, We Swore," Science Times in *The New York Times*, September 20, 2005, p. D6.

85 R. L. Trask, *Language: The Basics*, 2nd ed. (London: Routledge, 1995), p. 170, 179.

86 Based on Melinda G. Kramer, Glenn Leggett, and C. David Mead, *Prentice Hall Handbook for Writers*, 12th ed. (Englewood Cliffs, NJ: Prentice Hall, 1995), p. 272.

87 Robert Mayer, *How to Win Any Argument* (Franklin Lakes, NJ: Career Press, 2006), p. 187.

88 Joel Saltzman, *If You Can Talk, You Can Write* (New York: Time Warner, 1993), pp. 48–49.

89 David Crystal, *Language and the Internet* (Cambridge: Cambridge University Press, 2001), pp. 238–239, cited in Crispin Thurlow, Laura Lengel, and Alice Tomic, *Computer Mediated Communication: Social Interaction and the Internet* (London: Sage, 2004), p. 123.

90 Crispin Thurlow, Laura Lengel, and Alice Tomic, *Computer Mediated Communication: Social Interaction and the Internet* (London: Sage, 2004), pp. 124–125.

91 Crispin Thurlow, Laura Lengel, and Alice Tomic, *Computer Mediated Communication: Social Interaction and the Internet* (London: Sage, 2004), pp. 124–125.

92 For more about the Oxford Dictionaries Online, see The Oxford Dictionaries Online, http://oxforddictionaries.com/?ABTest=fonts.css&utm_expid=53203432-7.nIZ06w4jQO6CBLpDJCQ4Mg.1; Jenna Wortham, "Oxford Dictionaries Online Adds 'Selfie,' 'Emoji' and Other Tech-Orieneted Terms," Blog in *The New York Times*, August 28, 2013, http://bits.blogs.nytimes.com/2013/08/28/oxford-dictionaries-online-adds-selfie-emoji-and-other-tech-oriented-terms/?_r=0; Katy Steinmertz, "Dictionary Adds 'Badassery', 'Selfie' and 'Twerk,'" *Time NewFeed*, August 28, 2013, http://newsfeed.time.com/2013/08/28/dictionary-adds-badassery-selfie-and-twerk; Valerie Straus, "Twerk, MOOC, girl crush—Words Added to Oxford Dictionaries Online." *The Washington Post*, August 28, 2013, http://www.washingtonpost.com/blogs/answer-sheet/wp/2013/08/28/twerk-mooc-girl-crush-words-added-to-oxford-dictionaries-online.

93 Michael Dierda, "New Dictionary Words Are Oh So Ugh," *The Washington Post*, August 29, 2013, p. C3.

94 For additional examples and warnings about overuse of symbols, see Deborah Jude-York, Lauren D. David, and Susan L. Wise, *Virtual Teams: Breaking the Boundaries of Time and Place* (Menlo Park, CA: Crisp Learning, 2000), pp. 91–92.

95 Virginia Richmond and James C. McCroskey, *Communication Apprehension, Avoidance and Effectiveness*, 5th ed. (Boston: Allyn and Bacon, 1998). © 1998 by Pearson Education. Reprinted by permission of the publisher. See also John Daly and Michael Miller, "The Empirical Development of an Instrument to Measure Writing Apprehension," *Research in the Teaching of English* 12 (1975): 242–249.

Chapter 6

1 William Shakespeare, *As You Like It*, Act III, Scene V, 82. See Steven C. Scheer, "Whoever Loved That Loved Not at First Sight," *Words Matter*, March 2, 2008, http://stevencscheers.logspot.com/2008/03/whoever-loved-that-loved-not-at-first.html. Professor Scheer notes, "this famous line from Shakespeare's *As You Like It* is actually in quotation marks in the play. The line is a quote from Christopher Marlowe's *Hero and Leander*."

2 *Just One Look* is an R&B song first recorded by Doris Troy in 1963. Other versions were recorded by the Hollies, Lynda Carter, Lulu, Harry Nilsson, and Linda Ronstadt.

3 *In Your Eyes* was written and recorded by Peter Gabriel, British musician and former member and founder of the band Genesis. The song is in the 1986 album *So*, a nominee for Album of the Year for the 1987 Grammy Awards.

4 Ben Jones of the Face Research Laboratory, University of Aberdeen, Scotland quoted in James Randerson, "Love at First Sight Just Sex and Ego, Study Says," *The Guardian*, November 6, 2007, http://www.guardian.co.uk/science/2007/nov/07/; See also Ben Jones and Lisa DeBruine, Institute of Neuroscience and Psychology, University of Glasgow, Scotland, http://facelab.org; Claire R. Conway et al., "Evidence for Adaptive Design in Human Gaze Preference," *Proceedings of the Royal Society* (2008), 275: 63–69; Erina Lee, "Dating Do: Eye Contact!" *The Science of Love*, December 20, 2012, http://www.eharmony.com/blog/2012/12/20/dating-do-eye-contact; Deborah MacKenzie, "Eye Contact and a Smile Will Win You a Mate," *New Scientist*, November 7, 2007, http://www.newscientist.com/article/dn12886-eye-contact-and-a-smile-will-win-you-a-mate.html.

5 Nina-Jo Moore, Mark Hickson, III, and Don W. Stacks, *Nonverbal Communication, Studies and Application*, 5th ed. (New York: Oxford, 2010), p. 4.

6 Judee K. Burgoon and Aaron E. Bacue, "Nonverbal Communication Skills," in John O. Greene and Brant R. Burleson (Eds.), *Handbook of Communication and Social Interaction Skills* (Mahwah, NJ: Lawrence Erlbaum, 2003), pp. 208–209.

7 Judee K. Burgoon, Laura K. Guerroro, and Kory Floyd, *Nonverbal Communication* (Boston: Allyn & Bacon, 2010), p. 233.

8 From Sigmund Freud, *Fragment of Analysis of a Case of Hysteria*, Standard Edition, Volume 7, 1905, Chapter 2: The First Dream. Psychoanalytical-Electronic Publishing, http://www.pepweb.org/document.php?id=se.007.001a.

9 Judee Burgoon, "Truth, Lies, and Virtual Worlds," *The National Communication Association's Carroll C. Arnold Distinguished Lecture*, at the annual convention of the National Communication Association, Boston, November 2005.

10 Paul Ekman, *Telling Lies: Clues to Deceit in the Marketplace, Politics, and Marriage* (New York: W.W. Norton, 1992), p. 80.

11 H. Dan O'Hair and Michael J. Cody, "Deception," in William R. Cupach and Brian H. Spitzberg (Eds.), *The Dark Side of Interpersonal Communication* (Hillsdale, NJ: Lawrence Erlbaum Associates, 1994), p. 190.

12 Mark L. Knapp, *Lying and Deception in Human Interaction* (Boston: Pearson, 2008), pp. 217–218.

13 Benedict Carey, "Judging Honesty By Words, Not Fidgets," *The New York Times*, May 12, 2009, p. D4.

14 Mark L. Knapp, Judith A. Hall, and Terrence G. Horgan, *Nonverbal Communication in Human Interaction*, 8th ed. (Boston: Wadsworth, 2014), p. 15.

15 Paul Ekman, "Communication Through Nonverbal Behavior: A Source of Information About an Interpersonal Relationship," in Silvia S. Tomkins and C. E. Izard (Eds.), *Affect, Cognition, and Personality* (New York: Springer, 1965), p. 441. See also Paul Ekman and Wallace V. Friesen, "The Repertoire of Nonverbal Behavior: Categories, Origins, Usage and Codings," *Semiotica* 1 (1969): 1–20.

16 Paul Ekman, "Communication Through Nonverbal Behavior: A Source of Information About an Interpersonal Relationship," in Silvan S. Tompkins and C. E. Izard (Eds.), *Affect, Cognition and Personality* (New York: Springer, 1965), pp. 390–442.

17 From the Federal Reserve Bank of St. Louis, *The Regional Economist*, quoted in "Good Looks Can Mean Good Pay, Study Says," *The Baltimore Sun*, April 28, 2005, p. D1.

18 Angus Deaton, "Life at the Top: The Benefits of Height," 2009, http://www.-princeton.edu/~deaton/downloads/life_at_the_top_benefits_of_height_final_june_2009.pdf.

19 Judee K. Burgoon, David B. Buller, and W. Gill Woodall, *Nonverbal Communication: The Unspoken Dialog* (New York, McGraw-Hill, 1996), p. 286. See also Richard West and Lynn H. Turner, *Introducing Communication Theory* (Boston: McGraw Hill, 2007), pp. 152–153.

20 Virginia Peck Richmond, James C. McCroskey, and Mark L. Hickson III, *Nonverbal Behavior in Interpersonal Relationships*, 7th ed. (Boston: Pearson, 2012), p. 34.

21 Jo-Ellan Dimitrius and Mark Mazzarella, *Reading People: How to Understand People and Predict Their Behavior—Anytime, Anyplace* (New York: Ballantine, 1999), p. 52.

22 Jeannette Catsoulis, "Look but Don't Touch: It's All About the Hair," *The New York Times*, October 8, 2009, http://movies.nytimes.com/2009/10/09/movies/09hair.html; See also "Chris Rock, Official Trailer, *Good Hair*," *YouTube*, July 31, 2009, http://www.youtube.com/watch?v=1m-4qxz08So&noredirect=1.

23 Freezy, "Video: Sesame Street Makes 'I Love My Hair' for Young Black Girls," *FREESWORLD* (Marie 'Free' Wright), October 18, 2010, http://www.freesworld.com/2010/10/18/video-sesame-street-makes-i-love-my-hair-for-young-black-girls/.

24 Mark L. Knapp, Judith A. Hall, and Terrence G. Horgan, *Nonverbal Communication in Human Interaction*, 8th ed. (Boston: Wadsworth, 2014), p. 220.

25 Paul Ekman and Wallace V. Friesen, "Hand Movements," in Laura K. Guerrero, Joseph A. DeVito, and Michael L. Hecht (Eds.), *The Nonverbal Communication Reader: Classic and Contemporary Readings*, 2nd ed. (Long Grove, IL: Waveland Press, 2008), pp. 105–108. The original article, "Hand Movements," was published in the *Journal of Communication* 22 (1972): 353–374.

26 Roger E. Axtell, *Do's and Taboos Around the World*, 2nd ed. (New York: John Wiley and Sons, 1990), p. 47.

27 Tourism New Zealand, "Maori Culture," http://www.newzealand.com/travel/media/features/maori-culture/maori_ta-moko-significance_feature.cfm.

28 Virginia Peck Richmond, James C. McCroskey, and Mark L. Hickson III, *Nonverbal Behavior in Interpersonal Relationships*, 7th ed. (Boston: Pearson, 2012), p. 19.

29 The Week Staff, "America's Booming Tattoo Economy," *The Week*, September 20, 2012, http://theweek.com/article/index/233633/the-tattoo-economy-by-the-numbers. Sources: *Harris Interactive, Mental Floss, The Motley Fool, NBC News, Pew Research Center, Tattoo Info, The Wall Street Journal*.

30 The Week Staff, "America's Booming Tattoo Economy," *The Week*, September 20, 2012, http://theweek.com/article/index/233633/the-tattoo-economy-by-the-numbers. Sources: *Harris Interactive, Mental Floss, The Motley Fool, NBC News, Pew Research Center, Tattoo Info, The Wall Street Journal*.

31 Harris Poll. "Three in Ten Americans with Tattoos Say Having One Makes Them Feel Sexier," *HarrisInteractive*, February 12, 2008, http:harrisinteractive.com/harris_poll.

32 "Dress Codes, Tattoos and Piercings," June 4, 2008, Employee Rights Blog, http://employeeissues.com/blog/body-art-dress-code.

33 "Dress Codes, Tattoos and Piercings," June 4, 2008, Employee Rights Blog, http://employeeissues.com/blog/body-art-dress-code.

34 David Brooks, "Nonconformity Is Skin Deep," *The New York Times*, August 27, 2006, p. WK11.

35 Oren Dorell, "Cover Up Your Tattoos, Some Employees Told," *USA Today*, October 31, 2008, p. 3A.

[36]Laura K. Guerrero, Joseph A. DeVito, and Michael L. Hecht, "Section D. Contact Codes: Proxemics and Haptics," in Laura K. Guerrero, Joseph A. DeVito, and Michael L. Hecht (Eds.), *The Nonverbal Communication Reader: Classic and Contemporary Readings*, 2nd ed. (Long Grove, IL: Waveland Press, 2008), p. 174.

[37]Quoted in Benedict Carey, "Evidence That Little Touches Do Mean So Much," *The New York Times*, February 23, 2010, p. D5, http://www.nytimes.com/2010/02/23/health/23mind.html.

[38]Matthew J. Hertenstein et al., "Touch Communicates Distinct Emotions," *Emotion* 6 (2006): 552.

[39]Larry Smeltzer, John Waltman, and Donald Leonard, "Proxemics and Haptics in Managerial Communication" in Laura K. Guerrero and Michael L. Hecht (Eds.), *The Nonverbal Communication Reader: Classic and Contemporary Readings*, 3rd ed. (Long Grove, IL: Waveland Press, 2008), p. 190.

[40]Virginia Peck Richmond, James C. McCroskey, and Mark L. Hickson III, *Nonverbal Behavior in Interpersonal Relationships*, 7th ed. (Boston: Pearson, 2012), p. 189.

[41]Sumathi Reddy, "A Genuine Grin Can Help the Heart: Is Polite Facing Enough to Benefits?" *The Wall Street Journal*, February 25, 2013, p. D3, http://online.wsj.com/article/SB10001424127887323699704578326363601444362.html.

[42]Sumathi Reddy, "Stress-Busting Smile: A Genuine Grin Can Help the Heart; Is Polite Faking Enough to See Benefits?" *The Wall Street Journal*, February 25, 2013, p. D4, http://online.wsj.com/article/SB10001424127887323699704578326363601444362.html.

[43]Paul Ekman and Wallace V. Friesen, *Unmaking the Face: A Guide to Recognizing Emotions from Facial Cues* (Englewood Cliffs, NJ: Prentice Hall, 1975).

[44]Joseph B. Walther and K. P. D'Addario, "The Impacts of Emoticons on Message Interpretation in Computer-Mediated Communication" Paper presented at the meeting of the International Communication Association, Washington, DC, May 2001.

[45]Amy Ip, "The Impact of Emoticons on Affect Interpretation in Instant Messages," anysmile.com/doc/emoticon_paper.pdf.

[46]Thomas Mandel and Gerard Van der Leun, *Rules of the Net: Online Operating Instructions for Human Beings* (New York: Hyperion, 1996), p. 92.

[47]Gerald W. Grumet, "Eye Contact: The Core of Interpersonal Relatedness," in Laura K. Guerrero and Michael L. Hecht (Eds.), *The Nonverbal Communication Reader: Classic and Contemporary Readings*, 3rd ed. (Long Grove, IL: Waveland Press, 2008), pp. 125–126.

[48]Ben Jones and Lisa DeBruine, Institute of Neuroscience and Psychology, University of Glasgow, Scotland, http://facelab.org; James Randerson, "Love at First Sight Just Sex and Ego, Study Says," *The Guardian*, November 6, 2007, http://www.guardian.co.uk/science/2007/nov/07/.

[49]"Famous Quotes and Savings About Eyes," *Buzzle*, http://www.buzzle.com/articles/famous-quotes-and-sayings-about-eyes.html.

[50]Guo-Ming Chen and William J. Starosta, *Fundamentals of Intercultural Communication* (Boston: Allyn & Bacon, 1998), p. 91.

[51]Summary of eye behavior research from Virginia Peck Richmond, James C. McCroskey, and Mark L. Hickson III, *Nonverbal Behavior in Interpersonal Relations*, 7th ed. (Boston: Pearson, 2012), p. 102.

[52]Lyle V. Mayer, *Fundamentals of Voice and Diction*, 13th ed. (Boston: McGraw Hill, 2004), p. 229.

[53]Centers for Disease Control and Prevention, *Intimate Partner Violence: Fact Sheet*, http://www.cdc.gov/violenceprevention/pdf/IPV_factsheet-a.pdf.

[54]ABC News, "Battle of the Sexes: Spousal Abuse Cuts Both Ways," February 7, 2004, http://abcnews.go.com/sections/2020/dailynews/2020_batteredhusbands030207.html.

[55]Eric F. Sygnatur and Guy A. Toscano, "Work-Related Homicides: The Facts," *Compensation and Working Conditions*, Spring 2000, http://bls.gov/opub/cwc/archive/spring2000art1.pdf.

[56]National Communication Association, Credo for Ethical Communication, 1999, http://www.natcom.org/nca/Template2.asp?bid=374.

[57]Virginia Peck Richmond, James C. McCroskey, and Mark L. Hickson III, *Nonverbal Behavior in Interpersonal Relationships*, 7th ed. (Boston: Pearson, 2012), p. 108–110.

[58]Nina-Jo Moore, Mark Hickson, III, and Don W. Stacks, *Nonverbal Communication, Studies and Application*, 5th ed. (New York: Oxford, 2010), p. 293.

[59]Mark L. Knapp, Judith A. Hall, and Terrence G. Horgan, *Nonverbal Communication in Human Interaction*, 8th ed. (Boston: Wadsworth, 2014), pp. 94–97; Nina-Jo Moore, Mark Hickson, III, and Don W. Stacks, *Nonverbal Communication, Studies and Application*, 5th ed. (New York: Oxford, 2010), p. 117.

[60]Mark L. Knapp, Judith A. Hall, and Terrence G. Horgan, *Nonverbal Communication in Human Interaction*, 8th ed. (Boston: Wadsworth, 2014), pp. 94–97; Nina-Jo Moore, Mark Hickson, III, and Don W. Stacks, *Nonverbal Communication, Studies and Application*, 5th ed. (New York: Oxford, 2010), p. 117.

[61]Allan Pease and Barbara Pease, *The Definitive Book of Body Language* (New York: Bantam, 2004), pp. 193–194.

[62]Edward T. Hall, *The Hidden Dimension* (Garden City, NY: Doubleday, 1966).

[63]Judith Newman "Inside the Teenage Brain," *Parade Magazine*, November 28, 2010, http://www.parade.com/news/2010/11/28-inside-the-teenage-brain.html; See also National Institute of Mental Health, "Teenage Brain: A Work in Progress (Fact Sheet)," http://www.nimh.nih.gov/health/publications/teenage-brain-a-work-in-progress-fact-sheet/index.shtml.

[64]William D. S. Killgore and Deborah A. Yurgelun-Todd, "Neural Correlates of Emotional Intelligence in Adolescent Children," *Cognitive, Affective and Behavioral Neuroscience*, 7 (2007): 140–151; Deborah A. Yurgelun-Todd and William D. Killgore, "Fear-related Activity in the Prefrontal Cortex Increases with Age During Adolescence: A Preliminary MRI Study," *Neuroscience Letters* 406 (2006): 194–199.

[65]Interview: Deborah Yurgelun-Todd, "Inside the Teenage Brain," *Frontline*, January 31, 2002, http://www.pbs.org/wgbh/pages/frontline/shows/teenbrain/interviews/todd.html.

[66]Nina-Jo Moore, Mark Hickson, III, and Don W. Stacks, *Nonverbal Communication, Studies and Application*, 5th ed. (New York: Oxford, 2010), p. 192.

[67]Rita Gorawara-Bhat, Mary Ann Cook, and Greg A. Sachs, "Nonverbal Communication in Doctor-Elderly Patient Transactions (NDEPT): Development of a Tool," *Patient Education and Counseling* 66 (2007): 223–234. Quoted in Nina-Jo Moore, Mark Hickson III, Don W. Stacks, *Nonverbal Communication: Studies and Applications*, 5th ed. (New York: Oxford, 2010), p.193.

[68]Jeffrey D. Robinson, "Nonverbal Communication in Doctor-Patient Relationships," in Laura K. Guerrero and Michael L. Hecht (Eds.), *The Nonverbal Communication Reader: Classic and Contemporary Readings*, 3rd ed. (Long Grove, IL: Waveland Press, 2008), pp. 384–394. Summarized in Judee K. Burgoon, Laura K. Guerroro, and Kory Floyd, *Nonverbal Communication* (Boston: Allyn & Bacon, 2010), p. 323.

[69]Laura Landro, "The Talking Cure: Improving the Ways Doctors Communicate with Their Patients Can Lead to Better Health Care—and Lower Costs," *The Wall Street Journal*, April 9, 2013, pp. R1–R2.

[70]Stacy L. Young, Dawn M. Kelsey, and Alexander L. Lancaster, *Communication Currents* 6 (October 2011). The original article is: Stacy L. Young, Dawn M. Kelsey, and Alexander L. Lancaster, "Predicted Outcome Value of E-mail Communication: Factors That Foster Professional Relational Development Between Students and Teachers," *Communication Education* 60 (2011): 371–388.

[71]Virginia Peck Richmond, James C. McCroskey, and Mark L. Hickson III, *Nonverbal Behavior in Interpersonal Relationships*, 7th ed. (Boston: Pearson, 2012), pp. 263-283.

[72]Nina-Jo Moore, Mark Hickson, III, and Don W. Stacks, *Nonverbal Communication, Studies and Application*, 5th ed. (New York: Oxford, 2010), p. 375.

[73]Timothy G. Plax and Patricia Kearney, "Classroom Management: Contending with College Student Discipline," in Anita L. Vangelisti, John A. Daly, and Gustav W. Friedrich (Eds.), *Teaching Communication: Theory, Research, and Methods*, 2nd ed. (Mahwah, NJ: Lawrence Erlbaum, 1999), p. 276.

[74]Brian H. Spitzberg, "CSRS: The Conversational Skills Rating Scale—An Instructional Assessment of Interpersonal Competence," in the *NCA Diagnostic Series*, 2nd ed. (Washington, D.C.: National Communication Association, 2007). See applications to nonverbal communication in Brian H. Spitzberg, "Perspectives on Nonverbal Communication Skills," in Laura K. Guerrero and Michael L. Hecht (Eds.), *The Nonverbal Communication Reader: Classic and Contemporary Readings*, 3rd ed. (Long Grove, IL: Waveland Press, 2008), pp. 21–26.

Chapter 7

[1]Social Network, *Internet Movie Database* (IMDb), http://www.imdb.com/title/tt1285016/.

[2]Kirk Honeycutt, "The Social Network—Film Review," *Hollywood Reporter*, October 12, 2010, http://www.hollywoodreporter.com/movie/social-network/review/6050.

[3]Malcolm R. Parks, *Personal Relationships and Personal Networks* (Mahwah, NJ: Lawrence Erlbaum Associates, 2007), p. 1.

[4]Student Health Services, "Developing Healthy Relationships," University of Indianapolis, http://healthservices.uindy.edu/counseling/coRelation.php.

[5]David W. Johnson, *Reaching Out: Interpersonal Effectiveness and Self-Actualization*, 7th ed. (Boston: Allyn & Bacon, 2000), p. 12.

[6]Daniel Goleman, "'Friends for Life': An Emerging Biology of Emotional Healing," *The New York Times*, October 10, 2006, p. D5. For a more detailed examination of this phenomenon, see Daniel Goleman, *Social Intelligence* (New York: Bantam, 2006), p. 10.

[7]John M. Gottman with Joan De Claire, *The Relationship Cure* (New York: Three Rivers Press, 2001), p. 23.

[8]Henry Alford, "Twitter Shows Its Rude Side," *The New York Times*, April 28, 2013, p. ST2, http://www.nytimes.com/2013/04/28/fashion/nasty-comments-on-twitter.html?pagewanted=all&_r=0.

[9]See Kate Loveys, "5,000 Friends on Facebook: Scientists Prove 150 Is the Most We Can Cope With," *Daily Mail*, http://www.dailymail.co.uk/news/article-1245684/5-000-friends-Facebook-Scientists-prove-150-cope-with.html; Robin Dunbar, "You've Got to Have (150) Friends," *The New York Times*, December 26, 2010, http://www.nytimes.com/2010/12/26/opinion/26dunbar.html; Aleks Krotoski, "Dunbar: We Can Only Ever Have 150 Friends at Most," *The Guardian/Observer*, March 13, 2010; Note: Although some researchers have argued that the number may be double 150, it certainly does not approach the thousands of people social media users claim as friends.

[10]George Anders, "Oxford Scholar: Your 1,000 Friends on Facebook Are a Mirage," *Forbes*, July 18, 2012, http://www.forbes.com/sites/georgeanders/2012/07/18/oxford-scholar-facebook-wont-widen-your-social-circle.

[11]Path: The place for your personal life. https://path.com/about, 2013.

[12]Mike Isaac, "New Social Network Path = iPhone + Instagram + Facebook - 499,999,950 Friends," *Forbes*, November 14, 2010, http://www.forbes.com/sites/mikeisaac/2010/11/14/new-social-network-path-iphone-instagram-facebook-499999950-friends.

[13]Mike Isaac, "Path Does Not Spam Users: Dave Morin Talks About the Hyper-Growth Pains of a Personal Network," *All Things Considered*, May 6, 2013, http://allthingsd.com/20130506/the-hyper-growth-pains-of-path-the-personal-network.

[14]Michael Poh, "7 Telltale Signs of Facebook Addiction," *Hongkiat*, 2012, http://www.hongkiat.com/blog/facebook-addiction-signs.

[15]Michael W. Austin, "Facebook Addiction?," *Psychology Today*, February 20, 2012, www.psychologytoday.com/blog/ethics-everyone/201202/facebook-addiction.

[16]Based on James C. McCroskey and Thomas A. McCain, "The Measurement of Interpersonal Attraction," *Speech Monographs* 41 (1974): 261–266.

[17]William Schutz, *The Human Element: Productivity, Self-Esteem, and the Bottom Line* (San Francisco: Jossey-Bass, 1994).

[18]In more recent works, Schutz refers to this need as *openness*. However, we find that students understand this concept better when we use Schutz's original term—*affection*.

[19]Daniel Menaker, *A Good Talk: The Story and Skill of Conversation* (New York: Hatchette Book Groups, 2010), p. 1.

[20]Corry Huff, "The Telephone Is Social Media," 2013, http://www.coryhuff.com/the-telephone-is-social media.

[21]"What Drives Co-Workers Crazy," *The Week*, February 23, 2007, p. 40.

[22]"What Drives Co-Workers Crazy," *The Week*, February 23, 2007, p. 40.

[23]"What Drives Co-Workers Crazy," *The Week*, February 23, 2007, p. 40. See also "Proper Cell Phone Etiquette," www.cellphonecarriers.com/cell-phone-etiquette.html.

[24]Daniel Menaker, *A Good Talk: The Story and Skill of Conversation*, (New York: Hatchette Book Groups, 2010), p. 182.

[25]Maria J. O'Leary and Cynthia Gallois, "The Last Ten Turns in Conversations Between Friends and Strangers," in Laura K. Guerrero, Joseph A. DeVito, and Michael L. Hecht (Eds.), *The Nonverbal Communication Reader: Classic and Contemporary Readings*, 2nd ed. (Prospect Heights, IL: Waveland Press, 1999), pp. 415–421.

[26]Wendy Samter, "Friendship Interaction Skills Across the Life Span," in John O. Greene and Brant R. Burleson (Eds.), *Handbook of Communication and Social Interaction Skills* (Mahwah, NJ: Lawrence Erlbaum, 2003), p. 641.

[27]Sandra Petronio, *Boundaries of Privacy: Dialectics of Disclosure* (Albany: State University of New York Press, 2003), pp. 5–6.

[28]Wendy Samter, "Friendship Interaction Skills Across the Life Span," in John O. Greene and Brant R. Burleson (Eds.), *Handbook of Communication and Social Interaction Skills* (Mahwah, NJ: Lawrence Erlbaum, 2003), p. 662.

[29]William K. Rawlins, *Friendship Matters: Communication, Dialects, and the Life Course* (New York: Aldine De Gruyter, 1992), p. 181.

[30]Wendy Samter, "Friendship Interaction Skills Across the Life Span," in John O. Greene and Brant R. Burleson (Eds.), *Handbook of Communication and Social Interaction Skills* (Mahwah, NJ: Lawrence Erlbaum, 2003), p. 661.

[31]William K. Rawlins, *Friendship Matters: Communication, Dialects, and the Life Course*, (New York: Aldine De Gruyter, 1992), p. 105.

[32]Mark C. Knapp and Anita L. Vangelisti, *Interpersonal Communication and Human Relationships* (Boston: Allyn & Bacon, 1996), pp. 34–35.

[33]Kathryn Dindia and Lindsay Timmerman, "Accomplishing Romantic Relationships," in John O. Greene and Brant R. Burleson (Eds.), *Handbook of Communication and Social Interaction Skills* (Mahwah, NJ: Lawrence Erlbaum, 2003), pp. 694–697.

[34]Mark C. Knapp and Anita L. Vangelisti, *Interpersonal Communication and Human Relationships* (Boston: Allyn & Bacon, 1996), pp. 33–44.

[35]Richard Layard, *Happiness: Lessons from a New Science* (New York: Penguin Books, 2005), p. 66.

[36]Mark C. Knapp and Anita L. Vangelisti, *Interpersonal Communication and Human Relationships* (Boston: Allyn & Bacon, 1996), p. 34.

[37]Yageneh June Torbati, "Census: Fewer Than 10 Percent of City Households Are Nuclear Families," *The Baltimore Sun*, December 18, 2010, http://articles.baltimoresun.com/2010-12-18/news/bs-md-census-households-20101217_1_nuclear-families-census-data-young-professionals.

[38]Lynn H. Turner and Richard West, *Perspectives on Family Communication*, 2nd ed. (Boston: McGraw Hill, 2002), p. 8.

[39]Based on family types in Lynn H. Turner and Richard West, *Perspectives on Family Communication*, 2nd ed. (Boston: McGraw Hill, 2002), p. 33 and pp. 18–37.

[40]Judith R. Harris as quoted in several online chats and interviews. See *The Washington Post*'s online chat, September 30, 1998, http://discuss.washingtonpost.com/wp-srv/zforum/98/harris093098.html; *Edge 58*, June 29, 1999, www.edge.org/documents/archive/edge58.html.

[41]Judith Rich Harris, "Where Is the Child's Environment? A Group Socialization Theory of Development," *Psychological Review* 102 (1995): 462, 469.

[42]"Blame Your Peers, Not Your Parents, Authors Says," *APA Monitor*, October 1998, www.snc.edu/psych/korshavn/peer01.html.

[43]For analysis and criticism of Harris's research, see Craig H. Hart, Lloyd D. Newell, and Susanne Frost Olsen, "Parenting Skills and Social–Communicative Competences in Childhood," in John O. Greene and Brant R. Burleson (Eds.), *Handbook of Communication and Social Interaction Skills* (Mahwah, NJ: Lawrence Erlbaum, 2003), pp. 774–776.

[44]Janet Maslin, "But Will It All Make 'Tiger Mom' Happy?," *The New York Times*, January 20, 2011, http://www.nytimes.com/2011/01/20/books/20book.html?_r=1.

[45]David Brooks, "Amy Chua Is a Wimp," *The New York Times*, January 17, 2011, http://www.nytimes.com/2011/01/18/opinion/18brooks.html.

[46]Paul Tough, "The Character Test," *The New York Times Magazine*, September 18, 2011, p. 40, http://www.nytimes.com/2011/10/02/magazine/reply-all-the-character-test.html.

[47]Lynn H. Turner and Richard West, *Perspectives on Family Communication*, 2nd ed. (Boston: McGraw Hill, 2002), pp. 125–126.

[48]Lynn H. Turner and Richard West, *Perspectives on Family Communication*, 2nd ed. (Boston: McGraw Hill, 2002), pp. 126–127.

[49]Lynn H. Turner and Richard West, *Perspectives on Family Communication*, 2nd ed. (Boston: McGraw Hill, 2002), p. 134.

[50]Tina Rosenberg, "The Power of Talking to Baby," *The New York Times*, April 14, 2013, p. YT8, http://opinionator.blogs.nytimes.com/2013/04/10/the-power-of-talking-to-your-baby.

[51]Tina Rosenberg, "The Power of Talking to Baby," *The New York Times*, April 14, 2013, p. YT8, http://opinionator.blogs.nytimes.com/2013/04/10/the-power-of-talking-to-your-baby.

[52]Malcolm R. Parks, "Ideology in Interpersonal Communication: Off the Couch and into the World," in Michael Burgoon (Ed.), *Communication Yearbook 5* (New Brunswick, NJ: Transaction Books, 1982), pp. 79–107.

[53]Joseph Luft, *Group Process: An Introduction to Group Dynamics*, 3rd ed. (Palo Alto, CA: Mayfield, 1984).

[54]Joseph Luft, *Group Process: An Introduction to Group Dynamics*, 3rd ed. (Palo Alto, CA: Mayfield, 1984).

[55]David W. Johnson, *Reaching Out: Interpersonal Effectiveness and Self-Actualization*, 7th ed. (Boston: Allyn & Bacon, 2000), p. 47.

[56]Joseph Luft, *Group Process: An Introduction to Group Dynamics*, 3rd ed. (Palo Alto, CA: Mayfield, 1984).

[57]Joseph Luft, *Group Process: An Introduction to Group Dynamics*, 3rd ed. (Palo Alto, CA: Mayfield, 1984), pp. 58–59.

[58]For more information on self-disclosure skills, see David W. Johnson, *Reaching Out: Interpersonal Effectiveness and Self-Actualization*, 7th ed. (Boston: Allyn & Bacon, 2000), pp. 59–61.

[59]Irvin Altman and Dalmas Taylor, *Social Penetration: The Development of Interpersonal Relationships* (New York: Holt, Rinehart, and Winston, 1973).

[60]Walid A. Afifi and Laura K. Guerrero, "Motivations Underlying Topic Avoidance in Close Relationships," in Sandra Petronio (Ed.), *Balancing the Secrets of Private Disclosure* (Mahwah, NJ: Lawrence Erlbaum, 2000), p. 168.

[61]See *Shrek*, DreamWorks, 2003.

[62]David W. Johnson, *Reaching Out: Interpersonal Effectiveness and Self-Actualization*, 7th ed. (Boston: Allyn & Bacon, 2000), p. 61.

[63]Jack R. Gibb, "Defensive Communication," *Journal of Communication* 2 (1961): 141–148.

[64]The original Gibb article was published in 1961 without references or explanations of the research methodology. Although Gibb's climate categories are interesting, researchers have concluded, "the confidence placed in Gibb's theory of supportive and defensive communication as currently construed has been facile and empirically unwarranted." See Gordon Forward and Kathleen Czech, "Why (Most) Everything You Think You Know About Gibb's Supportive and Defensive Communication Climate May be Wrong and What To Do About It," Paper presented to the Small Group Communication Division at the National Communication Association Convention, San Diego, 2008, p. 16; Gordon L. Forward, Kathleen Czech, and Carmen M. Lee, "Assessing Gibb's Supportive and Defensive Communication Climate: An Examination of Measurement and Construct Validity," *Communication Research Reports* 28 (2011): 1–15.

[65]Based on Jack R. Gibb, "Defensive Communication," *Journal of Communication* 2 (1961): 141–148; See also http://lynn_meade.tripod.com/id61_m.htm.

[66]Robert Plutchik, *Emotions: A Psychoevolutionary Synthesis* (New York: Harper and Row, 1980).

[67]Robert Plutchik, "Emotions: A General Psychoevolutionary Theory," in K. R. Scherer and Paul Ekman (Eds.), *Approaches to Emotion* (Mahwah, NJ: Lawrence Erlbaum, 1984), p. 203.

[68]Daniel Goleman, *Working with Emotional Intelligence* (New York: Bantam Books, 1998), p. 317.

[69]Peter Salovey and John D. Mayer, "*Emotional Intelligence, Imagination, Cognition, and Personality* 9 (1990): 185-211. On p. 189, Salovey and Mayer define emotional intelligence as "the ability to monitor one's own and others' feelings and emotions, to discriminate among them and to use this information to guide one's thinking and actions."

[70]See Daniel Goleman, *Emotional Intelligence: Why It Can Matter More Than IQ* (New York: Bantam, 1995); Daniel Goleman, *Working with Emotional Intelligence* (New York: Bantam Books, 1998); Hendrie Weisinger, *Emotional Intelligence at Work* (San Francisco: Jossey-Bass, 1998).

[71]Daniel Goleman, *Emotional Intelligence: Why It Can Matter More Than IQ*, (New York: Bantam, 1995), pp. 27–28. See also Antonio R. Damasio, *Descartes' Error: Emotion, Reason, and the Human Brain* (New York: Quill, 2000).

[72]Daniel Goleman, *Emotional Intelligence: Why It Can Matter More Than IQ*, (New York: Bantam, 1995), pp. 27–28. See also Antonio R. Damasio, *Descartes' Error: Emotion, Reason, and the Human Brain* (New York: Quill, 2000).

[73]Terri Orbuch, "Relationship Rescue: Jealousy Can Eat Away at Happiness: Distinguishing Different Kinds of Jealousy," New Avenue, *Huffington Post*, July 2, 2012, http://www.huffingtonpost.com/2012/06/30/relationship-rescue-jealousy_n_1639878.html; Terri Orbuch, "Jealousy in New Relationships," The Love Doctor, *Psychology Today*, July 16, 2010, http://www.psychologytoday.com/blog/the-love-doctor/201007/jealousy-in-new-relationships; Jennifer L. Bevin, *The Communication of Jealousy* (New York: Peter Lang, 2013).

[74]Terri Orbuch, "Jealousy in New Relationships," The Love Doctor, *Psychology Today*, July 16, 2010, http://www.psychologytoday.com/blog/the-love-doctor/201007/jealousy-in-new-relationships.

[75]Cambridge University Press Media Release, "Hardwired for Jealousy: Stalkers' Brains Could Be Programmed for Obsession, New Research Shows," December 13, 1012, http://www.cambridge.org/about-us/media/press-releases/hardwired-jealousy-research.

[76]Laura K. Guerrero and Peter A. Andersen, "The Dark Side of Jealousy and Envy: Desire, Delusions, Desperation, and Destructive Communication," in Brian H. Spitzberg and William R. Cupach (Eds.), *The Dark Side of Close Relationships* (Mahwah, NJ: Lawrence Erlbaum Associates, 1998), pp. 55, 66.

[77]Brant R. Burleson, "Emotional Support Skills," in John O. Greene and Brant R. Burleson (Eds.), *Handbook of Communication and Social Interaction Skills* (Mahwah, NJ: Lawrence Erlbaum, 2003), p. 552.

[78]Terry Orbuch, "Relationships Rescue: Jealousy Can Eat Away at Happiness," Next Avenue, *Huffington Post*, July 2, 2012, http://www.huffingtonpost.com/2012/06/30/relationship-rescue-jealousy_n_1639878.html.

[79]Based on Laura K. Guerrero et al., "Coping with the Green-Eyed Monster: Conceptualizing and Measuring Communicative Responses to Romantic Jealousy," *Western Journal of Communication* 59 (1995): 270–304; Laura K. Guerrero and Walid Afifi, "Toward a Goal-Oriented Approach for Understanding Communicative Responses to Jealousy," *Western Journal of Communication* 63 (1999): 216–248. The three communication strategies are labeled as follows in these articles: Integrative Communication, Compensatory Restoration, and Negative Affect Expression.

[80]Terri Orbuch, "Relationship Rescue: Jealousy Can Eat Away At Happiness: Distinguishing Different Kinds of Jealousy," New Avenue, *Huffington Post*, July 2, 2012, http://www.huffingtonpost.com/2012/06/30/relationship-rescue-jealousy_n_1639878.html; Terri Orbuch, "Jealousy in New Relationships," The Love Doctor, *Psychology Today*, July 16, 2010, http://www.psychologytoday.com/blog/the-love-doctor/201007/jealousy-in-new-relationships; Jennifer L. Bevan, *The Communication of Jealousy* (New York: Peter Lang, 2013).

[81]Graham D. Bodie et al., "The Temporal Stability and Situational Contingency of Active-Empathic Listening," *Western Journal of Communication* 77 (2013): 126. See also Christopher C. Gearhart and Graham D. Bodie, "Active-Empathic Listening as a General Social Skill: Evidence from Bivariate and Canonical Correlations," *Communication Reports* 24 (2011): 86–98.

[82]Based on Graham D. Bodie et al, "The Temporal Stability and Situational Contingency of Active-Empathic Listening," *Western Journal of Communication* 77 (2013): 119.

[83]Brant R. Burleson, "Emotional Support Skills," in John O. Greene and Brant R. Burleson (Eds.), *Handbook of Communication and Social Interaction Skills* (Mahwah, NJ: Lawrence Erlbaum, 2003), pp. 589–681.

[84]Brant R. Burleson, Amanda J. Holmstrom, and Cristina M. Gilstrap, "Guys Can't Say *That* to Guys: Four Experiments Assessing the Normative Motivation Account for Deficiencies in the Emotional Support Provided by Men," *Communication Monographs* 72 (2005): 582.

[85]Susan M. Jones and John G. Wirtz, "How Does the Comforting Process Work? An Empirical Test of an Appraisal-Based Model of Comforting," *Human Communication Research* 32 (2006): 217.

[86]Brant R. Burleson, "Emotional Support Skills," in John O. Greene and Brant R. Burleson (Eds.), *Handbook of Communication and Social Interaction Skills* (Mahwah, NJ: Lawrence Erlbaum, 2003), p. 553.

[87]National Communication Association Credo for Ethical Communication, www.natcom.org/aboutNCA/Policies/Platform.html.

[88]Paula S. Tompkins, *Practicing Communication Ethics* (Boston: Allyn & Bacon, 2011), p. 83.

[89]Elaine E. Englehardt, "Introduction to Ethics in Interpersonal Communication," in Elaine E. Englehardt (Ed.), *Ethical Issues in Interpersonal Communication* (Fort Worth, TX: Harcourt, 2001), pp. 1–25; Carol Gilligan, "Images of Relationship," and Nel Noddings, "An Ethics of Care," in Elaine E. Englehardt (Ed.), *Ethical Issues in Interpersonal Communication* (Fort Worth, TX: Harcourt, 2001), pp. 88–96 and 96–103.

[90]Brant R. Burleson, "Emotional Support Skills," in John O. Greene and Brant R. Burleson (Eds.), *Handbook of Communication and Social Interaction Skills* (Mahwah, NJ: Lawrence Erlbaum, 2003), p. 583.

[91]Daniel Goleman, "Friends for Life: An Emerging Biology of Emotional Healing," *The New York Times*, October 10, 2006, p. D5. Also see, Daniel Goleman, *Social Intelligence* (New York: Bantam, 2006).

[92]Nicholas Bakalar, "Five-Second Touch Can Convey Specific Emotions, Study Finds," *The New York Times*, August 11, 2009, p. D3, http://www.nytimes.com/2009/08/11/science/11touch.html&gt.

[93]Daniel Goleman, *Social Intelligence* (New York: Bantam, 2006), p. 243.

[94]Martin S. Remland, *Nonverbal Communication in Everyday Life*, 2nd ed. (Boston: Houghton Mifflin, 2003), p. 330.

[95]Based on Daniel Goleman, *Working with Emotional Intelligence* (New York: Bantam Books, 1998), pp. 26, 27; Hendrie Weisinger, *Emotional Intelligence at Work* (San Francisco: Jossey-Bass, 1998); Daniel Goleman, *Emotional Intelligence: Why It Can Matter More Than IQ* (New York: Bantam, 1995).

Chapter 8

[1]Diane Vaughan, *Uncoupling: How Relationships Come Apart* (New York: Vintage, 1986), p. 3.

[2]Ellie Lisitsa, "The Positive Perspective: Dr. Gottman's Magic Ratio!" *The Gottman Institute Relationship Blog*, December 3, 2012, http://www.gottmanblog.com/2012/12/the-positive-perspective-dr-gottmans.html.

[3]Based on Richard West and Lynn H. Turner, *Introducing Communication Theory*, 2nd ed. (New York: McGraw-Hill, 2004), p. 215. See also Dominic A. Infante, Andrew S. Rancer, and Deanna F. Womack, *Building Communication Theory*, 4th ed. (Prospect Heights, IL: Waveland, 2003), pp. 212–214; Leslie A. Baxter, "Dialectical Contradictions in Relationships Development," *Journal of Social and Personal Relationships* 6 (1990): 69–88.

[4]Leslie A. Baxter and Barbara M. Montgomery, *Relating: Dialogues and Dialectics* (New York: Guilford Press, 1996), p. 19.

[5]Leslie A. Baxter and Barbara M. Montgomery, *Relating: Dialogues and Dialectics* (New York: Guilford Press, 1996), p. 5.

[6]See Leslie A. Baxter, "A Dialectical Perspective on Communication Strategies in Relationship Development," in Steve Duck (Ed.), *Handbook of Personal Relationships* (New York: Wiley, 1990), pp. 257–273.

[7]Lawrence B. Rosenfeld, "Overview of the Ways Privacy, Secrecy, and Disclosure Are Balanced in Today's Society," in Sandra Petronio (Ed.), *Balancing the Secrets of Private Disclosures* (Mahwah: NJ: Lawrence Erlbaum, 2000), p. 5.

[8]Richard West and Lynn H. Turner, *Introducing Communication Theory*, 3rd ed. (New York: McGraw-Hill, 2007), p. 203.

[9]Abigail A. Baird, *THINK Psychology* (Upper Saddle River, NJ: Prentice Hall, 2010), p. 4.

[10]Isabel B. Myers with Peter B. Myers, *Gifts Differing: Tenth Anniversary Edition* (Palo Alto, CA: Consulting Psychologists, 1990).

[11]Annie Murphy Paul, *The Cult of Personality* (New York: Free Press, 2004), pp. 125–127.

[12]Exercise caution in accepting and applying psychological theories as "laws" of interpersonal communication. Also note, "Most people's personalities, psychologists note, do not fall neatly into one category or another, but occupy some intermediate zone.... [Nor are these traits necessarily] inborn or immutable types," Annie Murphy Paul, *The Cult of Personality*, (New York: Free Press, 2004), pp. 125–127.

[13]Robert E. Levasseur, *Breakthrough Business Meetings: Shared Leadership in Action* (Holbrook, MA: Bob Adams, 1994), p. 79.

[14]Carl E. Larson and Frank M. J. LaFasto, *TeamWork: What Must Go Right/What Can Go Wrong* (Newbury Park, CA: Sage, 1989), p. 63.

[15]Otto Kroeger and Janet M. Thuesen, *Type Talk: Or How to Determine Your Personality Type and Change Your Life* (New York: Delacorte, 1988), p. 80.

[16]This non-validated instrument is a compilation of Myers-Briggs Type Indicator traits based on Isa N. Engleberg's analysis, background, and experience as a certified Myers-Briggs Type Indicator® trainer and a synthesis of MBTI resources (© Isa N. Engleberg). The authorized Myers-Briggs Type Indicator® instrument is for licensed use only by qualified professionals whose qualifications are on file and have been accepted by Consulting Psychologists Press, Inc.

[17]Dudley Weeks, *The Eight Essential Steps to Conflict Resolution*, (New York: Putnam, 1992), p. 7.

[18]Ronald T. Potter-Efron, *Work Rage: Preventing Anger and Resolving Conflict on the Job* (New York: Barnes and Noble Books, 2000), pp. 22–23.

[19]Kenneth Cloke and Joan Goldsmith, *Resolving Conflicts at Work: A Complete Guide for Everyone on the Job* (San Francisco: Jossey-Bass, 2000), p. 23.

[20]See Kenneth W. Thomas and Ralph W. Kilmann, "Developing a Forced-Choice Measure of Conflict-Handling Behavior: The MODE Instrument," *Educational Psychological Measurement* 37 (1977): 390–395; William W. Wilmot and Joyce L. Hocker, *Interpersonal Conflict*, 7th ed. (New York: McGraw-Hill, 2007), pp. 130–175; Dudley D. Cahn and Ruth Anna Abigail, *Managing Conflict Through Communication*, 5th ed. (Boston: Pearson, 2014), pp. 29–54.

[21]Isa N. Engleberg and Dianna R. Wynn, *Working in Groups: Communication Principles and Strategies*, 6th ed. (Boston: Pearson, 2013), p. 177, by permission of the publisher and authors. Based on Kenneth W. Thomas, *Intrinsic Motivation at Work: Building Energy and Commitment* (San Francisco: Berret-Koehler, 2000), p. 94.

[22]Daniel J. Canary and William R. Cupach, *Competencies in Interpersonal Conflict* (New York: McGraw-Hill, 1997), p. 133.

[23]Russell Copranzano, et al, "Disputant Reactions to Managerial Conflict Resolution Tactics: A Comparison Among Argentina, the Dominican Republic, Mexico, and the United States," *Group and Organization Management* 24 (1999): 131.

[24]Jerry Wisinski, *Resolving Conflicts on the Job* (New York: American Management Association, 1993), pp. 27–31.

[25]Adapted from Dudley D. Cahn and Ruth Anna Abigail, *Managing Conflict Through Communication*, 5th ed. (Boston: Pearson, 2014), pp. 84–87.

[26]Dominic A. Infante and Andrew S. Rancer, "A Conceptualization and Measure of Argumentativeness," *Journal of Personality Assessment* 46 (1982): 72–80. Reproduced by permission of Society for Personality Assessment. www.personality.org.

[27]Dominic A. Infante and Andrew S. Rancer, "A Conceptualization and Measure of Argumentativeness," *Journal of Personality Assessment* 46 (1982): 72–80.

[28]Daniel J. Canary and William R. Cupach, *Competencies in Interpersonal Conflict* (New York: McGraw-Hill, 1997), p. 58.

[29]Regina Fazio Maruca, "The Electronic Negotiator: A Conversation with Kathleen Valley," *Harvard Business Review*, January 2000, http://hbr.org/2000/01/the-electronic-negotiator/ar/pr.

[30]Quoted in Frances Caircross, *The Company of the Future* (Cambridge: Harvard Business School, 2002), p. 108.

³¹Kali Munro, "Conflict in Cyberspace: How to Resolve Conflict Online," 2002, http://users.rider.edu/~suler/psycyber/psycyber.html.

³²Jeanne Segal and Melinda Smith, "Conflict Resolution Skills," *Help Guide* (In Collaboration with Harvard Health Publications), March 2013, http://www.helpguide.org/mental/eq8_conflict_resolution.htm.

³³Jeanne Segal and Melinda Smith, "Conflict Resolution Skills," *Help Guide* (In Collaboration with Harvard Health Publications), March 2013, http://www.helpguide.org/mental/eq8_conflict_resolution.htm.

³⁴Jeanne Segal and Melinda Smith, "Conflict Resolution Skills," *Help Guide* (In Collaboration with Harvard Health Publications), March 2013, http://www.helpguide.org/mental/eq8_conflict_resolution.htm.

³⁵Jeanne Segal and Melinda Smith, "Anger Management," *Help Guide* (In collaboration with Harvard Health Publications), April 2013, http://www.helpguide.org/mental/anger_management_control_tips_techniques.htm.

³⁶Georg H. Eifert, Matthew McKay, and John P. Forsyth, *ACT on Life Not on Anger* (Oakland, CA: New Harbinger, 2006).

³⁷Georg H. Eifert, Matthew McKay, and John P. Forsyth, *ACT on Life Not on Anger* (Oakland, CA: New Harbinger, 2006), pp. 15, 16.

³⁸Georg H. Eifert, Matthew McKay, and John P. Forsyth, *ACT on Life Not on Anger* (Oakland, CA: New Harbinger, 2006), pp. 19, 20.

³⁹Georg H. Eifert, Matthew McKay, and John P. Forsyth, *ACT on Life Not on Anger* (Oakland, CA: New Harbinger, 2006), p. 21.

⁴⁰Jeanne Segal and Melinda Smith, "Anger Management," *Help Guide* (In collaboration with Harvard Health Publications), April 2013, http://www.helpguide.org/mental/anger_management_control_tips_techniques.htm.

⁴¹Bill DeFoore, *Anger: Deal with It, Heal with It, Stop It from Killing You* (Deerfield Beach, FL: Health Communications, 1991), p. 8.

⁴²Georg H. Eifert, Matthew McKay, and John P. Forsyth, *ACT on Life Not on Anger* (Oakland, CA: New Harbinger, 2006), p. 19.

⁴³Daniel J. Canary and William R. Cupach, *Competencies in Interpersonal Conflict* (New York: McGraw-Hill, 1997), p. 78.

⁴⁴Aristotle, *Nicomachean Ethics*, translated by W. D. Ross; revised by J. O. Urmson, in Jonathan Barnes (Ed.), *The Complete Works of Aristotle: The Revised Oxford Translation* (Princeton, NJ: Princeton University Press, 1984), p. 1776.

⁴⁵Based on studies suggesting guidelines for expressing anger: See William W. Wilmot and Joyce L. Hocker, *Interpersonal Conflict*, 5th ed. (New York: McGraw Hill, 1998), p. 227.

⁴⁶Carol Tavris, *Anger: The Misunderstood Emotion* (New York: Simon and Schuster, 1982), p. 253.

⁴⁷Kenneth Cloke and Joan Goldsmith, *Resolving Conflicts at Work: A Complete Guide for Everyone on the Job* (San Francisco: Jossey-Bass, 2000), pp. 109–110; *When and How to Apologize*, University of Nebraska Cooperative Extension and the Nebraska Health and Human Services System, http://extension.unl.edu/welfare/apology.htm.

⁴⁸William W. Wilmot and Joyce L. Hocker, *Interpersonal Conflict*, 5th ed. (New York: McGraw Hill, 1998), p. 228.

⁴⁹"Assertiveness," January 6, 2012, Adapted from Positive Coping Skills Toolbox, VA Mental Illness Research, Education, and Clinical Centers (MIRECC), http://www.athealth.com/Consumer/disorders/assertiveness.html.

⁵⁰Sharon Anthony Bower and Gordon H. Bower, *Asserting Yourself: A Practical Guide to Positive Change* (Cambridge, MA: Perseus Books, 1991), p. 9; See also, "Assertiveness," January 6, 2010, http://www.athealth.com/Consumer/disorders/assertiveness.html.

⁵¹Sharon Anthony Bower and Gordon H. Bower, *Asserting Yourself: A Practical Guide to Positive Change* (Cambridge, MA: Perseus Books, 1991), pp. 4–5.

⁵²"Assertiveness," January 6, 2012, Adapted from Positive Coping Skills Toolbox, VA Mental Illness Research, Education, and Clinical Centers (MIRECC), http://www.athealth.com/Consumer/disorders/assertiveness.html.

⁵³Madelyn Burley-Allen, *Managing Assertively: How to Improve Your People Skills* (New York: John Wiley, 1983), p. 45.

⁵⁴"Assertiveness," January 6, 2012, Adapted from Positive Coping Skills Toolbox, VA Mental Illness Research, Education, and Clinical Centers (MIRECC), http://www.athealth.com/Consumer/disorders/assertiveness.html.

⁵⁵Barbara Aufiero, "Characteristics of Passive-Aggressive Behavior," *LiveStrong*, March 28, 2011, http://www.livestrong.com/article/112076-characteristics-passive-aggressive-behavior.

⁵⁶Paula S. Tompkins, *Practicing Communication Ethics: Development, Discernment, and Decision Making* (Boston: Pearson, 2011), pp. 56–57.

⁵⁷Based on Sissela Bok, *Lying: Moral Choice in Public and Private Life* (New York: Vintage Books, 1978) in Paula S. Tompkins, *Practicing Communication Ethics: Development, Discernment, and Decision Making* (Boston: Pearson, 2011), pp. 56–57.

⁵⁸Sharon Anthony Bower and Gordon H. Bower, *Asserting Yourself: A Practical Guide to Positive Change* (Cambridge, MA: Preseus, 1991), p. 90. See also, "Assertiveness," athealth.com, January 6, 2010, http://www.athealth.com/Consumer/disorders/assertiveness.html.

⁵⁹Edmund J. Bourne, *The Anxiety and Phobia Workbook*, 5th ed. (Oakland, CA: Harbinger, 2010), p. 306.

⁶⁰Edmund J. Bourne, *The Anxiety and Phobia Workbook*, 5th ed. (Oakland, CA: Harbinger, 2010), p. 307. The example is adapted and written by the textbook authors.

⁶¹Edmund J. Bourne, *The Anxiety and Phobia Workbook*, 5th ed. (Oakland, CA: Harbinger, 2010), p. 307.

⁶²© Isa N. Engleberg, 2010.

Chapter 9

¹Pew Research Center, "Millennials: Confident. Connected. Open to Change," February 24, 2010, http://www.pewsocialtrends.org/2010/02/24/millennials-confident-connected-open-to-change. For the full report see Pew Research Center, *Millennials: A Portrait of the Net Generation*, February 2010, http://pewsocialtrends.org/files/2010/10/millennials-confident-connected-open-to-change.pdf.

²Paul Davidson, "Managers to Millennials: Jobs Interviews No Time to Text," *USA Today*, April 29, 2013, http://www.usatoday.com/story/money/business/2013/04/28/college-grads-job-interviews/2113505.

³Center for Professional Excellence at York College of Pennsylvania, *2013 Professionalism in the Workplace* Report, January 2013, http://www.ycp.edu/media/yorkwebsite/cpe/York-College-Professionalism-in-the-Workplace-Study-2013.pdf. This is the fourth annual survey of professionalism in the workplace conducted by York College of Pennsylvania's Center for Professional Excellence. Each year, people responsible for hiring new college graduates are surveyed to assess the state of professionalism in the workplace.

⁴Meghan Casserly, "Top Five Personality Traits Employers Hire Most," *Forbes*, October 4, 2012, http://www.forbes.com/sites/meghancasserly/2012/10/04/top-five-personality-traits-employers-hire-most.

⁵James M. Kouzes and Barry Z. Posner, *Encouraging the Heart: A Leader's Guide to Rewarding and Recognizing Others* (San Francisco: Jossey-Bass, 1999), p. 4.

⁶Matthew Gilbert, *Communication Miracles at Work: Effective Tools and Tips for Getting the Most from Your Work Relationships* (Berkeley, CA: Conari Press, 2002), p. 112.

⁷Matthew Gilbert, *Communication Miracles at Work: Effective Tools and Tips for Getting the Most from Your Work Relationships* (Berkeley, CA: Conari Press, 2002), p. 112.

⁸Based on a Gallop Poll reported in Teresa Amabile and Steven Kramer, "Do Happier People Work Harder," *The New York Times*, September 4, 2011, p. SR7.

⁹Daniel P. Modaff, Sue DeWine, and Jennifer A. Butler, *Organizational Communication: Foundations, Challenges, Misunderstandings* (Los Angeles, CA: Roxbury, 2008), p. 197.

¹⁰Daniel P. Modaff, Sue DeWine, and Jennifer A. Butler, *Organizational Communication: Foundations, Challenges, Misunderstandings* (Los Angeles, CA: Roxbury, 2008), p. 207.

¹¹Daniel P. Modaff, Sue DeWine, and Jennifer A. Butler, *Organizational Communication: Foundations, Challenges, Misunderstandings* (Los Angeles, CA: Roxbury, 2008), p. 206.

¹²Daniel P. Modaff, Sue DeWine, and Jennifer A. Butler, *Organizational Communication: Foundations, Challenges, Misunderstandings* (Los Angeles, CA: Roxbury, 2008), p. 198.

¹³Based on Daniel P. Modaff, Sue DeWine, and Jennifer A. Butler, *Organizational Communication: Foundations, Challenges, Misunderstandings* (Los Angeles, CA: Roxbury, 2008), pp. 236–237.

¹⁴Monica Tanase-Coles, "Empathy in Business: Indulgence or Invaluable?," *Forbes*, March 22, 2013, http://www.forbes.com/sites/ashoka/2013/03/22/empathy-in-business-indulgence-or-invaluable.

¹⁵Matthew Gilbert, *Communication Miracles at Work: Effective Tools and Tips for Getting the Most from Your Work Relationships* (Berkeley, CA: Conari Press, 2002), p. 153.

¹⁶Daniel P. Modaff, Sue DeWine, and Jennifer A. Butler, *Organizational Communication: Foundations, Challenges, Misunderstandings* (Los Angeles, CA: Roxbury, 2008), p. 157.

¹⁷Robert Longely, "Labor Studies of Attitudes Toward Work and Leisure: U.S. Workers Are Happy and Stress Is Over-stressed," August 1999, http://usgovinfo.about.com/od/censusandstatistics/a/labordaystudy.htm.

¹⁸Carley H. Dodd, *Managing Business and Professional Communication* (Boston: Allyn & Bacon, 2004), p. 40.

¹⁹Michael E. Pacanowsky and Nick O'Donnell-Trujillo, "Communication and Organizational Cultures," *Western Journal of Speech Communication* 46 (1982): 115–130; Michael E. Pacanowsky and Nick O'Donnell-Trujillo, *Communication Monographs* 50 (1983): 127–130.

²⁰Based on Carley H. Dodd, *Managing Business and Professional Communication* (Boston: Allyn & Bacon, 2004), pp. 169–170.

²¹Council of Better Business Bureaus, "Dealing with Unruly Customers," 2013, http://www.bbb.org/alerts/article.asp?ID=370.

²²Based on John Tschohl, Service Quality Institute, "Service, Not Servitude: Common Sense Is Critical Element of Customer Service," 2004, http://www.customer-service.com/articles/022502.cfm.

²³Joel Lovell, "Workplace Rumors Are True," *The New York Times*, December 10, 2006, http://www.nytimes.com/2006/12/10/magazine/10section4.t-9.html.

²⁴Joel Lovell, "Workplace Rumors Are True," *The New York Times*, December 10, 2006, http://www.nytimes.com/2006/12/10/magazine/10section4.t-9.html.

²⁵Rachel Devine, "Gossip at Work," *iVillage Work & Career*, October 30, 2000, http://www.ivillage.co.uk/gossip-work/83086.

²⁶Quoted in Samuel Greengard, "Gossip Poisons Business: HR Can Stop It," *Workforce*, July 15, 2001, http://www.workforce.com/articles/gossip-poisons-business-hr-can-stop-it.

²⁷Samuel Greengard, "Gossip Poisons Business: HR Can Stop It," *Workforce*, July 15, 2001, http://www.workforce.com/articles/gossip-poisons-business-hr-can-stop-it. "Rumor Has It—Dealing with Misinformation in the Workplace," *Entrepreneur*, September 1, 1997, http://www.entrepreneur.com/article/14590.

²⁸Rachel Devine, "Gossip at Work," *iVillage Work & Career*, October 30, 2000. http://www.ivillage.co.uk/gossip-work/83086; Carl Skooglund and Glenn Coleman, "Advice from the Ethics Office at Texas Instruments Corporation: Gossiping

notes

at Work," *Online Ethics Center for Engineering and Science* June 7, 2006, http://www.onlineethics.org/Resources/Cases/gossip.aspx; Muriel Solomon, *Working with Difficult People* (New York: Prentice Hall, 2002), pp. 125–126.

[29]Sean M. Horan and Rebecca M. Chory, "Understanding Work-Life Blending: Credibility Implications for Those Who Date at Work, *Communication Studies*, 62 (2011): 565; "Working It—L.A. Stories—Survey Data on Office Romances," *Los Angeles Business Journal*, May 27, 2002, http://los-angeles-business-journal.vlex.com/source/los-angeles-business-journal-2851/issue/2002/5/27.

[30]Sean M. Horan, "Adventures in Dating: Workplace Romance Motives," *Psychology Today*, June 5, 2013, http://www.psychologytoday.com/blog/adventures-in-dating/201306/workplace-romance-motives; "Romance in the Office is Common Occurrence," *Society for Industrial and Organizational Psychology*, 2013, http://www.siop.org/Media/News/office_romance.asp.

[31]Bill Leonard, "Workplace Romances Seem to Be Rule, Not Exception," *HR Magazine*, April 2001, http://www.findarticles.com/p/articles/mi_m3495/is_4_46/ai_73848276.

[32]"Study: 54 Percent of Companies Ban Facebook, Twitter at Work," *Wired.Com*, October 9, 2009, http://www.wired.com/epicenter/2009/10/study-54-of-companies-ban-facebook-twitter-at-work.

[33]Sharon Gaudin, "Study: Facebook Use Cuts Productivity at Work," *Computerworld*, July 22, 2009, www.computerworld.com/s/article/print/9139020/Study_54_of_companies_ban_Facebook_Twitter_at_work?taxonomyName=Web+2.0+and+Web+Apps&taxonomyId=16.

[34]Association of Corporate Counsel, "Workplace Challenges Associated with Employees' Social Media Use," *Legal Resources QuickCounsel*, http://www.acc.com/legalresources/quickcounsel/wcawesmu.cfm.

[35]Ed Piantek, "Flirting with Disaster," *Risk and Insurance*, May 1, 2000, http://www.findarticles.com/p/articles/mi_m0BJK/is_200_May/ai_62408701.

[36]Rieva Lesonsky, "Office Romances on the Rise Among Millennial Employees," *The Huffington Post*, April 9, 2012, http://www.huffingtonpost.com/2012/04/09/office-romances-on-the-rise-among-millennial-employees_n_1412190.html.

[37]U.S. Equal Employment Opportunity Commission, "Facts about Sexual Harassment," June 27, 2002, http://www.eeoc.gov/facts/fs-sex.html.

[38]Lawrence Downes, "How the Military Talks About Sexual Assault," *The New York Times*, May 26, 2013, http://takingnote.blogs.nytimes.com/2013/05/26/how-the-military-talks-about-sexual-assault; Ernesto Londoño, "Military Academies Report Increase in Sexual Assaults," *The Washington Post*, December 21, 2012, http://articles.washingtonpost.com/2012-12-21/world/36017489_1_sexual-assault-military-academies-defense-department-report.

[39]Deborah Ware Balogh, et al, "The Effects of Delayed Report and Motive for Reporting on Perceptions of Sexual Harassment," *Sex Roles: A Journal of Research*, 48, April 2003: 337–348.

[40]Ed Piantek, "Flirting with Disaster," *Risk and Insurance*, May 1, 2000, http://www.findarticles.com/p/articles/mi_m0BJK/is_200_May/ai_62408701.

[41]Nichole L. Torres, "Boys Will Not Be Boys: Lewdness and Rudeness Can Be a Mess for Your Business—Even Without Mixed Company," *Entrepreneur* 29, November 1, 2001: 16.

[42]Rebecca A. Thacker and Stephen F. Gohmann, "Male/Female Differences in Perceptions and Effects of Hostile Environment Sexual Harassment: 'Reasonable' Assumptions?" *Public Personnel Management*, September 22, 1993, http://www.allbusiness.com/human-resources/workforce-management/401746-1.html. See also Maria Rotundo, Dung-Hanh Nguyen, and Paul R. Sacket, "A Meta-analytic Review of Gender Differences in Perceptions of Sexual Harassment," *Journal of Applied Psychology* 86 (October 2001): 914–922.

[43]Julie A. Woodzicka and Marianne LaFrance, "Real Versus Imagined Gender Harassment," *Journal of Social Issues* 57 (Spring 2001): 15–30.

[44]Deborah Ware Balogh et al., "The Effects of Delayed Report and Motive for Reporting on Perceptions of Sexual Harassment," *Sex Roles*, 48 (2003): 337–348.

[45]Based on Daniel P. Modaff and Sue DeWine, *Organizational Communication: Foundations, Challenges, Misunderstandings* (Los Angeles, CA: Roxbury, 2002), p. 202.

[46]Daniel P. Modaff and Sue DeWine, *Organizational Communication: Foundations, Challenges, Misunderstandings* (Los Angeles, CA: Roxbury, 2002), p. 236.

[47]Cited in Matthew Gilbert, *Communication Miracles at Work: Effective Tools and Tips for Getting the Most from Your Work Relationships* (Berkeley, CA: Conari Press, 2002), p. 10; See also Humphrey Taylor, "The Mood of American Workers," *Harris Interactive*, January 19, 2000, http://www.harrisinteractive.com/harris_poll.

[48]Virginia Galt, "When Quitting a Job, Discretion Is the Better Part of Valor," http://www.theglobeandmail.com/report-on-business/when-quitting-a-job-discretion-is-the-better-part-of-valour/article996915.

[49]Hal Plotkin, "Introduction," *Dealing with Difficult People* (Boston: Harvard Business School, 2005), p. 1.

[50]Hal Plotkin, "How to Handle Difficult Behaviors," *Dealing with Difficult People* (Boston: Harvard Business School, 2005), pp. 132–137.

[51]Ken Cloke and Joan Goldsmith "How to Handle Difficult Behaviors," *Dealing with Difficult People* (Boston: Harvard Business School, 2005), pp. 66–67.

[52]Matt Villano, "What to Tell the Company as You Walk Out the Door," *The New York Times*, November 27, 2005, p. BU8. Quoting Jim Atkinson, regional vice president, Right Management Consultants, Broadview Heights, OH.

[53]Dawn Rosenberg McKay, "Job Loss: How to Cope," 2009, http://career-planning.about.com/od/jobloss/a/job_loss.htm.

[54]This definition is a composite of elements found in most academic definitions of an interview. See, for example, Larry Powell and Jonathan Amsbary, *Interviewing: Situations and Contexts* (Boston: Pearson/Allyn & Bacon, 2006), p. 1; Charles Stewart and William B. Cash, *Interviewing: Principles and Practices*, 10th ed. (New York: McGraw-Hill, 2003), p. 4; Jeanne Tessier Barone and Jo Young Switzer, *Interviewing Art and Skill* (Boston: Allyn & Bacon, 1995), p. 8.

[55]Richard Nelson Bolles, *What Color Is Your Parachute? A Practical Manual for Job-Hunters and Career-Changers* (Berkeley: Ten Speed Press, 2007), p. 78.

[56]Accountemps study displayed in *USA Today* Snapshots, "Most Common Job Interview Mistakes Noticed by Employers," *USA Today*, October 17, 2006, p. B1.

[57]Larry Powell and Jonathan Amsbary, *Interviewing: Situations and Contexts* (Boston: Pearson/Allyn & Bacon, 2006), p. 47; Wallace V. Schmidt and Roger N. Conaway, *Results-Oriented Interviewing: Principles, Practices, and Procedures* (Boston: Allyn & Bacon, 1998), p. 107; Charles Stewart and William B. Cash, *Interviewing: Principles and Practices*, 10th ed. (New York: McGraw-Hill, 2003), p. 245; *Job Link USA*, "Interview," http://www.joblink-usa.com/interview.htm; CollegeGrad.Com, "Candidate Interview Questions," http://www.collegegrad.com/jobsearch/16-15.shtml.

[58]"Lying: How Can You Protect Your Company?" *Your Workplace, Monthly Newsletter of Westaff*, http://www.westaff.com/yourworkplace/ywissues37_full.html.

[59]Daryl Koehn, University of St. Thomas Center for Business Ethics, "Rewriting History: Resume Falsification More Than a Passing Fiction," http://www.stthom.edu/cbes/resume.html.

[60]Donna Hemmila, "Tired of Lying, Cheating Job Applicants, Employers Calling in Detectives," *San Francisco Business Times* March 1, 1999, http://www.esrcheck.com/articles/Tired-of-lying-cheating-job--applicants-employers-calling-in-detectives.php; http://www.bizjournals.com/sanfrancisco/stories/1998/03/02/story6.html?page=2.

[61]Barbara Mende, "Employers Crack Down on Candidates Who Lie," *Wall Street Journal Career Journal*, http://www.careerjournal.com/jobhunting/resumes/20020606-mende.html.

[62]Wallace V. Schmidt and Conaway, *Results-Oriented Interviewing: Principles, Practices, and Procedures* (Boston: Allyn & Bacon, 1999), p. 84.

[63]Mary Heiberger and Julia Miller Vick, "How To Handle Difficult Interview Questions," *Chronicle of Higher Education*, January 22, 1999, http://chronicle.com/jobs/v45/i21/4521career.htm; Allison Doyle, "Illegal Interview Questions: Questions Employers Should Not Ask, 2013, http://jobsearch.about.com/od/interviewsnetworking/a/illegalinterv.htm.

[64]Charles J. Stewart and William B. Cash, Jr., *Interviewing: Principles and Practices*, 10th ed. (Boston: McGraw-Hill, 2003), pp. 254–255; "Candidate Interview Questions," http://www.collegegrad.com/jobsearch/16-15.shtml.

[65]Wallace V. Schmidt and Conaway, *Results-Oriented Interviewing: Principles, Practices, and Procedures* (Boston: Allyn & Bacon, 1999), pp. 100–111.

[66]Richard Nelson Bolles, *The 2007 What Color Is Your Parachute? A Practical Manual for Job-Hunters and Career-Changers* (Berkeley, CA: Ten Speed Press, 2007), p. 82.

[67]In addition to the books we've cited in this chapter, we also researched numerous web sites: Jacquelyn Smith, "The 13 Most Outrageous Job Interview Mistakes," *Forbes*, February 21, 2013, http://www.forbes.com/sites/jacquelynsmith/2013/02/21/the-13-most-outrageous-job-interview-mistakes; "The 7 Worst Job Interview Mistakes People Make," *The Fiscal Times*, May 15, 2013, http://www.thefiscaltimes.com/Articles/2013/05/15/The-7-Worst-Job-Interview-Job-Mistakes-People-Make.aspx#page1; Alison Doyle, "Most Common Interview Mistakes," About.com, Job Seeking, http://jobsearch.about.com/od/interview-mistakes/ss/most-common-interview-mistakes_2.htm; Dave Johnson, "10 Top Mistakes People Make in Job Interviews," *CBS MoneyWatch*, February 12, 2013, http://finance.yahoo.com/news/10-top-mistakes-people-make-in-job-interviews-190143044.html; Four Major Job Interview Mistakes to Avoid," May 9, 2013, http://www.ihcus.com/2013/05/09/four-major-job-interview-mistakes-to-avoid. Anna Davies, "7 Common Job Interview Mistakes, *Cosmopolitan*, 2012, http://www.cosmopolitan.com/advice/work-money/job-interview-mistakes#slide-2; Ryan Murphy, "Top Ten: Job Interview Mistakes," Ask Men, http://www.askmen.com/feeder/askmenRSS_article_print_2006.php?ID=1005465; Career and Employment Center, Fresno City College, https://www.jobs.fresnocitycollege.edu/Cmx_Content.aspx?cpId=38.

[68]Nate C. Hindman, "Millennials' Biggest Interview Mistake Is 'Inappropriate Attire,' According To Hiring Managers," *The Huffington Post*, September 25, 2012, http://www.huffingtonpost.com/2012/09/24/millenial-biggest-interview-mistake_n_1910103.html?view=print&comm_ref=false.

[69]Paul Davidson, "Managers to Millennials: Jobs Interviews No Time to Text," *USA Today*, April 29, 2013, http://www.usatoday.com/story/money/business/2013/04/28/college-grads-job-interviews/2113505.

[70]J. Maureen Henderson, "3 Ways Millennials Can Master Job Interviews," *Forbes*, May 6, 2013, http://www.forbes.com/sites/jmaureenhenderson/2013/05/06/3-ways-millennials-can-master-job-interviews.

[71]Anna Davies, "8 Common Job Interview Mistakes," *Cosmopolitan*, 2013, http://www.cosmopolitan.com/advice/work-money/job-interview-mistakes#slide-2.

[72]Alison Brod, president of Alison Brod PR, quoted in Anna Davies, "8 Common Job Interview Mistakes," *Cosmopolitan*, 2013, http://www.cosmopolitan.com/advice/work-money/job-interview-mistakes#slide-2.

[73]Career and Employment Center, Fresno City College, https://www.jobs.fresnocitycollege.edu/Cmx_Content.aspx?cpId=38.

[74]©Isa N. Engleberg.

Chapter 10

[1] See http://www.cirquedusoleil.com/en/home.aspx#/en/home/about.aspx; www.youtube.com/user/cirquedusoleil.

[2] Arupa Tesolin, "Igniting the Creative Spark at Cirque du Soleil—Arupa Tesolin Interviews Lyn Heward Creative Leader at Cirque," *Self Growth*, May 2008, http://www.selfgrowth.com/articles/Igniting_the_Creative_Spark_at_Cirque_du_Soleil.html. See also Vicki M. James, "Observations of Great Teamwork from Cirque Du Soleil," *Professional Project Services*, February 10, 2013, http://project-pro.us/2013/02/10/three-secrets-of-teamwork.

[3] Steve W. J. Kozlowski and Daniel R. Ilgen, "Enhancing the Effectiveness of Work Groups and Teams," *Psychological Science in the Public Interest* 7 (2006): 77.

[4] Peter D. Hart Research Associates, *How Should Colleges Prepare Students to Succeed in Today's Global Economy?* (Washington, DC: Peter D. Hart Research Associates, December 28, 2006), p. 2; See also Association of American Colleges and Universities, *College Learning for the New Global Age* (Washington, DC: Association of American Colleges and Universities, 2007).

[5] Patrick C. Kyllonen, *The Research Behind the ETS Personal Potential Index (PPI)*, Background Paper from the Educational Testing Service, 2008, http://www.ets.org/Media/Products/PPI/10411_PPI_bkgrd_report_RD4.pdf; Daniel S. de Vise, "New Index Will Score Graduate Students' Personality Tests," *The Washington Post*, July 10, 2009, p. A11.

[6] American Management Association "2010 Critical Skills Survey," quoted in Elaine Pofeldt, "Put Some Punch into Your Career," *Money*, May 2011, p. 24.

[7] Isa N. Engleberg and Dianna R. Wynn, *Working in Groups: Communication Principles and Strategies*, 6th ed. (Boston: Pearson, 2013), p. 3.

[8] Peter D. Hart Research Associates, *How Should Colleges Prepare Students to Succeed in Today's Global Economy?* (Washington, DC: Peter D. Hart Research Associates, December 2006), p. 7.

[9] Carl E. Larson and Frank M. J. LaFasto, *TeamWork: What Must Go Right/What Can Go Wrong* (Newbury Park, CA: Sage, 1989), p. 27.

[10] Jon R. Katzenbach and Douglas K. Smith, *The Wisdom of Teams: Creating the High-Performance Organization* (New York: HarperBusiness, 1999), p. 9.

[11] Robert B. Cialdini, "The Perils of Being the Best and the Brightest," *Becoming an Effective Leader* (Boston: Harvard Business School Press, 2005), pp. 174, 175.

[12] 3M Meeting Management Team with Jeannine Drew, *Mastering Meetings: Discovering the Hidden Potential of Effective Business Meetings* (New York: McGraw-Hill, 1994), p. 12.

[13] Steven G., Rogelberg, Linda Rhoades Shanock, and Cliff W. Scott, "Wasted Time and Money in Meetings: Increasing Return on Investment," *Small Group Communication* 43 (2012): 236–237.

[14] Linda Stewart, "Building Virtual Teams: Strategies for High Performance," *Forbes*, March 30, 2012, http://www.forbes.com/sites/ciocentral/2012/03/30/building-virtual-teams-strategies-for-high-performance.

[15] Susan B. Barnes, *Online Connections: Internet Interpersonal Relationships* (Cresskill, NJ: Hampton Press, 2001), p. 41.

[16] Isa N. Engleberg and Dianna R. Wynn, *Working in Groups: Communication Principles and Strategies*, 6th ed. (Boston: Pearson, 2013), pp. 268–271.

[17] Linda Stewart, "Building Virtual Teams: Strategies for High Performance," *Forbes*, March 30, 2012, http://www.forbes.com/sites/ciocentral/2012/03/30/building-virtual-teams-strategies-for-high-performance.

[18] Linda Stewart, "Building Virtual Teams: Strategies for High Performance," *Forbes*, March 30, 2012, http://www.forbes.com/sites/ciocentral/2012/03/30/building-virtual-teams-strategies-for-high-performance.

[19] Deborah L. Duarte and Nancy Tennant Snyder, *Mastering Virtual Teams*, 3rd ed. (San Francisco: Jossey-Bass, 2007), pp. 21, 158.

[20] Ernest G. Bormann, *Small Group Communication: Theory and Practice*, 3rd ed. (Edina, MN: Burgess, 1996), pp. 132–135, 181–183.

[21] Ernest G. Bormann, *Small Group Communication Theory and Practice*, 3rd ed. (Edina, MN: Burgess, 1996), pp. 134–135.

[22] Donald G. Ellis and B. Aubrey Fisher, *Small Group Decision Making: Communication and the Group Process*, 4th ed. (New York: McGraw-Hill, 1994), pp. 43–44.

[23] Rodney W. Napier and Matti K. Gershenfeld, *Groups: Theory and Experience*, 7th ed. (Boston: Houghton Mifflin, 2004), p. 182.

[24] Bruce W. Tuckman, "Developmental Sequence in Small Groups," *Psychological Bulletin* 63 (1965): 384–399. Tuckman's 1965 article is reprinted in *Group Facilitation: A Research and Applications Journal* 3 (Spring 2001), http://dennislearningcenter.osu.edu/references/Group%20DEV%20ARTICLE.doc. Note: Tuckman and Jensen identified a fifth stage—adjourning—in the 1970s. There is little research on the characteristics and behavior of members during this stage other than a decrease in interaction, and in some cases, separation anxiety. See Bruce Tuckman and Mary Ann Jensen, "Stages of Small-Group Development Revisited," *Group and Organization Studies* 2 (1977): 419–427.

[25] Artemis Change, Julie Duck, and Prashant Bordia, "Understanding the Multidimensionality of Group Development," *Small Group Research* 37 (2006): 329.

[26] Artemis Change, Julie Duck, and Prashant Bordia, "Understanding the Multidimensionality of Group Development," *Small Group Research* 37 (2006): 331, 337–338.

[27] Susan Wheelan and Nancy Brewer Danganan, "The Relationship Between the Internal Dynamics of Student Affairs Leadership Teams and Campus Leaders' Perceptions of the Effectiveness of Student Affairs Divisions," *Journal of Student Affairs Research and Practice* 40 (2002): 27.

[28] Susan Wheelan and Nancy Brewer Danganan, "The Relationship Between the Internal Dynamics of Student Affairs Leadership Teams and Campus Leaders' Perceptions of the Effectiveness of Student Affairs Divisions," *Journal of Student Affairs Research and Practice* 40 (2002): 96.

[29] Karen K. Jenn, "A Qualitative Analysis of Conflict Types and Dimensions in Organizational Groups," *Administrative Science Quarterly* 42 (1997): 540. See also Karen A. Jehn and Corine Bendersky, "Intragroup Conflict in Organizations: A Contingency Perspective on the Conflict-Outcome Relationship," in Barry Staw and Roderick Kramer (Eds.), *Research in Organizational Behavior*, Vol. 25 (Kidington, Oxford, UK: Elsevier, 2003), p. 540; Kristin J. Behfar et al., "Conflict in Small Groups: The Meaning and Consequences of Process Conflict," *Small Group Research* 42 (2011): 128.

[30] Kristin J. Behfar et al., "Conflict in Small Groups: The Meaning and Consequences of Process Conflict," *Small Group Research* 42 (2011): 136–137.

[31] Marvin E. Shaw, "Group Composition and Group Cohesiveness," in Robert S. Cathcart and Larry A. Samovar (Eds.), *Small Group Communication: A Reader*, 6th ed. (Dubuque, IA: Wm. C. Brown, 1992), pp. 214–220.

[32] Stanley M. Gully, Dennis J. Devine, and David J. Whitney, "A Meta-Analysis of Cohesion and Performance: Effects of Level of Analysis and Task Interdependence," *Small Group Research* 26: 497–521. Reprinted in *Small Group Research* 43 (2012): 718–719. Volume 43 of *Small Group Research* reprints four classic articles on group cohesion.

[33] Based on Ernest G. Bormann and Nancy Bormann, *Effective Small Group Communication*, 6th ed. (Edina, MN: Burgess, 1996), pp. 137–139.

[34] Patricia H. Andrews, "Group Conformity," in Robert S. Cathcart, Larry A. Samovar, and Linda D. Henman (Eds.), *Small Group Communication: Theory and Practice*, 7th ed. (Madison, WI: Brown and Benchmark, 1996), p. 185.

[35] Nicky Hayes, *Managing Teams: A Strategy for Success* (London: Thomson, 2004), p. 31.

[36] Kenneth D. Benne and Paul Sheats, "Functional Roles of Group Members," *Journal of Social Issues* 4 (1948): 41–49. We have modified the original Benne and Sheats list by adding or combining behaviors that we have observed, as well as roles identified by other writers and researchers.

[37] Kenneth D. Benne and Paul Sheats, "Functional Roles of Group Members," *Journal of Social Issues* 4 (1948): 41–49. We have modified the original Benne and Sheats list by adding or combining behaviors that we have observed, as well as roles identified by other writers and researchers.

[38] Kenneth D. Benne and Paul Sheats, "Functional Roles of Group Members," *Journal of Social Issues* 4 (1948): 41–49. We have modified the original Benne and Sheats list by adding or combining behaviors that we have observed, as well as roles identified by other writers and researchers.

[39] Based on Michael Doyle and David Straus, *How to Make Meetings Work* (New York: Jove, 1976), pp. 107–117. Several titles and behaviors are original contributions by the authors.

[40] James C. McCroskey and Virginia P. Richmond, "Correlates of Compulsive Communication: Quantitative and Qualitative Characteristics," *Communication Quarterly* 43 (1995): 39–52.

[41] Eric Harper et al, *The Leadership Secrets of Santa Claus: How to Get Big Things Done in YOUR "Workshop" ... All Year Long* (Dallas, TX: The Walk the Talk Company, 2003), pp. 78–79.

[42] Isa N. Engleberg and Dianna R. Wynn, *Working in Groups: Communication Principles and Strategies*, 3rd ed. (Boston: Houghton Mifflin, 2004), p. 207.

[43] Antony Bell, *Great Leadership: What It Is and What It Takes in a Complex World* (Mountain View, CA: Davies-Black, 2006), pp. 87, 91.

[44] Fred E. Feidler and Martin M. Chemers, *Improving Leadership Effectiveness: The Leader Match Concept*, 2nd ed. (New York: Wiley, 1984).

[45] See Joseph R. Santo, "Where the Fortune 50 CEOs Went to College," *Time*, August 15, 2006, http://www.time.com/time/printout/0,8816,1227055,00.html.

[46] Ivan G. Seidenberg, "Reference for Business," *Encyclopedia of Business*, 2nd edition, http://www.referenceforbusiness.com/biography/S-Z/Seidenberg-Ivan-G-1946.html.

[47] Matthew Miller, "The Wealthiest Black Americans," May 6, 2009, *Forbes*; http://www.forbes.com/sites/mfonobongnsehe/2013/03/05/the-black-billionaires-2013.

[48] "John Boehner, U.S. House Majority Leader," *Encyclopedia of World Biography*, http://www.notablebiographies.com/newsmakers2/2006-A-Ec/-Boehner-John-A.html.

[49] Based on material in Isa N. Engleberg and Dianna R. Wynn, *Working in Groups: Communication Principles and Strategies*, 6th ed. (Boston: Pearson, 2013), pp. 103–105.

[50] Edwin P. Hollander, *Leadership Dynamics: A Practical Guide to Effective Relationships* (New York: Macmillan, 1978), p. 53. See also a meta-analysis of this variable in Marianne Schmid Mast, "Dominance as Expressed and Inferred Through Speaking Time," *Human Communication Research* 28 (2002): 420–450.

[51] The 5-M Model of Leadership Effectiveness© is based, in part, on Martin M. Chemers's integrative theory of leadership, which identifies three functional aspects of leadership: image management, relationship development, and resource utilization. We have added two more functions—decision making and mentoring—and have incorporated more of a communication perspective into Chemers's view of leadership as a multifaceted process. See Martin M. Chemers, *An Integrative Theory of Leadership* (Mahwah, NJ: Lawrence Erlbaum, 1997), pp. 151–173. See also Isa N. Engleberg and Dianna R. Wynn, *Working in Groups: Communication Principles and Strategies*, 6th ed. (Boston: Pearson, 2013), pp. 113–117. © Isa N. Engleberg.

52 Orem Harari, *The Leadership Secrets of Colin Powell* (New York: McGraw-Hill, 2002), p. 249.

53 Mike Krzyzewski, "Coach K on How to Connect," *The Wall Street Journal*, July 16–17, 2011, p. C12.

54 Martin M. Chemers, *An Integrative Theory of Leadership* (Mahwah, NJ: Lawrence Erlbaum, 1997), p. 160.

55 Harvey Robbins and Michael Finley, *The New Why Teams Don't Work: What Goes Wrong and How to Make It Right* (San Francisco: Berrett-Koehler, 2000), p. 107.

56 Carol Tice, "Building the 21st Century Leader," *Entrepreneur*, February, 2007, pp. 66, 67.

57 Carol Tice, "Building the 21st Century Leader," *Entrepreneur*, February, 2007, p. 68.

58 Antony Bell, *Great Leadership: What It Is and What It Takes in a Complex World* (Mountain View, CA: Davies-Black, 2006), p. 67.

59 James M. Kouzes and Barry Z. Posner, *Credibility: How Leaders Gain and Lose It, Why People Demand It* (San Francisco: Jossey-Bass, 1993), pp. 230–231.

60 Susan B. Shimanoff and Mercilee M. Jenkins, "Leadership and Gender: Challenging Assumptions and Recognizing Resources," in Robert S. Cathcart, Larry A. Samovar, and Linda D. Henman (Eds.), *Small Group Communication: Theory and Practice*, 7th ed. (Madison, WI: Brown and Benchmark, 1996), p. 327.

61 Martin M. Chemers, *An Integrative Theory of Leadership* (Mahwah, NJ: Lawrence Erlbaum, 1997), p. 126.

Chapter 11

1 Fred Kaplan, "Barack Obama Killed Osama Bin Laden. Period," *Slate*, May, 2012, http://www.slate.com/articles/news_and_politics/politics/2012/05/barack_obama_s_decision_to_go_after_osama_bin_laden_how_the_president_overruled_his_advisers_in_ordering_the_assassination.html.

2 There are many excellent books and resources charting the decision-making processes involved in planning and conducting the raid on Osama bin Laden's compound. The account in this chapter is based on the following sources: Mark Bowden, *The Finish: The Killing of Osama bin Laden* (New York: Atlantic Monthly Press, 2012); John A. Gans, Jr., "Obama's Decision to Kill Bin Laden," *The Atlantic*, October 20, 2012, http://www.theatlantic.com/international/archive/2012/10/this-is-50-50-behind-obamas-decision-to-kill-bin-laden/263449/; Fred Kaplan, "Barack Obama Killed Osama Bin Laden. Period," *Slate*, May, 2012, http://www.slate.com/articles/news_and_politics/politics/2012/05/barack_obama_s_decision_to_go_after_osama_bin_laden_how_the_president_overruled_his_advisers_in_ordering_the_assassination.html; Peter Baker, Helen Cooper, and Mark Mazzetti, "Bin Laden Is Dead, Obama Says," *The New York Times*, May 2, 2001, http://www.nytimes.com/2011/05/02/world/asia/osama-bin-laden-is-killed.html?pagewanted=all.

3 Mark Bowden, *The Finish: The Killing of Osama bin Laden* (New York: Atlantic Monthly Press, 2012), p. 201.

4 John A. Gans, Jr., "Obama's Decision to Kill Bin Laden," *The Atlantic*, October 20, 2012, http://www.theatlantic.com/international/archive/2012/10/this-is-50-50-behind-obamas-decision-to-kill-bin-laden/263449/.

5 Rodney W. Napier and Matti K. Gershenfeld, *Groups: Theory and Experience*, 7th ed. (Boston: Houghton Mifflin, 2004), p. 291.

6 Peter R. Drucker, *The Effective Executive* (New York: HarperBusiness, 1967), p. 143.

7 Marshall Scott Poole, "Procedures for Managing Meetings: Social and Technological Innovation," in Richard A. Swanson and Bonnie Ogram Knapp (Eds.), *Innovative Meeting Management* (Austin, TX: 3M Meeting Management Institute, 1990), pp. 54–55.

8 Randy Y. Hirokawa, "Communication and Group Decision-Making Efficacy," in Robert S. Cathcart, Larry A. Samovar, and Linda D. Henman (Eds.), *Small Group Communication: Theory and Practice*, 7th ed. (Madison, WI: Brown and Benchmark, 1996), p. 108.

9 John Gastil, *Democracy in Small Groups: Participation, Decision Making, and Communication* (Philadelphia: New Society Publishers, 1993), p. 24.

10 This is a composite list based on several sources: Laura W. Black, "How People Communicate During Deliberative Events," in Tina Nabatchi et al. (Eds.), *Democracy in Motions: Evaluating the Practice and Impact of Deliberative Engagement* (Oxford: Oxford University Press, 2012), p. 61; Laura W. Black et al., "Self-Governance Through Group Discussion in Wikipedia: Measuring Deliberation in Online Groups, *Small Group Research* 42 (October, 2011): 597–601; John Gastil, *The Group in Society* (Los Angeles: Sage, 2010), pp. 248–252; John Gastil, *Democracy in Small Groups: Participation, Decision Making, and Communication* (Philadelphia: New Society Publishers, 1993), pp. 24–26.

11 Keith Sawyer, *Group Genius: The Creative Power of Collaboration* (New York: Basic Books, 2007), pp. 66–67. Sawyer attributes the story to Dale Carnegie.

12 Irving L. Janis, *Groupthink*, 2nd ed. (Boston: Houghton Mifflin, 1982), p. 9.

13 Irving L. Janis, *Groupthink*, 2nd ed. (Boston: Houghton Mifflin, 1982), p. 9.

14 John Gastil, *The Group in Society* (Los Angeles: Sage, 2010), p. 82.

15 John Gastil, *The Group in Society* (Los Angeles: Sage, 2010), p. 82.

16 Donelson R. Forsyth, *Group Dynamics*, 5th ed. (Belmont, CA: Wadsworth/Cengage, 2010), p. 342.

17 Julia T. Wood, "Alternative Methods of Group Decision Making," in Robert S. Cathcart and Larry A. Samovar (Eds.), *Small Group Communication: A Reader*, 6th ed. (Dubuque, IA: Wm. C. Brown, 1992), p. 159.

18 Donald G. Ellis and B. Aubrey Fisher, *Small Group Decision Making* (New York: McGraw-Hill, 1994), p. 142

19 John R. Katzenbach and Douglas K. Smith, *The Discipline of Teams* (New York: Wiley, 2001), p. 112.

20 John R. Katzenbach and Douglas K. Smith, *The Discipline of Teams* (New York: Wiley, 2001), p. 113.

21 Rodney W. Napier and Matti K. Gershenfeld, *Groups: Theory and Experience*, 7th ed. (Boston: Houghton Mifflin, 2004), p. 337.

22 Adapted from Karyn C. Rybacki and Donald J. Rybacki, *Advocacy and Opposition: An Introduction to Argumentation*, 4th ed. (Boston: Allyn & Bacon, 2000), pp. 11–15.

23 Randy Hirokawa and Roger Pace, "A Descriptive Investigation of the Possible Communication-Based Reasons for Effective and Ineffective Group Decision Making," *Communication Monographs* 50 (1983): 379.

24 Suzanne Scott and Reginald Bruce, "Decision Making Style: The Development of a New Measure," *Educational and Psychological Measurements* 55 (1995): 818–831; Reginald A. Bruce and Susanne G. Scott, "The Moderating Effective of Decision-Making Style on the Turnover Process: An Extension of Previous Research," http://cobweb2.louisville.edu/faculty/regbruce/bruce//research/japturn.htm; "Decision Making Styles," UCD Career Development Center, 2006, http://www.ucd.ie/careers/cms/decision/student_skills_decision_styleex.html.

25 Samer Khasawneh, Aiman Alomari, and Abdullah Abu-tineh, "Decision-Making Styles of Department Chairs at Public Jordanian Universities: A High-Expectancy Workforce," *Tertiariary Education and Management* 17 (2011): 311, https://eis.hu.edu.jo/deanshipfiles/pub103793271.pdf.

26 The authors of this textbook created this short decision-making style questionnaire. Longer, validated surveys are available from several sources: Reginald A. Bruce and Susanne G. Scott, "The Moderating Effective of Decision-Making Style on the Turnover Process: An Extension of Previous Research," http://cobweb2.louisville.edu/faculty/regbruce/bruce//research/japturn.htm; Suzanne Scott and Reginald Bruce, "Decision Making Style: The Development of a New Measure," *Educational and Psychological Measurements* 55 (1995): 818–831 "Decision Making Styles," UCD Career Development Center, 2006, http://www.ucd.ie/careers/cms/decision/student_skills_decision_styleex.html.

27 Based, in part, on Tom Kelley with Jonathan Littman, *The Art of Innovation: Lessons in Creativity from IDEO, America's Leading Design Firm* (New York: Currency, 2001), pp. 56–59. See also Rodney W. Napier and Matti K. Gershenfeld, *Groups: Theory and Experience*, 7th ed. (Boston: Houghton Mifflin, 2004), p. 321.

28 Alex F. Osborn, *Applied Imagination*, rev. ed. (New York: Scribner, 1957).

29 3M Meeting Management Team with Jeannine Drew, *Mastering Meetings: Discovering the Hidden Potential of Effective Business Meetings* (New York: McGraw-Hill, 1994), p. 59.

30 Tom Kelley with Jonathan Littman, *The Art of Innovation: Lessons in Creativity from IDEO, America's Leading Design Firm*, (New York: Currency, 2001), p. 55.

31 Tom Kelley with Jonathan Littman, *The Art of Innovation: Lessons in Creativity from IDEO, America's Leading Design Firm*, (New York: Currency, 2001), pp. 64–66.

32 Andre L. Delbecq, Andrew H. Van de Ven, and David H. Gustafson, *Group Techniques for Program Planning* (Glenview, IL: Scott, Foresman, 1975).

33 P. Keith Kelly, *Team Decision-Making Techniques* (Irvine, CA: Richard Chang Associates, 1994), p. 29.

34 P. Keith Kelly, *Team Decision-Making Techniques* (Irvine, CA: Richard Chang Associates, 1994), p. 29.

35 Andre L. Delbecq, Andrew H. Van de Ven, and David H. Gustafson, *Group Techniques for Program Planning* (Glenview, IL: Scott, Foresman, 1975), p. 8.

36 Andre L. Delbecq, Andrew H. Van de Ven, and David H. Gustafson, *Group Techniques for Program Planning* (Glenview, IL: Scott, Foresman, 1975), p. 8.

37 Tudor Rickards, "Brainstorming," in Mark A. Runco and Steven R. Pitzker (Eds.), *Encyclopedia of Creativity*, Vol. 1, Ae-h (San Diego: Academic Press, 1999), p. 222.

38 Craig E. Johnson and Michael Z. Hackman, *Creative Communication: Principles and Applications* (Prospect Heights, IL: Waveland, 1995), pp. 129–30; Tudor Rickards, "Brainstorming," in Mark A. Runco and Steven R. Pitzker (Eds.), *Encyclopedia of Creativity*, Vol. 1, Ae-h (San Diego: Academic Press, 1999): 219–228.

39 J. H. Jung, Younghwa Lee, and Rex Karsten, "The Moderating Effect of Intraversion-Introversion Differences on Group Idea Generation Performance," *Small Group Research* 43 (February 2012): 30, 31–34, 43–45.

40 Craig E. Johnson and Michael Z. Hackman, *Creative Communication: Principles and Applications* (Prospect Heights, IL: Waveland, 1995), p. 131.

41 Isa N. Engleberg and Dianna R. Wynn, *Working in Groups: Communication Principles and Strategies*, 6th ed. (Boston: Pearson, 2013), pp. 212–213.

42 Isa N. Engleberg and Dianna R. Wynn, *Working in Groups: Communication Principles and Strategies*, 6th ed. (Boston: Pearson, 2013); "Voting with Dots," http://www.albany.edu/cpr/gf/resources/Voting_with_dots.html; Kay Stevens, "Dotmocracy," *Better Evaluation*, November 2012, http://betterevaluation.org/evaluation-options/Dotmocracy; See also pages that explain dotmocracy's procedures, rules, and requirements on dotmocracy.org; "Multivoting," *Smart Learning*, 2012, http://www.smartlearningcommunity.net/sites/default/files/Multivoting.pdf.

43 See Kenneth E. Andersen, "Developments in Communication Ethics: The Ethics Commission, Code of Professional Responsibilities, and Credo for Ethical Communication," *Journal of the Association for Communication Administration* 29 (2000): 131–144. The Credo for Ethical Communication is also posted on the NCA Website (http://www.natcom.org).

44 John Dewey, *How We Think* (Boston: Heath, 1910).

[45]Based on Kathryn Sue et al., *Group Discussion: A Practical Guide to Participation and Leadership*, 3rd ed. (Prospect Heights, IL: Waveland Press, 2001), pp. 8–9. The authors present six steps in their standard-agenda model by combining solution suggestions and solution selection into one step. We have divided this step into separate functions given that the solution suggestion step may require creative thinking and brainstorming. Given that the solution evaluation and selection step may be the most difficult and controversial, it deserves a separate focus as well as different strategies and skills.

[46]Deborah L. Duarte and Nancy Tennant Snyder, *Mastering Virtual Teams*, 3rd ed. (San Francisco: Jossey-Bass, 2006), p. 171.

[47]Deborah L. Duarte and Nancy Tennant Snyder, *Mastering Virtual Teams*, 3rd ed. (San Francisco: Jossey-Bass, 2006), pp. 33–34, 168.

[48]Rodney W. Napier and Matti K. Gershenfeld, *Groups: Theory and Experience*, 7th ed. (Boston: Houghton Mifflin, 2004), p. 327.

[49]Luis L. Martins and Christina E. Shalley, "Creativity in Virtual Work: Effects of Demographic Differences," *Small Group Research* 4 (October 2011): 536, 551–553.

[50]Deborah L. Durarte and Nancy Tennant Snyder, *Mastering Virtual Teams*, 3rd ed. (San Francisco: Jossey Bass, 2006), p. 190. See also the "Virtual Groups: Developmental Tasks" feature in Isa N. Engleberg and Dianna R. Wynn, *Working in Groups: Communication Principles and Strategies*, 6th ed. (Boston: Pearson, 2013), p. 32.

[51]Craig R. Scott and C. Erik Timmerman, "Relating to Computer, Communication, and Communication-Mediated Communication Apprehension to New Communication Technology in the Workplace," *Communication Research* 32 (2005): 683–715; See also the "Virtual Groups: Confidence with Technology" feature in Isa N. Engleberg and Dianna R. Wynn, *Working in Groups: Communication Principles and Strategies*, 6th ed. (Boston: Pearson, 2013), p. 60.

[52]Isa N. Engleberg and Dianna R. Wynn, *Working in Groups: Communication Principles and Strategies*, 6th ed. (Boston: Pearson, 2013), pp. 116, 257, 266–288.

[53]Edward De Bono, *New Thinking for the New Millennium* (New York: Viking, 1999) quoted in Darrell Man, "Analysis Paralysis: When Root Cause Analysis Isn't the Way," *The TRIZ-Journal*, 2006, http://www.triz-journal.com.

[54]"Avoid Analysis Paralysis," *Infusion Insight*, http://www.infusionsoft.com/articles/65-infusion-insight/615-avoid-analysis-paralysis.

[55]A 2010 study quoted in Simone Kauffeld and Nale Lahmann-Willenbrock, "Meetings Matter: Effects of Team Meetings on Team and Organizational Success," *Small Group Research* 43 (April 2012): 131.

[56]"Office Communication Toolkit: 7 Common Employee Gripes," Special Report from *Business Management Daily*, September 22, 2009.

[57]Simone Kauffeld and Nale Lahmann-Willenbrock, "Meetings Matter: Effects of Team Meetings on Team and Organizational Success," *Small Group Research* 43 (April 2012): 131.

[58]Tyler Cowen, "On My Mind: In Favor of Face Time," *Forbes*, October 1, 2007, www.members.forbes.com/forbes/2007/1001/030.html.

[59]Karen Anderson, *Making Meetings Work: How to Plan and Conduct Effective Meetings* (West Des Moines, IA: American Media Publishing, 1997), p. 18.

[60]Sharon M. Lippincott, *Meetings: Do's, Don'ts, and Donuts* (Pittsburgh, PA: Lighthouse Point Press, 1994), p. 172.

[61]Isa N. Engleberg and Dianna R. Wynn, *Working in Groups: Communication Principles and Strategies*, 6th ed. (Boston: Pearson, 2013), pp. 252–253; Steven G. Rogelberg, Linda Rhoades Shannock, and Cliff W. Scott, "Wasted Time and Money in Meetings: Increasing Return on Investment," *Small Group Research* 43 (April 2012): 242; Susan M. Lippincott, *Meetings: Do's, Don'ts, and Donuts* (Pittsburgh, PA: Lighthouse Point Press, 1994), pp. 89–90.

[62]3M Meeting Management Team with Jeannine Drew, *Mastering Meetings: Discovering the Hidden Potential of Effective Business Meetings* (New York: McGraw-Hill, 1994), p. 78.

[63]Benjamin E. Barin et al., "Leading Group Meetings: Supervisors' Actions, Employee Behaviors, and Upward Perceptions," *Small Group Research* 43 (June 2012): 349.

[64]© Isa N. Engleberg.

Chapter 12

[1]The description of Cardinal Jorge Mario Bergoglio ascendancy to Pope Francis is based on several news sources including, most significantly, Stacy Meichtry and Alessandra Galloni, "Fifteen Days in Rome: How the Pope Was Picked," *The Wall Street Journal*, April 13, 2013, pp. C1–C2. (This article is available on the web at http://online.wsj.com/article/SB10001424127887324240804578416550744061538.html#printMode.) See also Wall Street Journal Staff, *Pope Francis: From the End of the World to Rome* (New York: HarperCollins, April 16, 2013); Rachel Donadio, "Cardinals Pick Bergoglio, Who Will Be Pope Francis," *The New York Times*, March 14, 2013, http://www.nytimes.com/2013/03/14/world/europe/cardinals-elect-new-pope.html?pagewanted=all; Jaweed Kaleem, "Pope Francis, Cardinal Jorge Mario Bergoglio of Buenos Aires, Elected Leader of Catholic Church," *The Huffington Post*, March 15, 2013, http://www.huffingtonpost.com/2013/03/13/pope-francis-cardinal-jorge-mario-bergoglio-_n_2855101.html.

[2]Martin McDermott, *Speak with Courage: 50+ Insider Strategies for Presenting with Confidence* (Boston: Bedford/St. Martin's, 2014), p. 34.

[3]John A. Daly, Anita L. Vangelisti, and David J. Weber, "Speech Anxiety Affects How People Prepare Speeches: A Protocol Analysis of the Preparation Process of Speaking," *Communication Monographs* 62 (1995): 283–398.

[4]John A. Daly, Anita L. Vangelisti, and David J. Weber, "Speech Anxiety Affects How People Prepare Speeches: A Protocol Analysis of the Preparation Process of Speaking," *Communication Monographs* 62 (1995): 396.

[5]Martin McDermott, *Speak with Courage: 50+ Insider Strategies for Presenting with Confidence* (Boston: Bedford/St. Martin's, 2014, pp. 32, 24.

[6]Isa N. Engleberg and John A. Daly, *Presentations in Everyday Life*, 3rd ed. (Boston: Pearson/Allyn & Bacon, 2009), p. 3 and Note 5 on p. 21; Isa N. Engleberg and John A. Daly, *Think Public Speaking* (Boston: Pearson, 2013), p. 4 and Notes 4 and 5 on p. 367.

[7]The complete, twenty-four-item survey is available in the *Instructor's Manual* that accompanies this textbook. Class results can be compared to those of both types of survey respondents: book buyers who speak professionally and students enrolled in a college public speaking course.

[8]Isa N. Engleberg and John A. Daly conducted the survey of book buyers in collaboration with the Market Research Department at Houghton Mifflin, a former publisher. Survey items included traditional topics usually covered in public speaking textbooks. Approximately 2,000 copies of a two-page questionnaire were mailed to individuals who had recently purchased a commercially available public speaking book and who had used a business address to secure the purchase. We received 281 usable questionnaires, resulting in a response rate of 11 percent. Respondents were geographically dispersed. Twenty-five percent worked in industry. Workers in government (10 percent), health (10 percent), and nonprofit organizations (10 percent) made up 30 percent of respondents. Nine percent came from the financial industry; another 9 percent worked in technology related industries. Approximately 25 percent of the respondents, including business owners and independent contractors, worked in "other" occupations. More recently, we administered a similar survey of college students enrolled in a basic public speaking course. Respondents attended various types of geographically dispersed institutions of higher education (community colleges, liberal arts colleges, and large universities). We received more than 600 usable questionnaires.

[9]Dorothy Leeds, *Power Speak: Engage, Inspire, and Stimulate Your Audience* (Franklin Lakes, NJ: Career Press, 2003), p. 47.

[10]Nancy Duarte, *HBR Guide to Persuasive Presentations* (Boston: Harvard Business Review Press, 2012), p. 19.

[11]Jerry Weissman, *Winning Strategies for Power Presentations* (Boston: Pearson, 2013) p. 20.

[12]Rushworth M. Kidder, "Trust: A Primer on Current Thinking," Institute for Global Ethics, http://www.globalethics.org/files/wp_trust_1222960968.pdf/21/.

[13]Milton Rokeach, *The Nature of Human Values* (New York: Free Press, 1973), p. 3.

[14]Nancy Duarte, *HBR Guide to Persuasive Presentations* (Boston: Harvard Business Review Press, 2012), pp. 21–23.

[15]Nancy Duarte, *HBR Guide to Persuasive Presentations* (Boston: Harvard Business Review Press, 2012), p. 4.

[16]Based on John A. Daly, *Advocacy: Championing Ideas and Influencing Others* (New Haven: Yale University Press, 2011), pp. 241–242.

[17]Gene Zelazny, *Say It with Presentations*, Revised (New York: McGraw-Hill, 2006), pp. 4–6.

[18]Isa N. Engleberg and John A. Daly, *Presentations in Everyday Life*, 3rd ed. (Boston: Pearson/Allyn & Bacon, 2009), p. 113; Isa N. Engleberg and John A. Daly, *Think Public Speaking* (Boston: Pearson, 2013), pp. 76–77.

[19]Isa N. Engleberg and John A. Daly, *Presentations in Everyday Life*, 3rd ed. (Boston: Pearson/Allyn & Bacon, 2009), p. 126; Isa N. Engleberg and John A. Daly, *Think Public Speaking* (Boston: Pearson, 2013), p. 86.

[20]Isa N. Engleberg and John A. Daly, *Presentations in Everyday Life*, 3rd ed. (Boston: Pearson/Allyn & Bacon, 2009), pp. 152–169; Isa N. Engleberg and John A. Daly, *Think Public Speaking* (Boston: Pearson, 2013), pp. 108–113.

[21]Based on Nancy Duarte, *HBR Guide to Persuasive Presentations* (Boston: Harvard Business Review Press, 2012), pp. 160–161.

[22]Andrea L. Foster, "Professor Avatar: In the Digital Universe of Second Life, Classroom Instruction Also Takes on a New Personality," *The Chronicle of Higher Education*, September 21, 2007, p. 24.

[23]Gene Zelazny, *Say It with Charts Complete Toolkit* (New York: McGraw-Hill, 2007), p. 33.

[24]Isa N. Engleberg and John A. Daly, *Presentations in Everyday Life*, 3rd ed. (Boston: Pearson/Allyn & Bacon, 2009), p. 370.

[25]Peggy Noonan, *Simply Speaking* (New York: HarperCollins, 1998), p. 10.

[26]Granville N. Toogood, *The Articulate Executive* (New York: McGraw-Hill, 1996), p. 93.

[27]Many websites explain and/or feature TED talks. For example, see "About TED," http://www.ted.com/pages/about; Kate Torgovnick "The 20 Most-Watched TED Talks," August 21, 2012, http://blog.ted.com/2012/08/21/the-20-most-watched-ted-talks-to-date; "Why Are TED Talks 18 Minutes Long?" *Digital Inspiration*, http://www.labnol.org/tech/ted-talk-18-minutes/12755.

[28]Granville N. Toogood, *The Articulate Executive* (New York: McGraw-Hill, 1996), pp. 94–95.

[29]Malcolm Kushner, *Successful Presentations for Dummies* (Foster City, CA: IDG Books Worldwide, 1997), p. 21.

[30]The earliest and most respected source describing the components of a speaker's credibility is Aristotle's *Rhetoric*. See Lane Cooper, *The Rhetoric of Aristotle*, (New York: Appleton-Century-Crofts, 1932), p. 92. Aristotle identified "intelligence, character, and good will" as "three things that gain our belief." Aristotle's observations have been verified and expanded. In addition to those qualities identified by

Aristotle, researchers have added variables such as objectivity, trustworthiness, co-orientation, dynamism, composure, likability, and extroversion. Research has consolidated these qualities into three well-accepted attributes: competence, character, and dynamism. We have used the term *charisma* in place of dynamism.

[31] Malcolm Kushner, *Successful Presentations for Dummies* (Foster City, CA: IDG Books Worldwide, 1997), p. 21.

[32] Nathan Crick, *Rhetorical Public Speaking* (Boston: Allyn & Bacon, 2011), p. 130.

[33] Lane Cooper, *The Rhetoric of Aristotle* (New York: Appleton-Century-Crofts, 1932), p. 7.

[34] Lane Cooper, *The Rhetoric of Aristotle* (New York: Appleton-Century-Crofts, 1932), pp. 8 and 9.

[35] James R. Andrews, Michael C. Leff, and Robert Terrill, *Reading Rhetorical Texts: An Introduction to Criticism* (Boston: Houghton Mifflin, 1998), p. 59.

[36] Nathan Crick, *Rhetorical Public Speaking* (Boston: Allyn & Bacon, 2011), p. 136.

[37] The examples of audience civility come from the following sources: M. Alex Johnson, "Clemson President Scolds Students, Fans for Booing Obama at Football Game," *U.S. News* on NBCNews.com, http://usnews.nbcnews.com/_news/2012/10/23/14647507-clemson-president-scolds-students-fans-for-booing-obama-at-football-game?lite; Sannon Travis, "Romney Draws Boos from NAACP, Support from Conservatives," *CNN Politics*, July 11, 2012, http://www.cnn.com/2012/07/11/politics/romney-naacp; Cileste Katz and Aliyah Shahid, "Gay Soldier Booed by GOP Debate Audience," *New York Daily News*, September 23, 2011, http://www.nydailynews.com/blogs/dailypolitics/2011/09/gay-soldier-booed-by-gop-debate-audience; Garance Frank-Ruta, "The Worst Fox News-Google Debate Moment: Audience Boos a Gay Soldier," *The Atlantic*, September 23, 2011, http://www.theatlantic.com/politics/archive/2011/09/the-worst-fox-news-google-debate-moment-audience-boos-a-gay-soldier/245547; "Paul Ryan Booed," September 21, 2011, http://www.cbsnews.com/video/watch/?id=7422526n.

[38] Dana Hinders, "Plagiarism Statistics," http://freelance-writing.lovetoknow.com/Plagiarism_Statistics.

[39] Isa N. Engleberg and John A. Daly, *Presentations in Everyday Life*, 3rd ed. (Boston: Pearson/Allyn & Bacon, 2009), p. 193; Isa N. Engleberg and John A. Daly, *Think Public Speaking* (Boston: Pearson, 2013), pp. 101 and 138.

[40] Suzanne Choney, "Steal This Report: College Plagiarism Up, Says Pew Report," *MSNBC*, August 30, 2011, http://www.pewinternet.org/Media-Mentions/2011/Steal-this-report-College-plagiarism-up-says-Pew-report.aspx.

[41] Dana Hinders, "Plagiarism Statistics," http://freelance-writing.lovetoknow.com/Plagiarism_Statistics.

[42] Blair Hornstine, "Stories, Essays Lack Attribution," *The Courier Post*, June 3, 2003, http://www.newworldencyclopedia.org/entry/Plagiarism#Famous_examples_and_accusations_of_plagiarism.

[43] Joseph C. Self, "The 'My Sweet Lord/He's So Fine' Plagiarism Suits," *The 901 Magazine*, 2003, http://abbeyrd.best.vwh.net/mysweet.htm; http://www.newworldencyclopedia.org/entry/Plagiarism#Famous_examples_and_accusations_of_plagiarism.

[44] Richard Byrne, "7 Resources for Detecting and Preventing Plagiarism," *Free Technology for Teachers*, August 24, 2010, http://www.freetech4teachers.com/2010/08/7-resources-for-detecting-and.html#.UcSd3djzsmY.

[45] "2013 Compare Best Online Plagiarism Checking Servers," *Plagiarism Checker Review*, http://plagiarism-checker-review.toptenreviews.com; Richard Byrne, "7 Resources for Detecting and Preventing Plagiarism," *Free Technology for Teachers*, August 24, 2010, http://www.freetech4teachers.com/2010/08/7-resources-for-detecting-and.html#.UcSd3djzsmY.

[46] © Isa N. Engleberg

Chapter 13

[1] Josephus Daniels, *The Wilson Era: Years of War and After, 1917–1923* (Westport, CN: Greenwood Publishing Group, 1974), p. 632.

[2] Nancy Duarte, *HBR Guide to Persuasive Presentations* (Boston: Harvard Business Review Press, 2012), p. 15.

[3] A classic overview of Cicero's contributions to rhetoric appears in Lester Thonssen and A. Craig Baird, *Speech Criticism: The Development of Standards for Rhetorical Appraisal* (New York: The Ronald Press, 1948), pp. 78–91. See also James L. Golden, Goodwin F. Berquist, and William E. Coleman, *The Rhetoric of Western Thought*, 4th ed. (Dubuque, IA: Kendall/Hunt, 1989).

[4] Center for Disease Control and Prevention, "Middle East Respiratory Virus (MERV)," July 26, 2013, http://www.cdc.gov/coronavirus; "As Novel Coronavirus Outbreak Continues, WHO, CDC Urge Heightened Vigilance," *American Academy of Family Physicians News*, May 23, 2013, http://www.aafp.org/news-now/health-of-the-public/20130523novelcoronavirus.html; "CDC Cautions Doctors About Deadly New Coronavirus," *American Medical News*, June 24, 2013, http://www.amednews.com/article/20130624/health/130629983/10.

[5] Clive Thompson, "Community Urinalysis," *The New York Times Magazine*, December 8, 2007, p. 62.

[6] Arne Duncan, "The Vision of Education Reform in the United States: Secretary Arne Duncan's Remarks to United Nations Educational, Scientific and Cultural Organization (UNESCO)," U.S. Department of Education, November 4, 2010, http://www.ed.gov/news/speeches/vision-education-reform-united-states-secretary-arne-duncans-remarks-united-nations-ed.

[7] Scott Jaschik, "A Stand Against Wikipedia," *Inside Higher Education*, January 26, 2007, http://www.insidehighered.com/news/2007/01/26/wiki. *Inside Higher Ed* is an online source for news, opinion and jobs for higher education.

[8] "Wikipedia vs Encyclopaedia: A Question of Trust? Are Online Resources Reliable or Should We Stick to Traditional Encyclopaedias?," *TechRadar*, April 21, 2008, http://www.techradar.com/news/internet/web/wikipedia-vs-encyclopaedia-a-question-of-trust-316163; See also the reference studies in http://en.wikipedia.org/wiki/Reliability_of_Wikipedia.

[9] Wikipedia provides a more detailed discussion of each guideline. For example, see http://en.wikipedia.org/wiki/Wikipedia:Neutral_point_of_view. "This page in a nutshell: Articles mustn't *take* sides, but should *explain* the sides, fairly and without bias. This applies to both what you say and how you say it."

[10] This brief summary is based on: *Evaluating Wikipedia Article Quality: Using Wikipedia* (San Francisco: Wikimedia Foundation), p. 4. See also http://bookshelf.wikimedia.org.

[11] "Criticism of Wikipedia," http://en.wikipedia.org/wiki/Criticism_of_Wikipedia.

[12] Carole Blair, "Civil Rights/Civil Sites: '. . . Until Justice Rolls Down Like Water,'" *The Carroll C. Arnold Distinguished Lecture*, National Communication Association Convention, November 2006 (Boston: Pearson/Allyn & Bacon, 2008), p. 2.

[13] Isa N. Engleberg, *The Principles of Public Presentation* (New York: Harper-Collins, 1994), p. 140.

[14] Daphne Duval Harrison, *Black Pearls: Blues Queens of the 1920s* (New Brunswick, NJ: Rutgers University Press, 1988).

[15] Vivian Hobbs, Commencement Address at Prince George's Community College, Largo, Maryland, 1991. See full manuscript in Isa N. Engleberg, *The Principles of Public Presentations* (New York: HarperCollins, 1994), pp. 339–341.

[16] Quoted in John A. Daly, *Advocacy: Championing Ideas and Influencing Others* (New Haven, CN: Yale University Press, 2011), p. 121.

[17] "Full Transcript and Videos: USDA Shirley Sherrod, NAACP, Breitbart, FOXNEWS," *FactReal*, Posted by FactReal on July 22, 2010; Updated by FactReal on July 26, 2010, http://factreal.wordpress.com/2010/07/22/full-transcript-videos-usda-shirley-sherrod-naacp-breitbart-foxnews.

[18] Bill O'Reilly, "The O'Reilly Factor," *Fox News*, *Media Matters for America*, July 21, 2010, http://mediamatters.org/iphone/research/201007210079.

[19] Matthew S. McGlone, "Contextomy: The Art of Quoting Out of Context," *Media Culture and Society* 27 (2005): 511–522.

[20] Dan Le Batard, *The Miami Herald*, September 24, 2004, www.miami.com/mld/miamiherald/sports/columnists/dan_le_batard/9745974.htm.

[21] Stella Ting-Toomey and Leeva C. Chung, *Understanding Intercultural Communication* (Los Angeles: Roxbury, 2005), pp. 189–190.

[22] Based on John Chafee with Christine McMahon and Barbara Stout, *Critical Thinking, Thoughtful Writing*, 2nd ed. (Boston: Houghton Mifflin, 2002), pp. 534–536, 614; Jim Kapoun "Teaching Undergrads Web Evaluation: A Guide for Library Instruction," *C&RL News*, July/August, 1998, pp. 522–523 cited in "Five Criteria for Evaluating Web Pages," Cornell University, http://olinuris.library.cornell.edu/print/4499 and http://olinuris.library.cornell.edu/ref/research/webcrit.html, Minor textual corrections, May 10, 2010. For more criteria questions and a worksheet see, Isa Engleberg and Dianna R. Wynn, "Assessing a Web Site Worksheet," *Instructor's Manual for THINK Communication*, 3rd ed. (Boston: Pearson, 2015).

[23] Michael M. Kepper with Robert E. Gunther, *I'd Rather Die Than Give a Speech* (Burr Ridge, IL: Irwin, 1994), p. 6.

[24] Classic research on the value of organizing a presentation was conducted in the 1960s and '70s. See Ernest C. Thompson, "An Experimental Investigation of the Relative Effectiveness of Organizational Structure in Oral Communication," *Southern Speech Journal* 26 (1960): 59–69; Ernest C. Thompson, "Some Effects of Message Structure on Listeners' Comprehension," *Speech Monographs* 34 (1967): 51–57; James C. McCroskey and R. Samuel Mehrley, "The Effects of Disorganization and Nonfluency on Attitude Change and Source Credibility," *Communication Monographs* 36 (1969): 13–21; Arlee Johnson, "A Preliminary Investigation of the Relationship Between Organization and Listener Comprehension," *Central States Speech Journal* 21 (1970): 104–107; and Christopher Spicer and Ronald E. Bassett, "The Effect of Organization on Learning from an Informative Message," *Southern Speech Communication Journal* 41 (1976): 290–299.

[25] Tony Buzon, *Use Both Sides of Your Brain*, 3rd ed. (New York: Plume, 1989).

[26] An annotated manuscript of Julie Borchard's "The Sound of Muzak" speech is available in Isa N. Engleberg and John A. Daly, *Presentations in Everyday Life*, 3rd ed. (Boston: Pearson/Allyn and Bacon, 2009), pp. 251–253. Ms. Borchard was a student and forensics team member at Prince George's Community College.

[27] Nancy Duarte, *HBR Guide to Persuasive Presentations* (Boston: Harvard Business Review Press, 2012), p. 30.

[28] What follows are a few of the websites that offer or review mind mapping software: http://www.boundlessat.com/Inspiration-9; http://www.examtime.com/mind-maps; http://www.mindmapper.com/main/main.asp; http://mind-mappingsoftwareblog.com/product-reviews; http://www.pcadvisor.co.uk/reviews/software/3442278/mindmup-review.

[29] Jerry Weissman, *Winning Strategies for Power Presentations* (Upper Saddle River, NJ: FT Press, 2013), p. 18.

[30] The Speech Framer was developed by Isa N. Engleberg as an alternative or supplement to outlining. See Isa N. Engleberg and John A. Daly, *Presentations in Everyday Life*, 3rd ed. (Boston: Pearson/Allyn and Bacon, 2009), pp. 217–218. © Isa N. Engleberg, 2003.

[31] Ms. Dunlap was an honors student at Prince George's Community College.

[32] Isa N. Engleberg and John A. Daly, *Presentations in Everyday Life*, 3rd ed. (Boston: Pearson/Allyn and Bacon, 2009), pp. 211–216; Isa N. Engleberg and John A. Daly, *Think Public Speaking* (Boston: Pearson, 2013), pp. 153–156.

[33] Lee Towe, *Why Didn't I Think of That? Creativity in the Workplace* (West Des Moines, IA: American Media, 1966), p. 7.

[34] Lee Towe, *Why Didn't I Think of That? Creativity in the Workplace* (West Des Moines, IA: American Media, 1966), pp. 9–11. Based on Ellis Paul Torrance, *The Torrance Tests of Creative Thinking Norms—Technical Manual Figural (Streamlined) Forms A & B.* (Bensenville, IL: Scholastic Testing Services, Inc., 1998). For a review of the test, see Kyng Hee Kim, "Can We Trust Creativity Tests? A Review of the Torrance Tests of Creative Thinking (TTCT)," *Creativity Research Journal* 18 (2006): 3–14. Note: We did not include one of Torrrance's criteria—Elaboration—because students often have difficulty understanding the meaning of this term in a communication context.

[35] Isa N. Engleberg and John A. Daly, *Presentations in Everyday Life*, 3rd ed. (Boston: Pearson/Allyn and Bacon, 2009), p. 216.

[36] Isa N. Engleberg and John A. Daly, *Presentations in Everyday Life*, 3rd ed. (Boston: Pearson/Allyn and Bacon, 2009), pp. 219–221; Isa N. Engleberg and John A. Daly, *Think Public Speaking* (Boston: Pearson, 2013), pp. 157–159.

[37] Isa N. Engleberg and John A. Daly, *Presentations in Everyday Life*, 3rd ed. (Boston: Pearson/Allyn and Bacon, 2009), pp. 228–239; Isa N. Engleberg and John A. Daly, *Think Public Speaking* (Boston: Pearson, 2013), pp. 168–172.

[38] Camille Dunlap, "Asleep at the Wheel," with permission from Ms. Dunlap, a former student at Prince George's Community College.

[39] Clare Kim, "U.S. Gun Deaths Since Newtown Exceed Iraq War Deaths," May 30, 2013, The Last Word with Lawrence O'Donnell, *MSNBC*, http://tv.msnbc.com/2013/05/30/u-s-gun-deaths-since-newtown-exceed-iraq-war-deaths.

[40] Matt Vasilogambros, "Gun Deaths Since Newtown Now Surpass Number of Americans Killed in Iraq," May 31, 2013, *National Journal*, http://www.nationaljournal.com/nationalsecurity/gun-deaths-since-newtown-now-surpass-number-of-americans-killed-in-iraq-20130530; Chris Kirk and Dan Kois, "How Many People Have Been Killed by Guns Since Newtown?" *Slate*, June 13, 2013, http://www.slate.com/articles/news_and_politics/crime/2012/12/gun_death_tally_every_american_gun_death_since_newtown_sandy_hook_shooting.html.

[41] Arne Duncan, National Science Teachers Association Conference, March 20, 2009, http://www.ed.gov/print/news/speeches/2009/03/03202009.html.

[42] Samuel E. Wood, Ellen Green Wood, and Denise Boyd, *The World of Psychology*, 6th ed. (Boston: Pearson/Allyn & Bacon, 2008), p. 204.

[43] Samuel E. Wood, Ellen Green Wood, and Denise Boyd, *The World of Psychology*, 6th ed. (Boston: Pearson/Allyn & Bacon, 2008), pp. 204–205.

[44] Based on information in Anna Quindlen, "The Failed Experiment," *Newsweek*, June 26, 2006, p. 64.

[45] For the complete text of King's "I Have a Dream" speech plus commentary, see James R. Andrews and David Zarefsky, *Contemporary American Voices: Significant Speech in American History, 1945–Present* (New York: Longman, 1992), pp. 78–81; See also Martin Luther King, Jr., "I Have a Dream," *American Rhetoric: Top 100 Speeches*, http://www.americanrhetoric.com/top100speechesall.html.

[46] David J. Dempsey, *Present Your Way to the Top* (New York: McGraw-Hill, 2010), pp. 78–79.

[47] Isa N. Engleberg and John A. Daly, *Presentations in Everyday Life*, 3rd ed. (Boston: Pearson/Allyn and Bacon, 2009), pp. 251–256; Isa N. Engleberg and John A. Daly, *Think Public Speaking* (Boston: Pearson, 2013), pp. 173–178.

[48] Marge Anderson, "Looking Through Our Window: The Value of Indian Culture," *Vital Speeches of the Day* 65 (1999): 633–634.

[49] Nancy Duarte, *HBR Guide to Persuasive Presentations* (Boston: Harvard Business Review Press, 2012), p. 39.

[50] Robert M. Franklin, "The Soul of Morehouse and the Future of the Mystique," President's Town Meeting, Morehouse College, April 21, 2009, http://themaroontiger.com/attachments/329_The%20Soul%20of%20Morehouse%20and%20the%20Future%20of%20the%20Mystique%20-%20abridged.pdf.

[51] David J. Dempsey, *Present Your Way to the Top* (New York: McGraw-Hill, 2010), p. 120.

Chapter 14

[1] Lou Cannon, *President Reagan: The Role of a Lifetime* (New York: Public Affairs, 2000), p. 20. Note: Reagan made this comment to Landon Parvin, one of his speechwriters.

[2] Lani Arredondo, *The McGraw-Hill 36-Hour Course: Business Presentations* (New York: McGraw-Hill, 1994), p. 147.

[3] Isa N. Engleberg and John A. Daly, *Presentation in Everyday Life*, 3rd ed. (Boston: Pearson/Allyn and Bacon, 2009), pp. 263–272; Isa N. Engleberg and John A. Daly, *Think Public Speaking* (Boston: Pearson, 2013), pp. 192–195. The CORE Speaking Styles, © Isa N. Engleberg, 2009.

[4] Jerry Della Femina, quoted in A. Jerome Jewler (Ed.), *Creative Strategy in Advertising*, 2nd ed. (Belmont, CA: Wadsworth, 1985), p. 41.

[5] John A. Daly, *Advocacy: Championing Ideas and Influencing Others* (New Haven: Yale University Press, 2010), p. 291. Based on research by Daniel Oppenheimer, "Consequences of Erudite Vernacular Utilized Irrespective of Necessity: Problems with Using Long Words Needlessly," *Applied Cognitive Psychology* 20 (2006): 139–156.

[6] John W. Bowers, "Some Correlates of Language Intensity," *Quarterly Journal of Speech* 50 (1964): 415–420.

[7] Based on Isa Engleberg and Ann Raimes, *Pocket Keys for Speakers* (Boston: Houghton Mifflin, 2004), pp. 191–193.

[8] George Lakoff, *Whose Freedom? The Battle Over America's Most Important Ideas* (New York: Farrar, Strauss and Giroux, 2006), p. 10.

[9] Max Atkinson, *Lend Me Your Ears* (New York: Oxford, 2005), p. 221.

[10] "Full Transcript and Videos: USDA Shirley Sherrod, NAACP, Breitbart, FOXNEWS," *FactReal*, July 26, 2010, http://factreal.wordpress.com/2010/07/22/full-transcript-videos-usda-shirley-sherrod-naacp-breitbart-foxnews/.

[11] Marcel Danesi and Paul Perron, *Analyzing Cultures: An Introduction and Handbook* (Bloomington, IN: Indiana University Press, 1999), p. 174.

[12] Isa N. Engleberg and John A. Daly, *Think Public Speaking* (Boston: Pearson, 2013), p. 194; Isa N. Engleberg and John A. Daly, *Presentation in Everyday Life*, 3rd ed. (Boston: Pearson/Allyn and Bacon, 2009), pp. 274–275.

[13] Nancy Duarte, *HBR Guide to Persuasive Presentations* (Boston: Harvard Business Review Press, 2012), p. 60.

[14] Associated Press, "Jerry Rice, Emmitt Smith enter HOF," August 8, 2010, http://sports.espn.go.com/nfl/halloffame10/news/story?id=5445640.

[15] Kathleen Hall Jamieson, *Eloquence in an Electronic Age: The Transformation of Political Speechmaking* (New York: Oxford University Press, 1988), pp. 81, 84.

[16] The full speech transcript is available at: http://www.independent.co.uk/news/world/asia/the-full-text-malala-yousafzais-speech-to-the-un-general-assembly-8706606.html. A video of the speech is available at http://www.youtube.com/watch?v=B5X70VyjU0g; See also Ashley Fantz, "Malala at U.N.: The Taliban Failed to Silence Us," *CNN*, July 12, 2013, http://www.cnn.com/2013/07/12/world/united-nations-malala/index.html.

[17] Geoffrey Brewer, "Snakes Top List of Americans' Fears," *Gallup News Service*, March 19, 2001, http://www.gallup.com/poll/1891/snakes-top-list-americans-fears.aspx.

[18] Lori J. Carrell and S. Clay Willmington, "The Relationship Between Self-Report Measures of Communication Apprehension and Trained Observers' Ratings of Communication Competence," *Communication Reports* 11 (1998): 87–95.

[19] Michael T. Motley and Jennifer L. Molloy, "An Efficacy Test of New Therapy ("Communication-Orientation Motivation") for Public Speaking Anxiety," *Journal of Applied Communication Research* 22 (1994): 44–58.

[20] Isa N. Engleberg and John A. Daly, *Think Public Speaking* (Boston: Pearson, 2013), pp. 224–225; Isa N. Engleberg and John A. Daly, *Presentation in Everyday Life*, 3rd ed. (Boston: Pearson/Allyn and Bacon, 2009), pp. 314–316.

[21] Isa N. Engleberg and John A. Daly, *Think Public Speaking* (Boston: Pearson, 2013), pp. 227–234; Isa N. Engleberg and John A. Daly, *Presentation in Everyday Life*, 3rd ed. (Boston: Pearson/Allyn and Bacon, 2009), pp. 319–329.

[22] Alice Baker, "Do Opera Singers Use Microphones?" *Opera Singer F.A.Q.*, 2003, http://digilander.libero.it/cmi/faq/faq.html; "Do Opera Singers Use Microphones During Performances?" February 11, 2013, http://jobstr.com/threads/show/1237-opera-singer.

[23] Susan D. Miller, *Be Heard the First Time: A Woman's Guide to Powerful Speaking* (Herndon, VA: Capital Books, 2006), p. 100.

[24] John A. Daly, *Advocacy: Championing Ideas and Influencing Others* (New Haven: Yale University Press, 2010), p. 298.

[25] Geraldine Barkworth, "Speaking Without Microphone-bia: A Fear of Microphones," *Goddess of Public Speaking*, April 16, 2011, http://www.goddessofpublicspeaking.com.au/blog/public-speaking/speaking-without-microphone-bia-%E2%80%9Ca-fear-of-microphones%E2%80%9D/.

[26] Ty Ford, *Ty Ford's Audio Bootcamp Field Guide* (Baltimore: Technique, Inc., 2004), p. 19.

[27] National Geographic for AP Special Features, "The 'Um' Factor: What People Say Between Thoughts," *The Baltimore Sun*, September 28, 1992, pp. 1D, 3D.

[28] Michael Erard, *Um: Slips, Stumbles, and Verbal Blunders, and What They Mean* (New York: Pantheon Books, 2007), p. 96.

[29] Isa N. Engleberg and John A. Daly, *Think Public Speaking* (Boston: Pearson, 2013), pp. 234–238; Isa N. Engleberg and John A. Daly, *Presentation in Everyday Life*, 3rd ed. (Boston: Pearson/Allyn and Bacon, 2009), pp. 328–337.

[30] Steven A. Beebe, "Eye Contact: A Nonverbal Determinant of Speaker Credibility," *The Speech Teacher* 23 (1974): 21–25.

[31] Mark L. Knapp, Judith A. Hall, and Terrence G. Horgan, *Nonverbal Communication in Human Interaction*, 8th ed. (Belmont, CA: Wadsworth/Cengage Learning, 2014), p. 258.

[32] Peggy Noonan, *Simply Speaking: How to Communicate Your Ideas with Style, Substance, and Clarity* (New York: HarperCollins, 1998), p. 206.

[33] Everett M. Rogers and Thomas M. Steinfatt, *Intercultural Communication* (Prospect Heights, IL: Waveland Press, 1999), p. 174.

[34] Everett M. Rogers and Thomas M. Steinfatt, *Intercultural Communication* (Prospect Heights, IL: Waveland Press, 1999), p. 172; Guo-Ming Chen and William J. Starosta, *Foundations of Intercultural Communication* (Boston: Allyn and Bacon, 1998), pp. 81–92.

[35] Lani Arredondo, *The McGraw-Hill 36-Hour Course: Business Presentations* (New York: McGraw-Hill, 1994), p. 238.

[36] Isa N. Engleberg and John A. Daly, *Think Public Speaking* (Boston: Pearson, 2013), pp. 244–258; Isa N. Engleberg and John A. Daly, *Presentation in Everyday Life*, 3rd ed. (Boston: Pearson/Allyn and Bacon, 2009), pp. 343–362.

[37] Janet Bozarth, *Better Than Bullet Points: Creating Engaging e-Learning with PowerPoint®* (San Francisco: Pfeiffer/Wiley, 2008), p. 3.

[38]Robin Williams, *The Non-Designer's Presentation Book: Principles for Effective Presentation Design* (Berkeley, CA: Peachpit Press, 2010), p. 136.

[39]Robin Williams, *The Non-Designer's Presentation Book: Principles for Effective Presentation Design* (Berkeley, CA: Peachpit Press, 2010), p. 137.

[40]Stephen M. Kosslyn, *Clear and to the Point: 8 Psychological Principles for Compelling PowerPoint Presentations* (New York: Oxford University Press, 2007), pp. 4–12; Richard E. Mayer, *Multimedia Learning*, 2nd ed. (New York: Cambridge University Press, 2009).

[41]John Daly and Anita Vangelisti, "Skillfully Instructing Learners: How Communicators Effectively Convey Messages," in John O. Greene and Brant R. Burleson (Eds.), *Handbook of Communication and Social Interaction Skills* (Mahwah, NJ: Lawrence Erlbaum Associates, 2003), p. 878.

[42]Cyndi Maxey and Kevin E. O'Connor, *Present Like a Pro* (New York: St. Martin's Griffin, 2006), p. 49.

[43]Isa N. Engleberg and John A. Daly, *Think Public Speaking* (Boston: Pearson, 2013), pp. 29–30; Isa N. Engleberg and John A. Daly, *Presentation in Everyday Life*, 3rd ed. (Boston: Pearson/Allyn and Bacon, 2009), pp. 37–39.

[44]Peggy Noonan, *Simply Speaking: How to Communicate Your Ideas with Style, Substance, and Clarity* (New York: HarperCollins, 1998), p. 9.

[45]Thomas K. Mira, *Speak Smart: The Art of Public Speaking* (New York: Random House, 1997), p. 91.

[46]"Remarks by the President at a Memorial Service for the Victims of the Shooting in Tucson, Arizona," The White House, Office of the Press Secretary, January 12, 2011, http://www.whitehouse.gov/the-press-office/2011/01/12/remarks-president-barack-obama-memorial-service-victims-shooting-tucson.

[47]Read a transcript of the Nick Jonas speech on "Diabetes Awareness" at the National Press Club, August 24, 2009, http://www.press.org/members/transcriptview.cfm?pdf=20090824_jonas.pdf; Watch and listen to the Nick Jonas speech on "Nick Jonas Discusses Juvenile Diabetes at the National Press Club, August 24, 2009," *YouTube*, http://www.youtube.com/watch?v=DyYOxzrJB4Y.

[48]Aung San Suu Kyi, "Freedom from Fear," 1990. Transcripts and video of this speech are available from a variety of web sources: http://www.famous-speeches-and-speech-topics.info/famous-speeches/aung-san-suu-kyi-speech-freedom-from-fear.htm; http://chnm.gmu.edu/wwh/p/119.html; http://www.youtube.com/watch?v=lukeAw6X2a8; http://eloquentwoman.blogspot.com/2012/06/famous-speech-friday-aung-san-suu-kyis.html.

Chapter 15

[1]Isa N. Engleberg and John A. Daly, *Think Public Speaking* (Boston: Pearson 2013), p. 264.

[2]James M. Lang, "Beyond Lecturing," *The Chronicle of Higher Education*, September 9, 2006, p. C4.

[3]James M. Lang, "Beyond Lecturing," *The Chronicle of Higher Education*, September 9, 2006, p. C4.

[4]Wilbert J. McKeachie, *Teaching Tips: Strategies, Research, and Theory for College and University Teachers*, 10th ed. (Boston: Houghton Mifflin, 1999), p. 70.

[5]Wilbert J. McKeachie, *Teaching Tips: Strategies, Research, and Theory for College and University Teachers*, 10th ed. (Boston: Houghton Mifflin, 1999), pp. 69–84.

[6]Sections of Chapters 12 through 16 are based on Isa N. Engleberg and John A. Daly, *Presentations in Everyday Life*, 3rd ed. (Boston: Pearson/Allyn and Bacon, 2009); Isa N. Engleberg and John A. Daly, *Think Public Speaking* (Boston: Pearson, 2013), Chapter 15.

[7]This section is based on the research and theory-building of Katherine E. Rowan, professor of communication at George Mason University. See Katherine E. Rowan, "Informing and Explaining Skills: Theory and Research on Informative Communication," in John O. Greene and Brant R. Burleson (Eds.), *Handbook of Communication and Social Interaction Skills* (Mahwah, NJ: Lawrence Erlbaum Associates, 2003), pp. 403–438; Katherine E. Rowan, "A New Pedagogy for Explanatory Public Speaking: Why Arrangement Should Not Substitute for Invention," *Communication Education* 44 (1995): 236–250.

[8]John A. Daly, *Advocacy: Championing Ideas and Influencing Others* (New Haven: Yale University Press, 2011), p. 246.

[9]Katherine E. Rowan, "A New Pedagogy for Explanatory Public Speaking: Why Arrangement Should Not Substitute for Invention," *Communication Education* 44 (1995): 242; Katherine E. Rowan, "Informing and Explaining Skills: Theory and Research on Informative Communication," in John O. Greene and Brant R. Burleson (Eds.), *Handbook of Communication and Social Interaction Skills* (Mahwah, NJ: Lawrence Erlbaum Associates, 2003), p. 411.

[10]Katherine E. Rowan, "A New Pedagogy for Explanatory Public Speaking: Why Arrangement Should Not Substitute for Invention," *Communication Education* 44 (1995): 241.

[11]Craig Silverman, "Major Breaking News Errors Giving Rise to New Responses in Boston Coverage," *The Poynter Institute*, April 18, 2013, http://www.poynter.org/latest-news/regret-the-error/210699/major-breaking-news-errors-giving-rise-to-new-responses-in-boston-coverage.

[12]Craig Silverman, "Major Breaking News Errors Giving Rise to New Responses in Boston Coverage," *The Poynter Institute*, April 18, 2013, http://www.poynter.org/latest-news/regret-the-error/210699/major-breaking-news-errors-giving-rise-to-new-responses-in-boston-coverage.

[13]Numerous news websites provided details about the poor reporting after the Boston Marathon Bombing: Alexis C. Madrigal, "It Wasn't Sunil Tripathi: The Anatomy of a Misfortunate Disaster," *The Atlantic*, April 19, 2013, http://www.theatlantic.com/technology/archive/2013/04/it-wasnt-sunil-tripathi-the-anatomy-of-a-misinformation-disaster/275155; L. V. Anderson, "Family of Missing Brown Student Updates Facebook Page With Touching New Message," *The Atlantic*, April 19, 2013, http://www.theatlantic.com/technology/archive/2013/04/it-wasnt-sunil-tripathi-the-anatomy-of-a-misinformation-disaster/275155; Dave Lee, "Boston Bombing: How Internet Detectives Got It Very Wrong," *BBC NEWS Technology*, April 19, 2013, http://www.bbc.co.uk/news/technology-22214511; Uttara Choudhury, "Sunil Tripathi, Wrongly Linked to Boston Attack, Died in River: Autopsy Report," *The Independent*, April 23, 2013.

[14]Alexis C. Madrigal, "It Wasn't Sunil Tripathi: The Anatomy of a Misfortunate Disaster," *The Atlantic*, April 19, 2013, http://www.theatlantic.com/technology/archive/2013/04/it-wasnt-sunil-tripathi-the-anatomy-of-a-misinformation-disaster/275155.

[15]Dave Lee, "Boston Bombing: How Internet Detectives Got It Very Wrong," *BBC NEWS Technology*, April 19, 2013, http://www.bbc.co.uk/news/technology-22214511.

[16]Dave Lee, "Boston Bombing: How Internet Detectives Got It Very Wrong," *BBC NEWS Technology*, April 19, 2013, http://www.bbc.co.uk/news/technology-22214511.

[17]http://www.lifestylelift.org/grammy-award-winner-debby-boone-named-lifestyle-lift-spokesperson-and-infomercial-talk-show-host.

[18]We researched numerous websites ranging from trainer sites to those assessing the value of workout DVDs: http://www.fitnessmagazine.com/workout/gear/dvds/10-best-workout-dvds; http://www.consumersearch.com/exercise-video-reivews; http://exercise.about.com/od/cardiomachinesources/tp/cardiovideos; http://www.womansday.com/health-fitness/workout-routines/10-best-fitness-dvds. http://www.jillianmichaelsbodyrevolution.com; http://www.doctoroz.com/videos/shaun-ts-miracle-15-minute-workout; http://beachbody.com/product/fitness_programs/10_minute_trainer_do.

[19]http://www.natcom.org/index.asp?bid=510.

[20]Isa N. Engleberg and John A. Daly, *Presentation in Everyday Life*, 3rd ed. (Boston: Pearson/Allyn and Bacon, 2009), pp. 3–4.

[21]Isa N. Engleberg and John A. Daly, *Presentation in Everyday Life*, 3rd ed. (Boston: Pearson/Allyn and Bacon, 2009), pp. 37–39; Isa N. Engleberg and John A. Daly, *Think Public Speaking* (Boston: Pearson, 2013), pp. 4, 29–30.

[22]Rives Collins and Pamela J. Cooper, *The Power of Story: Teaching Through Storytelling*, 2nd ed. (Boston: Allyn & Bacon, 1997), p. 2.

[23]Walter R. Fisher, *Human Communication as Narration: Toward a Philosophy of Reason, Value, and Action* (Columbia, SC: University of South Carolina Press, 1987), pp. 64, 65.

[24]Henry L. Roubicek, *So What's Your Story?* (Dubuque, IA: Kendall Hunt, 2011), p. 17.

[25]John A. Daly, *Advocacy: Championing Ideas and Influencing Others* (New Haven: Yale University Press, 2011), p 120.

[26]John A. Daly, *Advocacy: Championing Ideas and Influencing Others* (New Haven: Yale University Press, 2011), pp. 121–123.

[27]William Hendricks et al., *Secrets of Power Presentations* (Franklin Lakes, NJ: Career Press, 1996), p. 79.

[28]Research verifies that when stories are followed by a moral or epilogue, audiences are more likely to accept the message. See Rebekah et al., "An Examination of the Narrative Persuasion with Epilogue Through the Lens of the Elaboration Likelihood Model," *Communication Quarterly* 61 (2013): 431–445.

[29]Malcolm Kushner, *Successful Presentations for Dummies* (Foster City, CA: IDG Books, 1997), p. 79.

[30]Rives Collins and Pamela J. Cooper, *The Power of Story: Teaching Through Storytelling*, 2nd ed. (Boston: Allyn & Bacon, 1997), pp. 24–28; Isa Engleberg and John Daly, *Presentations in Everyday Life: Strategies for Effective Speaking*, 3rd ed. (Boston: Pearson/Allyn and Bacon, 2009), pp. 292–294.

[31]Walter R. Fisher, *Human Communication as Narration: Toward a Philosophy of Reason, Value, and Action* (Columbia, SC: University of South Carolina Press, 1987), p. 24.

[32]Walter R. Fisher, *Human Communication as Narration: Toward a Philosophy of Reason, Value, and Action* (Columbia, SC: University of South Carolina Press, 1987), p. 68.

[33]Candace Spigelman, "Argument and Evidence in the Case of the Personal," *College English* 64, Volume 1 (2001): 80–81.

[34]Walter Fisher, "Narrative as Human Communication Paradigm," in John Louis Lucaites, Celeste Michelle Condit, and Sally Caudill (Eds.), *Contemporary Rhetorical Theory* (New York: The Guilford Press, 1999), p. 272.

[35]Henry L. Roubicek, *So What's Your Story?* (Dubuque, IA: Kendall Hunt, 2011), p. 20.

[36]Based on Joanna Slan, *Using Stories and Humor: Grab Your Audience* (Boston: Allyn & Bacon, 1998), pp. 89–95, 116. See also Isa N. Engleberg and John A. Daly, *Presentation in Everyday Life*, 3rd ed. (Boston: Pearson/Allyn and Bacon, 2009), pp. 296–298; Isa N. Engleberg and John A. Daly, *Think Public Speaking* (Boston: Pearson, 2013), pp. 207–209.

[37]Based on Paul Galdone, *The Three Little Pigs* (New York: Houghton Mifflin, 1970).

[38]Malcolm Kushner, *Successful Presentations for Dummies* (Foster City, CA: IDG Books, 1997), p. 350.

[39]Gene Perret, *Using Humor for Effective Business Speaking* (New York: Sterling, 1989), pp. 19–26.

[40]Yang Lin and Patricia S. Hill, "Cross-Cultural Humor: A New Frontier for Intercultural Communication Research," in Rachel L. DiCiocolo (Ed.), *Humor Communication: Theory, Impact, and Outcomes* (Dubuque, IA: Kendall Hunt, 2012), p. 269.

[41]Ghu-Hai Chen and Rod A. Martin, "A Comparison of Humor Styles: Coping Humor, and Mental Health Between Chinese and Canadian University Students," *Humor—International Journal of Humor Research* 20 (2007): 209.

[42]Shahe S. Kazarian and Rod A. Martin "Humor Styles, Culture-Elated Personality, Well-Being, and Family Adjustment Among Armenians in Lebanon," *Humor—International Journal of Humor Research* 19 (2006): 405–423; Quoted in Yang Lin and Patricia S. Hill, "Cross-Cultural Humor: A New Frontier for Intercultural Communication Research," in Rachel L. DiCiocolo (Ed.), *Humor Communication: Theory, Impact, and Outcomes* (Dubuque, IA: Kendall Hunt, 2012).

[43]Gil Greengross "Laughing All the Way to the Bedroom: The Importance of Humor in Mating," *Humor Sapiens/Psychology Today*, May 1, 2011, http://www.psychologytoday.com/blog/humor-sapiens/201105/laughing-all-the-way-the-bedroom.

[44]Frank Cotham cartoon, Published in *The New Yorker*, February, 18, 2002, http://www.cartoonbank.com/2002/at-what-point-does-this-become-our-problem/invt/122039. Note: The winning caption is at the end of this web site: "At what point does this become our problem?" For more cartoon and winning captions, see *The New Yorker Cartoon Caption Contest Book* (Kansas City: Andrews McMeel Publishing, 2008).

[45]See Isa N. Engleberg and John A. Daly, *Presentations in Everyday Life*, 2nd ed. (Boston/Allyn and Bacon, 2005), pp. 313–315.

[46]Gil Greengross "Laughing All the Way to the Bedroom: The Importance of Humor in Mating," *Humor Sapiens/Psychology Today*, May 1, 2011, http://www.psychologytoday.com/blog/humor-sapiens/201105/laughing-all-the-way-the-bedroom.

[47]Summary of tips for using humor from Isa N. Engleberg and Dianna R. Wynn, *The Challenge of Communicating: Guiding Principles and Practices* (Pearson/Allyn & Bacon, 2008), p. 408; Joanna Slan, *Using Stories and Humor: Grab Your Audience* (Boston: Allyn & Bacon, 1998), pp. 170–172.

[48]Since developing this presentation, *CliffsNotes* has gone through several changes and traumas. In 1998, Cliff Hillegass sold Cliff'sNotes, Inc. to John Wiley & Sons, Inc. In May 2001, Mr. Hillegass passed away at the age of 83. In 2007, Cliff's Notes.com was relaunched with an updated design and notes for school subjects such as math, science, writing, foreign languages, history, and government. "A Brief History of CliffsNotes," http://www.cliffsnotes.com/WileyCDA/Section/A-Brief-History.id-305430.html. In 2012, Houghton Mifflin Harcourt acquired CliffsNotes, Inc.

Chapter 16

[1]See Jennifer Epstein, "Michelle Obama: 'Hadiya Pendleton was me, and I was her'," *Politico*, April 10, 2013, http://www.politico.com/politico44/2013/04/michelle-obama-hadiya-pendleton-was-me-and-i-was-her-161339.html; Paige Lavender, "Michelle Obama Tears Up During Gun Violence Speech in Chicago," *Huffington Post*, April 10, 2013, http://www.huffingtonpost.com/2013/04/10/michelle-obama-tears-up_n_3055104.html?view=print&comm_ref=false; Charyl Corley, "Michelle Obama Steps Into Gun Control Debate," *National Public Radio*, April 10, 2013, http://www.npr.org/blogs/itsallpolitics/2013/04/10/176822207/michelle-obama-steps-into-gun-control-debate.

[2]Office of the First Lady, "Remarks by the First Lady at the Joint Luncheon Meeting: Working Together to Address Youth Violence in Chicago," The White House, April 10, 2013, http://www.whitehouse.gov/the-press-office/2013/04/10/remarks-first-lady-joint-luncheon-meeting-working-together-address-youth.

[3]Lesley Kriewald, "The Power of Social Media," Texas A&M School of Engineering, 2013, http://engineering.tamu.edu/research/2012/the-power-of-social-media.

[4]Robert H. Gass and John S. Seiter, *Persuasion, Social Influence, and Compliance Gaining*, 4th ed. (Boston: Pearson, 2011), Preface and p. 13.

[5]A variation on the 1931 jazz standard "It Don't Mean a Thing (If It Ain't Got That Swing)" by Duke Ellington with lyrics by Irving Mills.

[6]Robert H. Gass and John S. Seiter, *Persuasion, Social Influence, and Compliance Gaining*, 4th ed. (Boston: Pearson, 2011), p. 198.

[7]William J. McGuire, "Inducing Resistance to Persuasion: Some Contemporary Approaches," in Leonard Berkowitz (Ed.), *Advances in Experimental Psychology* (New York: Academic Press, 1964), pp. 192–229.

[8]John A. Daly, *Advocacy: Championing Ideas and Influencing Others* (New Haven: Yale University Press, 2011), p. 222.

[9]Jack W. Brehm, *A Theory of Psychological Reactance* (New York: Academic Press, 1966). See also Michael Burgoon et al., "Revisiting the Theory of Psychological Reactance," in James Price Dillard and Michael Pfau (Eds.), *The Persuasion Handbook: Development in Theory and Practice* (Thousand Oaks, CA: Sage, 2002), pp. 213–232; James Price Dillard and Linda J. Marshall, "Persuasion as a Social Skill," in John O. Greene and Brant R. Burleson (Eds.), *Handbook of Communication and Social Interaction Skills* (Mahwah, NJ: Lawrence Erlbaum, 2003), pp. 500–501.

[10]Don Levine, "Booze Barriers," *Boulder Weekly*, September 7, 2000, http://www.boulderweekly.com/archive/090700/coverstory.html, p. 4.

[11]Don Levine, "Booze Barriers," *Boulder Weekly*, September 7, 2000, http://www.boulderweekly.com/archive/090700/coverstory.html, p. 4.

[12]Stephen Toulmin, *The Uses of Argument* (London: Cambridge University Press, 1958). See also Stephen Toulmin, Richard Rieke, and Allan Janik, *An Introduction to Reasoning* (New York: Macmillan, 1979).

[13]Thomas Sewell, "I Beg to Disagree: The Lost Art of Logical Arguments," *Naples Daily News*, (January 14, 2005), p. 9D.

[14]Fred D. White and Simone J. Billings, *The Well-Crafted Argument: A Guide and Reader*, 2nd ed. (Boston: Houghton Mifflin, 2005), p. 93.

[15]Charles U. Larson, *Persuasion: Reception and Responsibility*, 11th ed. (Belmont, CA: Thomson/Wadsworth, 2007), p. 185.

[16]Les Christie, "Number of People Without Health Insurance Climbs," *CNN Money* (A Service of *CNN*, *Fortune*, and *Money*) September 13, 20011, http://money.cnn.com/2011/09/13/news/economy/census_bureau_health_-insurance/index.htm.

[17]Charles U. Larson, *Persuasion: Reception and Responsibility*, 11th ed. (Belmont, CA: Thomson/Wadsworth, 2007), p. 58.

[18]Richard M. Perloff, *The Dynamics of Persuasion: Communication and Attitudes in the 21st Century*, 4th ed. (New York: Routledge/Taylor & Francis, 2010), pp. 204–206.

[19]Student speech from Authors' files printed with permission.

[20]Aristotle, *Rhetoric*, in Jonathan Barnes (Ed.), *The Complete Works of Aristotle: The Revised Oxford Translation*, Vol. 2 (Princeton, NJ: Princeton University Press, 1995), p. 2155.

[21]Michael Osborn, Suzanne Osborn, and Randall Osborn, *Public Speaking*, 8th ed. (Boston: Pearson/Allyn & Bacon, 2009), p. 380.

[22]Michael Osborn, Suzanne Osborn, and Randall Osborn, *Public Speaking*, 8th ed. (Boston: Pearson/Allyn & Bacon, 2009), p. 376.

[23]Richard Maxwell and Robert Dickman, *The Elements of Persuasion: Use Storytelling to Pitch Better, Sell Faster, and Win More Business* (New York: HarperCollins, 2007), p. 125.

[24]See Alexander Todorov, Shelley Chaiken, and Marlone D. Henderson, "The Heuristic-Systematic Model of Social Information Processing," in James Price Dillard and Michael Pfau (Eds.), *The Persuasion Handbook: Developments in Theory and Practice* (Thousand Oaks, CA: Sage, 2002), pp. 195–211; James Price Dillard and Linda J. Marshall. "Persuasion as a Social Skill," in John O. Greene and Brant R. Burleson (Eds.), *Handbook of Communication and Social Interaction Skills* (Mahwah, NJ: Lawrence Erlbaum, 2003), pp. 494–495.

[25]Andrew Breitbart, "John McCain: Tea Party Senators 'Wacko Birds'," *Tea Party*, March 8, 2013, http://www.teaparty.org/john-mccain-new-gop-guard-wacko-birds-21328; http://www.breitbart.com/Big-Government/2013/03/08/McCain-Paul-Cruz-Wacko.

[26]See "Appeal to Tradition," *Wikipedia*, for more examples, http://wiki.ironchariots.org/index.php?title=Appeal_to_tradition.

[27]Based on Patrick J. Hurley, *A Concise Introduction to Logic*, 8th ed. (Belmont, CA: Wadsworth Thomson Learning, 2003), pp. 172–174.

[28]Alan H. Monroe, *Principles and Types of Speech* (Chicago: Scott, Foresman, 1935).

[29]Based on Nicholas D. Kristof and Sheryl WuDunn, "The Women's Crusade," *The New York Times Magazine*, August 23, 2009, pp. 28–39. Kristof is an international journalist and advocate for women's rights.

[30]Sharon Shavitt and Michelle R. Nelson, "The Role of Attitude Functions in Persuasion and Social Judgment," in James Price Dillard and Michael Pfau (Eds.), *The Persuasion Handbook: Developments in Theory and Practice* (Thousand Oaks, CA: Sage, 2002), p. 150.

[31]Sharon Shavitt and Michelle R. Nelson, "The Role of Attitude Functions in Persuasion and Social Judgment," in James Price Dillard and Michael Pfau (Eds.), *The Persuasion Handbook: Developments in Theory and Practice* (Thousand Oaks, CA: Sage, 2002), p. 150.

[32]This presentation appeared in *Vital Speeches of the Day* 65 (August 1, 1999), pp. 633–634. See also Marge Anderson, "The Value of Native Culture," http://www.manataka.org/page848.html; http://udaisd.proboards.com/index.cgi?board=general&action=display&thread=38.

[33]Former Chief Executive Marjorie Anderson of the Mille Lacs Band of Ojibwe passed away June 29, 2013. She was nationally known as a leader in Indian gaming, tribal self-governance and tribal treaty rights. For more information see "Marge Anderson, Former Chief of Mille Lacs Band, Passes Away," *Mille Lacs County Times*, July 4, 2013, http://millelacscountytimes.com/2013/07/04/marge-anderson-former-chief-of-mille-lacs-band-passes-away.

credits

Text Credits

Chapter 1

p. 5: Carol Huang. "Facebook and Twitter Key to Arab Spring Uprising" The National, 6/6/11. p. 13: Reprinted by permission of the National Communication Association. p. 14: Reprinted by permission of the National Communication Association. p. 18: Reprinted by permission of the National Communication Association.

Chapter 2

p. 21: Based on Leon Festinger, "A Theory of Social Comparison Processes," Human Relations, 7 (1954): 117–140. p. 24: Robert Epstein in "The Truth about Online Dating," Scientific American Mind, January 30, 2007, p. 33. p. 27: Mark R. Leary and Robin M. Kowalski, "Impression Management: A Literature Review and Two-Component Model," Psychological Bulletin, 1990, 107, p. 34. Copyright © 1990 by The American Psychological Association. Adapted by permission. p. 35: James C. McCroskey, "Oral Communication Apprehension: Summary of Recent Theory and Research," Human Communication Research 4 (1977): 80. p. 38: Richmond, Virginia P., McCroskey, James C., Communication: Apprehension, Avoidance and Effectiveness, 5th Edition © 1998. Reprinted by permission of Pearson Education, Inc., Upper Saddle River, NJ.

Chapter 3

p. 42: LUSTIG, MYRON; KOESTER, JOLENE; INTERCULTURAL COMPETENCE, 7th Ed., © 2013. Reprinted and Electronically reproduced by permission of Pearson Education, Inc., Upper Saddle River, New Jersey. p. 44: Stephen Prothero, Religious Literacy: What Every American Needs to Know—And Doesn't (New York: HarperCollins, 2007), p. 11. p. 47: LUSTIG, MYRON; KOESTER, JOLENE; INTERCULTURAL COMPETENCE, 7th Ed., © 2013. Reprinted and Electronically reproduced by permission of Pearson Education, Inc., Upper Saddle River, New Jersey. p. 48: Geert Hofstede, Gert Jan Hofstede, and Michael Minkov, Cultures and Organizations: Software of the Mind: Intercultural Cooperation and Its Importance for Survival, 3rd ed. (New York: McGraw-Hill, 2010) pp 95–97. Copyright © 2010. Reprinted by permission of the author. p. 49: Geert Hofstede, Gert Jan Hofstede, and Michael Minkov, Cultures and Organizations: Software of the Mind: Intercultural Cooperation and Its Importance for Survival, 3rd ed. (New York: McGraw-Hill, 2010) pp 95–97. Copyright © 2010. Reprinted by permission of the author. p. 50: Based on Cheris Kramarae, Women and Men Speaking: Framework for Analysis (Rowley, MA: Newbury House, 1981). p. 51: Geert Hofstede, Gert Jan Hofstede, and Michael Minkov, Cultures and Organizations: Software of the Mind: Intercultural Cooperation and Its Importance for Survival, 3rd ed. (New York: McGraw-Hill, 2010) pp 95–97. Copyright © 2010. Reprinted by permission of the author. p. 55: Howard Giles et al., "Accommodation Theory: Communication, Context, and Consequence," in Contexts of Accommodation: Developments in Applied Sociolinguistics, ed. Howard Giles et al. (Cambridge: Cambridge University Press, 1991), pp. 1–68. Copyright © 1991 Maison de Sciences de l'Homme and Cambridge University Press. p. 56: Communication Research Reports: CRR by WORLD COMMUNICATION ASSOCIATION : WEST VIRGINIA UNIVERSITY Reproduced with permission of PUBLISHED BY THE WORLD COMMUNICATION ASSOCIATION I in the format republish in a book/textbook via Copyright Clearance Center. p. 59: Rita Hardiman, "White Racial Identity Development in the United States," in Race, Ethnicity and Self: Identity in Multicultural Perspective, ed. Elizabeth Pathy Salett and Dianne R. Koslow (Washington, DC: National MultiCultural Institute, 1994), pp. 130–31. p. 60: David Cay Johnston, "A Close Look at Your Bills 'Fine Print,'" September 20, 2012, Fresh Air, National Public Radio, http://www.npr.org/2012/09/20/161477162/a-close-look-at-your-bills-fine-print p. 60: Richard Nisbett, The Geography of Thought: How Asians and Westerners Think Differently . . . and Why (New York: Free Press, 2003), p. xiii. p. 60: Marvin Harris, Cows, Pigs, Wars, and Witches: The Riddles of Culture (New York: Vintage Books, 1975), p. 30.

Chapter 4

p. 59: Seth S. Horowitz, "The Science and Art of Listening," The New York Times, November 11, 2012, p. SR 2. p. 61: Based on Lynn O. Cooper and Trey Buchanan, "Listening Competency on Campus: A Psychometric Analysis of Student Learning, The International Journal of Listening, 24 (2010), pp. 141–163. p. 64: Based on Don Gabor, How to Start a Conversation and Make Friends (New York: Fireside, 2001), pp. 66–68. p. 67: Deborah Tannen, You Just Don't Understand: Women and Men in Conversation (New York: Ballantine Books, 1990), pp. 141–142.

Chapter 5

p. 78: Donna Smith, "Bullying: When Words Hurt," Disney Family.com, http://family.go.com/parenting/pkg-teen/article-766446-bullying-when-words-hurt p. 82: Marcel Danesi and Paul Perron, Analyzing Cultures: An Introduction and Handbook (Bloomington, IN: Indiana University Press, 1999), p. 61. p. 89: James V. O'Conner, Cuss Control: The Complete Book on How to Curb Your Cursing (New York: Three Rivers Press, 2000), pp. 18–27. p. 92: Richmond, Virginia P., McCroskey, James C., Communication: Apprehension, Avoidance and Effectiveness, 5th Edition. © 1998. Reprinted by permission of Pearson Education, Inc., Upper Saddle River, NJ.

Chapter 6

p. 97: The dark side of interpersonal communication by CUPACH, WILLIAM, R.; SPITZBERG, BRIAN H., Reproduced with permission of LAWRENCE ERLBAUM ASSOCIATES, INCORPORATED in the format Republish in a book via Copyright Clearance Center. p. 99: Mark L. Knapp, Judith A. Hall, and Terrence G. Horgan, Nonverbal Communication in Human Interaction, 8th ed. (Boston: Wadsworth, 2014), p. 15. p. 99: Paul Ekman, "Communication through Nonverbal Behavior: A Source of Information about an Interpersonal Relationship," in Silvia S. Tomkins and C. E. Izard (Eds.), Affect, Cognition, and Personality (New York: Springer, 1965) p. 101: Freezy, "Video: Sesame Street Makes 'I Love My Hair' for Young Black Girls." FREESWORLD (Marie 'Free' Wright), October 18, 2010, http://www.freesworld.com/2010/10/18/video-sesame-street-makes-i-love-my-hair-for-young-black-girls/. p. 106: Lyle V. Mayer, Fundamentals of Voice and Diction, 13th ed. , p. 229. Copyright © 2004 McGraw-Hill Education. Reprinted by permission of McGraw-Hill Education. p. 107: From Knapp/Hall/Horgan. Nonverbal Communication in Human Interaction, 8E. © 2014 Wadsworth, a part of Cengage Learning, Inc. Reproduced by permission. www.cengage.com/permissions. p. 110: Nina-Jo Moore, Mark Hickson, III, and Don W. Stacks, Nonverbal Communication, Studies and Application, 5th ed. (New York: Oxford, 2010), p. 192. p. 111: Brian H. Spitzberg, "CSRS: The Conversational Skills Rating Scale—An Instructional Assessment of Interpersonal Competence," in the NCA Diagnostic Series, 2nd ed. (Washington, D.C.: National Communication Association, 2007).

Chapter 7

p. 116: John M. Gottman with Joan De Claire, The Relationship Cure (New York: Three Rivers Press, 2001), p. 23. p. 117: William Schutz, The Human Element: Productivity, Self-Esteem, and the Bottom Line (San Francisco: Jossey-Bass, 1994). Copyright © 1994. Reprinted by permission of John Wiley & Sons. p. 117: Daniel Menaker, A Good Talk: The Story and Skill of Conversation (NY: Hatchette Book Groups, 2010), p. 1. p. 121: Knapp, Mark C. and Vangelisti, Anita L. Interpersonal Communication and Human Relationships, 5th Edition © 2005. Reprinted by permission of Pearson Education, Inc., Upper Saddle River, NJ. p. 121: Lynn H. Turner and Richard West, Perspectives on Family Communication, 2nd ed. (Boston: McGraw Hill, 2002), p. 8. p. 123: Joseph Luft, Group Process: An Introduction to Group Dynamics, 3rd ed. Copyright © 1984 McGraw-Hill Education. Reprinted by permission of McGraw-Hill Education. p. 127: Based on Robert Plutchik, Emotions: A Psychoevolutionary Synthesis (New York: Harper and Row, 1980). p. 127: Daniel Goleman, Working with Emotional Intelligence (New York: Bantam Books, 1998), p. 317. p. 128: Handbook of communication and social interaction skills by Greene, John, O.; Burleson, Brant Raney Reproduced with permission of LAWRENCE ERLBAUM ASSOCIATES INCORPORATED in the format Republish in a book via Copyright Clearance Center.

Chapter 8

p. 136: Relating: dialogues and dialectic by BAXTER, LESLIE A.; MONTGOMERY, BARBARA M. Reproduced with permission of GUILFORD PUBLICATIONS INCORPORATED in the format Republish in a book via Copyright Clearance Center. p. 145: Adapted from Dudley D. Cahn and Abigail, Ruth Anna, Managing Conflict through Communication, 3rd ed. © 2007. Reprinted by permission of Pearson Education Inc., Upper Saddle River, NJ. p. 146: Journal of Personality Assessment by SOCIETY FOR PERSONALITY ASSESSMENT Reproduced with permission of LAWRENCE ERLBAUM, ASSOCIATES, INC. in the format republish in a book/textbook via Copyright Clearance Center. p. 147: From Regina Fazio Maruca, "The Electronic Negotiator: A Conversation with Kathleen Valley," Harvard Business Review, January 2000. © 2000. Reprinted by permission of Harvard Business Publishing. p. 148: ACT on life not on anger: the new acceptance and commitment therapy guide to problem anger by Eifert, Georg H.; McKay, Matthew; Forsyth, John P. Reproduced with permission of New Harbinger Publications in the format Republish in a book via Copyright Clearance Center. p. 149: William W. Wilmot and Joyce L. Hocker, Interpersonal Conflict, 5th ed. Copyright © 1995 McGraw-Hill Education. Reprinted by permission of McGraw-Hill Education. p. 151: TOMPKINS, PAULA, S., PRACTICING COMMUNICATION ETHICS: DEVELOPMENT, DISCERNMENT, AND DECISION-MAKING, 1st Ed., © 2011. Reprinted and Electronically reproduced by permission of Pearson Education, Inc., Upper Saddle River, New Jersey. p. 152: From Asserting yourself: A Practical Guide to Positive Change by Sharon Anthony Bower and Gordon H. Bower, Copyright © 1991. Reprinted by permission of DeCapo Press, a member of the Perseus Books Group. p. 152: The anxiety and phobia workbook by Bourne, Edmund, J. Reproduced with permission of New harbinger Publications in the format Republish in a book via Copyright Clearance Center. p. 156: Laura K. Guerrero, "Coping with Hurtful Events" Communication Currents, Vol. 7, Issue 1, February 2012. Copyright © 2012 Reprinted by permission of the National Communication Association.

Chapter 9:

p. 159: Reprinted by permission of the Center for Professional Excellence. p. 160: MODAFF, DANIEL, P., BUTLER, JENNIFER, A., DEWINE, SUE, ORGANIZATIONAL COMMUNICATION: FOUNDATIONS, CHALLENGES, AND MISUNDERSTANDINGS, 2nd Ed., © 2008. Reprinted and electronically reproduced by PEARSON EDUCATION, One Lake Street, Upper Saddle River, New

Jersey 07458. p. 160: Based on Daniel P. Modaff, Sue DeWine, and Jennifer A. Butler, Organizational Communication: Foundations, Challenges, Misunderstandings (Los Angeles, CA: Roxbury, 2008). p. 162: Based on John Tschohl, Service Quality Institute, "Service, Not Servitude: Common Sense Is Critical Element of Customer Service," 2004, http://www.customer-service.com/articles/022502.cfm. p. 164: Sean M. Horan and Rebecca M. Chory, "Understanding Work-Life Blending: Credibility Implications for Those Who Date at Work," Communication Studies, 62 (2011), p. 565; p. 166: U.S. Equal Employment Opportunity Commission, "Facts about Sexual Harassment"(June 27, 2002), http://www.eeoc.gov/facts/fs-sex.html. p. 166: Lawrence Downes, "How the Military Talks About Sexual Assault, The New York Times, May 26, 2013, http://takingnote.blogs.nytimes.com/2013/05/26/how-the-military-talks-about-sexual-assault. p. 168: Hal Plotkin, "How to Handle Difficult Behaviors," Dealing with Difficult People , p. 132–137. Copyright © 2005 Reprinted by permission of Harvard Business Publishing. p. 175: Based on J. Maureen Henderson, "3 Ways Millennials Can Master Job Interviews," Forbes, May 6, 2013.

Chapter 10

p. 179: Arupa Tesolin, "Igniting the Creative Spark at Cirque du Soleil—Argupa Tesolin Interviews Lyn Heward Creative Leader at Cirque," Self Growth, May 2008. http://www.selfgrowth.com/articles/Igniting_the_Creative_Spark_at_Cirque_du_Soleil.html. p. 180: Steve W. J. Kozlowski and Daniel R. Ilgen (2006). "Enhancing the Effectiveness of Work Groups and Teams," Psychological Science in the Public Interest, 7 (3), p. 77. p. 183: Linda Stewart, "Building Virtual Teams: Strategies for High Performance," Forbes, March 30, 2012, http://www.forbes.com/sites/ciocentral/2012/03/30/building-virtual-teams-strategies-for-high-performance. p. 184: Based on Ernest G. Bormann, Small Group Communication: Theory and Practice, 3rd ed. (HarperCollins, 1990) pp. 132–135, 181–183. p. 184: Based on Ernest G. Bormann, Small Group Communication: Theory and Practice, 3rd ed. (HarperCollins, 1990) pp. 132–135, 181–183. p. 186: Based on Kristin J. Behfar, Elizabeth A. Mannix, Randall S. Peterson, and William M. Trochim, "Conflict in Small Groups: The Meaning and Consequences of Process Conflict," Small Group Research, 42 (2011), pp. 128, 136–137. p. 187: Definition of "norms", Patricia H Andrews, edited by Robert S Cathcart, edited by Larry A Samovar, edited by Linda D Henman, Patricia H. Andrews, "Group Conformity," in Small Group Communication: Theory and Practice, 7th ed., ed. Robert S. Cathcart, Larry A. Samovar, and Linda D. Henman (Madison, WI: Brown and Benchmark, 1996), p. 185., Cathcart, Robert S. p. 194: Orem Harari, The Leadership Secrets of Colin Powell (New York: McGraw-Hill, 2002), p. 249.

Chapter 11

p. 201: Randy Y. Hirokawa, "Communication and Group Decision-Making Efficacy," in Small Group Communication: Theory and Practice, 7th ed. (Madison, WI: Brown and Benchmark, 1996). p. 202: Irving L. Janis, Symptoms of Groupthink, Groupthink, 2nd ed. Boston: Houghton Mifflin, 1982, pp. 174–175). p. 202: Irving L. Janis, GROUPTHINK, p. 9. p. 204: Rodney Napier and Matti Gershenfeld, Groups: Theory and Experience, 7/e, pp 337. p. 204: John Katzenbach and Douglas Smith, The Disciplines of Teams, p113(2001). p. 205: Randy Hirokawa and Roger Pace, "A Descriptive Investigation of the Possible Communication-Based Reasons for Effective and Ineffective Group Decision Making," Communication Monographs 50 (1983): p. 379. p. 205: Based on Suzanne Scott and Reginald Bruce "Decision Making Style: The Development of a New Measure," Educational and Psychological Measurements 55 (1995): 818–831. p. 207: DELBECO, ANDRE L; VAN DE VEN, ANDREW, H.; GUSTAFSON, DAVID H., GROUP TECH PROGRAM PLANG, 1st Ed., © 1975. Reprinted and Electronically reproduced by permission of Pearson Education, Inc., Upper Saddle River, New Jersey. p. 211: Based on Karen Anderson, Making Meetings Work: How to Plan and conduct Effective Meetings, American Media Publishing, 1997. p. 18. p. 212: Sharon M. Lippincott, Meetings: Do's, Don'ts, and Donuts (Pittsburgh, PA: Lighthouse Point Press, 1994), p. 172. p. 214: 3M Meeting Management Team with Jeannine Drew, Mastering Meetings: Discovering the Hidden Potential of Effective Business Meetings (New York: McGraw-Hill, 1994), p. 78. p. 218: Adapted from Lyn M. Van Swol "Why Can't Groups Focus on New Information," Communication Currents, Vol. 4, Issue 2, April 2009.

Chapter 12

p. 221: From speak With Courage: 50 Insider Strategies for Presenting with Ease and Confidence by Martin McDermott. Copyright © 2015 by Bedford/St. Martin's. Reprinted with permission. p. 222: Dorothy Leeds, Power Speak: Engage, Inspire, and Stimulate Your Audience, Career Press (2003) p. 47. p. 222: Nancy Durarte, HBR Guide to Persuasive Presentations Harvard Business Review Press (2012), p 19. p. 230: ENGLEBERG, ISA, N.; DALY, JOHN, A., PRESENTATIONS IN EVERYDAY LIFE, 3rd Ed., © 2009. Reprinted and Electronically reproduced by permission of Pearson Education, Inc., Upper Saddle River, New Jersey. p. 233: Lane Cooper, The Rhetoric of Aristotle (New York: Appleton-Century-Crofts, 1932), p. 8 and 9. p. 233: Nathan Crick, Rhetorical Public Speaking (Allyn & Bacon, 2100, p. 136). p. 226: Gene Zelazny, Say It with Presentations, Revised. Copyright © 2006 McGraw-Hill Education. Reprinted with permission of McGraw-Hill Education.

Chapter 13

p. 239: From Nancy Duarte, HBR Guide to Persuasive Presentations, Harvard Business Review 2012, p. xv., 30,39. Copyright © 2012. Reprinted by permission of Harvard Business Publishing. p. 239: Josephus Daniels, The Wilson Era: Years of War and After, 1917–1923 (Westport, CN: Greenwood Publishing Group, 1974), p. 632. p. 240: Joanne Cantor, Mommy, I'm Scared. (1998 Mariner Books) p. 241: Scott Jaschik, "A Stand Against Wikipedia," Inside Higher Education, January 26, 2007, http://www.insidehighered.com/news/2007/01/26/wiki. p. 241: Carole Blair, "Civil Rights/Civil Sites: '. . . Until Justice Rolls Down Like Waters,'" The Carroll C. Arnold Distinguished Lecture, National Communication Association Convention, November 2006, p. 2. Copyright © 2006 Reprinted by permission of the

National Communication Association. p. 242: Isa N. Engleberg, The Principles of Public Presentation (New York: HarperCollins, 1994) p. 140. p. 242: Vivian Hobbs, Commencement Address at Prince George's Community College, Largo, Maryland, 1991. p. 242: Quoted in John A. Daly, Advocacy: Championing Ideas and Influencing Others (New Haven, CN: Yale University Press, 2011), p. 121. p. 243: Dan Le Batard, The Miamia Herald p. 243: Full Transcript and Videos: USDA Shirley Sherrod, NAACP, Breitbart, FOXNEWS," FactReal, Posted by FactReal on July 22, 2010; Updated by FactReal on 7/26/2010, http://factreal.wordpress.com/2010/07/22/full-transcript-videos-usda-shirley-sherrod-naacp-breitbart-foxnews. p. 243: Full Transcript and Videos: USDA Shirley Sherrod, NAACP, Breitbart, FOXNEWS," FactReal, Posted by FactReal on July 22, 2010; Updated by FactReal on 7/26/2010, http://factreal.wordpress.com/2010/07/22/full-transcript-videos-usda-shirley-sherrod-naacp-breitbart-foxnews. p. 244: Based on John Chafee with Christine McMahon and Barbara Stout, Critical Thinking, Thoughtful Writing, 2nd ed. (Boston: Houghton Mifflin, 2002), pp. 534–536, 614; Jim Kapoun "Teaching Undergrads Web Evaluation: A Guide for Library Instruction," C&RL News (July/August, 1998), pp. 522–523 cited in "Five Criteria for Evaluating Web Pages," Cornell University, http://olinuris.library.cornell.edu/print/4499 and http://olinuris.library.cornell.edu/ref/research/webcrit.html, Minor textual corrections, May 10, 2010. For more criteria questions and a worksheet see, Isa Engleberg and Dianna R. Wynn, "Assessing a Web Site Worksheet," Instructor's Manual for THINK Communication (Boston: Pearson/Allyn and Bacon, 2010). p. 245: Michael M. Kepper with Robert E. Gunther, I'd Rather Die Than Give a Speech (Burr Ridge, IL: Irwin, 1994), p. 6. p. 246: Arne Duncan, National Science Teachers Association Conference, March 20, 2009. http://www.ed.gov/print/news/speeches/2009/03/03202009.html. p. 253: Camille Dunlap, "Asleep at the Wheel," with permission from Camille Dunlap, a former student at Prince George's Community College. p. 256: Marge Anderson, "Looking through Our Window: The Value of Indian Culture,". p. 256: Reprinted by permission of Dr. Robert M. Franklin, President Emeritus, Morehouse College.

Chapter 14

p. 260: Lou Cannon, President Reagan: The Role of a Lifetime (New York: Public Affairs, 2000), p. 20. p. 261: Jerry Della Femina, quoted in Drewniany, Bonnie L. and Jewler, A. Jerome, Creative Strategy in Advertising, 2nd ed. (Belmont CA: Wadsworth, 1985). p. 263: http://www.independent.co.uk/news/world/asia/the-full-text-malala-yousafzais-speech-to-the-un-general-assembly-8706606.html. p. 271: Peggy Noonan, Simply Speaking: How to Communicate Your Ideas with Style, Substance, and Clarity (New York: HarperCollins, 1998), p. 206. p. 273: Janet Bozarth, Better than Bullet Points. p. 277: Peggy Noonan, Simply Speaking: How to Communicate Your Ideas with Style, Substance, and Clarity (New York: HarperCollins, 1998). p. 278: Reprinted by permission of NJJ Production, Inc.

Chapter 15

p. 283: John A. Daly, Advocacy: Championing Ideas and Influencing Others (New Haven: Yale University Press, 2011), p. 246. p. 285: Dave Lee, "Boston Bombing: How Internet Detectives Got It Very Wrong, BBC NEWS Technology, April 19, 2013, http://www.bbc.co.uk/news/technology-22214511. p. 285: Craig Silverman, "Major Breaking News Errors Giving Rise to New Responses in Boston Coverage," The Poynter Institute, April 18, 2013, http://www.poynter.org/latest-news/regret-the-error/210699/major-breaking-news-errors-giving-rise-to-new-responses-in-boston-coverage. p. 285: Alexis C. Madrigal, "It Wasn't Sunil Tripathi: The Anatomy of a Misfortunate Disaster," The Atlantic, April 19, 2013, http://www.theatlantic.com. p. 288: Henry L. Roubicek, So What's Your Story? (Dubuque, IA: Kendall Hunt, 2011), p. 17. p. 292: Gil Greengross "Laughing All the Way to the Bedroom: The Importance of Humor in Mating," Humor Sapiens/Psychology Today, May 1, 2011. p. 291: Gene Perret, Using Humor for Effective Business Speaking (1989) Sterling Publishing Company. p. 294: Reprinted by permission of John Sullivan.

Chapter 16

p. 302: Office of the First Lady, "Remarks by the First Lady at the Joint Luncheon Meeting: Working Together to Address Youth Violence in Chicago," The White House, April 10, 2013, http://www.whitehouse.gov/the-press-office/2013/04/10/remarks-first-lady-joint-luncheon-meeting-working-together-address-youth. p. 304: Lesley Kriewald, "The Power of Social Media," Texas A&M School of Engineering, 2013, http://engineering.tamu.edu/research/2012/the-power-of-social-media. p. 309: Les Christie, "Number of People Without Health Insurance Climbs," CNN Money (A Service of CNN, Fortunate, and Money) September 13, 20011, http://money.cnn.com/2011/09/13/news/economy/census_bureau_health_insurance/index.htm. p. 310: Based on Richard M. Perloff, The Dynamics of Persuasion: Communication and Attitudes in the 21st Century, 4th (New York: Routledge/Taylor & Francis, 2010), pp. 204–206. p. 317: Marge Anderson, from "Looking Through Our Window: The Value of Indian Culture" a speech delivered to the First Friday Club of the Twin Cities, March 5, 1999. Reprinted by permission of Marge Anderson, Chief Executive of the Mille Lacs Band of Ojibwe. p. 324: Reprinted by permission of the National Communication Association.

Photo Credits

Front Matter

vi: (top, left) Chris Fortuna/Riser/Getty Images; (top, right) moodboard/Alamy; vii: (top, left) Photo ITAR-TASS/Newscom; (top, right) Izabela Habur/E+/Getty Images; viii: (top, left) Monty Brinton/CBS/Getty Images; (top, right) Nathan King/Alamy; ix: (top, left) Pete Souza/White House Pool/Unimedia Images, Inc/Newscom; (top, right) Gregorio Borgia/AP Images; x: (top, left) Radius Images/Alamy; (top, right) t Rose Palmisano/ZUMA Press/Newscom; xi: (top, left) Mark Bowden/E+/Getty Images; (top, right) Brian Kersey/Upi/Newscom; xii: (top) Gregorio Borgia/AP Images; (center) ArenaCreative/Fotolia; xiv: (top, right) Peter Horree/Alamy; (center) Rex C. Curry/MCT/Newscom; (bottom) Malyshchyts Viktar/Fotolia; xvi: (top) Isa Engleberg; (bottom) Dianna Wynn

THINK COMMUNICATION FEATURES

Mediated Communication in Action

Think About Theory

Readings

Think Presentational Communication
Resources

test your knowledge ANSWERS

Chapter 1
1-c; 2-d; 3-b; 4-d; 5-c; 6-a; 7-a; 8-a; 9-c; 10-c

Chapter 2
1-d; 2-a; 3-c; 4-d; 5-a; 6-a; 7-b; 9-b; 9-b; 10-c

Chapter 3
1-c; 2-d; 3-d; 4-b; 5-a; 6-b; 7-d; 8-d

Chapter 4
1-d; 2-c; 3-d; 4-b; 5-c; 6-a; 7-d; 8-c

Chapter 5
1-b; 2-d; 3-b; 4-a; 5-c; 6-a; 7-a; 8-c; 9-d; 10-b

Chapter 6
1-b; 2-a; 3-a; 4-d; 5-c; 6-b; 7-c; 8-b

Chapter 7
1-b; 2-c; 3-d; 4-c; 5-a; 6-d; 7-a; 8-a; 9-c; 10-d

Chapter 8
1-c; 2-d; 3-b; 4-b; 5-a; 6-d; 7-d; 8-a

Chapter 9
1-d; 2-c; 3-c; 4-c; 5-b; 6-d

Chapter 10
1-c; 2-c; 3-a; 4-c; 5-b; 6-d; 7-a; 8-d

Chapter 11
1-d; 2-b; 3-a; 4-c; 5-d; 6-b: 7-b; 8-a; 9-d; 10-c

Chapter 12
1-a; 2-b; 3-b; 4-b; 5-b; 6-c; 7-c; 8-d; 9-c; 10-b

Chapter 13
1-c; 2-b; 3-c; 4-c; 5-a; 6-b; 7-d; 8-b; 9-a; 10-a

Chapter 14
1-a; 2-c; 3-c; 4-b; 5-c; 6-a; 7-d; 8-c; 9-c; 10-a

Chapter 15
1-d; 2-d; 3-d; 4-b; 5-a; 6-b; 7-b; 8-c; 9-d; 10-c

Chapter 16
1-b; 2-c; 3-d; 4-d; 5-b; 6-c; 7-d; 8-d